THE *unofficial* GUIDE®
TO Walt Disney World®

2026

BECKY GANDILLON
with **BOB SEHLINGER** *and* **LEN TESTA**

(Walt Disney World is officially known as Walt Disney World Resort.)

Please note that prices fluctuate in the course of time and that travel information changes under the impact of many factors that influence the travel industry. We therefore suggest that you email or call ahead for confirmation when making your travel plans. Every effort has been made to ensure the accuracy of information throughout this book, and the contents of this publication are believed to be correct at the time of printing. Nevertheless, the publishers cannot accept responsibility for errors or omissions, for changes in details given in this guide, or for the consequences of any reliance on the information provided by the same. Assessments of attractions and so forth are based upon the authors' own experiences; therefore, descriptions given in this guide necessarily contain an element of subjective opinion, which may not reflect the publisher's opinion or dictate a reader's own experience on another occasion. Readers are invited to write the publisher with ideas, comments, and suggestions for future editions.

The Unofficial Guides
An imprint of AdventureKEEN
2204 First Ave. S., Ste. 102
Birmingham, AL 35233

Copyright © 2026 by Robert W. Sehlinger. All rights reserved. No part of this publication may be reproduced, stored in a retrieval system, or transmitted in any form or by any means, electronic, mechanical, photocopying, recording, scanning, or otherwise, except as permitted under Section 107 or 108 of the 1976 United States Copyright Act, without either the prior written permission of the publisher or authorization through payment of the appropriate per-copy fee to the Copyright Clearance Center, 222 Rosewood Drive, Danvers, MA 01923; 978-750-8400; fax 978-646-8600; or at copyright.com. Requests to the publisher for permission should be addressed to AdventureKEEN, 2204 First Ave. S., Ste. 102, Birmingham, AL 35233; info@theunofficialguides.com.

To contact us from within the United States, please call 800-678-7006 or fax 877-374-9016. You may also email us at info@theunofficialguides.com. Reach us on social media at TheUnofficialGuides on Facebook, Instagram, Pinterest, and Threads; TheUGSeries on X; and TheUnofficialGuideSeries on YouTube.

AdventureKEEN also publishes its books in a variety of electronic formats. Some content that appears in print may not be available in electronic formats.

Unofficial Guide is a registered trademark of Keen Communications, LLC, in the United States and other countries and may not be used without written permission. All other trademarks are the property of their respective owners. Keen Communications, LLC, is not associated with any product or vendor mentioned in this book.

Cover design by Scott McGrew
Text design by Vertigo Design

ISBN: 978-1-62809-170-0 (pbk.); eISBN: 978-1-62809-171-7 (ebook)

Distributed by Publishers Group West

Manufactured in the United States of America

5 4 3 2 1

COME CHECK US OUT!

Supplement your valuable guidebook with tips, news, and deals by visiting our websites:

theunofficialguides.com
touringplans.com

Sign up for the *Unofficial Guide* newsletter for even more travel tips and special offers.

Join the conversation on social media:

 TheUGSeries   TheUnofficialGuides

 TheUnofficialGuides   TheUnofficialGuides

 TheUnofficialGuideSeries   TheUnofficialGuides

Other Unofficial Guides

The Disneyland Story: The Unofficial Guide to the Evolution of Walt Disney's Dream

Universal vs. Disney: The Unofficial Guide to American Theme Parks' Greatest Rivalry

The Unofficial Guide to Disney Cruise Line

The Unofficial Guide to Disneyland

The Unofficial Guide to Las Vegas

The Unofficial Guide to Universal Orlando

The Unofficial Guide to Washington, D.C.

LIST of MAPS and DIAGRAMS

Walt Disney World 12–13

DISNEY ACCOMMODATIONS
All-Star Resorts 162
Animal Kingdom Lodge & Villas 155
Art of Animation Resort 167
BoardWalk Inn & Villas 134
Caribbean Beach Resort 141
Contemporary Resort &
    Bay Lake Tower 124
Coronado Springs Resort 159
Disney Deluxe Resorts
    Room Diagrams 100
DVC Resorts Room Diagrams
    100–103
Disney Moderate Resorts
    Room Diagrams 103–104
Disney Value Resorts
    Room Diagrams 104
Fort Wilderness Resort &
    Campground, 170–171
Grand Floridian Resort & Spa
    and Grand Floridian Villas 112
Old Key West Resort 148
Polynesian Village Resort,
    Villas & Bungalows 116
Pop Century Resort 167
Port Orleans Resort–
    French Quarter 151
Port Orleans Resort–Riverside 150
Riviera Resort 141
Saratoga Springs Resort & Spa 144
Shades of Green 128
Swan, Swan Reserve & Dolphin 138
Treehouse Villas at Saratoga Springs
    Resort & Spa 145
Wilderness Lodge & Boulder Ridge/
    Copper Creek Villas 120
Yacht & Beach Club Resorts
    and Beach Club Villas 130

ORLANDO AREA
Disney Springs 500–501
Disney Springs Sneak Routes 350
I-4 & Walt Disney World Area 335
I-4 Sneak Routes 351
I-Drive Area Sneak Routes 352
Lodging Areas Around Walt Disney
    World 181
Lodging Areas 1 & 4: I-Drive &
    Universal 189
Lodging Area 2: Lake Buena Vista &
    the I-4 Corridor 191
Lodging Area 3: US 192 193
Rental-Home Developments
    Near WDW 184–185
South Orlando 10–11
US 192–Kissimmee Resort Area
    Sneak Routes 349

THEME PARKS
Blizzard Beach 488
Disney's Animal Kingdom 436–437
Disney's Hollywood Studios 460–461
EPCOT 406–407
The Magic Kingdom 366–367
Typhoon Lagoon 491

CONTENTS

List of Maps and Diagrams opposite page

Introduction 1
For the Love of Disney 1
Why Disney World Needs a 576-Page Guidebook 1
How to Use This Book 3

PART 1 Walt Disney World: An Overview 7
What Is Disney World? 7
  WHAT'S NEW AT WALT DISNEY WORLD 15

PART 2 Planning Before You Leave Home 19
Your Disney Trip-Planning Timeline 19
Planning Resources 23
When to Go to Walt Disney World 29
  WDW PHONE NUMBERS 37–38
  WDW ADDRESSES 38

PART 3 Making the Most of Your Time 39
Allocating Vacation Time 39
How to Avoid Long Waits in Line 43

PART 4 Making the Most of Your Money 60
Allocating Money 60
  WHAT YOU PAY AND WHAT YOU GET AT WDW 62–64
Walt Disney World Admission Tickets 66
  WDW THEME PARK TICKET OPTIONS 70–71
Optional Expenses 74

PART 5 Accommodations 77
The Basic Considerations 77
The Disney Resorts 82
  COST PER NIGHT OF DISNEY HOTEL ROOMS 94
Readers' Disney Resort Report Card 107
Walt Disney World Hotel Profiles 110
How to Evaluate a Walt Disney World Travel Package 178
Hotels Outside Walt Disney World 180
  HOTEL INFORMATION TABLE 194–199

CONTENTS

PART 6 Dining In and Around Walt Disney World 200
Our Approach to Dining: Reader Surveys Plus Expert Opinions 200
Where to Find Good Meals 202
Disney Dining 101 203
- **ADVANCE DINING RESERVATIONS: THE OFFICIAL LINE 208**
- **THE REALITY OF GETTING LAST-MINUTE DINING RESERVATIONS 209**

Character Dining 214
- **CHARACTER-MEAL HIT PARADE 216–217**

Disney Dining Suggestions 218
- **WALT DISNEY WORLD LOUNGES 228**

Counter-Service Mini-Profiles 229
Full-Service Restaurants in Depth 241
- **WDW RESTAURANTS BY CUISINE 242–245**

PART 7 Walt Disney World with Kids 289
Managing the Magic 289
Lost Children 302
Kids and Scary Stuff 304
- **SMALL-CHILD FRIGHT-POTENTIAL TABLE 305–306**

Waiting-in-Line Strategies for Young Children 307
- **ATTRACTION HEIGHT RESTRICTIONS 308**

The Disney Characters 310
- **WDW CHARACTER-GREETING VENUES 312**

Character Meals 313
Childcare 313
Special Kids' Programs 313
Birthdays and Special Occasions 314

PART 8 Tips for Varied Circumstances 315
Walt Disney World for Guests with Disabilities 315
- **QUIET SPOTS IN WALT DISNEY WORLD 317**

Walt Disney World for Pregnant Guests 321
Walt Disney World for Larger Guests 322
Walt Disney World for Older Guests 323
Walt Disney World for Couples 325
- **TIPS FOR GOING SOLO 327**

Walt Disney World for Singles 328
Odds and Ends 328

PART 9 Arriving and Getting Around 329
Getting to Walt Disney World 329
How to Travel Around the World 337
- **COMMUTING TIMES BY CAR VS. THE DISNEY TRANSPORTATION SYSTEM 341–341**

PART 10 Bare Necessities 355
Money, Etc. 355
In-Park Issues 356
Services 360

CONTENTS vii

PART 11 The Magic Kingdom 364
Overview 364
Arriving 364
Getting Oriented 368
Main Street, U.S.A. 374
Adventureland 377
Frontierland 379
Liberty Square 381
Fantasyland 382
Tomorrowland 390
Magic Kingdom Entertainment 394
Traffic Patterns in the Magic Kingdom 399
Magic Kingdom Touring Plans 401

PART 12 EPCOT 404
Overview 404
Arriving 405
Getting Oriented 409
Future World 413
World Showcase 421
EPCOT Entertainment 430
Traffic Patterns in EPCOT 433
EPCOT Touring Plan 433

PART 13 Disney's Animal Kingdom 435
Overview 435
Arriving 439
Getting Oriented 440
The Oasis 444
Discovery Island 444
Africa 447
Asia 450
Pandora—The World of Avatar 453
Animal Kingdom Entertainment 455
Traffic Patterns in Animal Kingdom 456
Animal Kingdom Touring Plan 457

PART 14 Disney's Hollywood Studios 458
Overview 458
Arriving 459
Getting Oriented 462
Hollywood and Sunset Boulevards 465
Echo Lake 470
Toy Story Land 472
Animation Courtyard 474
Star Wars: Galaxy's Edge 475
Disney's Hollywood Studios Entertainment 479
Disney's Hollywood Studios Touring Plan 479

PART 16 The Water Parks 480
Overview 480
Planning Your Day 482
> **SOGGY TIPS FROM A WATER-LOVING FAMILY 484–485**

Blizzard Beach 487
> **BLIZZARD BEACH ATTRACTIONS 489**

Typhoon Lagoon 489
> **TYPHOON LAGOON ATTRACTIONS 490**

Water-Park Touring Plans 493

PART 16 Behind-the-Scenes and VIP Tours 494
Behind the Scenes at the Magic Kingdom 494
Behind the Scenes at EPCOT 495
Behind the Scenes at Disney's Animal Kingdom 496
VIP Tours 496

PART 17 Disney Springs, Shopping, and Nightlife 496
Disney Springs 496
Shopping in Walt Disney World and Orlando 505
Nightlife at Walt Disney World Resorts 510

PART 18 Recreation and Spas 512
Run, Disney, Run 512
Treat Yourself in Walt Disney World 514
The Wilderness Must Be Explored 516
Big Competition at Miniature Golf 516
Skill Up! 517

Accommodations Index 519
Restaurant Index 525
Subject Index 529

TOURING PLANS 548
"Not a Touring Plan" Touring Plans 548
Clip-Out Touring Plans 551
Clip-Out Touring Plan Companions 569

INTRODUCTION

FOR *the* LOVE *of* DISNEY

THE UNOFFICIAL GUIDE TO WALT DISNEY WORLD has been helping families plan Disney vacations since 1986. Thousands of hours of research, millions of data points, and hundreds of hours of writing go into updating this guide every year. You've really got to love a place to put that much time and effort into studying it—and we do. Millions of you do too. We get comments like these every day via Instagram and email:

> *I was worried that even with all my planning, something would still go wrong, but this was the best vacation we've ever taken.*

> *Count me as a Disney skeptic—the most expensive place on earth and all that. But once my wife convinced me to take our "once in a lifetime trip" and I saw my kids' faces during fireworks and character meets, I'm converted. We'll be back. Soon.*

> *We just got back home, and we're already looking forward to planning our next trip. There's still so much to do!*

Disney's theme parks are among the most iconic and memorable vacation destinations in the world. They masterfully combine imagination and storytelling with cutting-edge technologies, all presented with a touch of pixie dust. Walt Disney World is also its own city, built from the ground up with a single purpose: to entertain, amaze, and inspire. And it's staffed by the best cast members on earth. Everything and everyone works together to make the magic happen.

WHY DISNEY WORLD NEEDS *a* 576-PAGE GUIDEBOOK

WE CAN SEE YOUR ANXIETY LEVEL RISING. What have I done? What am I getting myself into? Why in the world would I need a textbook-size tome of information, suggestions, recommendations, and—gulp—data for one family vacation? Is all this really necessary?

The thing that surprises most visitors is that a Walt Disney World vacation requires much more planning and effort than any other vacation they've taken. A lot of that has to do with scale and capacity. Some of the best experiences at Disney World simply don't have the capacity to serve the 60,000 people who visit the Magic Kingdom on an average day. The best restaurants can't handle that many people, and the best rides have queues that would spill out all over the whole park if everyone tried to experience them. This results in vastly different experiences for the visitors who do their homework and for those who don't. A reader from Georgia understands:

> *As we were scanning into the Magic Kingdom, we were next to a family who clearly not only had no plan but also had no clue what rides, experiences, or food options existed in the park. I wanted to give them a crash course so they didn't waste their time or money.*

But it's all going to be OK—even without graduate-level research and planning. If you love theme parks, Disney World is as good as it gets. If you arrive without knowing anything and make every possible mistake, there's a really good chance you'll still have a wonderful vacation. After all, you probably won't even know what you might be missing out on! All the planning we cover here is just to guard against as much disappointment as possible and to maximize your fun—while also minimizing the cost and the time you spend in lines.

The ultimate goals of this book are to help you avoid potential problems and to point out opportunities for that elusive "magic" that you might otherwise know about. We're here to help you turn what would already be a great vacation into a particularly amazing one.

A mom from Vermont who hadn't been to Disney since before the pandemic came back with this to say:

> *I consider myself to be a Disney expert. Been there, planned that. I only got this book as a backup. Wow, am I glad I did! So much changes over time that even this expert needs all the help she can get.*

WHAT SETS THIS BOOK APART?

THE ADVICE IN THIS BOOK is different from what you'll find by scrolling social media, random blog hunting, or reading other books, in three important ways: First, the team behind this book is totally independent of the Walt Disney Company, Walt Disney World, and all other parts of the Disney corporate organization. We don't get any free trips, gifts, special favors, invitations, or other compensation from Disney; we pay for everything we review. Disney doesn't request, influence, edit, or approve anything you'll read here. That means the advice in this book is honest—if a restaurant serves bad food, an experience isn't worth the cost, or a ride's wait is consistently too long, we say so. No need to guess at what the motivation behind our recommendations might be.

Second, we use data, science, and technology to help solve the problems that everyone encounters at Walt Disney World. The Disney theme parks are the ultimate problem-solving opportunity for numbers nerds and engineers like us: It's the most meticulously well-run environment anywhere. For example, lines for rides and restaurants that seem chaotic at first actually form in predictable ways at predictable times. That makes it possible to study and predict them.

You might be surprised that Disney-related questions like "How can I spend less time in line?" or "What rides should my kids try?" are active areas of research in schools around the world, and similar business problems pop up in corporate America every day. The authors, experts, and researchers who contribute to this book have years—even decades—of academic and professional experience in these areas and are using them to help you. And don't worry—we'll translate all that data and science into easy-to-understand, actionable advice.

The third way this book is different is the amount of time and money that goes into writing it. Over the years, we've spent millions of dollars and tens of thousands of hours reviewing and analyzing Disney World's hotels, rides, crowds, and restaurants. No other book or website commits the people, skills, or budget to do anything like the research you'll find here. The only other organization that does the same level of analysis on Disney World is Disney itself. And in this book, you'll learn plenty of things that they won't tell you.

HOW *to* USE THIS BOOK

THE BEST WAY TO USE THIS BOOK is to read the introduction and Part 1, then scan the table of contents to get a feel for the kinds of topics each chapter covers. Read fully the chapters that seem most important to you. Then, as you plan your trip, you can refer back to sections as they become relevant to you.

The chapters appear in roughly the order you'll need them for planning and then taking your trip. For example, Part 2 contains advice on what you need to know to start planning your trip. Then the next few chapters guide you through choosing a hotel, finding good places to eat, and picking the best rides and entertainment in the parks.

Each chapter starts with **Key Questions** (see below)—a list of FAQs visitors have, along with the page number where you can find the answers. Of course, each chapter answers more questions than the ones highlighted. You can skim each chapter's section headings to see if there are other topics that might be important to you.

> **KEY QUESTIONS ANSWERED IN THIS CHAPTER**
> - Where can I find a planning checklist and timeline? *(page 19)*
> - What are the six most important tips for avoiding lines at Disney World? *(page 43)*
> - What are Lightning Lane Multi Pass and Lightning Lane Single Pass, and how do I use them? *(page 53)*

Some subjects, such as how Disney accommodates guests in wheelchairs, are relevant across multiple parts of your vacation. These subjects are usually covered in depth in one chapter (in this case, Part 8), with cross-references in other chapters when they're needed.

Most topics are covered in great detail. For example, Disney World has hundreds of attractions, from simple spinners you might find at your local carnival to massive super-headliners. Understanding these rides and how they're run will help you decide what's worth your time.

INTRODUCTION

THE *UNOFFICIAL GUIDE* TEAM

ALLOW US TO INTRODUCE THE PEOPLE who work on this book, except for some of our dining critics, who shall remain anonymous:

- **BECKY GANDILLON** Author
- **BOB SEHLINGER** Coauthor
- **LEN TESTA** Coauthor
- **FRED HAZELTON** Statistician
- **JIM HILL** Disney Dish contributor
- **DAVID DAVIES** Webmaster, TouringPlans.com
- **TRAVIS BRYANT** Webmaster, TheUnofficialGuides.com

CONTRIBUTORS
Bella Cannuscio
Christina Harrison
Bob Jacobs
Seth Kubersky
Colin McManus
Brian McNichols
Liliane J. Opsomer
Amy Schinner
Laurel Stewart
Bethany Vinton
Deb Wills

DATA COLLECTORS
Chantale Brazeau
Christine Harrison
Giovanna Harrison
Ivonne Ramos
Darcie Vance
Rich Vosburgh
Kelly Whitman

EDITORIAL AND ART
- **KATE JOHNSON** Managing editor
- **ANNIE LONG** Layout
- **JENNA BARRON, EMILY BEAUMONT, HOLLY CROSS** Proofreaders
- **SCOTT McGREW** Cover design
- **STEVE JONES, CASSANDRA POERTNER** Cartography
- **POTOMAC INDEXING** Indexing (**Joanne Sprott,** team leader)

YOUR UNOFFICIAL WALT DISNEY WORLD TOOLBOX

WE REFER TO THIS GUIDE, AT 576 PAGES, as the "Big Book." It provides the detailed information that anyone traveling to Walt Disney World needs to plan a spectacular vacation. It's the cornerstone of your trip planning.

Two additional guides in the *Unofficial* series provide information for visitors who may want to combine their Disney World trip with a Disney cruise or a visit to nearby Universal Orlando:

The Unofficial Guide to Disney Cruise Line, by Tammy Whiting with Len Testa and Erin Foster, presents advice for first-time cruisers; money-saving tips for booking your cruise; detailed profiles for restaurants, shows, and nightclubs; deck plans; and thorough coverage of the ports visited by Disney Cruise Line.

The Unofficial Guide to Universal Orlando, by Seth Kubersky, is the most comprehensive guide to Universal Orlando Resort in print. At more than 400 pages, it's the perfect tool for understanding and enjoying Universal's ever-expanding complex of theme parks, a water park, resort hotels, nightclubs, and restaurants. The guide includes field-tested touring plans that will save you hours of standing in line.

CORRECTIONS, UPDATES, AND BREAKING NEWS

WE EXPECT THIS 2026 EDITION to be available through fall 2026. The first set of updates was started in the spring of 2025 and incorporates Disney's current operating procedures at press time.

But things can and do change at Walt Disney World all the time. Despite our best efforts at staying up-to-date, Disney could introduce significant changes to its theme parks and resorts soon after this book goes to print. For an up-to-date summary of changes made since publication, go to theugseries.com/wdwupdates.

There are two other good places to go if you want more real-time updates from our team. The first is Becky's Instagram account: @raisingminniemes, where she posts recent, data-driven information three times a week and a themed touring strategy once a week. The second is the Touring Plans blog (blog.touringplans.com), which has at least one article a day about Walt Disney World, Disney Cruise Line, or Universal Orlando.

LETTERS AND COMMENTS FROM READERS

MANY READERS WRITE IN with comments or to share their own tips. Their feedback is regularly incorporated into the *Guide* and contributes to its ongoing revision and improvement. If you write to us or complete our reader survey (see link below), we won't release your name or address to anyone. If you're willing to have your comments quoted in the *Guide*, be sure to tell us where you're from.

Speaking of comments, from the thousands of surveys we receive each year, a little over 10% contain comments. Of that 10%, an even smaller percentage are useful and well written. Quotable comments are like gold. If a comment hits the nail on the head, it's unlikely that we'll receive a more well-written and more insightful one. If a better comment hasn't been submitted recently, the older one remains in the next edition because it best serves our readers.

Online Reader Survey

TouringPlans.com hosts a questionnaire you can use to give feedback on your Walt Disney World visit. Access it at touringplans.com/walt-disney-world/survey. This questionnaire lets every member of your party, regardless of age, share what they think about attractions, hotels, restaurants, and more. This feedback is critical to the updating of this book and our recommendations.

You can also print out the reader survey and mail it to us at the following address:

Reader Survey
The Unofficial Guide to Walt Disney World
2204 First Ave. S., Ste. 102
Birmingham, AL 35233

Finally, if you'd like to review this book on Amazon, go to theugseries.com/2026reviews.

How to Contact the Authors

The best way to contact us is via email or social media:

Email: info@theunofficialguides.com
Facebook: TheUnofficialGuides | X: @TheUGSeries
Instagram: @theunofficialguides or @raisingminniemes (Becky)

You may also send us a letter at the physical address listed above. Please put your mailing address on both your letter and your envelope, as the two sometimes get separated. It's also a good idea to include your phone number in case we need to contact you.

Brad Huber developed the latest version of our Lines app. Todd Perlmutter, Bryan Klinck, and EJJ skillfully debugged the touring plan software. Lines' chat is moderated by the fabulous Weasus, missoverexcited, and PrincipalTinker. We'd also like to thank these folks who have assisted with fact-checking and research over the years: Robert Bloom, Shannon Bohn, Dani Dennison, Anne Densk, Alyssa Drake, Erin Foster, Scott Gustin, Jennifer Heymont, Erin Jenkins, Lauren Macvane, David McDonough, and Carlye Wisel. Thanks also to Jamie Holding and his GitHub repository (github.com/cubehouse/themeparks). Thanks to John Tierney, who knows more about DVC rentals and water treatment than any one human has a right to know. Finally, to everyone at Walt Disney Parks and Resorts who follows our research from a distance, even if they can't say it: We love you too. You are the reason that magic happens.

THE IMPORTANCE OF BEING SERIOUS

SOME READERS ARE SHOCKED that anyone would spend so much time on in-depth analysis of a theme park. But most people do research before buying a car or a major appliance, and a Disney vacation costs more than a dishwasher—and sometimes more than a used car!

On top of that, the Disney advertising machine is immensely powerful and prone to hyperbole. When Disney says its theme parks and restaurants are "world-class" and its artists are "legends," we think it's important to cut through the noise and help you understand what's real and what is marketing magic . . . or nonsense.

One of the ways we do that is to point out whether the things Disney is doing today meet the standards it has set for itself. When we say that Guardians of the Galaxy: Cosmic Rewind in EPCOT is the best roller coaster Disney has ever made, it's because we believe it meets the highest of Disney's ideals dating back to Walt himself—all wrapped up in an intense ride with technology (and characters) that Walt never envisioned. Likewise, if we complain about an immersive and cohesive trip through the Wild West being interrupted by a verdant green New Orleans bayou (see page 381), that's because it breaks the story that Disney itself worked so hard to tell. And at Disney, storytelling is key.

THE IMPORTANCE OF BEING GOOFY

WHAT MAKES WRITING ABOUT WALT DISNEY WORLD so much fun is that the Disney executives have to take everything so seriously. Day to day, they debate momentous decisions with far-reaching consequences: Should Mickey wear red or green or silver this holiday season? What possible color schemes can we come up with for our next batch in the never-ending parade of spirit jerseys? What "big anniversary" can we celebrate next? Do these Minnie ears look vulgar?

Unofficially, we think having a sense of humor is important. This guidebook has one, and it's probably necessary that you do too—not just to use this book but to have the most fun possible at Walt Disney World. Think of the *Unofficial Guide* as your private trainer getting your sense of humor in shape. It will help you understand the importance of being goofy.

PART 1

WALT DISNEY WORLD:
An Overview

KEY QUESTIONS ANSWERED IN THIS CHAPTER
- What is Walt Disney World? *(see below)*
- How big is Walt Disney World? *(see page 8)*
- What's the difference between the different theme parks? *(page 8)*
- What do these new words and acronyms mean? *(page 18)*

WHAT IS DISNEY WORLD?

WE MIGHT BE BIASED, but we think Walt Disney World (WDW), in Orlando, Florida, isn't just a theme park; it's *the* theme park. With its unmatched size, scope, quality, theming, and sheer ambition, it leaves every other amusement or theme park in the dust.

If you watch any sort of media, you're probably familiar with commercials for Disney's theme parks. These ads show picture-perfect moments of families bonding over holding Mickey-shaped balloons while they experience rides or meet characters. But 30-second snapshots don't exactly cover where to find those rides and characters, how long you'll stand in line, or how much money this magical visit will cost. That's where this book comes in. We give you all the information you need to know, in a format that you can refer back to as you continue to plan, book, and actually enjoy your vacation.

Let's start with the basics. Walt Disney World has four distinct theme parks. Chances are, when you think of Walt Disney World, your mind goes straight to the **Magic Kingdom**—the first one built and the one with the castle. The other three theme parks are **EPCOT, Disney's Animal Kingdom,** and **Disney's Hollywood Studios**—each with its own unique flavor of magic.

And that's just the beginning! Walt Disney World also features two water parks, **Blizzard Beach** and **Typhoon Lagoon;** over three dozen hotels; a campground; more than 100 restaurants; a massive year-round sports center; an outdoor mall/entertainment/hotel complex called **Disney Springs;** six convention centers; four golf courses; and enough spas, recreation options, and other activities to fill an entire vacation without ever setting foot in a park. Phew!

HOW BIG IS WALT DISNEY WORLD?

WALT DISNEY WORLD IS *MASSIVE*—it spans about 43 square miles of land area, roughly double the size of Manhattan, a bit smaller than Boston, and a bit larger than Miami.

The four theme parks aren't right next door to each other; they're separated by miles of barely developed Central Florida swampland. To get around, you'll either need a car or you'll have to rely on Walt Disney World's extensive transportation system. We're talking fleets of buses, boats, vans, monorails, and aerial gondolas (the Skyliner). Fun fact: Disney World's bus system is the third largest in Florida, behind Jacksonville's and Miami's. Its transportation system is so large (and complex) that much of Part 9 is dedicated to it.

With so much ground to cover and so much to see, it would take at least two weeks to thoroughly explore most of it. But realistically, two weeks at Disney is way outside the budget for most families. Don't worry—we'll help you maximize your time so that you can focus on the best the World has to offer for your trip.

To get your bearings, think of the four theme parks as mini hubs within Walt Disney World. For example, the **Magic Kingdom Resort Area** is about 7 square miles and contains the Magic Kingdom theme park plus its nearby hotels, restaurants, golf courses, and entertainment. Thinking in terms of these hub areas makes navigating WDW a little less overwhelming.

THE MAJOR THEME PARKS

The Magic Kingdom

Opened in 1971, the Magic Kingdom is the original Walt Disney World theme park—the "classic" park that echoes the charm of Disneyland, which came before it. Home to **Cinderella Castle,** this is where Disney magic really comes to life, with rides, shows, and entertainment centered around beloved Disney characters. While it's just one piece of the Walt Disney World puzzle, the Magic Kingdom remains its beating heart—and the most attended theme park in the world.

The Magic Kingdom is designed with six "lands" radiating out from a central hub. First you walk through **Main Street, U.S.A.,** which brings you from the park entrance to the hub, featuring the castle. Arranged clockwise around the hub are **Adventureland, Frontierland, Liberty Square, Fantasyland,** and **Tomorrowland.** Packed with more rides, shows, and entertainment than any other Disney park, the Magic Kingdom could easily fill two days of touring. But if time is tight, you can still hit the highlights in a full day of strategic exploring.

Three resorts—the **Contemporary, Grand Floridian,** and **Polynesian Village**—and their villa units (**Bay Lake Tower, The Villas at the Grand Floridian,** and **Disney's Polynesian Villas & Bungalows** and **Island Tower**) are connected to the Magic Kingdom by monorail and boat. Nearby, three other hotels—**Shades of Green** (for the US military and their families), **Wilderness Lodge** (including the **Boulder Ridge**

Villas and **Copper Creek Villas & Cabins**), and **Fort Wilderness Resort & Campground**—are accessible by boat and bus instead of monorail.

EPCOT

Opened in 1982, EPCOT is twice as big as the Magic Kingdom. The "front" (northern) part of the park is divided into three neighborhoods: **World Discovery, World Celebration,** and **World Nature.** Each features massive pavilions dedicated to human creativity, technological advancement, and the natural world. Meanwhile, **World Showcase,** the "back" (southern) part, encircles a 40-acre lagoon and highlights the architectural, social, and cultural traditions of nearly a dozen nations, with each country represented by its own pavilion. EPCOT recently underwent a major transformation aimed at becoming more family-friendly. The revitalization brought in more character experiences and created open spaces perfect for families with young children.

The EPCOT resorts are a dream for convenience seekers. Staying at **BoardWalk Inn & Villas, Dolphin, Swan, Swan Reserve, Yacht & Beach Club Resorts,** or **Beach Club Villas** puts you within a 5- to 15-minute walk of the International Gateway, EPCOT's secondary entrance, located in World Showcase. These resorts are also linked to EPCOT and Disney's Hollywood Studios by boat and walkway. EPCOT is connected to the Magic Kingdom and its hotels by monorail. An elevated gondola system called the **Skyliner** links EPCOT and Disney's Hollywood Studios to Disney's Pop Century, Art of Animation, Caribbean Beach, and Riviera Resorts. In case you can't tell, this is one of the most well-connected areas of Walt Disney World and is a personal favorite of Becky's because of its easy access to resorts, parks, and almost endless dining options.

Disney's Hollywood Studios

Opened in 1989, Disney's Hollywood Studios (DHS) is slightly larger than the Magic Kingdom and is divided into two distinct areas. Roughly half of the park celebrates the motion picture, music, and television industries. Here, visitors can stroll along re-creations of Hollywood and Sunset Boulevards from Hollywood's Golden Age, enjoy thrilling rides, watch musical performances, and experience an action-packed movie stunt show.

The other half of DHS features two immersive movie-themed lands, with one more on the way! **Toy Story Land,** which debuted in 2018, offers three themed rides suitable for children and two immersive dining options, all in a playful setting that makes you feel like you've shrunk to toy size. **Star Wars: Galaxy's Edge,** opened in 2019, transports guests to a galaxy far, far away with two state-of-the-art attractions that cater more to older children, teens, and adults. Construction on the third movie-themed land, **Monstropolis** (which will be roughly adjacent to Galaxy's Edge), began in 2025.

Guests can travel to or from DHS by bus or Skyliner but not by monorail. Visitors staying at EPCOT-area resorts have additional options, including walking or taking a boat. For those driving, ample parking is available in the DHS lot.

continued on page 14

10 PART 1 WALT DISNEY WORLD: AN OVERVIEW

South Orlando

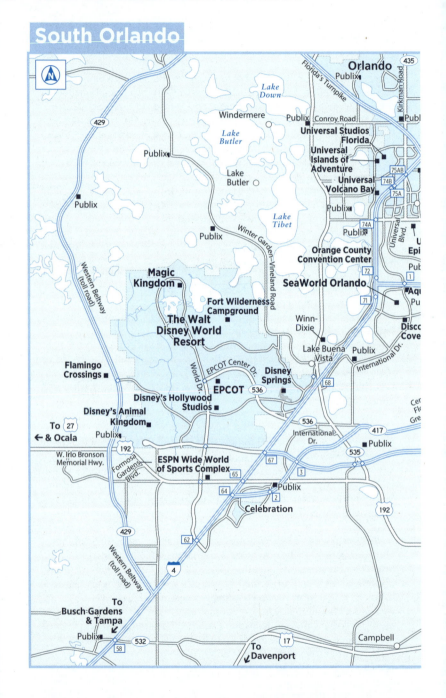

SOUTH ORLANDO MAP 11

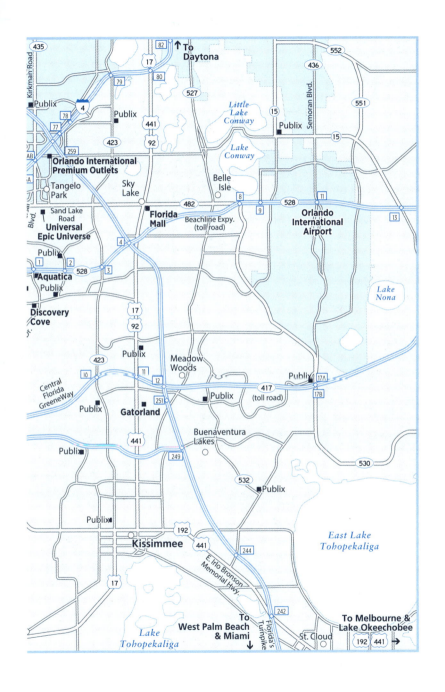

12 PART 1 WALT DISNEY WORLD: AN OVERVIEW

Walt Disney World

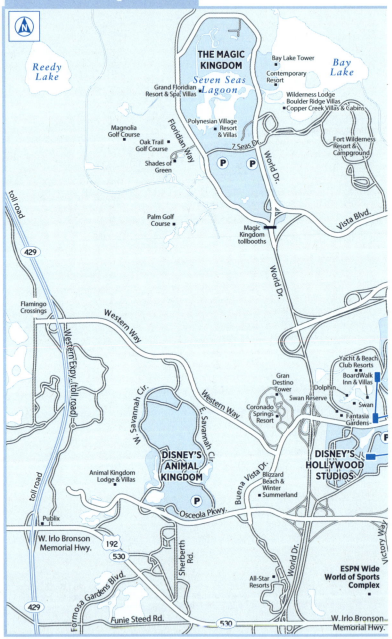

WALT DISNEY WORLD MAP 13

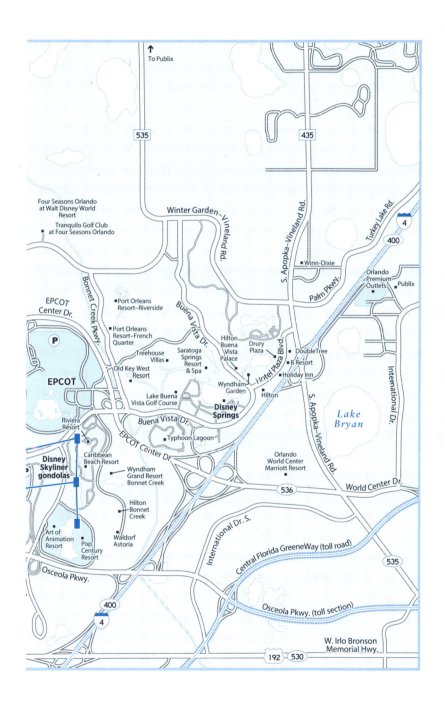

continued from page 9

Disney's Animal Kingdom

At about five times the size of the Magic Kingdom, Disney's Animal Kingdom is the largest park at Walt Disney World. It blends zoological exhibits with rides, shows, and live entertainment. The park is laid out in a hub-and-spoke configuration, similar to the Magic Kingdom. Visitors enter through a tropical rainforest that serves as "Main Street," leading to **Discovery Island,** the park's central hub. Dominated by the iconic 14-story-tall, hand-carved **Tree of Life,** Discovery Island offers services, shopping, and dining. From there, guests can access the themed areas: **Africa, Asia,** and **Pandora—The World of Avatar.** (Another area, **Tropical Americas,** will open in 2027. It will replace DinoLand U.S.A., which began closing in 2025).

Discovery Island and Africa opened in 1998, followed by Asia in 1999. Africa spans more than 100 acres by itself and is home to free-roaming herds in a re-creation of the Serengeti. Asia immerses guests in lush jungles and towering mountain landscapes.

Pandora, based on James Cameron's *Avatar* film franchise, wows visitors with its breathtaking scenery, including "floating mountains" and glow-in-the-dark plants replicated from the movie.

Animal Kingdom has its own parking lot and is connected to other Walt Disney World destinations by the Disney bus system. Although no hotels are within walking distance of Animal Kingdom, the **All-Star Resorts, Animal Kingdom Lodge & Villas, Coronado Springs Resort,** and others are located nearby.

THE WATER PARKS

DISNEY WORLD IS HOME TO TWO WATER PARKS: **Typhoon Lagoon** and **Blizzard Beach.** Opened in 1989, Typhoon Lagoon features a massive wave pool that produces 6-foot-tall waves, making it a favorite for both surfers and (strong) swimmers. Blizzard Beach opened in 1995 and offers wider variety of slides, including some of the most thrilling water attractions at Disney World. Both parks are meticulously themed, with immersive atmospheres that transport guests to either a snowy alpine escape or a tropical paradise. Each has its own parking lot and is accessible via the Disney bus system.

OTHER WALT DISNEY WORLD VENUES

Disney Springs

Themed as a charming Florida waterfront town, Disney Springs is divided into four distinct areas, each with its own shopping, dining, and entertainment: Marketplace, West Side, Town Center, and The Landing.

Marketplace, located on the east side, is home to the country's largest Disney merchandise store, along with upscale boutiques, specialty shops, and a variety of dining options. **West Side** offers a diverse mix of nightlife, shopping, dining, and entertainment, including a **Cirque du Soleil** show exclusive to Disney World. At the heart of Disney Springs, **Town Center** hosts a wide range of well-known brands, from

WHAT IS DISNEY WORLD?

WHAT'S NEW AT WALT DISNEY WORLD

LAST YEAR OR SO

- Disney's paid **Lightning Lane Multi Pass** and **Lightning Lane Single Pass** ride reservation systems debuted in 2024, replacing Genie+ (which had replaced FastPass+ in 2021).
- A major expansion of the **Polynesian Village Resort,** called **Island Tower,** for Disney Vacation Club members, opened on the Seven Seas Lagoon in 2024.
- **Lightning McQueen's Racing Academy** at **DHS** closed in 2024 to make way for a new stage show, **Disney Villains: Unfairly Ever After,** set to open in summer 2025.
- Two new lounges are opening in 2025: **Pirates of the Caribbean tavern** in the **Magic Kingdom** and **Geo-82,** a lounge at **Spaceship Earth** in **EPCOT.**
- The **Disney Starlight: Dream the Night Away** evening parade will debut in the **Magic Kingdom** in summer 2025.
- A reimagined version of **Test Track** opened in **EPCOT** in late summer 2025.
- *Zootopia: Better Zoogether* will debut in **Animal Kingdom**'s **Tree of Life** theater in winter 2025.

LAST 2 YEARS

- **Tiana's Bayou Adventure,** a retheming of the Splash Mountain log-flume ride, opened in the **Magic Kingdom**'s Frontierland in 2024.
- **The Cabins at Fort Wilderness** were replaced with newer units, and the resort became a Disney Vacation Club property in 2024.

LAST 5 YEARS

- The **Early Theme Park Entry** and **Extended Evening Theme Park Hours** programs debuted, replacing the Extra Magic Hours program.
- The **Magic Kingdom's** nighttime show, *Disney Enchantment,* closed in 2023.
- **Tron Lightcycle/Run,** an outdoor roller coaster, opened in the **Magic Kingdom**'s Tomorrowland in 2023.
- **Journey of Water, Inspired by Moana** (an outdoor interactive water-play area) and *Luminous* (a new fireworks show) opened in **EPCOT** in 2023.
- **Guardians of the Galaxy: Cosmic Rewind,** the world's longest indoor roller coaster, opened in **EPCOT** in 2022.
- **Remy's Ratatouille Adventure,** a ride based on the Pixar film *Ratatouille,* opened in **EPCOT** in 2021.
- **EPCOT**'s nighttime show, *Harmonious,* closed in 2023.
- The **Star Wars: Galactic Starcruiser** immersive hotel experience closed in 2023.

LAST 10 YEARS

- **DHS** opened **Toy Story Land** (with **Alien Swirling Saucers** and **Slinky Dog Dash**) and **Star Wars: Galaxy's Edge** (with **Star Wars: Rise of the Resistance** and *Millennium Falcon: Smugglers Run*).
- **Mickey & Minnie's Runaway Railway,** an immersive 3D ride through the new Mickey Mouse cartoon universe, also opened in **DHS.**
- **EPCOT** unveiled the food-and-arts-themed **International Festival of the Arts,** which takes place in January and February.
- **Disney's Animal Kingdom** added its sixth land, **Pandora—The World of Avatar,** featuring **Avatar Flight of Passage** (a thrilling flight simulator) and **Na'vi River Journey,** a gentle boat ride. The adventurous restaurant **Tiffins** and its accompanying **Nomad Lounge** also opened.
- **Disney's Riviera Resort,** a Disney Vacation Club property, opened in 2019, along with the **Disney Skyliner** elevated gondola system.
- **Disney's Coronado Springs Resort** opened the 15-story **Gran Destino Tower** in 2019, with more-upscale guest rooms and dining options.

Anthropologie and Free People to Levi's and Under Armour. It feels like an upscale outdoor outlet mall—just don't expect outlet pricing. Finally, **The Landing,** perched along the waterfront, offers even more shopping and arguably the best dining options in Disney Springs.

Guests of Disney resort hotels and theme parks can reach Disney Springs using Disney transportation. For those who choose to drive, there are three multistory parking garages, with short walks to shopping and dining locations of your choosing.

Disney's BoardWalk

Located near EPCOT, the BoardWalk is an idealized re-creation of a 1930s East Coast waterfront resort. It offers upscale restaurants, shops and galleries, and a cake shop. In the evening, a DJ dance club (for guests age 21 and up) joins the lineup. A dueling piano bar closed in 2025, and a replacement hadn't been announced at press time. Visiting the Board-Walk is free, but adults-only areas may require a cover charge.

This area is anchored by the **BoardWalk Inn & Villas** and is located within walking distance of the EPCOT resorts, EPCOT's International Gateway entrance, and Disney's Hollywood Studios. Boat transportation is available to and from EPCOT and Hollywood Studios, the Skyliner connects the BoardWalk to the Studios and the hotels on its route, and buses serve other Walt Disney World locations.

WHAT'S NEW AT WALT DISNEY WORLD

Disneyland is something that will never be finished. It's something that I can keep developing. It will be a live, breathing thing that will need change.

—Walt Disney

WHAT WALT SAID OF DISNEYLAND is also true of Disney World. The table on the previous page shows all the major changes that have taken place at Walt Disney World in the last 1, 2, 5, and 10 years.

THE PEOPLE OF WALT DISNEY WORLD

DISNEY'S EMPLOYEES are called **cast members.** These are the people who can make or break a vacation with their service. Fortunately, cast members often go the extra mile to make your visit special, as the following readers share.

First, from Texas grandmother who almost had a schedule disaster:

My 5-year-old granddaughter REALLY wanted to ride Rock 'n' Roller Coaster. We made a Lightning Lane reservation, knowing she might not be tall enough. We got to the ride, and the sweet cast member helped measure her. She just made it. We started scanning our bands . . . only to realize we had gotten confused about the time and had missed the return window by hours. The cast member let us all go on it since we were all so excited. The wait would have been well over an hour otherwise!

And a mom from Illinois had this to relate:

During our babymoon at Disney, a PhotoPass cast member created an unforgettable moment for us. After snapping a few shots, he smiled and asked, "Can we get creative?" What followed was

> *a magical whirlwind as he led us to unique spots, capturing photos we'd never have dreamed of. It was unplanned, unexpected, and beautifully spontaneous—one of those rare moments of pure Disney magic that we'll treasure forever.*

A family from Indiana was impressed with how Disney handled logistics for them during a medical emergency:

> *My family has been to Disney eight times in the past 20 years, and we have never had any emergencies or problems during any of our stays, until the most recent stay, in November 2024. My mom ended up in the hospital on the second night. My dad was with her during the day and then coming back to the resort to sleep. I was in charge of figuring out logistics for our room reservations. I walked up to a cast member at the concierge at French Quarter and immediately burst into tears. I was so stressed out about a huge emergency happening so far from home and also wondering if my mom was going to make it back to Indiana. She hugged me, gave me a ton of tissues, and led me to a seating area off to the side where we could talk. She was able to extend our rooms and gave us the most discounted rate on those extra days (Florida-resident rate for standard view, instead of our actual river- and garden-view rooms). And she gave my parents complementary tickets for the park days that they missed.*

On the other end of the spectrum, a big celebration turned even more magical for this family from California:

> *This May, I celebrated being a five-year breast cancer survivor with my family at Disney World. During our Animal Kingdom day, one of the cast members saw our matching shirts as we boarded Flight of Passage. After we rode, they stopped us and asked if we would all like to ride again. We were so honored and assumed that would be all, but after we got off the second ride, the cast member then personally walked us "backstage" and directly onto Na'vi River Journey. By the time we got off, she had already added two more Magical Experience passes to all of our tickets. I'll never forget the joy on my mom's face as she not only got to experience Disney magic but also got to do it with her healthy "little girl."*

Interacting with cast members is our favorite part of a Disney vacation. They love their jobs and are passionate about making vacations magical for the people they serve. Unfortunately, their day-to-day is also generally pretty difficult, thanks to guests with high expectations, sometimes unreasonable demands, and vacation-induced anxiety that makes them occasionally act unpleasantly toward cast members. We encourage every guest to practice compassion and curiosity when interacting with cast members. Aim to make their jobs easier by listening and being kind. We promise that they're doing their best to keep you safe, well fed, and happy.

POCKET TRANSLATOR FOR COMMON DISNEY ABBREVIATIONS

IT MAY COME AS A SURPRISE to many, but Walt Disney World has its own somewhat peculiar language. On the next page are some abbreviations and slang you're likely to encounter, both in this guide and in the larger Disney community.

PART 1 WALT DISNEY WORLD: AN OVERVIEW

COMMON ABBREVIATIONS	
ADR Advance Dining Reservation	**ETPE** Early Theme Park Entry (formerly Morning Extra Magic Hours, or Morning EMH)
BG Boarding group (may be used for newer rides)	**EETPH** Extended Evening Theme Park Hours (formerly Evening Extra Magic Hours, or Evening EMH)
CM Cast member	**I-DRIVE** International Drive (a major Orlando thoroughfare)
DCL Disney Cruise Line	**MDE** My Disney Experience mobile app
DHS Disney's Hollywood Studios	**TTC** Ticket and Transportation Center
DTS Disney Transportation System	**WDI** Walt Disney Imagineering
DVC Disney Vacation Club	**WDW** Walt Disney World

THE DISNEY LEXICON IN A NUTSHELL
ATTRACTION Ride or theater show
ATTRACTION HOST Ride operator
BACKSTAGE Behind the scenes, out of view of customers
CAST MEMBER Employee
CHARACTER Disney character impersonated by an employee
COSTUME Work attire or uniform
DARK RIDE Indoor ride
FACE CHARACTER A character who doesn't wear a head-covering costume (such as Snow White, Cinderella, and Jasmine)
GREETER Cast member positioned at an attraction entrance
GUEST Customer/visitor
HIDDEN MICKEY Frontal silhouette of Mickey's head worked subtly into the design of buildings, railings, golf greens, attractions, and just about anything else
OFF-SITE HOTEL/RESORT A hotel or resort located outside of Walt Disney World's boundaries
ON-SITE HOTEL/RESORT A hotel or resort located inside Walt Disney World's boundaries and served by the Disney Transportation System
ONSTAGE In full view of customers
PRESHOW Entertainment at an attraction before the feature presentation
SOFT OPENING The opening of a park or attraction before its stated opening date

PART 2

PLANNING *before* YOU LEAVE HOME

KEY QUESTIONS ANSWERED IN THIS CHAPTER

- Where can I find a planning checklist and timeline? *(see below)*
- What is My Disney Experience, and how do I use it? *(page 23)*
- When is Disney World least crowded and most crowded? *(page 31)*
- What are Early Theme Park Entry and Extended Evening Theme Park Hours, and how do I use them? *(pages 34–36)*
- What special events are scheduled while I'm at Walt Disney World? *(page 32)*
- How can I contact someone at Disney with questions? *(page 37)*

Visiting Walt Disney World is a bit like childbirth—you never really believe what people tell you, but once you have been through it yourself, you know exactly what they were saying!

—Hilary Wolfe, a mother and
Unofficial Guide reader from Wales

YOUR DISNEY TRIP-PLANNING TIMELINE

THE QUICK-START GUIDE TO USING THE *GUIDE*

AS YOU PLAN YOUR DISNEY VACATION, you'll encounter several date-specific milestones. For example, you can make Disney dining reservations starting 60 days before your arrival. To help you stay on track, the comprehensive timeline on the next few pages outlines key research, decisions, and tasks involved in planning your trip. Each milestone references the relevant sections of this book and additional resources for more detailed information.

Most Disney trips involve about a dozen important dates to remember. If you've started planning more than 11 months in advance, you'll have plenty of time to prepare before those dates arrive. If your trip is just a couple of months away, you'll need to move through the timeline quickly to secure your reservations and plans.

Is all this planning really necessary? Yes! In-demand experiences, like dining at a popular character meal, often book up quickly due to limited capacity. Without reservations, you could miss out entirely. Dining reservations are especially critical if you want to secure spots at popular restaurants. Other bookings, such as those for ride reservations, spa treatments, or recreational activities, are important to consider too. The earlier you start your research and make reservations, the better your chances of getting everything on your wish list.

How to Plan in a Hurry

We get variations on this comment a lot:

> *AH! Our first Disney trip is in three weeks, and I just found out about the Unofficial Guide. I had no idea about all the research and reservations I needed to do! Am I too late?*

You'll be fine. You'll still want to go through the timeline; you'll just work through the steps a little (or much) quicker.

9–12 Months Before Your Trip

You may already have a general idea of when you want to visit Disney World. The overall cost of the trip, however, often takes people by surprise. Take a couple of evenings to plan a budget and an approximate time of year to travel, and to narrow down your hotel choices.

- **Establish a budget.** See pages 62–64 for an idea of how much Disney vacation you can get for $1,500–$4,000, for various family sizes. You can also go to disneyworld.disney.go.com and put in some sample dates to see package prices without purchasing.
- **Figure out when to go and where to stay.** Begin researching resorts (see Part 5) and the best times of year to visit (see page 29).
- **Brush up on discounts.** Disney releases certain discounts around the same time every year. Check theugseries.com/wdw-discounts for a list of these regular discounts, when they're usually announced, and the travel dates they cover. Also see the section on hotel discounts beginning on page 70.
- **Create an account at My Disney Experience** (see page 23). You'll need it to make hotel, dining, and (potentially) ride reservations later.
- **Make a preliminary Disney hotel reservation.** This typically requires a deposit equal to one night's cost and guarantees you a room. Staying on-site gets you early and (at select resorts) late access to the theme parks, offering a substantial advantage in avoiding long lines (see pages 34–36). You can change or cancel without penalty for several months while you continue your research.
- **Disney Vacation Club (DVC)** members can make reservations at their home resort starting 11 months before their trip. See page 85 for information on how to rent points from a DVC member.
- **Investigate whether trip insurance makes sense for your situation.** It is almost certainly worthwhile, especially if you'll be traveling to Disney World during peak hurricane season (August and September). Third-party policies, such as those from insuremytrip.com, are usually cheaper than Disney's trip insurance and are often more comprehensive. In the post-pandemic era, almost all trips should be insured for trip cancellation or interruption, and for medical emergencies.

- **If you're not a US citizen, make sure your family's passports and visas are in order.** Passports typically need to be valid for six months beyond your travel dates. An electronic US visa is typically good for two years from the date of issue, if you need one. See esta.cbp.dhs.gov/esta to check whether your country participates in the US's visa waiver program. You must apply for a visa (or waiver) at least 72 hours prior to arrival.

7–9 Months Before Your Trip

Now is the time to start thinking about how many park days you'll want and locking in your tickets.

- **Purchase your park tickets** at least this far in advance (see page 66 for ticket and add-on details). TouringPlans' Least Expensive Ticket Calculator (touringplans.com/walt-disney-world/ticket-calculator) will help you find the best discounts on Disney tickets. This helps you lock in prices before any potential increases—ticket prices usually go up in October of each year, so it's best to purchase before then.
- **Link your tickets to your My Disney Experience account** so that all tickets and reservations are linked.
- **Disney Vacation Club** members can make resort reservations outside their home resort starting seven months before their trip.
- **Start thinking about which parks you want to visit on each day.** This will help determine if you need Park Hopper tickets and will help inform where you'll make dining and ride reservations.

4–6 Months Before Your Trip

Get familiar with Disney's rides, shows, and attractions, and start planning what you'll see each day.

- **Review the attractions and shows** in the Magic Kingdom (see page 364), EPCOT (see page 507), Disney's Animal Kingdom (see page 544), and Disney's Hollywood Studios (see page 574).
- **Make a list of must-see attractions in each park.** If you're unsure whether your child should experience a particular attraction, see the Small-Child Fright-Potential Table on pages 305–306. See page 308 for a list of height requirements for the attractions.
- **Review our touring plans** (see pages 548–568) and use them to begin putting together a touring strategy for each park. You can also use the software at touringplans.com/walt-disney-world/touring-plans.

180 Days Before Your Trip

Use this time to research Disney's restaurants and dining options.

- **Get familiar with Disney World restaurants** (see Part 6) so you're ready when Disney's dining reservation system opens at your 60-day mark. You can also check touringplans.com/walt-disney-world/dining for current restaurant ratings, menus, and prices at every Disney restaurant, all searchable.
- **Get familiar with the Disney Dining Plan** (see page 205). If you're planning to stay at a Disney hotel, you'll need to figure out whether the plan will save you money on the meals you're interested in.

120 Days Before Your Trip

As your vacation approaches, it's time to make concrete arrangements for your days in the theme parks.

- **Save money on stroller rentals in the parks** (if you'll need one) by renting from a third-party company; see page 300 for our recommendations. You can also **save on wheelchair and ECV rentals** this way; see page 318 for details and recommendations.

60 Days Before Your Trip

Now you can start making restaurant, tour, spa, and other reservations.

- **Make reservations for table-service dining** beginning at 6 a.m. Eastern time to book online (disneyworld.disney.go.com/dining) or 7 a.m. to book by phone: ☎ 407-WDW-DINE (939-3463). If you're staying at a Walt Disney World resort, you can make reservations for up to 10 days of your trip starting today. You have a better chance of getting what you want by using the website instead of calling and by booking popular dining locations for later in your trip. See page 207 for more tips.

- **Make reservations for the following** online or by phone:
  Theme park tours: ☎ 407-WDW-TOUR (939-8687)
  Recreational activities such as boating: ☎ 407-WDW-PLAY (939-7529)
  Spa treatments: ☎ 407-WDW-SPAS (939-7727)
  Bibbidi Bobbidi Boutique: ☎ 407-WDW-STYL (939-7895)

- **Start a walking regimen** to prepare for the 7-10 miles per day you may be walking in the parks. See page 293 for more on that.

- **Start online check-in** at disneyworld.disney.go.com/trip/online-check-in, if you're staying at a Disney hotel. Doing this in advance means you'll be able to head directly to your hotel room upon arrival, without having to stop at the front desk.

45 Days Before Your Trip

- **Final payment for room-only reservations is due** if you book online within 45 days of arrival (payment of room-only reservations booked farther out isn't due until check-in).

- **Order your MagicBands** (see page 73), if desired.

- **If you're flying,** make arrangements for your transfer between the airport and your hotel (see page 329).

- **If you want to switch resorts or make more dining reservations,** now is a good time to check on both.

30 Days Out

- **Send your room request to Disney.** TouringPlans can do this for you automatically (see page 26) if you have a paid account. If you don't, you can call ☎ 407-939-1936 or do it via online chat.

- **Final payment for Disney vacation packages is due.**

- **Sign up for Disney's Disability Access Service (DAS)** if needed. See page 316 for more details.

- **Confirm park hours** and finish preliminary touring plans.

- **Download the Lines app** if you'd like to follow a touring plan and get updates while in the parks.

- **Arrange to stop delivery of mail and newspapers.**

- **Arrange for pet or house sitters.**

- **If you decide not to go to Disney World,** you typically have 30 days to cancel most Disney vacation packages without a penalty; room-only reservations can be canceled without a penalty until 8 days before your trip. See page 82 for a review of Disney's cancellation policies.

2 Weeks Out

- **Arrange grocery delivery to your resort** (see page 362).

- If you're flying to the US from another country, complete the **Advance Passenger Information and Secure Flight** (**APIS**) process at least 72 hours before your flight. You should be able to do this through your airline's website; otherwise, make sure your travel agent has your information. You'll need to provide the address where you'll be staying, so have that information handy when you complete the form.
- Check that you have enough prescription medication.
- If you're staying at a Disney Good Neighbor hotel, ensure your hotel reservation appears in the "Resort Hotel" section of the My Disney Experience app or website. This is how Disney knows you're eligible for Early Theme Park Entry or Extended Evening Theme Park Hours (see pages 34–36).

8 Days Out

- For 2026 arrivals, this is typically your last chance to **cancel Disney room-only reservations** without penalty. Call ☎ 407-W-DISNEY (407-934-7639).

7 Days Out

- If you're staying at a Disney resort, you can **begin purchasing Lightning Lane Multi Pass (LLMP) and Lightning Lane Single Pass (LLSP) and making ride reservations** for up to 14 days of your trip at 7 a.m. Eastern time on the My Disney Experience app.

6 Days Out

- Check the weather forecast.
- **Start packing.** Good shoes are especially important. It's always a good idea to be prepared for heat and rain.

4 Days Out

- **Purchase Disney's Memory Maker photo package** (see page 360) at least three days in advance to ensure that all photos are linked as soon as you arrive. You'll also get a discount if you buy your package in advance.

3 Days Out

- If you're staying off-site, you can **begin purchasing Lightning Lane Multi Pass (LLMP) and Lightning Lane Single Pass (LLSP) and making ride reservations** for up to the length of your date-based ticket at 7 a.m. Eastern time on the My Disney Experience app.

The Day Before

- Check in for your flight online.
- **Finish your Disney resort online check-in,** if you haven't already done so, at disneyworld.disney.go.com/trip/online-check-in.
- **Cancel any unneeded reservations** for dining, babysitting, or pet-sitting.
- Do one last check of park hours and weather.

PLANNING RESOURCES

DISNEY ONLINE: OFFICIAL AND OTHERWISE

A SUITE OF TECHNOLOGY ENHANCEMENTS to Disney's theme parks and hotels, known as **MyMagic+**, is designed to streamline your vacation. Central to this is the optional wristband (**MagicBand**) that functions as your admission ticket, hotel key, and method of payment. MyMagic+ also integrates with Disney's dining and ride reservation systems. It allows you to make detailed decisions about every day of your trip, sometimes months in advance, if you want to visit popular attractions and avoid long waits. Dining reservations, for instance, essentially require you to know the exact time you want to eat, and where, two months before you arrive.

The Walt Disney World website (disneyworld.disney.go.com) and the **My Disney Experience** (**MDE**) mobile app are the glue that binds all of these systems together. Because you must plan so much before you leave home, the next section covers the basics of both the app and the website. MagicBand information starts on page 73. Details on Disney's ride reservation systems—**Lightning Lane Multi Pass, Lightning Lane Single Pass,** and Disney's other way of waiting in lines, called **boarding groups** or **virtual queues**—start on page 52. Finally, Disney's itinerary-planning service, **Genie,** which you absolutely should *not* use, is described on pages 58–59.

My Disney Experience on the Disney World Website

The web version of MDE (disneyworld.disney.go.com/plan) allows you to make hotel, dining, ride, and some recreation reservations; buy admission; and get park hours, attraction information, and much more.

TECHNICAL PROBLEMS Disney World's website is so unreliable that most visitors are familiar with the various "broken" page screens, and some even keep track of how many times they encounter "Stitch ate my page" vs. "The Seven Dwarfs are working on it." If you run into technical issues on Disney's website, the first thing to do is try using your browser's private or incognito mode. Disney's website often places so many cookies on your computer that it breaks its own systems. If that doesn't work and human intervention is required, call ☎ 407-939-4357 in the US or ☎ 0800-169-0749 in the UK for help.

Be careful about when you call for help if something goes wrong. Days when big events or new promotions get released can be plagued by multi-hour waits on the phones. On most regular days, though, your wait will be minimal.

BEFORE YOU BEGIN Set aside at least 30–40 minutes to complete the process of setting up your vacation in My Disney Experience. Make sure you have the following items on hand:

- A valid admission ticket or confirmation number for everyone in your group
- Your hotel reservation number, if you're staying on-site (including the Swan, Swan Reserve, Dolphin, and Disney Springs hotels)
- A computer, smartphone, or tablet connected to the internet
- An email account that you can access easily while traveling
- The dates, times, and confirmation numbers of any dining or recreation reservations you've already made

If you're coordinating travel plans with friends or family who live elsewhere, you'll also need the following information:

- The names and (optional) email addresses of the people you're traveling with
- The dates and times of any dining or recreation reservations they've made

GETTING STARTED Go to disneyworld.disney.go.com/plan and click "Create Account." You'll be asked for your email address, along with your name, billing address, and birth date. (Disney uses your billing

PLANNING RESOURCES

address to send your hotel-reservation information, if applicable, and to charge your credit card for anything you purchase.)

Once you've created an account, the website will display a page with links to other steps in the planning process. These steps are described next. If the website shows you different screens and options when you sign in, click the "My Disney Experience" icon in the upper-right corner of the page and look for similar wording.

DISNEY HOTEL INFORMATION If you're staying at a Disney hotel, select "Resort Hotel," then "Link Reservation." Enter your reservation number. This associates your MDE account with your hotel stay in Disney's computer systems. If you've booked a travel package that includes theme park admission, Disney's system will automatically link the admission to your MDE account, allowing you to skip the "Linking Tickets" step. If you've booked a Disney hotel through a third-party site like Priceline, that site should send you a Disney reservation number to use here. It can take up to a week for third-party sites to send Disney your information, so be patient and plan ahead.

REGISTER FRIENDS AND FAMILY Click the "Family & Friends" icon, then enter the names and ages of everyone traveling with you. You can do this later, too, but you'll need this information when you make your dining and ride reservations.

LINKING TICKETS Before you can make some types of reservations, you will need to have purchased theme park tickets for every member of your group and linked them to MDE profiles.

If you haven't purchased your tickets, come back to this section when you have. Once you've purchased tickets, click the "Park Tickets" widget, then click on "Link Tickets," and follow the instructions.

MAKING DINING RESERVATIONS In My Disney Experience, click the "Dining" icon, then the "Make a Reservation" link. (You may have to reenter your travel dates.) First, you'll need to indicate how many people are dining. Then you'll choose a date and a time range for when you'd like to dine. A list of every available Walt Disney World dining location will be displayed. Use the filtering criteria at the top of the page to narrow down the list. Once you've settled on a restaurant, click the time of the reservation you'd like to book. To complete your reservation, you'll also need to enter a credit card number to hold your reservation. If you want to make other dining reservations, you'll need to repeat this process for each one.

If you know the restaurant where you want to eat, you can search for it in the search bar at the top, then click "Check Availability" on its page (rather than scrolling through the whole list of every available dining location).

unofficial **TIP**
Download the MDE app several weeks before your trip. Tap around until you know how to find wait times, make reservations, and anything else you might want to do during your park days.

My Disney Experience Mobile App

In addition to its website, Disney offers an app called My Disney Experience. It includes park hours; attraction operating hours, descriptions, and wait times; restaurant hours, descriptions, and menus; the ability to make dining and ride reservations; GPS-based directions; counter-service meal ordering; locations of park photographers and restrooms; wait times for buses if you're at a resort; and more.

TOURINGPLANS WEBSITE

IN ADDITION TO THIS GUIDE AND DISNEY'S RESOURCES, we recommend that you visit our sister website, **TouringPlans.com**. The blog posts there can keep you up-to-date on breaking news and even more data for your Walt Disney World vacation.

TouringPlans.com complements and supplements the information in this book, and it provides real-time personalized services that are impossible to build into a book. The book is your comprehensive reference guide; TouringPlans.com is your personal concierge. You can sign up for free at touringplans.com/walt-disney-world/join/basic.

With that free access, you'll be able to create custom touring plans, follow them in the parks, and get updates to them if conditions change while you're there. You'll also find current information on attractions, shows, restaurants, crowds, park hours, and more. A few of the site's features require a $25-per-year subscription fee to access, such as a detailed, day-by-day crowd calendar and a service that sends your hotel-room request directly to Disney.

Below is a brief rundown of some things you'll find on the site:

TICKET DISCOUNTS A free, customizable search helps you find the cheapest tickets for your specific trip dates and needs.

CUSTOM TOURING PLANS Some of the best and most well-tested touring plans are found in the *Unofficial Guides*. They've been used by millions of families over the years, usually with excellent results. That said, they often depend on arriving at the park early, and they're built to accommodate the general public. Your family or traveling party might want to visit different attractions or tour only in the afternoon and evening. In those cases, and for others with unique circumstances, you can build a custom touring plan online.

A DETAILED 365-DAY CROWD CALENDAR FOR EACH THEME PARK Subscribers can see which parks should be the least crowded every day of their trip, using a 1–10 scale. You can also view historical crowd data and check the accuracy of the predictions.

HOTEL-ROOM VIEWS AND ROOM-REQUEST SERVICE TouringPlans.com has photos of the views from every Disney-owned hotel room in Walt Disney World—more than 35,000 images in all—and it'll give you the exact wording to use to request a specific room. If you're a subscriber, it'll even automatically email your request to Disney 30 days before you arrive.

Disney tries to accommodate your request, but sometimes it can't make it work. Just remember that it's a request and not a guarantee.

ANSWERS TO YOUR TRIP-PLANNING QUESTIONS The TouringPlans online community includes tens of thousands of Disney fans and repeat travelers willing to help with your vacation plans. Ask questions in the forum and offer your own helpful tips.

LINES APP This in-park app, designed to accompany you in the park, provides ride and park information that Disney doesn't, including:

TOURINGPLANS.COM BENEFITS

BENEFIT	NO ACCOUNT	BASIC (FREE) ACCESS	SUBSCRIBER ACCESS
• Online articles and resources	•	•	•
• Ticket Calculator	•	•	•
• Menu search	•	•	•
• Access to your custom touring plans in the Lines mobile app	•	•	•
• Room Finder (photos of the view from every room at Disney's resorts)	•	•	ad-free
• Access to TouringPlans forums	read only	contribute	ad-free
• Crowd calendar access	3 days	3 days	365 days
• Planning Dashboard (select parks, make notes, and get email reminders)		•	•
• Create custom touring plans for future dates		•	•
• Optimize your custom touring plans while touring		•	•
• Access to more than 100 premium touring plans			•
• Hotel-room request service			•
• View posted and TouringPlans' predicted actual wait times			•
• Access to Lines Chat on your mobile device			•

- **Predicted and actual wait times at attractions.** Lines is the only Disney app that displays both posted wait times and the estimated actual wait times. The wait time posted outside of a ride is sometimes much longer than the actual wait time.
- **"Ride now or wait" recommendations.** Lines shows you whether ride wait times are likely to get longer or shorter.
- **Real-time updates while you're in a park.** Lines automatically updates your custom touring plan to reflect actual crowd conditions at a given moment. You can also restart your plan and add or change attractions, breaks, meals, and more.

The *Unofficial Guide* and TouringPlans.com, along with the Lines app, are designed to work together as a comprehensive planning and touring resource.

This mom from Missouri used all the tools available to her:

> The Unofficial Guide *was the perfect place to start planning our vacation (actually our honeymoon). After reading the book, I had a good idea of what hotels I was interested in, and I had must-do and must-eat places somewhat picked out. I then took the knowledge from the book and switched to the website to personalize our touring plans and use as a reference when needed. The book and the website together made our trip INCREDIBLE.*

Our website, **TheUnofficialGuides.com,** is dedicated to news about our guidebooks and features a blog with posts from *Unofficial Guide* authors. You can also sign up for the **"Unofficial Guides Newsletter,"** which contains more travel tips. We also recommend that you check out the following:

1. **Walt Disney World Resort vacation-planning videos.** You can watch online videos advertising Walt Disney World's offerings at plandisney.disney.go.com/plandisney-video-library.
2. *Guide for Guests with Disabilities.* An overview of services and options for guests with disabilities is available at disneyworld.disney.go.com/guest-services/guests-with-disabilities, at Guest Relations when entering the parks, at resort front desks, and at wheelchair-rental areas (for locations, see the "Services" sidebar in each theme park chapter).

Other Recommended Websites

Searching online for Disney World information is like navigating a giant haystack for a tiny needle: You may find a lot of junk before you get to what you need. Before you decide to just burn it all away, check out these websites, which we've found to be the most helpful and user-friendly.

BEST Q&A SITE planDisney (formerly the Walt Disney World's Moms Panel) is made up of Disney World veterans chosen from among more than 10,000 applicants each year. The panelists have a website, plandisney.disney.go.com, where they offer tips and discuss how to plan a Disney World vacation. Several panelists have specialized experience in areas such as runDisney or traveling with sports groups. Some speak languages other than English, too. Search for previously answered questions, or submit your own.

BEST MONEY-SAVING SITE MouseSavers (mousesavers.com) keeps an updated list of discounts that can be used at Disney World resorts, separated into categories such as "For Everyone," "For Annual Pass Holders," and "For Disney Visa Card Holders." Anyone who calls or books online can use a current discount. The savings can be considerable—as much as 40%. The site also offers deals on tickets, rental cars, and non-Disney hotels in the area, along with a calendar showing when Disney sales typically launch.

BEST SITE FOR CAR-RENTAL DEALS AutoSlash (autoslash.com) will search its database of over 1,000 current coupon and discount codes for every car company in Orlando to find you the best deal—and they continue tracking after you book so you are assured the lowest rate possible. See pages 331–334 for more on renting a car for your Disney World vacation.

BEST DISNEY DINING RESERVATION FINDERS You'll sometimes find that the one dining reservation you care most about is the one you can't get. There are paid and free tools to alert you when a reservation becomes available. If you want to stick to free options, **Mouse Dining** (mousedining.com) is good for frequent email-checkers. The **Stakeout** app is better if you like an in-app experience (but you only get one free search). **Thrill Data** (see below) has unlimited free searches, but in our experience has returned available reservations way outside of our requested times.

MORE DISNEY DATA Thrill Data (thrill-data.com) has an amazing amount of Disney data, often presented in different ways than what you'll find at Touring Plans or in the Lines app. Because different people consume data in different ways, you may find one or the other more to your personal taste. Some of our favorite Thrill Data visualizations include virtual queue callbacks—so you can plan ahead for when your boarding group might get called—and Lightning Lane reservation availability for every attraction 21 days out.

BEST DISNEY DISCUSSION BOARDS There are tons of these; among the most active boards are **disboards.com; forums.wdwmagic.com; forum.touringplans.com;** and, for Brits, **thedibb.co.uk** (*DIBB* stands for "Disney Information Bulletin Board").

WHEN *to* GO *to* WALT DISNEY WORLD

SELECTING THE TIME OF YEAR FOR YOUR VISIT

WALT DISNEY WORLD IS BUSIEST from the weekend before Christmas Day until the first full weekend in January. The next-busiest times are spring break (early March–early April, plus the week before Easter when Easter is later); Thanksgiving week; and February during Presidents' Day and Mardi Gras. You'll also see shorter bursts of crowds on three-day weekends, such as Columbus Day and Veterans Day. Jersey Week, typically around the second week of November, sees an influx of families from the East Coast.

The least busy time *historically* is Labor Day through early October. In addition, the last two weeks of October and the first week of November are usually less crowded than average, as are the weeks after Thanksgiving and before Christmas. The weeks between late April and Memorial Day have lower crowds than the weeks on either side.

The biggest rule of thumb is that Walt Disney World is less crowded (and less expensive) when most kids are in school. That said, summer heat has become more and more effective at driving guests away from visiting Orlando in June, July, and August. Summer has almost

WALT DISNEY WORLD CLIMATE												
	JAN	FEB	MAR	APR	MAY	JUN	JUL	AUG	SEP	OCT	NOV	DEC
AVERAGE DAILY HIGH												
	70°F	73°F	77°F	82°F	86°F	88°F	89°F	89°F	86°F	82°F	76°F	72°F
AVERAGE DAILY MAX HEAT INDEX (COMBINED EFFECT OF HEAT AND HUMIDITY)												
	70°F	73°F	78°F	85°F	93°F	103°F	109°F	110°F	105°F	92°F	77°F	72°F
AVERAGE DAILY TEMPERATURE												
	60°F	63°F	67°F	72°F	77°F	80°F	81°F	81°F	79°F	74°F	67°F	63°F
AVERAGE DAILY HUMIDITY												
	71%	68%	65%	64%	65%	75%	79%	80%	80%	73%	71%	73%
AVERAGE MONTHLY RAINFALL												
	2.2"	2.0"	2.5"	2.2"	2.8"	6.2"	6.2"	6.7"	5.6"	2.7"	1.4"	2.0"
NUMBER OF DAYS OF RAIN PER MONTH												
	5	5	5	5	7	14	16	17	14	8	4	4

Source: climate-data.org

become the new offseason. If you can tolerate the heat, it's a newly enticing time to visit. Disney has also been releasing more deals for the summer season to tempt visitors.

In short: Disney World can be busy at any time, thanks to special events and targeted discounts, and you'll need to look beyond the time of year to pinpoint the least crowded dates. For a calendar of scheduled events, visit theugseries.com/wdwevents.

DON'T FORGET AUGUST Kids go back to school pretty early in Florida (and in a lot of other places). This makes mid- to late August a good time for families who can't vacation during the school year . . . and don't mind the oppressive heat.

A New Jersey mother of two school-age children spells it out:

> *The end of August is the PERFECT time to go (just watch out for hurricanes; it's the season). There were virtually no wait times, 20 minutes at the most.*

PLANNING FOR FLORIDA WEATHER

> *Why is the world's best theme park in the world's worst climate?*
>
> —A reader from Oregon

LONG BEFORE WALT DISNEY WORLD EXISTED, tourists visited Florida year-round to enjoy the warmer climate. The best weather months are generally November through March (see the table on the previous page). Fall is typically dry, while spring and summer are wet. Rain is possible anytime, usually in the form of scattered thunderstorms; an entire day lost to steady rain is rare.

SUMMER TEMPERATURES CAN FEEL LIKE 120°F If your weather app says it's 95°F in Orlando, be aware that it's warmer when you're standing in the sun, and hotter still if you are on blacktop or wearing dark-colored clothing.

Florida's humidity makes the heat feel worse because it prevents your sweat from evaporating to cool you off. During summer in the Magic Kingdom, you'll commonly experience Heat Indexes ("feels-like" temperatures) above 110°F, and we've measured highs of 122°F. How hot is that? A steak cooked rare is considered done at 130°F.

Be prepared for the heat, or you will pay the price. Organize your day so that you have frequent indoor breaks for attractions, shows, or meals and snacks. Stay hydrated—always have access to water! I also like to carry electrolyte packets (like Liquid IV) and mix them into my water once a day if I've been sweating a lot. And with all the humidity, a neck fan or handheld fan can make an incredible amount of difference in how you feel throughout the day.

RAIN HAPPENS A rainy day at Disney is still better than a sunny day at home, but it can be a pain if you're not prepared for it. Evaluate whether everyone in your party would prefer ponchos or rain jackets to wear around a rainy park (I like the coverage of ponchos, but my family find them to be too clingy). Invest in a portable umbrella that is built to withstand wind as well as rain (it can also provide shade).

Wear shoes that will dry out quickly and be comfortable even when wet. If I know we're headed into a rainy day, I'll pack a fresh pair of socks for every family member in a ziplock bag inside my park bag. Fresh, dry footwear in the middle of the day is a luxury. On particularly wet days, you could even invest in a locker rental. Put dry shoes and socks for everyone in the locker and change into them when things clear up or when you can't stand the soggy footwear anymore.

CROWD CALENDAR

DISNEY WORLD'S ATTENDANCE has been almost 50 million guests per year since the pandemic—an average of around 137,000 guests per day. That makes tips for avoiding crowds invaluable. Besides which month or week to visit, you should also think about the best park to visit on each day of your stay. For example, when it's not "party season" in the Magic Kingdom (parties close the park early periodically from August through December), it's almost always most crowded on Mondays, when many families begin their weeklong vacations.

Disney regularly tinkers with things like resort discounts, park capacity, and park hours to entice more people to visit or adjust capacity if attendance is looking sparse. Because of that, it's not possible to include an accurate calendar of crowds in this book; it would be outdated before it even went to print. To stay updated, you can find a calendar covering the next year at touringplans.com /walt-disney-world/crowd-calendar. For each date, you'll find a crowd-level index based on a 1–10 scale, with 1 being least crowded and 10 being most crowded. The calendar is based on how long you'll wait in line and takes into account all holidays, special events, and more, as described in the next section. It's not always 100% accurate, but it can give you an idea of general crowd trends.

There is a subscription fee for full access, but owners of the current edition of this guide are eligible for a discount on the subscription. See page 26 for more information about TouringPlans.com.

Just because a park is predicted to be a crowd level 1 or 2 doesn't mean it will be empty—even on a "slow" day, you will certainly see posted wait times of 1 hour or more for popular rides such as **Seven Dwarfs Mine Train** and **Tron Lightcycle/Run** in the Magic Kingdom, **Avatar Flight of Passage** in Disney's Animal Kingdom, **Remy's Ratatouille Adventure** and **Frozen Ever After** in EPCOT, and **Star Wars: Rise of the Resistance** and **Slinky Dog Dash** in DHS.

HOW TOURINGPLANS DETERMINES CROWD LEVELS AND BEST DAYS Several factors contribute to the models used to predict both crowd levels and the best days to visit each theme park.

Data used to predict crowd levels:

- Recent wait times, which are given high importance
- Historical theme park hours from the same time period in past years
- Future hotel-room bookings in the Orlando area
- Disney's special-events calendar (for example, the Magic Kingdom's Halloween and Christmas parties)
- Federal legal holidays in the United States
- Public-school schedules, weighted by distance from Florida and tourism rates

TouringPlans also collects thousands of wait times from rides in Walt Disney World daily, including posted and actual times. *Popular Science* did a nice article several years ago on the data science behind their predictions; read it at popsci.com/touring-plan-app-disney-lines.

SPRING BREAK AND HOLIDAY CROWDS

FOR MANY FAMILIES, visiting Disney World during a busy time is unavoidable. The good news is that with the right knowledge and a solid strategy, you can still have a fantastic trip—even in the crowds. Don't stress too much if your vacation dates align with peak times. This book is packed with tips to help you navigate the parks and make the most of your visit no matter the crowd level.

Disney World sees its highest demand during holiday periods and school breaks because that's when most people have the flexibility to travel. If you're planning to visit during spring break or a major holiday, it's important to understand that the parks have a limited guest capacity. Disney prioritizes park entry for guests staying at Disney hotels and guests with date-specific tickets purchased in advance. In the post-pandemic era, it's rare for parks to fill up, but it does happen, especially around New Year's.

Christmas and New Year's at the Theme Parks

Don't expect to see every attraction at a park in a single day during this busiest time of the year. That said, **Disney's Animal Kingdom** is usually the least crowded park during the holidays, especially New Year's Eve, when it closes earlier than the other parks. **EPCOT** is another good option. With about twice the acreage and typically lower crowds than the Magic Kingdom, it offers more space to spread out and plenty of non-queue activities to help you avoid being overwhelmed by wait times.

New Year's Eve is the busiest day of the year in the Magic Kingdom. To manage the crowds, Disney stages its New Year's Eve fireworks on both December 30 and December 31. This gives you the option to enjoy the show without the full New Year's Eve crowd—or to catch fireworks in multiple parks. If you stay until midnight on the 31st, be prepared for significant delays getting back to your hotel by bus or car—it can take 1–3 hours.

To make things easier, consider booking a room at a Magic Kingdom monorail resort with walking path access (the **Contemporary** or **Grand Floridian**). While these accommodations will be pricey, the convenience is unmatched.

If you're visiting EPCOT or the Studios for New Year's Eve, we recommend the **BoardWalk Inn, BoardWalk Villas, Yacht Club, Beach Club, Swan, Swan Reserve,** or **Dolphin**. All are within walking distance of those parks, saving you the long waits for buses or the Skyliner, which will have a long wait even when running at full capacity.

THE WALT DISNEY WORLD CALENDAR

DISNEY CELEBRATES SPECIAL EVENTS throughout the year. Some events commemorate major holidays, while others are designed by Disney to boost attendance during otherwise slow times of year.

JANUARY Usually held the second weekend after New Year's, the **Walt Disney World Marathon** attracts thousands of runners and their families every year. It's scheduled for January 7–11 in 2026. You can find information on all Disney running events at rundisney.com. Also see page 512 for more on runDisney events.

Another winter event is the **EPCOT International Festival of the Arts.** Running from the second or third full week of January until almost the end of February, the festival (which is included as part of your park admission) highlights the visual, performing, and culinary arts, with live performances, creative cuisine, and workshops where you can build your own creative skills. See pages 219, 221, and 511 for more information.

FEBRUARY Black History Month is celebrated throughout Walt Disney World with displays, artisans, storytellers, and entertainers.

In 2026, **Presidents' Day** is Monday, February 16, and **Mardi Gras** is Tuesday, February 17. That combination plus **Valentine's Day** will create a very crowded weekend and first half of the week.

MARCH The **EPCOT International Flower & Garden Festival,** which runs March–May, showcases exotic floral displays—the 30 million blooms from some 1,200 species will make your eyes pop. The festival also features food and beverage kiosks, making it more like fall's International Food & Wine Festival (see August, below), only with impressive Disney-themed topiaries.

APRIL Easter is April 5, 2026. That's going to lead to a condensed spring break season from mid-March through early April. Expect crowds to be much higher during that period than in the weeks later in April.

MAY Memorial Day (Monday, May 25, 2026) signals the official start of summer and family vacation season. But realistically, locals are more likely than out-of-town visitors to attend during this long weekend.

JUNE Gay Days, an unofficial gathering of LGBTQ people from around the world, has been happening annually since 1991. Gay Days can draw more than 100,000 visitors to the Orlando area. For more information, visit gaydays.com.

JULY July Fourth used to be one of the most crowded seasons of the year, but thanks to the incredibly hot weather and the increasing interest in other parts of the year, that is no longer the case. In fact, this may be the least crowded major holiday other than Labor Day (see September).

AUGUST The **EPCOT International Food & Wine Festival** is usually held from August to late November and represents cuisines from around the world. It used to include demonstrations, wine seminars, tastings, and more, but recently it's been more about food booths and a concert series. See page 34, 218, 221–222, and 511 for more information.

Mickey's Not-So-Scary Halloween Party, in the Magic Kingdom, is typically held on select nights between mid-August and November 1, 7 p.m.–midnight. Ticket holders can get into the park starting at 4 p.m. The festivities include trick-or-treating in costume, parades, live music, stage shows, and a fireworks show. See page 75 for more information on this popular event.

SEPTEMBER The weeks before and after **Labor Day** (the first Monday of the month) tend to be the least crowded time to visit Disney World.

OCTOBER Indigenous Peoples' Day is on October 12, 2026. Many schools organize fall breaks or long weekends in early or mid-October, and this can lead to larger crowds during this part of the month.

NOVEMBER The **Wine and Dine Half-Marathon** early in this month revolves around a 13.1-mile race that ends with a nighttime party amid the EPCOT International Food & Wine Festival. **Veterans Day** and **Jersey Week** (when many East Coast schools have several days or an entire week off) also occur in early November, significantly boosting crowds for a week. **Thanksgiving,** (Thursday, November 26, 2026) also creates a crush of crowds that disappear very quickly following the holiday.

The annual **Disney Parks Christmas Day Parade,** televised on December 25, is usually filmed in the Magic Kingdom in November. The parade ties up pedestrian traffic on Main Street, U.S.A., all day. In the past few years, taping has happened between November 9 and 12.

DECEMBER EPCOT's holiday celebration, the **International Festival of the Holidays,** typically runs from late November to late December and includes food booths similar to those found in World Showcase during the Festival of the Arts, the Food & Wine Festival, and the Flower & Garden Festival.

Disney's Very Merry Christmas Party takes place in the Magic Kingdom on select evenings in November and December, 7 p.m.–midnight (after regular hours; ticket holders can get into the park starting at 4 p.m.). The event includes attractions; stage shows featuring Disney characters; unlimited complimentary snacks and drinks, a holiday-themed fireworks show, carolers, "a magical snowfall on Main Street," white lights on Cinderella Castle, and live entertainment.

Jollywood Nights debuted in Hollywood Studios in 2023 as counterprogramming to the Magic Kingdom's wildly popular Christmas party. The DHS event is focused on food and entertainment, but there are no complimentary snacks like at Magic Kingdom.

EARLY THEME PARK ENTRY

EARLY THEME PARK ENTRY (aka Early Entry or ETPE) is a valuable perk for guests staying at **Disney resort hotels,** including the **Swan, Dolphin,** and **Swan Reserve; Shades of Green;** the **Four Seasons; Disney Springs hotels;** and **Hilton hotels in Bonnet Creek.** This benefit allows eligible guests to enter any Disney theme park 30 minutes before official park opening every day. While 30 minutes may not seem like much, it can make the difference between a smooth, enjoyable park day and one spent in long lines.

WHAT'S REQUIRED? To use Early Entry, you'll need a valid theme park ticket or MagicBand, and your hotel or resort reservation needs to be linked to your My Disney Experience account.

DISNEY SPRINGS AND GOOD NEIGHBOR HOTELS Guests at eligible Disney Springs hotels and Disney Good Neighbor hotels (see table on page 80) are also eligible for Early Entry. But Disney's computer systems sometimes fail to recognize these reservations, which can lead to confusion at the park entrance. To avoid issues, make sure your reservation number is linked in MDE at least one week before your trip. Be prepared with proof of your stay, such as a hotel key or confirmation email, in case the system doesn't sync.

If a problem arises at the gate, cast members can often resolve it with verification, but your experience may vary. We've heard stories of families being asked to call hotels to get confirmation upon entry. On one of our recent stays at the Swan, scanning in for Early Entry worked every day of the trip other than the very last one at EPCOT. On that morning, the cast member just asked us what our hotel was and to produce a key. After that, we were allowed in.

HOW DOES EARLY ENTRY WORK? Early Entry allows eligible guests to enter any park 30 minutes before the general public, with select attractions open during this time. In the Magic Kingdom, for example, you should find attractions open in Fantasyland and Tomorrowland. In Hollywood Studios and EPCOT, most attractions with lines (not character greetings) are open during Early Entry. In Animal Kingdom, all attractions with lines, other than Kilimanjaro Safaris, open early.

To make the most of this valuable benefit, arrive at the park entrance 60–90 minutes before official opening. The earlier you arrive, the closer you'll be to the front of the Early Entry crowd. Note that Disney often opens the gates slightly (or significantly) earlier than the 30-minute mark, giving you even more time in the park.

During holidays and other busy times, some parks open to regular guests at 8 a.m. and Early Entry begins at 7:30 a.m., so you'll need to be at the park entrance no later than 7 a.m. You won't be alone in doing this, but because relatively few people are willing to get up that early for a theme park, your first few hours in the parks will be (wait for it) magical.

How Early Entry Affects Attendance at the Theme Parks

Early Entry is offered at every park, every day, giving resort guests a valuable opportunity to get a head start on popular attractions. Off-site guests, on the other hand, will face longer lines at headliners as they enter the park after on-site guests have already begun their day.

If you're staying at an eligible resort, remember these three things about Early Entry:

1. The Magic Kingdom has more attractions open for Early Entry than any other park, but few are super-headliners. As a result, crowds don't disperse as much as in other parks. Downtime or delays early in the day at Seven Dwarfs Mine Train can significantly reduce the value of Early Entry here.

2. Hollywood Studios doesn't have as many rides as the Magic Kingdom, but the whole park is open for Early Entry, and there are many high-wait attractions to choose from. That helps spread out crowds and means you have many ways to save time. We think Hollywood Studios offers the best value for Early Entry of any park.

3. Early Entry is a great advantage at top attractions, and many thousands of guests will know that. If you're heading for a newer or very popular ride, arrive even earlier than you might think necessary to be at the front of the Early Entry crowd.

WHAT'S THE CATCH? The disadvantage of Early Entry for on-site guests is the early wake-up time required to make the most of it. For off-site guests, the disadvantage is more significant: They're guaranteed to be behind thousands of on-site guests at every park, every day. On crowded days, popular attractions that are open during Early Entry, such as Avatar Flight of Passage, will easily have lines that are over an hour long by the time the first off-site guest even sets foot in the park.

To help mitigate the impact of Early Entry on off-site guests, this book includes off-site versions of most touring plans. However, even with an optimized plan, off-site guests should expect to spend several more hours in line each day compared to on-site guests due to the head start Early Entry provides.

EXTENDED EVENING THEME PARK HOURS

EXTENDED EVENING THEME PARK HOURS (EETPH) is a post-closing perk that is similar to Early Entry but is offered far less frequently and to a much smaller group of guests. Available only to guests staying at **Deluxe or Disney Vacation Club (DVC) resorts,** EETPH typically occurs one or two nights per week at select parks. During these events, eligible guests can enjoy two extra hours in the park after it closes to the general public. For example, if the Magic Kingdom closes at 9 p.m., EETPH allows Deluxe and DVC guests to stay and enjoy attractions until 11 p.m.

During EETPH, Disney sets up checkpoints throughout the park, such as at the entrance to each attraction, to verify that only eligible guests participate. Cast members will scan your MagicBand or ticket to confirm your resort stay.

The main advantage of EETPH is that a very limited number of guests qualify, resulting in exceptionally short lines. In late December 2022, we managed to see 10 attractions in the Magic Kingdom during EETPH, waiting a total of 31 minutes in line. In comparison, those same 10 attractions would've taken almost 7 hours to see during that day. In EPCOT, it's a little harder to take advantage of the extra hours because the major attractions are so far apart. And on the rare occasions when Animal Kingdom offers EETPH, Expedition Everest and Avatar Flight of Passage are typically walk-on attractions for the second hour.

WALT DISNEY WORLD PHONE NUMBERS

WDW PHONE NUMBERS

DISNEY RESORTS

- All-Star Movies Resort ☎ 407-939-7000
- All-Star Music Resort ☎ 407-939-6000
- All-Star Sports Resort ☎ 407-939-5000
- BoardWalk Inn and Villas ☎ 407-939-6200
- Caribbean Beach Resort ☎ 407-934-3400
- Contemporary Resort and Bay Lake Tower ☎ 407-824-1000
- Coronado Springs Resort ☎ 407-939-1000
- Fort Wilderness Resort & Campground ☎ 407-824-2900
- Grand Floridian Resort & Spa/Grand Floridian Villas ☎ 407-824-3000
- Old Key West Resort ☎ 407-827-7700
- Polynesian Village Resort ☎ 407-824-2000
- Polynesian Village Villas ☎ 407-824-3500
- Pop Century Resort ☎ 407-938-4000
- Port Orleans Resort–French Quarter ☎ 407-934-5000
- Port Orleans Resort–Riverside ☎ 407-934-6000
- Riviera Resort ☎ 407-828-7030
- Saratoga Springs Resort & Spa, Treehouse Villas ☎ 407-827-1100
- Shades of Green ☎ 407-824-3400 or 407-824-3600
- Walt Disney World Dolphin ☎ 407-934-4000
- Walt Disney World Swan ☎ 407-934-3000
- Walt Disney World Swan Reserve ☎ 407-934-3000
- Yacht Club Resort ☎ 407-934-7000
- Wilderness Lodge/Boulder Ridge & Copper Creek Villas ☎ 407-824-3200

GENERAL

- Blizzard Beach Information ☎ 407-560-3400
- General Information ☎ 407-824-4321 or 407-824-2222
- General Information for Deaf and Hard-of-Hearing Guests (TTY) ☎ 407-827-5141
- Convention Information ☎ 321-939-7129
- Disney Institute ☎ 321-939-4600
- Disney Springs Information ☎ 407-939-5277
- Group Camping ☎ 407-939-7807
- Guided Tour Information ☎ 407-939-8687
- Guided VIP Solo Tours ☎ 407-560-4033
- Lost and Found *(for articles lost yesterday or before; for same day, go to Guest Relations, front desk, or disneyworld.com/lostandfound)* ☎ 407-824-4245
- Merchandise Guest Services ☎ 877-560-6477
- Outdoor Recreation Reservations and Information ☎ 407-939-7529
- Resort Dining ☎ 407-939-3463

continued on next page

WDW PHONE NUMBERS (continued)

GENERAL (continued)

- Security ☎ 407-560-7959 (routine); ☎ 407-560-1990 (urgent)
- Special Requests for Guests with Disabilities ☎ 407-560-2547 (voice)
- Typhoon Lagoon Information ☎ 407-939-5277
- Walt Disney Travel Company ☎ 407-939-6244
- Walt Disney World Ticket Inquiries ☎ 407-934-7639
- Weather Information ☎ 407-827-4545

HEALTHCARE AND EMERGENCIES

- Advent Health Centra Care (urgent-care clinic) ☎ 407-390-1888 (Kissimmee); ☎ 407-934-2273 (Lake Buena Vista); ☎ 407-291-8975 (Universal–Dr. Phillips)
- Wrecker Service (7 a.m.–11 p.m.; if closed, call Security) ☎ 407-824-0976

RECREATION AND ENTERTAINMENT

- AMC Disney Springs 24 Dine-In Theatres ☎ 407-827-1308
- ESPN Wide World of Sports Complex ☎ 407-939-1500
- Fantasia Gardens and Fairways Miniature Golf ☎ 407-560-4870
- Golf Reservations and Information ☎ 407-939-4653
- House of Blues Tickets and Information ☎ 407-934-2583
- Winter Summerland Miniature Golf ☎ 407-560-3000

RESERVATIONS

- Accommodations/Central Reservations ☎ 407-934-7639
- Advance Dining Reservations ☎ 407-939-3463
- Car Rentals ☎ 407-824-3470, ext. 1
- Telecommunication for the Deaf Reservations (TTY) ☎ 407-827-5141

WDW ADDRESSES

GENERAL INFORMATION
WDW Guest Communications
PO Box 10040, Lake Buena Vista, FL 32830-0040
☎ 407-560-2544
wdw.guest.communications@disneyworld.com or guest.services@disneyworld.com
General online help: disneyworld.disney.go.com/help/email

CONVENTION AND BANQUET INFORMATION (aka Group Sales)
Walt Disney World Resort South
PO Box 10000, Lake Buena Vista, FL 32830-1000
☎ 321-939-7129; disneymeetings.com

DISNEY IMAGINATION CAMPUS (youth programs)
☎ 321-939-7560; disneycampus.com

WALT DISNEY WORLD TICKET MAIL ORDER
☎ 407-566-4985; ticket.inquiries@disneyworld.com

PART 3
MAKING *the* MOST *of* YOUR TIME

KEY QUESTIONS ANSWERED IN THIS CHAPTER

- How long does it take to see Walt Disney World? *(see below)*
- What are standby queues, boarding groups/virtual queues, Lightning Lane Multi Pass, Lightning Lane Single Pass, and Lightning Lane Premier Pass, and how do I use them? *(page 51)*
- What are the six most important tips for avoiding lines at Walt Disney World? *(page 43)*
- What are touring plans, and how do I use them? *(page 46)*

ALLOCATING VACATION TIME

FINDING THE RIGHT PACE

A WHIRLWIND TOUR of Disney's four theme parks and two water parks takes at least **six full days** and a level of physical and emotional stamina typically only needed for running a marathon. A family from New Jersey thought we were exaggerating just to make sure people were a little prepared. But when they returned from vacation, they sent us this note remarking on their progress, as tracked by their fitness app:

> *Never have we ever closed so many circles! I was astounded that every park day we logged between 25,000 and 30,000 steps!*

You'll quickly figure out that at Walt Disney World, less is more. Take the parks in small doses, with time for swimming and/or rest and relaxation in between. Forcing yourself to go too fast or too long will just make everyone cranky and tired. It's exhausting to get up with the sun and run around a theme park for 10–12 hours day after day. Sooner or later (usually sooner), you'll hit a wall. To avoid that, use one or both of these tips:

1. Take at least a morning off (preferably an entire day) after two consecutive days in the parks.
2. Return to your hotel for at least a 2-hour break each day you're in the parks.

Getting to the park early is often the key to avoiding long waits, so have a balance of early days, late nights, and time off.

This Virginia family recommends taking it slow and easy:

We spent eight days in Disney, and it was totally worth it. A longer trip, believe it or not, eliminates the happy death march—we cut our stress by 90%. Each day, we took some sort of break: a morning swim, an afternoon nap, a sit-down snack in a restaurant. The end result was that the kids got to see/ride everything they wanted without exhausting themselves (or us)—or spending most of their days in line. And we had almost zero tantrums (really!).

WHICH PARK SHOULD YOU SEE FIRST?

IT DEPENDS! You'll want to consider the time of year you visit, the length of your stay, and who you're traveling with.

If you start in the **Magic Kingdom,** you start your trip off with the wow factor. This is the classic Disney day. But you could be overwhelmed trying to cram this busiest park into your first day when you're still adjusting to Disney vacation mode.

EPCOT is designed to help you learn and to see and appreciate other perspectives. It has great food and plenty of entertainment that doesn't require waiting in lines. But it's also the park that requires the most walking and could wear you out before your vacation has even really begun.

Disney's Hollywood Studios has some of the best individual attractions of any park, which can make it a hit with the thrill seekers or *Star Wars* fans in your family. But it also has the highest average wait times, which add up to a significant risk of starting your vacation on a frustrating note.

Animal Kingdom is the most relaxed of any park—and the hottest. You could start with the relaxing day or save it for later in your vacation when you need a breather.

HOURS OF OPERATION

THE DISNEY WORLD WEBSITE typically publishes park hours around 60–75 days in advance, but schedule adjustments can happen at any time, including the day of your visit. Check disneyworld.disney.go.com or the My Disney Experience app for exact hours before you arrive. Off-season, parks may be open as few as 9 hours (9 a.m.–6 p.m.), while at busy times (particularly holidays) they may operate for more than 13 hours. The parks used to have much more staggered opening times, but recently it seems that most parks open at 9 a.m. during the offseason, with a little variation during busier times. If a park opens earlier than 9, you can bet that Disney expects it to be crowded and is trying to expand park hours to absorb crowds.

Opening Time

When you search Disney's website for park hours, you'll usually find the times at which the park is open to the general public. For example, when Disney says the Magic Kingdom is open from 9 a.m. to 9 p.m., that means the gates open to all ticket holders at 9 a.m. However, Early Theme Park Entry (see page 34) means it opens at 8:30 a.m. for Disney resort guests. Disney often opens the parks to these guests even earlier—especially Hollywood Studios and Magic Kingdom, which have several holding areas throughout the park where guests wait until attractions are running. But because off-site guests aren't eligible for Early Entry, they are likely to be held at the park entrance until the official opening time, regardless of when on-site guests are admitted.

Closing Time

Attraction queues shut down at approximately the official closing time. Some shopping venues, such as Main Street, U.S.A., in the Magic Kingdom, stay open 30–60 minutes after the rest of the park has closed. And many dining venues offer reservations up until closing time, so the parks remain walkable until those last meals wrap up and people wander out.

THE PRACTICALITY OF RETURNING TO YOUR HOTEL FOR REST

MANY READERS ASK ABOUT the practicality of leaving the theme park for a nap or a swim at their resort—a midday rest is a great way to keep energy up during your Disney vacation.

In Part 5, you'll find a table that lists the commuting times to each of the Disney theme parks from many popular hotels within 20 miles of Walt Disney World (see pages 340–341). That's a great starting point, but driving time is not all you need to know. You also have to factor in the time to get to your car from the theme park.

At Animal Kingdom, Hollywood Studios, and EPCOT, you can get to your car in the parking lot in about 15–20 minutes. From the Magic Kingdom, it will take you 40–50 minutes. Obviously, if you're at the farthest point from the park entrance, it will take even longer. Once in your car, you'll be able to commute to most US 192 hotels, all Disney World resorts, all Lake Buena Vista hotels, and most hotels along the I-4 corridor and south International Drive (I-Drive) in 20 minutes or less. It will take about the same time to reach hotels on I-Drive north of Sand Lake Road and in the Universal Orlando area. So, for most people, the one-way commute, including walking from the park entrance, will average 40–45 minutes.

That means if you want your kids to have a 90-minute nap in the room, you'll need to make time for 45 minutes of park-to-resort time, 90 minutes of rest, another 45 minutes of resort-to-park time, plus any wind-down and get-ready-again time you may need. *Bottom line:* Plan for 3–4 hours outside the park for an hour-and-a-half nap.

ARRIVAL AND DEPARTURE DAYS: WHAT TO DO WHEN YOU HAVE ONLY HALF A DAY

ON ARRIVAL AND DEPARTURE DAYS, you will probably have only part of a day for touring or other vacation activities. It's a common problem: You touch down in Orlando around noon, excited and ready to go—but where?

The first question: Do you feel comfortable using a full day's admission when you have less than a full day to tour? The incremental cost to add another day is under $20 if you're visiting for four or more days, but it's $90 for one to three days (see the table on pages 70–71 for the breakdown). The crowd level that day, your arrival time, and the parks' closing times are all important factors to consider.

Opting for a Partial Day at the Theme Parks

If you decide to use one day's admission on a half day or less, refer to the **Lines** app or the posted wait times in the My Disney Experience app to see the least crowded park to visit.

One option—if you can reach the park before 1 p.m. and stay until closing (usually 6 or 7 p.m.)—is Disney's Animal Kingdom, which sees significantly lower crowds in the afternoon and early evening compared to any other park. You'll find shorter lines for Avatar Flight of Passage, Kilimanjaro Safaris, and Expedition Everest in the late afternoon on all but the busiest days of the year. You just won't have time to do all of the shows or entertainment during one afternoon.

Another option is to experience EPCOT's World Showcase, where crowds and lines don't particularly matter (apart from Frozen Ever After and Remy's Ratatouille Adventure). Enjoy great food and entertainment, and come back on another park day for attractions.

Whenever you arrive at a theme park after noon, you should go to higher-capacity attractions where wait times are relatively shorter, even during the most crowded part of the day. The clip-out Touring Plan Companions in the back of the book offer recommended times to visit each attraction so you can find attractions that might work with your schedule for a midday arrival. Although the lines for these attractions may seem long, they move quickly.

Alternatives to the Theme Parks on Arrival Day

Before you head out for fun on arrival day, you can check in and unpack, and you could detour to the grocery or convenience store to buy snacks, drinks, and breakfast food. At all Disney resorts and many non-Disney hotels, you can't occupy your room until after 3 p.m. (4 p.m. for DVC resorts); however, many properties will check you in and store your luggage before that.

The least expensive way to spend your arrival day is to check in, unpack, do your chores, and relax at your resort's swimming pool.

Another daytime option is a trip to a **water park** (see Part 15). In the summer of 2026, this will be an even more worthwhile option, because booking a room or vacation package through Disney gets you into a water park for free on your arrival day.

If none of the above options sound appealing, consider entertainment and dining at **Disney Springs** (page 498) or **minigolf** (page 516).

In the Evening

Dinner provides a great opportunity to plan the next day's activities. If you're hungry for entertainment, too, consider **Disney Springs**, which includes **Cirque du Soleil** (see page 499); **Raglan Road,** an Irish pub with live music and good food (see page 271); and other diversions.

Departure Days

Departure days don't seem to cause as much indecision as arrival days. If you want to visit a theme park on your departure day, get up early and be at a park when it opens. If you have plenty of time, check out of your hotel and store your luggage with the bell desk or in your car. Or, if you can arrange a late checkout, you might want to return to your hotel for a shower and change of clothes before your trip home. Departure day is a great time to plan a longer breakfast or brunch at a resort, especially if you want a chance to explore one of the Deluxe or DVC resorts that offer great dining options.

HOW *to* AVOID LONG WAITS *in* LINE

LONG LINES ARE USUALLY THE TOP COMPLAINT from theme park guests—not the quality of the rides, the cost, or the food. That's exactly why one of the main purposes of the *Unofficial Guide* is to save you time in line. It's what the book is most famous for and what most of our work revolves around.

Disney has gone on record saying the average Magic Kingdom guest experiences around 10 of that park's 50-ish attractions in a one-day visit, about one ride per hour. Disney considers everything from headliner rides (like Tiana's Bayou Adventure) to evening fireworks to the Main Street, U.S.A., piano player as one of those 10. Using the advice and touring plans in this book, we're confident that you can see 20 or more attractions in the same amount of time. In fact, Becky's family averages 25 attractions per Magic Kingdom day on their family vacations. How do they do that? By minimizing waiting.

There are six keys to avoiding long lines at Disney World. We elaborate on each of these in the remainder of this chapter.

1. Decide in advance what you really want to see (see below).
2. Arrive early (see next page).
3. Know what to expect when you arrive (see page 45).
4. Use a touring plan (see page 46).
5. Understand how standby queues, Lightning Lane Multi Pass, and Lightning Lane Single Pass work (see page 53).
6. Use the single-rider line if one is available (see page 59).

DECIDE IN ADVANCE WHAT YOU REALLY WANT TO SEE

DISNEY'S ATTRACTIONS OFFER SOMETHING for everyone, from midway-type rides like you'd find at your local carnival to cutting-edge experiences you won't find anywhere else. To help you decide which to see, Parts 11–14 provide detailed descriptions of each theme park and its attractions. In each description, we include an evaluation with our insights and an overall star rating, as well as guest ratings based on feedback from other Disney visitors, also expressed as star ratings based on age group (preschool, grade school, teens, young adults, over 30, and over 65). To give you a clear understanding of the size and scope of each attraction, we've organized them into the following categories:

SUPER-HEADLINERS The best attractions the theme park has to offer. These are Disney's crown jewels, showcasing the latest in attraction technology and design. When you return from your trip, these are the rides and experiences everyone will ask if you rode.

HEADLINERS Multimillion-dollar, fully immersive adventures and theater presentations that combine modern technology and detailed theming with impressive special effects. These are also must-dos.

MAJOR ATTRACTIONS Solid crowd-pleasers that may feature cutting-edge technology, or larger-scale experiences from an earlier era of design. While not as advanced as headliners, they offer engaging and memorable adventures.

MINOR ATTRACTIONS Midway-type rides, small "dark" rides (cars on a track, zigzagging through the dark), small theater presentations, transportation rides, and elaborate walk-through attractions. These attractions often have shorter waits and provide light entertainment.

DIVERSIONS Exhibits, both passive and interactive, including playgrounds or walk-throughs (such as EPCOT's **Journey of Water, Inspired by Moana**). These often offer the chance to slow down and explore.

While not every attraction fits perfectly into these categories, this system provides a helpful way to compare and prioritize them during your visit.

A Word About Disney Thrill Rides

Keep an open mind about Disney's "thrill rides." Compared to rides at other theme parks, Disney's attractions are generally quite tame, with more emphasis on theme, atmosphere, and special effects than on extreme motion or speed. While it's always wise to take Disney's pre-ride warnings seriously, it's worth noting that even **Frozen Ever After** is classified as a thrill ride, simply because it has a small drop. That drop is so gentle, however, that thousands of Disney's youngest visitors ride it every day without issue.

That said, some attractions deliver more intense thrills. **Expedition Everest, Rock 'n' Roller Coaster,** and **Tron Lightcycle/Run** are serious coasters, and they're faster and more intense than **Space Mountain** or **Big Thunder Mountain Railroad.**

If you're prone to motion sickness, **Mission: Space,** a high-tech spinning simulation ride in EPCOT, is a toss-up (pun intended). It absolutely has the potential to ruin your day, as do the spinning **Guardians of the Galaxy: Cosmic Rewind,** also in EPCOT, and the **Star Tours** flight simulator in Disney's Hollywood Studios.

ARRIVE EARLY! ARRIVE EARLY! ARRIVE EARLY!

THIS IS THE MOST RELIABLE WAY to efficiently tour the parks and avoid long lines. Early mornings always guarantee fewer people in the parks and lower wait times. For example, in the Magic Kingdom, the same four rides you can experience in 1 hour if you arrive for Early Entry can take as long as 3 hours after 10:30 a.m.

Start your day right by eating breakfast before you arrive. Don't waste prime touring time sitting in a restaurant or waiting in line to order food. If you arrive before Early Entry begins, consider packing a small breakfast to eat while you wait for attractions to open. This is what Becky does for her kids. It gets them out of the room quicker, lands them farther ahead of the Early Entry crowds, and gives the kids something to do besides sitting around getting bored.

Being inside the park and past the tapstiles before official opening gives you a major head start. While others are still fumbling with their tickets or figuring out how the tapstiles work, the lucky few (hundreds) already in the park are heading for their first attraction. With a good plan, you'll probably be on your second ride before many have even entered the park—and you'll stay ahead of them all day.

The earlier a park opens, the greater your advantage can be. Most vacationers simply don't want to wake up early enough to arrive before park opening; many fewer people are willing to make an 8 a.m. opening than a 9 a.m. opening. If you visit during the offseason and are staying at a Disney resort, aim to arrive at the tapstiles 60 minutes before official opening (to take advantage of the Early Entry benefit for Disney hotel guests). If you're staying off-site, arrive 30 minutes before official opening to get into the park as soon as it officially opens.

> **unofficial TIP**
> To save time, hold your bag away from your body as you walk through the security screening. This lowers the chance that you'll get selected for a bag check. If you have an umbrella packed away, take it out and hold it separately.

During holiday periods, on-site guests should arrive about 75 minutes early, before official park opening, and off-site guests should arrive about 45 minutes before park opening. By *arrive*, we mean be through security and at the tapstiles.

Many readers share their experiences about getting to the parks before opening, such as this mom from Tennessee:

> I didn't want to believe the hype about rope drop [park opening]. It's too difficult to get everyone up and to the parks that early on vacation! But on the one day I was able to get us there on time, we experienced double what we were able to do on any other day. Next Disney vacation, everyone has an early bedtime so we can do more rope drops!

It's important to note that Disney's Early Theme Park Entry program (see page 34) almost eliminates the rope-drop advantage for off-site guests, as there will already be thousands of people in line in front of them by the time they're admitted. The one exception is the Magic Kingdom, where Adventureland, Frontierland, and Liberty Square don't open until regular park opening anyway, so you can be at the front of the pack to get to those attractions.

If getting the kids up earlier than usual causes crankiness that will put a damper on your day, don't worry—you'll have a great time no matter when you get to the park. Many families with sleepy children have found that it's better to accept the relative inefficiencies of arriving at the park a bit late than to jar the children out of their routine. A mom of teens from Mississippi agrees:

> I would have loved to experience the uncrowded early morning in the parks, but it wasn't worth the surly attitudes of our teenage crew. They were more than happy to stay up late, so we would try to avoid long lines during the day and then go to the big headliners in the last hour the park was open instead.

KNOW WHAT TO EXPECT WHEN YOU ARRIVE

ARRIVING BEFORE PARK OPENING is key for most touring plans. Here's what you'll need to know about Disney's opening procedures.

TRANSPORTATION Disney's transportation options—buses, boats, the Skyliner, and the monorails—begin operating about 90 minutes before official park opening. If you're driving, parking lots typically open about 1 hour before the park does.

ENTRANCE PROCESS Each park has an entrance plaza just outside of the tapstiles, where guests will wait until the park begins admitting them. To prevent overcrowding at the tapstiles, Disney allows on-site guests to enter the park 30–60 minutes before official opening time. Off-site guests may be directed to a holding area until official opening.

ROPE DROP Once inside, on-site guests are held at designated points within the park in a process known as rope drop. Attractions typically begin running at the advertised Early Entry or official opening time, and guests are then allowed to proceed directly to their first ride. On crowded days, attractions may begin running even earlier.

USE A TOURING PLAN

RESEARCH SHOWS THAT a key factor in theme parks visitors' satisfaction is the number of attractions they can experience during their visit. To help you have the most enjoyable and efficient park days, this book includes field-tested touring plans. These step-by-step itineraries are designed to maximize the number of attractions you experience while minimizing wait times.

If you follow the touring plans in this book, you can save 4 hours or more of standing in line during a full park day, and you'll see more attractions than if you try to tour the parks on your own. How? Data! Numbers and math are powerful tools.

You may be surprised to learn that avoiding lines in theme parks is a lot like the challenges faced by companies such as FedEx and UPS. For them, it's about delivering packages efficiently; for you, it's about navigating rides and attractions. The principles are the same: You're the driver, the attractions are the stops, and the time you spend walking or waiting in line is the travel time between deliveries.

Because this kind of situation is common in the business world, it gets studied and solved widely in schools and corporations, mainly in the fields of mathematics, operations research, and computer science. Bob used his experience teaching college operations research to come up with the first Disney touring plans in this book. Years later, Bob helped Len while Len was writing his master's thesis on efficient computer techniques for this kind of problem. Then Len brought Becky into the TouringPlans crew while she was (and still is) solving related problems for companies around the country for years in her "real job" as a data and analytics consultant.

To summarize: In the decades since we started this journey, our team of data scientists, programmers, and researchers has been focused on figuring out how to avoid lines at Disney World.

This research has been recognized by both the travel industry and academe, having been cited by such diverse sources as *Popular Science*, *The Atlanta Journal-Constitution*, *The Dallas Morning News*, the Mathematical Association of America, *Money*, *The New York Times*, Operations Research Forum, *Travel Weekly*, *USA Today*, and

Wired, along with the BBC, CBS News, Fox News, and the Travel Channel. The methodology behind the touring plans was also used as a case study in the book *Numbers Rule Your World,* by Kaiser Fung, an expert in business analytics and data visualization.

So, at its core, a touring plan is a step-by-step guide to avoiding lines. But it's also the product of obsessive Disney-data fans combining advanced math, rigorous testing, and a passion for helping you make the most of your Disney vacation.

We get a ton of reader mail commenting on touring plans. A mom from Kentucky had this to say:

> If there is one cult in this world I could join, it would be the staff of the *Unofficial Guide.* I tell everyone going to Disney to use this book and the awesome app. Years ago, we tried to convince friends to use the book, but they were scared off by the highly structured nature of the touring plans. We happened to see them at Disney during a late summer afternoon. Our family had enjoyed a full day with lots of rides and no more than a 20-minute wait. They had been on two total rides, standing in line over 1½ hours each time. They were miserable and already considering escaping back to the hotel.

A mom from Arkansas with plenty of Disney experience gave the touring plans a shot:

> This is our fifth family trip to WDW, and this was my first time to use a touring plan. I have read the books and been a member of Lines for years. However, I never bought into the demands of the touring plan. After this last trip, I am officially a fan! I cannot express to you how much better our trip was since we followed a plan. We accomplished more in the first hour of Magic Kingdom than we used to accomplish in 3 hours. My family will use touring plans from now on.

Variables That Affect the Success of the Touring Plans

How much time you'll save with any of the plans can be affected how early you arrive at the parks; how quickly you move from attraction to attraction; how many breaks you take; when, where, and how you eat (counter service vs. table service); whether you have strollers to park; and other factors, such as **Rider Switch.** Even though it's key for enabling parents to experience attractions that their child is too short to ride, Rider Switch (see page 307) can keep families with little ones from moving quickly through height-restricted attractions.

UNEXPECTED RIDE CLOSURES Some things are beyond your control. A perfect example of this is rides that don't open on time or suddenly stop running at some point during the day. For example, when **Tiana's Bayou Adventure** first opened in the Magic Kingdom in the summer of 2024, it was unexpectedly unavailable about 30% of the time for its first two months in operation. It would frequently open hours later than the rest of the park and then break down again later in the afternoon or evening.

Even with the best data and tools at Becky's disposal, plus plenty of experience with new attractions, it took her three different trips to the Magic Kingdom to finally be able to ride Tiana because its extensive downtime kept preventing her from riding, even when she successfully joined virtual queues *and* purchased Lightning Lane Multi Pass.

Attractions with regular reliability issues can be especially difficult to plan around and to experience during your park day. Tiana still averages more than an hour of downtime every day (as of early 2025). **Kali River Rapids, Rise of the Resistance, Seven Dwarfs Mine Train, Space Mountain,** and **Test Track** (pre-refurbishment) all make the naughty list for averaging more than an hour of downtime every day. Not only can this throw off your plan if the attraction isn't running when you get to it in your touring plan, but it could also mean that you wait for a while only to be kicked out of line when the attraction breaks down. You don't get to ride, and you wasted time in line.

On bad days, multiple headliner attractions break down simultaneously, as this reader from Connecticut experienced:

> *What took tons of time was down attractions. It seems like almost everything was down: Kilimanjaro Safaris at Animal Kingdom; Soarin', Spaceship Earth, and Remy's Ratatouille Adventure when we visited EPCOT; and Rise of the Resistance and Smugglers Run at the Studios.*
>
> *At least Smugglers Run handled it well. They gave us a pass to reride without waiting. In the welcome video when we rerode, the guy said, "Oh, I didn't expect you to come back after the incident. Good to see you again." That was amazing.*

RIDE BREAKDOWNS AND LIGHTNING LANE All of Disney's least reliable rides happen to use Lightning Lane. This combination of frequent downtime and Lightning Lane usage significantly worsens standby times across the park. Here's why:

When a popular ride like Tiana's Bayou Adventure breaks down for 2 hours, thousands of guests who would've ridden it end up going to another attraction instead—like Space Mountain, Seven Dwarfs Mine Train, or Tron Lightcycle/Run. About half of those displaced Tiana guests were using Lightning Lane, and Disney allows them to use that reservation at almost any other attraction. But those other attractions already have long standby lines thanks to the displaced non–Lightning Lane guests. The only way to fit the Lightning Lane guests from Tiana into other Lightning Lanes is to put them ahead of standby guests (by prioritizing Lightning Lane over standby when loading the ride). This pushes standby wait times even higher—all because an entirely different ride broke down.

This creates a vicious cycle. Some frustrated guests may decide to purchase Lightning Lane Multi Pass (LLMP) to avoid the growing lines. As more people join Lightning Lanes, subsequent ride breakdowns make the problem worse because even more guests are redirected to the Lightning Lanes, further increasing standby wait times.

Because of this, if you're determined to experience an unreliable super-headliner like Rise of the Resistance, it's wise to purchase Lightning Lane Single Pass for it on medium and high crowd days. Rise, specifically, is notoriously unreliable. And when it breaks down, Disney usually kicks out everyone in line and tells them to try back "later" when the ride is running again. (This process is called "dumping the queue.") If you're a particularly unlucky standby guest, you

HOW TO AVOID LONG WAITS IN LINE

ATTRACTIONS THAT FREQUENTLY EXPERIENCE OUTAGES		
ATTRACTION AND THEME PARK	AVERAGE DOWNTIME PER DAY (IN MINUTES)	LIKELIHOOD RIDE IS DOWN AT SOME POINT DURING THE DAY
TIANA'S BAYOU ADVENTURE *Magic Kingdom*	105	75%
STAR WARS: RISE OF THE RESISTANCE *Hollywood Studios*	75	75%
TEST TRACK *EPCOT**	65	70%
KALI RIVER RAPIDS *Animal Kingdom*	65	60%
SPACE MOUNTAIN *Magic Kingdom*	65	60%
SEVEN DWARFS MINE TRAIN *Magic Kingdom*	60	70%
REMY'S RATATOUILLE ADVENTURE *EPCOT*	55	70%
EXPEDITION EVEREST *Animal Kingdom*	55	65%
SLINKY DOG DASH *Hollywood Studios*	55	55%
ROCK 'N' ROLLER COASTER *Hollywood Studios*	55	55%

* Test Track downtime is based on pre-refurbishment data and may not reflect what will happen in 2026.

can spend an hour in line, get dumped, come back later, and repeat the same frustration. At least if you purchase Lightning Lane access for it, you'll be able to come back to the Lightning Lane whenever you want.

The touring plans in this book account for ride reliability when determining which attractions you should visit first. And if you're following a touring plan on the Lines app, you can tap "Optimize" at any time to have the plan adjust automatically to avoid the problem areas or attractions.

If you're following a printed touring plan, it's safe to assume that a ride outage will affect your plan. Our advice is to check the My Disney Experience or Lines app for current wait times throughout the rest of the park and adjust your plan accordingly.

WEATHER One variable we can't predict accurately within a book is the weather. When lightning or heavy rains are nearby, Disney will close many (if not all) outdoor rides for safety. The effect on ride wait times when this happens is similar to having a whole set of unexpected ride breakdowns at once. Indoor attractions become incredibly popular, or people cut their losses and leave the park. If you're prepared for the rain (see page 30), you can navigate these crowd patterns and experience lower waits overall.

Customize Your Touring Plans

The attractions included in this book's touring plans are the most popular, as determined by more than 1 million reader surveys. If you've never been to Walt Disney World, we suggest using these plans as a starting point. They're designed to help you see the best Disney attractions with as little waiting in line as possible and have been used successfully by thousands of families.

If you are a repeat visitor (or you visit the same park more than once during your trip), your favorite attractions may be different than the ones included in the plans. One way to customize the plans is to go to **TouringPlans.com** to create personalized versions. Tell the software the date, time, and park you've chosen to visit, along with the attractions you want to see. Your custom plan will tell you, for your specific travel date, the exact order in which you should visit attractions to minimize your waits in line.

Some changes to the included touring plans are easy to make without creating a totally custom version. If a plan calls for an attraction you're not interested in, simply skip it and move on to the next one. You can also substitute similar attractions in the same area of the park. For example, if a plan says that you should ride Dumbo and you'd rather not, but you would enjoy the Mad Tea Party (which is not in the plan), then go ahead and substitute that for Dumbo. As long as the substitution is an attraction that has a similar wait time and duration and is near the attraction called for in the touring plan, the overall effectiveness of the plan won't be affected.

What to Do If You Lose the Thread

If unforeseen events interrupt a plan:

1. If you're following a touring plan in the Lines app, just mark any attractions you've already done as completed and tap "Optimize" when you're ready to start touring again. The app will figure out the best possible plan for the remainder of your day.
2. If you're following a printed touring plan, skip a step on the plan for every 20 minutes you're delayed. For example, if your kid gets distracted by Tomorrowland Speedway and demands to ride, and you lose 40 minutes to that endeavor, skip two steps and pick up from there.
3. Forget the plan and organize the remainder of your day using the standby wait times listed in the My Disney Experience or Lines app, or consult the Clip-Out Touring Plan Companions starting on page 569.

"Bouncing Around"

Disney generally tries to place its most popular rides on opposite sides of the park. In the Magic Kingdom, for example, these attractions are positioned almost as far apart as possible—in the north, east, and west corners of the park—so that guests are more evenly distributed throughout the park and throughout the day.

It's often possible to save a lot of time in line by walking all the way across the park to catch one of these rides when crowds are low. Some readers object to this crisscrossing. A woman from Georgia, told us she "got dizzy from all the bouncing around." Believe us, we empathize. In general, the plans recommend crossing the park only if it'll save you more than 1 minute in line for every 1 minute of extra walking.

If you want to experience headliner attractions in one day at any park without long waits, you almost certainly have to crisscross the park early in the morning before they all develop lines. Otherwise, you can hit one or two early and then try to hop in line for another right before the park closes.

Touring Plan Rejection

It's always best to stick to the plan if possible, especially in the mornings, if you're visiting during busy times. The consequence of touring spontaneity during peak season is hours of standing in line. However, some folks don't respond well to the rigidity of a touring plan. No amount of time saved in line is worth family strife and arguments on vacation. And not everyone's vacation style lends itself to following step-by-step plans all day, every day. Be flexible. Have fun. Know yourself and your party and what makes you happy.

One of our all-time favorite letters came from a Nebraska couple. One of them was a planner, and one clearly wasn't. They were both experienced negotiators, as their letter shows:

> We created our own 4.25-by-5.5-inch guidebook for our trip that included a number of pages from TouringPlans.com. This was the first page:

THE TYPE-A SPOUSE'S BILL OF RIGHTS
1. We will not see everything in one vacation.
2. Len Testa will not be vacationing with us. His plans don't schedule time for benches. Ours may.
3. We may deviate from the touring plans at some point. Really.
4. Even if it isn't on the Disney Dining Plan, a funnel cake or other snack may be purchased without a grouchy face from the non-purchasing spouse.
5. Sometimes, sitting by the pool may sound more fun than going to a park, show, or other scheduled event. On this vacation, that will be fine.
6. "But I thought we were going to . . . " is a phrase that must be stricken from the discussion of any plans that had not been previously discussed as a couple.
7. Other items may be added as circumstances dictate at the parks.

> *It was a much happier vacation with these generally understood principles in writing.*

How Early Theme Park Entry, Extended Evening Theme Park Hours, and Special Events Work with the Touring Plans

With Early Theme Park Entry, Disney resort guests are admitted to all four Disney theme parks at least 30 minutes before official park opening. Off-site guests who enter the parks at official opening will find thousands of on-site guests already ahead of them in lines.

The touring plans in this book help you make the most of that extra time if you're staying on-site. And to mitigate the effect of Early Entry on off-site guests, there are also off-site versions of the plans.

During Extended Evening Theme Park Hours (see page 36) and After Hours events (see page 76), crowds are typically so low that a touring plan isn't needed—just head to the nearest attraction that interests you. If you need any strategy, it's to save headliners for later in the night. Generally, Halloween and Christmas parties will also have low wait times at attractions. Parties tend to attract guests who are interested in the special entertainment.

METHODS OF WAITING IN LINE AT WALT DISNEY WORLD

PRIOR TO 2021, Disney ran a *free* ride reservation system called FastPass+ that allowed visitors to reserve a spot on an attraction for a specific day and time. You could book a reservation at a specific ride, for a specific 1-hour time window, up to two months before your trip.

In 2021, Disney decided to monetize this process by charging to avoid waits. The result was Genie+, an unprecedented, unpopular, and unwieldy system for navigating the theme parks and utilizing queues called Lightning Lanes.

In mid-2024, Disney supposedly responded to guest feedback by once again overhauling the paid ride reservation system. It did away with Genie+ in favor of Lightning Lane Multi Pass and Lightning Lane Single Pass, which are just as expensive but have slightly easier-to-understand rules and advance booking similar to FastPass+. In late 2024, Disney added Lightning Lane Premier Pass to the lineup. There are now at least five processes for waiting in line at rides (six if you count VIP tours!). Each method has its own set of rules, often put in place for Disney's benefit, not yours.

Here are the ways you can wait in line at Walt Disney World:

STANDBY QUEUES This is the way most people are familiar with: You get in a line for a ride, and you wait until it's your turn to ride. It doesn't cost anything, and the wait-time sign in front of the attraction gives you some idea of how long you're going to be waiting, even if it's not 100% accurate.

COST: Free with park admission

BOARDING GROUPS/VIRTUAL QUEUES A boarding group, or virtual queue, is a virtual line without a guaranteed return time. They're typically used at new, popular rides with some expected unreliability. Here's how it works: At exactly 7 a.m. on the day of your visit, you'll use the My Disney Experience (MDE) app to request a boarding group. If you're successful, you'll get a boarding group number and a rough estimate of how long you must wait until your group is called.

If the ride is running smoothly, boarding groups typically start getting called within 30 minutes of park opening, beginning with boarding group 1. The MDE app will display the current range of boarding groups that are able to ride. When your group is called, the app will alert you so you can return.

Boarding groups are used at rides that Disney thinks are likely to break down often, or where it wants to control the length of the standby line. Because new rides may not have worked out all their bugs, Disney isn't confident it can give guests a specific time to ride. For example, suppose Disney gave you a specific time of 1–2 p.m. to ride Tiana's Bayou Adventure. If Tiana's breaks down and is unavailable between 1 and 2 p.m., then at 2 p.m., the ride must accommodate everyone who didn't get to ride between 1 and 2, plus everyone who was scheduled to ride between 2 and 3 p.m. There's not enough ride capacity to do that (and Disney doesn't want to run the ride at half capacity in anticipation of breakdowns either). Boarding groups solve this problem by not attaching a specific return time to your virtual wait. Instead you're assigned a group, and you hope the ride is reliable enough that your group gets called and you get to ride. No guarantee.

Note: At press time, no attractions at Walt Disney World were using virtual queues, but this may change as new, popular attractions open.

COST: Free with park admission

HOW TO AVOID LONG WAITS IN LINE

RIDE RESERVATION SYSTEM DEFINITIONS	
LIGHTNING LANE	An alternative to the standby line at some rides. Comes in three flavors: Multi Pass, Single Pass, and Premier Pass.
LIGHTNING LANE MULTI PASS (LLMP)	A way of using the Lightning Lane at most (but not all) of the popular rides in each park, for a single additional upcharge per person, per day.
LIGHTNING LANE SINGLE PASS (LLSP)	Another way of using the Lighting Lane, available for a per-attraction fee, for one or two of the most popular rides in each park. It's a way for Disney to charge more than it would for Lightning Lane Multi Pass while shortening the lines at a park's top attractions.
LIGHTNING LANE PREMIER PASS (LLPP)	Yet another option for using the Lightning Lane, this time without having to make reservations. Pay a large amount of money for a single park on a single day, and you can use each Lightning Lane once, at a time of your choosing.

LIGHTNING LANE MULTI PASS (previously FastPass+ and Genie+) Lightning Lane Multi Pass (LLMP, or "limp") is a paid version of Disney's former FastPass+ system. Built as a feature in the MDE app, it costs $16–$39 per person, per day. The price varies by day and by park: LLMP costs more on busier days and at more popular parks.

Paying for LLMP lets you make reservations to skip the standby line. The first three of these reservations are **advance selections** that you make at the time of purchase. At every park other than Animal Kingdom, one of these three selections can be at a **Tier 1** attraction, and the other two must be **Tier 2** attractions (see table on next page). Animal Kingdom has no tiers. You'll make your advance selections, and then Disney will make suggestions on what it thinks the best available return times are for those attractions on that day. You have the opportunity to modify any of the three return times before finalizing your purchase.

If you are staying on-site, you can purchase LLMP beginning 7 days before you check in at your resort, and you can make your advance selections when you purchase. You can purchase LLMP for any day of your visit (as long as your visit is 14 days or less).

If you're staying off-site, you'll have to wait until 3 days before the first day of your date-specific ticket to purchase LLMP and make your advance selections. This puts off-site guests at a significant disadvantage, as popular attractions will already be "sold out" before that 3-day window. But similar to resort guests, off-site guests can also make LLMP purchases and advance selections for the entire length of their ticket. If you're an Annual Pass holder without a resort reservation, you can make LLMP purchases and advance selections up to 3 days before your park reservation or any "good-to-go" day (when park reservations aren't required).

Disney can limit the number of guests who purchase LLMP. While that doesn't happen often, if you want to be absolutely certain you have it, you should make your LLMP purchases as early as possible. This also helps you get the best advance selection return times. Clever Disney, creating some FOMO and a sense of urgency where they didn't exist with Genie+!

Making the best advance selections requires quite a bit of strategy. Your Tier 1 selection should absolutely be the attraction that will save

LIGHTNING LANE MULTI PASS ATTRACTIONS AND ADVANCE SELECTION TIERS

MAGIC KINGDOM

TIER 1

• Big Thunder Mountain Railroad *(reopens in 2026)* • Jungle Cruise • Peter Pan's Flight • Space Mountain • Tiana's Bayou Adventure

TIER 2

• The Barnstormer • Buzz Lightyear's Space Ranger Spin • Dumbo the Flying Elephant • The Haunted Mansion • It's a Small World • Mad Tea Party • The Magic Carpets of Aladdin • The Many Adventures of Winnie the Pooh • *Mickey's PhilharMagic* • *Monsters, Inc. Laugh Floor* • Pirates of the Caribbean • Tomorrowland Speedway • Under the Sea—Journey of the Little Mermaid

EPCOT

TIER 1

• Frozen Ever After • Remy's Ratatouille Adventure • Soarin' Around the World • Test Track (likely LLMP and possibly LLSP upon reopening)

TIER 2

• Disney & Pixar Short Film Festival • Journey into Imagination with Figment • Living with the Land • Mission: Space • The Seas with Nemo & Friends • Spaceship Earth • *Turtle Talk with Crush*

ANIMAL KINGDOM *(no tiers)*

• Expedition Everest • *Feathered Friends in Flight!* • *Festival of the Lion King* • Finding Nemo: The Big Blue . . . and Beyond! • Kali River Rapids • Kilimanjaro Safaris • Na'vi River Journey

DISNEY'S HOLLYWOOD STUDIOS

TIER 1

• Mickey & Minnie's Runaway Railway • *Millennium Falcon:* Smugglers Run • Rock 'n' Roller Coaster • Slinky Dog Dash

TIER 2

• Alien Swirling Saucers • *Beauty and the Beast—Live on Stage* • *Disney Junior Play and Dance!* • *For the First Time in Forever—A Frozen Sing-Along Celebration* • *Indiana Jones Epic Stunt Spectacular!* • Star Tours—The Adventures Continue • The Twilight Zone Tower of Terror • Toy Story Mania!

---

you the most time. But your Tier 2 selections are trickier—one needs to happen as early in the day as possible so that you can "unlock" more reservations (see below). The other can be a great time-saver.

When your return window opens, you'll go to the attraction and use the Lightning Lane—a separate line that's faster than the standby line. Guests in this line are given priority to board. As soon as you pass all Lightning Lane tapstiles, you'll "unlock" a new reservation, and you can book any other attraction in the park with available return times (and where you haven't already used the Lightning Lane). Almost all popular attractions offer LLMP (or **Lightning Lane Single Pass**; see page 56).

With LLMP, Disney appears to normally allocate 50% of a ride's hourly capacity to Lightning Lane users. But because LLMP costs real money, we also think Disney has set an upper goal on how long people will wait in the Lightning Lane—something like "no more than 10 minutes." And that means if the Lightning Lane gets backed up, Disney will take up to 99 guests from that line for every 1 guest it takes from the standby line. If you're in the standby line when that happens, it can be endlessly frustrating.

The number of available Lightning Lane reservations is limited, so LLMP doesn't eliminate the need to wake up early. If you get to the park early and use your first reservation quickly, you have the opportunity to begin booking other popular attractions before they sell out for the day. The quicker your start, the more use you get out of LLMP.

IS LLMP WORTH THE COST? It all depends. We recommend using LLMP in the Magic Kingdom under most crowd conditions (just not on low-crowd party days) and in Disney's Hollywood Studios on medium or high crowd days, if you are confident in your ability to get good same-day reservations. However, we can't say that a family of four should spend $120 (or even $80) on LLMP in EPCOT or Animal Kingdom: EPCOT has fewer rides, and they're spaced far apart, which limits the amount of time you'd save using LLMP beyond what you could save just by showing up early and hitting the key attractions first. And Animal Kingdom has few enough attractions with long waits that you can easily follow a touring plan to avoid waits without paying.

For specific advice on how best to use LLMP at each park, read the LLMP section in that park's chapter (Parts 11–14).

Reader comments about LLMP vary but generally focus on comparing it to Genie+, reservation availability, and the amount of time spent staring at a phone.

A reader from Indiana says:

I felt like I got used to Genie+ and could stack up reservations and have a wait-free evening . . . even if I didn't land in Orlando until noon. Now, if I want to use LLMP, I have to start my day early. It just doesn't match with how I like to visit Disney.

Also regarding phone usage, a visitor from Georgia says:

I miss the days when my phone was running out of battery because I was taking pictures of my kids enjoying the parks and making memories. On our most recent trip, I went through two [portable chargers] a day, almost all thanks to scrolling through ride reservations and constantly refreshing. What happened to my family time?

The bad news: Disney says that about 50% of park guests are using these reservations, which earns the company hundreds of millions of dollars per year ($720 million between October 2021 and June 2024, to be specific). Because of this, we don't think LLMP is going away or getting cheaper anytime soon.

COST: $16–$39 per person per day

Lightning Lane Multi Pass (LLMP) Guidelines

- Valid park tickets or Annual Passes are required to obtain Lightning Lane return times.
- When you purchase LLMP, you may make three ride reservations for the day you're going to use it. The price is based on the park where the reservations are made. At Animal Kingdom, you can reserve any three attractions. At the other parks, you can pick either three Tier 2 attractions or one Tier 1 attraction plus two Tier 2 attractions (see table on opposite page).
- When you make your advance selections, Disney will automatically select return times for you. You have a limited amount of time to attempt to manually edit those return times before you finalize your purchase.
- Once you use any ride reservation (or your return window passes without you redeeming the reservation), you unlock a new reservation. For this

- reason, you should almost never have more than three reservations at a time. The popular Genie+ strategy of "stacking" isn't possible with LLMP.
- After you use your first Lightning Lane reservation, any future reservations during the day can be made at any of the four WDW theme parks. That means all LLMP purchases are technically multipark purchases, but they are priced according to the park where you make your advance selections.
- Don't make a LLMP reservation unless it can save you 20 minutes or more at an attraction or if a nearby ride is distributing immediate return times.
- Always check the return period before obtaining your reservation. Keep an eye out for attractions where the Lightning Lane return time is immediate, or at least faster than the standby wait.
- On-site guests can purchase LLMP and make ride reservations for their entire trip (of 14 days or less) at 7 a.m. Eastern time 7 days before their resort check-in. Off-site guests can purchase LLMP and make ride reservations for their entire date-based ticket length at 7 a.m. 3 days before the first day of their ticket. Annual Pass holders without a resort reservation can purchase LLMP and make ride reservations at 7 a.m. 3 days before any park reservation or good-to-go day.
- If you're not staying on-site, don't count on Lightning Lane being available for popular attractions when your booking window opens during busier times of year. This especially applies to **Slinky Dog Dash, Tower of Terror, Toy Story Mania!, Remy's Ratatouille Adventure,** and to a slightly lesser extent **Frozen Ever After** and **Test Track.**
- Everyone in your party must have their own Lightning Lane return time. Reservations are tied to each individual ticket and may not be transferred.
- Be mindful of your Lightning Lane return time and plan accordingly. You may use your LLMP return time 5 minutes before its start time and up to 119 minutes after it expires. This unadvertised grace period is typically the only exception to your return window.
- Attractions typically do not dispense Lightning Lane reservations while they are closed for technical difficulties or special events.
- If an attraction is unavailable due to technical difficulties during your return window, your Lightning Lane automatically converts to a **replacement pass.** Replacement passes remain valid for use until closing time at that attraction (if it reopens) or at selected other Lightning Lane attractions in the same park. If the original return window was near closing time, the replacement pass may be valid the next day.
- You may want to pick one member of your party to handle everyone's tickets and Lightning Lane reservations on their phone. This gives your group the option of splitting up while retaining access to each other's plans; however, each person must still use their own ticket to enter the park or redeem Lightning Lane reservations.

LIGHTNING LANE SINGLE PASS (LLSP) You'll have to pay separately to skip the line at a new or popular ride, even if you've already purchased LLMP. If you want to avoid a potential 2-hour wait at Avatar Flight of Passage or Tron, Disney will offer you a chance to ride at a price, by using Lightning Lane Single Pass (LLSP, or "lisp").

Purchasing a LLSP in MDE is straightforward. Passes are sold per person, and guests are limited to **two per day.** The advance-booking timing rules are the same as those for LLMP. When it's your time to ride, you'll use the Lightning Lane to board.

You don't need to purchase LLMP to purchase LLSP. Likewise, purchasing LLSP does not get you access to the other LLMP attractions.

At press time, these were the LLSP attractions in each park:

HOW TO AVOID LONG WAITS IN LINE

LIGHTNING LANE SINGLE PASS (LLSP) SAVINGS ANALYSIS

ATTRACTION	AVERAGE MINUTES IN LINE SAVED	HIGHEST COST	COST PER SAVED MINUTE/HOUR
AVATAR FLIGHT OF PASSAGE *Animal Kingdom*	41	$18	$0.44/$26
GUARDIANS OF THE GALAXY *EPCOT*	47	$19	$0.47/$24
SEVEN DWARFS MINE TRAIN *Magic Kingdom*	27	$14	$0.52/$31
STAR WARS: RISE OF THE RESISTANCE *Hollywood Studios*	37	$25	$0.68/$41
TRON LIGHTCYCLE/RUN *Magic Kingdom*	44	$22	$0.50/$30

- **MAGIC KINGDOM** Seven Dwarfs Mine Train and Tron Lightcycle/Run
- **EPCOT** Guardians of the Galaxy: Cosmic Rewind
- **HOLLYWOOD STUDIOS** Star Wars: Rise of the Resistance
- **ANIMAL KINGDOM** Avatar Flight of Passage

> **COST:** Varies by attraction, day of year, and time of day. The lowest cost we've seen recently for a LLSP is $10, at Seven Dwarfs Mine Train. The highest (so far) is $25 at Rise of the Resistance. We expect these prices to increase because reservations have been selling out regularly at current prices.

IS LLSP WORTH THE COST? For certain rides. The table above shows how much time you're likely to save at each LLSP attraction on an average day, along with the maximum cost we've seen for that LLSP. As a rough estimate, the highest-priced one-day park ticket costs about $17 per hour in the park (assuming $199 over 12 hours). So, any LLSP that costs less than $17 per hour saved is a good deal. No LLSP meets that criterion under average crowd conditions. You're typically paying for the convenience of a "guaranteed" ride time more than time savings.

LIGHTNING LANE PREMIER PASS (PP) At the end of 2024, Disney surprised everyone by announcing yet another way to skip lines. Anyone can purchase it, but the price is *steep*. If you even have to ask about the cost, this product is not for you.

PP is a prepackaged set of every LLMP and LLSP attraction in a single park. You can use the Lightning Lane at each of these attractions once in a park day, and you don't have to make any reservations—just show up! But you can't repeat any attractions, trade any out, or park-hop. And you'll pay a lot for the privilege of just walking up to Lightning Lanes—a minimum of $329 per person per day at Magic Kingdom, for example.

IS PP WORTH IT? Again, if you're even asking that question, you are not the audience for this product. And that's OK. There is no way to make PP make sense from a budget vs. time-saving perspective. In fact, if you have a large party, it could actually be cheaper to do a VIP tour—and that comes with a tour guide, free snacks, reserved seating for fireworks and parades, park-hopping, and rerides. But if you don't care about budget and just want the convenience of using a Lightning Lane without a reservation, then PP is for you.

> **COST:** Varies by park and day, from $129 per person per day at Animal Kingdom to $449 per person per day at Magic Kingdom.

DISNEY GENIE (MINUS THE PLUS) Disney announced the "free Genie" itinerary-planning feature of the MDE app in 2019 and said little more about it for the next two years. Originally, Genie sounded a lot like our computer-optimized touring plans: You'd tell Genie what rides you wanted to ride, and Genie would plan your day to minimize your wait in line.

But that's not at all what Genie does. In fact, Genie is one of the worst products Disney has ever produced. Its real purpose isn't to plan your day—because it doesn't. It's to serve Disney's park management needs. To understand why requires a little background.

Back in the days of FastPass+, the widespread use of the free reservations adeptly spread crowds away from headliners (where they had reservations anyway) toward typically lower-wait attractions where guests spent their time in line until they could use those reservations.

Now consider LLMP instead. It costs money, so fewer people use it. That means Disney loses the all-important crowd distribution that FastPass+ provided. The risk to Disney's operations is that guests just queue up for Disney's best, most popular rides, resulting in long lines, while other attractions sit underused.

That's where free Genie comes in—it suggests lower-rated, less popular attractions to guests who wouldn't have otherwise visited and directs crowds away from the parks' most popular attractions. This has been proven repeatedly in our field-testing. For example, Len tested Genie one day in Hollywood Studios. Arriving at 8:30 a.m., in time for Early Entry, Len fired up the Genie app to get Genie's recommendations. Here was the morning itinerary Genie suggested:

9:30 A.M. Ride Toy Story Mania!

10:20 A.M. Buy a *Star Wars* droid in Galaxy's Edge.

11:10 A.M. Eat lunch at Ronto Roasters.

That's right: Genie knew Len was in the park at 8:30 a.m. At that hour, waits at Tower of Terror, Rock 'n' Roller Coaster, and Toy Story Mania! were well below 5 minutes (another researcher rode them to check). Despite no lines at these headliners, Genie suggested just one ride in the first 3½ hours Len was in the park.

Genie also tried to upsell Len on the benefits of Lightning Lane purchases available at the time and suggested he buy a $100 *Star Wars* droid. All told, Genie immediately suggested three ways for Len to spend money before noon, but only one ride.

Somehow, it got worse. When Len declined Genie's suggestion to buy a droid at 10:20 a.m., Genie then suggested these attractions:

- *Walt Disney Presents*
- *Disney Junior Play and Dance!*
- Lightning McQueen's Racing Academy
- Alien Swirling Saucers

Genie suggested that Len—a middle-aged man touring alone—see two stage shows for small children or go on a midway-style spinner also for small children. These are also four of the lowest-rated attractions in the park.

The afternoon portion of Len's Genie's itinerary looked like this:

12:10 P.M. Ride *Millennium Falcon:* Smugglers Run.
2:00 P.M. Experience Star Tours—The Adventures Continue.
2:35 P.M. Ride Star Wars: Rise of the Resistance (using standby line).
4:30 P.M. Ride Alien Swirling Saucers.
5:35 P.M. See *Muppet*Vision 3D.*
6:00 P.M. Eat dinner at ABC Commissary.
6:40 P.M. See the *Vacation Fun* Mickey Mouse movie.
7:30 P.M. Ride The Twilight Zone Tower of Terror.
8:45 P.M. Watch the *Wonderful World of Animation* projection show.

Rise of the Resistance broke down before Len could ride it, and Genie swapped Rise for Slinky Dog Dash. Even though Rise resumed operation shortly after, Genie never suggested it to Len again.

Note that Genie's initial 12½-hour plan didn't include Mickey & Minnie's Runaway Railway, Slinky Dog Dash, or Rock 'n' Roller Coaster—some of the park's highest-rated attractions for his age group. And while Len eventually got on Slinky, he missed out on Rise of the Resistance. So in a full day in the park, with plenty of time, Len experienced just three of the top five rides.

What happened to Len in the Studios isn't unusual: In every park where we've tried Genie, it asked us for preferences and produced an itinerary that ignored all or most of those choices.

Other readers have chimed in with similar experiences. Here's one from a family from Wisconsin:

> *We were VERY disappointed with the new Genie app. It was tedious to use, not intuitive, and showed us things we could care less about and could not remove from our screens. How many times in a day must we tell the app that we don't want to go to Swiss Family Treehouse?*

We've heard that guest satisfaction survey results for Genie are terrible. That's not surprising. As we see it, Genie is two parts crowd control for Disney park operations, two parts upselling engine, and *maybe* one part planning app. Genie is unlikely to get you to all of a park's highest-rated attractions. Needless to say, we don't think it's a substitute for a good touring plan. We don't recommend it. To anyone. Ever.

COST: The basic version of Genie is free. It is still not worth using.

USE THE SINGLE-RIDER LINE *(if available)*

THIS TIME-SAVER, a line for individuals riding alone, is available at **Test Track** and **Remy's Ratatouille Adventure** in EPCOT, **Expedition Everest** in Animal Kingdom, and *Millennium Falcon:* **Smugglers Run, Rock 'n' Roller Coaster,** and **Star Wars: Rise of the Resistance** at Hollywood Studios. The objective is to fill odd spaces left by groups that don't quite fill the ride vehicle. Because there aren't many singles and most groups are unwilling to split up, single-rider lines are almost always incredibly short. The one exception is at Rock 'n' Roller Coaster, where the single-rider line will regularly close when it's longer than the standby queue.

PART 4

MAKING *the* MOST *of* YOUR MONEY

KEY QUESTIONS ANSWERED IN THIS CHAPTER

- What kind(s) of tickets do I need for Disney World? *(page 66)*
- Where can I find ticket discounts? *(page 70)*
- What are MagicBands, and how do they work? *(page 73)*
- Which special events are worth the extra cost? *(page 74)*

The least surprising part of our trip was the large number of "Most Expensive Day Ever" shirts that we saw around the parks.

—A reader from Georgia

ALLOCATING MONEY

HOW MUCH DOES A DISNEY VACATION COST?

EVERY YEAR, WE HEAR FROM thousands of families who are either planning or just back from a Disney vacation, and we talk with travel agents who hear from thousands more. What generally surprises these families the most is how much their trip ends up costing.

To help you avoid that surprise, we've created the table on pages 62–64. It shows how much Disney vacation you get for $1,500, $2,000, $3,000, and $4,000, for families of various sizes. Each price category contains a list of hotel options (off-site budget, Disney Value, Disney Moderate, or Disney Deluxe) and meal types (counter service or table service). These options illustrate the trade-offs you should consider when planning your trip—and there *will* be trade-offs. Here's an example for a family of two adults and one child with a $2,000 budget, excluding transportation:

OPTION A One full day at a Disney theme park, one table-service meal and one counter-service meal per person, and two nights at a Deluxe resort

OPTION B Two full days at Disney theme parks, two table-service meals and two counter-service meals per person, and three nights at a budget off-site motel

In this case, and in general, your choice is between (1) a nicer hotel or (2) a longer trip (more time in the parks) at a cheaper hotel. You might also get better meals if you cut costs in other categories.

If you'd like to plug in your own numbers, you can download our spreadsheet at theugseries.com/wdwyouget. Ticket prices are based on Disney's February 2025 costs and include tax. All hotel prices are quoted for summer nights in 2025 and include tax. What you'll pay may vary, depending on what time of year you visit.

Here are the assumptions we made to go along with actual prices from Disney's website:

- Children are ages 3-9; adults are age 10 and up.
- One night at a non-Disney budget hotel—the **Quality Inn & Suites by the Parks**—booked through the hotel, costs $127.
- One night at any of **Disney's All-Star Resorts** (all had the cheapest Disney Value resort rates at the time) costs $223 on the WDW website.
- One night at **Disney's Coronado Springs Resort** (the cheapest Disney Moderate resort at the time) costs $323 using Disney's website.
- One night in a studio at **Disney's Saratoga Springs Resort** (the cheapest Disney Deluxe/Disney Vacation Club resort at the time) costs $543 using Disney's website.
- Resort prices represent **rack rates,** or the price without any discount. Frequently, you could travel during seasons when Disney is offering room discounts and pay less than what is listed here.
- A day's worth of counter-service meals (two counter-service meals), plus a snack, costs $63 for adults and $31 for kids.
- A day's worth of table-service meals (one counter-service meal and one table-service meal), plus a snack, costs $99 for adults and $52 for kids.

For most trips in these price ranges, theme park admission ranges from 35% to 60% of the cost of a trip, regardless of family size. If you're not staying at a Disney Deluxe resort, it's safe to assume that theme park admission costs will take half of your budget (again, excluding transportation).

It's a different story for off-site hotels, which lack services like free shuttles and extra time in the theme parks. Excellent third-party resorts, such as the **Sheraton Vistana** and **Marriott's Harbour Lake,** offer *two-bedroom* rooms at rates up to 65% less than those of Disney's cheapest *one-bedroom* rooms at Deluxe resorts. And local Airbnb or Vrbo options can offer even more space for even less. But if you pick one of these off-site locations, make sure to factor in the cost of a car, parking, and gas.

How to Save Over $600 on Your Trip

In this book, you'll find many techniques for saving money on a Walt Disney World vacation, including finding an inexpensive hotel, discounts on park tickets, and budget-friendly restaurants. But sometimes you can do all of that and *still* need to cut your overall costs to stay within your budget.

Let's go over some "bonus" things you can do to potentially save more than $600 on your Disney vacation. For each of these tips,

continued on page 64

WHAT YOU PAY AND WHAT YOU GET AT WDW

2 ADULTS/$4,000

BUDGET OPTION ($4,009)
- 8 days theme park admission, parking
- 8 nights at a budget off-site motel
- 12 CS meals, 4 TS meals per person

VALUE OPTION ($3,966)
- 6 days theme park admission
- 7 nights at a Disney Value resort
- 9 CS meals, 3 TS meals per person

MODERATE OPTION ($4,004)
- 5 days theme park admission
- 6 nights at a Disney Moderate resort
- 9 CS meals, 1 TS meal per person

DELUXE OPTION ($3,729)
- 3 days theme park admission
- 4 nights at a Disney Deluxe resort
- 5 CS meal, 3 TS meals per person

2 ADULTS, 2 KIDS/$4,000

BUDGET OPTION ($3,999)
- 5 days theme park admission, parking
- 5 nights at a budget off-site motel
- 7 CS meals, 1 TS meal per person

VALUE OPTION ($4,064)
- 4 days theme park admission
- 4 nights at a Disney Value resort
- 8 CS meals per person

MODERATE OPTION ($3,979)
- 3 days theme park admission
- 4 nights at a Disney Moderate resort
- 4 CS meal, 2 TS meals per person

DELUXE OPTION ($4,087)
- 3 days theme park admission
- 3 nights at a Disney Deluxe resort
- 6 CS meals per person

2 ADULTS, 1 KID/$4,000

BUDGET OPTION ($4,039)
- 6 days theme park admission, parking
- 6 nights at a budget off-site motel
- 11 CS meals, 1 TS meal per person

VALUE OPTION ($3,942)
- 4 days theme park admission
- 5 nights at a Disney Value resort
- 4 CS meals, 4 TS meals per person

MODERATE OPTION ($4,069)
- 4 days theme park admission
- 5 nights at a Disney Moderate resort
- 8 CS meals per person

DELUXE OPTION ($4,073)
- 3 days theme park admission
- 4 nights at a Disney Deluxe resort
- 3 CS meals, 3 TS meals per person

3 ADULTS/$4,000

BUDGET OPTION ($3,957)
- 5 days theme park admission, parking
- 6 nights at a budget off-site motel
- 7 CS meals, 1 TS meal per person

VALUE OPTION ($3,933)
- 5 days theme park admission
- 5 nights at a Disney Value resort
- 6 CS meals, 2 TS meals per person

MODERATE OPTION ($4,002)
- 4 days theme park admission
- 4 nights at a Disney Moderate resort
- 7 CS meals, 1 TS meal per person

DELUXE OPTION ($3,963)
- 3 days theme park admission
- 3 nights at a Disney Deluxe resort
- 3 CS meals, 3 TS meals per person

3 ADULTS, 1 KID/$4,000

BUDGET OPTION ($4,034)
- 4 days theme park admission, parking
- 5 nights at a budget off-site motel
- 8 CS meals per person

VALUE OPTION ($3,850)
- 3 days theme park admission
- 4 nights at a Disney Value resort
- 3 CS meals, 3 TS meals per person

MODERATE OPTION ($3,992)
- 3 days theme park admission
- 4 nights at a Disney Moderate resort
- 4 CS meals, 2 TS meals per person

DELUXE OPTION ($3,614)
- 2 days theme park admission
- 3 nights at a Disney Deluxe resort
- 2 CS meals, 2 TS meals per person

2 ADULTS/$3,000

BUDGET OPTION ($2,926)
- 5 days theme park admission, parking
- 6 nights at a budget off-site motel
- 9 CS meals, 1 TS meal per person

VALUE OPTION ($3,076)
- 4 days theme park admission
- 6 nights at a Disney Value resort
- 8 CS meals per person

MODERATE OPTION ($3,028)
- 4 days theme park admission
- 4 nights at a Disney Moderate resort
- 8 CS meals per person

DELUXE OPTION ($2,971)
- 3 days theme park admission
- 3 nights at a Disney Deluxe resort
- 6 CS meals per person

2 ADULTS, 2 KIDS/$3,000

BUDGET OPTION ($3,025)
- 3 days theme park admission, parking
- 4 nights at a budget off-site motel
- 6 CS meals per person

VALUE OPTION ($3,127)
- 3 days theme park admission
- 3 nights at a Disney Value resort
- 6 CS meals per person

MODERATE OPTION ($2,851)
- 2 days theme park admission
- 3 nights at a Disney Moderate resort
- 2 CS meals, 2 TS meals per person

DELUXE OPTION ($2,968)
- 2 days theme park admission
- 2 nights at a Disney Deluxe resort
- 2 CS meals, 2 TS meals per person

CS = counter service (aka quick service)   TS = table service (aka full service)

WHAT YOU PAY AND WHAT YOU GET AT WDW *(continued)*

2 ADULTS, 1 KID/$3,000

BUDGET OPTION ($3,167)
- 4 days theme park admission, parking
- 5 nights at a budget off-site motel
- 8 CS meals per person

VALUE OPTION ($2,979)
- 3 days theme park admission
- 4 nights at a Disney Value resort
- 4 CS meals, 2 TS meals per person

MODERATE OPTION ($2,962)
- 3 days theme park admission
- 3 nights at a Disney Moderate resort
- 5 CS meals, 1 TS meal per person

DELUXE OPTION ($3,000)
- 2 days theme park admission
- 3 nights at a Disney Deluxe resort
- 3 CS meals, 1 TS meal per person

3 ADULTS/$3,000

BUDGET OPTION ($2,921)
- 3 days theme park admission, parking
- 5 nights at a budget off-site motel
- 4 CS meals, 2 TS meals per person

VALUE OPTION ($3,013)
- 3 days theme park admission
- 4 nights at a Disney Value resort
- 3 CS meals, 1 TS meal per person

MODERATE OPTION ($2,982)
- 3 days theme park admission
- 3 nights at a Disney Moderate resort
- 6 CS meals per person

DELUXE OPTION ($2,982)
- 2 days theme park admission
- 3 nights at a Disney Deluxe resort
- 4 CS meals per person

3 ADULTS, 1 KID/$3,000

BUDGET OPTION ($3,011)
- 3 days theme park admission, parking
- 3 nights at a budget off-site motel
- 3 TS meals per person

VALUE OPTION ($3,005)
- 2 days theme park admission
- 3 nights at a Disney Value resort
- 3 CS meals, 3 TS meals per person

MODERATE OPTION ($2,955)
- 2 days theme park admission
- 3 nights at a Disney Moderate resort
- 2 CS meals, 2 TS meals per person

DELUXE OPTION ($2,943)
- 2 days theme park admission
- 1 night at a Disney Deluxe resort
- 3 CS meals, 1 TS meal per person

2 ADULTS/$2,000

BUDGET OPTION ($1,981)
- 3 days theme park admission, parking
- 4 nights at a budget off-site motel
- 5 CS meals, 1 TS meal per person

VALUE OPTION ($2,012)
- 3 days theme park admission
- 3 nights at a Disney Value resort
- 6 CS meals per person

MODERATE OPTION ($2,014)
- 2 days theme park admission
- 3 nights at a Disney Moderate resort
- 2 CS meals, 2 TS meals per person

DELUXE OPTION ($1,988)
- 2 days theme park admission
- 2 nights at a Disney Deluxe resort
- 2 CS meals, 2 TS meals per person

2 ADULTS, 2 KIDS/$2,000

BUDGET OPTION ($2,073)
- 2 days theme park admission, parking
- 3 nights at a budget off-site motel
- 2 CS meals, 2 TS meals per person

VALUE OPTION ($2,099)
- 2 days theme park admission
- 2 nights at a Disney Value resort
- 4 CS meals per person

MODERATE OPTION ($1,616)
- 1 day theme park admission
- 2 nights at a Disney Moderate resort
- 2 CS meals per person

DELUXE OPTION ($2,056)
- 1 day theme park admission
- 2 nights at a Disney Deluxe resort
- 1 CS meal, 1 TS meal per person

2 ADULTS, 1 KID/$2,000

BUDGET OPTION ($1,883)
- 2 days theme park admission, parking
- 3 nights at a budget off-site motel
- 2 CS meals, 2 TS meals per person

VALUE OPTION ($1,947)
- 2 days theme park admission
- 3 nights at a Disney Value resort
- 4 CS meals per person

MODERATE OPTION ($2,016)
- 2 days theme park admission
- 1 night at a Disney Moderate resort
- 3 CS meals, 1 TS meal per person

DELUXE OPTION ($1,840)
- 1 day theme park admission
- 2 nights at a Disney Deluxe resort
- 1 CS meal, 1 TS meal per person

3 ADULTS/$2,000

BUDGET OPTION ($1,987)
- 2 days theme park admission, parking
- 3 nights at a budget off-site motel
- 2 CS meals, 2 TS meals per person

VALUE OPTION ($2,023)
- 2 days theme park admission
- 3 nights at a Disney Value resort
- 4 CS meals per person

MODERATE OPTION ($1,999)
- 2 days theme park admission
- 2 nights at a Disney Moderate resort
- 4 CS meals per person

DELUXE OPTION ($1,892)
- 1 day theme park admission
- 2 nights at a Disney Deluxe resort
- 1 CS meal, 1 TS meal per person

CS = counter service (aka quick service)   TS = table service (aka full service)

continued on next page

WHAT YOU PAY AND WHAT YOU GET AT WDW (continued)

3 ADULTS, 1 KID/$2,000

BUDGET OPTION ($2,021)
- 2 days theme park admission, parking
- 2 nights at a budget off-site motel
- 4 CS meals per person

VALUE OPTION ($1,469)
- 1 day theme park admission
- 2 nights at a Disney Value resort
- 1 CS meal, 1 TS meal per person

MODERATE OPTION ($1,668)
- 1 day theme park admission
- 2 nights at a Disney Moderate resort
- 1 CS meal, 1 TS meal per person

DELUXE OPTION ($1,565)
- 1 day theme park admission
- 1 night at a Disney Deluxe resort
- 1 CS meal, 1 TS meal per person

2 ADULTS/$1,500

BUDGET OPTION ($1,465)
- 2 days theme park admission, parking
- 3 nights at a budget off-site motel
- 2 CS meals, 2 TS meals per person

VALUE OPTION ($1,491)
- 2 days theme park admission
- 2 nights at a Disney Value resort
- 2 CS meals, 2 TS meals per person

MODERATE OPTION ($1,548)
- 2 days theme park admission
- 2 nights at a Disney Moderate resort
- 4 CS meals per person

DELUXE OPTION ($1,080)
- 1 day theme park admission
- 1 night at a Disney Deluxe resort
- 2 CS meals, 2 TS meals per person

2 ADULTS, 2 KIDS/$1,500

BUDGET OPTION ($1,243)
- 1 day theme park admission, parking
- 2 nights at a budget off-site motel
- 1 CS meal, 1 TS meal per person

VALUE OPTION ($1,416)
- 1 day theme park admission
- 2 nights at a Disney Value resort
- 1 CS meal, 1 TS meal per person

MODERATE OPTION ($1,501)
- 1 day theme park admission
- 2 nights at a Disney Moderate resort
- 2 CS meals per person

DELUXE OPTION ($1,512)
- 1 day theme park admission
- 1 night at a Disney Deluxe resort
- 1 CS meal, 1 TS meal per person

2 ADULTS, 1 KID/$1,500

BUDGET OPTION ($1,571)
- 2 days theme park admission, parking
- 2 nights at a budget off-site motel
- 4 CS meals per person

VALUE OPTION ($1,200)
- 1 day theme park admission
- 2 nights at a Disney Value resort
- 1 CS meal, 1 TS meal per person

MODERATE OPTION ($1,400)
- 1 day theme park admission
- 2 nights at a Disney Moderate resort
- 1 CS meal, 1 TS meal per person

DELUXE OPTION ($1,296)
- 1 day theme park admission
- 1 night at a Disney Deluxe resort
- 1 CS meal, 1 TS meal per person

3 ADULTS/$1,500

BUDGET OPTION ($1,079)
- 1 day theme park admission, parking
- 2 nights at a budget off-site motel
- 1 CS meal, 1 TS meal per person

VALUE OPTION ($1,252)
- 1 day theme park admission
- 2 nights at a Disney Value resort
- 1 CS meal, 1 TS meal per person

MODERATE OPTION ($1,452)
- 1 day theme park admission
- 2 nights at a Disney Moderate resort
- 1 CS meal, 1 TS meal per person

DELUXE OPTION ($1,349)
- 1 day theme park admission
- 1 night at a Disney Deluxe resort
- 1 CS meal, 1 TS meal per person

3 ADULTS, 1 KID/$1,500

BUDGET OPTION ($1,295)
- 1 day theme park admission, parking
- 2 nights at a budget off-site motel
- 1 CS meal, 1 TS meal per person

VALUE OPTION ($1,469)
- 1 day theme park admission
- 2 nights at a Disney Value resort
- 1 CS meal, 1 TS meal per person

MODERATE OPTION ($1,540)
- 1 day theme park admission
- 2 nights at a Disney Moderate resort
- 2 CS meals per person

DELUXE OPTION ($1,436)
- 1 day theme park admission
- 1 night at a Disney Deluxe resort
- 1 CS meal, 1 TS meal per person

CS = counter service (aka quick service)   TS = table service (aka full service)

continued from page 61

assume a family of four traveling to Walt Disney World for a one-week (six-day, seven-night) vacation. Our sample family includes two adults and two children, ages 4 and 7.

ALLOCATING MONEY

TIP 1: RESEARCH AND PREPARE FOR THE WEATHER
It can rain at Disney World at any time of year, and it can get unbearably hot and surprisingly cold. Bring your own rain ponchos, sweatshirts, and/or neck fans instead of purchasing them in the parks.

Don't buy 2 adult ponchos x $12 and 2 kids' ponchos x $10 in the parks = **$44**
Do buy 4 ponchos at local dollar store or online = **$5**
SAVINGS $44 − $5 = **$39**

Don't buy 2 adult sweatshirts x $60 and 2 kids' sweatshirts x $40 in the parks = **$200** (*ouch*)
Do bring your own from home, or buy 4 Disney sweatshirts outside the parks ($25/adult and $15/kid) = **$80**
SAVINGS $200 − $80 = **$120**

Don't buy 2 neck fans for the family to share x $30 in the parks = **$60**
Do buy 2 neck fans in advance x $16 = **$32**
SAVINGS $60 − $32 = **$28**

TIP 2: BUY TICKETS IN ADVANCE . . . FAR IN ADVANCE
Disney is pretty predictable about raising ticket prices every year. The good news is this lets you plan ahead and purchase your park tickets in advance.

Don't wait until a couple of months out to buy park tickets
Do buy tickets in advance either from Disney or from one of our recommended ticket wholesalers (see page 69)
AVERAGE SAVINGS $25 x 4 tickets = **$100**

TIP 3: BRING YOUR OWN STROLLER OR RENT FROM A THIRD PARTY (RATHER THAN DISNEY)
Our sample family wants a stroller for their 4-year-old in the parks. Disney strollers are cheap but bulky and uncomfortable. They'll do in a pinch, but you can do better for your money.

Don't rent a stroller for $13 per day (length-of-stay rate) x 6 days = **$78**
Do buy 1 umbrella stroller outside the parks (much more comfortable and convenient) = **$32**
Or rent 1 Baby Jogger City Mini stroller or similar from a third party (*much* more comfortable and convenient; see page 300) = **$75**
SAVINGS $3 to $46, plus whining avoidance

TIP 4: STAY HYDRATED FOR FREE
All Disney restaurants (not food carts) will give you a free cup of ice water. Instead of wasting money on bottled water or sugary drinks, this is an easy way to save some cash. For our sample family, let's assume that everyone wants to drink something other than water at breakfast and that the kids' meals will include a drink at lunch and dinner. Only the adults will drink free water, and we'll assume they each skip one bottled water and one soda per day.

Don't buy 1 soda and 1 bottled water at $4.49 each x 2 adults x 6 days = **$108**
Do drink free water instead = **$0**
SAVINGS $108 − $0 = **$108**

TIP 5: BRING YOUR OWN SNACKS AND SODAS
It's amazing how much you can save by bringing your own snacks and drinks into the park. You can bring them from home or have groceries delivered to your resort. Consider choosing fun things that are different from what you

would normally feed your kids at home so that the snacks are still a treat, just less expensive.

Don't buy 1 snack at $6 each and 1 soda at $4.49 each x 4 people x 6 days = **$252**
Do bring your own snacks and sodas = **$60**
SAVINGS $252 - $60 = **$192**

TIP 6: EAT BREAKFAST IN YOUR ROOM
This not only saves you time but could also save you a small fortune. As with snacks and sodas, you can bring them from home or have groceries delivered. It's quick, easy, and cheap.

Don't buy one $13 breakfast platter + one $7 yogurt parfait + two $8 kids' Mickey waffle meals + four $3.79 milks x 6 days = **$307**
Do bring your own breakfast, including paper bowls, napkins, plastic spoons, cereal, breakfast pastries, mini doughnuts, cereal bars, fruit, juice, and milk = **$90**
SAVINGS $307 - $90 = **$217**

TOTAL SAVINGS **$647-$782** *($108-$131 per day)*

Three More Tips

1. Buy your tickets online from one of the sellers listed on page 69. Get tickets only for the number of days you plan to visit, skipping any add-ons. You can even time your tickets to take advantage of date-based pricing (see below).

2. Rent a condo or vacation home close to the parks if you want more space for less money. You'll have a longer and less convenient commute to the parks, but you'll get much more bang for your buck. Just check traffic patterns using a mapping app that displays traffic, such as Google Maps, before you book. Look up your potential vacation rental's address at park opening and closing times to see what traffic you might encounter when driving to and from the parks.

3. Buy discounted Disney apparel and souvenirs from one of Orlando's two **Disney Character Warehouse** outlets (theugseries.com/disneyoutlets). Or stop by **Primark** on your way back to MCO at the end of your trip. Even better, purchase for kids beforehand, then surprise them during the vacation. They'll still be excited about souvenirs, and you will avoid Disney gift shop sticker shock.

WALT DISNEY WORLD ADMISSION TICKETS

DISNEY OFFERS THOUSANDS of theme park ticket options, ranging from the humble (yet somehow still expensive) **1-Day Base Ticket,** which is good for a single day's entry into one Disney theme park, to the blinged-out **Incredi-Pass,** which is good for 365 days of admission into every Disney theme park and more attractions. See pages 70–71 for a summary of the most common admission types.

DATE-BASED PRICING

DISNEY USES DATE-BASED PRICING for theme park tickets, meaning prices fluctuate depending on the date, similar to the way you could pay more or less for hotels and flights depending on when you want to travel. Additionally, 1-day tickets for the Magic Kingdom usually cost more than tickets for the other parks.

Tickets are generally most expensive when kids are out of school: Christmas and other holidays, spring break, and summer vacation. Less-expensive tickets are available during nonholiday periods when kids are in school and during peak hurricane season in September.

Your ticket price depends on the first date you plan to visit a theme park or water park. Your final price will be based on that starting date, the number of days you plan to visit theme parks or water parks, and whether you plan to visit more than one theme park per day.

If you reschedule your vacation from days when tickets are more expensive to days when they are less expensive, Disney will not refund the difference in price—but they will charge you the difference if you need to move from less expensive to more expensive days.

TICKET ADD-ONS

THREE TICKET ADD-ON OPTIONS are available with your park admission, each at an additional cost:

PARK HOPPER This add-on is the one you'll need if you want to visit more than one theme park per day. The cost is usually $90–$100 on top of the base ticket price. The longer your stay, the less it costs per day. For example, as an add-on to a 7-Day Base Ticket, the flat fee works out to around $14 a day for park-hopping privileges; as an add-on to a 2-Day Base Ticket, the fee is more like $45 a day. If you want to be able to change parks after lunch or hit up EPCOT every night for dining, this is the add-on you need. Keep in mind that you can't choose to park-hop for just a day or two and not pay for park-hopping on other days. It's all-or-nothing.

WATER PARK AND SPORTS This $75 (including tax) option provides daily entry to **Blizzard Beach, Typhoon Lagoon, Oak Trail Golf Course, Fantasia Gardens and Fairways** and **Winter Summerland** minigolf, and the **ESPN Wide World of Sports Complex.**

PARK HOPPER PLUS The Park Hopper Plus (PHP) option combines the Park Hopper and Water Park and Sports add-ons. It costs $90–$122 more than a base ticket, including tax, which is cheaper than the combined cost of the two options purchased separately.

You can't change how many Park Hopper/Water Park/PHP admissions you can buy with either option; the number is fixed, and unused days are not refundable. You can, however, skip Park Hopper/Water Park/PHP entirely and buy an individual admission to any of the venues listed under "Water Park and Sports" above—that may be the best deal if you won't be park-hopping and want to visit just Typhoon Lagoon and/or Blizzard Beach one time.

If you buy a ticket but then decide later that you want to add the Park Hopper/PHP option, you can do so. But Disney doesn't prorate the cost: If you add Park Hopper/PHP on the last day of your trip, you'll pay the same price as if you'd bought it before you left home.

WHEN TICKETS EXPIRE
(for tickets dated August 13, 2021, and later)

ALONG WITH IMPLEMENTING date-based pricing, Disney has shortened the amount of time you have to use your tickets. If you haven't been to Disney in several years, you're used to all tickets expiring 14 days from the date of first use. Ticket expiration is now based on how many days you're visiting the theme parks and water parks, as shown in the table below.

WHEN TICKETS EXPIRE										
DAYS ON BASE TICKET	1	2	3	4	5	6	7	8	9	10
DAYS TILL TICKET EXPIRES FROM FIRST USE *(without Park Hopper Plus)*	Expires after first use	4	5	7	8	9	10	12	13	14
DAYS TILL TICKET EXPIRES FROM FIRST USE *(with Park Hopper Plus)*	1	5	6	8	9	10	11	13	14	15

For example, if you purchase a basic 4-Day Base Ticket and specify that you'll start using it on June 1, 2026, you must complete your four theme park visits by midnight on June 7, 2026. *Once you start using your ticket, any unused admissions expire even if you don't use them.*

If you purchase a ticket and don't use any of it before it expires, you can apply the amount paid for that ticket toward the purchase of a new ticket at current prices, provided the new ticket's price is the same as (or more than) that of the expired ticket.

ANNUAL PASSES

ANNUAL PASSES PROVIDE UNLIMITED USE of the major theme parks for one year. Pass holders can add water park access for $105. Four versions are available (prices are for age 3 and up and include tax):

- The **Pixie Dust Pass** ($469; Florida residents only) lets you have up to three simultaneous park reservations. The Pixie Dust Pass has the most blockout dates, or dates when the pass cannot be used (almost all weekends are off-limits, plus a week or two around every major holiday and chunks of time around minor holidays).
- The **Pirate Pass** ($829; Florida residents only) includes four simultaneous park reservations. It has fewer weekend blockout dates than the Pixie Dust Pass but retains blockout dates for every major and minor holiday.
- The **Sorcerer Pass** ($1,079; Florida residents and Disney Vacation Club members only) includes five simultaneous park reservations. The only blockout dates are the Wednesday–Saturday around Thanksgiving, and the two weeks surrounding Christmas and New Year's.
- The **Incredi-Pass** ($1,549; available to everyone) includes five simultaneous park reservations and has no blockout dates.

Note that while park reservations are no longer required for date-based tickets, they are still required for certain types of admission, including Annual Passes.

Annual Pass holders also get some perks, including free parking; hotel, dining, and merchandise discounts; and seasonal offers such as a dedicated entrance line at the parks. They can also visit the parks after 2 p.m. without needing a reservation (except on Saturdays and Sundays in the Magic Kingdom). Beginning in 2024, Annual Pass holders were also given "good-to-go" days when no park reservations were needed at all. Annual Passes are not valid for special events. See disneyworld.disney.go.com/passes for details.

WHERE TO PURCHASE DISNEY WORLD TICKETS

TICKETS ARE AVAILABLE at Disney World resorts and theme parks, Disney Store locations, and Disney World's website (disneyworld.disney.go.com) for the prices shown on pages 70–71. (If you purchase on arrival at the park, you will incur a $21.30-per-ticket surcharge for tickets of three days or longer.)

If you're trying to keep your vacation costs to an absolute minimum, consider using a **third-party wholesaler,** such as **Boardwalk Ticketing** (boardwalkticketing.com) or **Tripster** (tripster.com), especially for trips of three or more park days. All tickets are brand-new, and the savings can easily exceed $200 for a family of four. Tripster offers discounted tickets for almost all Central Florida attractions, including Walt Disney World, Universal, and SeaWorld. Boardwalk Ticketing offers them only for Disney. Discounts for the major theme parks range from about 6% to 12%; tickets for other attractions are more deeply discounted.

*un*official **TIP**
If you order physical tickets in advance, allow enough time for them to be mailed to your home.

Third-party wholesalers will provide you with electronic tickets just like Disney does, so you'll be able to make hotel, dining, and ride reservations through the My Disney Experience website, though you may have to wait up to a week to do so when ordering from a third party (see page 69).

You might be wondering why Disney gives third-party wholesalers discounts on tickets. Here's the strategy: Disney knows most visitors will pay full price for tickets, so there's no incentive to offer them a discount. However, Disney also knows that there are other shoppers who will visit only if they can get a deal. Disney uses third-party wholesalers to offer discounted tickets to those shoppers, so it doesn't have to offer discounts to the general public. It's a win–win–win: The discount shoppers get their deal, Disney maximizes its revenue, and third-party companies earn a little bit too.

Where *Not* to Buy Tickets and Passes

In addition to the many authorized resellers of Disney admissions, there are quite a few unauthorized ones. They buy up unused days on legitimately purchased park passes and resell them as if they were brand-new.

These resellers insist that you specify the exact days you plan to use the ticket. They already know, of course, how many days are left on the pass and when it expires. If you tell them that you plan to use it tomorrow and the next two days, then they'll sell you a ticket that has three days left on it and expires in three days. Because they don't tell you this, you might assume that the usual five-day expiration period applies from the date of first use. If you skip

*un*official **TIP**
Also steer clear of tickets offered on eBay and Craigslist.

WDW THEME PARK TICKET OPTIONS

	1-DAY	2-DAY	3-DAY	4-DAY	5-DAY
USE WITHIN:	1 DAY	4 DAYS	5 DAYS	7 DAYS	8 DAYS
BASE TICKET AGES 3-9					
ALL PARKS: $121-$207		$252-$374	$377-$551	$498-$701	$528-$784
	–	($126-$187/day)	($126-$184/day)	($125-$175/day)	($106-$157/day)
BASE TICKET AGE 10+					
ALL PARKS: $127-$212		$264-$383	$395-$566	$507-$720	$551-$807
	–	($132-$192/day)	($132-$189/day)	($127-$180/day)	($110-$161/day)

Base Ticket admits guest to one theme park each day of use. Tickets must be used within the number of days shown in the "Use Within" row above.

PARK HOPPER

AGES 3-9: $191-$286		$332-$464	$457-$641	$589-$802	$619-$885
AGE 10+: $196-$292		$344-$474	$475-$656	$597-$821	$641-$908

Park Hopper option entitles guest to visit more than one theme park on each day of use. See below for details.

WATER PARK AND SPORTS

AGES 3-9: NOT SOLD		$327-$448	$452-$625	$573-$775	$603-$858
AGE 10+: NOT SOLD		$334-$458	$470-$640	$581-$794	$625-$882

Water Park and Sports entitles you to a specified number of visits (between 1 and 10) to a choice of entertainment and recreation venues. It's a flat $70 fee to add to any ticket for any age and any ticket length.

PARK HOPPER PLUS

AGES 3-9: $212-$308		$355-$486	$478-$662	$610-$823	$640-$906
AGE 10+: $217-$313		$376-$495	$496-$677	$619-$842	$662-$930
	1 visit	2 visits	3 visits	4 visits	5 visits

Park Hopper Plus option entitles guest to a specified number of visits (1-10) to a choice of entertainment and recreation venues, plus the Park Hopper option above. PHP tickets expire 1 day later than the "Use Within" days above.

a day instead of using the pass on the next three consecutive days, you'll find out that it expires before you thought it would.

HOW TO SAVE MONEY ON DISNEY WORLD TICKETS

DISNEY'S DATE-BASED PRICING SCHEME is the most complicated system ever used for ticket purchases. It is so complicated, in fact, that the TouringPlans team wrote a computer program to analyze all of the options and look for loopholes in the pricing rules. Their **Ticket Price Comparison Tool** (theugseries.com/ug-ticketcalculator), aggregates ticket prices from Disney, as well as a number of online ticket vendors. To try it, answer a few questions about the size of your party and the parks you intend to visit, and the calculator will identify your four cheapest ticket options. It will also show you how much you'll save versus buying at the gate.

The program will also make recommendations for considerations other than price. For example, Annual Passes might cost more, but Disney often offers substantial resort discounts and other deals to Annual Pass holders. These resort discounts, especially during the off-season, can more than offset the price of the pass.

WALT DISNEY WORLD ADMISSION TICKETS

NOTE: ALL TICKET AND ADD-ON PRICES INCLUDE 6.5% SALES TAX.

	6-DAY	7-DAY	8-DAY	9-DAY	10-DAY
	9 DAYS	10 DAYS	12 DAYS	13 DAYS	14 DAYS
BASE TICKET AGES 3–9					
	$547–$832	$568–$853	$601–$883	$623–$892	$641–$922
	($92–$139/day)	($81–$122/day)	($75–$110/day)	($69–$99/day)	($64–$92/day)
BASE TICKET AGE 10+					
	$571–$855	$591–$879	$625–$907	$649–$928	$668–$948
	($95–$143/day)	($84–$126/day)	($78–$113/day)	($72–$103/day)	($67–$95/day)
Park choices are Magic Kingdom, EPCOT, Disney's Hollywood Studios, or Disney's Animal Kingdom.					
PARK HOPPER					
	$638–$933 / $661–$956	$658–$954 / $682–$980	$691–$984 / $716–$1,009	$714–$1,004 / $739–$1,033	$732–$1,023 / $758–$1,049
Park choices are any combination of Magic Kingdom, EPCOT, Disney's Hollywood Studios, or Disney's Animal Kingdom on each day of use.					
WATER PARK AND SPORTS					
	$622–$906 / $645–$930	$642–$928 / $666–$953	$675–$957 / $700–$982	$698–$978 / $723–$1,002	$716–$997 / $742–$1,022
Choices are Disney's Blizzard Beach water park, Disney's Typhoon Lagoon water park, Oak Trail Golf Course, ESPN Wide World of Sports Complex, and Fantasia Gardens and Fairways or Winter Summerland minigolf.					
PARK HOPPER PLUS					
	$659–$954 / $683–$978	$679–$976 / $703–$1,001	$712–$1,005 / $737–$1,030	$735–$1,026 / $760–$1,054	$753–$1,045 / $780–$1,070
	6 visits	7 visits	8 visits	9 visits	10 visits
Choices are Disney's Blizzard Beach water park, Disney's Typhoon Lagoon water park, Oak Trail Golf Course, ESPN Wide World of Sports Complex, or Fantasia Gardens and Fairways or Winter Summerland minigolf.					

If you'd rather do your own research, here's everything you'll need to consider:

1. BUY PARK TICKETS BEFORE YOU GET TO THE PARKS. As mentioned, if you buy at the theme parks, Disney adds a surcharge of $21.30 to park tickets with three or more days of admission.

2. BUY FROM A THIRD-PARTY WHOLESALER. As noted on page 69, Disney contracts with third-party ticket vendors to offer discounts to consumers who'll visit only if they can get a deal.

3. MEMBERS OF THE US MILITARY AND FLORIDA RESIDENTS GET SPECIAL DISCOUNTS. One of Disney's recent deals for US military personnel included a 4-Day Park Hopper for $350, a savings of almost $400 compared to the regular price at the time. Florida resident deals abounded beginning in 2025, with flexible four-day tickets for a steep discount too.

4. SET YOUR TICKET'S START DATE EARLIER THAN YOUR ARRIVAL DATE. Suppose you're visiting for a long weekend (Thursday–Sunday) and you're buying four-day tickets. You'd naturally pick Thursday as your ticket's start date. But remember that four-day park tickets are valid for seven days. If you're visiting at the start of a busy (that is, expensive) season, setting your ticket start date to a couple of days before you arrive can save you money. Try setting your start date for Tuesday or Wednesday to see if the price is lower.

5. IF YOU'RE VISITING ONLY ONE WATER PARK, buy a separate water park ticket instead of purchasing the Water Park and Sports add-on. The break-even point on the Water Park and Sports option is two water park visits.

6. VISIT A WATER PARK ON YOUR FIRST FULL DAY. Say your trip starts at the end of a busy period and you're already planning one water park visit. Visiting the water park on your first day allows you to set your theme park start date one day later, potentially saving money on your date-based ticket.

Ticket Deals for United Kingdom Residents

In the United Kingdom, Disney offers advance-purchase tickets that aren't available in the United States. As we went to press, you could get 14-Day **Magic Tickets** starting at £539 for adults and £519 for kids—around the same price as a 7-Day Magic Ticket. Magic Tickets provide unlimited admission to major and minor parks, along with park-hopping privileges. They expire 14 days after first use. To find out more, call ☎ 0800-169-0730 from the UK or visit disneyholidays.co.uk/walt-disney-world or the **Disney Information Bulletin Board** (thedibb.co.uk).

Discounts for Certain Groups and Individuals

CONVENTION-GOERS Disney World, Universal Orlando, SeaWorld, and other Orlando-area parks sometimes set up a web link where you can purchase discounted afternoon and evening admissions. This link should be included in your convention materials.

DISNEY CORPORATE SPONSORS If you work for one of these companies, you may be eligible for discounted admissions or perks at the parks. Check with your workplace's employee-benefits office.

DISNEY IMAGINATION CAMPUS Disney runs educational programs for K–12 students; these programs also offer ticket discounts (with restrictions). Visit disneycampus.com.

DISNEY VACATION CLUB Members can sometimes use points to pay for certain types of Annual Passes.

FLORIDA RESIDENTS get substantial savings on most tickets. You'll need to prove Florida residency with a valid driver's license or state identification card.

MILITARY, DEPARTMENT OF DEFENSE, CIVIL SERVICE Active-duty and retired military, Department of Defense (DOD) civilian employees, some civil-service employees, and dependents of these groups can buy Disney multiday admissions at a discount. Military personnel can buy discounted admission for nonmilitary guests if the military member accompanies the nonmilitary guest. If a group seeks the discount, at least half of the group's members must be eligible.

WALT DISNEY WORLD ADMISSION TICKETS

DISNEY TICKET PRICE INCREASES

DISNEY USUALLY RAISES TICKET PRICES once or twice a year. Hikes were announced in October 2024, February and December 2022, February 2020, March 2019, February and September 2018, and February 2014–2017.

Prices on all tickets went up an average of almost 7% in 2024, 9% in 2022, 6% in 2020, 4% in 2019, 9% in 2018, and 7% in 2017. For your budget, assume an increase of 5%–10% per year to be safe if you're planning ahead.

unofficial **TIP**
Save money on tickets by purchasing them before the next price increase.

FOR ADDITIONAL INFORMATION ON TICKETS

IF YOU HAVE A QUESTION regarding tickets that can be addressed only with a person-to-person conversation, call **Disney Ticket Inquiries** at ☎ 407-934-7639 or email ticket.inquiries@disneyworld.com. If you call, be aware that you may spend considerable time on hold; if you email, it can take up to three days to get a response. Fortunately, the ticket section of the Disney World website, disneyworld.disney.go.com/tickets, is straightforward in showing how ticket prices break down.

TICKETS AND MAGICBANDS

WE'VE USED THE WORD *TICKET* to describe that thing you carry around as proof of your admission purchase. In fact, there are three forms of Disney admission media—none of which is a paper ticket.

One admission medium, the **MagicBand**, is a wristband about the size and shape of a small wristwatch. It contains a tiny radio frequency identification (RFID) chip that stores a link to the record of your admission purchase in Disney's computers. Your MagicBand also functions as your Disney hotel-room key, and it can (optionally) work as a credit card for most food and merchandise purchases.

Disney seems to be phasing out sales of MagicBands and is instead attempting to only sell the newer generation, called **MagicBand+**. These are available for purchase for around $25–$40 if you are staying on-site, or $35–$50 if you are staying off-site. MagicBand+ does everything the original MagicBand does, but it will also light up and make sounds during certain interactions, like entering the park, waving at a statue, or watching a nighttime spectacular.

Each member of your family gets their own MagicBand with a unique serial number. The wristbands are removable, adjustable, and waterproof. You can choose your colors and designs when you order them at the Disney World website. Even more designs are available throughout the parks and at shopdisney.com.

Along with the wristband, each family member will be asked to select a four-digit PIN for purchases.

If you don't want a MagicBand, you're staying off-property, or you bought your admission from a third-party vendor, your second "ticket" option is a plastic **Key to the World** (**KTTW**) **Card,** which is the size of a credit card and has an embedded RFID chip.

Your third option is to use the **My Disney Experience** (**MDE**) app on your Bluetooth-enabled smartphone. This option allows you to tap your smartphone or smartwatch for admission at park entrances, the same way you tap your phone for payments at stores and restaurants.

Of the three options, we think the MagicBands and KTTW Cards are the fastest and easiest to use. The main problem with using the MDE app is that it takes much longer to pull out your phone, open the app, and find the right screen to do what you want. And that's assuming you don't have to connect to Wi-Fi, log into the app, or remember your password.

RFID for Payment, Lightning Lanes, Hotel-Room Access, and Photos

Disney's hotel-room doors have RFID readers, allowing you to enter your room simply by tapping your wristband or KTTW Card against the reader or by telling the MDE app to open the door. RFID readers are also installed at virtually every Disney cash register on-property, allowing you to pay for food, drinks, ride reservations, and souvenirs by tapping your MagicBand/KTTW Card against the reader. For in-person purchases, you'll be asked to verify your identity by entering your PIN on a small keypad. As mentioned, the MDE app requires that you enable Bluetooth transmitting and receiving for tickets, photos, ride reservations, and payments.

unofficial **TIP**
Disney strongly encourages guests to use contactless methods of payment while in the World. These include MagicBands, ApplePay, Google Pay, credit cards, and debit cards.

If you're using Disney's **Memory Maker** service (see page 360), your MagicBand or KTTW Card serves as the link between your photos and your MDE account. Each photographer carries an RFID reader on which you tap your MagicBand, KTTW Card, or phone after having your photo taken. The computers that run the Memory Maker system will link your photos to your account, and you'll be able to view them on the Disney World website or in the app.

Disney's onboard ride-photo computers also incorporate RFID technology. As you start down the big drop near the finale of Tiana's Bayou Adventure, for example, sensors read the serial number on your MagicBand (or detect the Bluetooth signal sent from the MDE app) and pass it to Tiana's cameras. When those cameras capture your family plunging past the photo spot, they attach your MagicBands' serial numbers to the photo, allowing you to see your ride photos after you've returned home. Because ride sensors may not pick up the signal from an RFID card or a phone sitting in a wallet or purse, we recommend using MagicBands if you want to be sure your on-ride photos are captured. MagicBand+ seems to work better for this purpose than the older generation.

OPTIONAL EXPENSES

WHICH SPECIAL EVENTS ARE WORTH THE MONEY?

AS A WAY TO "SELL" THE SAME THEME PARK RIDES multiple times per day, Disney constantly experiments with offers of extra time in the parks that require buying separate admission. For example, before the pandemic, the Magic Kingdom hosted a preopening event, regular park hours, and then another event after the park closed to regular guests, all on the same day.

The scope of the events varies: Evening events typically include most of a park's attractions. Holiday-themed events are held in the evening and include special entertainment, parades, fireworks, and decorations in addition to access to almost all of the park's rides; complimentary snacks are offered at certain events.

Disney restricts the number of tickets sold for these events, from a few thousand for After Hours events to less than 30,000 (we've heard) for Halloween and Christmas parties in the Magic Kingdom. As a result, wait times for rides at most of these events are usually no more than 15 minutes. Superpopular rides, such as Seven Dwarfs Mine Train or Slinky Dog Dash, will undoubtedly have longer waits, but they'll still be much shorter than waits during the day. What you're paying for, therefore, is shorter lines (in addition to other entertainment or snacks).

We think all of these events have some value to guests with limited time. To help you decide whether they are worth the cost, we've summarized each below, in the (rough) order we recommend them.

1. MICKEY'S NOT-SO-SCARY HALLOWEEN PARTY (Magic Kingdom; select days mid-August–November 1, 7 p.m.–midnight, with ticketed guests allowed into the park starting at 4 p.m.; ticket prices were $119–$199 per person in 2024). With holiday-themed characters and performers, the Magic Kingdom's Halloween parade is the best in Walt Disney World—and something you'll only see at the party. The event also includes decorations throughout the park; special (often rare) character greetings; fireworks; and occasional, light rethemeing of a few attractions, plus a boatload of candy.

2. DISNEY'S VERY MERRY CHRISTMAS PARTY (Magic Kingdom; select days early November–late December, 7 p.m.–midnight, with ticketed guests allowed into the park starting at 4 p.m.; ticket prices were $169–$219 per person in 2024). Like the Halloween party, the Christmas party offers holiday decorations and a special parade and fireworks, plus unique shows and live performances by Disney characters. However, some of the Christmas party entertainment (like the parade) is shown during the week of Christmas during normal park hours and is not exclusive to the party. We rank the Halloween party higher because it offers more for a lower price, but the Christmas party is admittedly pure magic.

3. JOLLYWOOD NIGHTS (Disney's Hollywood Studios; select days early November–late December, 7:30 p.m.–12:30 a.m., with ticketed guests allowed into the park starting at 6 p.m.; ticket prices were $159–$179 per person in 2024). This is the only holiday party offered at Walt Disney World that doesn't include complimentary snacks. But it has unique characters, unbelievably good stage shows, immersive holiday décor, incredible food options, and walk-ons for most of the popular Hollywood Studios attractions. Between 2023 and 2024, it added a full hour of party time, an ice-skating show, and a dance party without an increase in price. This is Becky's personal favorite event that Disney offers, but it's not geared toward kids/families, so we've ranked it below the two Magic Kingdom options.

4. MAGIC KINGDOM AFTER HOURS (Magic Kingdom; 3 hours after regular park closing; select Mondays and Thursdays; $175–$185 per person). Yes, it's up to $185 for 3 hours in the park (and it's $10–$20 more expensive than the same dates a year earlier), but the high cost keeps crowds low. Most rides will have wait times of 5 minutes or less, meaning that the number of rides you can visit depends largely on how fast you can walk between them and how long the rides last. Becky and her husband did After Hours at Magic Kingdom, and during the 1.5 hours before closing and the 3 event hours, they did 20 attractions, saw fireworks, and took PhotoPass photos. That's a full day in 4.5 hours.

5. DISNEY'S HOLLYWOOD STUDIOS AFTER HOURS (Disney's Hollywood Studios; 3 hours after regular park closing; typically Wednesday but day of the week varies; $155–$185 per person in 2025). If you can't get up early for **Rise of the Resistance** and you're not a single rider, this is the easiest way to experience the ride (multiple times!) with short waits. Plus, nighttime rides on **Tower of Terror** and **Slinky Dog Dash** are vastly different than daytime rides. The price is high, but the waits are the lowest you'll experience at Hollywood Studios.

6. EPCOT AFTER HOURS (EPCOT; 3 hours after regular park closing; typically Thursday, but day of the week varies; $155–$175 per person in 2025). As at Hollywood Studios, this is the way to see the park's headliners without long lines. Waits are usually so short that the limiting factor for how many rides you'll experience is likely to be the walking distance between **Remy's** and **Guardians of the Galaxy**. Because rides are so spread out and there are fewer long-wait attractions to absorb crowds, we think EPCOT After Hours is the least worthwhile of the major theme park After Hours options.

7. DISNEY H2O GLOW AFTER HOURS (Typhoon Lagoon; 3 hours after regular park closing; typically Saturdays mid-May–early September, but day of the week varies; $75–$85 per person in 2024). During months with warmer nights, Disney offers after-hours admission to Typhoon Lagoon. Besides the glow-in-the-dark visuals at the wave pool, this event offers some of the shortest lines you'll likely find at a Disney water park.

PART 5

ACCOMMODATIONS

KEY QUESTIONS ANSWERED IN THIS CHAPTER

- What are the pros and cons of staying at a Disney resort? *(page 79)*
- What kinds of hotels are represented at Walt Disney World? *(page 82)*
- Where can I find hotel discounts? How do they work? *(page 84)*
- Which Disney resort should I choose? *(page 88)*
- What amenities are offered at Disney resorts? *(page 96)*
- What do the rooms at Disney resorts look like? *(page 100)*
- What are some simple tips for booking my hotel online? *(page 179)*

The BASIC CONSIDERATIONS

LOCATING A SUITABLE HOTEL OR CONDO is critical to planning any Walt Disney World vacation. The first question is whether you should stay at a hotel inside Disney World (**on-site**) or outside Disney World (**off-site**).

Around 86% of *Unofficial Guide* readers stay on-site during their trip. On top of the convenience and the amenities, readers say they enjoy "being in the Disney bubble"—that is, the special magic and convenience associated with staying inside the World. "I feel more a part of everything and less like a visitor," one guest writes. We get it, and we agree.

> *unofficial* **TIP**
> In general, your first choice for lodging should be an on-site resort. The extra cost is generally more than offset by the room quality, amenities, transportation, and theme park benefits.

The primary reasons to stay off-site are cost and space. Walt Disney World room rates vary from about $150 on a slow weeknight at what Disney calls its Value resorts to more than $2,000 per night during the holidays at its Deluxe properties. Clean, bare-bones motel rooms off-site can be had for as little as $70 a night (though you will have to make some compromises at that price point). It's sometimes possible to get an off-site hotel room comparable to one at a Disney Moderate resort for half the cost during holidays, or a room twice the size for the same money, all within a 15-minute drive of the parks.

There are advantages to staying outside Disney World and driving or taking a hotel shuttle to the theme parks. Meals can be less expensive, and rooming outside the World makes you more likely to visit other Orlando-area attractions and dining spots. **Universal Studios, Universal Islands of Adventure,** the **Kennedy Space Center Visitor Complex, SeaWorld,** and **Gatorland** are well worth your attention.

Because Walt Disney World is so large, some off-property hotels are actually closer in both time and distance to some of the theme parks than other Disney resorts are. Our Hotel Information Table on pages 194–199 includes commuting times from the Disney resorts and select non-Disney hotels.

If you're looking for the cheapest room possible on the premise that "it's just a place to sleep," please read our comments on page 180 first. Our research indicates that most people are happier *not* booking the cheapest room, even when taking the extra cost into account.

THE LATEST IN LODGING

AT THE TIME OF THIS WRITING, Disney was offering significant hotel discounts throughout 2025. With many attractions (and entire lands) going down for construction and new lands being built-out over the next several years, Disney will probably continue to discount rooms to give people an incentive to visit. This means you may be able to stretch your lodging budget.

Speaking of stretching your budget, if you're planning to stay at a Disney Moderate or Deluxe resort, it's possible to get an equivalent or superior room by renting **Disney Vacation Club** (**DVC**) points instead of paying cash (see pages 85–86). For example, it can be less expensive to rent points for a one-bedroom villa in Animal Kingdom Lodge than to pay cash for a smaller standard room at a Value resort. Likewise, renting points for a two-bedroom villa at the Grand Floridian is often less expensive than paying cash for a standard room at one of the resort's outer buildings. If renting DVC points for an on-site room is still outside your budget, see "The Best Off-Site Hotels for Families," page 180, for the best alternatives.

THE BENEFITS OF STAYING IN THE WORLD

GUESTS WHO STAY ON DISNEY PROPERTY enjoy privileges and amenities unavailable to those staying off-site. Though some of these perks are advertising gimmicks, others are real and valuable. Here are the benefits and what they mean:

1. CONVENIENCE Commuting to the theme parks using the Disney transportation system is easy (though not always fast), especially if you stay at a resort that offers monorail, boat, or Skyliner access.

2. EARLY ACCESS TO ATTRACTION AND RESTAURANT RESERVATIONS Guests at Disney resorts can make LLMP and LLSP reservations starting 7 days before check-in; off-site guests must wait until 3 days before their dated park ticket. Guests staying on-property can also make dining reservations 60 days before they arrive and then an additional 10 days into their trip.

3. EARLY THEME PARK ENTRY Disney resort guests—along with guests of the **Swan, Dolphin, Swan Reserve, Shades of Green, Signia by Hilton Orlando Bonnet Creek, Waldorf Astoria Orlando, Four Seasons Orlando,** and **Disney Springs Resort Area** hotels—enjoy extra time in the theme parks not available to off-site guests. In many cases, this means shorter waits in line for Disney's most popular rides. See page 34 for details.

4. EXTENDED EVENING THEME PARK HOURS Guests staying at Disney Deluxe resorts and DVC properties, plus the **Dolphin, Swan, Swan Reserve,** and **Shades of Green,** get two extra hours in the theme parks after they close to regular guests. At the time of this writing, Extended Evening Theme Park Hours were offered one or two days per week in various parks. See page 36 for details.

5. FREE PARKING Disney resort guests pay nothing to park in theme park lots—this saves you $30 per day. Likewise, Disney doesn't charge a fee for overnight parking at its resorts, unlike most off-site hotels.

6. GOLFING PRIVILEGES Disney resort guests can get priority tee times at the on-property golf courses.

7. NO RESORT FEES Unlike many hotels outside of Walt Disney World, the on-site resorts don't charge a nightly resort fee on top of their advertised rates.

THE PROS AND CONS OF STAYING ON-SITE

1. COST You should expect to pay **$150–$175 per night** (including taxes and fees), depending on time of year, for a clean, safe, well-maintained hotel room near Disney World. In or near this price range, on-site hotels come out ahead. Rooms at **Pop Century Resort,** for example, cost $183–$450 (before discounts) throughout the year. For even less, you could stay at the **All-Star Resorts,** all of which have been refurbished to look and feel almost exactly like the rooms at Pop Century. Still, for Skyliner access, we prefer Pop Century even with its slightly higher cost.

Off-site hotels and homes are often better deals for families looking for more space, or high-end lodging and service, for the same money. For instance, Disney's cheapest family suite, at the **All-Star Music Resort,** sleeps six and costs $350–$716 per night. A comparable room at the **Sonesta ES Suites Lake Buena Vista** costs around $189–$304 per night, depending on the time of year. Renting a three-bedroom condo in Kissimmee is even cheaper: around $160–$260 per night. In 2024, my (Becky's) family spent four nights at a two-bedroom condo in Oakwater Resort for less than $100 a night. We had two bedrooms, two bathrooms, two walk-in closets, laundry machines, a full kitchen, and a living room. And we were less than 15 minutes from any of the theme parks! You can afford a longer trip with those savings—a fact that more than offsets the on-site perks.

Similarly, the cheapest room at Disney's flagship **Grand Floridian Resort & Spa** costs about $780–$1,280. The cheapest room at the **Four Seasons Resort Orlando** (near the Magic Kingdom) is $70 above the upper end of that range. But the Four Seasons room is larger and better in every way, with restaurants generally as good as the Grand Floridian's, along with superior customer service. And the pools are like their own water park.

DISNEY VS. OFF-SITE HOTEL PRIVILEGES AT A GLANCE

HOTEL	LLMP AND LLSP RESERVATIONS	RESTAURANT RESERVATIONS	EARLY THEME PARK ENTRY	EXTENDED EVENING HOURS
Disney resort hotels and Disney Vacation Club (DVC) properties	7 days before check-in	Up to 70 days out	Yes	Deluxe, DVC only
Disney Springs Resort Area (DSRA) hotels*	3 days before park ticket begins	60 days out	Yes	No
Four Seasons Resort Orlando at Walt Disney World Resort	3 days before park ticket begins	60 days out	Yes	No
Shades of Green Resort	7 days before check-in	60 days out	Yes	Yes
Signia by Hilton Orlando Bonnet Creek	3 days before park ticket begins	60 days out	Yes	No
Swan, Dolphin, and Swan Reserve	7 days before check-in	60 days out	Yes	Yes
Waldorf Astoria Orlando	3 days before park ticket begins	60 days out	Yes	No
Non-Disney hotels	3 days before park ticket begins	60 days out	No	No

* DoubleTree Suites by Hilton, Drury Plaza Hotel Orlando, Hilton Orlando Buena Vista Palace, Hilton Orlando Lake Buena Vista, Holiday Inn Orlando–Disney Springs, Renaissance Orlando Resort and Spa (formerly B Resort & Spa), and Wyndham Garden Lake Buena Vista

Note: All table-service restaurants at Disney Springs and the Swan, Dolphin, and Swan Reserve are independently owned and run, as are a handful of other restaurants around the parks (such as Patina Restaurant Group's Tutto Italia and Via Napoli in EPCOT). These non-Disney-owned restaurants take Advance Dining Reservations, and many also accept reservations directly or through OpenTable.com.

While we think Disney's least expensive hotels are worth the extra cost versus staying off-site, we receive plenty of negative reader comments. The vast majority are about the lack of value found at Disney's more expensive hotels. A reader from Illinois is an example:

> Before the pandemic, we stayed on-site at Disney resorts every time. I'm planning our first trip back, and I just don't think paying on-site prices makes sense anymore. No Magical Express from the airport, no more free Fastpass+ selections. And we're not early risers, so Early Entry won't help us either.

Quite frankly, we agree that Disney's Deluxe hotels—the Grand Floridian and Contemporary in particular—are overpriced. At both of these locations, what you're paying for is the ability to walk to the Magic Kingdom.

The Hotel Information Table on pages 194–199 includes the cost range for both on-site and select off-site hotels at a glance.

2. EASE OF ACCESS Even if you stay in the Walt Disney World bubble, you're dependent on some mode of transportation. It may be less stressful to use the Disney transportation system, but, with the exception of getting to the Magic Kingdom, the fastest, most efficient, most flexible way to get around is usually by car. If you're in EPCOT, for example, and you want to take your cranky kids back to the Contemporary Resort for a nap, forget the monorail; you'll get back much faster by car.

The Disney transportation system is like most public transportation with its pros and cons, and users must expect inconveniences, including vehicles that arrive and depart on *their* schedule, not yours; the occasional need to transfer; multiple stops; time lost loading and unloading passengers; and other people just as desperate to catch a ride as you are.

If you plan to have a car, traffic on I-4 is the largest potential problem with staying at an off-site hotel, especially if you're coming or going during rush hours. The closer your off-site hotel is to Disney property, the less risk there is in being stuck in I-4 traffic. Secondary roads, such as Turkey Lake Road, Palm Parkway, International Drive, and Universal Boulevard, can help get you around that traffic.

A Kentucky dad was pleasantly surprised by the short commute:

My wife read in another guidebook that it can take 2 hours to commute to the parks if you stay outside Walt Disney World. I guess it could take 2 hours if you stayed in Tampa, but from our hotel on US 192, we could commute to any of the parks except the Magic Kingdom *and* have at least one ride under our belt in about an hour.

For commuting times from our recommended off-site hotels, see our Hotel Information Table on pages 194–199.

3. FOOD COSTS A few off-site hotels' prices include some sort of free breakfast, ranging from fruit and pastries to pancakes, microwavable waffles, bacon, and eggs. The Disney hotels don't. Depending on how hungry your family is in the morning, eating breakfast at your off-site hotel can save you a minimum of $6–$16 per person, per day versus breakfast in the parks. Or you can get groceries delivered to wherever you're staying. My family does grocery delivery to our room whether we're staying off-site or on-site, and it saves us a significant amount of money, especially on breakfast foods.

4. YOUNG CHILDREN Although the hassle of commuting to most off-site hotels is only slightly (if at all) greater than that of commuting to Disney hotels, a definite peace of mind results from staying in the World. Disney resorts are used to catering to kids, much more so than any hotels in the "real world."

5. SPLITTING UP If you're in a party that will probably split up to tour (as frequently happens in families with teens or children of widely varying ages), staying in the World offers more transportation options and, thus, more independence. Mom and Dad can take the car and return to the hotel for a relaxed dinner and early bedtime while the teens remain in the park for extra rides.

6. VISITING OTHER ORLANDO-AREA ATTRACTIONS If you also plan to visit Universal Orlando, SeaWorld, the Kennedy Space Center, or other area attractions, it may be more convenient to stay off-site or to split your stay.

The DISNEY RESORTS

DISNEY RESORTS 101

BEFORE YOU MAKE ANY DECISIONS, let's go over the basics about Disney resorts.

Disney has four main categories of resorts: **Value, Moderate, Deluxe,** and **DVC Villa.** It's a handy system that we'll use in discussing both Disney and off-site hotels. A fifth category, **Campground,** is exclusive to the campsites at **Fort Wilderness Resort.**

Value resorts are the least expensive Disney-owned hotels. They also have the smallest rooms and most limited amenities.

Moderate resorts are a step up from the Values in guest-room quality, amenities, and cost.

Deluxe resorts are Disney's top-of-the-line hotels, boasting extensive theming; luxurious rooms; and superior on-site dining, recreation, and services.

Disney Vacation Club (DVC) resorts (or DVC Villas) offer suites, some with full kitchens. DVC resorts—several of which are attached to Deluxe resorts—equal or surpass Deluxe resorts in quality. They can also be a better value, depending on how you book.

MAKING RESERVATIONS Whether you book your room through Disney, a travel agent, the internet, a tour operator, or an organization like AAA, you can often save by reserving the room by itself, instead of as part of a vacation package. This is known as a **room-only reservation.** We share the advantages and disadvantages of buying a package on page 178, but we can go ahead and tell you now that Disney World packages at list price rarely save you any money.

We always recommend that you book your trip through a travel agent or the Walt Disney World website (disneyworld.disney.go.com) instead of calling the Disney Reservation Center (DRC). Not only is booking online much faster than booking by phone, but DRC reservationists are also focused on selling you a Walt Disney Travel Company package. Even if you insist that all you want is the room, they'll try to persuade you to bundle it with some small extra, like a minigolf pass, so that your purchase can be counted as a package—this lets Disney apply various restrictions and cancellation policies that you wouldn't be saddled with if you bought just the room by itself. Also keep in mind that DRC and Walt Disney Travel Company representatives don't have detailed personal knowledge of the resorts.

*un*official **TIP**
If you must book by phone, call before 11 a.m. or after 3 p.m. Eastern time.

If for some reason you must book your vacation on the phone, a careful shopper from Indiana advises both wariness and toughness:

> Making reservations through 407-W-DISNEY is like buying a car: You need to know the sales tricks, have a firm idea of what you want, and be prepared to walk away if you don't get it at a price you're willing to pay.

CANCELLATION POLICIES Regarding cancellation, know that there are some trade-offs. If you book a package and then cancel 2–29 days before arrival, you lose your $200 deposit. If you cancel a day or less before arrival, you lose the entire package cost. If you reserve only a room and cancel fewer than eight days before arrival (a new stricter policy in 2025—it used to be five days), you lose your deposit of one night's room charge. Further, if you want to change your package's details—such as adjusting travel dates, moving to a cheaper resort, or adding a discount code—30 days or fewer before your trip, Disney imposes a $50 fee, plus a $15 processing fee.

YOUR HOTEL-ROOM VIEW Rates at Disney hotels vary by season (see pages 84–85) and from room to room according to view. Beyond your choice of resort and your travel dates, the biggest factor in how much you'll pay is the view you choose.

Standard view, the most ambiguous category, crops up at almost every Disney resort. It's usually interpreted as a view of infrastructure or unremarkable scenery. Animal Kingdom Lodge, for example, has savanna views, water views, and standard views. Savanna views overlook the replicated African veldt, water views overlook the swimming pool, and value and standard views usually offer stunning vistas of . . . rooftops and parking lots.

Each resort has its own definition of **water view.** At the Grand Floridian, for example, rooms with views of Seven Seas Lagoon are sensibly called "lagoon view" rooms, while those with views of the marina or pools are lumped together with other "resort view" rooms (no standard-view rooms here). Yacht Club Resort, like the Grand Floridian, is on a lake and has a pool and a marina. Here, lake and quiet pool views are both water-view rooms, but you have to upgrade to Club Level to get a guaranteed view of Stormalong Bay! And at Wilderness Lodge, a water view could be the pool, a waterfall, Bay Lake, or even Copper Creek.

For many readers, a good view is essential to enjoying their room. Getting the view you want, however, doesn't necessarily mean that you'll have the *experience* you want, as a New York couple points out:

> *We stayed in the Conch Key building at the Grand Floridian. The view was lovely, but we could hear the boat's horn blasting every 20 minutes, 7 a.m.–midnight. It was obnoxious and kept us up.*

TouringPlans.com's **Hotel Room Views** project uses more than 35,000 photos to show the view from every Disney-owned hotel room in Walt Disney World, plus instructions on how to request each room. It also has interactive maps for every building in every resort, so you can search for rooms by cost, view, walking distance, noise, accessibility, and more. Visit touringplans.com/walt-disney-world/hotels to see photos of the rooms we recommend in this chapter.

HOW TO GET THE ROOM YOU WANT Disney won't guarantee a specific room when you book but will post your request on your reservation record. One easy way to make a request is to use the Hotel Room Views tool described above. Select the room you want, and your request will be automatically emailed to Disney 30 days before you arrive. Alternatively, you can call the resort or Reservation Center or use the chat feature on the MDE website to have room requests added to your reservation.

Our experience and reader comments indicate that making a request with just a single room number doesn't work well. Often that one room isn't available, and you've given no additional information as to why that room was preferable. To increase your odds of getting the room you want, tell the reservationist (or your travel agent) *to the letter* what characteristics and amenities you desire.

> *unofficial* **TIP**
> A week or two before you arrive, call your resort's front desk. Call late in the evening when they're not so busy and reconfirm the requests that by now should be appearing in their computer system.

Be politely assertive when speaking to any Disney agent. Specify the type of view you're looking for. Similarly, state clearly such preferences as a particular floor, a room near dining, or one away from elevators and ice machines. If you have a long list of preferences, type it in order of importance and email, fax, or snail-mail it to the hotel. Include your contact information and your reservation-confirmation number. Be brief, though: Disney's reservation system has a limited amount of space to store what you write.

In this chapter, you'll find the information needed for each resort to frame your requests, including a resort map and our recommendations for specific rooms or buildings.

Readers say the hotel-room request service works about two out of three times. Disney's room assigners tell us that the most common reasons for not getting the exact room requested are as follows:

- **Someone is already in the requested room.** This is common during holidays and other busy times. It helps to list several alternatives.
- **Asking to get into your room early (before 3 or 4 p.m.).** Unless you say otherwise, the front desk will assume that any room currently available overrides your earlier requests.
- **Listing only rooms that are more expensive than the one you paid for.** It doesn't hurt to ask for an upgrade, but make sure you've given the room assigners a fallback option based on what you've bought.
- **Unclear requests.** Make sure your requests are *succinct* and *realistic*.

HOW TO GET DISCOUNTS ON LODGING

THERE ARE SO MANY GUEST ROOMS in and around Disney World that competition is brisk, and everyone, including Disney, cuts deals to fill them. Disney, however, has a unique way of managing its room inventory. To uphold the brand integrity of its hotels, Disney prefers to use enticements rather than discounts. For example, in the past Disney has included a Free Dining benefit if you reserved a certain number of nights at rack rate and has offered special deals only by email or in-room pamphlet to returning guests. Consequently, many of the "normal" strategies for getting discounted rates at most hotels don't work well for Disney hotels.

Note: Discounts may be limited to a certain number of rooms or certain dates. Rooms at deep discounts tend to get snatched up quickly, so don't take too long to decide what you want to do.

1. HUNT FOR SEASONAL SAVINGS. Save 15%–35% per night or more on a Disney hotel room by visiting during the slower times of year.

However, Disney has so many "seasons" in its calendar that it's hard to keep up; plus, the dates for each season vary among resorts. Disney also changes the price of its hotel rooms with the day of the week, charging more for the same room on Friday and Saturday nights. The rate hikes can range from $13 to over $100 per room, per night. It may require some legwork and being flexible on your travel dates, but there are usually deals to be found.

2. DON'T STOP LOOKING Even after booking, keep an eye out for discounts that could be applied to your reservation. A family from Massachusetts benefited from their continued research:

> I booked our trip online with Disney using a special-offer discount we had received in the mail. Two months before our trip, and after I had already paid in full, Disney ran a special that was even better than the one I had booked. I gave them a call, and they politely, quickly, and efficiently credited the difference.

Specials can include discounts on vacation packages in addition to discounts on rooms. Discounts on park admission or dining packages can be substantial, depending on the number of people in your traveling party or where you're staying.

3. READ THE BANNERS ON DISNEY'S WEBSITE As we went to press, Disney's website listed all the discounts running for the general public. The trick is knowing where to look. In Disney's case, visit disneyworld.disney.go.com/resorts. The link to the discounts page is found in the banner above all of your search information—where you'll be tempted to just scroll past to get to where you want.

4. INVESTIGATE INTERNET SELLERS **Expedia** (expedia.com), **Hotwire** (hotwire.com), **Priceline** (priceline.com) and its **Express Deals** section (theugseries.com/priceline-express), and **Travelocity** (travelocity.com) offer discounted rooms at Disney hotels. Most price breaks are in the 7%–25% range. *Always check these websites' prices against Disney's.*

5. RENT DISNEY VACATION CLUB POINTS The **Disney Vacation Club** (**DVC**) is Disney's time-share program. There are 13 DVC resorts: **Animal Kingdom Villas, Bay Lake Tower at the Contemporary Resort, Beach Club Villas, BoardWalk Villas, Boulder Ridge Villas, The Cabins at Fort Wilderness, Copper Creek Villas & Cabins, Grand Floridian Villas, Old Key West Resort, Polynesian Villas & Bungalows, Riviera Resort, Saratoga Springs Resort & Spa,** and **Treehouse Villas at Saratoga Springs.**

DVC members buy an allotment of annual "points" that they use to pay for their Disney accommodations. Sometimes members opt to "rent" (sell) their points instead of using them. Though Disney is not involved in the transaction, it allows this practice. The typical rental rate is $15–$19 per point, depending on the resort and time of year, when you deal with members directly; third-party brokers charge $18–$21 per point for hosting the buying-and-selling market and offering credit card payments.

Last-minute deals can bring the price down to the $8–$12 range. For example, in late 2023 we booked a last-minute offer for a standard-view, two-bedroom Animal Kingdom Villa for around $300 per night, all-in. Disney's rack rate for the room was $1,151, so the DVC points represented almost a 75% discount. At other times, we've stayed in studios at Animal Kingdom Lodge for $90 per night (in September) and at the Polynesian for $170 per night (in January).

Staying in a savanna-view studio for six nights during summer 2025 in Animal Kingdom Lodge & Villas currently costs $3,303 if you're paying with cash. The same room costs a DVC member 74 points. If you rented those points at $18 per point, that studio would cost you $1,332—a savings of almost $2,000. Put another way: That $1,332 bill would be cheaper than a room at any on-site resort (other than the All-Stars) for the same night.

Likewise, you can gain a lot more space for the same budget by renting points. If you're a family of five or six, a two-bedroom villa in Animal Kingdom Lodge sleeps eight. While it could cost around $576 per night (at $18 per point), a family suite at Art of Animation costs $590 (without discounts). For $14 *less* per night, you get more than double the space—1,173 square feet in Animal Kingdom versus 565 at Art of Animation—and better amenities.

LAST-MINUTE DVC DEALS The website **DVCReservations.com** emails a newsletter roughly every week with steeply discounted DVC rooms available within the next 90 days. These discounts are, by a wide margin, the best generally available deals you can find on Disney hotel rooms: typically 35%–60% off Disney's rates. We've seen plenty of instances where the least expensive room on-property was a 376-square-foot DVC rental villa at Old Key West or Saratoga Springs, not a 260-square-foot Value resort room such as Pop Century or the All-Stars.

RENTING POINTS FROM AN OWNER VS. A THIRD PARTY When renting points, you have two options: Deal directly with a DVC member or go through a third-party broker. For a fixed rate of around $18–$21 per point, **David's Vacation Club Rentals** (dvcrequest.com) will match your request for a specific resort and dates to its available supply. David's per-point rate is higher than if you did the legwork yourself, but they take requests months in advance, and they notify you as soon as something becomes available; plus, they take credit cards.

In addition to David's, some readers, like this one from Missouri, have had good results with the **DVC Rental Store** (dvcrentalstore.com):

> We rented DVC points for this trip through the DVC Rental Store, and we had a wonderful experience. Unlike David's, they don't make you pay the entire cost upon booking. For our stay at Boulder Ridge Villas, we paid just over half what we were planning to pay for the Wilderness Lodge.

When you deal directly with the DVC member, you pay the member directly, such as by certified check (few members take credit cards). The member makes a reservation in your name and pays Disney the requisite number of points. Arrangements vary, but again, the going rate is around $15–$19 per point. Trust is required from both parties. Usually, your reservation is documented by a confirmation sent from Disney to the owner and then passed along to you. Though the deal you cut is strictly up to you and the owner, you should always insist on receiving the confirmation number before making more than a one-night deposit.

We suggest checking one of the online Disney discussion boards (such as Disboards.com) if you're not picky about where you stay and when you go and you're willing to put in the effort to ask around. If you're trying to book a particular resort, especially during a busy time of year, it's usually easier to just use an established third-party site.

6. CRACK THE (PIN) CODE Disney maintains a list of recent visitors, as well as those who have inquired about a Disney World vacation. During slow times of the year, Disney will send these folks personalized discounts by direct mail or email. Each offer is uniquely identified by a long string of letters and numbers called a PIN code. This code is required to get the discount—thus, it can't be shared—and Disney will verify that the street or email address that the code was sent to is yours.

unofficial **TIP**
To enhance your chances of receiving a PIN-code offer, you need to get your name and street or email address into the Disney system.

To get your name into the Disney system for a PIN code, call ☎ 407-W-DISNEY (934-7639) and request written info. If you've been to Disney World before, your name and address will, of course, already be on record, but you won't be as likely to receive a PIN-code offer as you would by calling and requesting that information be mailed to you.

Or go to disneyworld.disney.go.com and sign up to automatically be sent offers and news at your email address. You might also consider getting a **Disney Rewards Visa card,** which entitles you to exclusive discounts (visit disneyrewards.com for details). One version of the card is free, and the other has a $49 annual fee.

7. DISNEY-SPECIALIST TRAVEL AGENTS Disney vacations are so popular that entire travel agencies specialize only in Disney theme park trips and cruises. Even large, general-travel agencies such as AAA often have dedicated agents with specialized, up-to-date knowledge of what's going on at the parks.

Three obvious situations where it makes sense to use a travel agent are as follows:

1. This is one of your first trips to Walt Disney World and you'd like to talk to someone objective in person.
2. You're looking to save time in evaluating several different scenarios, such as which of two discounts saves the most money.
3. You want someone else to keep checking for a better deal than what you already have.

We can't emphasize enough how much time (and money) a travel agent will save you in those last two scenarios. If you're trying to compare, say, the cost difference between a Value and a Moderate resort with a particular discount that may not be available at all resorts on all dates, you could easily spend an hour working through different combinations to find the best deal. We think most people give up long before finishing, potentially wasting a lot of money. Good travel agents will do this for you at no charge (because they earn a commission from Disney when you book through them).

8. ORGANIZATIONS AND AUTO CLUBS Disney has developed time-limited programs with some auto clubs and organizations. AAA, for example, can often offer discounts on hotels and packages comparable to those Disney offers its Annual Pass holders. Such deals come and go, but the market suggests there will be more. If you're a member of AARP, AAA, or any travel or auto club, ask whether the group has a program before shopping elsewhere.

9. ROOM UPGRADES Sometimes a room upgrade is as good as a discount. If you're visiting Disney World during a slower time, book the least expensive room your discounts will allow. When checking in, ask politely about being upgraded to a room with a more expensive view. A fair percentage of the time, you'll get one at no additional charge or at a deep discount. Understand, however, that a room upgrade should be considered a favor. Hotels are under no obligation to upgrade you, so if your request is not met, accept the decision graciously.

10. MILITARY DISCOUNTS Shades of Green, an Armed Forces Recreation Center resort located near the Grand Floridian Resort & Spa, offers luxury accommodations at rates based on a service member's rank, as well as attraction tickets to the theme parks (see profile on page 126). For rates and other information, call ☎ 888-593-2242 or visit shadesofgreen.org.

11. YEAR-ROUND DISCOUNTS AT MARRIOTT RESORTS Members of the military, government workers, teachers, nurses, and AAA members can save on rooms at the Dolphin, Swan, and Swan Reserve (when space is available, of course). Plus, Marriott Bonvoy members can use points to book stays. Call ☎ 888-828-8850, or visit swandolphin.com and click on "Special Offers."

CHOOSING A WALT DISNEY WORLD RESORT

IF YOU WANT TO STAY IN THE WORLD but don't know which hotel to choose, the most important factors to consider are as follows:

1. Room quality (see below)
2. Transportation (see page 91)
3. Cost (see page 91)
4. Pools and amenities (see page 92)
5. Location/distance from parks (see page 93)
6. Theme (see page 95)
7. Dining options (see page 97)
8. Room size (see page 98)

1. ROOM QUALITY Many Disney hotel rooms are among the best designed anywhere. Plus, they're much better maintained than the average hotel room in Orlando. All rooms have minifridges and free, reliable Wi-Fi, along with coffee makers.

As Disney refurbishes its hotel rooms, it also reexamines how modern families use these spaces. As a simple example, new rooms typically have 5–10 built-in USB charging ports to accommodate everyone's cell phones and tablets, and beds have plenty of space for storing large empty suitcases underneath.

Not surprisingly, many readers rate Disney's Deluxe and DVC rooms highest for quality, but some Value and Moderate rooms rate

ROOM-QUALITY RATINGS FOR THE DISNEY RESORTS

SHADES OF GREEN | 96	PORT ORLEANS FRENCH QUARTER | 88
RIVIERA | 95	BAY LAKE TOWER | 88
SARATOGA SPRINGS RESORT | 91	BOARDWALK INN | 88
ANIMAL KINGDOM VILLAS–KIDANI VILLAGE | 90	BOARDWALK VILLAS | 88
GRAND FLORIDIAN VILLAS (*studio*) | 90	WILDERNESS LODGE | 87
BEACH CLUB VILLAS | 90	SWAN | 87
GRAND FLORIDIAN RESORT | 90	POLYNESIAN VILLAS & BUNGALOWS | 87
ANIMAL KINGDOM LODGE–JAMBO HOUSE | 90	POLYNESIAN VILLAGE RESORT | 86
COPPER CREEK VILLAS | 90	ART OF ANIMATION | 86
ANIMAL KINGDOM VILLAS—JAMBO HOUSE | 89	PORT ORLEANS RIVERSIDE | 86
	CONTEMPORARY | 86
OLD KEY WEST | 89	DOLPHIN | 83
BOULDER RIDGE VILLAS | 89	BEACH CLUB RESORT | 83
CORONADO SPRINGS | 89	ALL-STAR SPORTS | 83
CABINS AT FORT WILDERNESS | 89	CARIBBEAN BEACH | 83
SWAN RESERVE | 89	ALL-STAR MUSIC | 82
	ALL-STAR MOVIES | 81
YACHT CLUB | 88	POP CENTURY | 79

Treehouse Villas did not receive enough surveys to rate.

even higher. The text that follows provides context for these room-quality ratings. In addition, the table above shows how the Walt Disney World resorts stack up as far as room quality.

VALUE RESORTS Room quality in this category is highest at **Art of Animation,** where rooms are clean and functional. But because the resort opened in 2012, they're not old enough to need the updates that the other Value resorts have received. This can make them feel dated in comparison. Quality also varies within the resort: Family suites score *much* higher than the standard *Little Mermaid* rooms.

Room quality for the **All Stars Resorts** is in the middle of the pack for the Disney Value resorts. The entire room configuration has changed in the last few years. Carpet has been replaced with vinyl plank flooring. Queen beds are standard, and king beds are available. In rooms with two queen beds, one bed can fold into the wall when not in use, exposing a table; this frees up around 36 square feet of space in these 260-square-foot rooms—a 14% increase. In addition, bathrooms are brighter and more open, and more storage is available in the living areas. **Pop Century** falls to the bottom of the list this year because its updates happened a while ago, and people consistently rate the family suites at Art of Animation higher than the normal rooms at Pop Century. Thankfully, all the rooms there are scheduled to be refreshed from mid-2025 through early 2026.

MODERATE RESORTS Readers rate the rooms at **Coronado Springs** the highest of any Moderate resort. These rooms have been modernized with vinyl plank flooring, plenty of desk space, excellent lighting, and doors separating the bathroom area from the main living space. The resort's **Gran Destino Tower** is Disney's most recent addition to the

Moderate category. It offers some of the best-designed bathrooms in its category. Even better, Gran Destino's Club Level rooms—with access to the fabulous private **Chronos Club** lounge—are the cheapest Club Level rooms on Disney property. If you're looking to try one of these rooms, Gran Destino is a great place to start.

Readers rate the rooms at **Port Orleans French Quarter** the second-highest. All of the rooms were refurbished in 2024 or 2025, resulting in rooms that feel new and fresh, with plenty of storage and outlets.

Port Orleans Riverside and **Caribbean Beach** have the lowest-rated Moderate rooms. All rooms in Riverside have vinyl plank flooring. One section, Alligator Bayou, has an updated bathroom design and a new drop-down twin bed for a child. However, the furniture design in these rooms is rustic (to fit the theming) and lacks the modern conveniences found in the updated Value resorts. Riverside is scheduled to start receiving room refurbishments after French Quarter, so if you stay here in 2026, request a refurbished room.

Caribbean Beach recently got a welcome upgrade, including a conversion of its *Pirates of the Caribbean*–themed rooms in the Trinidad section to a *Little Mermaid* theme. These updates use lighter, brighter color schemes and bring foldout and drop-down bed options to rooms that previously had two fixed beds. Like the renovations at the Value resorts, this update modernized and increased the functionality of the rooms at Caribbean Beach. Our one word of caution is that, because of the resort's size, many Caribbean Beach renovation efforts are stopped before all rooms are finished. We believe this happened again with the most recent renovations, so if you're booking here, ask for a refurbished room.

DELUXE RESORTS Rooms at the **Grand Floridian** and **Animal Kingdom Lodge (Jambo House)** are rated the highest in this category. Both score 90 for room quality, but the two are very different. Grand Floridian rooms were recently refurbished and have light colors and furnishings. Rooms at Jambo House are smaller and not as new but have incredible theming, and having animals right outside your balcony is an additional selling point.

Other above-average Deluxe rooms are found at **Swan Reserve, Yacht Club,** and **BoardWalk Inn. Shades of Green** is also considered a Deluxe resort, for those who qualify to stay there. It's rated higher for room quality than any other WDW resort. Rooms that rate average (or just slightly below) are found at **Wilderness Lodge, Swan, Polynesian,** and **Contemporary.** The lowest-rated Deluxe rooms are found at the **Dolphin** and **Beach Club.**

Animal Kingdom Lodge & Villas, BoardWalk Inn, Contemporary, Grand Floridian, Polynesian Village, Wilderness Lodge, and **Yacht & Beach Club Resorts,** in addition to the Moderate **Gran Destino Tower,** boast **Club Level** (concierge) floors. Benefits include personalized trip planning and a lounge stocked with small bites to graze on. This New Jersey reader, however, found the snacks to be on the skimpy side:

> *We found the Club Level food offerings limited and carefully metered out. Tiny plates were replenished slowly. Given that Club Level is a significant extra expense, we didn't appreciate being told how much we could eat and when.*

DVC RESORTS Some of Disney's highest-rated rooms are found at its time-share resorts. Topping the list are **Riviera Resort** (one of the newest DVC properties) and **Saratoga Springs** (one of the oldest). Riviera's above-average on-site dining and Skyliner access to EPCOT and Hollywood Studios make it a positive—and pricey—addition to Disney's resort lineup. The large, stylish rooms are, in our opinion, some of the best of any Disney-owned hotel. Saratoga Springs coming in second place is a more curious result.

Almost all other DVC resorts have rooms rated above average: **Animal Kingdom Lodge–Kidani Village, Grand Floridian Villas, Beach Club Villas, Copper Creek Villas & Cabins at Wilderness Lodge, Old Key West, Boulder Ridge Villas at Wilderness Lodge, Cabins at Fort Wilderness, Bay Lake Tower,** and **BoardWalk Villas.** The only DVC resort that falls below average is the **Polynesian Villas & Bungalows.**

2. TRANSPORTATION If you'll be driving, your Disney hotel's transportation isn't especially important unless you plan to spend most of your time in the Magic Kingdom (because almost any Disney transportation beats parking at the Transportation and Ticket Center). If you haven't decided whether you want a car for your Disney vacation, see "How to Travel Around the World" (page 337).

The resorts that our readers rate highest for Disney transportation are **Polynesian Village, Riviera,** and **Grand Floridian.** The Polynesian and Grand Floridian connect to the Magic Kingdom and EPCOT by monorail. These resorts use buses to get to other destinations on Disney property. The Riviera connects to Caribbean Beach, Pop Century, and Art of Animation Resorts; Disney's Hollywood Studios; and EPCOT via the Skyliner and uses buses to get to other on-property locations.

The resorts that our readers rated below average for transportation are the **Swan** and **Dolphin;** the **Cabins at Fort Wilderness;** and **Shades of Green.** The bus service at Fort Wilderness is next-level difficult, with not just multiple stops, like at other resorts, but also totally separate internal bus loops, which increases the time it takes to get where you're going. The non-Disney bus service at the Swan and Dolphin runs less often than Disney's buses, and it drops guests off at the Transportation and Ticket Center, not the Magic Kingdom park entrance. And Shades of Green recently lost its walking path to the Magic Kingdom, which makes a huge difference.

unofficial **TIP**
If you plan to use Disney transportation to visit all four theme parks and one or both water parks, book a centrally located resort with good transportation connections, such as the EPCOT resorts (page 129) or the Riviera, Caribbean Beach, Art of Animation, Pop Century, or Polynesian Resorts.

3. COST Hotel rooms start as low as $133 a night at the All-Stars and top out above $2,100 for many DVC villas. The table on page 94 shows the cost per night for various Disney hotel rooms.

Disney's **Value resorts** are the least expensive on-site hotels. Because they're popular, they have four separate, unofficial price categories:

- The **All-Star Resorts** are Disney's oldest and least expensive Value resorts. But they've all received refurbishments that make them manageable, if not ideal.

- **Pop Century Resort** sits in the middle of the Value price range—about 20% per night more than the All-Stars. It's the most popular Disney World resort among *Unofficial Guide* readers.
- **Art of Animation Resort** has the largest rooms, best food court, and best pools in the Value category. Standard rooms cost about $100 per night more than those at the All-Stars.
- Two-room **Family Suites** are available at the All-Star Music and Art of Animation Resorts, from around $350 to $1,000 per night, including tax.

While the All-Stars and Pop Century are older and less expensive than AOA, they've had extensive room renovations that make them among the most attractive and functional on-property. In terms of room quality, they're better and cheaper than AOA's standard rooms.

The next most expensive tier includes Disney's **Moderate resorts.** Like the Values, these have different price points:

- **Coronado Springs Resort** (excluding Gran Destino Tower) has the cheapest rooms in the Moderate category. It's large, with multiple bus stops, and has low-rated on-site dining.
- **Port Orleans Riverside** and **Port Orleans French Quarter** are only slightly more expensive. They are the favorite of many repeat visitors.
- **Caribbean Beach Resort** got a bump in popularity (and price) when it got access to two Skyliner stations.
- **Gran Destino Tower,** a 15-story tower located on the grounds of Coronado Springs Resort, is the newest entry in the Moderate category. Its Club Level rooms are the least expensive of their type in Walt Disney World.

Rates at Disney's **Deluxe resorts** vary depending on room size and the resort's location relative to the theme parks:

- The **Walt Disney World Swan, Dolphin,** and **Swan Reserve** are usually the least expensive Deluxe hotel rooms on-property. They're not owned by Disney, and they cater to convention traffic as much as families, giving them a different feel from the other hotels. These hotels are within walking distance of EPCOT and Disney's Hollywood Studios.
- The smallest and least expensive Disney-owned Deluxe hotel rooms are found at **Wilderness Lodge** and **Animal Kingdom Lodge.** Both have excellent theming; Animal Kingdom Lodge has excellent dining as well.
- The next tier of Deluxe prices applies to the EPCOT resorts: the **Yacht & Beach Club Resorts** and **BoardWalk Inn.** These are arranged around Crescent Lake, with a short walk to EPCOT and a slightly longer walk (or Skyliner ride) to Disney's Hollywood Studios.
- Even more expensive are the **Polynesian Village** and **Contemporary Resorts.** Both opened in 1971 and are a short walk or monorail ride from the Magic Kingdom and EPCOT. The Polynesian has excellent theming. Along with its easy access to two theme parks, its location makes it easy to visit any hotel restaurant along the Magic Kingdom monorail loop.
- Finally, Disney's most expensive standard hotel rooms are found at the **Grand Floridian Resort & Spa,** Disney World's flagship hotel.

4. POOLS AND AMENITIES Disney's **Yacht & Beach Club Resorts** share the highest-rated pool in Walt Disney World. Called **Stormalong Bay,** it includes a lazy river with a sand bottom and an elaborate waterslide that begins from a pirate ship beached on Crescent Lake. Stormalong Bay is so popular that guests must show proof they're staying at the resort before being admitted to the pool area.

The **Riviera**'s pools also get top marks from readers. With two pools and a kids' water-play area, there's plenty of space for guests to relax. In the middle of the pools is **Bar Riva,** with shade and beverages for adults. Becky thinks Bar Riva is so good, she takes the Skyliner over for lunch when she's spending the day in Hollywood Studios.

The Lava Pool at the **Polynesian Village Resort** rates barely below Stormalong Bay and is generally less crowded. It's also a better layout for keeping track of your kids. **Trader Sam's Tiki Terrace,** the **Pineapple Lanai,** and **Captain Cooks** are all steps away.

If you don't want to pay for Deluxe accommodations, the pools at **Art of Animation** are also rated above average. These are well themed and have convenient bar and food options.

Readers rate the pools at **Contemporary, All-Stars, Pop Century,** and **Fort Wilderness** as below average. All of these have relatively generic pools that are often crowded.

See the table on page 95 for specific resort pool ratings and the table on page 96 for a summary of the amenities at each resort.

5. LOCATION AND DISTANCE FROM THE THEME PARKS Once you've determined your budget, think about what you want to do at Disney World. Will you go to all four theme parks or concentrate on one or two?

The resorts closest to the Magic Kingdom include the **Grand Floridian** and its **Villas;** the **Contemporary** and **Bay Lake Tower;** and the **Polynesian Village, Villas & Bungalows.** All are served by the monorail and walking paths, so staying at one of these resorts also gets you access to more dining options, many of which are among the World's best.

Next closest to the Magic Kingdom are **Wilderness Lodge & Boulder Ridge/Copper Creek Villas** and **Fort Wilderness Resort & Campground.** They are linked to the Magic Kingdom (and the Contemporary) by boat and to everywhere else in Disney World by bus service (rather convoluted bus service from Fort Wilderness).

The most centrally located hotels in Walt Disney World are the **EPCOT resorts—BoardWalk Inn, BoardWalk Villas, Yacht & Beach Club Resorts, Beach Club Villas, Swan, Dolphin,** and **Swan Reserve.** These resorts are within easy walking distance of Disney's Hollywood Studios and EPCOT's International Gateway. Besides giving you easy theme park access, staying at one of these hotels gets you access to a wide variety of restaurants. EPCOT hotels are best for guests planning to spend most of their time in EPCOT or Disney's Hollywood Studios.

Caribbean Beach, Riviera, Pop Century, and **Art of Animation** are just south and east of EPCOT and the Studios. All are connected to EPCOT and DHS by the Skyliner and to everything else by bus.

The Disney resorts along Bonnet Creek, which offer quick access to Disney Springs and its top restaurants, include **Old Key West, Saratoga Springs** and its **Treehouse Villas,** and the two **Port Orleans Resorts.** On an adjacent 70-acre parcel of non-Disney land called **Bonnet Creek Resort** are the **Waldorf Astoria Orlando;** the **Signia by Hilton Orlando Bonnet Creek;** and two Wyndham properties, **Club Wyndham Bonnet Creek** and its more luxurious sibling, **Wyndham Grand Orlando Resort Bonnet Creek.**

2025 COST PER NIGHT OF DISNEY HOTEL ROOMS (rack rates)

Rates are for standard rooms except as noted.

ALL-STAR RESORTS	$133–$305
ALL-STAR MUSIC RESORT FAMILY SUITES	$350–$716
ANIMAL KINGDOM LODGE	$506–$1,231
ANIMAL KINGDOM VILLAS (studio, Jambo House/Kidani Village)	$506–$1,209
ART OF ANIMATION FAMILY SUITES	$497–$992
ART OF ANIMATION RESORT	$217–$425
BAY LAKE TOWER AT CONTEMPORARY RESORT (studio)	$721–$1,480
BEACH CLUB RESORT	$621–$1,289
BEACH CLUB VILLAS (studio)	$621–$1,117
BOARDWALK INN	$667–$1,235
BOARDWALK VILLAS (studio)	$667–$1,230
BOULDER RIDGE VILLAS (studio)	$546–$1,008
CARIBBEAN BEACH RESORT	$317–$612
CONTEMPORARY RESORT	$609–$1,480
COPPER CREEK VILLAS & CABINS (studio)	$546–$1,008
CORONADO SPRINGS RESORT	$260–$605
FORT WILDERNESS RESORT & CAMPGROUND (cabins)	$485–$1,015
GRAN DESTINO TOWER AT CORONADO SPRINGS RESORT	$328–$684
GRAND FLORIDIAN RESORT & SPA	$824–$1,773
GRAND FLORIDIAN VILLAS (studio)	$824–$1,764
OLD KEY WEST RESORT (studio)	$488–$825
POLYNESIAN VILLAGE RESORT	$734–$1,711
POLYNESIAN VILLAS & BUNGALOWS (studio)	$734–$1,796
POP CENTURY RESORT	$183–$450
PORT ORLEANS RESORTS—FRENCH QUARTER AND RIVERSIDE	$289–$603
RIVIERA RESORT (studio)	$752–$1,359
SARATOGA SPRINGS RESORT & SPA (studio)	$489–$939
SHADES OF GREEN	$179–$277
WALT DISNEY WORLD DOLPHIN	$234–$534
WALT DISNEY WORLD SWAN	$252–$468
WALT DISNEY WORLD SWAN RESERVE	$314–$578
TREEHOUSE VILLAS	$1,187–$2,276
WILDERNESS LODGE	$546–$1,252
YACHT CLUB RESORT	$622–$1,215

The Bonnet Creek Resort area walks the line between on- and off-property: The hotels are as close to the theme parks as Disney's own, offer transportation to the parks and Disney Springs, and are every bit as good as Disney's best—often at around half the price. Further muddying the waters, guests of the Signia and Waldorf Astoria get Early

AUTHORS' RATINGS FOR THE DISNEY RESORT POOLS

1. **YACHT & BEACH CLUB RESORTS & BEACH CLUB VILLAS** (shared complex) ★★★★★
2. **ANIMAL KINGDOM VILLAS** (Kidani Village) ★★★★½
3. **POLYNESIAN VILLAGE, VILLAS & BUNGALOWS** ★★★★½
4. **RIVIERA RESORT** ★★★★½
5. **WILDERNESS LODGE & BOULDER RIDGE/COPPER CREEK VILLAS** ★★★★½
6. **ANIMAL KINGDOM LODGE & VILLAS** (Jambo House) ★★★★
7. **ART OF ANIMATION RESORT** ★★★★
8. **CARIBBEAN BEACH RESORT** ★★★★
9. **CORONADO SPRINGS RESORT/GRAN DESTINO TOWER** ★★★★
10. **OLD KEY WEST RESORT** ★★★★
11. **PORT ORLEANS RESORTS** ★★★★
12. **SARATOGA SPRINGS RESORT & SPA/TREEHOUSE VILLAS** ★★★★
13. **SHADES OF GREEN** ★★★★
14. **BOARDWALK INN & VILLAS** ★★★½
15. **CONTEMPORARY RESORT/BAY LAKE TOWER** ★★★½
16. **GRAND FLORIDIAN RESORT & SPA, VILLAS** ★★★½
17. **WALT DISNEY WORLD SWAN, DOLPHIN, AND SWAN RESERVE** ★★★½
18. **ALL-STAR RESORTS** ★★★
19. **FORT WILDERNESS RESORT & CAMPGROUND** ★★★
20. **POP CENTURY RESORT** ★★★

Theme Park Entry privileges (as do guests of the **Four Seasons Resort Orlando,** adjacent to Fort Wilderness Resort).

6. THEME With a few exceptions, each Disney resort is designed to evoke a special place or period of history. Some resorts carry off their theming better than others, and some themes are more exciting. See the table on page 98 for a list of the resorts' themes.

unofficial **TIP**
If you stay at an EPCOT resort, you have more than 30 restaurants within a 12-minute walk.

Readers rate the resorts in the next four paragraphs tops for theming:

Animal Kingdom Lodge replicates the grand safari lodges of Kenya and Tanzania and overlooks its own African-style savanna. By far the most exotic Disney resort, the lodge and its villas are great for both couples on romantic getaways and families with children.

Wilderness Lodge is visually extraordinary, reminiscent of a grand early-20th-century national-park lodge. The lobby opens eight stories to a timbered ceiling supported by giant columns of bundled logs. The lodge and its **Boulder Ridge Villas** and **Copper Creek Villas & Cabins** are a great choice for couples and seniors and are fun for children.

Likewise dramatic, the **Polynesian Village Resort** and **Polynesian Villas & Bungalows** convey the feeling of the Pacific Islands. They're great for couples and families. Many waterfront rooms on upper floors offer a perfect view of Cinderella Castle and the Magic Kingdom fireworks across Seven Seas Lagoon. In general, these theme scores apply only to the "main" resort, and not to the newer Island Tower.

DISNEY RESORT AMENITIES

RESORT	SUITES	CONCIERGE FLOOR	NUMBER OF ROOMS	ROOM SERVICE (full)	FITNESS CENTER
ALL-STAR RESORTS	•	–	5,406	–	–
ANIMAL KINGDOM LODGE	•	•	972	•	•
ANIMAL KINGDOM VILLAS	•	•*	458	•	•
ART OF ANIMATION RESORT	•	–	1,984	–	–
BAY LAKE TOWER	•	–	295	•	•
BEACH CLUB VILLAS	•	–	282	•	•
BOARDWALK INN	•	•	378	•	•
BOARDWALK VILLAS	•	–	532	•	•
CARIBBEAN BEACH RESORT	–	–	1,536	–	–
CONTEMPORARY RESORT	•	•	655	•	•
CORONADO SPRINGS RESORT	•	•	1,839	•	•
DOLPHIN	•	–	1,509	•	•
FORT WILDERNESS CABINS	–	–	409	–	–
GRAN DESTINO TOWER	•	•	545	•	–
GRAND FLORIDIAN RESORT & SPA, VILLAS	•	•	1,016	•	•
OLD KEY WEST RESORT	•	–	761	–	•
POLYNESIAN VILLAGE, VILLAS & BUNGALOWS	•	•	1,134	•	•**
POP CENTURY RESORT	–	–	2,880	–	–
PORT ORLEANS RESORT	–	–	3,056	–	–
RIVIERA RESORT	–	–	300	•	•
SARATOGA SPRINGS RESORT & SPA	•	–	1,260	–	•
SHADES OF GREEN	•	–	586	•	•
SWAN	•	–	758	•	•
SWAN RESERVE	•	–	349	•	•
TREEHOUSE VILLAS	•	–	60	–	•
WILDERNESS LODGE, BOULDER RIDGE/COPPER CREEK VILLAS	•	•	889	•	•
YACHT & BEACH CLUB RESORTS	•	•	1,211	•	•

* Jambo House only   ** Island Tower only

Art of Animation exhibits a strong commitment to theme, both outside and inside. If you or one of your kids is a big fan of *The Little Mermaid*, *Cars*, *The Lion King*, or *Finding Nemo*, you can't beat these immersive rooms and suites.

Unofficial Guide readers rate the following resorts as below average for theming: the **All-Star Resorts**; **Pop Century**; **Saratoga Springs**; the **Contemporary Resort** and **Bay Lake Tower**; and the **Swan**, **Swan Reserve**, and **Dolphin**.

The **All-Star Resorts** have 15 themed areas: 5 celebrate sports (surfing, basketball, tennis, football, and baseball), 5 relate to films, and 5 have musical motifs. The resort's design, with entrances shaped like giant Dalmatians, Coke cups, footballs, and the like, is somewhat adolescent, sacrificing grace and beauty for energy and novelty.

Pop Century Resort is pretty much a clone of the All-Star Resorts, only here the giant icons symbolize decades of the 20th century (Big Wheels, 45-rpm records, and such).

Saratoga Springs Resort & Spa, supposedly representative of an upstate New York country retreat, looks like what you'd get if you crossed the Beach Club with Wilderness Lodge. Mostly it's known as "the horse resort."

The **Contemporary Resort** and its **Bay Lake Tower** and the **Swan, Swan Reserve,** and **Dolphin** are essentially themeless though architecturally interesting. The original Contemporary is a 15-story A-frame building with monorails running through the middle. An update in 2021 added characters from Pixar's *The Incredibles.* The Swan and Dolphin are massive yet whimsical; designed by Michael Graves, they're excellent examples of early-1990s "entertainment architecture," but they lack any references to Disney theme parks, films, or characters.

7. DINING OPTIONS If high-quality dining is a top priority for your Walt Disney World trip, **Animal Kingdom Lodge** and the **Grand Floridian** are excellent choices. Three of Walt Disney World's top sit-down restaurants are found in Animal Kingdom Lodge: **Jiko—The Cooking Place, Sanaa,** and **Boma—Flavors of Africa.** The Grand Floridian holds Walt Disney World's very best restaurant, **Victoria & Albert's,** and five of its other restaurants all place near the top of our reader surveys.

The best resorts for dining quality *and* selection are the EPCOT resorts: **BoardWalk Inn & Villas, Dolphin, Swan, Swan Reserve, Yacht and Beach Club Resorts,** and **Beach Club Villas.** Each has decent sit-down restaurants, and each is within easy walking distance of the others as well as the dining options available in World Showcase. However, on-site quick-service options are limited, and readers rate these hotels below average for quick-service options. If quick, simple breakfasts and lunches are what you're after, stay elsewhere.

The only other hotels in Disney World with similar access to a concentrated area of good restaurants are in the **Disney Springs Resort Area. DoubleTree Suites, Drury Plaza Hotel, Hilton Orlando Buena Vista Palace, Hilton Orlando Lake Buena Vista, Holiday Inn Orlando, Renaissance Orlando Resort and Spa,** and **Wyndham Garden Lake Buena Vista** are all within walking distance of restaurants in Disney Springs. As with the EPCOT resorts, though, many readers complain about the difficulty they have finding quick, tasty breakfast and lunch options at these hotels.

Hotels rated as below average for dining include **Fort Wilderness Resort & Campground,** all of the **Value resorts, Saratoga Springs, Old Key West,** and **BoardWalk Inn & Villas.** Because Fort Wilderness caters primarily to guests who are cooking for themselves, on-site dining options are limited, and not just in terms of the menu selections: The restaurants' remote location, near the shore of Bay Lake, makes them a hassle to get to from most parts of the resort—so unless you're renting a bike or golf cart, count on a *long* walk or bus ride to get something to eat.

Disney's operation of the Value resort restaurants clearly indicates that they want you to eat in the parks. And Old Key West and Saratoga Springs haven't received much dining love since they

THEMES AT THE DISNEY RESORTS	
ALL-STAR RESORTS	Movies, music, and sports
ANIMAL KINGDOM LODGE & VILLAS	African game preserve
ART OF ANIMATION RESORT	Disney's animated films
BAY LAKE TOWER	Upscale, ultramodern urban hotel
BEACH CLUB RESORT & VILLAS	New England beach club of the 1870s
BOARDWALK INN	East Coast boardwalk hotel of the early 1900s
BOARDWALK VILLAS	East Coast beach cottage of the early 1900s
CARIBBEAN BEACH RESORT	Caribbean islands
CONTEMPORARY RESORT	The future as perceived by past and present generations
CORONADO SPRINGS RESORT	Northern Mexico and the American Southwest
GRAN DESTINO TOWER	Spanish/Moorish influences
GRAND FLORIDIAN RESORT & SPA, VILLAS	Turn-of-the-20th-century luxury hotel
OLD KEY WEST RESORT	Relaxed Florida Keys vibe
POLYNESIAN VILLAGE RESORT, VILLAS & BUNGALOWS	Hawaii–South Seas with Moana
POP CENTURY RESORT	Pop-culture icons from various decades of the 20th century
PORT ORLEANS FRENCH QUARTER	Turn-of-the-19th-century New Orleans
PORT ORLEANS RIVERSIDE	Old Louisiana bayou-side retreat
RIVIERA RESORT	Mediterranean beach resort in the South of France
SARATOGA SPRINGS RESORT & SPA	1880s Victorian lake
WALT DISNEY WORLD DOLPHIN	"Modern" (early 1990s) Florida resort
WALT DISNEY WORLD SWAN	What modern looked like 30 years ago
WALT DISNEY WORLD SWAN RESERVE	True 21st-century design aesthetic
TREEHOUSE VILLAS	Disney-rustic vacation homes with modern amenities
WILDERNESS LODGE, VILLAS	Grand national-park lodge of the early 20th century
YACHT CLUB RESORT	New England seashore hotel of the 1880s

opened. The one surprise here is BoardWalk Inn. Table-service dining here actually rates pretty well, but the food court (quick-service) scores are so low that it drags the overall dining average down.

8. ROOM SIZE How much space you get inside a Disney hotel room almost always depends on how much you pay. The size of a standard (or studio) room at Disney's resorts varies from 260 square feet at the Value resorts to 440 square feet at the Deluxe **Grand Floridian Resort** to 460 square feet for a studio at the **Polynesian Villas** DVC resort. The diagrams on pages 100–104 show the size and layout of typical rooms at each Disney property.

It's no surprise that readers rate larger rooms better than smaller ones. At the top of this list are rooms at **Old Key West,** Disney's first DVC resort, which are larger than most. Also scoring well are the rooms at the **Grand Floridian Villas**—we're not kidding when we say that the showers here are large enough that you might consider sleeping in them to get away from a snoring partner. And although they don't score well in most other categories, the rooms at the **Cabins at Fort Wilderness Resort** and Saratoga Springs' **Treehouse Villas** are popular with readers in terms of sheer space.

It's not surprising that the resorts rated lowest for room size are the Value options. But the Swan and Dolphin also sneak into that grouping.

Standard rooms at the **Riviera Resort** include a two-person, 225-square-foot Tower Studio that's so small that the only bed is a queen fold-down. They're almost certainly the worst rooms on-property, and we recommend skipping them. Another skip is the Duo Studio at the **Polynesian**'s new **Island Tower.** They're 262 square feet and feel "lighter" than the Tower Studios, but the bed has a thin, uncomfortable mattress, and the prices are astronomical for what you get.

STANDARD ROOMS THAT SLEEP FIVE (plus one child under age 3 in a crib) are found at the following resorts:

- **DELUXE** Beach Club, BoardWalk Inn, Contemporary, Grand Floridian, Polynesian Village, Yacht Club
- **MODERATE** Caribbean Beach, Port Orleans Riverside (Alligator Bayou only)

FAMILY SUITES sleep six people and are found exclusively at **All-Star Music** and **Art of Animation Resorts.** The All-Star versions are basically two Value rooms stuck together; those at Art of Animation, however, were designed from the ground up and are slightly larger (and nicer). Family Suites at both resorts have two bathrooms.

The **Cabins at Fort Wilderness Resort** also sleep six, but they have just one bathroom each.

HOW WE INSPECT HOTELS

WE EVALUATE SEVERAL HUNDRED hotels in the Walt Disney World area to compile the *Unofficial Guide*'s list of lodging choices. If a hotel has been renovated or has refurbished its guest rooms, we reinspect it, along with any new hotels, for the next edition of the *Guide*. Hotels reporting no improvements are rechecked every two years. We inspect most Disney-owned hotels every 6–12 months, and no less than once every couple of years.

That doesn't mean we don't need your help. We can't be everywhere all at once. If you notice something new or especially great or terrible about a WDW resort (or nearby hotel), send Becky a message on Instagram (@raisingminniemes) or email beckyg@touringplans.com so that we can be sure to check it out.

Pipe Down Out There!

The most common complaint that Walt Disney World–area hotel guests make regarding their rooms is excessive noise. A well-designed room blocks noise coming from both your neighbor's television and the pool across the resort.

The hotels with the best exterior soundproofing are **Contemporary, Grand Floridian, Gran Destino Tower, Saratoga Springs, Riviera,** and **Yacht Club.** Hotels with the least exterior soundproofing are **All-Star Movies, Art of Animation**'s *Little Mermaid* rooms, **Caribbean Beach,** both **Port Orleans Resorts,** and **Polynesian** (except the villas).

The **Riviera** and **Gran Destino Tower** are newer resorts, and it looks like Disney specifically addressed soundproofing when installing those exterior doors. At the other end of the list, the **Polynesian Village** and **Port Orleans Resorts** have performed consistently poorly in our tests

continued on page 105

DISNEY DELUXE RESORTS*

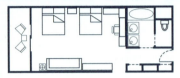

CONTEMPORARY RESORT
394 square feet; accommodates 5 guests plus 1 child under age 3 in a crib

POLYNESIAN VILLAGE RESORT
415 square feet; accommodates 5 guests plus 1 child under age 3 in a crib

BOARDWALK INN
371 square feet; accommodates 5 guests plus 1 child under age 3 in a crib

GRAND FLORIDIAN RESORT & SPA
440 square feet; accommodates 5 guests plus 1 child under age 3 in a crib

BEACH CLUB RESORT
381 square feet; accommodates 5 guests plus 1 child under age 3 in a crib

YACHT CLUB RESORT
381 square feet; accommodates 5 guests plus 1 child under age 3 in a crib

WILDERNESS LODGE
344 square feet; accommodates 4 guests plus 1 child under age 3 in a crib

ANIMAL KINGDOM LODGE
344 square feet; accommodates 4 guests plus 1 child under age 3 in a crib

* *Typical room*

DVC RESORTS

ANIMAL KINGDOM VILLAS–JAMBO HOUSE
Studio: 316–365 square feet *(gray area)*
1-bedroom: 629–710 sf
2-bedroom: 945–1,075 sf
Grand Villa: 2,349 square feet

ANIMAL KINGDOM VILLAS–KIDANI VILLAGE
Studio: 366 square feet *(gray area)*
1-bedroom: 807 square feet
2-bedroom: 1,173 square feet
Grand Villa: 2,201 square feet

Note: *Diagrams are not to scale.*

THE DISNEY RESORTS: ROOM DIAGRAMS 101

DVC RESORTS (continued)

BAY LAKE TOWER
Studio: 339 square feet *(gray area)*;
1-bedroom: 803 sf; **2-bedroom:** 1,152 sf
Grand Villa: 2,044 square feet

OLD KEY WEST RESORT
Studio: 376 square feet *(gray area)*;
1-bedroom: 942 square feet; **2-bedroom:** 1,333 square feet; **Grand Villa:** 2,202 square feet

BEACH CLUB VILLAS
Studio: 356 square feet *(gray area)*
1-bedroom: 726 square feet
2-bedroom: 1,083 square feet

BOARDWALK VILLAS
Studio: 412 square feet *(gray area)*;
1-bedroom: 814 square feet; **2-bedroom:** 1,236 square feet; **Grand Villa:** 2,491 square feet

GRAND FLORIDIAN VILLAS
Studio: 374 square feet *(gray area)*
1-bedroom: 844 square feet
2-bedroom lock-off: 1,232 square feet

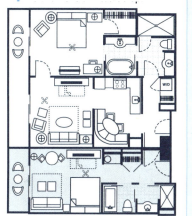

DVC GUEST-OCCUPANCY LIMITS

- **Studios:** 4 at all except: Boulder Ridge Villas (5), Grand Floridian (5), Polynesian (5), and Riviera (2 for Tower Studios, 5 for Deluxe Studios)
- **1-bedroom villas:** 4 at Beach Club, Saratoga Springs, and Boulder Ridge; 4 or 5 in Animal Kingdom Lodge (Jambo House); 5 everywhere else
- **2-bedroom villas and bungalows:** 8 or 9 in Animal Kingdom Lodge & Villas (Jambo House); 9 in Animal Kingdom Villas (Kidani Village), Bay Lake Tower, Riviera, BoardWalk, and Old Key West; 9 or 10 at Grand Floridian; 8 everywhere else
- **3-bedroom and Grand Villas:** 9 at Treehouse Villas; 12 everywhere else

  Note: To all these limits you may add 1 child under age 3 in a crib.

Note: *Diagrams are not to scale.*

DVC RESORTS *(continued)*

SARATOGA SPRINGS RESORT & SPA
Studio: 355 square feet *(gray area)*
1-bedroom: 714 square feet
2-bedroom: 1,075 square feet
Grand Villa: 2,113 square feet

TREEHOUSE VILLAS
3-bedroom: 1,074 square feet

POLYNESIAN BUNGALOWS
1,650 square feet
(see next page for villas)

BOULDER RIDGE VILLAS
Studio: 356 square feet *(gray area)*
1-bedroom: 727 square feet
2-bedroom: 1,080 square feet

COPPER CREEK VILLAS & CABINS
Studio (sleeps 4): 345 square feet *(gray area)*
1-bedroom (sleeps 4): 761 square feet
2-bedroom (sleeps 8): 1,105 square feet
Cabin (2 bedrooms; sleeps 8): 1,737 square feet
Grand Villa (3 bedrooms; sleeps 12): 3,204 square feet

Note: *Diagrams are not to scale.*

THE DISNEY RESORTS: ROOM DIAGRAMS

DVC RESORTS (continued)

RIVIERA RESORT
Deluxe Studio:
423 square feet *(gray area)*
1-bedroom: 813 square feet
2-bedroom lock-off:
1,246 square feet
3-bedroom:
2,530 square feet

RIVIERA RESORT, TOWER STUDIO
225 square feet; accommodates 2 guests plus 1 child under age 3 in a crib

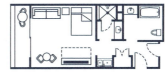

POLYNESIAN VILLAS
Studio: 460 square feet

THE CABINS AT FORT WILDERNESS RESORT
504 square feet; accommodate 6 guests plus 1 child under age 3 in a crib

ISLAND TOWER, DUO STUDIO
262 square feet; accommodates 2 guests plus 1 child under age 3 in a crib

ISLAND TOWER, DELUXE STUDIO
378–447 square feet; accommodates 4 guests plus 1 child under age 3 in a crib

DISNEY MODERATE RESORTS

CORONADO SPRINGS RESORT, GRAN DESTINO TOWER
Typical room, 375 square feet; accommodates 4 guests plus 1 child under age 3 in a crib

Note: *Diagrams are not to scale.*

MODERATE RESORTS (continued)

CORONADO SPRINGS RESORT
Typical room, 314 square feet; accommodates 4 guests plus 1 child under age 3 in a crib

CARIBBEAN BEACH RESORT
Typical room, 314 square feet; accommodates 5 guests plus 1 child under age 3 in a crib

PORT ORLEANS RESORT–FRENCH QUARTER
Typical room, 314 square feet; accommodates 4 guests plus 1 child under age 3 in a crib

PORT ORLEANS RESORT–RIVERSIDE
Typical room, 314 square feet; accommodates 5 guests plus 1 child under age 3 in a crib. Alligator Bayou has 54-inch-long trundle bed for child at no extra charge.

DISNEY VALUE RESORTS

ART OF ANIMATION RESORT, *FINDING NEMO* FAMILY SUITE
Typical suite, 565 square feet; accommodates 6 guests plus 1 child under age 3 in a crib

ART OF ANIMATION RESORT, *LITTLE MERMAID* STANDARD ROOM
Typical room, 277 square feet; accommodates 4 guests plus 1 child under age 3 in a crib

ALL-STAR RESORTS
Typical room, 260 square feet; accommodates 4 guests plus 1 child under age 3 in a crib

ALL-STAR RESORTS FAMILY SUITE
Typical suite, 520 square feet; accommodates 6 guests plus 1 child under age 3 in a crib

POP CENTURY RESORT
Typical room, 260 square feet; accommodates 4 guests plus 1 child under age 3 in a crib

Note: *Diagrams are not to scale.*

continued from page 99

over the years. Your best bet at the Polynesian or Port Orleans might be to ask for a remote corner room without a connecting interior door.

Room soundproofing, however, is only half the story; the other half is location, particularly as it relates to people outside your room. A pool-view room at any resort, for instance, is likely to pick up a lot more noise than an upper-floor corner room.

With all these factors in mind, we set out to determine the amount of external noise affecting every single room at Walt Disney World. We took into account factors including the floor level, pedestrian traffic, proximity to public spaces, and number of nearby rooms.

Take the northwest-facing rooms in buildings 4 and 5 of Disney's **All-Star Music Resort:** They overlook the extreme end of a parking lot, well away from most public spaces. There's little pedestrian traffic here, and the rooms themselves are well soundproofed—a recipe for quiet, or so we thought. But as it turns out, the remoteness of this location isn't lost on Disney: It's where the diesel buses are warmed up in the morning before servicing the three All-Stars.

Our research indicates that quiet rooms can be found in almost any resort, regardless of price point. For readers who put peace and quiet at the top of their lists, we've listed the 12 quietest spots among all WDW resorts in the table 106.

Let There Be Light!

In addition to sound, we measure the amount of light available in three key areas of each hotel room: at the bathroom vanity or sink, at the desk or work area, and in bed. The good news is that Disney has been steadily improving the lighting throughout most of its resorts. The **Contemporary** sets the standard: Light at the desk measures well above the recommended level for office or school work. Light at the bathroom vanity is brighter than normal daylight. Other resorts with good lighting include the **Riviera, Polynesian Village, Wilderness Lodge,** and **All-Stars.** Resorts that didn't do well in our lighting test include **Port Orleans Riverside** (but we'll see if the 2025 refurbishment helps). If you think you'll need to get work done while vacationing at Walt Disney World, consider staying at a hotel with good lighting.

Check-In and Checkout

Up to 60 days before you arrive, you can log on to mydisneyexperience.com to complete the check-in process. Depending on how much information you provide before your trip, your resort check-in can be eliminated or streamlined considerably.

> *unofficial* **TIP**
> Check the MDE app before you get in a long check-in line—sometimes the app will be updated with your room number even if you didn't get a text or email alert.

DIRECT-TO-ROOM CHECK-IN If you provide the website with a credit card number, a PIN for purchases, and your arrival and departure times, Disney will send you an email or text confirming that your check-in is complete. When your room number is available, Disney will send that to you, allowing you to go straight to your room without stopping at the front desk.

QUIETEST ROOMS AT WALT DISNEY WORLD
ALL-STAR MUSIC West-facing rooms in buildings 5 and 6
ALL-STAR SPORTS West-facing rooms in building 3; north-facing rooms in building 2
BAY LAKE TOWER All of these rooms are among the quietest in WDW
BEACH CLUB Easternmost hallways, rooms facing east
BEACH CLUB VILLAS Rooms facing southeast
BOARDWALK INN All rooms facing courtyard, just east of main lobby
BOULDER RIDGE VILLAS Southernmost part of the building, water-view rooms facing east
CARIBBEAN BEACH Trinidad South, buildings 35 and 38, rooms facing the lake (west)
PORT ORLEANS FRENCH QUARTER Building 1, rooms facing water; building 7, north wing, rooms facing water; building 6, north wing, rooms facing water
PORT ORLEANS RIVERSIDE Alligator Bayou, buildings 26 and 28, rooms facing east; Acadian House, north wings, rooms facing west
TREEHOUSE VILLAS Any room is good
WILDERNESS LODGE/COPPER CREEK VILLAS Middle of northernmost wing, rooms facing northwest (woods)

ONLINE CHECK-IN If you've checked in online but you haven't added a credit card or PIN to your account, you'll still be able to bypass the regular check-in desk and head for the Online Check-In Desk to finish the check-in process. *Note:* Online check-in should be completed at least 24 hours before you arrive.

AT THE FRONT DESK At the Value resorts, such as All-Star Sports, Disney has separate check-in areas for large tour groups and sports teams, leaving the huge main check-in desk free for regular travelers. A cast member also roams the lobby and can issue an "all hands on deck" alert when lines develop. The arrival of a busload of guests can sometimes overwhelm the front desk at Deluxe resorts, which have smaller front desks and fewer agents, but this is the exception rather than the rule. If your room is unavailable when you arrive, Disney will offer to call or text you when it's ready.

On your checkout day, your bill will be prepared and emailed or made available in My Disney Experience. If everything is in order, you can simply pack up and depart. But beware—on a recent trip, our family left for breakfast at another resort but didn't check out. When we got back to our room to use bathrooms and grab a few snacks we left in the fridge, housekeeping was already cleaning the room! This isn't supposed to happen, but it's a possibility.

EARLY CHECK-IN Official check-in time is 3 p.m. at Disney hotels and 4 p.m. for DVC villas. If you check in early and you ask for a room that's ready, that request will cancel out any previous one you've made.

HOUSEKEEPING SERVICE As of 2025, Disney's housekeeping service visits rooms every other day at Value and Moderate resorts and daily at Deluxe resorts. If you book a DVC resort at a cash rate, you will receive daily housekeeping service (except at the Cabins at Fort Wilderness, which are serviced every other day). If you book a DVC resort using points (including point rental), housekeeping will visit on the fourth and eighth days of your stay.

AUTHORS' PICKS FOR DISNEY RESORTS
ADULTS
VALUE: Pop Century For the efficient room designs and Skyliner access
MODERATE: Port Orleans French Quarter For its small size, updated rooms, quiet resort, and beignets
DELUXE: Wilderness Lodge For its just-right balance of location, amenities, and food
GROUPS OF 5 OR MORE
VALUE: All-Star Music The newest suites, with two baths, are 33% less than the suites at Art of Animation.
MODERATE: Caribbean Beach Book a fifth-sleeper room and request a location near a Skyliner station.
DELUXE: Old Key West Book a two-bedroom villa with DVC rental points.
FAMILIES WITH YOUNG KIDS
VALUE: Art of Animation For its delightful outdoor decorations and themed pools
MODERATE: Caribbean Beach For its fun colors and pool, plus Skyliner access to two parks
DELUXE: Animal Kingdom Lodge For the fantastic scenery and chances to see animals
FAMILIES WITH OLDER KIDS
VALUE: Pop Century For the lively pool scene that's conducive to meeting new friends; the teen-friendly food court; and Art of Animation's food court, which is within walking distance
MODERATE: Port Orleans Riverside There is plenty of opportunity to independently explore at this large resort.
DELUXE: Yacht & Beach Clubs For Stormalong Bay and easy access to two parks

PARKING POLICIES Disney offers free overnight parking at its resorts for guests who are staying there. Day guests who visit the Disney resorts to eat, shop, use recreational facilities, and the like can park there for free (valet parking costs extra). Guests staying at the **Campsites at Fort Wilderness Resort** get a parking space for one vehicle. Day parking in the theme parks is also free for guests staying on-property.

READERS' DISNEY RESORT REPORT CARD

EACH YEAR, SEVERAL THOUSAND READERS send in responses to our surveys. The Readers' 2025 Disney Resort Report Card, on pages 108–109, documents their opinions of the Walt Disney World resorts as well as the Swan, Dolphin, and Swan Reserve hotels.

In the **% Stay Again** and **% Rec to Friends** columns, we list the percentage of readers responding "Definitely" to the questions "Would you stay at this hotel again?" and "Would you recommend this hotel to a friend?" For this edition, percentages of 94 or above in response to the first question and 73 or above in response to the second are considered **Above Average;** percentages of 89 or below in response to the first question and 62 or below in response to the second are considered **Below Average.** In the hotel profiles on the following pages, we include these two percentages, plus the overall reader rating expressed as a letter grade, from the Report Card.

continued on page 110

READERS' 2025 DISNEY RESORT REPORT CARD

RESORT	PAGE	NO. OF SURVEYS	% STAY AGAIN	% REC TO FRIENDS
VALUE				
ALL-STAR MOVIES RESORT	160	78	82	48
ALL-STAR MUSIC RESORT	160	87	86	40
ALL-STAR SPORTS RESORT	160	95	87	53
ART OF ANIMATION RESORT	166	129	89	65
CAMPSITES AT FORT WILDERNESS	169	25	100	83
POP CENTURY RESORT	165	472	94	65
MODERATE				
CARIBBEAN BEACH RESORT	139	288	91	54
CORONADO SPRINGS RESORT	157	180	95	72
PORT ORLEANS FRENCH QUARTER	150	167	96	80
PORT ORLEANS RIVERSIDE	152	169	88	63
DELUXE				
ANIMAL KINGDOM LODGE	153	121	95	76
BEACH CLUB RESORT	129	135	89	64
BOARDWALK INN	133	101	95	77
CONTEMPORARY RESORT	123	90	85	60
GRAND FLORIDIAN RESORT & SPA	110	120	87	70
POLYNESIAN VILLAGE RESORT	114	98	95	66
SHADES OF GREEN	126	23	100	87
WALT DISNEY WORLD DOLPHIN	136	66	91	54
WALT DISNEY WORLD SWAN	136	55	90	60
WALT DISNEY WORLD SWAN RESERVE	136	26	88	72
WILDERNESS LODGE	119	113	95	82
YACHT CLUB RESORT	129	103	96	78
DELUXE VILLA (DVC)				
ANIMAL KINGDOM VILLAS–JAMBO HOUSE	153	58	96	74
ANIMAL KINGDOM VILLAS–KIDANI VILLAGE	156	113	86	61
BAY LAKE TOWER AT THE CONTEMPORARY	125	116	97	71
BEACH CLUB VILLAS	132	101	94	73
BOARDWALK VILLAS	135	143	96	76
BOULDER RIDGE VILLAS	122	75	94	72
CABINS AT FORT WILDERNESS	172	27	85	63
COPPER CREEK VILLAS & CABINS AT WILDERNESS LODGE	122	65	97	77
OLD KEY WEST RESORT	147	135	94	71
POLYNESIAN VILLAS & BUNGALOWS	117	116	88	64
RIVIERA RESORT	142	116	96	89
SARATOGA SPRINGS RESORT & SPA	143	184	91	54
VILLAS AT THE GRAND FLORIDIAN	113	53	94	77
Average for Disney Hotels			92	67
Average for Off-Site Hotels			80	60

Treehouse Villas at Saratoga Springs Resort (page 146) did not have enough surveys to rate for this edition.

READERS' 2025 DISNEY RESORT REPORT CARD

ROOM QUALITY	CHECK-IN EFFICIENCY	QUIETNESS OF ROOM	PARKS TRANSPORT	POOL	STAFF	DINING	OVERALL
B-	A-	B-	B-	C+	A	D	B
B-	A-	B-	C+	C	A-	D+	B-
B	A	B-	B	C+	B+	D+	B
B	A-	B	A-	B	A-	D+	B+
B-	A	B-	B-	C	A	D-	A+
C+	A-	C	A-	C	A-	D+	B+
B-	A-	B	A-	B-	A-	D+	B
B+	A-	B	C	B-	A-	C	A-
B+	A	B+	B+	B	A-	C-	A-
B	A-	B+	C	B	A-	C-	B+
B+	A	B	C	B+	A-	B-	A
B	A-	C	A-	A-	B+	C-	B+
B+	A-	B-	A-	C	A-	D	A
B	A-	B-	B+	C	B	C	B+
B+	A-	B	A-	B-	A	C-	A-
B	A-	C+	A	B+	A-	C	B+
A	A+	A-	B+	A-	A-	D	A-
B	B	B	B-	C+	B-	D	B
B+	A-	B	C+	C+	A	D	A-
B+	A-	B-	C+	C	B+	D	A-
B+	A-	B	B	B	A-	C	A
B+	A	B	A-	A-	A-	C-	A-
B+	A-	B+	C	B-	A	B-	A-
A-	A-	B+	C	B	A	C	B+
B+	A	A-	B+	C	B+	C	A-
A-	A	A-	A-	A-	A-	C-	B
B+	A	B-	A-	B	A-	D+	A-
B+	A	A-	B	B+	A	C	A
B+	A	A	C	D+	B+	D-	A-
B+	A-	B	B	B+	A	C	A
B+	A	B	C	B	A	C-	B+
B	A-	B-	B+	B	A-	C	B+
A	A	A	A	B+	A	C	A
A-	A-	A-	C	B	A	D	B+
A-	B+	B	A-	B-	A-	C+	A-
B+	**A-**	**B**	**B**	**B-**	**A-**	**C-**	**A-**
B	**B**	**B**	**D**	**D**	**B**	**D-**	**B-**

continued from page 107

Room Quality reflects readers' satisfaction with their rooms, while **Check-In Efficiency** rates the speed and ease of check-in. **Quietness of Room** measures how well insulated from external noise guests perceive their rooms to be. **Parks Transport** rates Disney's bus, boat, Skyliner, and/or monorail service to and from the resorts. **Pool** reflects readers' satisfaction with the resorts' swimming pools. **Staff** measures the friendliness and helpfulness of the resort's employees, and **Dining** rates the overall food quality and value.

Off-site hotels are, on average, rated slightly lower than Disney resorts, with problems noted in food courts and transportation. We think these ratings justify what Disney charges at its resorts.

Putting It All Together: Reader Picks for Best and Worst Resorts

Taking the top spots for satisfaction ratings this year are two resorts on opposite ends of the spectrum: **Riviera Resort** and the **Campsites at Fort Wilderness.** Riviera is well connected to other resorts and two parks and has beautiful rooms. The Campsites offer the lowest price point of any on-site option and the ability to stay in the comfort of your own RV (or a rented one) for a potentially longer vacation. Just below these is **Wilderness Lodge** (and its DVC counterparts). These three resorts are highly rated in every category except food, where they score just above average.

After a brief rebound last year, the lowest-rated Disney resorts are **All-Star Movies** and **All-Star Music** (but not Sports). Both are rated low for their pools, dining options, and noise level in rooms.

WALT DISNEY WORLD RESORT PROFILES

THE MAGIC KINGDOM RESORTS
Disney's Grand Floridian Resort & Spa
(See map on page 112. See **theugseries.com/grand-floridian** *and* **theugseries.com/gf-villas** *for extended coverage.)*

STRENGTHS	WEAKNESSES
• High staff-to-guest ratio	• Most expensive WDW resort
• Excellent dining options for adults	• Public areas often blocked by wedding parties
• Large rooms with daybeds	
• Excellent on-site spa	• Noise from Magic Kingdom, boat horns, and whistles
• Fun *Alice in Wonderland*-themed splash area for kids	
	• The lobby is insanely crowded during certain holidays
• Boat and monorail transportation to the Magic Kingdom, plus a pedestrian walkway	• Bus transportation may be shared by the other monorail resorts
• Diverse recreational options	
• Close to Palm, Magnolia, and Oak Trail Golf Courses	

Unofficial Guide **Reader-Survey Results**

Percentage of readers who'd stay here again	**87%** (*Below Average*)
Percentage of readers who'd recommend this resort to a friend	**70%** (*Average*)
Overall reader rating	**A−**

QUICK TAKE: *The Grand Floridian is the quintessential Walt Disney World resort. Unfortunately, the cost reflects this. And during Christmas and Easter, crowds viewing the elaborate holiday displays in the lobby can negatively affect your experience.*

WALT DISNEY WORLD'S FLAGSHIP HOTEL is inspired by grand Victorian resorts such as the Hotel del Coronado in San Diego and Mount Washington Resort in New Hampshire. The complex of four- and five-story buildings integrates verandas, intricate latticework, dormers, and turrets beneath a red-shingled roof to capture the feeling of a 19th-century ocean resort. Covering 40 acres along Seven Seas Lagoon, it offers lovely pools, white-sand beaches, and a marina.

After a refresh in 2024, the 867 guest rooms now feature shades of blues, whites, and tans. Lighter furniture, walls, and hardwood floors make the already large rooms seems lighter and more spacious than ever. The textured headboards and large rug add luxury without feeling stuffy. A typical room is 440 square feet (dormer rooms are smaller) and is furnished with two queen beds, a daybed, and a small desk with chair. Many rooms have balconies. All rooms have a Keurig coffee maker, a large dresser with minifridge, and a wall-mounted TV.

Bathrooms are large, with plenty of counter space, pretty fixtures, and fluffy towels. Under-sink storage is lacking. Water pressure in the shower is probably less than what you get at home but it does the job.

The hotel is connected directly to the Magic Kingdom by monorail, boat, and a pedestrian walkway, and to other Disney World destinations by bus. Walking time to the monorail-, boat-, and bus-loading areas from the most remote guest rooms is about 7–10 minutes. It takes about 15–20 minutes on the pedestrian walkway to get to the Magic Kingdom tapstiles.

The resort has many highly rated table-service restaurants. Add to that everything accessible via the monorail, and you have very impressive dining selections. The main building displays life-size gingerbread houses at Christmas, which brings noise and crowds to the lobby. During this season, waits for the monorail can balloon up to 90 minutes.

The Grand Floridian's **Senses Spa,** modeled after the spas on the Disney Cruise Line ships, is one of the best in the Orlando area. In addition, the resort's pools are nice, if not incredibly exciting. The **Courtyard Pool** has a zero-entry ramp for small children to splash in. An *Alice in Wonderland*–themed splash area sits between the main building and the villas.

The grounds are a lovely place to walk around in the evening, with romantic lighting and charming background music.

Most of the reader comments we get about the Grand Floridian are positive. From a North Carolina mother of two preschoolers:

> *The Grand Floridian pool with the waterslide was a big hit with our kids. They also loved taking the boat across the lagoon to return from the Magic Kingdom.*

Grand Floridian Resort & Spa and Grand Floridian Villas

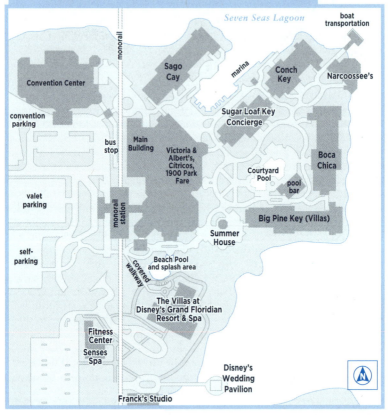

GOOD (AND NOT-SO-GOOD) ROOMS AT THE GRAND FLORIDIAN *(See* theugseries.com/gf-views *for photos.)* The resort is spread over a peninsula that juts into Seven Seas Lagoon. In addition to the main building, there are five rectangular outer buildings, one of which (**Big Pine Key**) contains the villas. Grand Floridian room numbers are coded. Take room 7213: 7 is the building number, 2 is the floor, and 13 is the room number. Most of the rooms have a balcony, and most balconies are enclosed by a rail that affords good visibility. Dormer rooms, just beneath the roof in each building, have smaller enclosed balconies that limit visibility when you're seated. Most dormer rooms, however, have vaulted ceilings and a coziness that compensates for the less desirable balconies.

If you want to be near the bus and monorail, most of the restaurants, and shopping, ask for a room in the main building. It's the highest-rated building at this resort. The best rooms are **4322–4329** and **4422–4429**, which have full balconies and overlook the lagoon in the direction of the beach and the Polynesian Village. Other excellent main-building rooms are **4401–4409**, with full balconies overlooking the marina and an unobstructed view of Cinderella Castle across the lagoon.

Of the four outer guest-room buildings, **Boca Chica** and **Conch Key** have one long side facing the lagoon and the other facing inner courtyards and swimming pools. At Conch Key, full-balcony rooms **7229–7231, 7328, 7329, 7331, 7425–7429,** and **7431** offer vistas across the lagoon to the Magic Kingdom and castle. Less expensive rooms in the same building that offer good marina views are **7212, 7312, 7412–7415, 7417, 7419, 7421, 7513–7515,** and **7517**. In Boca Chica, ask for a lagoon-view room on the first, second, or third floor. Avoid garden-view rooms in this building if possible.

The other two guest-room buildings, **Sugar Loaf Key** (Club Level) and **Sago Cay,** face each other across the marina. The opposite side of Sugar Loaf Key faces a courtyard, while the other side of Sago Cay faces a finger of the lagoon and a forested area. These views are pleasant but not in the same league as those listed previously. Exceptions are end rooms in Sago Cay that have a view of the lagoon and Cinderella Castle (rooms **5139, 5144, 5145, 5242–5245,** and **5342–5345**).

THE VILLAS AT DISNEY'S GRAND FLORIDIAN RESORT & SPA

Unofficial Guide **Reader-Survey Results**

Percentage of readers who'd stay here again	**94%** (*Above Average*)
Percentage of readers who'd recommend this resort to a friend	**77%** (*Above Average*)
Overall reader rating	**A–**

THIS DISNEY VACATION CLUB PROPERTY opened in the fall of 2013. Readers consistently rate it as one of the best resorts in Walt Disney World, and it's the absolute favorite of many.

Decorated like close siblings to the refurbished resort rooms, the villas are well-appointed. Most have vaulted living-room ceilings and faux-wood balconies or porches. Those balconies stretch the entire length of the room, giving everyone enough space for a good view.

Studios have a kitchenette with minifridge, sink, and drip coffee maker, while the larger rooms have full kitchens. Those feature a stainless steel range, with the dishwasher and refrigerator tucked behind white wood panels that match the glass-door cabinets. Other amenities in the full kitchens include a full-size coffee maker, a toaster, frying pans, and the usual set of plates, glasses, cups, and cutlery. Also in the kitchen are a banquette seat and a table with room for six.

The living room has a sofa that seats three comfortably, an upholstered chair and ottoman, a coffee table, and a large flat-screen TV. The sofa converts into a bed that sleeps two; a cabinet below the TV hides a small pull-down bed. We'd use these beds for kids, not adults.

Studio rooms have a queen bed in addition to the folding options listed above. One-bedroom villas have a king bed along with the folding options; two-bedroom villas have a king bed in one room and two queen beds in the other, plus the folding options; the Grand Villa's third bedroom has an additional two queen beds.

The one- and two-bedroom units and the Grand Villa bedrooms are outfitted with a large writing desk, a flat-screen TV with DVD player, two nightstands with convenient outlets, and a side chair. They also have large walk-in closets.

Bathrooms are large, with marble tile and flat-screen TVs built into the mirrors. Studio bathrooms have a separate toilet and shower area; in the one-bedroom configuration, a tub and dressing area sit adjacent to the bedroom. The bathroom and shower are connected by a pocket door, allowing two groups of people to get dressed at the same time. The tiled shower is so large that it could function as another bedroom if that was ever a need. It has a rain showerhead mounted in the ceiling in addition to a wall-mounted faucet.

The villas have their own well-located parking lot but no dining in their buildings. Within walking distance, however, are the restaurants of both the main Grand Floridian building and Polynesian Village. Room service is available from the Grand Floridian's in-room-dining menu.

GOOD (AND NOT-SO-GOOD) ROOMS AT THE GRAND FLORIDIAN VILLAS *(See* theugseries.com/gf-villa-views *for photos.)* Rooms **1X14, 1X16,** and **1X18** face the Magic Kingdom and have views of Space Mountain and the castle; **1X14** has perhaps the best views of any room in the villas. (*X* indicates the floor number.)

Even-numbered rooms **1X02–1X12** face west, toward the Polynesian Village and Seven Seas Lagoon, and afford a good view of the nightly water pageant as it floats by.

South-facing rooms in Big Pine Key look out over Seven Seas Lagoon, although mature trees and landscaping partially block those views from many upper-floor rooms. Rooms **9X41–9X47** may have views of the Magic Kingdom fireworks.

Disney's Polynesian Village Resort, Villas & Bungalows

(See map on page 116. See theugseries.com/ug-poly *and* theugseries.com/poly-villas *for extended coverage.)*

STRENGTHS	
• Walking distance to EPCOT monorail	• Close to Palm, Magnolia, and Oak Trail Golf Courses
• Most family-friendly dining on the monorail loop	**WEAKNESSES**
• Fun South Seas theme	• No spa or exercise facilities (guests can use those at the Grand Floridian or in the Island Tower)
• Boat and monorail transportation to the Magic Kingdom	• Noise from boat horns and whistles
• Among the best Club Levels of the Deluxe resorts	• Bus transportation could be shared with other monorail-loop resorts

Unofficial Guide Reader-Survey Results
(resort only; see page 117 for villa/bungalow ratings)

Percentage of readers who'd stay here again	95% *(Above Average)*
Percentage of readers who'd recommend this resort to a friend	66% *(Average)*
Overall reader rating	B+

SOUTH PACIFIC TROPICS ABOUND at this Deluxe resort, which consists of two- and three-story Hawaiian longhouses situated around the four-story **Great Ceremonial House,** which contains restaurants, shops, and an atrium lobby with slate floors and tropical plants. Buildings feature wood accents, including exposed roof beams and tribal-inspired geometric inlays.

Spread across 39 acres along Seven Seas Lagoon, the resort has 480 standard hotel rooms and three white-sand beaches. Its pool complex likewise captures the South Pacific theme. There is no dedicated fitness center, but guests are welcome to use the fitness center in the new **Island Tower** (see page 118) or the Grand Floridian's facilities, just a quarter-mile walk (bonus workout!) or 2-minute monorail ride away. Landscaping is superb—garden-view rooms are generally superior to equivalent rooms at other resorts.

The most recent room refurbishments were completed in summer 2021, adding bright, island-themed murals and subtle references to characters from Disney's *Moana*. We're always suspicious when Disney adds characters to anything because we've had bad experiences with that in the past (RIP Maelstrom). But this is one of Disney's better room-renovation projects in recent memory, and the *Moana* additions work well with the resort's theme. Most rooms have two queen beds, a sofa, a reading chair, a large dresser with plenty of shelf space, and a wall-mounted TV. A minifridge and coffee maker sit between two large closets near the doorway and opposite the bathroom area. The closets are spacious and light. Lighting is good throughout the room, including by the desk and beds.

The Poly's bathrooms have two large sinks that offer plenty of counter space. A spacious, glass-enclosed shower provides good-to-excellent water pressure. The new bathroom layout includes a door between the toilet and sink area, plus another separating the entire bathroom from the rest of the room. This allows three people to get dressed in privacy at once.

The resort has an on-site monorail station, and all rooms are within easy walking distance of the Transportation and Ticket Center, with access to the EPCOT monorail. Bus service is available to other Disney destinations, and boat service takes you to the Magic Kingdom. Walking time to the bus and on-site monorail stations is 7–10 minutes at most. The pedestrian walkway between the Poly and the Grand Floridian continues to the Magic Kingdom—it's about 1.5 miles from the farthest point at the Poly to the Magic Kingdom tapstiles.

The Poly's transportation options are a major draw:

We stay at the Polynesian Village because it offers the best transportation. You can walk to a direct monorail to both the Magic Kingdom and EPCOT, the water taxi can be a fast option, and the bus service to other parks is fairly direct.

A Maryland family found the room soundproofing lacking, confirming our own research:

We took towels from the pool and stuffed them under the door to deaden the noise coming from the connecting room.

The Polynesian Village has two lounges, with **Trader Sam's Grog Grotto** being the most popular. Modeled after the famed bar of the same name at the Disneyland Hotel, it serves whimsical (and potent) cocktails and tasty appetizers, along with interactive art and "artifacts" stuffed into every available inch of space. During busier times of the year, it can take several hours to get a table at Trader Sam's, so we don't recommend it. **Tambu Lounge** is less well known but rated better overall.

PART 5 ACCOMMODATIONS

Polynesian Village Resort, Villas & Bungalows

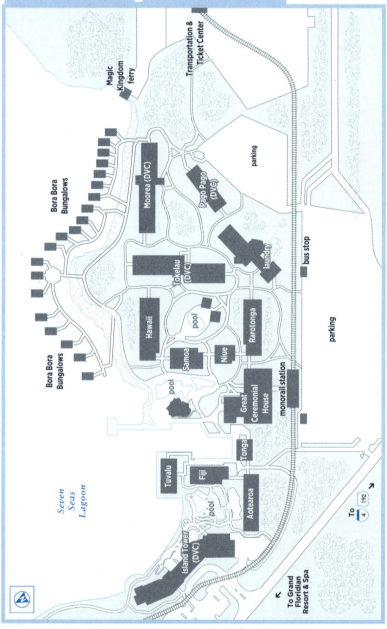

GOOD (AND NOT-SO-GOOD) ROOMS AT POLYNESIAN VILLAGE RESORT *(See theugseries.com/poly-views for photos.)* The resort's eight guest room buildings, or longhouses, are spread between the monorail on one side and Seven Seas Lagoon on the other. All buildings have first-floor patios and third-floor balconies. The older buildings, which contain about half of the resort's rooms, have faux balconies on their second floors. (The newer buildings offer full balconies on both the second and third floors, and patios on the first.) If space is important, ask for a first-floor room because patios are roomier than balconies. But if views are important, ask for a third-floor room, as mature vegetation blocks the views from some patios.

The Great Ceremonial House contains most of the restaurants and shops, the lobby, guest services, and bus and monorail stations. Of the longhouses most convenient to it—**Tuvalu, Fiji, Aotearoa, Tonga, Rarotonga, Niue,** and **Samoa**—Fiji and Samoa offer views of the swimming complex, a small marina, or inner gardens. There are no lagoon views from any of the above, except for indirect views from the upper floors of Fiji, Samoa, and Tuvalu; Aotearoa; and a tunnel view from Tonga. Samoa is still a good choice for families because it's close to the main swimming complex. The 22-room Niue is the highest-rated building at the Polynesian. You won't get views of the Magic Kingdom, but Niue is centrally located between both pools and the Great Ceremonial House.

You can specifically request a lagoon- or Magic Kingdom–view room at the Polynesian Village, if you're willing to pay extra. The best of these rooms are on the third floor in **Tuvalu** and, if you're staying in a Club Level (concierge) room, the third floor in **Hawaii.**

In addition to the second-floor rooms with faux balconies, we also advise against booking the monorail-side (south-facing) rooms in **Rarotonga** and **Aotearoa.** The monorail runs within spitting distance, which is awkward and noisy.

Many first-floor rooms in **Hawaii (1501–1518)** are garden- or lagoon-view rooms; their scenery is blocked by the overwater bungalows. However, these rooms still offer a chance to see the evening fireworks and are a little less expensive than similar rooms on higher floors.

POLYNESIAN VILLAS & BUNGALOWS

Unofficial Guide **Reader-Survey Results**

Percentage of readers who'd stay here again	**88%** (*Below Average*)
Percentage of readers who'd recommend this resort to a friend	**64%** (*Average*)
Overall reader rating	**B+**

THE TOKELAU, MOOREA, AND PAGO PAGO longhouses hold DVC studio rooms that sleep five and are the largest studios in Walt Disney World's DVC inventory. They also have two bathrooms: The smaller bath has a small sink and step-in shower; the larger has a toilet, sink, and bath/shower combination. This allows three people to get ready simultaneously. The studios also include kitchenettes.

The Polynesian's 20 over-the-water **Bora Bora Bungalows** sit in front of Hawaii, Tokelau, and Moorea. Connected to land by a wood walkway, these two-bedroom bungalows offer stunning views of the Magic Kingdom fireworks and of Seven Seas Lagoon and its nightly Electrical Water Pageant. Not surprisingly, those stunning views come with stunning prices—up to $6,100 per night.

The bungalows are well built, with top-notch design elements from top to bottom. The bedrooms are spacious, the bathrooms are gorgeous, and the open kitchen design works wonderfully. The doorbell even plays a different chime every time you ring it. And yeah, the views are spectacular.

However, the bungalows have two fatal flaws: price and noise. Regarding the first, they cost an average of 146 DVC points for a one-night stay, roughly equivalent to $2,920 at the time of this writing. Check-in is at 4 p.m. and checkout at 11 a.m., so a 19-hour stay costs about $154 an hour. That's assuming you get your room assigned on time and don't leave early.

And then there's the ferry horn. A ferry leaves about every 12 minutes, from 30 minutes before Early Entry begins until an hour after the parks close. Every time a ferry departs, it sounds a warning horn. The sound is like an air-raid siren: loud enough to stop indoor conversation in its tracks. Reading, watching TV, getting a baby to nap, sleeping before one of those late-park-close nights? Forget it. If you're determined to stay here, shoot for **bungalows 7001–7005,** which are farthest from the TTC.

The Polynesian Villas have a separate parking lot close to their longhouses. Dining and transportation are shared with the main resort.

NEW DVC BUILDING Opened in December 2024, **Island Tower** is part of the Polynesian Villas' DVC complex. This new 10-story building is situated between the Fiji/Aotearoa buildings and the Wedding Pavilion at the Grand Floridian, right by Seven Seas Lagoon. It offers deluxe studios, one- and two-bedroom villas, and a new room type: **Duo Studios.** These studios are 262 square feet (roughly the size of a Value resort room) and only sleep two people in a queen-size Murphy bed.

There is a lot to love about the new Island Tower. The public spaces are beautiful, especially the four "terrace gardens" on floors 3–6. These are open-air areas where you can relax and take in views of Seven Seas Lagoon (on floors 3 and 5) or the monorail track, road, and golf course (on floors 4 and 6). The lobby is stunning too. If aesthetics are what matters to you, you won't be disappointed.

But that's where the good news ends. If you care more about the logistics of your WDW stay, the Island Tower leaves much to be desired. There is no transportation, front desk, or bell services desk in the tower. Instead, you have to walk over to the Great Ceremonial House for those things (including grocery deliveries). In the rooms, there are surprisingly few outlets for charging devices. At press time, you couldn't even get coffee for refillable mugs without walking over to the Great Ceremonial House.

And you pay an astronomical amount for having to deal with these headaches: The rack rate for a Duo Studio (again, with 262 square feet and only a Murphy bed) facing the parking lot is $700/night. At the time of this writing, the tower was only a couple of months old; it's possible Disney will take all the "constructive" feedback it's getting and implement some changes.

GOOD (AND NOT-SO-GOOD) ROOMS AT THE POLYNESIAN VILLAS Because there are a few quirks in the way Disney categorizes room views in the villas, it's possible to snag a Magic Kingdom view from a garden-view room. The second- and third-floor rooms in **Tokelau (2901–2928,**

2939–2948, 3901–3928, and **3939–3948**) offer the best shot at getting side views of Cinderella Castle and the fireworks, although palm trees may block many second-floor views. First-floor rooms also have landscaping blocking most views; on the upside, the patios provide room to move to find a better spot. Overall, Tokelau is the highest-rated DVC building at the Polynesian Villas.

The second and third floors in **Moorea** have rooms with lagoon and Magic Kingdom views; those that face north see the Magic Kingdom. Avoid **Pago Pago**'s southeast-facing rooms (**1X01–1X12**)—these look onto the parking lot and monorail. (*X* indicates the floor number.)

If you plan to spend a lot of time in EPCOT, **Moorea** and **Pago Pago** are good choices because they're within easy walking distance of the TTC and the EPCOT monorail. Even if you're going to the Magic Kingdom, it's a short walk from Moorea and Pago Pago to the TTC and its Magic Kingdom monorail.

In the **Island Tower,** theme park–view rooms are the most expensive type. If you want to make the most of what you're paying, request a room that ends in an even number between 32 and 58 (**8X32-8X58**). These rooms have the most direct views of the Magic Kingdom and the rest of the lagoon.

Disney's Wilderness Lodge, Boulder Ridge Villas, and Copper Creek Villas & Cabins

(See map on page 120. See **theugseries.com/wilderness-lodge, theugseries.com/boulder,** *and* **theugseries.com/copper** *for extended coverage.)*

STRENGTHS	WEAKNESSES
• National park lodge theme is beautiful and well executed	• Transportation to Magic Kingdom is by bus or boat only
• Along with Animal Kingdom Lodge, it's the least expensive Disney Deluxe resort	• Noise from the main building's lobby can be heard inside nearby rooms
• Close to recreational options at Fort Wilderness	• Bus transportation to the Magic Kingdom is sometimes shared with Fort Wilderness
• Great views from guest rooms	• Smallest rooms and baths of Disney's Deluxe resorts
• The villas have an exceptionally peaceful location and public areas	

***Unofficial Guide** Reader-Survey Results (Wilderness Lodge only; see page 122 for Copper Creek Villas & Cabins and Boulder Ridge Villas)*

Percentage of readers who'd stay here again	**95%** *(Above Average)*
Percentage of readers who'd recommend this resort to a friend	**82%** *(Above Average)*
Overall reader rating	**A**

QUICK TAKE: *With their recent renovations, the Copper Creek Villas are the new top pick here, followed by rooms in the main building.*

THIS DELUXE RESORT is inspired by grand, rustic Arts and Crafts lodges of the early 20th century, like The Ahwahnee in Yosemite National Park. Situated on the shore of Bay Lake, Wilderness Lodge consists of an eight-story central building plus two seven-story guest wings, a wing of studio and one- and two-bedroom condominiums, and 26 lakeside cabins. The hotel features exposed timber columns, log cabin–style facades, and dormer windows, along with an 82-foot-tall stone fireplace in the lobby.

Wilderness Lodge, Boulder Ridge Villas, and Copper Creek Villas & Cabins

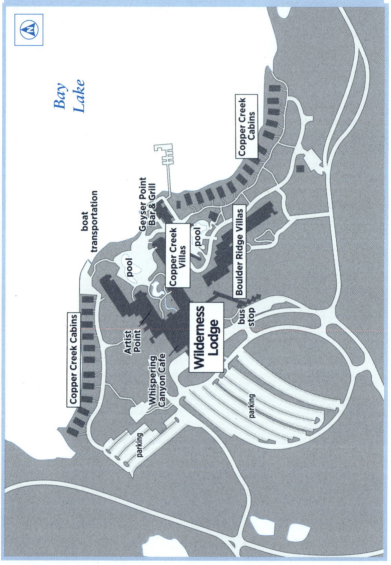

Outside, there's a beach, a reliable geyser, and a pool complex modeled on a mountain stream.

This book uses the admittedly clunky "Wilderness Lodge, Boulder Ridge Villas, and Copper Creek Villas & Cabins" to refer to the entire complex, including its DVC units, which are available to the general public when not being used by DVC members. Here's what the various names mean:

- **Disney's Wilderness Lodge** The resort component of the main building (the lodge), which opened in 1994
- **Boulder Ridge Villas** DVC rooms in an adjacent building, opened in 2000
- **Copper Creek Villas & Cabins** DVC rooms in the main building (Copper Creek Villas) and the lakeside cabins, both opened in 2017

The Deluxe guest rooms in the lodge were refurbished during the pandemic closures. More storage space, lots of outlets, and better lighting were added, and dark wood paneling was swapped out for soft headboards and lighter walls with woodsy Disney touches.

Typical rooms have two queen beds or a single king bed. All rooms have a table and chairs, a dresser, a TV, a double vanity just outside the bathroom, a minifridge, and a coffee maker. Rooms on the ground floor have patios; rooms above have balconies.

The pool area features a children's water-play area and a pool bar.

Dining choices consist of two full-service restaurants (Story Book Dining at Artist Point with Snow White and Whispering Canyon Cafe), plus the outdoor **Geyser Point Bar & Grill**. More dining is available via a short boat ride to the Contemporary or Fort Wilderness.

This lodge is a very popular place to stay during the holiday season, with a towering tree dominating the already breathtaking lobby. But it doesn't attract the crowds of gawkers like the Grand Floridian does, so you'll still get to enjoy your rocking chair by the fire in peace.

The resort is connected to the Magic Kingdom by boat or bus and to other parks by bus. Your best bet for catching the first boat is to send someone out to the boat dock about 90 minutes before the Magic Kingdom's official opening time. If a line has started to form but has fewer than 30 people, get in line. If the line is longer than that, consider taking a bus or using a ride-sharing app. Boat service may be suspended during storms, so if it's raining or rain looks likely, Disney will provide buses. Walking time to the buses and boats from the most remote rooms is 5–8 minutes.

A mom from Oklahoma says that transportation is a big weakness:

> During our most recent stay, transportation from Wilderness Lodge to the parks was the worst we have ever experienced in all our trips to WDW. We waited more than an hour for a boat to the Magic Kingdom; then, after it finally showed up and loaded, we made an unexplained trip to Fort Wilderness and loaded 26 more people. It took 90 minutes to get to the Magic Kingdom!

GOOD (AND NOT-SO-GOOD) ROOMS AT WILDERNESS LODGE *(See* theugseries.com/ug-wild-views *for photos.)* The lodge is shaped like a very blocky letter U. The main entrance and lobby are at the bottom of the U. Next are middle wings that connect the lobby to the parallel end sections, which extend to the open part of the U. The U's open end flanks pools and gardens and overlooks Bay Lake (sometimes indirectly). Avoid rooms on the fourth, fifth, and sixth floors that end with numbers 67–99; these overlook the main lobby and pick up any noise there.

The better rooms are on floors four, five, and six, toward the U's open end. Rooms **4000–4003, 5000–5003,** and **6000–6003** offer a direct frontal view of Bay Lake through some tall trees. Facing inward, odd-numbered rooms **4005–4023, 5005–5023,** and **6005–6023** face the courtyard but have excellent indirect lake views. Even-numbered rooms **5004–5034** and **6004–6034** face the Copper Creek Cabins, the woodlands northwest of the lodge, and the Magic Kingdom.

Odd-numbered rooms **5035–5041** and **6035–6041** offer a direct but distant view of the lake, with pools and gardens in the foreground.

COPPER CREEK VILLAS & CABINS

Unofficial Guide **Reader-Survey Results**

Percentage of readers who'd stay here again	**97%** (*Above Average*)
Percentage of readers who'd recommend this resort to a friend	**77%** (*Above Average*)
Overall reader rating	**A**

SOME ROOMS IN THE LODGE'S MAIN BUILDING are DVC units—Disney calls these Copper Creek Villas. Options include studios and one-, two-, and three-bedroom villas. The studios have kitchenettes, while most one- and two-bedroom villas have full kitchens. At the time of this writing, Copper Creek Villas were scheduled to receive a refurbishment in mid- to late 2025. We fully expect the results of this refurbishment to make these the best rooms in the Wilderness Lodge complex, even though no details were available prior to publication.

The floor plan of the cabins is similar to that of the Bora Bora Bungalows at the Polynesian. Room quality and views are excellent—they'd *better* be, at around $5,100 per night in peak season.

We prefer the cabins to the bungalows, thanks to their slightly lower price and lack of ferry horns, as does this Iowa reader:

> *Loved the cabin at Copper Creek—better value than the Polynesian bungalows. Quiet and well arranged, but close to everything.*

GOOD (AND NOT-SO-GOOD) ROOMS AT COPPER CREEK VILLAS AND CABINS (*See* theugseries.com/copper-views *for photos.*) Avoid rooms **X100–X106,** which overlook the lobby. Odd-numbered rooms **X107–X133** face the interior courtyard and pool. Studios numbered **X119** have a view of the lake in the distance. Even-numbered rooms **X108–X134** face Boulder Ridge Villas, a garden area, and woods. (*X* indicates the floor number.) Rooms on the sixth floor are high enough for you to see the lake past Boulder Ridge and Copper Creek Cabins.

Guests in cabins **8001–8006** get to watch boats glide to the Magic Kingdom, while cabins **8023–8026** offer excellent fireworks views.

BOULDER RIDGE VILLAS

Unofficial Guide **Reader-Survey Results**

Percentage of readers who'd stay here again	**94%** (*Above Average*)
Percentage of readers who'd recommend this resort to a friend	**72%** (*Average*)
Overall reader rating	**A**

ALSO PART OF DVC, the 136 Boulder Ridge Villas are studio and one- and two-bedroom units in a freestanding building to the right (southeast) of the lodge. Studios have kitchenettes, and one- and two-bedroom villas have full kitchens. The recently updated décor is inspired by Native American design and makes the rooms feel lighter and larger than before. Boulder Ridge has its own pool but shares restaurants and other amenities with the main lodge.

Boulder Ridge Villas' studios have fold-down beds (other than the fifth floor, which has sleeper sofas). All of its villas have armoires and flat-screen TVs, and one- and two-bedroom units have stainless steel kitchen appliances. The renovated rooms are a perfect blend of inspiration from Disney characters, Native American art, and national parks. It sounds like a lot, but the integration is masterfully done.

The excellent theming and layout of the rooms, along with the relative peace and quiet away from the main lobby, makes these perfect accommodations for families looking for more relaxation.

GOOD (AND NOT-SO-GOOD) ROOMS AT BOULDER RIDGE VILLAS See **theugseries.com/boulder-views** *for photos.*) Except for a few rooms overlooking the pool, these rooms offer woodland views. The best are odd-numbered rooms **X531–X563** on floors three through five, which open to the northeast side of the resort. Rooms on the opposite side of the same wing offer similar views, but with some roads and parking lots visible, plus traffic noise.

Disney's Contemporary Resort & Bay Lake Tower

(See map on page 124. See **theugseries.com/ug-comtemporary** and **theugseries.com/ug-blt** for extended coverage.)

THIS 655-ROOM DELUXE RESORT'S A-frame design permits the Magic Kingdom monorail to pass through the cavernous atrium. The 90-foot mosaic is a 1971 work by Disney animator and artist Mary Blair. The off-white central tower is augmented by the three-story **South Garden Wing,** fronting Bay Lake, to the south and by **Bay Lake Tower,** a 295-room, 15-story DVC development, to the north.

STRENGTHS	WEAKNESSES
• The only hotel the monorail goes *through*	• Overpriced, especially "theme park-view" rooms that mostly overlook parking lots
• Large rooms with views of Bay Lake	• Décor generally feels lazy and uninspired
• Bay Lake Tower rooms are among the quietest in all of Walt Disney World	• Very small studios in Bay Lake Tower sleep no more than two people comfortably
• Easy walk to the Magic Kingdom	• Bus transportation may be shared by the other monorail resorts
• Excellent staff/service	
• Best DVC lounge on WDW property	
• Recreation options on Bay Lake	

Unofficial Guide Reader-Survey Results (Contemporary Resort only; see page 125 for Bay Lake Tower ratings)

Percentage of readers who'd stay here again	**85%** (*Below Average*)
Percentage of readers who'd recommend this resort to a friend	**60%** (*Below Average*)
Overall reader rating	**B+**

Standard rooms in the A-frame (**Contemporary Tower**) afford fantastic views of Bay Lake or the Magic Kingdom, and all have balconies. At 394 square feet each, they're only slightly smaller than equivalent rooms at the Grand Floridian Resort.

Rooms in the Contemporary Tower received a refurbishment in the summer of 2021 that added characters from Pixar's *The Incredibles* films. Off-white walls, bedspreads, and flooring are paired with carpets and sofas in bold reds and other *Incredibles*-esque colors. All rooms include a minifridge and coffee maker. There's plenty of storage

Contemporary Resort & Bay Lake Tower

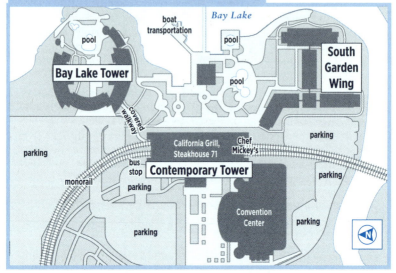

space and spots to plug in chargers. The beds are Sealy Posturepedic pillow-tops, which are very comfortable. Soundproofing from outdoor noise has been improved.

Bathrooms feature a continuous countertop featuring two sinks and plenty of storage. The shower/tub combination is enclosed by glass sliders. It's one of the nicest bathrooms in any Disney Deluxe resort. Likewise, the bathroom door is a midcentury-appropriate (and space-saving) slider. References to *The Incredibles* are found around the room. If you're looking at photos of these rooms online, note that we think they look better in person.

Our main criticism of the Contemporary's look is that it's devoid of imagination. Disney had the opportunity to transform it into one of America's great midcentury-themed hotels, and it didn't. Instead, it recycled the same generic ideas it has been putting into every recent hotel. Compare the look of the rooms themselves to the midcentury masterpiece Steakhouse 71 in the same building. That restaurant pops with a uniquely Disney but decidedly stylish feel. We wish the same vibe extended throughout the resort and the rooms. What's the point of being a storytelling company if you're phoning it in at your flagship hotels?

Dining options abound at the Contemporary. On the first floor is **Steakhouse 71,** specializing in grilled meats (or pancakes in the morning). The counter-service **Contempo Café** on the fourth floor's Grand Canyon Concourse serves upscale sandwiches, salads, and flatbread pizzas. **Chef Mickey's,** also on the fourth floor, hosts a popular character buffet. On the 15th floor, **California Grill** serves sophisticated contemporary American cuisine.

The pool has slides for kids and cabanas for rent. The Contemporary is within easy walking distance of the Magic Kingdom; monorail transportation is available to both the Magic Kingdom and EPCOT (via transfer), and other destinations can be accessed by bus or boat. Walking time to the transportation loading areas is 6–9 minutes or less.

GOOD (AND NOT-SO-GOOD) ROOMS AT THE CONTEMPORARY RESORT
(See **theugseries.com/contemporary-views** *for photos.)* Rooms in the Contemporary Tower overlook Bay Lake on one side and the parking lot, with Seven Seas Lagoon and the Magic Kingdom in the background, on the other. Except for most second- and third-floor rooms in the South Garden Wing, all have balconies. If you stay on the Magic Kingdom side, ask for a room on the ninth floor or higher, where the views of the parking lot are less distracting. On the Bay Lake side, the view is fine from all floors, though higher floors are preferable.

In the South Garden Wing, all ground-floor rooms have patios. Only end rooms on the second and third floors facing Bay Lake have full balconies; all other rooms have balconies that are just a foot deep. Keep in mind that the South Garden Wing is a fair walk from the restaurants, shops, front desk, guest services, and monorail station in the A-frame. This makes them more peaceful but less convenient.

There's a lot of boat traffic in the lake and canal alongside the South Garden Wing. Nearest the lake, and quietest, are rooms **6116–6123**, **6216–6223**, and **6316–6323**. At the water's edge, but noisier, are rooms **6107–6115, 6207–6215,** and **6307–6315**. Flanking the canal connecting Bay Lake and Seven Seas Lagoon are rooms **5128–5151, 5228–5251,** and **5328–5351**. All of these have nice canal and lake views, which subject them to some daytime noise from passing watercraft, but the whole area is exceptionally quiet at night.

Avoid rooms ending with numbers **52–70**; almost all of these look directly onto a parking lot.

BAY LAKE TOWER AT DISNEY'S CONTEMPORARY RESORT

Unofficial Guide **Reader-Survey Results**

Percentage of readers who'd stay here again	97% (*Above Average*)
Percentage of readers who'd recommend this resort to a friend	71% (*Average*)
Overall reader rating	A–

OPENED IN 2009, this 15-story, 295-unit DVC resort consists of studios and one- and two-bedroom villas, as well as two-story, three-bedroom Grand Villas with views of Bay Lake and the Magic Kingdom. Laid out in a semicircle, Bay Lake Tower is connected to the Contemporary by an elevated, covered outdoor walkway and shares the main resort's monorail service and dining options.

Rooms have flat-screen TVs, minifridges, microwaves, and coffee makers. Brightly colored accessories, paintings, and accent walls complement an otherwise-neutral color scheme. Wood tables and granite countertops add a natural touch. Each room has a private balcony or patio. Rooms in this building are among the quietest on Disney property.

Studios sleep up to four people and include one queen-size bed and one double sleeper sofa. The part of the studio with the bed, sofa, and TV measures about 170 square feet and feels small with even two people; four would be a squeeze.

One-bedroom villas sleep five people (the living room's chair and sofa fold out to sleep three) and provide a formal kitchen, a second bathroom, and a living room in addition to the studio bedroom.

The two-bedroom villas sleep nine and include all the kitchen amenities found in a one-bedroom, plus an extra bathroom. One of the baths is attached to a second bedroom with two queen beds or a queen plus a sleeper sofa. As with the one-bedrooms, a sofa bed and sleeper chair in the living room provide extra places to snooze, though they're best suited for small children. Bathrooms in the two-bedroom villas are a bit more spacious than those in the one-bedrooms.

The two-story Grand Villas sleep 12 and include four bathrooms, the same main-bedroom layout, and two bedrooms with two queen beds apiece. An upstairs seating area overlooking the main floor provides a sleeper sofa and chair. Two-story windows offer unparalleled views of Bay Lake or the Magic Kingdom, with prices to match.

Bay Lake Tower has its own check-in desk, as well as its own private pool and pool bar, plus a small fire pit on the beach. Its **Top of the World Lounge** is one of the best bars on Disney property, and it admits only DVC owners and their guests.

This Minnesota family of four loved the views:

> We had a studio with a Magic Kingdom view. The balcony was a private oasis where my husband and I would relax and watch the fireworks together after the kids were asleep. On our second night, he looked at me and said, "We're always going to stay here."

GOOD (AND NOT-SO-GOOD) ROOMS AT BAY LAKE TOWER *(See* theugseries.com/blt-views *for photos.)* If you're paying for a Magic Kingdom view, request a room on an upper level—above the seventh floor, at least—so you're not looking out at the parking lot. Even-numbered rooms **XX06–XX16** have the best viewing angle of the park. Rooms **XX24–XX30** may technically be described as having theme park views, but they're angled toward the Contemporary, and you have to turn the other way to see the park. (*X* indicates the floor number.)

The rooms on the lake side of Bay Lake Tower have views of EPCOT's fireworks and more, as a reader from Washington found out:

> I could watch the fireworks from our balcony (OK, the bed), and that was cool, but really the best part was being able to see Spaceship Earth lit up. Beautiful! More of this, please, Disney.

Shades of Green

(See map on page 128. See theugseries.com/ug-shades *for extended coverage.)*

STRENGTHS	WEAKNESSES
• Large guest rooms	• No theming and nondescript room décor
• Discount tickets and rooms for military personnel with ID	• Limited on-site dining
	• Limited bus service
• Quiet setting	• Daily parking fee ($17)
• Views of golf course from guest rooms	• No free parking at theme parks
• Convenient self-parking	
• Swimming complex, fitness center	

Unofficial Guide Reader-Survey Results

Percentage of readers who'd stay here again	100% (*Above Average*)
Percentage of readers who'd recommend this resort to a friend	87% (*Above Average*)
Overall reader rating	**A−**

ORIGINALLY OWNED BY DISNEY, Shades of Green was called The Golf Resort when it opened in 1973 and was renamed The Disney Inn in 1986. In 1994 Disney reached an agreement with the U.S. Army Family and Morale, Welfare, and Recreation Command (Army MWR) to lease the property as an official Armed Forces Recreation Center. In 1996 the Army MWR purchased the property outright; Disney still owns the land on which the resort is located.

Shades of Green is open to active and retired US service members (including reservists) and their families, among other qualifying groups. Civilians may accompany eligible military personnel as their guests. (For details and a list of the required documentation for each group, see shadesofgreen.org/about-shades-green/eligibility.)

Shades of Green consists of one three-story and one five-story building nestled among three golf courses that are open to Disney guests. At 455 square feet each, the 586 guest rooms here are some of the largest on Disney property.

The resort's website states that Shades of Green is comparable to a Disney Deluxe resort. While the rooms are large and immaculately maintained—not to mention a great value for those who qualify to stay here—it lacks the wow factor found at many Deluxe resorts. The dining options and transportation are adequate. Service, on the other hand, is great—definitely up to the Deluxe standard.

Standard rooms have two queen-size beds, a single sleeper sofa, a minifridge, a table and two chairs, and a TV. Junior suites sleep six with three queen beds, one in the living area. Family suites sleep eight with two queen beds, a queen sleeper sofa, and a king bed; these suites also have two bathrooms. All rooms have a patio or balcony.

A mom from Indiana makes the case for exploring all of your lodging options:

While it's true that Shades of Green is often a good deal, military families should still do some comparison shopping. Room rates are tiered based on rank—the higher your rank, the higher the rate. Definitely check into military rates at Disney properties, and also check out the **Armed Forces Vacation Club** *for condos near WDW [see afvclub.com for participating Orlando-area properties]. We rented a two-bedroom, two-bath condo with a full kitchen and pool for seven nights, and it cost us less than two nights at a Disney hotel.*

Shades of Green has two pools. The **Mill Pond Pool** features a tiered waterslide, while the **Magnolia Pool** has a zero-entry feature as well as a splash-and-play area and hot tubs.

Restaurants include **Mangino's,** an Italian eatery; the **Garden Gallery** buffet; two quick-service options (**Express Café** and **Java Café**); and **Evergreens,** a sports bar and grill. The **Army & Air Force Exchange Service** sells Disney merchandise in addition to snacks, soft drinks, alcohol, tobacco, and over-the-counter medicines.

Shades of Green

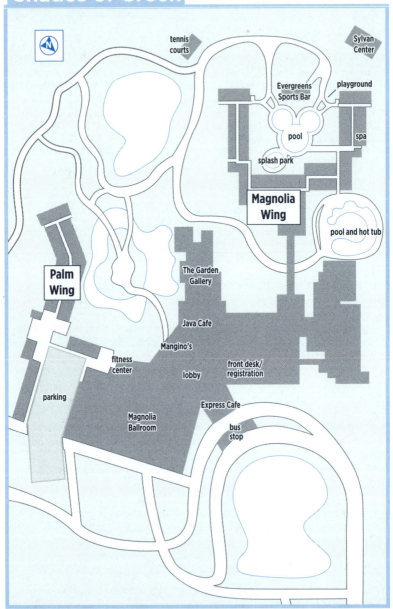

Transportation to all theme parks is by bus; a transfer is required to almost all destinations. Walking time to the bus-loading area from the most remote rooms is about 5 minutes. Readers such as this Ohio woman report that bus service is a sore spot:

Please stress to your readers how awful the transportation system is—there is no direct access to the Magic Kingdom or EPCOT, and the buses that go directly to the other parks run only once an hour. If you want to go back to your room midday, plan for an hour to an hour and a half of travel time there and then back to the park.

Shades of Green used to have a walking path to the Magic Kingdom, but it has closed and is not expected to reopen.

You don't have to worry much about bad room views or locations here. Except for a small number that overlook the entrance road and parking lot, most offer views of the golf courses or the swimming area.

THE EPCOT RESORTS

THE EPCOT RESORTS ARE POSITIONED around Crescent Lake between EPCOT and Disney's Hollywood Studios (closer to EPCOT). Both theme parks are accessible by boat, via Skyliner, and on foot. None of the resorts offer transportation to EPCOT's main entrance, and it's 0.7–1.1 miles to walk there, depending on the hotel and route. The **Skyliner** (see page 344) connects EPCOT's International Gateway with Hollywood Studios. If you're staying at the Beach Club Resort, taking the Skyliner may be faster than walking.

Disney's Yacht & Beach Club Resorts and Beach Club Villas

(See map on page 130. See **theugseries.com/ug-yacht, theugseries.com/ug-beach,** *and* **theugseries.com/bc-villas** *for extended coverage.)*

STRENGTHS	WEAKNESSES
• Stormalong Bay, the best-rated pool complex of any Walt Disney World resort	• Views and balcony size are hit-or-miss
• Walking distance to EPCOT's International Gateway	• Bus service to Magic Kingdom, Animal Kingdom, water parks, and Disney Springs may be shared with other EPCOT resorts
• Boat and Skyliner transportation to DHS	• No three-bedroom Grand Villas
• Close to BoardWalk and EPCOT dining	• Villas have fewer baths per bedroom than newer DVC properties and no lake views
• Well-themed public spaces	
• Bright and attractive guest rooms	

Unofficial Guide Reader-Survey Results *(resorts only; see page 132 for villa ratings)*

Percentage of readers who'd stay here again **Yacht: 96%** (*Above Average*); **Beach: 89%** (*Below Average*)
Percentage of readers who'd recommend to a friend **Yacht: 78%** (*Above Average*); **Beach: 64%** (*Average*)
Overall reader rating **Yacht: A–; Beach: B+**

THESE ADJOINING DELUXE RESORTS are very similar, so we've grouped them together. Both have clapboard facades with whitewashed wood trim. The Yacht Club is painted a subdued gray, while the Beach Club is a brighter blue. The Yacht Club has a nautical theme with model ships and antique navigational instruments in public areas. The Beach Club has plenty of beach scenes in seafoam green and white. Both have themed lobbies, with a giant globe in the Yacht Club's and sea horse fixtures in the Beach Club's. The resorts face the 25-acre Crescent Lake and share an elaborate swimming complex, **Stormalong Bay.**

There are 635 rooms and 21 suites at the Yacht Club and 576 rooms at the Beach Club, plus 282 studio and one- and two-bedroom

Yacht & Beach Club Resorts and Beach Club Villas

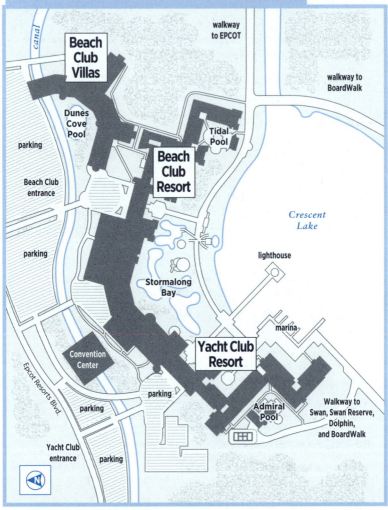

DVC units at the Beach Club Villas. Most rooms are 381 square feet and have two queen-size beds, a sofa, a desk and chair, a dresser, a wall-mounted TV, a minifridge, and a coffee maker. The Yacht Club's rooms are decorated in white, with blue and brass accents and vinyl plank flooring, while the Beach Club's feature summery tans and blues, with vinyl plank flooring. Some rooms have full balconies, and many rooms have mini balconies.

A reader from California appreciates the Yacht Club's rooms:

The rooms at Yacht Club are lovely. The [hard] floors are not noisy at all—if we had neighbors above us, we never heard them. Soundproofing on the balcony is good.

Both resorts provide excellent service. Nine restaurants and lounges are within easy walking distance, and Beach Club has an expanded grab-and-go area for quick snacks.

Transportation from these resorts to other destinations is by bus, boat, or Skyliner. Walking time to the transportation loading areas from the most remote rooms is 7 minutes.

Although the Yacht & Beach Club are situated along Crescent Lake, opposite Disney's BoardWalk, only a relatively small percentage of rooms directly overlook the lake—many additional rooms have lake views from the side but actually face a courtyard or garden. To complicate matters, the resorts don't differentiate between a room with a lake view and one overlooking a swimming pool, pond, or canal. There's only one category for anything wet: water view. To see specific views from these rooms, go to theugseries.com/yacht-views or theugseries.com/beach-views.

The Beach Club consists of a long main building with several wings protruding toward Crescent Lake. The main building and the various wings range from three to five stories. Most rooms have full or mini balconies or, on the ground floor, patios. Full balconies are big enough for a couple of chairs, while mini balconies are about 6 inches deep. Top-floor rooms often have enclosed balconies set into the roof. Unless you're standing, visibility is somewhat limited from these dormer balconies.

We receive a lot of comments about the Yacht & Beach Club Resorts. First, from a Massachusetts mom:

This was the first time we stayed at the Beach Club, and for us, the amazing pool complex was worth the extra money. Several nights, we climbed to the top of the waterslide as the sun was setting, and it was an incredible sight—truly a memorable experience!

Another family had a chillier experience, however:

Families with kids should not stay at the Beach Club during the winter. Based on an experience at the Polynesian Village in December, we anticipated that Stormalong Bay would be warm enough to swim in. It was not. This was a terrible disappointment to our kids. The resort's location is divine (I loved walking to France for breakfast), but the pool situation made me bitter about the cost of this place.

GOOD (AND NOT-SO-GOOD) ROOMS AT THE BEACH CLUB RESORT *(See* theugseries.com/beach-views *for photos.)* The Beach Club's best views are from rooms that have full balconies and from those that overlook the lake. The woods-facing rooms are the resort's most peaceful accommodations. They are the nearest to EPCOT's International Gateway entrance if you're walking but the farthest from the resort's main pool area, lobby, and restaurants.

Of the remaining rooms, most face courtyards, with some providing indirect views of the lake and others overlooking parking lots and the resort's front entrance.

Heads-up: The Beach Club will charge you for a water view if there's so much as a birdbath in sight. If you're going to spend the money, get a *real* water view.

- **Water-view rooms with full balconies facing the lake:** Odd-numbered rooms **2641–2645;** suite **2647;** rooms **3501–3507;** odd-numbered rooms **4607–4623,** and odd-numbered Club Level rooms **5699–5725**
- **Standard-view rooms with full balconies facing the woods and EPCOT:** Even-numbered rooms **2528–2530, 2578–2596, 3512–3530,** and **4532–4596**

GOOD (AND NOT-SO-GOOD) ROOMS AT THE YACHT CLUB RESORT *(See* theugseries.com/yacht-views *for photos.)* All Yacht Club rooms offer full balconies or, on the ground floor, patios. Rooms with the best views are as follows (the higher the last three digits in the room number, the closer to the lobby, main pool area, and restaurants):

- **Rooms with full balconies facing the lake, with the BoardWalk Inn in the background:** Odd-numbered rooms **2001–2009, 2043–2065, 2123–2137, 2157–2163; 3001–3009, 3043–3065, 3123–3137, 3157–3163; 4057–4065, 4123–4137, 4157–4163;** or Club Level rooms **5161, 5163,** or **5241**
- **Fifth-floor rooms directly facing EPCOT: 5195–5199** or **5153**
- **Standard-view fourth-floor rooms facing EPCOT: 4195–4199** or **4153**

BEACH CLUB VILLAS

Unofficial Guide **Reader-Survey Results**

Percentage of readers who'd stay here again	**94%** (*Average*)
Percentage of readers who'd recommend this resort to a friend	**73%** (*Above Average*)
Overall reader rating	**B**

THIS DISNEY VACATION CLUB PROPERTY is supposedly inspired by grand Atlantic seaside homes of the early 20th century. But really, there's little to differentiate the Beach Club Villas from the Yacht & Beach Club Resorts, or from the parts of the BoardWalk Inn & Villas that aren't on the BoardWalk.

Configured roughly in the shape of a fat slingshot, the Beach Club Villas are set back away from the lake. Arrayed in connected four- and five-story taffy-blue sections topped with cupolas, the villas are adorned with white woodwork and slat-railed balconies. The effect is clean and breezy but not much else.

Studios have a kitchenette, a queen bed, a single pull-down bed, and a Murphy bed, and one- and two-bedroom villas have full kitchens. The rooms are a bit small but attractively decorated in blues and corals after a refurbishment completed in late 2023.

The Beach Club Villas have their own modest swimming pool but otherwise share the restaurants, facilities, and transportation options of the adjoining Yacht & Beach Club Resorts. The villas' biggest weakness is that they offer no lake views.

GOOD (AND NOT-SO-GOOD) ROOMS AT THE BEACH CLUB VILLAS *(See* theugseries.com/bc-villas-views *for photos.)* Although the studios and villas are attractive and livable, the location of the Beach Club Villas—between parking lots, roads, and canals—leaves much to be desired. Only southeast-facing rooms provide both a scenic landscape (woods) and relative relief from traffic noise. The noise probably won't bother you if you're indoors with the balcony door closed, but for the money you pay to stay at the villas, you can easily find nicer, quieter accommodations elsewhere on Disney property. If you choose to stay at the Beach Club Villas, go for odd-numbered rooms **225–251, 325–351, 425–451,** and **525–551.**

Disney's BoardWalk Inn & Villas

(See map on page 134. See **theugseries.com/bw-inn** and **theugseries.com/bw-villas** for extended coverage.)

STRENGTHS	WEAKNESSES
• Walking distance to EPCOT's International Gateway and Disney's Hollywood Studios	• Long, confusing hallways
	• Limited quick-service dining options suitable for kids
• Unique garden suites	• Not as many rooms overlook the BoardWalk as you might think
• Great dining options for adults	
• Large fitness center	• Bus service to Magic Kingdom, Animal Kingdom, water parks, and Disney Springs may be shared with other EPCOT resorts
• Recently refurbished rooms	
	• BoardWalk Villas have fewer baths per bedroom than newer DVC properties

Unofficial Guide **Reader-Survey Results** *(inn only; see page 135 for villa ratings)*

Percentage of readers who'd stay here again	**95%** *(Above Average)*
Percentage of readers who'd recommend this resort to a friend	**77%** *(Above Average)*
Overall reader rating	**A**

ON CRESCENT LAKE ACROSS from the Yacht & Beach Club Resorts, the BoardWalk Inn is another Disney Deluxe resort. The complex is a detailed replica of an early-20th-century East Coast beach boardwalk. Facades of hotels, diners, and shops create an inviting and exciting waterfront skyline. In reality, the BoardWalk Inn & Villas comprise a single integrated structure behind the facades. Restaurants and shops occupy the boardwalk level, while accommodations rise to six stories above. The inn and villas share a pool featuring an old-fashioned amusement park theme; there are also two quiet pools for adults.

The inn's 378 Deluxe rooms measure 371 square feet each. Most have two queen beds, a sofa, a minifridge, a coffee maker, and a ceiling fan. The décor, updated in 2023 and 2024, includes yellow wallpaper, vinyl plank flooring, and neutral curtains. Closet space exceeds that of rooms in other Deluxe resorts. Most rooms have balconies. This room refurbishment seems to have made a huge impact at BoardWalk Inn, which went from below average in most rankings in the prior edition to above average in most categories this year.

The complex is within walking distance of EPCOT and is connected to other destinations by bus and boat. Walking time to transportation loading areas from the most remote rooms is 5–6 minutes. It's about a 5-minute walk to the Skyliner's International Gateway station at EPCOT, if you'd rather use that to get to Disney's Hollywood Studios. We'll also provide a warning that, even though we consider ourselves experts at navigating the WDW parks and resort, we frequently get lost or turned around in the labyrinthine hallways in the BoardWalk Inn and Villas. It's worse on the villas side, but be sure to get a cast member to help you navigate when you check in.

An Iowa family was surprised by the low number of rooms on the actual BoardWalk:

> *We were surprised that so relatively few rooms at the BoardWalk Inn have interesting views. The one couple in our group who actually had a view of the BoardWalk said it was noisy.*

BoardWalk Inn & Villas

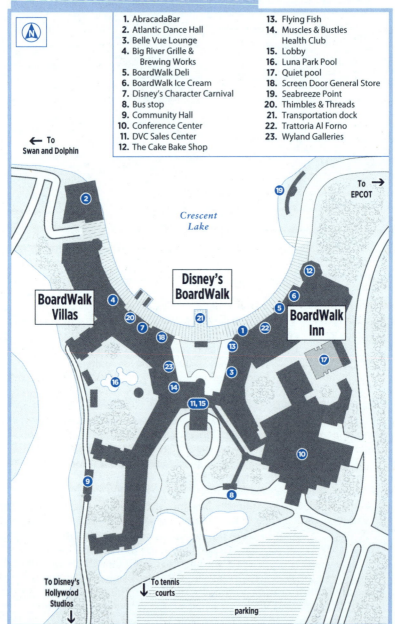

1. AbracadaBar
2. Atlantic Dance Hall
3. Belle Vue Lounge
4. Big River Grille & Brewing Works
5. BoardWalk Deli
6. BoardWalk Ice Cream
7. Disney's Character Carnival
8. Bus stop
9. Community Hall
10. Conference Center
11. DVC Sales Center
12. The Cake Bake Shop
13. Flying Fish
14. Muscles & Bustles Health Club
15. Lobby
16. Luna Park Pool
17. Quiet pool
18. Screen Door General Store
19. Seabreeze Point
20. Thimbles & Threads
21. Transportation dock
22. Trattoria Al Forno
23. Wyland Galleries

GOOD (AND NOT-SO-GOOD) ROOMS AT THE BOARDWALK INN *(See theugseries.com/bw-inn-views for photos.)* At BoardWalk Inn, views of the canal or pool are considered resort view. But if you book a BoardWalk Villa, the same canal and pool are called standard, garden, or pool view, and the view of the BoardWalk is called BoardWalk view.

Most rooms have a balcony or patio, although balconies on the standard upper-floor rooms alternate between large and medium in size. The BoardWalk Inn and its villas each share about half the frontage on the promenade, which overlooks Crescent Lake. The promenade's clubs, stores, and attractions are spread about equally between the two sections, leading to similar levels of noise and commotion. However, the inn side is closer to EPCOT and the nearby access road; this means easier access to that theme park but also more road noise. Otherwise, the inn is actually less noisy than the more expensive villas; there's one tranquil, enclosed courtyard and another half-enclosed area with a quiet pool (where BoardWalk's Garden Suites are located).

There are many rooms to avoid at the inn, starting with rooms overlooking the access roads and parking lots, and rooms looking down onto the roof of the resort's adjacent conference center. And although the aforementioned quiet rooms face courtyards, the views are pretty ho-hum. When you get right down to it, the only rooms with decent views are those fronting the promenade and lake, specifically odd-numbered rooms **3213–3259** and **4213–4259**. We've been told by Disney insiders that most of these rooms are reserved more than 10 months ahead.

BOARDWALK VILLAS

Unofficial Guide Reader-Survey Results

Percentage of readers who'd stay here again	96% (*Above Average*)
Percentage of readers who'd recommend this resort to a friend	76% (*Above Average*)
Overall reader rating	A–

THE 532 BOARDWALK VILLAS are decorated in white, tan, and blue (popular colors along Crescent Lake), with white tile in the kitchens and baths. Villas measure 412–2,491 square feet (studio through three-bedroom) and sleep 4–12. Many villas have full kitchens, laundry rooms, and whirlpool tubs; most rooms have balconies.

All the villas were refurbished in 2023–2024, resulting in increased scores across all room-related survey questions. Studios now feature a queen bed, a Murphy bed, and a pull-down single bed under the TV. Instead of a full table and chairs, there is a coffee table with pull-up top and some ottomans. This helps the room feel more spacious but does remove some mealtime functionality.

GOOD (AND NOT-SO-GOOD) ROOMS AT THE BOARDWALK VILLAS *(See theugseries.com/bw-villas-views for photos.)* Like the inn, the villas offer only a handful of rooms with good views. Odd-numbered rooms **3001–3047, 4001–4047,** and **5001–5047** afford dynamic views of the promenade and Crescent Lake, with EPCOT in the background. Rooms **X05, X07, X13, X15, X29,** and **X31** are studios (*X* indicates the floor number). They're a little noisy if you open your balcony door but otherwise offer a glimpse of one of Walt Disney World's more happening places.

Promenade-facing villa rooms have the same noise issues as their inn counterparts. The midsection of the canal-facing villas looks out onto the **Luna Park Pool,** which gets extremely noisy during the day. Some quieter villas located away from the promenade have views of the canal and a partially enclosed quiet pool. Rooms on the opposite side of this wing are almost as quiet, but they face the parking lot.

Walt Disney World Swan, Dolphin, and Swan Reserve

(See map on page 138. See **theugseries.com/swan, theugseries.com/dolphin,** *and* **theugseries.com/swan-reserve** *for extended coverage.)*

QUICK TAKE: *A respectable percentage of readers said they would stay here again. All things considered, however, these resorts rate below average among the Disney resorts. But if you're part of Marriott's loyalty program or you find a good price, they can be a great option thanks to their location and on-site perks.*

STRENGTHS	WEAKNESSES
• Best-priced location on Crescent Lake	• Presence of conventioneers may be off-putting to vacationing families
• The hotels participate in Marriott's loyalty program	• Daily resort fee ($50/night, plus tax) and parking fee ($35/night)
• Good on-site and nearby dining	• No Disney Dining Plan
• Only hotels within walking distance of minigolf (Fantasia Gardens)	• Non-Disney bus service runs less often than that of other resorts (and drops off at the TTC for Magic Kingdom)
• Large variety of upscale restaurants	
• On-site car rental (Alamo, National)	• Architecture that was on the cutting edge decades ago now looks dated and cheesy (Swan, Dolphin)
• Very nice pool complex	
• Walking distance to EPCOT's International Gateway and Disney's Hollywood Studios	• Self-parking is distant from the hotels' entrances
	• Spotty front-desk staffing (Swan/Dolphin)

Unofficial Guide **Reader-Survey Results**

Percentage of readers who'd stay here again **Swan: 90%** (*Average*); **Dolphin: 91%** (*Average*); **Swan Reserve: 88%** (*Below Average*)
Percentage of readers who'd recommend this resort to a friend **Swan: 60%** (*Below Average*); **Dolphin: 54%** (*Below Average*); **Swan Reserve: 72%** (*Average*)
Overall reader rating **Swan: A-; Dolphin: B; Swan Reserve: A-**

OPENED IN 1990, THE SWAN AND DOLPHIN face each other on either side of an inlet of Crescent Lake. The Swan Reserve is located across the street. Although they're inside Walt Disney World and Disney handles their reservations, they are independently managed and can also be booked directly at swandolphin.com or marriott.com. Because these hotels aren't run by Disney, service—especially wait time at the front desk—is less relentlessly "magical" than at other resorts.

All three resorts are served by bus transportation to the theme parks and participate in Early Entry and Extended Evening Theme Park Hours, but they don't participate in the Disney Dining Plan.

The Dolphin's main building is a 27-story turquoise triangle. This central building, with large wings extending from both sides and four smaller arms from its rear, is attached to a large conference center. Perched on the roof, at the edge of each main wing, are two 56-foot-tall dolphins with their tails in the air. The Swan's gently arching main building rises 12 stories and is flanked by two 7-story towers, with two 47-foot-tall swans adorning its roof.

In late 2024, the resorts announced a major refurbishment, including a refresh of all guest rooms. This work is expected to continue into 2026, but if you get a refreshed room, you may find improved cleanliness and functionality.

The Dolphin's rooms incorporate neutral walls, light wood, blue-gray carpeting, and taupe draperies. Oversize upholstered headboards frame the plush Westin Heavenly Beds, and minimal art adorns the walls. A dresser and a desk with a chair round out the furnishings. Note that the Dolphin's beds are either doubles or kings (no queens). All rooms at the Dolphin have coffee makers, and some have balconies. The baths in most rooms have step-in showers.

The Swan's standard rooms are remarkably similar to the Dolphin's. In fact, if you look up pictures of both, you might not even be able to tell the difference. But the Swan does have one thing in its favor: queen- or king-size Heavenly Beds, which make for ultracomfy sleeping. A flat-screen TV sits on the dresser. The bathrooms—small for Disney—have step-in showers and limited counter space.

Be warned: Both resorts will nickel-and-dime you with fees. Each tacks on a $50-per-day resort fee and another $35 per day for self-parking. Whatever rate you're quoted at either resort, count on another $100 per day in miscellaneous fees.

The two hotels collectively house more than a dozen restaurants and lounges and are within easy walking distance of EPCOT and the BoardWalk. They're also connected to other destinations by bus and boat. Walking time from the most remote rooms to the transportation loading areas is 7–9 minutes.

The Swan and Dolphin don't use Disney bus transportation between their hotels and Disney's theme parks and water parks. Buses going to the Magic Kingdom will drop you off at the Transportation and Ticket Center, where you'll have to take a boat, monorail, or bus to get to the Magic Kingdom (Disney buses will drop you off right at the park entrance). We recommend walking to the nearest Disney bus stop (at the BoardWalk or the Yacht or Beach Club Resort) instead of relying on Swan/Dolphin buses.

These readers from Texas say that of the two, the Swan is slightly easier to navigate:

> *While the Dolphin is closer to EPCOT, we prefer the Swan because it's easier and more straightforward to walk from the hotel to the park and vice versa. The Dolphin has a very narrow, winding sidewalk that doesn't look like it gets much traffic.*

This New Hampshire couple gives the pool area high marks:

> *Neither the Disney nor the Swan and Dolphin website depicts how great the pool complex is. Not only are there multiple pools, a waterslide, and maybe the best poolside bar in all of Disney World, there's also a wonderfully green, restful grotto-in-tropical-forest theme.*

SWAN RESERVE This 14-story hotel opened in 2021 and is adjacent to Disney's Fantasia Gardens and Fairways minigolf course. It has 349 guest rooms and suites, some with views of either EPCOT or

Swan, Swan Reserve & Dolphin

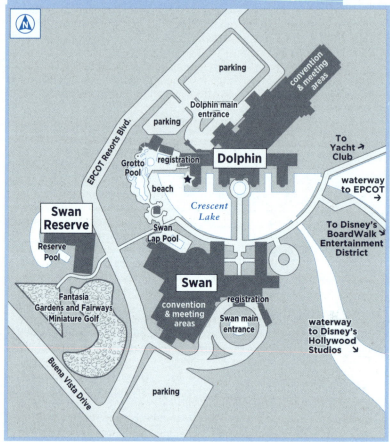

Hollywood Studios. Standard rooms sleep four and are around 330 square feet, roughly the same as a Disney Moderate.

Our stays at the Swan Reserve have been excellent. The newer rooms mean that beds are comfortable and the bathrooms functional. It's even possible to see theme park fireworks from some rooms. And in Becky's experience as a Marriott Bonvoy Elite member, it's been easier to get free room upgrades here than at the Swan or Dolphin.

As a smaller resort, the Swan Reserve has just one full-service restaurant, **Amare**. That can be a problem on busy nights, since Amare handles not only its own orders but also those from the bar, the pool, and room service. Still, it gets stellar reviews from readers.

The Swan Reserve has a stylish pool and a fitness center. Bus service is provided to Disney's theme parks, water parks, and Disney Springs, and the Swan and Dolphin are a short walk across the street. Even though it's a slightly longer walk to the parks or the bigger pool complex, we love the newer rooms and smaller size of the Swan Reserve compared to the Swan or Dolphin.

GOOD (AND NOT-SO-GOOD) ROOMS AT THE SWAN AND DOLPHIN

Note: The Swan and Dolphin are configured very differently, and because of their irregular shapes, it's easier to discuss groups of rooms in relation to exterior landmarks and compass directions rather than by room numbers. When speaking with a reservationist, use the following tips and descriptions.

SWAN **East-facing rooms** offer prime views, particularly in the upper half of the seven-story wing above **Il Mulino** restaurant. From this vantage point, you overlook a canal and Disney's BoardWalk, with EPCOT in the distance. Balcony rooms on floors five, six, and seven cost an additional $50 or more per night. The best rooms with views of EPCOT are **626** and **726**.

The worst views are from the **west-facing rooms** above the fourth floor, but rooms **680–691** offer nice pool views.

Above the Swan's main entrance, **south-facing rooms** overlook the parking lot, with forest and Hollywood Studios in the distance. However, the canal is also visible to the east. Note that these rooms do not have balconies.

DOLPHIN If you want a view of something besides a parking lot, your choices are relatively few. Rooms with pleasant views are in the four arms on the rear of the building. Rooms on all arms have balconies on floors one through four, and alternating balconies or windows on floors five through nine.

One of the Dolphin's best views overlooks the **Grotto Pool**, on the far west side of the building. An artificial beach with a small waterfall is visible from rooms at the very end of the large west wing. None of these rooms have a balcony.

The **Crescent Lake** side of the arm closest to the lake offers the best views. You have an unobstructed view of the lake and the EPCOT fireworks; a fine BoardWalk view for people-watching; and, from higher floors, a view of the beach at Beach Club Resort. There's ferry noise, but these rooms still have the most going for them. The best of the best here are rooms **8015, 7015, 5015, 4015,** and **3015.**

SWAN RESERVE Almost all the rooms here can have great views, as long as you stay on a high enough floor. Aim for floor nine or higher, where you'll typically get views of EPCOT or Hollywood Studios.

Disney's Caribbean Beach Resort

(See map on page 141. See theugseries.com/caribbean *for extended coverage.)*

STRENGTHS	WEAKNESSES
• Colorful Caribbean theme	• Check-in is far from most of the resort
• Lakefront setting	• Dining gets low marks from readers
• Large food court	• Multiple bus stops make it slow to go to Disney Springs, Animal Kingdom, and Magic Kingdom
• Skyliner access	
• Some buildings are within walking distance of the excellent dining options at the Riviera	• Some "villages" are a good distance from restaurants and shops
	• No elevators
• Child-size Murphy beds in select rooms increase capacity to five people	

Unofficial Guide Reader-Survey Results

Percentage of readers who'd stay here again	91% (*Average*)
Percentage of readers who'd recommend this resort to a friend	54% (*Below Average*)
Overall reader rating	B

OPENED IN 1998, CARIBBEAN BEACH WAS DISNEY'S first Moderate resort. It features two dozen colorful, two-story motel-style buildings, organized into five sections named after Caribbean islands: **Aruba, Barbados, Jamaica, Martinique,** and **Trinidad.**

Most of the 1,536 guest rooms measure 314 square feet and have two queen beds. Rooms are decorated in neutral beach tones with bright tropical accents, along with dark wood and rattan furnishings. The vanity area is separated from the main room by a sliding door, and the toilet and shower are behind another sliding door, allowing up to three people to get ready at once. Amenities include a dresser, a small table with chairs, a minifridge, a coffee maker, a TV, and plenty of storage. The front doors of each room open onto exterior hallways, so there are no private balconies here.

Rooms in Trinidad used to be pirate themed, but they've been recently refurbished with a very light under-the-sea theme, with lighter colors and an updated layout. The theme impacts some artwork but not much else. Each room has one fixed bed, a sofa that converts into a Murphy bed, and another single-size Murphy bed, creating more space in these rooms than any other area of Caribbean Beach. Bathrooms, lighting, and storage have also been improved, making these some of the best rooms in the resort from a functionality perspective (if not from a location perspective). If you're staying at Caribbean Beach and don't mind being slightly removed from the rest of the resort and its amenities, request an updated Trinidad room for a more modern feel.

The **Old Port Royale** serves as the resort's main hub, where you'll find check-in, dining, and shopping. Dining options include a food court with counter-service and grab-and-go meals, as well as **Sebastian's Bistro,** a waterfront sit-down restaurant. On-site dining here receives mixed reviews from readers, and many guests prefer walking to the highly rated restaurants at the neighboring **Riviera Resort** instead.

Caribbean Beach offers bus transportation to all Disney World destinations and **Skyliner** access to EPCOT and Disney's Hollywood Studios. The resort has two Skyliner stations: one south of Jamaica and another north of Aruba at Riviera Resort, providing quick and convenient transportation to the parks.

Walking time to the transportation-loading area from Caribbean Beach's most remote rooms is 7–9 minutes, and readers rate Disney bus service here as below average. Seriously consider bringing a car—this couple from Missouri wishes they had:

> *Caribbean Beach's bus service is horrendous. It often felt like there was only one bus running at a time, and we experienced several 30-plus-minute waits. The bus circled the entire resort—which is huge—before it headed out, so if you were unlucky enough to be at one of the last stops during a rush to the parks, the bus would pass right by if it was full. On multiple occasions, we arrived at the bus*

Caribbean Beach Resort & Riviera Resort

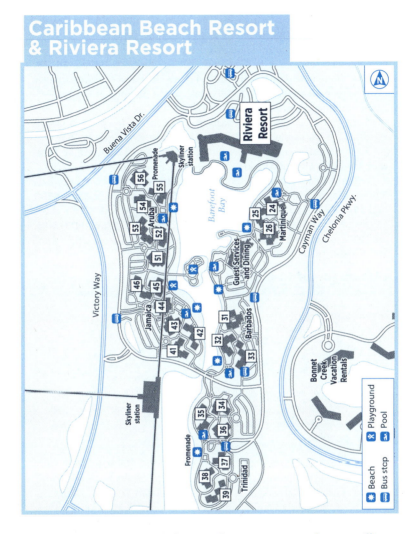

stop an hour or more before our dining reservations, but we still found ourselves running past the park gates to make it to the restaurant on time!

GOOD (AND NOT-SO-GOOD) ROOMS AT CARIBBEAN BEACH RESORT (See theugseries.com/caribbean-views *for photos.*) The five "islands," or groups of buildings clustered around Barefoot Bay, are nearly all identical. The two-story motel-style structures are arranged in various ways to face courtyards, pools, the bay, and so forth. The landscaping features lots of ferns and palm trees, especially in the courtyards.

In general, corner rooms are preferable because they have more windows. Beyond that, your choice depends on how close you want to be to Old Port Royale's check-in desk and restaurants, the Skyliner, pools, parking lots, or beaches on Barefoot Bay. Each island has direct access to at least one beach, playground, bus stop, and parking lot.

Martinique, next to the main pool and playground at Old Port Royale, is also close to the Riviera and its superior dining options.

Aruba and Jamaica are similar to Martinique, but guests must cross a footbridge from here to Old Port Royale. **Aruba buildings 54, 55,** and **56,** along with Jamaica building 41, are closest to the two Skyliner stations. **Jamaica building 43,** also close to the Skyliner, is the highest-rated building at Caribbean Beach.

With just three buildings, **Barbados** gets noise from surrounding roads and from rambunctious kids at Old Port Royale next door.

The quietest island, and the farthest from resort facilities, is **Trinidad.** It has its own playground and the newest rooms.

When it comes to views, you'll probably want a view of the bay. Rooms that have a bay view are **4246-4252** in **Jamaica** or **5256-5260** and **5541-5548** (but not **5542** or **5545**) in **Aruba.** If you don't mind the sun in your eyes during early evening, rooms **2254-2256, 2413-2416,** and **2445-2448** in Martinique are good bets, as are lake-facing rooms **3533-3534, 3853-3858,** and **3949** in Trinidad.

Disney's Riviera Resort

(See map on page 141. See **theugseries.com/riviera** *for extended coverage.)*

STRENGTHS	WEAKNESSES
• Stylish, well-appointed rooms	• Expensive
• Skyliner access	• Limited theming
• On-site dining and bar	• Tower studios are small and dark
• Children's play area near main pool	

Unofficial Guide Reader-Survey Results

Percentage of readers who'd stay here again	**96%** *(Above Average)*
Percentage of readers who'd recommend this resort to a friend	**89%** *(Above Average)*
Overall reader rating	**A**

ONE OF WALT DISNEY WORLD'S TOP-RATED RESORTS, Riviera Resort is inspired by the elegance of a beach retreat in the South of France. Though it sits directly next to Caribbean Beach, a Moderate resort, it is designed to feel as upscale as the Grand Floridian, with service, amenities, and prices to match. The nine-story tower houses 300 rooms, including studios and one-, two-, and three-bedroom villas.

The Riviera also offers a somewhat unique **tower studio,** which accommodates only two guests. (Disney has since implemented the same concept at the Polynesian's new Island Tower.) At just 225 square feet, these are the smallest rooms at Disney. They offer only a Murphy bed, and they feel cramped, dim, and very overpriced. Honestly, the bathroom is the most well lit and cheerful space in the room. For what you would pay here, there are far better options elsewhere.

Other rooms at the Riviera are some of the best designed at Disney, featuring a bright, modern aesthetic with white walls, neutral-toned furniture, and herringbone-patterned plank flooring. Deluxe studios have kitchenettes, while larger villas have full kitchens. The result is a comfortable, airy space, though the theming leans more toward generic luxury hotel than immersive Disney resort.

The Riviera's proximity to EPCOT and Disney's Hollywood Studios gives park-facing rooms on higher floors great views of nighttime entertainment, but Disney charges a premium for these views: Depending on date and view, rates run $443–$814 per night for the undesirable tower studios; $665–$1,250 for deluxe studios; $934–$1,800 for one-bedroom villas; $1,477–$2,800 for two-bedroom units; and $2,956–$5,165 for three-bedroom villas.

Dining is a highlight, with a mix of high-quality options. **Primo Piatto** is an excellent counter-service eatery with grab-and-go options, and **Le Petit Café** serves coffee and pastries in the morning and wine in the evening. **Bar Riva** is an upscale pool bar and so much more. It has a big menu of dishes not found elsewhere on-property. We love it so much that during a Hollywood Studios park day, we'll take the Skyliner over to eat lunch there rather than staying in the park. And finally, **Topolino's Terrace,** the table-service restaurant, is a Disney Signature venue that serves fixed-price character breakfasts for kids (this is one of our family's favorites) and upscale dinners for grown-ups.

Other amenities include two pools and a fitness center. The main **Riviera Pool** offers play areas for children, while the **Beau Soleil Pool** is the quiet pool. Riviera Resort is connected to EPCOT and Hollywood Studios by **Skyliner** and to the rest of the World by bus.

GOOD (AND NOT-SO-GOOD) ROOMS AT RIVIERA RESORT Oddly, standard-view rooms face EPCOT, and preferred-view rooms look out across Barefoot Bay toward Caribbean Beach. If you book a preferred room, ask for one in the west wing, facing south. You should have a direct view of the quiet pool, the bay, and the Skyliner. If you book a standard view, higher floors offer better views. Rooms ending in **odd numbers between 25 and 35** have the most direct views of EPCOT, and rooms ending in **odd numbers between 07 and 17** offer views of Hollywood Studios and EPCOT.

THE BONNET CREEK RESORTS

Not to be confused with the Disney resorts that follow, the **Bonnet Creek Resort** *is a 70-acre hotel, golf, and convention complex located along Bonnet Creek. Although it's adjacent to and accessible from Walt Disney World, that resort is not owned by Disney.*

Disney's Saratoga Springs Resort & Spa and Treehouse Villas at Disney's Saratoga Springs Resort & Spa

(See maps on pages 144 and 145. See theugseries.com/saratoga and theugseries.com/treehouse for extended coverage.)

DISNEY'S SARATOGA SPRINGS RESORT & SPA

STRENGTHS	
• Often available at discounted rates	• Only WDW-owned resort with dedicated golf course
• Multiple well-themed quiet pools	**WEAKNESSES**
• Closest resort to Disney Springs	• On-site dining is limited
• Boat service to Disney Springs	• Theme feels dull or dated
• Convenient parking for nearly all buildings	• Fewer baths per bedroom than newer DVC properties
• Excellent fitness center	

Saratoga Springs Resort & Spa

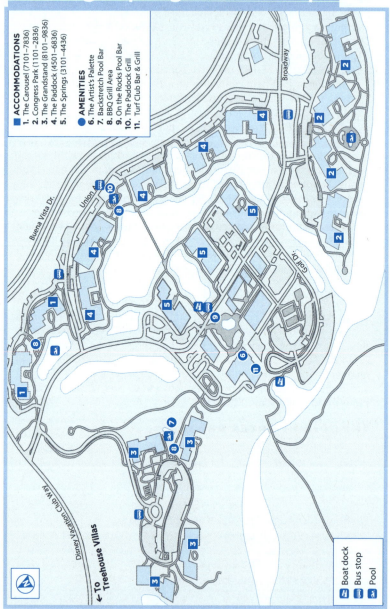

ACCOMMODATIONS
1. The Carousel (7101–7836)
2. Congress Park (1101–2836)
3. The Grandstand (8101–9836)
4. The Paddock (4501–6836)
5. The Springs (3101–4436)

AMENITIES
6. The Artist's Palette
7. Backstretch Pool Bar
8. BBQ Grill Area
9. On the Rocks Pool Bar
10. The Paddock Grill
11. Turf Club Bar & Grill

Boat dock
Bus stop
Pool

Unofficial Guide Reader-Survey Results (resort & spa only)

Percentage of readers who who'd stay here again	91%	(Average)
Percentage of readers who'd recommend this resort to a friend	54%	(Below Average)
Overall reader rating	B+	

WDW RESORT PROFILES: BONNET CREEK   145

Treehouse Villas at Saratoga Springs Resort & Spa

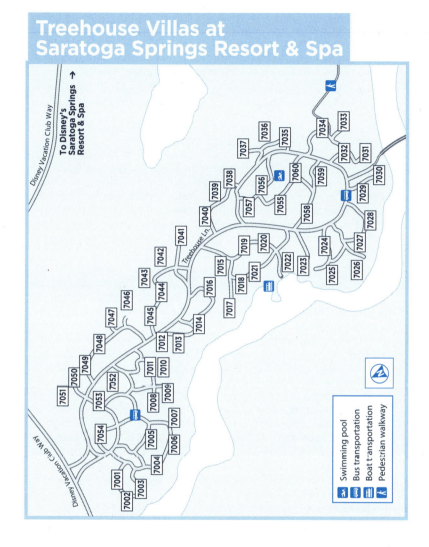

A DISNEY VACATION CLUB (DVC) RESORT, Saratoga Springs is themed as a Victorian-era retreat in upstate New York. Located across the lake from Disney Springs, it features 1,260 studio and villa accommodations. An adjacent 60-unit DVC complex, **Treehouse Villas at Disney's Saratoga Springs Resort & Spa,** opened in 2009.

The rooms lean toward a neutral, modern design, with faux-teak vinyl flooring in the living areas, dark-brown patterned carpets in the bedrooms, white kitchen cabinets, and stainless steel appliances. Furniture is sleek and minimalistic, but overall the resort lacks distinct theming. It could easily be mistaken for almost any upscale hotel. Single Murphy beds (most appropriate for children) are available under the wall-mounted TVs in the living rooms. Bathrooms are spacious in most villas but feel tighter in studios.

Saratoga Springs offers multiple ways to access Disney Springs: buses, boat service, and even a walking path.

The resort gets a lot of critical reviews from guests citing underwhelming theming, limited on-site dining, and difficult transportation. A couple from Indiana had a variety of complaints:

> *Saratoga Springs is our least favorite resort. We didn't enjoy the theming, and unless you have a car, getting around by bus is a real hassle. The food court is very small and the food expensive. Also, checkout was very slow, and our room seemed smaller than comparable rooms at BoardWalk Villas and Old Key West.*

On the positive side, guests also highlight the quiet atmosphere, proximity to Disney Springs, and top-tier fitness center. The fitness center is by far the best at Disney World. Unfortunately, the highly rated **Senses Spa** remains closed, though its counterpart at the Grand Floridian has reopened. Saratoga Springs is also the only Disney resort with direct access to a golf course (which surrounds the resort on three sides), making it an appealing choice for golfers.

GOOD (AND NOT-SO-GOOD) ROOMS AT SARATOGA SPRINGS RESORT & SPA *(See* theugseries.com/ss-views *for photos.)* This resort's sprawling size puts some of its best rooms far from the main lobby, restaurants, and shops. If you don't have a car, the best rooms are those in **The Springs,** numbered **3101–3436** and **3501–3836.** Ask for a room toward the northeast side of these buildings (away from the lobby), as the southwest rooms border a busy road. Avoid rooms **4101–4436**—a pedestrian walkway running behind the patios gets a lot of use in the early morning by guests who are heading to breakfast.

If you have a car or don't mind a longer walk to the lobby, rooms **1101–1436** and **2501–2836** in **Congress Park** offer quietness, a view of Disney Springs, and a relatively short walk to the bus stop. Also good are rooms **4501–4826, 6101–6436,** and **6501–6836** in **The Paddock.** Most of these rooms offer the shortest walks to Disney Springs. In The Paddock, avoid rooms on the northeast side of its **5101–5435** building and those on the northwest side of its **5501–5836** building—these border a swimming pool and bus stop.

If you're not concerned with the amenities of a specific room, ask for **building 16** in the **Grandstand** section. A short walk from the Carriage House, it's the top-rated building at Saratoga Springs.

TREEHOUSE VILLAS *(not enough surveys to rate)*

STRENGTHS	WEAKNESSES
• Spacious stand-alone three-bedroom villas	• Far from Saratoga Springs services such as check-in and dining
• Quiet location (but without much to do)	• Lackluster pool
• Innovative round design feels more spacious than other villas with the same square footage	• Limited number of units
	• Only two baths per villa
	• Bus travelers connect through Saratoga Springs

TUCKED BETWEEN Old Key West Resort and the Grandstand section of Saratoga Springs, the Treehouse Villas offer a unique, secluded lodging option. This 60-villa complex has its own separate entrance off Disney Vacation Club Way, giving it a private, retreat-like atmosphere. Each eight-sided villa is raised 10 feet off the ground on stilts, with ramps for wheelchair access. Surrounded by dense forest, these 1,072-square-foot villas have three bedrooms and two full bathrooms, plus more sleeping surfaces in the living room, making them an excellent choice for larger groups. Villas can sleep up to nine guests, similar to comparably sized villas at other DVC resorts. Two bedrooms have a queen bed; the third bedroom has bunk beds; and the living room has a sofa bed and foldout chair, all of which would be best for children.

The interior emphasizes natural materials, with stone floors in the kitchen, granite countertops, and rustic-stained wood furniture. Bunk beds, end tables, and picture frames are all crafted from rough-hewn logs, adding to the treehouse feel. Bathrooms feel modern with tile finishes but have a very compact design. The shower in the primary bathroom is especially cramped; tilt down to grab a bottle of shampoo, and you could bang your head on the side of the tub.

The three-bedroom treehouses usually cost about $70–$350 more per night than a comparable two-bedroom villa and $600–$700 *less* than a standard three-bedroom villa elsewhere at Saratoga Springs. For larger parties, the treehouses can be a great value. A New Jersey family thinks a stay at Treehouse Villas is money well spent:

> We give Treehouse Villas five stars for value. With nine people in our party, our villa saved us about $700–$1,000 per night. The three bedrooms and pullout couch comfortably slept our group. Plus, having a great eat-in kitchen helped us save money on breakfast.

While a walking path connects the Treehouse Villas to the rest of Saratoga Springs, transportation remains a significant drawback. There are two dedicated bus stops, but guests must transfer at the main resort to reach the parks. This Rhode Island reader felt stranded:

> Transportation is abhorrent—and I actually had some idea what to expect (i.e., taking one bus at the villas to another bus at the main resort). The treehouses are nice in and of themselves, but I would suggest not staying here if going to the parks is your main objective.

GOOD (AND NOT-SO-GOOD) ROOMS AT TREEHOUSE VILLAS *(See* theugseries.com/th-views *for photos.)* Numbers **7024-7034** and **7058-7060** are closest to one of the villas' two dedicated bus stops and the walkway to Saratoga Springs; numbers **7026-7033** also have water views. Treehouses **7001-7011** and **7045-7054** are closest to the other bus stop; treehouses **7020-7023** are closest to the boat docks. Finally, treehouses **7035-7037, 7055, 7056,** and **7060** surround the pool.

Disney's Old Key West Resort

(See map on page 148. See theugseries.com/okw *for extended coverage.)*

OLD KEY WEST WAS THE FIRST Disney Vacation Club property, and it remains a fan favorite for its spacious rooms, laid-back atmosphere, and easy access to parking. A Pennsylvania reader even calls it Walt Disney World's best-kept secret:

Old Key West Resort

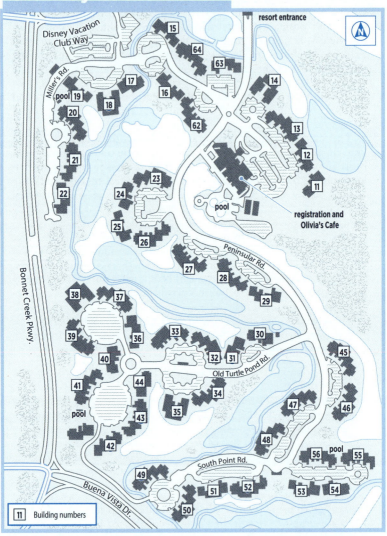

Old Key West has the most spacious rooms and the easiest access to your car—right outside your door! There are a number of small, almost private pools, so you don't have to go to the main pool.

The resort is designed to resemble a tropical Key West neighborhood, with two- and three-story buildings that have pastel facades, white trim, and shutters. Everything is laid out like a subdivision, wrapping around a golf course and Bonnet Creek, with clusters of buildings forming small, quiet communities. **Conch Flats Community Hall** is the resort's hub, housing the check-in area, a full-service restaurant, the fitness center, a marina, and the general store. Each cluster of

OLD KEY WEST RESORT

STRENGTHS	WEAKNESSES
• Largest villas of the DVC resorts	• Multiple bus stops increase travel time
• Often available at discounted rates or as a DVC rental	• No elevators in most buildings
	• Highway noise
• Close to Lake Buena Vista Golf Course	• Fewer baths per bedroom than newer DVC properties
• Boat service to Disney Springs	
• Convenient parking	• Mediocre on-site dining

Unofficial Guide Reader-Survey Results

Percentage of readers who'd stay here again	94% (*Average*)
Percentage of readers who'd recommend this resort to a friend	71% (*Average*)
Overall reader rating	B+

buildings has its own quiet pool, while the main pool at Conch Flats Community Hall features a waterslide shaped like a giant sandcastle.

Old Key West boasts some of the largest rooms in the World, and all were refurbished in 2018. Studios are 376 square feet and have two queen beds, a table and chairs, and an extra vanity outside the bathroom. One-bedroom villas are 942 square feet and have a king bed in the main bedroom and a queen sleeper sofa in the living room, along with a full kitchen and a laundry room. Two-bedroom villas are 1,333 square feet, with a king bed in one bedroom, two queens in the other, and a queen sleeper sofa and foldout chair in the living room, along with a full kitchen and a laundry room.

The décor is best described as a light beach theme with subtle Disney touches. Any room larger than a studio has vinyl plank flooring instead of carpet. And each room has a private balcony with views of the golf course, landscaping, or waterways. These are some of the most peaceful views on Disney property.

Old Key West's biggest drawbacks are transportation and limited dining options. Disney Springs is accessible by boat or bus, while other parks and locations are accessible only by bus, with multiple internal stops that can add as much as 15 minutes to your travel time. Walking time to the bus stops from the most remote rooms can take up to 6 minutes.

GOOD (AND NOT-SO-GOOD) ROOMS AT OLD KEY WEST RESORT (*See* theugseries.com/okw-views *for photos.*) Old Key West is huge, with 49 three-story villa buildings spread over about 100 acres. Views are nice from almost all of the villas; all multiroom villas and some studios have a large balcony furnished with a table and chairs.

Because the resort is bordered by busy Bonnet Creek Parkway and even busier Buena Vista Drive, the best villas are those located as far from the road noise as possible. For a lovely river view, ask for **building 45** or **46** (building 45 is the highest rated at Old Key West). For nice lake and golf-course views away from roads and close to restaurants, recreation, the marina, the main swimming complex, and shopping, ask for **building 13**. Nearby, **buildings 11** and **12** are likewise quiet and convenient; they offer primarily golf-course views. Avoid **buildings 19–22, 38, 39, 41, 42,** and **49–54**, which border Bonnet Creek Parkway and Buena Vista Drive.

Port Orleans Resort–Riverside

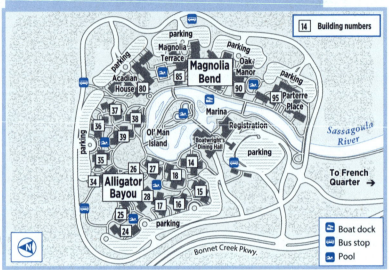

Disney's Port Orleans Resort: French Quarter and Riverside
(See maps above and opposite. See **theugseries.com/riverside** and **theugseries.com/frq** for extended coverage.)

A MODERATE RESORT, Port Orleans is divided into two large sections. The smaller, southern part is called the **French Quarter,** and the larger section is **Riverside.** French Quarter is this year's top-rated Moderate resort, both overall and in terms of readers who said they'd stay there again and readers who would recommend it to a friend.

PORT ORLEANS RESORT–FRENCH QUARTER

STRENGTHS	WEAKNESSES
• Excellent staff/service	• Boring pool
• Most compact of the Moderate resorts, with only one bus stop	• Shares bus service with Port Orleans Riverside during slower times of year
• Live entertainment in Scat Cat's Club	• No table-service dining
• Recently refurbished rooms	
• Beignets!	

Unofficial Guide Reader-Survey Results
(French Quarter only; see page 152 for Riverside)

Percentage of readers who'd stay here again	96% (Above Average)
Percentage of readers who'd recommend this resort to a friend	80% (Above Average)
Overall reader rating	A-

WITH SEVEN THREE-STORY GUEST BUILDINGS along Disney's artificial Sassagoula River, Port Orleans French Quarter brings a Disney-fied version of New Orleans' Vieux Carre to Walt Disney World. It's consistently a reader favorite, with many rating it above several Deluxe resorts.

The pink-and-blue buildings, complete with wrought-iron railings, shutters, and old-fashioned lampposts, create a charming, Mardi

Port Orleans Resort–French Quarter

Gras–inspired atmosphere. The resort's main building, **The Mint**, houses check-in and the food court, featuring a vibrant mural and vintage bank-teller windows. Outside, **Doubloon Lagoon** (the main pool) offers a colorful sea-serpent slide with Neptune at the helm.

All guest rooms were refurbished in 2024 and 2025, and the new rooms are some of the best in all of Disney World. Light flooring, walls, and furniture are brightened with pops of color and pattern in pillows, art, and other accents. There are plenty of outlets, and light *Princess and the Frog* theming helps reinforce both the New Orleans and uniquely Disney feel of these rooms.

The biggest downside here is the lack of a table-service restaurant. The food court is the only dining option, and it can get crowded, especially during peak mealtimes. The closest sit-down spot is at Port Orleans Riverside, a 15-minute walk away.

Buses serve as the primary mode of transportation to Disney locations. Thankfully, there is only one stop, and the walking distance from the farthest rooms is just 5 minutes or less. Boat transportation to Disney Springs is also available.

GOOD (AND NOT-SO-GOOD) ROOMS AT PORT ORLEANS FRENCH QUARTER *(See* theugseries.com/frq-views *for photos.)* The best views are from rooms facing the river and a pine forest on the opposite bank. Below are the best river-view rooms in each building:

BUILDING 1: 1127-1132, 1227-1232 (a tree blocks some of the view in **1229** and **1230**), and **1327-1332**

BUILDING 2: 2227-2232 (landscaping blocks some of the view in **2129** and **2130**), and **2327-2332**

BUILDING 5: 5118-5123, 5218-5225, and **5318-5325**

BUILDING 6: 6123-6129, 6138-6139, 6145-6148, 6223-6226, 6233-6240, 6245-6248, 6323-6329, 6335-6340, and **6345-6348**

BUILDING 7: 7142-7147, 7242-7247, and **7342-7347**

If you're not overly concerned with the specific room you get, the highest-rated building at French Quarter is **building 6**—in fact, it's the third-highest-rated building in Walt Disney World.

PORT ORLEANS RESORT–RIVERSIDE

STRENGTHS	
• Interesting narrative to theming	• Good place to walk or run for fitness
• Disney princess–themed rooms in Magnolia Bend	• Recreation options (bikes, boats)
	WEAKNESSES
• Live entertainment in River Roost Lounge	• Multiple bus stops; may share service with Port Orleans French Quarter during slower times of year
• Availability of fifth-sleeper rooms	
• Highly rated feature pool	• This is a *large* resort, with many buildings very far from check-in and dining

Unofficial Guide Reader-Survey Results	
Percentage of readers who'd stay here again	88% (*Below Average*)
Percentage of readers who'd recommend this resort to a friend	63% (*Average*)
Overall reader rating	B+

INSPIRED BY 19TH-CENTURY LOUISIANA RIVER COMMUNITIES, Port Orleans Riverside, like Port Orleans French Quarter, sits along the Sassagoula River. It offers two distinct themes: **Magnolia Bend** features three-story plantation-style mansions, and **Alligator Bayou** embraces a rustic, two-story tin-roofed lodge aesthetic. The resort's main pool is found on **Ol' Man Island,** just a bridge away from the main building, which houses check-in, the gift shop, the **Riverside Mill** food court, and **Boatwright's Dining Hall** (the resort's table-service restaurant). The main building even has a working cotton press powered by a 32-foot water wheel.

Each of Riverside's 2,048 rooms is 314 square feet. Most provide one king or two queen beds, a table and two chairs, a minifridge, a coffee maker, and two pedestal sinks outside the bathroom.

Disney refurbished rooms in Alligator Bayou in 2019. These sleep five people; the fifth bed is a Murphy-style fold-down suitable for kids only. Rooms feature hickory-branch tables and vinyl plank flooring. Bathrooms have increased shelf space and a curtain separator that allows three people to get dressed privately at the same time.

Magnolia Bend's more traditional rooms have begun to feel outdated, but they are scheduled to be refurbished in 2025 and 2026. The **Oak Manor** and **Parterre Place** complexes contain exclusively princess-themed Royal Guest Rooms, which cost up to $75 more per night than standard rooms.

Disney buses link Riverside to all Disney World destinations. Walking time to the bus-loading areas from the most remote rooms is 5 minutes or less. Unfortunately, bus service is one of readers' biggest gripes about Riverside. From a Delaware mom:

> *Port Orleans Riverside has some of the worst bus service on-property. One day a bus to a park takes 20 minutes; two days later, going to the exact same park, you will experience a long, leisurely drive around the loop, then make a stopover at French Quarter,*

followed by finally getting to the park about 45 minutes later or more. Utter madness!

Additionally, the resort's size can be overwhelming to some guests, as this reader from Florida writes:

It was our first extended stay at Port Orleans Riverside, and we found the resort to be too big and the pathways too confusing. We were situated half a mile from the lobby/food court, which made taking advantage of our refillable mugs a somewhat arduous task.

Riverside is so large that you might consider getting around via bicycle, if that's an option for your party.

GOOD (AND NOT-SO-GOOD) ROOMS AT PORT ORLEANS RIVERSIDE *(See* theugseries.com/riverside-views *for photos.)* Because rooms here are spread across 20 buildings, room selection is very important.

Magnolia Bend consists of four three-story, grand plantation–style complexes: **Acadian House, Magnolia Terrace, Oak Manor,** and **Parterre Place.** The best views are from the third-floor river side of Acadian House (**building 80**), which overlooks the river and Ol' Man Island: rooms **8414–8419.** Farther south, Parterre Place (**building 95**) has a number of rooms facing the river, but most views are blocked by trees or extend to the parking lot on the opposite shore. Try **9537–9540, 9573–9576, 9737–9739,** or **9773–9776.** In general, with the few previous exceptions, if you want a nice river view, opt for **Port Orleans French Quarter.**

Alligator Bayou, the other part of Port Orleans Riverside, forms an arch around the resort's northern half. These 16 smaller, two-story guest-room buildings, set among pine groves and abundant gardens, offer a cozy alternative to Magnolia Bend. If you want a river view, ask for a second-story water-view room in **building 27** or **38. Building 14** also offers some river-view rooms and is convenient to shops, the front desk, and the restaurant, but it's in a noisy, high-traffic area. A good compromise for families is **building 18**. It's insulated from traffic and noise by landscaping, but it's also next to a satellite swimming pool and within an easy walk of the lobby and restaurant.

Disney's official map for Port Orleans Riverside shows two green areas north of the river bend in Alligator Bayou—these are dried-up lakes that are now richly forested with pine trees. Though out of sight of water, these offer the most peaceful and serene accommodations in the entire Port Orleans Resort. In this area, we recommend **buildings 26, 25,** and **39,** in that order. Note that these buildings are somewhat distant from the resort's central facilities, and there's no adjacent parking. In Alligator Bayou, avoid **buildings 15, 16, 17,** and **24,** all of which are subject to traffic noise from nearby Bonnet Creek Parkway.

THE ANIMAL KINGDOM RESORTS
Disney's Animal Kingdom Lodge & Villas: Jambo House and Kidani Village

(See map on page 155. See **theugseries.com/ak-lodge, theugseries.com/jambo -villas,** *and* **theugseries.com/kidani-villas** *for extended coverage.)*

ANIMAL KINGDOM LODGE AND VILLAS–JAMBO HOUSE

STRENGTHS	WEAKNESSES
• Magnificent lobby	• Few counter-service dining options
• Excellent on-site dining options	• Most villas here are smaller than those at Kidani Village
• Large, beautiful feature pool	
• On-site cultural and nature programs	• Rooms are among the smallest of the Deluxe resorts
• Best theming of any Disney hotel	
• Animals!	• Bus transportation required to reach any theme park

QUICK TAKE: *Jambo House is among the best Disney resorts. It has easy access to three of the table-service restaurants rated highest in our reader surveys. If it's in your budget, Animal Kingdom Lodge & Villas is one of the first on-site resorts you should consider.*

TUCKED INTO THE SOUTHWESTERNMOST CORNER OF THE WORLD, Animal Kingdom Lodge sits right next to Disney's Animal Kingdom theme park. Opened in 2001, the resort is divided into two sections: **Jambo House,** which has standard deluxe rooms and DVC studios and villas, and **Kidani Village,** which has all-DVC studios and villas.

Unofficial Guide **Reader-Survey Results**
(Jambo House only; see page 157 for Kidani Village)

Percentage of readers who'd stay here again	**Lodge: 95%; Villas: 96%** *(both Above Average)*
Percentage of readers who'd recommend this resort to a friend	**Lodge: 76%; Villas: 74%** *(both Above Average)*
Overall reader rating	**Lodge: A; Villas: A–**

DESIGNED BY PETER DOMINICK (who also designed Wilderness Lodge), Jambo House blends African tribal architecture with the rustic grandeur of national-park lodges. Five-story, thatched-roof wings extend out from a stunning central lobby, creating panoramic views of a 21-acre savanna featuring streams, elevated rock outcrops, and more than 200 free-roaming animals and 30 species of birds.

Jambo House has 972 guest rooms. The standard deluxe rooms measure 344 square feet, with hand-carved furnishings, vibrant African-inspired décor, and modern amenities. Each room offers a TV, a table with two chairs, a minifridge, and a coffee maker. Almost all rooms have full balconies, and bathrooms offer double sinks.

Jambo House also has DVC studios and one-, two-, and three-bedroom villas. Most are slightly smaller than at neighboring Kidani Village—anywhere from 50 square feet smaller for a studio to more than 200 square feet smaller for a two-bedroom villa. The three-bedroom Grand Villas at Jambo House are an exception, larger than those at Kidani by 148 square feet.

Jambo's standard and studio rooms sleep four, Club Level rooms sleep five, and multibedroom villas sleep more. A Tennessee mom loved everything but the room size:

> *We wanted to love staying in Animal Kingdom Lodge. We found the setting unique, the staff exceptional, and the common areas breathtakingly gorgeous. Loved all three table-service restaurants. Location wasn't an issue since we had a car, and the pool was fabulous.*

Animal Kingdom Lodge & Villas

However, the rooms are really small for the price. We were especially dismayed at the commode/shower area—we had to sit on the commode in order to have room to shut the door. Unfortunately, the room size and bathrooms dropped us from "love" to "like."

Jambo house is home to some of Disney World's best dining, with all three table-service restaurants ranking near the top of guest favorites. **Jiko—The Cooking Place** is an elegant signature restaurant featuring twin wood-burning ovens and upscale African-inspired dishes. **Boma—Flavors of Africa** offers a buffet for breakfast and dinner, with an open kitchen, a wood-burning grill, and rotisserie cooking under thatched roofs. (**Sanaa**, the third restaurant, is a short walk away at Kidani Village.) **Victoria Falls**, a delightful mezzanine lounge overlooking Boma, rounds out the hotel's sit-down service. **The Mara**, the lone quick-service place, can get crowded, even with extended hours.

Uzima Springs Pool Bar serves drinks, salads, and snacks next to the resort's huge, elaborate pool.

A family from Connecticut found the resort's restaurants a draw:

> The restaurants in Animal Kingdom Lodge are great. We had lunch at Sanaa, which featured fantastic food and awesome views of the animals on the savanna. The Mara's counter-service options were way better than anything we found in the Magic Kingdom.

In addition to strong theming and excellent dining, Animal Kingdom Lodge offers a wide array of activities and amenities. **Uzima Springs Pool** is a huge, tropical-themed pool with waterslides and a zero-entry design. There are also nightly campfires and outdoor movies. Savanna-viewing areas are spread throughout the resort, allowing guests to see African wildlife up close. And the 1-hour **Starlight Safari** ($76–$89 per person; ages 8 and up) takes guests out onto the savanna nightly at 8:30 and 10 p.m. to see the animals at their most active.

Jambo House is one of the most remote resorts at Disney World. Bus service is the only form of transportation. We strongly recommend having a car if you stay here, as rides to the parks can feel long.

GOOD (AND NOT-SO-GOOD) ROOMS AT JAMBO HOUSE *(See theugseries.com/ak-views for photos.)* A quick look at the resort map makes it clear where to find the best rooms and villas at Jambo House. The **Kudu Trail** and **Zebra Trail** wings form a semicircle around the central savanna, offering the most stunning wildlife views. Each wing consists of five buildings that curve around the savanna, while two additional buildings extend outward.

The best rooms—on **floors three and four,** facing into the circle—are high enough to overlook the entire savanna yet low enough to let you appreciate the ground-level detail of this amazing wildlife exhibit.

Second-floor rooms really can't take in the panorama, and fifth-floor rooms are a little too high for good views of the animals. Most of the fourth-floor rooms in Jambo House are reserved for Club Level guests, and the fifth and sixth floors house the DVC units. Rooms in the **Zebra Trail** section are rated higher by readers, on average, than those in any other section of Jambo House.

Lower-rated rooms are found in the two smaller wings, **Ostrich Trail** and **Giraffe Trail,** branching from either side of the lodge near the main entrance. Some rooms on the north side of Ostrich Trail overlook a small savanna. Most rooms overlook the front entrance. Least desirable is Giraffe Trail, extending from the right side of the lobby: Its rooms overlook either the pool (water view) or the resort entrance (standard view).

ANIMAL KINGDOM VILLAS–KIDANI VILLAGE

STRENGTHS	
• Nice pool with excellent splash area	• Close to Jambo House amenities and restaurants
• Underground parking close to elevators	**WEAKNESSES**
• Beautiful, understated lobby	• Savanna views can be hit-or-miss
• Sanaa restaurant is an *Unofficial Guide* favorite	• Erratic bus service
• Great fitness room	• No quick-service dining options other than pool bar

Unofficial Guide Reader-Survey Results

Percentage of readers who'd stay here again	86% (*Below Average*)
Percentage of readers who'd recommend this resort to a friend	61% (*Below Average*)
Overall reader rating	A-

KIDANI VILLAGE, A SEPARATE BUILDING shaped like a backward 3, is an all-DVC resort with 324 villas, its own private savanna; a well-themed pool and splash zone; and **Sanaa**, a highly rated table-service restaurant. Additional amenities include a fitness center; an arcade; a gift shop; and sports courts for tennis, shuffleboard, and basketball. A half-mile walking trail (or internal shuttle) connects Kidani Village to Jambo House. And DVC guests at either location can use amenities at both resorts.

Kidani Village offers studios and one-, two-, and three-bedroom villas. Most rooms (except the three-bedroom villas) are larger than their counterparts at Jambo House. A standout feature is that any room larger than a studio has an extra bathroom, making it more convenient for larger groups. One-bedroom villas sleep five guests, while two-bedroom villas can accommodate up to nine guests.

Rooms at Kidani Village are scheduled for extensive refurbishment beginning in October 2025. This is expected to be a major overhaul.

Kidani Village is Becky's family's favorite resort. It's quiet and relaxed, and the lobby and rooms have a smaller, more personal feel than Jambo House's. Kidani's distance from Jambo House makes it feel especially remote.

GOOD (AND NOT-SO-GOOD) UNITS AT KIDANI VILLAGE *(See* theugseries.com/kidani-views *for photos.)* The best views at Kidani Village are from the north-facing units near the bottom and middle of the backward 3. Try rooms **7X38–7X44, 7X46–7X52, 7X06–7X11, 7X68–7X82,** and **7X61–7X67** (X indicates the floor number). These overlook the savanna next to Jambo House's Kudu Trail rooms and beyond into undeveloped woods. West- and south-facing units in the bottom half of Kidani Village overlook the parking lot; west-facing units in the top half have either pool or savanna views.

Disney's Coronado Springs Resort
(See map on page 159. See theugseries.com/coronado *for extended coverage.*)

STRENGTHS	WEAKNESSES
• Most sophisticated room décor of the Moderate resorts	• Dining options rated low by readers
• Setting is beautiful at night	• Presence of conventioneers may be off-putting to vacationing families
• Themed swimming area with waterslides	• Some rooms are a long distance from check-in, lobby, and restaurants
• On-site business center	
• Best public Wi-Fi at any Disney resort	• Multiple bus stops

Unofficial Guide Reader-Survey Results

Percentage of readers who'd stay here again	95% (*Above Average*)
Percentage of readers who'd recommend this resort to a friend	72% (*Average*)
Overall reader rating	A-

LOCATED NEAR ANIMAL KINGDOM, Coronado Springs Resort is Disney's only midpriced convention hotel. Inspired by northern Mexico and the American Southwest, the resort is divided into four themed sections. The two- and three-story **Ranchos** resemble Southwestern cattle ranches, while the two-story **Cabanas** are modeled after Mexican beach resorts. The multistory **Casitas** embody elements of Spanish Colonial architecture. The 15-floor **Gran Destino Tower** hosts the resort's main lobby and its most upscale accommodations. Sprawling around a 22-acre lake, the resort has three small pools and one large swimming complex. The main pool features a reproduction of a Mayan step pyramid with a cascading waterfall.

Most of the 1,839 rooms in the Ranchos, Cabanas, and Casitas measure 314 square feet and have two queen beds, a desk with a spacious working area, a chair, a minifridge, a coffee maker, and a vanity outside the bathroom. Sliding doors divide the main living area from the sinks, allowing three people to get dressed privately at the same time. Bathrooms have plenty of storage. Rooms are decorated with a subtle Southwestern theme. None of the rooms have balconies.

The 545 rooms in Gran Destino Tower range from standard hotel rooms to deluxe, one-bedroom, and presidential suites. Even the standard rooms are almost 20% larger than those in the other sections. They have vinyl plank flooring, large windows, good lighting, and lots of desk and storage space; rooms are also equipped with a minifridge and a Keurig coffee maker. Bathrooms have plentiful lighting and shelf space, two sinks, a huge shower, and separate vanity and toilet areas, allowing three people to get dressed privately at the same time. While beautifully designed, these rooms have minimal theming. They could easily fit into almost any other Disney resort. The public areas showcase a vibrant mix of Spanish and Moorish design, with bold colors and large, open spaces.

One of Gran Destino's biggest draws is its relatively affordable Club Level. Booking a room here gets you access to the **Chronos Club** lounge, which offers stunning views, great food throughout the day, and exceptional service. Rates for these rooms are typically $100–$300 per night cheaper than for any other Club Level room on Disney property, making it one of the best values for a premium experience at Disney World.

Coronado Springs has four full-service restaurants and a food court, plus two bars. Still, dining capacity, choices, quality, and value are not where they need to be for a resort this big. We recommend having a car to expand your dining options. But if you're eating onsite, we recommend just two locations: **Toledo—Tapas, Steak & Seafood,** located in Gran Destino Tower, serves Spanish-inspired dishes and is featured in the *Michelin Guide*. An overwater bar called **Three Bridges Bar & Grill** sits in the middle of the lake, connected to the resort by—you guessed it—three bridges.

The resort is connected to other Disney destinations by bus only. Walking time from the most remote rooms to the bus stop is 8–10 minutes. Bus service is the other of Coronado Springs' weaknesses. This Oklahoma family's comments are representative:

> *The buses took at least 30–45 minutes to arrive at the parks and/or resort. The queues for the bus would be filled with guests, and they still wouldn't send another.*

Coronado Springs Resort

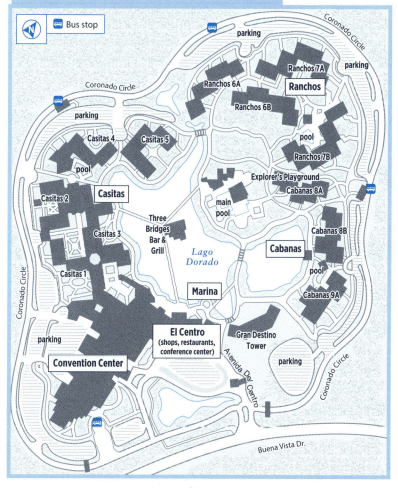

A Virginia mother had a different experience:

Coronado Springs was absolutely fabulous. The staff was friendly, the kids loved the pool, and we all loved the market. It was nice and quiet at night. There were many convention guests, but they didn't interfere with our trip.

Coronado Springs was the Disney Moderate resort of choice for this Kansas family:

On our previous three trips, we stayed at Pop Century, and I was curious if a Moderate resort was worth the extra money. At first the size of Coronado Springs was daunting, but we quickly settled into a routine and figured out the bus routes (bus service was really the only major drawback). The room was spacious, and the door separating the living area from the bath vanity was very useful because I was able to get ready in the morning without waking the kids. The kids really enjoyed the pool area, and I thought it was better themed than Pop Century. Overall, I thought the resort was worth the price difference.

GOOD (AND NOT-SO-GOOD) ROOMS AT CORONADO SPRINGS RESORT *(See* **theugseries.com/csr-views** *for photos.)* As convention hotels go, Coronado Springs is an oddity. At comparable hotels, everything is centrally located and the guest rooms are close to each other. Here, the rooms are spread around a huge lake, called **Lago Dorado.** If you're in a room on the opposite side of the lake from the meeting and dining areas, you'll need to plan on an 11- to 15-minute hike every time you leave your room.

Coronado Springs' main lobby is in Gran Destino Tower. West of the tower is **El Centro**, which contains shops, restaurants, and a conference center. If you think of Coronado Springs as a clock face, El Centro is at the 6 o'clock position. Moving clockwise around the lake, the **Casitas** are located in the 7–9 o'clock positions. For a good view of Lago Dorado, book one of these rooms:

3220-3223, 3241-3259, 3267-3273, or **3281-3287**

3320-3383 (*except* **3324, 3330-3335, 3360-3365, 3374-3380,** and **3384-3387**)

3420-3423, 3425-3429, 3436-3459, 3466-3473, 3480-3482, or **3487**

4461-4464

5202-5212

5303-5304 or **5311-5312**

5400-5402, 5405-5410, 5413, or **5423-5463** (*except* 5450)

Next come the **Ranchos,** which are set back from the lake at 11, 12, and 1 o'clock. The desert theme translates to lots of cactus and gravel, not much water or shade, and almost no good views. The Ranchos are a hike from everything but the main swimming area. We recommend avoiding this area.

The **Cabanas** are at 2, 3, and 4 o'clock. Lake-view rooms we recommend here include the following: **8129-8131** and **8142-8147; 8500-8510, 8550-8553,** and **8573** (*except* **8505, 8507,** and **8509**). Specific rooms aside, Cabanas **building 8C** (rooms **8800-8993**) is the highest-rated building at the resort.

Finally, **Gran Destino Tower** is at 5 o'clock, close to El Centro. Even-numbered rooms face EPCOT and Hollywood Studios, and guests on upper floors can see those parks' fireworks shows. Odd-numbered rooms at Gran Destino have a view of the resort's lake.

Disney's All-Star Resorts: Movies, Music, and Sports

(See map on page 162. See **theugseries.com/all-stars** *for extended coverage.)*

STRENGTHS	WEAKNESSES
• Least expensive of the Disney resorts	• Most likely Disney resorts to host large groups of teenagers
• Family suites at All-Star Music are less expensive than at Disney's Art of Animation Resort	• Room soundproofing is poor; bring a white-noise machine
• Convenient parking	• No full-service dining; food courts often overwhelmed at mealtimes
• Lots of pools	• All three resorts share buses during slower times of year; bus stops often crowded

> *Unofficial Guide* Reader-Survey Results
>
> Percentage of readers who'd stay here again:
> **Movies: 82%** (*Below Average*); **Music: 86%** (*Below Average*); **Sports: 87%** (*Below Average*)
>
> Percentage of readers who'd recommend this resort to a friend:
> **Movies: 48%** (*Below Average*); **Music: 40%** (*Below Average*); **Sports: 53%** (*Below Average*)
>
> Overall reader rating: **Movies: B; Music: B–; Sports: B**

DISNEY'S FIRST TAKE ON a budget-friendly resort is anything but subtle. Each of the three All-Star Resorts (Music, Movies, and Sports) features oversize, Pop Art–style icons that reinforce its theme. The 30 three-story buildings sprawl across a large property, and each resort has its own lobby, food court, check-in, and transportation areas. But because all three resorts sit immediately next to one other, some buildings that are technically part of one resort are actually closer to the lobby and amenities of another resort. For example, we recently stayed in the corner of building 3 at All-Star Movies, but the All-Star Music lobby was just steps away.

The facade of **All-Star Sports** features huge sports equipment: The towering football helmets, tennis rackets, and baseball bats are taller than the buildings they adorn. **All-Star Music** features 40-foot guitars, maracas, and saxophones, while **All-Star Movies** showcases giant popcorn boxes and iconic Disney film characters and props.

The lobbies are loud (in both decibels and brightness) and colorful, with large white stars adorning the walls. Tiled flooring and mostly empty walls (other than the stars) add to the echo chamber. Each lobby has an area where kids can watch Disney music videos or movies while parents check in.

Each resort has two main pools; Music's are shaped like musical instruments (the **Piano Pool** and the guitar-shaped **Calypso Pool**), and one of Movies' pools is star-shaped. All six pools feature replicas of Disney characters, some shooting water pistols.

At 260 square feet, standard rooms at the All-Star Resorts are among the smallest at Walt Disney World. They're similar in size to those at Pop Century but slightly smaller than Art of Animation's standard rooms. While the compact layout can be challenging for a family of four, room refurbishments that replaced one standard bed in each room with a Murphy bed have greatly improved functionality.

Each room includes vinyl plank flooring, sleek modern storage units, queen beds (with one folding into the wall to convert into a table), 10 USB outlets, and a coffee maker. Space is open under the bed for storage. The bathrooms have sliding glass doors and tile walls. The vanity area is vastly improved, with modular shelving, better lighting, and increased counter space. Another sliding door separates the bath from the main living space, allowing three people to get ready in privacy at the same time.

While we think the refurbishments are a big improvement overall, there's always an unexpected miss or two in a renovation. This reader from New Hampshire found a couple:

> *The updated rooms have a couple of downsides. One is no water pressure in the shower. And the thermostat is behind the coffee station, so it's impossible to see the temperature or which buttons you're hitting.*

All-Star Resorts

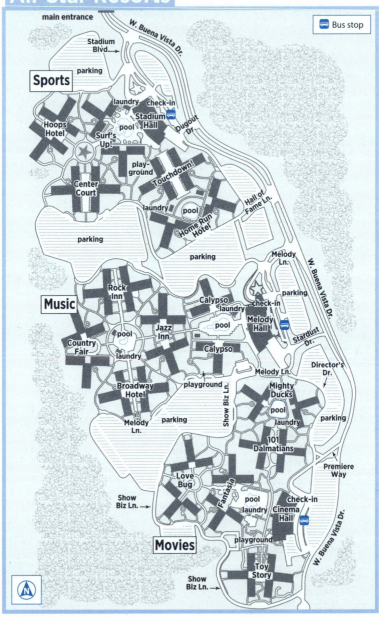

Due to the low staff-to-guest ratio, service at these resorts is mediocre. Also, there are no table-service restaurants (there is, however, a McDonald's about a quarter mile away, with sidewalk access). Food courts are functional and generally efficient, but they lack variety. And they can still get crowded during peak mealtimes. Bus service to the theme parks and water parks is well run. Walking time to the bus stop from the most remote guest rooms is about 8 minutes.

All-Star Sports and Music are the noisiest Disney resorts; we use a white-noise app or request a box fan when we stay here. Be aware, however, that while the All-Stars suffer in terms of noise when compared with other Disney properties, you're better off here than at most hotels you'll find in Kissimmee or Lake Buena Vista for $150 per night or less.

We receive a lot of letters commenting on the All-Star Resorts. An Indiana family loved their renovated room:

> *Our hotel room had so many storage shelves! Even though it was super small, we could be organized with our stuff for the week. I wish all hotels were like that! There were shelves next to each bed (along with plenty of outlets), shelves inside the bathroom, and shelves in the main bedroom. It was great. The fridge should be called a cooler. It didn't really keep stuff cold, but cool.*

A Canadian family had a not-so-positive experience:

> *The* Guide *didn't prepare us for the large groups of students who take over the resorts. They're very noisy and pushy when it comes to getting on buses. Our scariest experience was when we tried getting on a bus and got mobbed by about 100 students.*

ALL-STAR MUSIC FAMILY SUITES All-Star Music offers 192 family suites in the Jazz and Calypso buildings, each measuring 520 square feet. That makes them larger than Fort Wilderness Cabins but slightly smaller than Art of Animation's family suites. Each suite features a queen bed in the bedroom and a pull-out sleeper sofa in the living area. The kitchenette has a full-size fridge, a microwave, and a coffee maker. There are also two bathrooms, multiple flat-screen TVs, and a sliding door that separates the bedroom from the living space.

unofficial **TIP**
Music 5654 may be the best room at the All-Star Resorts. This third-floor corner room overlooks a small pond in a wooded area behind the resort. See theugseries.com/music-5654 to see the view.

Reader comments about the Family Suites are generally positive, albeit measured. From an Illinois family of five:

> *We found the All-Star Music Family Suite to be very roomy. Our teenagers and preteen were quite comfortable on the pull-out sofa. Having the two bathrooms was a must, and the kitchen area had lots of shelf space for the food we had delivered from Garden Grocer [see pages 362–363]. Our only complaint is that from 7:30 a.m. until midnight there's music playing. The rooms are soundproofed but not enough; we had to use earplugs.*

GOOD (AND NOT-SO-GOOD) ROOMS AT THE ALL-STAR RESORTS *(See* **theugseries.com/movies-views, theugseries.com/music-views,** *and* **theugseries.com/sports-views** *for photos.)* Although the layouts of the All-Star Resorts' Movies, Music, and Sports sections are different, the buildings are identical T-shaped, three-story, three-winged structures. They are grouped into pairs, generally facing each other and sharing a common subtheme (for example, there's a *Toy Story* pair in the Movies section and a Broadway pair in the Music section). In addition to being named by their theme, the buildings are numbered 1–10 in each section. Rooms are accessed via a motel-style outdoor walkway, and each building has an elevator.

Parking is plentiful, all of it in sprawling lots buffering the three sections. A room near a parking lot means easier loading and unloading but also unsightly views of the lot. The resort offers luggage service, but it often takes up to an hour for your bags to arrive.

To avoid a parking-lot view, you can request a room facing a courtyard or pool. The trade-off is noise—the sound of cars starting in the parking lot pales in comparison to shrieking children in the pool. The themed facade decorations are placed on the buildings' widest face—the top of the T—which is also the side facing the pool or courtyard. In some cases, as with the surfboards in the Sports section, these significantly obstruct the view. Floodlights are also trained on these facades, so if you step out of your room at night to view the action below, looking down may result in temporary blindness.

If you choose an All-Star Resort because you'd rather spend time and money at the parks than at your resort, then you should book a room near the bus stop, your link to the rest of the World. Note that the buses leave from the central public buildings of each section, which are located near the larger, noisier pools. If you're planning to return to your room for an afternoon nap, request a room farther away from the pools. Also consider an upper-story room to minimize foot traffic past your door. If you're only concerned with the highest-rated building in each resort (rather than the best rooms or specific amenities), here are the top-rated buildings at the All-Stars, according to our reader surveys:

- **All-Star Movies** Building 10 (*Toy Story*) and buildings 7 and 6 (*Love Bug*)
- **All-Star Music** Building 1 (Calypso)
- **All-Star Sports** Buildings 10 and 7 (Touchdown!)

On the other hand, if you choose an All-Star for its kid-friendliness, consider staying near the action. A bottom-floor room provides easy access to the pool, and a room looking out onto a courtyard or pool allows you to keep an eye on your children when they're playing outside. Opt for a section and building with a theme that appeals to your kids. If you're staying in Home Run Hotel, for instance, don't forget the ball and gloves to maximize the experience. Older elementary- and middle-school children will probably want to spend hotel time in or near the bigger pools.

Playgrounds are tucked behind Cinema Hall, next to building 9, in **All-Star Movies;** between the backs of buildings 9 and 10 in **All-Star Music;** and between buildings 6 and 7 in **All-Star Sports.** Rooms facing these are ideal for families with children too young or timid for the often-chaotic larger pools. In All-Star Movies, the playground is closer to the food court than to any rooms.

For travelers without young children, the best bets for privacy and quiet are rooms in buildings that overlook the forest behind the resort: **buildings 2** and **3** in **All-Star Sports** and **buildings 5** and **6** in **All-Star Music.**

WDW RESORT PROFILES: ANIMAL KINGDOM

Disney's Pop Century Resort
(See map on page 167. See theugseries.com/pop for extended coverage.)

STRENGTHS	WEAKNESSES
• Theming is fun for anyone over 40	• Room soundproofing is poor; bring a white-noise machine
• Our favorite pool bar of the Value resorts	
• Just one bus stop	• Theming may be lost on kids and teens
• Skyliner connection to DHS and EPCOT	• Small rooms that are the same size as All-Stars' but slightly more expensive
• Stylish, modern room design	
• Convenient parking	

Unofficial Guide Reader-Survey Results

Percentage of readers who'd stay here again	**94%** *(Above Average)*
Percentage of readers who'd recommend this resort to a friend	**65%** *(Average)*
Overall reader rating	**B+**

NOTE: *More* Unofficial Guide *readers stay at Pop Century than any other Disney resort.*

LOCATED ON CENTURY DRIVE, near the ESPN Wide World of Sports Complex, Pop Century is a Value resort that follows the same motel-style layout as the All-Star resorts. Its theming is what sets it apart. This resort celebrates the fads and pop culture of the 20th century, with building-size icons like Big Wheels and cans of Play-Doh, plus silhouettes of people dancing through the decades.

Pop Century's compact 260-square-foot guest rooms are thoughtfully designed, with modern, space-saving features. Each room features vinyl plank flooring and two beds, one of which can fold up to be used as a table and create more floor space. There is a wall-mounted TV with built-in shelving and an updated bathroom with plenty of counter and shelf space, plus a shower with glass doors. And the rates here make it one of Disney's most affordable resorts; only the All-Stars are typically priced lower.

One thing to consider about the rooms at Pop Century is that we receive many complaints from readers about poor soundproofing between them. We recommend bringing a white-noise machine, using a white noise app, or requesting a box fan to run in the room. A Wisconsin family had this to say:

> *The remodeled room was very nice. We liked the Murphy bed and extra bathroom counter space. The only downside was when we left the parks in the afternoon to take a nap, the loudspeaker in the pool area made it hard to rest in our room nearby.*

The public areas feature 20th-century furniture and décor with a nostalgic feel. The food court, bar, playground, pools, and so on emulate the All-Star versions in size and location. There are also outdoor games like a giant Twister board. A lake separating Pop Century from Disney's Art of Animation Resort (AOA) offers water views, and a bridge provides easy walking access between the two resorts.

Pop Century has a combination dining–shopping area featuring the resort's gift shop and fast-food concessions. AOA's food court is a short walk over a bridge from many Pop rooms; at press time, however, both food courts had the same selection. Because of the limited dining options at this resort, we recommend traveling to eat elsewhere, either by car or Skyliner.

Pop Century is connected to the rest of Walt Disney World by bus and Skyliner. Readers rate the bus service relatively low. Pop Century shares a Skyliner station with AOA. The Skyliner connects these two resorts with Caribbean Beach and Riviera Resorts, and it's the main Disney transportation to Disney's Hollywood Studios and EPCOT. (Disney adds bus service to EPCOT and DHS during busy times and when the Skyliner isn't running.) On average, the Skyliner is more efficient than the bus for traveling between these resorts and the theme parks.

A reader from Georgia likes Pop Century for several reasons:

(1) There's a lake and a view of fireworks. (2) The courtyards have Twister and neat pools for little children. (3) Pop's dinner entrées are among the best bargains and the best food anywhere. (4) The layout is convenient to the food court. (5) Bus transportation is better than anywhere else, including the Grand Floridian! (6) Where else do the cast members do the shag to oldies?

GOOD (AND NOT-SO-GOOD) ROOMS AT POP CENTURY RESORT *(See* **theugseries.com/pop-views** *for photos.)* The best rooms for both view and convenience are the lake-view rooms in **buildings 4** and **5** in the **1960s** area. Another option, though with a less compelling view, would be rooms in the same building facing east, toward the registration and food-court building. The next-best choices would be the east-facing rooms of **building 3** in the **1950s** and of **building 6** in the **1970s**. Avoid south-facing rooms in the **1980s** (**building 7**) and the **1990s** (**building 8**); both are echo chambers for noise from nearby Osceola Parkway.

Disney's Art of Animation Resort

(See **theugseries.com/aoa** *for extended coverage.)*

STRENGTHS	
• Exceptional theming, particularly the *Cars* and *Lion King* areas	• Walking trail around Hourglass Lake and connecting bridge to Pop Century
• Best pool of the Value resorts	**WEAKNESSES**
• Family Suites are innovatively designed and themed	• Most expensive Value resort
	• Poor in-room cell reception
• Skyliner connection to DHS and EPCOT	• Standard rooms are rarely discounted
• Just one bus stop	• Poor soundproofing

Unofficial Guide Reader-Survey Results

Percentage of readers who'd stay here again	**89%** *(Below Average)*
Percentage of readers who'd recommend this resort to a friend	**65%** *(Average)*
Overall reader rating	**B+**

DISNEY'S ART OF ANIMATION sits across Hourglass Lake from Pop Century and is another one of Disney's Value resorts. Like other resorts in this category, it has standard rooms housed in four-story buildings with exterior-facing walkways, along with themed pools and a food court. But what sets Art of Animation apart is that the majority of its accommodations are family suites. The resort offers 1,120 suites and 864 standard rooms. And the suite buildings have interior hallways instead of exterior walkways.

Pop Century Resort & Art of Animation Resort

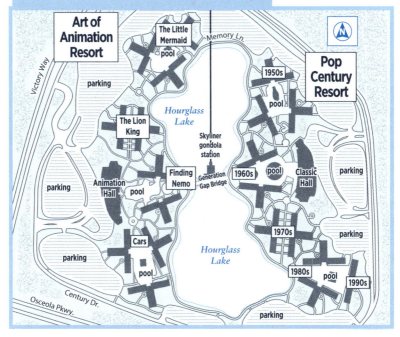

Family suites are around 565 square feet, roughly the size of two standard rooms combined. Each suite has a main bedroom, a living room, two full bathrooms, and a kitchenette with a minifridge, microwave, and coffee maker. Sleeping arrangements are a queen bed in the bedroom, a sleeper sofa, and a living room table that converts into a full-size bed. The bedroom and living room have flat-screen TVs.

Many families find the second bathroom to be a major convenience, especially for larger groups. This family from Texas appreciated that the second bathroom sped things up in the morning:

> *With two teenagers, the extra space and second bathroom were absolutely worth the additional cost. Imagine being able to get ready for a park day twice as fast!*

Standard rooms at Art of Animation are slightly larger than those at other Value resorts, coming in at 277 square feet. These rooms offer either one king bed or two doubles, along with a flat-screen TV, a minifridge, and a small table with chairs.

The theming draws from four Disney animated films: *Cars, Finding Nemo, The Lion King,* and *The Little Mermaid.* All but the *Little Mermaid*–themed rooms are suites. Each section is decorated with oversize, colorful icons representing characters and scenes from the films. The *Cars* buildings, for example, each display a four-story panoramic vista of the American desert, with the movie's iconic characters in the middle, while the *Lion King* buildings capture a vibrant jungle scene.

Readers frequently complain, however, about the long walk from the *Little Mermaid*–themed buildings to the main resort amenities. A tired reader from Illinois offered this:

There are only two reasons to stay in a Little Mermaid *room at Art of Animation: (1) There is a die-hard* Little Mermaid *fan in your party who will make your trip miserable if you don't get this room. (2) You don't feel you will walk enough in the parks and you want to add an extra-long trek to/from the bus, main pool, restaurant, gift shop, and front desk.*

Art of Animation has three themed pools, the largest being **The Big Blue Pool,** which is inspired by *Finding Nemo* and features underwater speakers playing music. Like the other Value resorts, Art of Animation has a central building—**Animation Hall**—which houses check-in, the food court (**Landscape of Flavors**), a gift shop, and an arcade.

While the resort is colorful and very kid-friendly, it has also won over many adults. A New Jersey reader says:

I was skeptical about Art of Animation. From pictures, it looked like it was going to be a child's dream but not necessarily an adult's. I was wrong—it's incredible! For a Value resort, it feels more like a Deluxe. The room was awesome—great layout, and having two bathrooms was so nice. The Big Blue Pool and the Cozy Cone Pool are great. Landscape of Flavors impressed me too—so many options for fresh, delicious comfort food as well as exotic fare.

Transportation from Art of Animation to EPCOT and Hollywood Studios is primarily via the Skyliner. However, lines for the Skyliner can start forming as early as 90 minutes before park opening. Disney does add buses to EPCOT and Hollywood Studios during busy times and when the Skyliner isn't operating. For access to the rest of Walt Disney World, guests must rely on Disney's bus system.

Another consistent issue at Art of Animation is slow Wi-Fi speeds. This Texas reader ran some tests:

*The Disney Wi-Fi speeds in the room (*Lion King *building 10) and by the pool were consistently around 25 Mbps download and 25 Mbps upload. When I stepped just outside our building, I got Disney Wi-Fi speeds of around 10 Mbps, but when I turned off Wi-Fi and used AT&T cellular, I actually got around 95 Mbps downloading.*

We also get many comments about noise and soundproofing issues at Art of Animation.

GOOD (AND NOT-SO-GOOD) ROOMS AT ART OF ANIMATION *(See* **theugseries.com/aoa-views** *for photos.)* The quietest suites are south- and east-facing rooms in **buildings 3** (*Cars*), **4** (*Finding Nemo*), and **6** (*The Lion King*). The quietest standard rooms are east-facing rooms in **building 8** and south-facing rooms in **building 7** (both *The Little Mermaid*). Avoid northwest-facing rooms in **building 1** (*Cars*) and southwest-facing rooms in **building 10** (*The Lion King*), which face the Disney bus route and Art of Animation's bus stops. The *Little Mermaid* buildings (7 and 8) are the lowest-rated at the resort, probably in part because they also have the smallest rooms. Ratings for the all-suite buildings tend to be very close, with the *Lion King* buildings (6 and 10) rated slightly higher than the others.

CAMPING AT WALT DISNEY WORLD

Fort Wilderness Resort & Campground
(See map on pages 170-171.)

STRENGTHS	WEAKNESSES
• Children's play areas	• Isolated location
• Best recreational options at WDW	• Complicated bus service
• Special day and evening programs	• Confusing campground layout
• Campsite amenities	• Lack of privacy
• Shower and toilet facilities	• Very limited on-site dining options
• *Hoop-Dee-Doo Musical Revue* show	• Crowding at beaches and pools
• Convenient self-parking	• Extreme distance to store and restaurant facilities from many cabins and campsites

Unofficial Guide Reader-Survey Results

Percentage of readers who'd stay here again: **Cabins: 85%** (*Below Average*); **Campsites: 100%** (*Above Average*)

Percentage of readers who'd recommend this resort to a friend: **Cabins: 63%** (*Average*); **Campsites: 83%** (*Above Average*)

Overall reader rating: **Cabins: A−; Campsites: A+**

DISNEY'S ONLY CAMPGROUND offers tent and RV camping, as well as fully equipped, air-conditioned cabins that can be rented through the Disney Vacation Club (DVC).

Tent/Pop-Up campsites ($76–$199/night depending on the season) provide water, electricity, and cable TV. **Full Hook-Up** campsites ($116–$242 per night) have all of the above amenities and accommodate large RVs. **Preferred** campsites for tents and RVs ($128–$270 per night) add sewer connections. **Premium** campsites ($138–$280 per night) add an extra-large concrete parking pad. Parking for one vehicle is included in the nightly rate. All campsites accommodate up to 10 people. Sites are level and include picnic tables, waste containers, grills, and free Wi-Fi. Fires are prohibited except in grills. Pets are permitted in some loops for a $5 fee per night.

Campsites are arranged on loops accessible from one of three main roads. There are 28 loops, with loops **100–2100** for tent and RV campers and loops **2200–2800** offering DVC cabins. RV sites are roomy—Premium and Full Hook-Up campsites can accommodate RVs more than 45 feet long—but tent campers will probably feel a bit cramped. (Note that tent stakes cannot be used at the Premium sites due to the concrete.) On any given day, at least 90% of campers are in RVs.

Fort Wilderness offers the widest variety of recreational facilities and activities of any Disney resort. Among them are two arcades; nightly campfire programs; Disney movies; a dinner theater; two swimming pools; a beach; walking paths; bike, boat, and golf-cart rentals; horseback riding; wagon rides; archery lessons; panning for gems; and tennis, basketball, and volleyball courts. There are multiple

continued on page 172

Fort Wilderness Resort & Campground

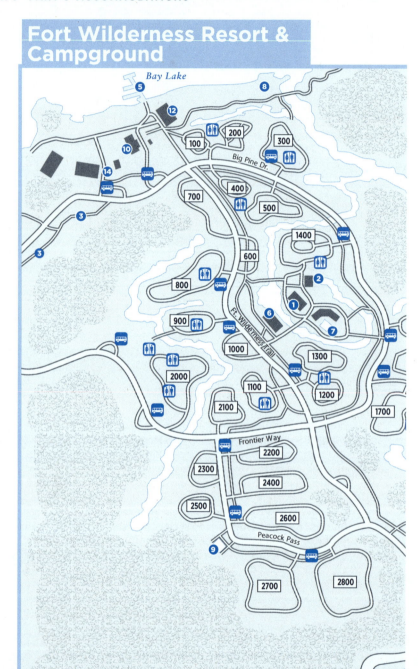

FORT WILDERNESS RESORT & CAMPGROUND MAP

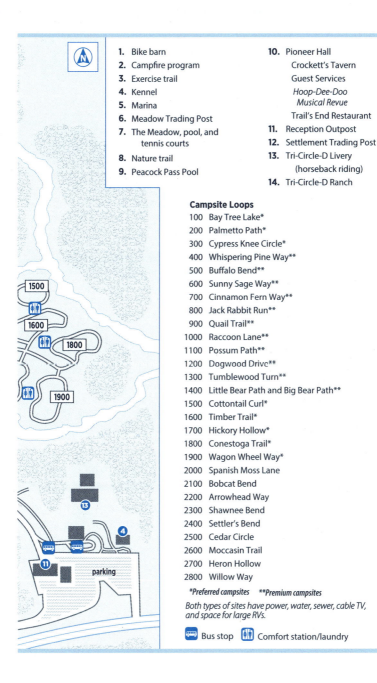

1. Bike barn
2. Campfire program
3. Exercise trail
4. Kennel
5. Marina
6. Meadow Trading Post
7. The Meadow, pool, and tennis courts
8. Nature trail
9. Peacock Pass Pool
10. Pioneer Hall
    Crockett's Tavern
    Guest Services
    Hoop-Dee-Doo Musical Revue
    Trail's End Restaurant
11. Reception Outpost
12. Settlement Trading Post
13. Tri-Circle-D Livery (horseback riding)
14. Tri-Circle-D Ranch

Campsite Loops

100	Bay Tree Lake*	
200	Palmetto Path*	
300	Cypress Knee Circle*	
400	Whispering Pine Way**	
500	Buffalo Bend**	
600	Sunny Sage Way**	
700	Cinnamon Fern Way**	
800	Jack Rabbit Run**	
900	Quail Trail**	
1000	Raccoon Lane**	
1100	Possum Path**	
1200	Dogwood Drive**	
1300	Tumblewood Turn**	
1400	Little Bear Path and Big Bear Path**	
1500	Cottontail Curl*	
1600	Timber Trail*	
1700	Hickory Hollow*	
1800	Conestoga Trail*	
1900	Wagon Wheel Way*	
2000	Spanish Moss Lane	
2100	Bobcat Bend	
2200	Arrowhead Way	
2300	Shawnee Bend	
2400	Settler's Bend	
2500	Cedar Circle	
2600	Moccasin Trail	
2700	Heron Hollow	
2800	Willow Way	

*Preferred campsites **Premium campsites
Both types of sites have power, water, sewer, cable TV, and space for large RVs.

🚌 Bus stop   🚻 Comfort station/laundry

continued from page 169

dining options, but they are far removed from most campsites. Comfort stations with toilets, showers, pay phones, ice machines, and laundry facilities are within walking distance of all campsites.

Access to the Magic Kingdom is by boat from Fort Wilderness Landing and to EPCOT by bus, with a transfer at the Transportation and Ticket Center (TTC) to the EPCOT monorail. During thunderstorms, boat service may be suspended, and Disney will provide buses. An alternate route to the Magic Kingdom is by bus to the TTC, then by monorail or ferry to the park. You can also take a boat to Wilderness Lodge and the Contemporary Resort. Transportation to all other Disney destinations is by bus. Motor traffic within the campground is permitted only when entering or exiting. Get around within the campground by bus, golf cart, or bike—the latter two are available for rent.

If you can't get a DVC cabin, don't own an RV, and don't want to stay in a tent, there are several Disney-approved vendors that rent RVs to guests. We recommend **Ohana Camper Rental** (ohanacamper rentalllc.com). All you have to do is book the campsite and the RV. Then James and Alicia will set everything up for you and give you a quick orientation, including tips for how to make the most of your time at Fort Wilderness. You won't have to worry about setup, hookup, or tear-down, and you get more space and separate sleeping areas for less than you would pay for a Disney resort room.

For tent and RV campers, there's a trade-off between sites that are convenient to amenities and those that are scenic, shady, and quiet. RVers who prefer to be near guest services, the marina, the beach, and the restaurants should go for loops **100, 200, 700,** and **400** (in that order—loop 100 is the highest rated at Fort Wilderness). Loops near the campground's secondary facility area, with a pool, a trading post, bike and golf-cart rentals, and a campfire program, are **1400, 1300, 600, 1000,** and **1500,** in order of preference.

If you're looking for a tranquil, scenic setting among mature trees, we recommend loops **1800, 1900, 1700,** and **1600,** in that order, and west-side sites on the **700** loop. The only loop offering both a lovely setting and proximity to key amenities is **300**. The best loops for tents and pop-up campers are **1500** and **2000,** with 1500 being nearest a swimming pool, a convenience store, and the campfire program.

Avoid most sites within 40 yards of the loop entrance—these are almost always near one of the main traffic paths. Sites on the outside of the loop are almost always preferable to those in the center. All sites are back-in, and the loop access roads are pretty tight and narrow.

Fort Wilderness Cabins

In 2024, Disney converted the Fort Wilderness Cabins to a DVC resort. All 364 cabins were replaced. These new structures look more like modern tiny houses than log cabins, with lots of windows. The footprint stays about the same, with one bedroom, one bathroom, and sleeping accommodations for six people.

Cabins offer a queen bed and bunk bed in the bedroom and a Murphy bed in the living room. The small bathroom has a walk-in shower.

All cabins have air-conditioning, TVs, full kitchens, and dining tables. Housekeeping is provided every other day. A New York family writes:

> We stayed at Fort Wilderness in a cabin because (1) we wanted a separate bedroom area; (2) we wanted a kitchen; (3) our kids are very lively, and the cabins were apart from each other so we wouldn't disturb other guests; and (4) we thought the kids might meet other children to play with. The cabins worked out just right for us. The kids had a ball chasing the little lizards and frogs, kicking around pinecones, sitting on the deck to eat ice pops, and sleeping in bunk beds.

A mother of two from Virginia is also a fan:

> This is the only resort where you're encouraged to go outside and play! You can bike, swim, hike the nature trail, ride a horse, rent a boat, play volleyball, go to the beach, attend a character sing-along and marshmallow roast followed by a classic Disney movie, enjoy multiple playgrounds, play tennis, take a romantic carriage ride, take your first pony ride, and see a wild turkey. Don't forget the view of the fireworks from the beach or the up-close water light parade. With all of this stuff, much of it free or very affordable, who needs the parks?

Bus service at Fort Wilderness leaves much to be desired—in fact, we wouldn't stay there unless we had a car. To go anywhere, you first have to catch an internal bus that makes many, many stops. If your destination is outside Fort Wilderness, you then must transfer to a second bus. To complicate things, buses serving destinations outside the campground depart from two locations, the **Reception Outpost** and **Pioneer Hall.** This means you must keep track of which destinations each transfer center serves. A Washington, DC, family of five writes:

> We generally enjoyed our cabin at Fort Wilderness. It was spacious, with bunk beds for the kids, a separate room for the parents to sleep, and a kitchen. We were very surprised and disappointed, though, when we figured out that we couldn't get anywhere in the resort in a timely fashion without either bikes or a golf cart—otherwise, you spend your day waiting for buses. A quick trip to the pool or the counter-service diner was impossible.

INDEPENDENT HOTELS OF THE DISNEY SPRINGS RESORT AREA

THE FIRST SIX HOTELS of the Disney Springs Resort Area (DSRA) were built when Disney had far fewer resorts of its own. These properties (**DoubleTree Suites by Hilton Orlando–Disney Springs Area, Hilton Orlando Buena Vista Palace, Hilton Orlando Lake Buena Vista, Holiday Inn Orlando–Disney Springs Area, Renaissance Orlando Resort and Spa,** and **Wyndham Garden Lake Buena Vista**) are run by major hotel chains and have little to no theming. The Buena Vista Palace stands out as a more upscale option (with a price to match), but several of these hotels now cater more to convention and business travelers than to vacationing families. A seventh hotel, the **Drury Plaza Hotel Orlando,** opened in late 2022.

The main advantages to staying in the DSRA are as follows:

- The ability to pay for your stay with hotel rewards points
- Access to Early Theme Park Entry benefits
- Being within walking distance of Disney Springs

The Wyndham Garden, Buena Vista Palace, and Holiday Inn are an easy 5- to 15-minute walk from the Marketplace, on the east end of Disney Springs. Guests at DoubleTree Suites, Drury Plaza, and Renaissance Orlando Resort and Spa are about 10 minutes farther.

All DSRA hotels provide shuttles to the Disney parks, but because they use private transportation companies, service is far less reliable than Disney's buses. Shuttles run on inconsistent schedules, may skip certain parks, and can leave guests waiting for up to an hour. A Colorado family of five, for example, found that the Hilton Orlando Lake Buena Vista's shuttle service fell short:

The transportation was unreliable. It did a better job of getting guests back to the hotel from the park than getting them to the park from the hotel. Shuttles from the hotel were randomly timed and went repeatedly to the same parks—skipping others and leaving guests to wait for up to an hour.

For guests with a car, these hotels are only slightly farther from the parks than some Disney-owned resorts. And despite their business-friendly focus, many still try to appeal to vacationing families. Some have pool complexes that rival Disney's, while others offer food courts, all-suite accommodations, and organized kids' activities. All have Disney ticket counters and gift shops, but several have outdated rooms that don't compare well to their Disney counterparts.

The Value Proposition

The benefits that Disney extends to the DSRA hotels—such as Early Theme Park Entry—add to the value of staying in the DSRA, especially for guests who can take advantage of hotel reward programs. Some properties, such as the **Drury Plaza,** offer free hot breakfast—a substantial savings for large families. That said, because of the lack of midday dining options and the poor shuttle service, many readers would be better off at **Disney's Pop Century.**

For those using hotel reward points to pay for their stay, the savings can be substantial—anywhere from $600 to $1,000 per week compared to staying at Pop Century. Also, the **DoubleTree**'s 540-square-foot suites are a standout, offering far more space than a comparable Disney suite for a much lower price, making it an easy decision for those booking with points.

One thing to keep in mind when comparing rates is that DSRA hotels often exclude tax, parking, and resort fees from their advertised prices. These extra charges can add $25–$75 per night to your stay, so be sure to check the total cost before booking (see table on page 176).

DoubleTree Suites by Hilton Orlando–Disney Springs Area ★★½

2305 Hotel Plaza Blvd. | ☎ 407-934-1000 | doubletreeguestsuites.com

LOCATED WITHIN WALKING DISTANCE OF DISNEY SPRINGS, this massive white building isn't much to look at, but it's the only all-suite resort on Disney property. What it lacks in atmosphere it makes up for in space and practicality. The 229 suites are well sized for families. Amenities include a safe, a hair dryer, a minifridge, a microwave, a coffee maker, a foldout sofa bed, and two TVs.

Kids can enjoy a free chocolate-chip cookie at check-in and a small playground. The resort offers a heated pool, children's pool, and whirlpool spa. But traffic noise from I-4 can be heard from the pool deck. Other amenities include a tiny fitness center, a game room, four tennis courts, and an outdoor bar. The **EverGreen Cafe** serves breakfast, lunch, and dinner.

Of all the DSRA hotels, the DoubleTree is the farthest from Disney Springs. It's about half a mile to the closest entrance and a full mile to its center, so expect a 15- to 20-minute walk each way. Transportation to the Magic Kingdom is also inconvenient because the hotel's shuttle drops guests at the Transportation and Ticket Center instead of the park entrance, adding even more travel time.

Drury Plaza Hotel Orlando ★★★½

2000 Hotel Plaza Blvd. | ☎ 407-560-6111 | druryplazahotelorlando.com

ONE OF THE NEWEST ADDITIONS to the DSRA area, the Drury opened in late 2022 and quickly became one of the better values in this part of Walt Disney World. While it lacks elaborate theming, it stands out with modern, well-designed rooms and a list of included amenities that set it apart from other DSRA properties. Drury Plaza offers 604 rooms and suites, all featuring comfortable beds, a minifridge, a microwave, a coffee maker, and a 55-inch flat-screen TV. The suites include a separate living area with a sofa bed, making them a solid choice for families looking for more space.

One of the biggest perks of staying here is the complimentary hot breakfast buffet, a rare offering and a big potential money-saver for families. Guests can also participate in a free evening "5:30 kickback" reception with snacks and drinks, including alcoholic beverages for adults. There's a heated pool with a kids' splash zone, two whirlpools, a fire pit, and a large fitness center. On-site dining includes **The Kitchen + Bar,** which serves lunch and dinner, and a convenience store for grab-and-go items. Perhaps most important of all is that there is no resort fee, which helps keep costs more reasonable compared to other DSRA hotels.

The location is about a 10-minute walk to the Marketplace side of Disney Springs. Complimentary shuttle service runs to all four Disney theme parks—though, like other DSRA hotels, the schedule isn't as frequent or convenient as Disney's own transportation. And at Magic Kingdom you will get dropped off at the Transportation and Ticket Center instead of the park entrance.

Hilton Orlando Buena Vista Palace ★★★

1900 E. Buena Vista Drive | ☎ 407-827-2727 | buenavistapalace.com

HILTON BOUGHT THIS PROPERTY in 2016 and invested substantially in renovating it. It markets the property as a luxury option in the DSRA area, with its high-rise tower, lagoon-style pool, and direct pedestrian bridge to Disney Springs. While the location is undeniably convenient, the rates (plus $74 in nightly resort and parking fees) often make staying at a Disney Moderate resort a better choice.

The hotel features more than 1,000 rooms and suites, all with modern furnishings. Rooms in the main tower offer better views and interiors that feel

AMENITIES AT THE DSRA RESORTS					
HOTEL	CHILDREN'S PROGRAMS	DINING	KID-FRIENDLY	POOL(S)	RECREATION
DOUBLETREE SUITES	None	★★	★★★	★★½	★★½
DRURY PLAZA HOTEL ORLANDO	None	★★½	★★½	★★★	★★★
HILTON ORLANDO BUENA VISTA PALACE	★★½	★★	★★★½	★★★½	★★★★
HILTON ORLANDO LBV	None	★★½	★★½	★★★	★★½
HOLIDAY INN ORLANDO	★★★	★★	★★	★★★	★★
RENAISSANCE ORLANDO	None	★★½	★★½	★★★	★★★
WYNDHAM GARDEN LBV	★★	★★½	★★★	★★★	★★★

WHAT IT COSTS TO STAY IN THE DSRA	
HOTEL	NIGHTLY RATE
DOUBLETREE SUITES BY HILTON ORLANDO	$131–$297
DRURY PLAZA HOTEL	$170–$430
HILTON ORLANDO BUENA VISTA PALACE	$172–$354
HILTON ORLANDO LAKE BUENA VISTA	$189–$361
HOLIDAY INN ORLANDO–DISNEY SPRINGS AREA	$134–$241
RENAISSANCE ORLANDO	$159–$374
WYNDHAM GARDEN LAKE BUENA VISTA	$160–$220

ADDITIONAL FEES AT THE DSRA RESORTS (excludes tax)				
HOTEL	SELF-PARKING	RESORT FEE	INTERNET	TOTAL PER DAY
DOUBLETREE SUITES	$25	$26	Free*	$51
DRURY PLAZA HOTEL	$25	None	Free	$25
HILTON ORLANDO BUENA VISTA PALACE	$35	$39	Free	$74
HILTON ORLANDO LBV	$35	$39	Free	$74
HOLIDAY INN ORLANDO	$25	$39	Free	$64
RENAISSANCE ORLANDO	$30	$45	Free	$75
WYNDHAM GARDEN LBV	$25	$36	Free	$61

* After joining the free Hilton Honors program

more updated. But those in the lower-rise Island buildings feel more dated and even a little run-down. Suites provide extra space, but the price difference rarely justifies the upgrade. Guest reviews mention lackluster housekeeping and inconsistent service, which can make the high price tag feel even steeper.

Where this Hilton stands out is its outdoor recreation. One of the main draws is the large pool complex, which includes a zero-entry pool, a lazy river, and poolside cabanas. The **Shades Bar & Grill** offers poolside dining, and the resort also has a marketplace for grab-and-go food, a Starbucks, and **Letter-Press,** its full-service restaurant. But even with all those options, most guests opt for the short walk over to Disney Springs for meals.

Hilton Orlando Lake Buena Vista–Disney Springs Area ★★★

1751 Hotel Plaza Blvd. | ☎ 407-827-4000 | hilton-wdwv.com

THE ROOMS AT THIS HILTON are clean, comfortable, and some of the closest to Disney Springs, with a pedestrian bridge connecting guests directly to the Marketplace side. However, as is the case at Buena Vista Palace, high nightly rates, resort fees, and parking charges make this hotel a questionable value, especially when compared to Disney's own Moderate resorts, which often cost less and include better perks.

The hotel offers 814 rooms and suites, which look and feel like a standard business hotel rather than a vacation property. Service can also be hit-or-miss, with guests mentioning slow front-desk service.

Like the Buena Vista Palace, pools and dining are both highlights here. There are two heated pools, a whirlpool spa, and a poolside bar. Dining options include **Benihana, Mainstreet Market** (for grab-and-go food), and the casual **Covington Mill** restaurant. But once again, most guests opt for the short walk over to Disney Springs for dining instead.

Holiday Inn Orlando–Disney Springs Resort Area ★★★½

1805 Hotel Plaza Blvd. | ☎ 407-828-8888 | hiorlando.com

LAST RENOVATED IN 2018, the Holiday Inn offers one of the better values among the DSRA hotels. Rooms are comfortable and modern, and the resort is in a good location. While it lacks Disney theming, it's a well-run, family-friendly hotel that delivers a balance of affordability and convenience. If Disney's Value resorts are sold out, this could be a good alternative.

The hotel offers 360-square-foot rooms with pillow-top beds and a 49- or 55-inch flat-screen TV. The well-maintained rooms are cleaner and more modern than those at many nearby budget hotels. The bathrooms are nice, too, with granite countertops and showerheads that offer a choice of comfort sprays. **Palm Breezes Restaurant** serves breakfast and dinner at reasonable prices. The grab-and-go in the lobby sells snacks and sandwiches. Other amenities include a large zero-entry pool and a whirlpool spa.

Renaissance Orlando Resort and Spa ★★
(formerly B Resort & Spa)

1905 Hotel Plaza Blvd. | ☎ 407-282-2828 | theugseries.com/renaissance-orlando

THE RENAISSANCE ORLANDO aims to offer modern accommodations and an upscale feel in the DSRA, but it falls short in several key areas. While the location is fine and the rooms are stylish, inconsistent service, frequent maintenance issues (especially with air-conditioning), and added fees make it a less appealing choice compared to other options in the area. The resort underwent a major rebranding and renovation in 2024, with rooms now featuring sleek, contemporary décor.

The fitness center is serviceable but unremarkable, and while the outdoor pool area is nice, it doesn't compare to those at Disney resorts or other resorts in the area. There's a small on-site restaurant and bar, but dining options are limited, and the lack of a food court means you'll likely be making the hike over to Disney Springs to eat. Unless you find a deeply discounted rate, this resort feels like a mid-tier-at-best hotel with a higher-end price tag. Even if you're part of the Marriott Bonvoy program, you should use your points at the **Walt Disney World Swan, Dolphin,** or **Swan Reserve** instead.

Wyndham Garden Lake Buena Vista ★★½

1850-B Hotel Plaza Blvd. | ☎ 407-842-6644 | wyndhamlakebuenavista.com

THE MAIN REASON TO STAY here is the short walk to Disney Springs. You can also almost always find rock-bottom prices on sites like Priceline. The lobby is bright and airy, and rooms are larger than most, with in-room refrigerators. That said, every time we've stayed here, there have been some maintenance or cleanliness issues, including, most recently, trouble locking the door and multiple dead mosquitoes in a supposedly just-cleaned room. Even for a rate under $100, we won't mess around with safety issues.

Pool-facing rooms in the hotel's wings can be noisy during summer. Elevators are unusually slow—it's faster to walk to the second and third floors, if you are able. As with most off-site resorts, transportation and quick-service dining options score low. Also, readers rate staff service here lower than that at any other resort, Disney-owned or not.

HOW *to* EVALUATE *a* WALT DISNEY WORLD TRAVEL PACKAGE

HUNDREDS OF WALT DISNEY WORLD vacation packages are offered each year. Some are created by the Walt Disney Travel Company, and others are offered through airlines, travel agents, and wholesalers. Most include lodging at or near Disney World, plus theme park tickets, but the details and value vary widely. Prices will be highest during holiday weeks and mid-February through Easter, but you can find great off-season deals, especially at off-site hotels.

Many ads for packages boast something like "5 Days at Walt Disney World from $845." The key word is *from*: That price almost always includes the least expensive lodging, dates, and ticket options. If you want a more desirable hotel, extra perks, or more convenience, expect the price to climb significantly.

Packages can include all sorts of hotels, from dependable Disney resorts to off-property locations of varying quality. Before booking, do some research. Find out when the hotel was last renovated, and verify how close it is to Disney World. If you won't have a car, confirm that the hotel's shuttle service is frequent and reliable.

While package deals sometimes offer savings, they're often bundled with extras that inflate the total price. The best value comes when a package costs less than booking everything separately and you're not paying for anything you wouldn't have purchased anyway. If the total price of the package and individual components is about the same, a package may still be worth it for the convenience of having everything prearranged for you. However, in many cases, you'll save money by booking your hotel, tickets, and transportation separately.

WALT DISNEY TRAVEL COMPANY PACKAGES

DISNEY'S VACATION PACKAGES follow the same pricing structure as its theme park tickets. The longer you stay, the less you'll pay per day.

HOW TO EVALUATE A WDW TRAVEL PACKAGE

Every package starts with a room and theme park tickets, which can be customized based on the number of days you plan to visit the parks. Tickets range from 2 to 10 days (1-day tickets aren't eligible for packages), and the per-day cost decreases with longer stays. See page 66 for details about ticket pricing.

One advantage of Disney's packages is flexibility. You don't need to buy tickets for every day of your hotel stay. If you're staying 7 nights but plan to visit the parks on only 5 days, you can purchase a 5-day ticket instead of paying for days you won't use. You also don't have to commit to extras like Park Hopper in advance because those can be added later if you decide you need or want them.

A basic Disney travel package includes:

- A room at a Disney resort for at least one night, with pricing based on resort category
- Theme park tickets for 2–10 days, customized to match your plans
- Unlimited use of the Disney transportation system
- Free day parking at the theme parks

unofficial **TIP**
Disney vacation packages may include dining plans and sweeteners such as a free round of minigolf and discounts on spa treatments, salon services, and recreational activities like water sports.

Booking Online vs. by Phone

It's much faster to book a Disney resort room online than it is to call Disney reservations (☎ 407-W-DISNEY [934-7639]). If you call, you'll be subjected to a minute or so of recordings covering recent park announcements—press 0 to skip this. Next, you'll go through about 5–10 minutes of answering more than a dozen recorded questions, asking you everything from your name and home address to your favorite color (only kidding about that last one). Slog on through, though, if you actually want to make a reservation. There doesn't seem to be a way to bypass these questions.

DOING THE MATH

COMPARING A DISNEY TRAVEL PACKAGE with purchasing the package components separately is a breeze.

1. Pick a Disney resort and decide how many nights you want to stay.
2. Plan your park days to determine how many days of admission you'll need.
3. When you have both of those things lined up, go online or call the Disney Reservation Center (DRC) at ☎ 407-W-DISNEY (934-7639) and price a package *including tax* for your selected resort and dates. The package will include both admission and lodging. If you're open to working with a Disney-savvy travel agent (we always recommend it), getting a quote from them can help you find any available discounts.
4. To compare costs, check the *room-only* rates for the same resort and dates, either online or by calling Disney. While you're at it, ask about any special room discounts that might apply. Then separately price out your theme park tickets, including tax, making sure to check for any ticket deals. See page 69 for information about saving money on tickets by purchasing from third parties.
5. Add the room-only rates and the ticket prices. Compare this sum to the quote for the package.
6. Keep an eye out for any deals that get released as you're comparing prices or even after you book. Cancellation windows are pretty flexible until eight days before you travel, so you might be able to save money by rebooking.

THROW ME A LINE!

IF YOU BUY A PACKAGE FROM DISNEY, don't expect the reservationists to help you sort out your options. Generally, they respond only to your specific questions, ducking queries that require an opinion. A reader from Illinois complains:

> My wife made two phone calls, and the representatives were very courteous, but they answered only the questions posed and were not eager to give advice on what might be most cost-effective. I feel a person could spend 8 hours on the phone with WDW reps and not have any more input than you get from reading the literature.

HOTELS *outside* WALT DISNEY WORLD

SELECTING AND BOOKING A HOTEL OUTSIDE WALT DISNEY WORLD

LODGING COSTS OUTSIDE Disney World vary greatly. If you shop around, you can find a clean motel with a pool within 20 minutes of the World for as low as $70 a night with tax. But at that price point, you often have to make compromises in either safety or functionality, or both. Really, $120 a night is the new $70 a night if you don't want to make those compromises. There are four primary areas to consider:

1. INTERNATIONAL DRIVE (I-DRIVE) AREA This area about 15–25 minutes northeast of Disney World offers a wide selection of hotels and restaurants. Prices range from $55 to over $400 per night. The chief drawback is the traffic. The stretch of I-Drive between Kirkman and Sand Lake Roads is often gridlocked, especially during morning and evening rush hours. A frequent visitor from New York shared:

> When I visited Disney World last summer, we wasted huge chunks of time in traffic on I-Drive. Our hotel was in the section between the big McDonald's at Sand Lake Road and Volcano Bay at Universal Boulevard. There are practically no left-turn lanes in this section, so anyone turning left can hold up traffic for a long time.

I-Drive hotels are listed on the **Visit Orlando** website: visitorlando.com/places-to-stay (click "International Drive Area").

2. LAKE BUENA VISTA AND THE I-4 CORRIDOR A number of hotels are found along FL 535 and along I-4 between Disney World and I-4's intersection with Florida's Turnpike. This area offers easy interstate access and is close to many restaurants, including those on I-Drive. The **Visit Orlando** website (visitorlando.com) lists most of them.

3. US 192 (IRLO BRONSON MEMORIAL HIGHWAY) This is the highway to Kissimmee, southeast of Walt Disney World. In addition to large full-service hotels, some small, privately owned motels often offer a good value. Dining options are plentiful, but traffic west of the Maingate can get heavy. To avoid congestion east of the Maingate between mile markers 8 and 13, use Osceola Parkway, which runs parallel to US 192 and provides a direct route into Disney World near Animal Kingdom.

HOTELS OUTSIDE WALT DISNEY WORLD

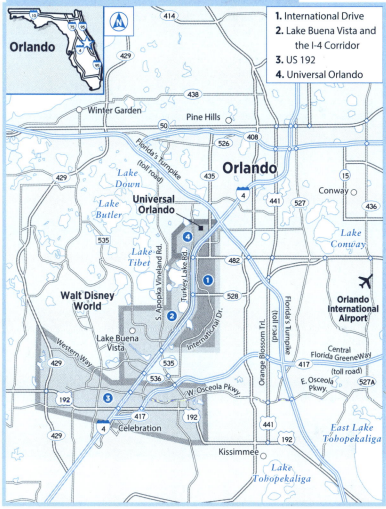

Lodging Areas Around Walt Disney World

1. International Drive
2. Lake Buena Vista and the I-4 Corridor
3. US 192
4. Universal Orlando

Hotels in this area are listed on the **Experience Kissimmee** website (experiencekissimmee.com). This area also includes Disney's value-priced **Flamingo Crossings** resort complex (see page 192).

4. UNIVERSAL ORLANDO AREA In the triangular area bordered by I-4 to the southeast, Vineland Road to the north, and Turkey Lake Road to the west are Universal Orlando and the hotels most convenient to it. Running north–south through the triangle is **Kirkman Road,** which connects to I-4. Unlike I-Drive, traffic here is much lighter, and interstate connections are convenient in both directions. This area is a good option if you plan to split your time between Walt Disney World and Universal Orlando.

DRIVING TIME TO THE PARKS

OUR HOTEL INFORMATION TABLE on pages 194–199 shows the estimated commuting time to the Disney theme parks from various hotels. Those times represent an average of several test runs. Your actual time may be shorter or longer depending on traffic, road construction (if any), and delays at traffic signals.

One important takeaway from the table is that physical proximity isn't always the best predictor of commuting time. For example, hotels on Major Boulevard near Universal Orlando are farther from Disney parks in terms of distance, yet they often have faster commutes than some closer hotels. That's because they have direct access to I-4, cutting down on stop-and-go traffic.

Keep in mind that these commuting times only cover the drive from your hotel to the entrance of the parking lot at each park. They do not include the time needed to park, pay the parking fee, and travel from the lot to the park entrance. Once you park, plan for additional time to reach the actual park entrance. For the Magic Kingdom, add 20–30 minutes for security and either the monorail or ferry from the Transportation and Ticket Center. At EPCOT, add 7–10 minutes to walk from the parking lot. At Hollywood Studios and Animal Kingdom, allow 5–15 minutes to get from the lot to the gate. If you haven't purchased tickets, expect another 10–20 minutes at the ticket booths before entering. For the full picture of commuting within Disney property, including Disney transportation versus driving, refer to the Door-to-Door Commuting Times table on pages 340–341.

HOTEL SHOPPING

OTAS **Online travel agencies** (**OTAs**) sell travel products from a wide assortment of suppliers, often at deep discounts. These sites include **Travelocity, Orbitz, Priceline, Expedia, Hotels.com,** and **Hotwire.**

More Hotel-Hunting Resources

NEW, INDEPENDENT, AND BOUTIQUE-HOTEL DEALS While chain hotels worry about sales costs and profit margins, independent and boutique hotels are concerned about making themselves known to the public. The market is huge, and it's increasingly hard for such hotels to get noticed.

Independent and boutique hotels work on the premise that if they can get you through the front door, you'll become a loyal customer; thus, deep discounts are part of their marketing plan.

AIRBNB This service (airbnb.com) and the similar **Vrbo** (vrbo.com) connect travelers with owner-hosted alternative lodging all over the world, from spare bedrooms in people's homes to private apartments and vacation homes. The incentives Disney offers for staying on-site are hard to beat. That said, Kissimmee is a rapidly growing market for rental services, and you can often find a two-bedroom condo that is a 10-minute drive from most Disney parks for roughly the same price as an on-site Value resort.

Be Careful Out There: Hotel Scams

In a persuasive scam that has been hitting hotels all over the country, a guest receives a phone call from someone claiming that a computer glitch has occurred and that the hotel needs the guest's credit card information again to expedite checkout. Here's what you need to know: A legit hotel won't ask you to provide sensitive information over the phone. If this happens to you, hang up and contact hotel security.

Another scam involves websites that look official and may include the logos of well-known hotel brands. The scammers will sell you a room, paid for in advance with your credit card, and then send you a credible-looking confirmation email. Problem is, they never made the booking *or* they made the booking but failed to pay the hotel.

CONDOMINIUMS AND VACATION HOMES

BECAUSE CONDOS TEND TO BE part of large developments (many of which are time-shares), they usually have amenities that rival those of high-end hotels. Expect features like swimming pools, playgrounds, arcades, fitness centers, and on-site maintenance. Vacation homes managed by rental companies also offer support, though the responsiveness can vary significantly between companies.

Vacation homes tend to be more private and fully self-contained than condos, often featuring a small swimming pool, a hot tub, a garage, a family room, and even a game room or home theater. Both condos and vacation homes usually include full kitchens, laundry rooms, and multiple TVs. However, while almost all rental homes have private pools, they rarely have backyards, meaning kids will mostly be limited to indoor or poolside play.

Time-share condos tend to all have uniform furniture and décor, while individually owned condos and vacation homes reflect the personal taste of their owners. High-rise condos may offer impressive views, while vacation homes, often in suburban subdivisions, typically lack scenic surroundings.

Many readers, such as this New Jersey family of five, rave about the space, privacy, and value of renting a condo or vacation home.

> *I cannot stress enough how important it is if you have a large family (more than two kids) to rent a house for your stay. We stayed at Windsor Hills Resort, 1.5 miles from the Disney Maingate. It took us about 10 minutes to drive there in the a.m., and we had no traffic issues at all.*

How the Vacation-Home Market Works

In the Walt Disney World area, there are more than 26,000 rental homes, including stand-alone homes, single-owner condos, and townhomes. Almost all the rental homes are occupied by their owners for at least a week or two each year; the rest of the year, owners make the homes available for rent. Some owners deal directly with renters, while others use a property-management company.

Incredibly, about 700 property-management companies operate in the Walt Disney World market. This suggests that the lowest rate of all can be obtained by dealing directly with owners, thus eliminating

PART 5 ACCOMMODATIONS

Rental-Home Developments Near WDW

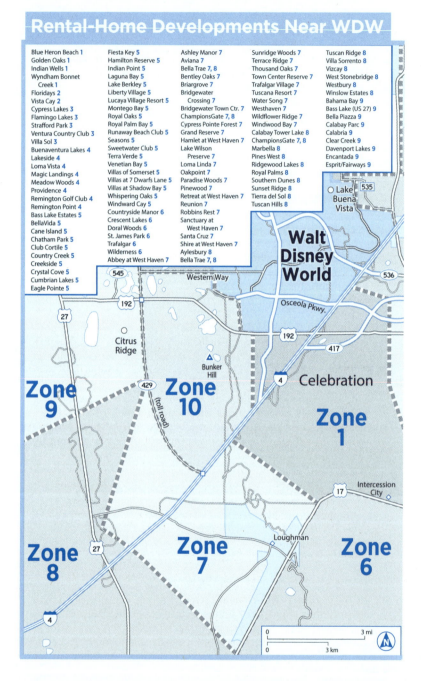

Blue Heron Beach 1
Golden Oaks 1
Indian Wells 1
Wyndham Bonnet Creek 1
Floridays 2
Vista Cay 2
Cypress Lakes 3
Flamingo Lakes 3
Strafford Park 3
Ventura Country Club 3
Villa Sol 3
Buenaventura Lakes 4
Lakeside 4
Loma Vista 4
Magic Landings 4
Meadow Woods 4
Providence 4
Remington Golf Club 4
Remington Point 4
Bass Lake Estates 5
BellaVida 5
Cane Island 5
Chatham Park 5
Club Cortile 5
Country Creek 5
Creekside 5
Crystal Cove 5
Cumbrian Lakes 5
Eagle Pointe 5

Fiesta Key 5
Hamilton Reserve 5
Indian Point 5
Laguna Bay 5
Lake Berkley 5
Liberty Village 5
Lucaya Village Resort 5
Montego Bay 5
Royal Oaks 5
Royal Palm Bay 5
Runaway Beach Club 5
Seasons 5
Sweetwater Club 5
Terra Verde 5
Venetian Bay 5
Villas of Somerset 5
Villas at 7 Dwarfs Lane 5
Villas at Shadow Bay 5
Whispering Oaks 5
Windward Cay 5
Countryside Manor 6
Crescent Lakes 6
Doral Woods 6
St. James Park 6
Trafalgar 6
Wilderness 6
Abbey at West Haven 7

Ashley Manor 7
Aviana 7
Bella Trae 7, 8
Bentley Oaks 7
Briargrove 7
Bridgewater Crossing 7
Bridgewater Town Ctr. 7
ChampionsGate 7, 8
Cypress Pointe Forest 7
Grand Reserve 7
Hamlet at West Haven 7
Lake Wilson Preserve 7
Loma Linda 7
Oakpoint 7
Paradise Woods 7
Pinewood 7
Retreat at West Haven 7
Reunion 7
Robbins Rest 7
Sanctuary at West Haven 7
Santa Cruz 7
Shire at West Haven 7
Aylesbury 8
Bella Trae 7, 8

Sunridge Woods 7
Terrace Ridge 7
Thousand Oaks 7
Town Center Reserve 7
Trafalgar Village 7
Tuscana Resort 7
Water Song 7
Westhaven 7
Wildflower Ridge 7
Windwood Bay 7
Calabay Tower Lake 8
ChampionsGate 7, 8
Marbella 8
Pines West 8
Ridgewood Lakes 8
Royal Palms 8
Southern Dunes 8
Sunset Ridge 8
Tierra del Sol 8
Tuscan Hills 8

Tuscan Ridge 8
Villa Sorrento 8
Vizcay 8
West Stonebridge 8
Westbury 8
Winslow Estates 8
Bahama Bay 9
Bass Lake (US 27) 9
Bella Piazza 9
Calabay Parc 9
Calabria 9
Clear Creek 9
Davenport Lakes 9
Encantada 9
Esprit/Fairways 9

an intermediary. If you're interested in pursuing this route, try finding a condo association's Facebook page (such as Windsor Hills) and connecting with owners that way.

MAP OF RENTAL-HOME DEVELOPMENTS NEAR WDW

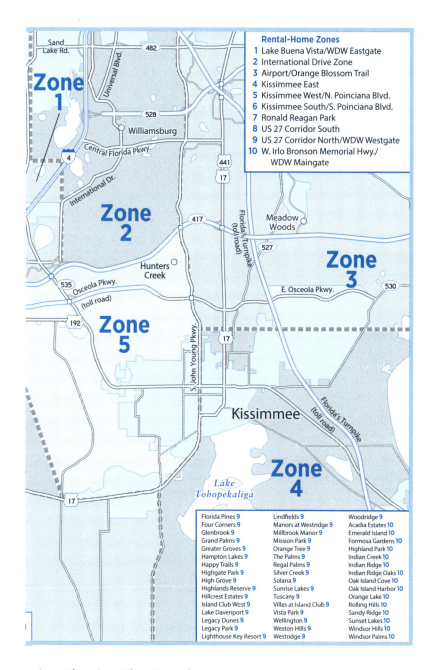

Location, Location, Location

The best vacation home is one that's within easy commuting distance of the theme parks (see map above). If you plan to spend most of your time in the World, the best selection of vacation homes is along **US 192,** south of the park.

To get the most from a vacation home, you need to be close enough to commute in 20 minutes or less to your Orlando destination. This will allow for naps, quiet time, swimming, and money-saving meals you prepare yourself.

Recommended Websites

After checking out dozens of sites, here are a few we recommend.

Florida Dream Homes (floridadreamhomes.com) has a good reputation for customer service and has photos of and information about the homes in its online inventory.

Vrbo (Vacation Rentals by Owner; vrbo.com) is a nationwide vacation-home listing service that puts prospective renters in direct contact with owners. The site is straightforward and always lists a large number of rental properties.

Visit Orlando (visitorlando.com) is the website to check if you're interested in renting a condominium at one of the many time-share developments (click on "Places to Stay" at the site's home page). You can call the developments directly, but going through this site allows you to bypass sales departments and escape their high-pressure invitations to sit through sales presentations. The site also lists hotels, vacation homes, and campgrounds.

THE BEST OFF-SITE HOTELS FOR FAMILIES

WHAT MAKES A SUPER FAMILY HOTEL? For starters, you should look for spacious rooms, free breakfast, an in-room fridge, a great pool, and activities for kids. Narrowed from hundreds of properties, the hotels profiled in the next section, listed by zone and alphabetically, are the best we've found in each area of Orlando. Some are expensive, others are more reasonable, and some are a bargain. All understand a family's needs.

The best square footage for your lodging dollar is often found in a suite. Suites have the advantage of separate bedrooms, allowing tired family members to rest while others stay up.

unofficial **TIP**
Check the resort's room photos to make sure you're booking an actual suite with multiple rooms. Some hotels with *suites* in their name or *all-suite* in their description are little more than slightly larger, single-space-for-everyone rooms with a microwave.

Unofficial Guide readers give low ratings to most off-site hotels' park-transportation options. Though all hotels profiled in the following pages offer some type of shuttle to the theme parks, some offer very limited service, so be sure to research the shuttle schedule before you book. Likewise, most off-site hotels' restaurants won't meet the needs of a family staying for a week, so plan to eat elsewhere.

For the hotels profiled on the following pages, we haven't included detailed descriptions, as we have for the Disney-owned resorts. This is because experiences at off-site hotels are much more variable. If you choose to stay off-site, make sure to do your own research into these recommended options.

I-DRIVE & UNIVERSAL AREAS

IF YOU PLAN ON SPENDING most of your vacation at the new Universal Epic Universe, then the new **Universal's Stella Nova Resort, Universal's Terra Luna Resort,** and **Universal's Helios Grand Hotel** should be your first choices for lodging. Full profiles of many of the following resorts can be found in *The Unofficial Guide to Universal Orlando.*

Hard Rock Hotel Orlando ★★★★

5800 Universal Blvd. | ☎ 407-503-2000 | hardrockhotels.com/orlando
Rate per night $555–$960. **Pool** ★★★★. **Shuttle to parks** Yes (Universal parks, SeaWorld, Aquatica). **Maximum number of occupants per room** 4 (king)/5 (2 queens). **Comments** Pets welcome ($100 flat fee, 2 max). Parking $31/day.

Loews Portofino Bay Hotel at Universal Orlando ★★★★½

5601 Universal Blvd. | ☎ 407-503-1000 | loewshotels.com/portofino-bay-hotel
Rate per night $531–$984. **Pools** ★★★★. **Shuttle to parks** Yes (Universal parks, SeaWorld, Aquatica). **Maximum number of occupants per room** 3 (king)/5 (2 queens). **Comments** Pets welcome ($100 flat fee, 2 max). Parking $31/day.

Loews Royal Pacific Resort at Universal Orlando ★★★★

6300 Hollywood Way | ☎ 407-503-3000 | loewshotels.com/royal-pacific-resort
Rate per night $458–$650. **Pools** ★★★★. **Shuttle to parks** Yes (Universal parks, SeaWorld, Aquatica). **Maximum number of occupants per room** 3 (king)/5 (2 queens). **Comments** Pets welcome ($100 flat fee, 2 max). Parking $31/day.

Loews Sapphire Falls Resort at Universal Orlando ★★★★

6601 Adventure Way | ☎ 407-503-5000 | loewshotels.com/sapphire-falls-resort
Rate per night $254–$305. **Pools** ★★★★. **Shuttle to parks** Yes (Universal parks, SeaWorld, Aquatica). **Maximum number of occupants per room** 3 (king)/5 (2 queens). **Comments** Pets welcome ($100 flat fee, 2 max). Parking $31/day.

Sheraton Vistana Villages Resort Villas, I-Drive/Orlando ★★★½

12401 International Dr. | ☎ 407-238-5000 | theugseries.com/vistana-villages
Rate per night $125–$249. **Pool** ★★★★. **Shuttle to parks** No. **Maximum number of occupants per room** 6 (2-bedroom suite).

Universal's Aventura Hotel ★★★½

6725 Adventure Way | ☎ 407-503-6000 | loewshotels.com/universals-aventura-hotel
Rate per night Standard rooms, $205–$250; Kids' Suites, $327–$501. **Pools** ★★★. **Shuttle to parks** Yes (Universal, SeaWorld, Aquatica). **Maximum number of occupants per room** 4 (2 queens or king with pullout)/6 (Kids' Suites). **Comments** Parking $21/day.

Universal's Cabana Bay Beach Resort ★★★½

6550 Adventure Way | ☎ 407-503-4000 | loewshotels.com/cabana-bay-hotel
Rate per night Standard rooms, $205–$250; suites, $263–$315. **Pools** ★★★★½. **Shuttle to parks** Yes (Universal, SeaWorld, Aquatica). **Maximum number of occupants per room** 4 (standard)/6 (suite). **Comments** Parking $21/day.

Universal's Endless Summer Resort ★★★½

Dockside Inn and Suites: 7125 Universal Blvd. | ☎ 407-503-8000 | loewshotels.com/dockside-inn-and-suites
Surfside Inn and Suites: 7000 Universal Blvd. | ☎ 407-503-7000 | loewshotels.com/surfside-inn-and-suites
Rate per night Standard rooms, $161–$193; suites, $210–$253. **Pools** ★★★. **Shuttle to parks** Yes (Universal, SeaWorld, Aquatica). **Maximum number of occupants per room** 4 (standard)/6 (suites). **Comments** Parking $17/day.

Universal's Helios Grand Hotel ★★★★½

8505 S. Kirkman Road | ☎ 888-430-4999 | loewshotels.com/helios-grand-hotel
Rate per night $300–$600. **Pools** ★★★. **Shuttle to parks** Yes (Universal, SeaWorld, Aquatica). **Maximum number of occupants per room** 5 (2 queens)/3 (king). **Comments** Parking $36/day.

Universal's Stella Nova and Terra Luna Resorts ★★★½

Stella Nova: 4500 Epic Blvd. | ☎ 888-273-1311 | loewshotels.com/stella-nova-resort
Terra Luna: 5500 Epic Blvd. | ☎ 888-273-1311 | loewshotels.com/terra-luna-resort
Rate per night $134–$225. **Pools** ★★★. **Shuttle to parks** Yes (Universal, SeaWorld, Aquatica). **Maximum number of occupants per room** 4 (2 queens). **Comments** Parking $30/day.

LAKE BUENA VISTA & I-4 CORRIDOR

Evermore Orlando Resort ★★★★½

1590 Evermore Way | ☎ 407-239-4700 | evermoreresort.com
Rate per night $499–$1,102. **Pool** ★★★★★. **Shuttle to parks** Yes. **Maximum number of occupants per room** 4 (Conrad hotel on-site) to 32 (11-bedroom homes). **Comments** This newer resort near the Four Seasons caters to a similar clientele. It has hotel rooms, flats, villas, and homes, plus its own water park. Variable resort fee.

Four Seasons Resort Orlando at Walt Disney World Resort ★★★★★

10100 Dream Tree Blvd. | ☎ 407-313-7777 | fourseasons.com/orlando
Rate per night $1,350–$2,715. **Pools** ★★★★★. **Shuttle to parks** Yes. **Maximum number of occupants per room** 4 (3 adults, or 2 adults plus 2 children). **Comments** The best deluxe hotel rooms, staff service, and pool complex in Walt Disney World, if not Orlando. Character breakfast on Thursday and Saturday (with reservation).

Marriott's Harbour Lake ★★★★

7102 Grand Horizons Blvd. | ☎ 407-465-6100 | theugseries.com/harbour-lake
Rate per night 1-bedroom villas, $229–$459; 2-bedroom villas, $259–$499. **Pool** ★★★★. **Shuttle to parks** No. **Maximum number of occupants per room** 4 (1-bedroom)/8 (2-bedroom). **Comments** Rated significantly higher than other suite hotels in the area.

HOTELS OUTSIDE WALT DISNEY WORLD 189

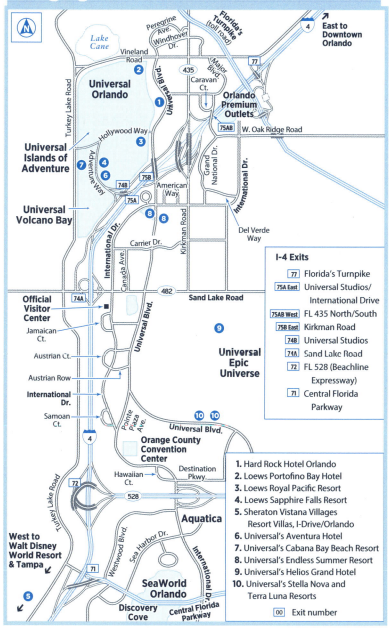

Sheraton Vistana Resort Villas
Lake Buena Vista/Orlando ★★★

8800 Vistana Centre Dr. | ☎ 407-239-3100 | theugseries.com/sheraton-vistana
Rate per night 1-bedroom, $161–$329; 2-bedroom, $219–$389. **Pools** ★★★½. **Shuttle to parks** Yes (Disney). **Maximum number of occupants per villa** 4 (1-bedroom)/8 (2-bedroom). **Comments** These villas are time-shares but are also rented nightly.

Signia by Hilton Orlando Bonnet Creek ★★★½

14100 Bonnet Creek Resort Lane | ☎ 407-597-3600 | hiltonbonnetcreek.com
Rate per night $251–$454. **Pool** ★★★★½. **Shuttle to parks** Yes (Disney). **Maximum number of occupants per room** 4. **Comments** $50/night resort fee. Parking $36/day. Guests are eligible for Early Theme Park Entry benefits.

Sonesta ES Suites Lake Buena Vista ★★★½

8751 Suiteside Dr. | ☎ 407-238-0777 | theugseries.com/sonesta
Rate per night 1-bedroom, $163–$254; 2-bedroom, $189–$304. **Pool** ★★★. **Shuttle to parks** Yes (Disney, Universal); fee applies. **Maximum number of occupants per room** 4 (1-bedroom)/8 (2-bedroom). **Comments** Parking $15/day.

Waldorf Astoria Orlando ★★★★½

14200 Bonnet Creek Resort Lane | ☎ 407-597-5500 | waldorfastoriaorlando.com
Rate per night $407–$854. **Pool** ★★★★. **Shuttle to parks** Yes (Disney). **Maximum number of occupants per room** 4 plus child in crib. **Comments** $50/night resort fee.

US 192 AREA

Gaylord Palms Resort & Convention Center ★★★★

6000 W. Osceola Pkwy. | ☎ 407-586-0000 | gaylordpalms.com
Rate per night $331–$854. **Pool** ★★★★. **Shuttle to parks** Yes (Disney, free; other parks, fee applies). **Maximum number of occupants per room** 4. **Comments** $45/night resort fee. Parking $38/day.

Holiday Inn Club Vacations at Orange Lake Resort ★★★

8505 W. Irlo Bronson Memorial Hwy. (US 192) | ☎ 407-477-7025 | theugseries.com/hi-orange-lake
Rate per night $149–$215. **Pools** ★★★★. **Shuttle to parks** Yes (fee applies). **Maximum number of occupants per room** Varies. **Comments** This is a time-share property, but you can rent directly through the resort. $39/night resort fee.

Margaritaville Resort Orlando ★★★½

8000 Fins Up Circle | ☎ 407-479-0350 | theugseries.com/margarita-orlando
Rate per night Hotel rooms, $201–$279; cottages (1–8 bedrooms), $249–$2,220. **Pool** ★★★★. **Shuttle to parks** No. **Maximum number of occupants per room** 2 (room); 18 (cottage). **Comments** $40/night resort fee. $75/night pet fee ($300 maximum) in hotel, $40/night pet fee in cottages.

Polynesian Isles Resort (Diamond Resorts) ★★★★

3045 Polynesian Isles Blvd. | ☎ 407-396-1622 | polynesianisle.com
Rate per night 1-bedroom villas, $137–$306; 2-bedroom villas, $187–$364. **Pool** ★★★½. **Shuttle to parks** No. **Maximum number of occupants per room** 4 (1-bedroom)/6 (2-bedroom), plus child in crib. **Comments** $15/night resort fee.

HOTELS OUTSIDE WALT DISNEY WORLD

Lodging Area 2: Lake Buena Vista & the I-4 Corridor

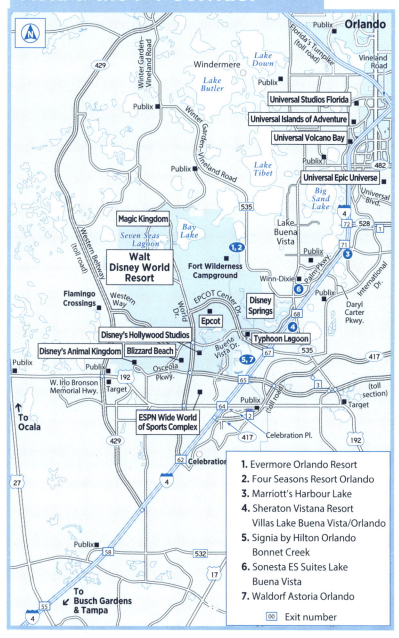

1. Evermore Orlando Resort
2. Four Seasons Resort Orlando
3. Marriott's Harbour Lake
4. Sheraton Vistana Resort Villas Lake Buena Vista/Orlando
5. Signia by Hilton Orlando Bonnet Creek
6. Sonesta ES Suites Lake Buena Vista
7. Waldorf Astoria Orlando

00 Exit number

FLAMINGO CROSSINGS

FLAMINGO CROSSINGS IS LOCATED at the intersection of US 429 and Western Way—less than 60 seconds west of Disney property by car (see map on opposite page). There are five hotels in this area. Two are Hilton properties: **Home2Suites** and **Homewood Suites.** Three are Marriott brands: **Residence Inn, SpringHill Suites,** and the extended-stay **TownePlace Suites.** All have between 220 and 300 rooms.

The brand-related hotels are adjacent and share parking, a huge pool complex, and gyms. Other amenities include practice fields and facilities for the sports groups that participate in events at the ESPN Wide World of Sports Complex. The lobbies are always abuzz with color-coordinated teens either preparing for or unwinding from some event.

In addition to being close to Disney property, the Flamingo Crossings hotels are about a 10-minute drive to a wide variety of retailers on US 192, including Publix, Super Target, and tons of restaurants.

Home2Suites by Hilton ★★★

341 Flagler Ave. | ☎ 407-993-3999 | theugseries.com/fc-home2

Rate per night $177–$280. **Pool** ★★★★. **Shuttle to parks** Yes (Magic Kingdom only, $5). **Maximum number of occupants per room** 6, plus child in crib.

Homewood Suites by Hilton ★★★½

411 Flagler Ave. | ☎ 407-993-3011 | theugseries.com/fc-homewood

Rate per night $177–$280. **Pool** ★★★★. **Shuttle to parks** Yes (Magic Kingdom only, $5). **Maximum number of occupants per room** 4 (1-bedroom suite with king and pull-out beds)/5 (1-bedroom suite with 2 queen and pullout beds), plus child in crib.

Residence Inn ★★★½

2111 Flagler Ave. | ☎ 407-993-3233 | theugseries.com/fc-res-inn

Rate per night Studios, $139–$209; 1-bedroom suites, $219–$343; 2-bedroom suites, $324–$433. **Pool** ★★★★. **Shuttle to parks** No. **Maximum number of occupants per room** 2 (studio)/6 (1-bedroom suite with pull-out sofa)/8 (2-bedroom suite with pull-out sofa).

SpringHill Suites ★★★

13279 Hartzog Road | ☎ 407-507-1200 | theugseries.com/fc-springhill

Rate per night $141–$285. **Pool** ★★★★. **Shuttle to parks** Yes (Magic Kingdom only, $5). **Maximum number of occupants per room** 6, plus child in crib.

TownePlace Suites ★★★

13295 Hartzog Road | ☎ 407-507-1300 | theugseries.com/fc-towne

Rate per night $114–$189. **Pool** ★★★★. **Shuttle to parks** Yes (Magic Kingdom only, $5). **Maximum number of occupants per room** 3 (1-bedroom suite)/5 (2-bedroom suite with 2 queen and pullout beds), plus child in crib.

HOTELS OUTSIDE WALT DISNEY WORLD 193

Lodging Area 3: US 192

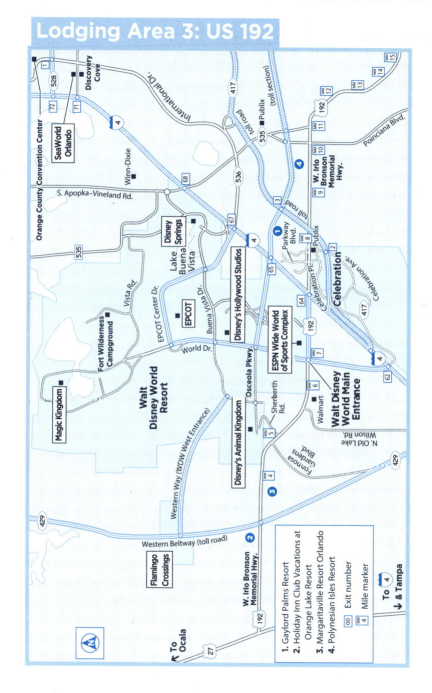

HOTEL INFORMATION TABLE

Bay Lake Tower at Disney's Contemporary Resort
(studios) ★★★★
4600 N. World Dr.
Lake Buena Vista, FL 32830
☎ 407-824-1000
theugseries.com/wdw-bay

LOCATION	WDW
ROOM QUALITY	88
COST ($ = $100)	$+ x 8
DAILY RESORT FEE	None
COMMUTING TIMES TO PARKS *(in minutes)*	
MAGIC KINGDOM	Monorail
EPCOT	09:30
ANIMAL KINGDOM	13:15
DHS	12:15

Boulder Ridge Villas at Disney's Wilderness Lodge (studios)
★★★★
901 Timberline Dr.
Lake Buena Vista, FL 32830
☎ 407-824-3200
theugseries.com/wdw-brv

LOCATION	WDW
ROOM QUALITY	89
COST ($ = $100)	$+ x 6
DAILY RESORT FEE	None
COMMUTING TIMES TO PARKS *(in minutes)*	
MAGIC KINGDOM	Ferry
EPCOT	08:00
ANIMAL KINGDOM	12:15
DHS	10:30

The Cabins at Disney's Fort Wilderness Resort ★★★★
4510 N. Fort Wilderness Trl.
Lake Buena Vista, FL 32830
☎ 407-824-2900
theugseries.com/wdw-cabin

LOCATION	WDW
ROOM QUALITY	89
COST ($ = $100)	$+ x 6
DAILY RESORT FEE	None
COMMUTING TIMES TO PARKS *(in minutes)*	
MAGIC KINGDOM	13:15
EPCOT	08:30
ANIMAL KINGDOM	17:00
DHS	11:00

Disney's All-Star Sports Resort
★★★
1701 W. Buena Vista Dr.
Lake Buena Vista, FL 32830
☎ 407-939-5000
theugseries.com/wdw-assp

LOCATION	WDW
ROOM QUALITY	83
COST ($ = $100)	$$+
DAILY RESORT FEE	None
COMMUTING TIMES TO PARKS *(in minutes)*	
MAGIC KINGDOM	14:00
EPCOT	08:00
ANIMAL KINGDOM	07:00
DHS	08:00

Disney's Animal Kingdom Lodge
★★★★
2901 W. Osceola Pkwy.
Lake Buena Vista, FL 32830
☎ 407-938-3000
theugseries.com/wdw-akl

LOCATION	WDW
ROOM QUALITY	90
COST ($ = $100)	$+ x 6
DAILY RESORT FEE	None
COMMUTING TIMES TO PARKS *(in minutes)*	
MAGIC KINGDOM	17:15
EPCOT	10:45
ANIMAL KINGDOM	03:30
DHS	11:15

Disney's Animal Kingdom Villas
(Jambo House, studios) ★★★★
2901 W. Osceola Pkwy.
Lake Buena Vista, FL 32830
☎ 407-938-3000
theugseries.com/wdw-jam

LOCATION	WDW
ROOM QUALITY	89
COST ($ = $100)	$+ x 6
DAILY RESORT FEE	None
COMMUTING TIMES TO PARKS *(in minutes)*	
MAGIC KINGDOM	17:15
EPCOT	10:45
ANIMAL KINGDOM	03:30
DHS	11:15

Disney's Beach Club Villas (studios)
★★★★
1800 EPCOT Resorts Blvd.
Lake Buena Vista, FL 32830
☎ 407-934-8000
theugseries.com/wdw-bcv

LOCATION	WDW
ROOM QUALITY	90
COST ($ = $100)	$+ x 7
DAILY RESORT FEE	None
COMMUTING TIMES TO PARKS *(in minutes)*	
MAGIC KINGDOM	12:00
EPCOT	Walk or boat
ANIMAL KINGDOM	12:30
DHS	Walk or Skyliner (19:00)

Disney's BoardWalk Inn ★★★★
2101 N. EPCOT Resorts Blvd.
Lake Buena Vista, FL 32830
☎ 407-939-6200
theugseries.com/wdw-bwi

LOCATION	WDW
ROOM QUALITY	88
COST ($ = $100)	$+ x 7
DAILY RESORT FEE	None
COMMUTING TIMES TO PARKS *(in minutes)*	
MAGIC KINGDOM	10:15
EPCOT	Walk or boat
ANIMAL KINGDOM	09:45
DHS	Walk or Skyliner (19:00)

Disney's BoardWalk Villas ★★★★
2101 N. EPCOT Resorts Blvd.
Lake Buena Vista, FL 32830
☎ 407-939-6200
theugseries.com/wdw-bwv

LOCATION	WDW
ROOM QUALITY	88
COST ($ = $100)	$+ x 7
DAILY RESORT FEE	None
COMMUTING TIMES TO PARKS *(in minutes)*	
MAGIC KINGDOM	10:15
EPCOT	Walk or boat
ANIMAL KINGDOM	09:45
DHS	Walk or Skyliner (19:00)

Disney's Grand Floridian Resort & Spa ★★★★½
4401 Floridian Way
Lake Buena Vista, FL 32830
☎ 407-824-3000
theugseries.com/wdw-flo

LOCATION	WDW
ROOM QUALITY	90
COST ($ = $100)	$+ x 9
DAILY RESORT FEE	None
COMMUTING TIMES TO PARKS *(in minutes)*	
MAGIC KINGDOM	Monorail
EPCOT	06:45
ANIMAL KINGDOM	10:45
DHS	08:15

Disney's Old Key West Resort
★★★★
1510 North Cove Road
Lake Buena Vista, FL 32830
☎ 407-827-7700
theugseries.com/wdw-okw

LOCATION	WDW
ROOM QUALITY	89
COST ($ = $100)	$+ x 5
DAILY RESORT FEE	None
COMMUTING TIMES TO PARKS *(in minutes)*	
MAGIC KINGDOM	12:45
EPCOT	08:00
ANIMAL KINGDOM	12:30
DHS	09:30

Disney's Polynesian Village Resort
★★★★½
1600 Seven Seas Dr.
Lake Buena Vista, FL 32830
☎ 407-824-2000
theugseries.com/wdw-poly

LOCATION	WDW
ROOM QUALITY	86
COST ($ = $100)	$+ x 8
DAILY RESORT FEE	None
COMMUTING TIMES TO PARKS *(in minutes)*	
MAGIC KINGDOM	Monorail
EPCOT	07:00
ANIMAL KINGDOM	09:15
DHS	08:30

* Irlo Bronson Memorial Highway   ** Not enough surveys or too new to rate

HOTEL INFORMATION TABLE

Copper Creek Villas & Cabins at Disney's Wilderness Lodge
(studios) ★★★★
901 Timberline Dr.
Lake Buena Vista, FL 32830
☎ 407-824-3200
theugseries.com/wdw-ccv

LOCATION	WDW
ROOM QUALITY	90
COST ($ = $100)	$+ x 6
DAILY RESORT FEE	None
COMMUTING TIMES TO PARKS (in minutes)	
MAGIC KINGDOM	Ferry
EPCOT	08:00
ANIMAL KINGDOM	12:15
DHS	10:30

Disney's All-Star Movies Resort
★★★
1901 W. Buena Vista Dr.
Lake Buena Vista, FL 32830
☎ 407-939-7000
theugseries.com/wdw-asmo

LOCATION	WDW
ROOM QUALITY	81
COST ($ = $100)	$$+
DAILY RESORT FEE	None
COMMUTING TIMES TO PARKS (in minutes)	
MAGIC KINGDOM	16:00
EPCOT	09:00
ANIMAL KINGDOM	08:00
DHS	09:00

Disney's All-Star Music Resort
★★★
1801 W. Buena Vista Dr.
Lake Buena Vista, FL 32830
☎ 407-939-6000
theugseries.com/wdw-asmu

LOCATION	WDW
ROOM QUALITY	82
COST ($ = $100)	$$+
DAILY RESORT FEE	None
COMMUTING TIMES TO PARKS (in minutes)	
MAGIC KINGDOM	15:00
EPCOT	09:00
ANIMAL KINGDOM	08:00
DHS	09:00

Disney's Animal Kingdom Villas
(Kidani Village, studios) ★★★★
3701 W. Osceola Pkwy.
Bay Lake, FL 32830
☎ 407-938-7400
theugseries.com/wdw-kid

LOCATION	WDW
ROOM QUALITY	90
COST ($ = $100)	$+ x 6
DAILY RESORT FEE	None
COMMUTING TIMES TO PARKS (in minutes)	
MAGIC KINGDOM	18:15
EPCOT	11:45
ANIMAL KINGDOM	04:15
DHS	12:15

Disney's Art of Animation Resort
★★★½
1850 Animation Way
Lake Buena Vista, FL 32830
☎ 407-938-7000
theugseries.com/wdw-aoa

LOCATION	WDW
ROOM QUALITY	86
COST ($ = $100)	$$+
DAILY RESORT FEE	None
COMMUTING TIMES TO PARKS (in minutes)	
MAGIC KINGDOM	11:45
EPCOT	Skyliner (15:00)
ANIMAL KINGDOM	08:15
DHS	Skyliner (10:00)

Disney's Beach Club Resort
★★★★
1800 EPCOT Resorts Blvd.
Lake Buena Vista, FL 32830
☎ 407-934-8000
theugseries.com/wdw-bcr

LOCATION	WDW
ROOM QUALITY	83
COST ($ = $100)	$+ x 7
DAILY RESORT FEE	None
COMMUTING TIMES TO PARKS (in minutes)	
MAGIC KINGDOM	12:00
EPCOT	Walk or boat
ANIMAL KINGDOM	12:30
DHS	Walk or Skyliner (19:00)

Disney's Caribbean Beach Resort
★★★½
1114 Cayman Way
Lake Buena Vista, FL 32830
☎ 407-934-3400
theugseries.com/wdw-cbr

LOCATION	WDW
ROOM QUALITY	83
COST ($ = $100)	$$$+
DAILY RESORT FEE	None
COMMUTING TIMES TO PARKS (in minutes)	
MAGIC KINGDOM	14:15
EPCOT	Skyliner (12:00)
ANIMAL KINGDOM	10:00
DHS	Skyliner (7:00)

Disney's Contemporary Resort
★★★★
4600 N. World Dr.
Lake Buena Vista, FL 32830
☎ 407-824-1000
theugseries.com/wdw-con

LOCATION	WDW
ROOM QUALITY	86
COST ($ = $100)	$+ x 7
DAILY RESORT FEE	None
COMMUTING TIMES TO PARKS (in minutes)	
MAGIC KINGDOM	Monorail
EPCOT	09:30
ANIMAL KINGDOM	13:15
DHS	12:15

Disney's Coronado Springs Resort
★★★★
1000 W. Buena Vista Dr.
Lake Buena Vista, FL 32830
☎ 407-939-1000
theugseries.com/wdw-csr

LOCATION	WDW
ROOM QUALITY	89
COST ($ = $100)	$$$+
DAILY RESORT FEE	None
COMMUTING TIMES TO PARKS (in minutes)	
MAGIC KINGDOM	11:15
EPCOT	06:00
ANIMAL KINGDOM	07:15
DHS	05:15

Disney's Polynesian Villas & Bungalows
(studios) ★★★★½
1600 Seven Seas Dr.
Lake Buena Vista, FL 32830
☎ 407-824-2000
theugseries.com/wdw-pvb

LOCATION	WDW
ROOM QUALITY	87
COST ($ = $100)	$+ x 8
DAILY RESORT FEE	None
COMMUTING TIMES TO PARKS (in minutes)	
MAGIC KINGDOM	Monorail
EPCOT	07:00
ANIMAL KINGDOM	09:15
DHS	08:30

Disney's Pop Century Resort
★★★
1050 Century Dr.
Lake Buena Vista, FL 32830
☎ 407-938-4000
theugseries.com/wdw-pop

LOCATION	WDW
ROOM QUALITY	79
COST ($ = $100)	$$+
DAILY RESORT FEE	None
COMMUTING TIMES TO PARKS (in minutes)	
MAGIC KINGDOM	13:30
EPCOT	Skyliner (15:00)
ANIMAL KINGDOM	09:15
DHS	Skyliner (10:00)

Disney's Port Orleans Resort–French Quarter
★★★½
2201 Orleans Dr.
Lake Buena Vista, FL 32830
☎ 407-934-5000
theugseries.com/wdw-frq

LOCATION	WDW
ROOM QUALITY	88
COST ($ = $100)	$$$+
DAILY RESORT FEE	None
COMMUTING TIMES TO PARKS (in minutes)	
MAGIC KINGDOM	11:00
EPCOT	08:00
ANIMAL KINGDOM	11:15
DHS	10:30

Note: Commuting times represent only the driving time to and from the parking lot entrance. You'll need to add some time (varies by park) for paying your parking fee and parking. See page 182 for details.

PART 5 ACCOMMODATIONS

HOTEL INFORMATION TABLE (continued)

Disney's Port Orleans Resort–Riverside ★★★½
1251 Riverside Dr.
Lake Buena Vista, FL 32830
☎ 407-934-6000
theugseries.com/wdw-por

LOCATION	WDW
ROOM QUALITY	86
COST ($ = $100)	$$$+
DAILY RESORT FEE	None
COMMUTING TIMES TO PARKS (in minutes):	
MAGIC KINGDOM	10:30
EPCOT	08:00
ANIMAL KINGDOM	11:45
DHS	09:30

Disney's Riviera Resort ★★★★½
1080 Esplanade Ave.
Lake Buena Vista, FL 32830
☎ 407-828-7030
theugseries.com/wdw-riv

LOCATION	WDW
ROOM QUALITY	95
COST ($ = $100)	$+ x 8
DAILY RESORT FEE	None
COMMUTING TIMES TO PARKS (in minutes):	
MAGIC KINGDOM	12:00
EPCOT	Skyliner (08:00)
ANIMAL KINGDOM	09:15
DHS	Skyliner (14:00)

Disney's Saratoga Springs Resort & Spa ★★★★
1960 Broadway
Lake Buena Vista, FL 32830
☎ 407-827-1100
theugseries.com/wdw-ssr

LOCATION	WDW
ROOM QUALITY	91
COST ($ = $100)	$+ x 5
DAILY RESORT FEE	None
COMMUTING TIMES TO PARKS (in minutes):	
MAGIC KINGDOM	13:45
EPCOT	08:45
ANIMAL KINGDOM	15:15
DHS	12:30

Drury Plaza Hotel Orlando ★★★½
2000 Hotel Plaza Blvd.
Lake Buena Vista, FL 32830
☎ 407-560-6111
druryplazahotelorlando.com

LOCATION	WDW
ROOM QUALITY	93
COST ($ = $100)	$$$+
DAILY RESORT FEE	None
COMMUTING TIMES TO PARKS (in minutes):	
MAGIC KINGDOM	14:45
EPCOT	09:00
ANIMAL KINGDOM	11:00
DHS	11:30

Evermore Orlando Resort ★★★★
1590 Evermore Way
☎ 407-239-4700
evermoreresort.com

LOCATION	WDW
ROOM QUALITY	**
COST ($ = $100)	$+ x 5
DAILY RESORT FEE	Varies
COMMUTING TIMES TO PARKS (in minutes):	
MAGIC KINGDOM	16:00
EPCOT	13:00
ANIMAL KINGDOM	17:00
DHS	16:00

Four Seasons Resort Orlando at Walt Disney World Resort ★★★★★
10100 Dream Tree Blvd.
Lake Buena Vista, FL 32836
☎ 407-313-7777
fourseasons.com/orlando

LOCATION	WDW
ROOM QUALITY	96
COST ($ = $100)	$+ x 14
DAILY RESORT FEE	None
COMMUTING TIMES TO PARKS (in minutes):	
MAGIC KINGDOM	10:00
EPCOT	09:00
ANIMAL KINGDOM	14:00
DHS	13:00

Hilton Orlando Lake Buena Vista–Disney Springs Area ★★★
1751 Hotel Plaza Blvd.
Lake Buena Vista, FL 32830
☎ 407-827-4000
hilton-wdwv.com

LOCATION	WDW
ROOM QUALITY	79
COST ($ = $100)	$$+
DAILY RESORT FEE	$39
COMMUTING TIMES TO PARKS (in minutes):	
MAGIC KINGDOM	13:00
EPCOT	08:00
ANIMAL KINGDOM	13:15
DHS	09:15

Holiday Inn Club Vacations at Orange Lake Resort ★★★
8505 W. US 192*
Kissimmee, FL 34747
☎ 407-477-7025
theugseries.com/hi-orange-lake

LOCATION	3
ROOM QUALITY	**
COST ($ = $100)	$$+
DAILY RESORT FEE	$39
COMMUTING TIMES TO PARKS (in minutes):	
MAGIC KINGDOM	22:00
EPCOT	19:15
ANIMAL KINGDOM	15:15
DHS	17:15

Holiday Inn Orlando–Disney Springs Resort Area ★★★½
1805 Hotel Plaza Blvd.
Lake Buena Vista, FL 32830
☎ 407-828-8888
hiorlando.com

LOCATION	WDW
ROOM QUALITY	82
COST ($ = $100)	$$
DAILY RESORT FEE	$39
COMMUTING TIMES TO PARKS (in minutes):	
MAGIC KINGDOM	12:15
EPCOT	10:00
ANIMAL KINGDOM	10:15
DHS	10:30

Loews Royal Pacific Resort at Universal Orlando ★★★★
6300 Hollywood Way
Orlando, FL 32819
☎ 407-503-3000
loewshotels.com/royal-pacific-resort

LOCATION	4
ROOM QUALITY	84
COST ($ = $100)	$+ x 5
DAILY RESORT FEE	None
COMMUTING TIMES TO PARKS (in minutes):	
MAGIC KINGDOM	21:45
EPCOT	18:15
ANIMAL KINGDOM	20:15
DHS	19:45

Loews Sapphire Falls Resort at Universal Orlando ★★★★
6601 Adventure Way
Orlando, FL 32819
☎ 407-503-5000
loewshotels.com/sapphire-falls-resort

LOCATION	4
ROOM QUALITY	87
COST ($ = $100)	$ x 4
DAILY RESORT FEE	None
COMMUTING TIMES TO PARKS (in minutes):	
MAGIC KINGDOM	20:00
EPCOT	16:15
ANIMAL KINGDOM	18:15
DHS	17:45

Margaritaville Resort Orlando ★★★½
8000 Fins Up Circle
Kissimmee, FL 34747
☎ 407-479-0750
theugseries.com/margarita-orlando

LOCATION	3
ROOM QUALITY	**
COST ($ = $100)	$$+
DAILY RESORT FEE	$40
COMMUTING TIMES TO PARKS (in minutes):	
MAGIC KINGDOM	19:00
EPCOT	15:45
ANIMAL KINGDOM	15:00
DHS	14:00

* Irlo Bronson Memorial Highway ** Not enough surveys or too new to rate

HOTEL INFORMATION TABLE

Disney's Wilderness Lodge ★★★★
901 Timberline Dr.
Lake Buena Vista, FL 32830
☎ 407-824-3200
theugseries.com/wdw-wil

LOCATION	WDW
ROOM QUALITY	87
COST ($ = $100)	$+ x 6
DAILY RESORT FEE	None
COMMUTING TIMES TO PARKS	*(in minutes):*
MAGIC KINGDOM	Ferry
EPCOT	08:00
ANIMAL KINGDOM	12:15
DHS	10:30

Disney's Yacht Club Resort ★★★★
1700 EPCOT Resorts Blvd.
Lake Buena Vista, FL 32830
☎ 407-934-7000
theugseries.com/wdw-ycr

LOCATION	WDW
ROOM QUALITY	88
COST ($ = $100)	$+ x 7
DAILY RESORT FEE	None
COMMUTING TIMES TO PARKS	*(in minutes):*
MAGIC KINGDOM	11:15
EPCOT	07:15
ANIMAL KINGDOM	10:45
DHS	05:15

DoubleTree Suites by Hilton Orlando–Disney Springs Area ★★½
2305 Hotel Plaza Blvd.
Lake Buena Vista, FL 32830
☎ 407-934-1000
doubletreeguestsuites.com

LOCATION	WDW
ROOM QUALITY	87
COST ($ = $100)	$$
DAILY RESORT FEE	$26
COMMUTING TIMES TO PARKS	*(in minutes):*
MAGIC KINGDOM	13:00
EPCOT	08:30
ANIMAL KINGDOM	11:30
DHS	11:00

Gaylord Palms Resort & Convention Center ★★★★
6000 W. Osceola Pkwy.
Kissimmee, FL 34746
☎ 407-586-0000
gaylordpalms.com

LOCATION	3
ROOM QUALITY	**
COST ($ = $100)	$$$$+
DAILY RESORT FEE	$45
COMMUTING TIMES TO PARKS	*(in minutes):*
MAGIC KINGDOM	11:00
EPCOT	07:45
ANIMAL KINGDOM	07:00
DHS	07:15

Hard Rock Hotel Orlando ★★★★
5800 Universal Blvd.
Orlando, FL 32819
☎ 407-503-2000
hardrockhotels.com/orlando

LOCATION	4
ROOM QUALITY	84
COST ($ = $100)	$+ x 6
DAILY RESORT FEE	None
COMMUTING TIMES TO PARKS	*(in minutes):*
MAGIC KINGDOM	24:00
EPCOT	19:00
ANIMAL KINGDOM	21:00
DHS	20:30

Hilton Orlando Buena Vista Palace ★★★
1900 E. Buena Vista Dr.
Lake Buena Vista, FL 32830
☎ 407-827-2727
buenavistapalace.com

LOCATION	WDW
ROOM QUALITY	87
COST ($ = $100)	$$$+
DAILY RESORT FEE	$39
COMMUTING TIMES TO PARKS	*(in minutes):*
MAGIC KINGDOM	13:00
EPCOT	08:00
ANIMAL KINGDOM	13:15
DHS	09:15

Home2Suites by Hilton Orlando at Flamingo Crossings Town Center ★★★
341 Flagler Ave.
Winter Garden, FL 34787
☎ 407-993-3999
theugseries.com/fc-home2

LOCATION	2
ROOM QUALITY	**
COST ($ = $100)	$$$-
DAILY RESORT FEE	None
COMMUTING TIMES TO PARKS	*(in minutes):*
MAGIC KINGDOM	16:45
EPCOT	13:00
ANIMAL KINGDOM	12:00
DHS	11:30

Homewood Suites by Hilton at Flamingo Crossings ★★★½
411 Flagler Ave.
Winter Garden, FL 34787
☎ 407-993-3011
theugseries.com/fc-homewood

LOCATION	2
ROOM QUALITY	**
COST ($ = $100)	$$$-
DAILY RESORT FEE	None
COMMUTING TIMES TO PARKS	*(in minutes):*
MAGIC KINGDOM	17:00
EPCOT	13:00
ANIMAL KINGDOM	11:00
DHS	12:00

Loews Portofino Bay Hotel at Universal Orlando ★★★★½
5601 Universal Blvd.
Orlando, FL 32819
☎ 407-503-1000
loewshotels.com/portofino-bay-hotel

LOCATION	4
ROOM QUALITY	87
COST ($ = $100)	$ x 6
DAILY RESORT FEE	None
COMMUTING TIMES TO PARKS	*(in minutes):*
MAGIC KINGDOM	24:00
EPCOT	19:45
ANIMAL KINGDOM	22:15
DHS	22:15

Marriott's Harbour Lake ★★★★
7102 Grand Horizons Blvd.
Orlando, FL 32821
☎ 407-465-6100
theugseries.com/harbour-lake

LOCATION	2
ROOM QUALITY	**
COST ($ = $100)	$$+
DAILY RESORT FEE	None
COMMUTING TIMES TO PARKS	*(in minutes):*
MAGIC KINGDOM	17:00
EPCOT	13:45
ANIMAL KINGDOM	15:45
DHS	15:15

Polynesian Isles Resort (Diamond Resorts) ★★★★
3045 Polynesian Isles Blvd.
Kissimmee, FL 34746
☎ 407-396-1622
polynesianisle.com

LOCATION	3
ROOM QUALITY	**
COST ($ = $100)	$$-$$$
DAILY RESORT FEE	$15
COMMUTING TIMES TO PARKS	*(in minutes):*
MAGIC KINGDOM	17:15
EPCOT	13:15
ANIMAL KINGDOM	13:30
DHS	14:00

Renaissance Orlando Resort and Spa (formerly B Resort & Spa) ★★
1905 Hotel Plaza Blvd.
Lake Buena Vista, FL 32830
☎ 407-828-2828
theugseries.com/renaissance-orlando

LOCATION	WDW
ROOM QUALITY	76
COST ($ = $100)	$$+
DAILY RESORT FEE	$45
COMMUTING TIMES TO PARKS	*(in minutes):*
MAGIC KINGDOM	12:45
EPCOT	09:00
ANIMAL KINGDOM	11:15
DHS	10:45

Note: Commuting times represent only the driving time to and from the entrance of the parking lot. Add some time (varies by park) for paying your parking fee and parking. See page 182 for details.

HOTEL INFORMATION TABLE (continued)

Residence Inn Orlando Flamingo Crossings Town Center ★★★½
2111 Flagler Ave.
Winter Garden, FL 34787
☎ 407-993-3233
theugseries.com/fc-res-inn

LOCATION	2
ROOM QUALITY	**
COST ($ = $100)	$+
DAILY RESORT FEE	None
COMMUTING TIMES TO PARKS (in minutes):	
MAGIC KINGDOM	17:00
EPCOT	09:15
ANIMAL KINGDOM	13:00
DHS	13:00

Shades of Green ★★★★
1950 W. Magnolia Palm Dr.
Lake Buena Vista, FL 32830
☎ 407-824-3400
shadesofgreen.org

LOCATION	WDW
ROOM QUALITY	94
COST ($ = $100)	$+
DAILY RESORT FEE	None
COMMUTING TIMES TO PARKS (in minutes):	
MAGIC KINGDOM	06:30
EPCOT	07:45
ANIMAL KINGDOM	11:00
DHS	10:15

Sheraton Vistana Resort Villas, Lake Buena Vista ★★★
8800 Vistana Centre Dr.
Orlando, FL 32821
☎ 407-239-3100
theugseries.com/sheraton-vistana

LOCATION	2
ROOM QUALITY	**
COST ($ = $100)	$$+
DAILY RESORT FEE	None
COMMUTING TIMES TO PARKS (in minutes):	
MAGIC KINGDOM	11:15
EPCOT	07:00
ANIMAL KINGDOM	11:15
DHS	09:45

SpringHill Suites Orlando at Flamingo Crossings ★★★
13279 Hartzog Road
Winter Garden, FL 34787
☎ 407-507-1200
theugseries.com/fc-springhill

LOCATION	2
ROOM QUALITY	**
COST ($ = $100)	$+
DAILY RESORT FEE	None
COMMUTING TIMES TO PARKS (in minutes):	
MAGIC KINGDOM	16:00
EPCOT	13:00
ANIMAL KINGDOM	11:30
DHS	11:15

TownePlace Suites Orlando at Flamingo Crossings ★★★
13295 Hartzog Road
Winter Garden, FL 34787
☎ 407-507-1300
theugseries.com/fc-towne

LOCATION	2
ROOM QUALITY	**
COST ($ = $100)	$+
DAILY RESORT FEE	None
COMMUTING TIMES TO PARKS (in minutes):	
MAGIC KINGDOM	16:00
EPCOT	13:00
ANIMAL KINGDOM	11:30
DHS	11:15

Treehouse Villas at Disney's Saratoga Springs Resort & Spa ★★★★
1960 Broadway
Lake Buena Vista, FL 32830
☎ 407-827-1100
theugseries.com/wdw-ssr

LOCATION	WDW
ROOM QUALITY	94
COST ($ = $100)	$+ x 15
DAILY RESORT FEE	None
COMMUTING TIMES TO PARKS (in minutes):	
MAGIC KINGDOM	10:45
EPCOT	07:15
ANIMAL KINGDOM	11:45
DHS	09:30

Universal's Endless Summer Resort: Surfside Inn & Suites ★★★½
7000 Universal Blvd.
Orlando, FL 32819
☎ 407-503-7000
loewshotels.com/surfside-inn-and-suites

LOCATION	4
ROOM QUALITY	86
COST ($ = $100)	$+
DAILY RESORT FEE	None
COMMUTING TIMES TO PARKS (in minutes):	
MAGIC KINGDOM	23:00
EPCOT	18:00
ANIMAL KINGDOM	18:00
DHS	17:00

The Villas at Disney's Grand Floridian Resort & Spa ★★★★★
4401 Floridian Way
Lake Buena Vista, FL 32830
☎ 407-824-3000
theugseries.com/wdw-gfv

LOCATION	WDW
ROOM QUALITY	90
COST ($ = $100)	$+ x 10
DAILY RESORT FEE	None
COMMUTING TIMES TO PARKS (in minutes):	
MAGIC KINGDOM	Monorail
EPCOT	06:45
ANIMAL KINGDOM	10:45
DHS	08:15

Waldorf Astoria Orlando ★★★★½
14200 Bonnet Creek Resort Lane
Orlando, FL 32821
☎ 407-597-5500
waldorfastoriaorlando.com

LOCATION	WDW
ROOM QUALITY	**
COST ($ = $100)	$+ x 5
DAILY RESORT FEE	$50
COMMUTING TIMES TO PARKS (in minutes):	
MAGIC KINGDOM	16:00
EPCOT	12:00
ANIMAL KINGDOM	14:15
DHS	10:15

Wyndham Garden Lake Buena Vista ★★★½
1850-B Hotel Plaza Blvd.
Lake Buena Vista, FL 32830
☎ 407-842-6644
wyndhamlakebuenavista.com

LOCATION	WDW
ROOM QUALITY	83
COST ($ = $100)	$+
DAILY RESORT FEE	$36
COMMUTING TIMES TO PARKS (in minutes):	
MAGIC KINGDOM	4:15
EPCOT	09:45
ANIMAL KINGDOM	14:45
DHS	12:15

Universal's Helios Grand Hotel
★★★★½
8505 S. Kirkman Road
Orlando, FL 32819
☎ 689-218-1000
loewshotels.com/helios-grand-hotel

LOCATION	4
ROOM QUALITY	**
COST ($ = $100)	Unavailable
DAILY RESORT FEE	None
COMMUTING TIMES TO PARKS (in minutes):	
MAGIC KINGDOM	15:15
EPCOT	16:45
ANIMAL KINGDOM	19:45
DHS	17:15

Universal's Stella Nova Hotel
★★★½
4500 Epic Blvd.
Orlando, FL 32819
☎ 689-218-2000
loewshotels.com/stella-nova-resort

LOCATION	4
ROOM QUALITY	76
COST ($ = $100)	$+
DAILY RESORT FEE	None
COMMUTING TIMES TO PARKS (in minutes):	
MAGIC KINGDOM	17:15
EPCOT	15:45
ANIMAL KINGDOM	19:45
DHS	17:15

* Irlo Bronson Memorial Highway ** Not enough surveys or too new to rate

HOTEL INFORMATION TABLE

Sheraton Vistana Villages Resort Villas, I-Drive/Orlando ★★★½
12401 International Dr.
Orlando, FL 32821
☎ 407-238-5000
theugseries.com/vistana-villages

LOCATION	1
ROOM QUALITY	**
COST ($ = $100)	$$+
DAILY RESORT FEE	None
COMMUTING TIMES TO PARKS (in minutes):	
MAGIC KINGDOM	20:15
EPCOT	17:30
ANIMAL KINGDOM	19:30
DHS	19:00

Signia by Hilton Orlando Bonnet Creek ★★★½
14100 Bonnet Creek Resort Lane
Orlando, FL 32821
☎ 407-597-3600
hiltonbonnetcreek.com

LOCATION	WDW
ROOM QUALITY	**
COST ($ = $100)	$$+
DAILY RESORT FEE	$50
COMMUTING TIMES TO PARKS (in minutes):	
MAGIC KINGDOM	14:00
EPCOT	09:45
ANIMAL KINGDOM	13:30
DHS	08:30

Sonesta ES Suites Lake Buena Vista ★★★½
8751 Suiteside Dr.
Orlando, FL 32836
☎ 407-238-0777
theugseries.com/sonesta

LOCATION	2
ROOM QUALITY	**
COST ($ = $100)	$+
DAILY RESORT FEE	None
COMMUTING TIMES TO PARKS (in minutes):	
MAGIC KINGDOM	17:00
EPCOT	15:00
ANIMAL KINGDOM	16:00
DHS	15:00

Universal's Aventura Hotel ★★★½
6725 Adventure Way
Orlando, FL 32819
☎ 407-503-6000
loewshotels.com/universals-aventura-hotel

LOCATION	4
ROOM QUALITY	86
COST ($ = $100)	$$+
DAILY RESORT FEE	None
COMMUTING TIMES TO PARKS (in minutes):	
MAGIC KINGDOM	20:00
EPCOT	16:00
ANIMAL KINGDOM	18:00
DHS	18:00

Universal's Cabana Bay Beach Resort ★★★½
6550 Adventure Way
Orlando, FL 32819
☎ 407-503-4000
loewshotels.com/cabana-bay-hotel

LOCATION	4
ROOM QUALITY	84
COST ($ = $100)	$$+
DAILY RESORT FEE	None
COMMUTING TIMES TO PARKS (in minutes):	
MAGIC KINGDOM	20:00
EPCOT	16:00
ANIMAL KINGDOM	18:00
DHS	18:00

Universal's Endless Summer Resort: Dockside Inn & Suites ★★★½
7125 Universal Blvd.
Orlando, FL 32819
☎ 407-503-8000
loewshotels.com/dockside-inn-and-suites

LOCATION	4
ROOM QUALITY	81
COST ($ = $100)	$+
DAILY RESORT FEE	None
COMMUTING TIMES TO PARKS (in minutes):	
MAGIC KINGDOM	22:00
EPCOT	17:00
ANIMAL KINGDOM	17:00
DHS	17:00

Walt Disney World Dolphin ★★★½
1500 EPCOT Resorts Blvd.
Lake Buena Vista, FL 32830
☎ 407-934-4000
swandolphin.com

LOCATION	WDW
ROOM QUALITY	83
COST ($ = $100)	$$$+
DAILY RESORT FEE	$50
COMMUTING TIMES TO PARKS (in minutes):	
MAGIC KINGDOM	08:45
EPCOT	Walk or boat
ANIMAL KINGDOM	09:15
DHS	Walk or Skyliner (19:00)

Walt Disney World Swan ★★★½
1200 EPCOT Resorts Blvd.
Lake Buena Vista, FL 32830
☎ 407-934-3000
swandolphin.com

LOCATION	WDW
ROOM QUALITY	86
COST ($ = $100)	$$$+
DAILY RESORT FEE	$50
COMMUTING TIMES TO PARKS (in minutes):	
MAGIC KINGDOM	08:45
EPCOT	Walk or boat
ANIMAL KINGDOM	09:15
DHS	Walk or Skyliner (19:00)

Walt Disney World Swan Reserve ★★★★
1255 EPCOT Resorts Blvd.
Lake Buena Vista, FL 32830
☎ 407-934-3000
swandolphin.com

LOCATION	WDW
ROOM QUALITY	91
COST ($ = $100)	$$$+
DAILY RESORT FEE	$50
COMMUTING TIMES TO PARKS (in minutes):	
MAGIC KINGDOM	08:45
EPCOT	Walk or boat
ANIMAL KINGDOM	09:15
DHS	Walk or Skyliner (19:00)

Universal's Terra Luna Hotel ★★★½
5500 Epic Blvd.
Orlando, FL 32819
☎ 689-218-3000
loewshotels.com/stella-nova-resort

LOCATION	4
ROOM QUALITY	**
COST ($ = $100)	$+
DAILY RESORT FEE	None
COMMUTING TIMES TO PARKS (in minutes):	
MAGIC KINGDOM	16:15
EPCOT	14:45
ANIMAL KINGDOM	18:45
DHS	16:15

Note: Commuting times represent only the driving time to and from the entrance of the parking lot. Add some time (varies by park) for paying your parking fee and parking. See page 182 for details.

PART 6

DINING *in* AND *around* WALT DISNEY WORLD

KEY QUESTIONS ANSWERED IN THIS CHAPTER

- What are the best restaurants in Walt Disney World? *(page 202)*
- What kinds of restaurants are in Walt Disney World? *(page 203)*
- Is the Disney Dining Plan worth it? *(page 205)*
- Do I need to make reservations for Disney's restaurants? *(page 207)*
- How and when should I make reservations? *(page 208)*
- Do I need a theme park ticket to eat at a restaurant inside a Disney theme park? *(page 212)*

THIS SECTION AIMS TO HELP YOU FIND GREAT FOOD worth the effort of getting a reservation and the price you'll pay. More than 200 restaurants—including around 90 table-service establishments, around 30 of which are in the theme parks—operate within Walt Disney World. These restaurants offer exceptional variety, serving everything from Moroccan lamb to Texas barbecue, but not every meal justifies its cost. With our help you can navigate the options and discover the best dining choices in every corner of the World.

OUR APPROACH *to* DINING:
Reader Surveys plus Expert Opinions

WHAT MAKES THIS BOOK'S DINING COVERAGE STAND OUT? At the *Unofficial Guide*, we begin with reviews from experts in Disney dining and then factor in feedback we get from tens of thousands of real guests. We've received more than 27,000 surveys about Walt Disney World restaurants in the past year, and more than 1 million since 2018. That's likely more than Yelp and TripAdvisor *combined*.

It's important to know that our experts and authors don't get any invites from Disney for things like opening nights (which tend not to reflect the average experience), and we pay for all of our own food. That keeps our opinions unbiased so you have a realistic representation of what you, too, might encounter at these same locations.

Here's how to use the reader surveys and critical reviews together: **If a restaurant has earned ratings of 90% or higher in our reader surveys and at least four stars (table service) or a B or better (counter service) from our experts, it's a solid choice.** Chances are good that you'll enjoy your meal. In EPCOT, for example, France's counter-service **Les Halles Boulangerie–Patisserie** and Italy's table-service **Via Napoli Ristorante e Pizzeria** both meet these high standards.

On the other hand, think twice before dining at restaurants with ratings of 80% or lower in our reader surveys and either three stars or less (table service) or a C or lower (counter service) from our experts. That said, personal preferences matter. You might love a type of food or dining atmosphere that doesn't appeal to the "average" visitor. And 80% satisfaction is still a lot of happy diners. But with limited vacation time and budget, it usually makes sense to prioritize higher-rated options.

When reader ratings don't align with our analysis, check the review for an explanation. A good example is **Boatwright's Dining Hall** at Port Orleans Riverside. It scored a 97% reader satisfaction rating this year but only gets two stars from our experts. That's because guests staying at Port Orleans tend to be pleased with the convenience, but it's not destination dining. If you're already at the resort, it's fine. But there's no reason to go out of your way for it.

Although we work hard to be fair, accurate, and thoughtful in our assessments, many readers, like this one from Pennsylvania, have a less nuanced perspective:

> Most of the food at Walt Disney World is OK. You pay more than you should, but it's more convenient to eat in Disney World than to try to find cheaper restaurants somewhere else.

As you read, keep in mind that researching and reviewing restaurants is no straightforward endeavor—it's endlessly complicated by personal tastes. Read our reviews through the lens of your own preferences and priorities.

Because reader feedback is just as important as expert reviews, we encourage you to share your thoughts by completing a reader survey at touringplans.com/walt-disney-world/survey. Or you can reach out by mail, email, or Instagram (see page 5). Your input helps keep this guide as accurate and useful as possible.

SURVEY RESULTS DEMYSTIFIED

FOR BOTH COUNTER-SERVICE and table-service restaurants, we list reader-survey results for each restaurant profiled, expressed as a percentage of positive (+) responses.

The average positive rating for all Disney counter-service restaurants is **89.3%**. And we get so many surveys every year that we're 98% confident that average is between 89.1% and 89.5%. Statistically, that means these ratings are highly reliable, giving you a solid basis for deciding whether a restaurant is worth your time and money.

Along with an average positive rating for each restaurant, we include a category description to put the percentage in context. The table below lists those categories and their corresponding average positive ratings:

OUR DINING SURVEY RATINGS SYSTEM		
CATEGORY	**COUNTER-SERVICE RESTAURANTS** *(average positive rating)*	**TABLE-SERVICE RESTAURANTS** *(average positive rating)*
EXCEPTIONAL	100%	98% or higher
MUCH ABOVE AVERAGE	96%–98%	95%–97%
ABOVE AVERAGE	92%–95%	92%–94%
AVERAGE	88%–91%	89%–91%
BELOW AVERAGE	83%–87%	84%–88%
MUCH BELOW AVERAGE	76%–82%	78%–83%
DO NOT VISIT	75% or lower	77% or lower

WHERE TO FIND GOOD MEALS

SOME OF THE BEST TABLE-SERVICE RESTAURANTS are found at Disney's Animal Kingdom Lodge, Disney's Grand Floridian Resort & Spa, and Disney Springs.

Animal Kingdom Lodge is home to a few of Disney's best restaurants: **Boma—Flavors of Africa** (No. 9 out of almost 100 table-service restaurants), is a beloved buffet featuring a mix of African-inspired and familiar dishes. **Jiko—The Cooking Place** ranks even higher, landing at No. 4. **Sanaa** blends African and Indian flavors, serving its famous bread service with a variety of flavorful dips.

At the **Grand Floridian, Victoria & Albert's** is Disney's crown jewel and the ultimate fine dining experience. It has won 20 consecutive AAA Five Diamond Awards, and it earned both a Michelin star and a Michelin Special Service Award in 2024. The food and service are unparalleled. The resort is also home to **Cítricos, Narcoossee's, Grand Floridian Cafe,** and the **1900 Park Fare** character buffet.

Within walking distance are the **Polynesian Village Resort**'s **Kona Cafe,** with excellent breakfast options, and **'Ohana,** with family-style dining at breakfast and dinner. The **Contemporary Resort**'s **California Grill** is a short monorail ride away too. If dining is a priority and these resorts fit your budget, staying at one of them could be worthwhile.

Disney Springs has the highest concentration of great restaurants on-property. The family-friendly **Raglan Road,** offering a lively atmosphere and a diverse menu, has held the No. 1 spot for table-service dining two years in a row. Other highlights include **Chef Art Smith's Homecomin'** (No. 6), with outstanding fried chicken, tasty cocktails, and rich desserts. For seafood and steaks, try **The Boathouse.**

Disney Springs also has some of the World's top counter-service spots, including the Indian fusion spot **Eet** (No. 1 in this category), **Salt & Straw** (for unique ice-cream flavors), and **Blaze Fast-Fire'd Pizza.**

For tapas, there are two standout choices at Disney, and both are in Disney Springs. **Wine Bar George,** run by a master sommelier, offers expertly paired small plates and wine selections. **Jaleo,** from celebrity chef José Andrés, serves modern Spanish cuisine with an extensive and reasonably priced menu, including a tasting menu for those who want to sample a bit of everything.

If the dining at Disney Springs sounds good to you, consider staying at **Disney's Saratoga Springs Resort & Spa.** Many of the buildings are within walking distance of the shopping and dining district.

If you're after in-park dining, the food in **Disney's Animal Kingdom** and **EPCOT** gets the highest marks.

DISNEY DINING 101

WALT DISNEY WORLD RESTAURANT CATEGORIES

FOOD AND BEVERAGE OPTIONS at Walt Disney World are defined by service, price, and convenience and are categorized as follows.

TABLE-SERVICE RESTAURANTS Table-service restaurants, also called **full-service** and **sit-down** restaurants, are found in all four theme parks, the Disney resorts (except Value resorts and Port Orleans French Quarter), and Disney Springs. Disney operates most of the restaurants in the theme parks and its hotels, with contractors or franchisees operating the rest. **Advance Dining Reservations** (see page 207) are recommended for all table-service restaurants.

CHARACTER MEALS Thirteen WDW restaurants offer character dining, where guests can meet Disney characters during their meal. Seven are buffets, and six offer either a family-style fixed menu (all tables get the same food) or a limited à la carte menu. All fixed-menu locations have a kids' menu featuring items like hot dogs, burgers, chicken nuggets, pizza, and mac and cheese. Advance Dining Reservations are strongly recommended for character meals.

BUFFETS AND FAMILY-STYLE RESTAURANTS Disney buffets are self-serve and all-you-care-to-eat and include kid-friendly offerings such as chicken nuggets, pizza, and fries. Family-style restaurants follow a similar approach but with food brought directly to the table. At EPCOT's **Garden Grill,** for example, your party will receive several platters piled high with meats and sides, with the option to request more (or less) of any item. We've tried all of Disney's family-style restaurants, and while many offer surprisingly good food in generous portions, some fall short. If you're considering one, it's worth checking ratings and reviews to find the best option.

Most credit cards are accepted at Disney's full-service restaurants. An automatic 18% gratuity is added to the bill for parties of six or more, but when tipping is at your discretion, a North Carolina reader urges generosity with servers:

> I've seen diners leave a dollar or two per person. I've also heard of people protesting Disney's prices by leaving a small tip or none at all. This is unacceptable—these servers keep your drinks full, keep your plates clean, and check on you constantly. They deserve at least 15%–18%. If you can't afford to tip, you shouldn't eat there.

DISNEY RESORT FOOD COURTS: READER-SURVEY RATINGS		
RESORT	**FOOD COURT**	**POSITIVE RATING**
All-Star Movies	World Premier Food Court	77% (*Much Below Average*)
All-Star Music	Intermission Food Court	88% (*Average*)
All-Star Sports	End Zone Food Court	79% (*Much Below Average*)
Art of Animation	Landscape of Flavors	88% (*Average*)
Caribbean Beach	Centertown Market	91% (*Average*)
Coronado Springs	El Mercado de Coronado Food Court	85% (*Below Average*)
Fort Wilderness	P & J's Southern Takeout	85% (*Below Average*)
Pop Century	Everything POP	69% (*Do Not Visit*)*
Port Orleans French Quarter	Sassagoula Floatworks & Food Factory	86% (*Below Average*)
Port Orleans Riverside	Riverside Mill Food Court	79% (*Much Below Average*)

* During part of the survey period, Everything POP was significantly impacted by refurbishment, which led to many low scores.

FOOD COURTS Featuring several counter-service eateries under one roof, food courts can be found at Disney's Moderate and Value resorts (see table above). If you're staying at one of these resorts, you're likely to eat there at least once or twice a day for convenience. The closest thing to a food court inside the theme parks is **Sunshine Seasons** in EPCOT (see page 234). Reservations are not available at food courts. In recent years, Disney has simplified and standardized the food court menus across all its resorts, leading to a noticeable drop in reader satisfaction ratings. While food courts remain a quick and easy option, they no longer offer as much variety or quality.

QUICK SERVICE Also called **counter service,** quick-service food is plentiful at all four theme parks, the BoardWalk, and Disney Springs. You'll find staples like hot dogs, hamburgers, chicken sandwiches, salads, and pizza almost everywhere. Menus often include specialty items that match the area. At EPCOT's Germany Pavilion, for example, you'll find bratwurst and beer; in Frontierland in the Magic Kingdom, vendors sell smoked turkey legs.

Most quick-service restaurants serve combo meals, but you can order just an entrée to save money. Quick-service prices are fairly consistent from park to park. You can expect to pay the same for your coffee or hot dog in Disney's Animal Kingdom as you would in Disney's Hollywood Studios (see table on page 231).

No matter where you choose to eat, here are a couple of quick tips to save some time:

- If mobile ordering is available, place your order 30–45 minutes before you want to eat; that will allow the restaurant time to prepare your food before you arrive, and it will reduce your wait. During busier times of the year, you may need to submit orders 1–2 hours in advance, just to be safe.
- Consider eating before noon or after 1 p.m., when it will be easier to find open tables at quick-service restaurants.

FAST CASUAL Somewhere between quick-service and table-service dining, Disney's fast-casual restaurants offer a step up from standard burgers and fries. The best-known example inside the theme parks is

Satu'li Canteen (see page 236) in Animal Kingdom. It's consistently one of the highest-rated dining options at Walt Disney World.

VENDOR FOOD Vendor carts abound in all four theme parks, Disney Springs, and the BoardWalk. Offerings include popcorn, ice-cream bars, churros, soft drinks, bottled water, and fresh fruit. Prices include tax; many vendors accept credit cards, charges to your room at a Disney resort, and the Disney Dining Plan (see below). A few may take cash only (look for a sign near the register).

DISNEY DINING PLANS

BEGINNING IN 2024, prepaid dining plans returned as part of Walt Disney World vacation packages. There are two tiers of the Disney Dining Plan: the **Quick Service Disney Dining Plan** and the **Disney Dining Plan**. Both allow you to prepay for meals as part of your package. In exchange, you'll get a certain number of meal and snack credits per day to be used at participating locations. One important note: Gratuity is not included, which means that even if you pay entirely with dining credits, you still need to tip out of pocket at table-service restaurants.

Here's a breakdown of how meals and snacks are defined:

- A **counter-service meal** includes an entrée, a side, and a beverage (which may be alcoholic, where available).
- A **table-service meal** includes an entrée (with sides, if included in the menu item), a dessert, and a beverage (which may be alcoholic, where available). You can also substitute the dessert for a side salad, cup of soup, or fruit plate, which is certainly healthier but less fun—and almost always less cost-effective.
- A **snack** can be one of many items sold at snack carts, or even side items, hand-scooped ice cream, and many other options. All of these will be noted with a special symbol on the menu so you know what qualifies.

New for 2026: Kids ages 3–9 get a free Disney Dining Plan with their vacation package if the adults in their room pay for the plan. This offer is combinable with other discounts, like room-only or ticket-only deals.

QUICK-SERVICE DINING PLAN This plan includes two quick-service meals per night, one snack per night, and one refillable drink mug per person on the room reservation. At press time, the plan cost $61 per adult, per night and $25 per child, per night.

DISNEY DINING PLAN (AKA TABLE-SERVICE DINING PLAN) This plan includes one quick-service meal per night, one table-service meal per night, one snack per night, and one refillable drink mug per person on the room reservation. At press time, the plan cost $99 per adult, per night and $31 per child, per night. Your eyes did not deceive you. That's almost $100 per adult, per night.

Dining Plan Value

In order to decide whether the dining plan is worth the cost, we need to establish the value of its credits. For this analysis, we assume that:

1. Snacks are worth an average of $6.
2. The refillable mug is essentially a free throw-in. You might use it, you might not. It doesn't significantly impact the value of the plan.

CHANCE OF SAVING MONEY WITH A DINING PLAN				
DRINK ORDERED	**DINING PLAN/MEAL**			
	COUNTER-SERVICE BREAKFAST	COUNTER-SERVICE LUNCH OR DINNER	TABLE-SERVICE BREAKFAST	TABLE-SERVICE LUNCH OR DINNER
COCKTAIL	14%	49%	2%	8%
WINE	0%	22%	1%	5%
BEER	0%	4%	0%	3%
SPECIALTY BEVERAGE* OR SODA	0%	1%	0%	1%
WATER	0%	0%	0%	0%

* Includes artisanal milkshakes, fresh smoothies, premium hot chocolate, coffee, tea, juice, and milk.

With those assumptions in mind, we calculated the value of an adult quick-service (QS) credit and an adult table-service (TS) credit. A quick-service credit is worth $28, and a table-service credit is worth $66. That means if you're using the dining plan, you need to order meals and drinks that total at least those amounts to break even. Anything less, and you're paying Disney more than the meal is worth.

With the value of a credit established, we analyzed every Disney menu to see how often a meal will at least match what you paid for the credit. Disney assumes no one is going to go through all that trouble, but we did, by figuring out prices of desserts, different types of beverages, and every entrée on-property. The table above walks you through the various chances you have of breaking even or "beating" Disney by using a dining plan.

For example, if you order a quick-service breakfast with a cocktail (good luck finding one), you'll save money by using the dining plan only 2% of the time. If you prefer wine or beer with your breakfast (again, good luck), that chance drops to 1%. If you prefer a specialty beverage (like coffee, juice, or milk) or soda with your breakfast, there is one quick-service breakfast option that will save you money on the dining plan—one, in all of Walt Disney World. If you stick to free tap water, there are no quick-service breakfast entrées that will allow you to break even by using the dining plan.

Across all meals, not a single scenario offers a better than 50% chance of saving money with the dining plan. You've probably heard the saying "the house always wins" when it comes to gambling, and the same applies here. If you just randomly order meals without strategizing, you will statistically lose money by paying for the dining plan instead of paying out of pocket.

Some guests are almost guaranteed to lose money on the dining plan. Those are families with nondrinkers and anyone between the ages of 10 and 20. These groups only have a 1% chance of ordering any meals that justify the plan's cost.

Is it possible to beat Disney by using the dining plan? Absolutely. You'll need to consistently order the most expensive entrées and drinks to maximize the value of your credits. You'll also need to secure reservations at the handful of restaurants where the plan works in your favor. And you'll be competing with every other guest who has done the same research and is also trying to book those high-value meals. Even if you optimize every meal, you're still paying out of pocket for gratuities, which adds up quickly. If you're considering the dining plan for convenience, understand that you may still be spending more than if you paid as you went. Bottom line: Unless you're willing to plan every meal strategically and drink lots of alcohol, the dining plan is unlikely to save you money.

In fact, this year we pulled the average value of the food and beverages you're most likely to get with your dining plan credits. Assuming you drink alcohol, the average Quick-Service Dining Plan user will lose $11–$14 per day compared to paying out of pocket, and the average Table-Service Dining Plan user will lose $23–$26 per day compared to paying out of pocket. If you don't drink alcohol or are between the ages of 10 and 20, those losses go up to $24–$26 per day on the QS plan and $36–$38 per day on the TS plan!

Becky's Recommended Dining Plan Alternative

Want to prepay for your meals and save money without being locked into the rules of the dining plan? Consider using Disney gift cards purchased at a discount. For example, at Target you can save 5% on gift cards by using the Target RedCard. Other retailers offer similar deals. Once we start planning a Disney vacation, we gradually stock up on gift cards, picking up $50 or $100 cards during routine shopping trips. By the time our trip rolls around, we've set aside enough to cover all our meals, including gratuity. This way, we have 100% chance of saving money on our food, and we can eat wherever and order whatever we'd like, without feeling pressured to maximize value by choosing the most expensive meal or ordering a cocktail every time.

ADVANCE DINING RESERVATIONS

BOOKING A TABLE-SERVICE RESERVATION at Disney World isn't as easy as making one elsewhere. With hundreds of guests competing for spots the moment they become available, securing a table at popular restaurants can be a real challenge. In fact, Disney's most in-demand restaurants can run out of reservations months in advance. And most Disney restaurants hold no tables at all for walk-in guests. That means if you want to dine at a specific restaurant, you'll need to book as early as possible—typically 60 days before your visit. This section breaks down how the reservation system works and what you need to know to increase your chances of getting the meals you want.

Behind the Scenes at Advance Dining Reservations

Disney's **Advance Dining Reservation** (**ADR**) system doesn't assign you to a specific table. Instead, it works on a template (or time-slot) system, based on how long guests typically spend at each restaurant.

Here's a simplified example of how it works: Let's say guests at Coral Reef Restaurant stay seated for an average of 70 minutes. After adding 5 minutes for cleaning the table, each table turns over every 75 minutes. Disney's central dining reservation system (**CDRS**) uses this data to manage availability for both online and phone reservations. Thus, when you book a table for four at 6:15 p.m., CDRS marks one

> ## ADVANCE DINING RESERVATIONS
> ### The Official Line
> YOU CAN RESERVE THE FOLLOWING up to 60 days in advance:
> - **ALL DISNEY TABLE-SERVICE RESTAURANTS** and character-dining venues
> - **FANTASMIC! DINING PACKAGE** in Disney's Hollywood Studios
> - **HOOP-DEE-DOO MUSICAL REVUE** at Fort Wilderness Resort & Campground
> - **OGA'S CANTINA** at Star Wars: Galaxy's Edge in Disney's Hollywood Studios
>
> Guests staying at Disney-owned resorts may make dining reservations for the entire length of their stay—up to 10 days—all at once when they are 60 days from check-in.

table as unavailable until 7:30 p.m. This process continues for all time slots, ensuring that every seat is filled as efficiently as possible.

What does all this mean for you? The good news is that if you have a reservation, you'll typically wait less than 20 minutes to be seated during peak hours. But if you arrive without a reservation, expect to wait 45–75 minutes . . . or to be told that there are no tables available. While walk-ins sometimes get lucky (see page 210), you should never count on it. Booking in advance is the best way to secure a table at Disney's most popular restaurants.

NO-SHOW PENALTIES Disney restaurants charge a no-show fee of $10–$25 per person (or $100 per person in the case of **Monsieur Paul** at EPCOT and **Victoria & Albert's** at the Grand Floridian). This has reduced the no-show rate to virtually zero, and these restaurants are booked every day according to their actual capacity. Note the following, however:

- Only one person needs to dine at the restaurant for Disney to consider your reservation fulfilled, even if you have a reservation for more people.
- You can cancel up to 2 hours before your reservation time.

GETTING ADVANCE DINING RESERVATIONS AT POPULAR RESTAURANTS

GETTING A RESERVATION at a high-demand restaurant requires some strategy and quick action. One of the toughest spots to book right now is EPCOT's **Space 220**. Why? Like the nearby Coral Reef, it offers a visually stunning setting. But its newness and well-executed theme make it one of the most sought-after dining locations on-property. That being said, keep in mind that reader and author ratings for Space 220 are low, so it may not be worth the effort.

The easiest and fastest way to book is to go to disneyworld.disney.go.com/dining, where reservations open at 6 a.m. Eastern time, a full hour before phone reservations open. If you live on the West Coast, this means waking up before 3 a.m., but when demand is high, early action is key.

To improve your chances, follow these steps:

- **Practice in advance!** Get familiar with Disney's reservation system a few days before your booking window opens.
- **Create a My Disney Experience account** (see page 23), if you haven't already, and save your credit card information to speed up the process.
- **Be online at 5:57 a.m. Eastern** and start searching before the clock hits 6. The system updates in real time, so you'll see availability as soon as it opens.

THE REALITY OF GETTING LAST-MINUTE DINING RESERVATIONS

IF YOUR VACATION is more than 60 days out and you want to dine at a popular venue, following our advice on pages 208–210 will get you the table you want more than 80% of the time. The longer you wait, the more effort you'll have to put in to find a reservation. The list below shows the restaurants where capacity and demand make finding a last-minute reservation more difficult.

- **AKERSHUS ROYAL BANQUET HALL** *(EPCOT)* Reservations are somewhat easier to get for lunch than dinner.
- **BEACHES & CREAM SODA SHOP** *(Beach Club)* It's not the food or the atmosphere but the limited seating that makes getting reservations difficult.
- **THE BOATHOUSE** *(Disney Springs)* Highly rated by readers. Dinner reservations from 5–9 p.m. are the most difficult to get.
- **CHEF ART SMITH'S HOMECOMIN'** *(Disney Springs)* One of Disney Springs' best restaurants. Your options might be lunch, or dinner after 10 p.m.
- **CHEF MICKEY'S** *(Contemporary Resort)* Neither the food nor the venue is anything special. The draw is the Disney characters.
- **SPACE 220** *(EPCOT)* The draw here is the setting, inside a simulated space station, rather than the food.

- **Use filters on the dining search** to limit the number of results, which helps reduce the time you spend scrolling through options.
- **Be flexible with party size.** Large groups are harder to seat, so try booking multiple smaller tables instead, if you're willing to split up.

Advance Dining Reservations for **Cinderella's Royal Table,** the *Fantasmic!* **Dining Package** (see page 467) and the *Hoop-Dee-Doo Musical Revue* dinner show (see page 226) require full prepayment with a credit card at the time of booking. For these, the reservation name cannot be changed after booking. However, you can cancel for a full refund by calling ☎ 407-WDW-DINE at least 48 hours in advance (compared to the 2-hour window for standard reservations). Disney may make exceptions for emergencies.

If you don't have access to a computer or smartphone at 5:45 a.m., your next best option is calling ☎ 407-WDW-DINE at 6:45 a.m. Eastern. However, you'll be an hour behind online users, and high call volume may cause you to be placed on hold.

If you are planning to use the Disney Dining Plan to pay for a *Fantasmic!* Dining Package, Cinderella's Royal Table, or *Hoop-Dee-Doo Musical Revue,* you may be better off reserving by phone anyway. The online system may not recognize your table-service credits, but you can book and pay with a credit card, then call ☎ 407-WDW-DINE after 6:45 a.m. to have the charge refunded and apply your dining plan credits instead.

NEVER, NEVER, NEVER GIVE UP Not getting what you want the first time you try doesn't mean the end of the story. A woman from Tennessee advises persistence:

> *I started trying to get a reservation at Be Our Guest Restaurant about a month out from our vacation. By checking the website whenever I thought of it—morning, noon, and night—I ended up getting not only a lunch reservation but a dinner reservation!*

LAST-MINUTE DINING RESERVATIONS Because Advance Dining Reservations require a credit card and no-shows incur a fee, cancellations happen regularly. Plans change, and as long as guests cancel within the allowed time frame, they avoid penalties. That frees up tables for others. Your best chance at snagging a last-minute reservation is to check disneyworld.disney.go.com/dining late in the evening the night before you want to dine. Many guests review their schedules before bed and drop reservations they no longer need, creating new availability for anyone quick enough to grab it.

***STILL* CAN'T GET A RESERVATION?** If you can't get one online or by phone, try for a walk-in table on the day you want to dine. It's a long shot but not impossible—especially between 2:30 and 4:30 p.m. or during a restaurant's final hour of service. Your chances improve during slower seasons or on cold or rainy days, when fewer guests are willing to venture out. There are also some websites and apps you can use to alert you when a reservation becomes available. See page 28 for our picks.

Table-service restaurants inside the theme parks are usually the strictest about walk-ins. Even if a restaurant looks quiet, you may still need to use the My Disney Experience app or visit Guest Services to check for availability. Some locations now display their walk-up wait times in the MDE app, allowing you to join a walk-up list directly from your phone if space is available.

ALSO CHECK OPENTABLE If you're struggling to book a Disney dining reservation, it's worth checking **OpenTable** (opentable.com or the mobile app). Several Disney World restaurants accept reservations through this platform, though availability can change.

One major perk of using OpenTable is that some restaurants won't charge a no-show fee if you miss your reservation, unlike Disney's system. However, OpenTable does track no-shows. If you fail to show up for four reservations within a year, your account will be suspended. Fortunately, modifying or canceling reservations through OpenTable is quick and easy, so be sure to update your plans if you can't make it.

WALT DISNEY WORLD RESTAURANTS BOOKABLE WITH OPENTABLE (subject to change)

DISNEY RESORTS

• **The Cake Bake Shop** and **Flying Fish** BoardWalk • **Jiko—The Cooking Place** Animal Kingdom Lodge–Jambo House

DISNEY SPRINGS

• **The Boathouse, Enzo's Hideaway, Maria & Enzo's Ristorante, Morimoto Asia, Paddlefish, Paradiso 37, Raglan Road Irish Pub & Restaurant, STK Orlando, Terralina Crafted Italian,** and **Wine Bar George** The Landing • **The Edison, Frontera Cocina,** and **Planet Hollywood** Town Center • **Jaleo, Splitsville Dining Room,** and **Summer House on the Lake** West Side

DOLPHIN, SWAN, AND SWAN RESERVE

• **Amare** Swan Reserve • **Il Mulino New York** and **Kimonos** Swan • **Rosa Mexicano** and **Todd English's Bluezoo** Dolphin

FORT WILDERNESS AREA

• **Capa, Plancha,** and **Ravello** Four Seasons Resort Orlando

DISNEY DINING 101

RESTAURANT RECOMMENDATIONS BY TYPE OF DINING
Courtesy of The Main St Dish *podcast*

IF YOU'RE LOOKING FOR	TRY
CHARACTER DINING	• **Akershus Royal Banquet Hall** (Norway, EPCOT) Princess dining at its finest. The menu is based on Norwegian cooking but also features some standard American dishes. • **Ravello** (Four Seasons Resort Orlando) The hidden gem of character dining. Serves one of the best character breakfasts in Disney a few times a week. Higher quality compared to other Disney buffets. Photo Pass is included with breakfast, and you can order bottomless mimosas! • **Topolino's Terrace** (Riviera Resort) Elevated food on the top floor of the resort. Characters appear only during breakfast. This is easily one of the hardest dining reservations to get.
DINING THAT DESERVES MORE HYPE	• **Le Cellier Steakhouse** (Canada, EPCOT) The ultimate meal for steak lovers. The phenomenal menu includes some of the best bites in Disney World, from Canadian classics like the Signature Poutine to steakhouse classics like the 28-ounce rib eye. • **Rosa Mexicano** (Dolphin) Serving breakfast, lunch, and dinner, this spot is worth the walk from EPCOT. Try the churro Mickey waffles for breakfast. For lunch and dinner, they serve up Mexican food and delicious margaritas. • **Sebastian's Bistro** (Caribbean Beach Resort) A hidden family-style gem featuring Caribbean flavors. Standouts include pull-apart rolls with caramelized onion jam and guava butter and pineapple-coconut bread pudding with caramel sauce.
THEMED DINING	• **Hoop-Dee-Doo Musical Review** (Fort Wilderness Resort & Campground) This frontier-style dinner show is a prepaid reservation with three showtimes and three seating categories. Along with singing and dancing, enjoy all-you-can-eat fried chicken and barbecue pork. • **Roundup Rodeo BBQ** (DHS) Dine and play as one of Andy's toys! Enjoy a family-style meal of barbecue meats paired with classic sides and selection of sauces. They also have great plant-based options. • **Space 220** (EPCOT) An immersive experience where a space elevator takes you to a dining area with a panoramic view of Earth from 220 miles above. A prix-fixe menu is offered for lunch and dinner. Lounge seating, with great bites and fun cocktails, is available by separate reservation.
SEAFOOD	• **The Boathouse** (Disney Springs) The focus this waterside spot gives to fresh seafood is apparent. No matter the time of day, there are always great options on the menu. • **Narcoossee's** (Grand Floridian Resort & Spa) Excellent seafood in a great location right by the Magic Kingdom. The atmosphere is light and airy, and the food outstanding. The wraparound porch is a great spot to watch fireworks.
FINE DINING	• **Capa** (Four Seasons Resort Orlando) A Spanish-style steakhouse with slightly more casual fine dining. The A5 Wagyu is always a great option, and there are plenty of tapas and sides to accompany the meal. • **Victoria & Albert's** (Grand Floridian Resort & Spa) The best of the best when it comes to dining at Disney World. No detail is missed, from the moment you walk in to your last drop of coffee. This is a dining experience.

THEME PARK RESTAURANTS AND ADMISSION

SOME FIRST-TIME VISITORS to Walt Disney World are surprised to learn that admission to a theme park is required to dine at any restaurant inside a park. The lone exception is **Rainforest Cafe** in Animal Kingdom, which can be entered from the parking lot just outside the park; you must have valid park tickets, however, if you want to enter Animal Kingdom.

Before booking a dining reservation, double-check the restaurant's location, especially if you weren't planning to visit a theme park that day. If you've already spent time in one park earlier in the day but your dining reservation is in a different park, you'll need a **Park Hopper** ticket (see page 67) to enter the second park for your meal.

DRESS

DRESS IS INFORMAL at most theme park restaurants, but Disney has a recommended dress code for some of its nicer resort restaurants, where "guests are expected to dress in attire that adheres to the restaurant's sophisticated and upscale aesthetic." Clothing needs to be clean, neat, and in good condition. No swimwear is allowed. Restaurants with this dress code are **Jiko—The Cooking Place** in Animal Kingdom Lodge, **Flying Fish** at the BoardWalk, **California Grill** at the Contemporary Resort, **Monsieur Paul** at EPCOT's France Pavilion, **Takumi-Tei** at EPCOT's Japan Pavilion, **Cítricos** and **Narcoossee's** at the Grand Floridian Resort & Spa, **Yachtsman Steakhouse** at the Yacht Club Resort, **Todd English's Bluezoo** at the Dolphin, **Il Mulino** at the Swan, and **Topolino's Terrace** at the Riviera Resort. **Victoria & Albert's** at the Grand Floridian is the only Disney restaurant with an even stricter dress code, requiring "semi-formal or formal attire."

FOOD ALLERGIES AND DIETARY NEEDS

IF YOU HAVE SPECIAL DIETARY NEEDS, make them known when you make reservations. For detailed information, see page 319.

Healthful Food at Walt Disney World

Healthy choices such as fresh fruit are available at most fast-food counters and from vendors. Vegetarians, people who have diabetes, those requiring kosher meals, and anyone trying to eat healthfully should have no trouble finding something that meets their needs, though options may be limited.

TABLE-SERVICE RESTAURANT TIPS AND TRICKS

BEFORE YOU BEGIN EATING your way through the World, you need to know a few things:

1. Theme park restaurants often rush their customers to make room for the next group of diners. Dining at high speed may appeal to a family with young, restless children, but for people wanting to relax, it can be more like eating in a pressure chamber than fine dining.
2. Disney restaurants have comparatively few tables for parties of two. If you're a duo, you might have to wait longer to be seated.

3. At full-service Disney restaurants, an automatic gratuity of 18% is added to your tab for parties of six or more—even at buffets where you serve yourself.

While the inflation-adjusted peak cost of a one-day theme park ticket has increased about 115% since 2010, the average lunch entrée price at Le Cellier has gone from around $22 to around $56—an increase of 155%. For reference, the average cost of a meal in a US restaurant went up 45% during the same time, according to the Federal Reserve Bank of St. Louis. This comment from a Louisiana mom spells it out:

> Disney keeps pushing prices up and up. For us, the sky is NOT the limit. We won't be back.

MOBILE ORDERING

DISNEY STRONGLY ENCOURAGES mobile ordering at most in-park counter-service restaurants. Through the MDE app, you can place an order, pay online, choose a pickup time, and notify the restaurant when you arrive. Once your food is ready, the app will direct you to a specific window or pickup area. You can see participating locations in the app.

Because wait times can be long, plan ahead. It often takes 30 minutes or more for restaurants to prepare your order, plus another 5–10 minutes for pickup. During most of the year, place your order 30–45 minutes before you want to eat. During peak times like holidays, ordering 1–2 hours in advance is a safer bet.

TIPS FOR SAVING TIME AND MONEY

EVEN IF YOU ONLY ORDER counter-service meals, you lose a lot of time getting food in the parks—and the costs can add up fast (see table on page 231). Here are some ways to maximize your savings:

1. Eat breakfast before you arrive, either at a restaurant outside the World or from a stocked fridge or cooler in your room. This will save you a ton of time and money.
2. After a good breakfast, bring your own snacks into the parks.
3. All theme park restaurants are busiest between 11:30 a.m. and 2:15 p.m. for lunch and between 6 and 9 p.m. for dinner. Avoid trying to eat during these hours, especially noon–1 p.m.
4. If you're short on time and the park is closing early, just stay until closing and eat dinner at your resort or Disney Springs. If the park stays open late, eat dinner at about 4:30 or 5 p.m. at the restaurant of your choice. You should sneak in just ahead of the dinner crowd.

This Missouri mom shares some of her own tips:

> Each child had a belt bag of his own, which he filled from a special box of goodies each day with things like packages of crackers and cheese and packets of peanuts and raisins. Each child also had a small, rectangular plastic water bottle that could hang on the belt. We filled these at water fountains before getting into lines.
>
> We left the park before noon; ate sandwiches, chips, and soda in the room; and napped. We purchased our evening meal in the park at a counter-service eatery. We budgeted for both morning and evening snacks from a vendor but often didn't need them.

CHARACTER DINING

CHARACTER DINING IS AVAILABLE at 13 restaurants across Walt Disney World. These meals are in high demand, and reservations for popular times can be difficult to secure. For more details on booking hard-to-get dining reservations, see "Getting Advance Dining Reservations at Popular Restaurants" (page 208).

WHAT TO EXPECT

CHARACTER BREAKFASTS ARE SERVED FAMILY-STYLE (in large skillets or platters), buffet-style, or à la carte. The typical breakfast includes scrambled eggs; bacon and sausage; potato casserole; waffles, pancakes, or French toast; biscuits, rolls, or pastries; and fruit. All locations offer kid-friendly and adult options, so buffets or menus will offer everything from burgers and mac and cheese to prime rib, broiled seafood, and other dishes inspired by the restaurant's theme. Characters circulate around the room while you eat, stopping at each table to sign autographs, take photos, and interact with guests. They move slowly enough that everyone will get a chance to meet them.

WHEN TO GO

ATTENDING A RESORT'S CHARACTER BREAKFAST usually prevents you from arriving at the theme parks in time for opening. Because early morning is best for touring and you don't want to burn daylight lingering over breakfast, we suggest the following strategies:

1. Go to a character dinner or lunch instead of breakfast. It will be a nice break.
2. Schedule the first seating for lunch, typically 11 or 11:30 a.m. Have a light breakfast before you head to the parks for opening, hit the most popular attractions until 10:45–11:15 a.m., and then head for lunch. That should keep you fueled until dinnertime, especially if you eat another light snack in the afternoon.
3. Go on arrival or departure day. The day you arrive and check in is good for a character dinner—not only is it a good way to ease into your trip, but it can also help your children get acquainted with how they'll encounter characters in the parks. Similarly, scheduling a character breakfast on checkout day, before you head for the airport or begin your drive home, is a nice way to cap off the trip.
4. Go on a rest day. If you plan to stay five or more days, you'll probably take a day or a half day off from touring to rest or do something else. These are perfect days for a character meal.

Many websites recommend booking the first character breakfast of the day so that you can enter the park before everyone else. Unfortunately, with the new park entry stages that have been implemented since the pandemic, you won't be ahead of anyone. Guests are allowed into every park before they actually open, and you'll be held with everyone else because early reservations now almost always align with the beginning of Early Entry.

HOW TO CHOOSE A CHARACTER MEAL

MANY READERS ASK FOR ADVICE about character meals. These questions from a Tennessee mom are typical:

CHARACTER DINING

What's the best way to figure out which character meal to reserve? Do we base it on food? On which characters are available? On where I can find a reservation? Are any of them that much better than the others?

In fact, some *are* better, sometimes much better. When we evaluate character meals, we look for the following:

1. THE CHARACTERS The meals feature a diverse assortment of characters. See our **Character-Meal Hit Parade** table on pages 216–217 to find out which characters are assigned to each meal.

2. ATTENTION FROM THE CHARACTERS At all character meals, Disney characters circulate among diners. How much time a character spends in camera range of you and your kids depends mostly on the ratio of characters to guests. The more characters and fewer guests, the better. Because many venues never fill to capacity, the character-to-guest ratios in our table have been adjusted to reflect average attendance. Even so, there's quite a range. The best ratio currently is at **Ravello**, where there are regularly fewer than 30 guests to every character. But Ravello can be a little logistically difficult, so your next-best options are **Artist Point, Garden Grill, Cinderella's Royal Table,** and **Topolino's Terrace**, where there's about one character to every 46 guests.

The worst ratio is theoretically at Animal Kingdom's **Tusker House**, where the ratio could be as low as one character for every 96 guests. We say *theoretically* because in practice the tables are usually not 100% full, so you get a slightly better ratio.

A Vermont mom gives the characters high marks:

My kids are all about the characters. I love that for them but sometimes hate skipping other attractions to stand in yet another character line. By paying for a few strategic character meals, we can knock out a bunch of important characters at once without waiting in multiple lines throughout our day.

3. THE SETTING The atmosphere at character meals varies widely. Some have imaginative, immersive settings, while others feel more like a school cafeteria. Ambience is rated on a scale of one to five stars, with five being the best. There are a few standouts worth mentioning: **Garden Grill** in The Land in EPCOT is a slowly revolving restaurant overlooking several scenes from the Living with the Land boat ride. Also in EPCOT, **Princess Storybook Dining** is held in the castlelike Akershus Royal Banquet Hall in the Norway Pavilion. Though **Chef Mickey's** at the Contemporary Resort may not have the most inspired décor, it has a great view of the monorail passing through the hotel.

4. THE FOOD Although some food served at character meals is remarkably good, most is just average. To help you sort everything out, we rate the food at each character meal in the Character-Meal Hit Parade table using a five-star scale.

Most restaurants offer a buffet or family-style service in which all hot items are served from the same pot or skillet. A Texas mom notes:

The family-style meals are much better for character dining—at a buffet, you're scared to leave your table in case you miss a character or other action.

CHARACTER-MEAL HIT PARADE

1. AKERSHUS ROYAL BANQUET HALL   EPCOT
- **MEALS SERVED** Breakfast, lunch, and dinner • **SETTING** ★★★★
- **CHARACTERS** 4–6 Disney princesses chosen from among Ariel, Belle, Jasmine, Tiana, Snow White, Aurora, Mulan, and Cinderella
- **TYPE OF SERVICE** Family-style (all you care to eat)
- **FOOD VARIETY & QUALITY** ★★★½ • **NOISE LEVEL** Moderate
- **CHARACTER-GUEST RATIO** 1:54

2. ARTIST POINT   WILDERNESS LODGE
- **MEAL SERVED** Dinner • **SETTING** ★★★½
- **CHARACTERS** Snow White, Dopey, Grumpy, the Evil Queen
- **TYPE OF SERVICE** Fixed menu with several choices
- **FOOD VARIETY & QUALITY** ★★★★½
- **NOISE LEVEL** Loud • **CHARACTER-GUEST RATIO** 1:35

3. CAPE MAY CAFE   BEACH CLUB RESORT
- **MEAL SERVED** Breakfast • **SETTING** ★★★
- **CHARACTERS** Goofy, Donald, Minnie, Daisy
- **TYPE OF SERVICE** Buffet • **FOOD VARIETY & QUALITY** ★★★
- **NOISE LEVEL** Moderate • **CHARACTER-GUEST RATIO** 1:67

4. CHEF MICKEY'S   CONTEMPORARY RESORT
- **MEALS SERVED** Breakfast and dinner • **SETTING** ★★★
- **CHARACTERS** Mickey, Minnie, Donald, Goofy, Pluto
- **TYPE OF SERVICE** Buffet • **FOOD VARIETY & QUALITY** ★★½
- **NOISE LEVEL** Very loud • **CHARACTER-GUEST RATIO** 1:56

5. CINDERELLA'S ROYAL TABLE   MAGIC KINGDOM
- **MEALS SERVED** Breakfast, lunch, and dinner • **SETTING** ★★★★½
- **CHARACTERS** Some combination of Cinderella, Ariel, Aurora, Belle, Jasmine, Snow White, and Fairy Godmother
- **TYPE OF SERVICE** Fixed menu • **FOOD VARIETY & QUALITY** ★★★
- **NOISE LEVEL** Quiet • **CHARACTER-GUEST RATIO** 1:45

6. THE CRYSTAL PALACE   MAGIC KINGDOM
- **MEALS SERVED** Breakfast, lunch, and dinner • **SETTING** ★★★
- **CHARACTERS** Pooh, Eeyore, Piglet, Tigger • **TYPE OF SERVICE** Buffet
- **FOOD VARIETY & QUALITY** Breakfast ★★½   Lunch and dinner ★★★
- **NOISE LEVEL** Very loud
- **CHARACTER-GUEST RATIO** Breakfast, 1:67; lunch and dinner, 1:89

7. GARDEN GRILL RESTAURANT   EPCOT
- **MEALS SERVED** Breakfast, lunch, and dinner • **SETTING** ★★★★
- **CHARACTERS** Mickey, Pluto, Chip 'n' Dale • **TYPE OF SERVICE** Family-style
- **FOOD VARIETY & QUALITY** Breakfast ★★★½   Lunch and dinner ★★★
- **NOISE LEVEL** Very quiet • **CHARACTER-GUEST RATIO** 1:46

8. HOLLYWOOD & VINE   DISNEY'S HOLLYWOOD STUDIOS
- **MEALS SERVED** Breakfast, lunch, and dinner • **SETTING** ★★½
- **CHARACTERS** *Breakfast:* Disney Junior characters *Lunch and dinner:* Minnie, Mickey, Goofy, Pluto, Donald (and sometimes Daisy)
- **TYPE OF SERVICE** Buffet • **FOOD VARIETY & QUALITY** ★★★½
- **NOISE LEVEL** Moderate • **CHARACTER-GUEST RATIO** 1:71

Characters are subject to change, so check before you go.

CHARACTER DINING

CHARACTER-MEAL HIT PARADE

9. 'OHANA   POLYNESIAN VILLAGE RESORT
- **MEAL SERVED** Breakfast • **SETTING** ★★★
- **CHARACTERS** Lilo and Stitch, Mickey, Pluto
- **TYPE OF SERVICE** Family-style
- **FOOD VARIETY & QUALITY** ★★★ • **NOISE LEVEL** Loud
- **CHARACTER-GUEST RATIO** 1:67

10. 1900 PARK FARE   GRAND FLORIDIAN RESORT
- **MEALS SERVED** Breakfast and dinner • **SETTING** ★★½
- **CHARACTERS** Cinderella, Aladdin as Prince Ali (but see page 268), Mirabel, Tiana in her Bayou Adventure outfit, and Snow White
- **TYPE OF SERVICE** Buffet
- **FOOD VARIETY & QUALITY** Breakfast ★★½   Dinner ★★★½
- **NOISE LEVEL** Moderate • **CHARACTER-GUEST RATIO** 1:55

11. RAVELLO   FOUR SEASONS RESORT ORLANDO
- **MEAL SERVED** Breakfast • **SETTING** ★★★
- **CHARACTERS** Mickey, Minnie, Goofy • **TYPE OF SERVICE** Buffet
- **FOOD VARIETY & QUALITY** ★★★★½ • **NOISE LEVEL** Quiet
- **CHARACTER-GUEST RATIO** 1:30

12. TUSKER HOUSE RESTAURANT   DISNEY'S ANIMAL KINGDOM
- **MEALS SERVED** Breakfast, lunch, and dinner • **SETTING** ★★★
- **CHARACTERS** Donald, Daisy, Mickey, Goofy, Pluto • **TYPE OF SERVICE** Buffet
- **FOOD VARIETY & QUALITY** ★★★½ • **NOISE LEVEL** Loud
- **CHARACTER-GUEST RATIO** 1:96

13. TOPOLINO'S TERRACE   RIVIERA RESORT
- **MEAL SERVED** Breakfast • **SETTING** ★★★★
- **CHARACTERS** Mickey, Minnie, Donald, Daisy
- **TYPE OF SERVICE** Fixed menu • **FOOD VARIETY & QUALITY** ★★★★
- **NOISE LEVEL** Moderate • **CHARACTER-GUEST RATIO** 1:45

Characters are subject to change, so check before you go.

5. NOISE If you want to eat in peace, character meals are usually a bad choice. That said, some are much noisier than others. Our table gives you an idea of what to expect.

6. WHICH MEAL? Although breakfasts seem to be the most popular, character lunches and dinners are usually more practical because they don't interfere with early-morning touring. During hot weather, a character lunch can be a welcome break.

7. COST Dinners and lunches cost more than breakfasts. Meal prices vary considerably from the least expensive to the most expensive restaurant. Breakfasts run $49–$74 for adults and $30–$45 for kids ages 3–9. For character lunches and dinners, expect to pay around $62–$88 for adults and $41–$52 for kids. Little ones age 2 years and younger eat free.

8. ADVANCE DINING RESERVATIONS See "Advance Dining Reservations: The Official Line," page 208, for details. If you don't get what you want at first, keep trying, advises a London mother of two:

> *When a booking window opens, many people overbook and then either get buyer's remorse or find alternative bookings and cancel. When my booking window first opened, I was able to book barely 20% of what I wanted, but within two to three weeks I had 100%.*

9. "FRIENDS" Some character meals advertise a main character and a varying cast of "friends"—for example, "Pooh and friends," meaning Eeyore, Piglet, and Tigger, or some combination thereof, or "Mickey and friends" with some assortment chosen from among Minnie, Goofy, Pluto, Donald, Daisy, Chip, and Dale.

10. CINDY'S ROYAL RUSH Most character meals are leisurely affairs, and you can usually stay as long as you want. However, because Cinderella's Royal Table in the Magic Kingdom is in such high demand, the restaurant does everything it can to move you through, as this European mother of a 5-year-old can attest:

> *We dined a lot, did three character meals and a few Signature restaurants, and every meal was awesome except for lunch with Cinderella. It was a rushed affair. We had barely sat down when the appetizers were thrown on our table, the princesses each spent just a few seconds with our daughter—almost no interaction—and the side dishes were cold. We were out of there within 40 minutes and felt very stressed. Considering the price, I cannot recommend it.*

DISNEY DINING SUGGESTIONS

HERE ARE OUR SUGGESTIONS for dining at each of the major theme parks. If you want to minimize the impact on your park day, consider dining late—the restaurants continue to serve after the park's official closing time.

THE MAGIC KINGDOM

THE BEST TABLE-SERVICE RESTAURANTS are **Liberty Tree Tavern** (94%/Above Average) in Liberty Square and **Jungle Navigation Co. Ltd. Skipper Canteen** (91%/Average) in Adventureland. Liberty Tree serves standard American family-style meals, while Skipper Canteen serves more-diverse cuisines in a Jungle Cruise–themed environment.

The big draw at the pricey **Cinderella's Royal Table** (93%/Above Average) is the setting—the food is just fine. **The Plaza Restaurant** (86%/Below Average) on Main Street serves passable meals at more moderate prices than at other higher-rated sit-down restaurants.

unofficial **TIP**
All Magic Kingdom table-service restaurants serve beer and wine with dinner.

The most in-demand restaurant in the Magic Kingdom is **Be Our Guest** (87%/Below Average) in Fantasyland; unfortunately, the entire dining experience has declined substantially, while the prices have increased. You're not missing anything—it's an especially poor value—and we hope Disney does something about it soon. Likewise, quality at **The Crystal Palace** (90%/Average) is relatively low. Additionally, avoid **Tony's Town Square** (81%/Much Below Average) on Main Street and (if it's open) **The Diamond Horseshoe** (71%/Do Not Visit)—these two are among the worst restaurants in Walt Disney World parks.

DISNEY DINING SUGGESTIONS

> **TOP MAGIC KINGDOM SNACKS**
> *Courtesy of* The Main St Dish *podcast*
>
> - **Spring Rolls** (Spring Roll Cart, Adventureland) You can always find the Cheeseburger Spring Roll, and there's usually a second flavor that is switched out occasionally.
> - **Pineapple Upside Down Cake** (Aloha Isle, Adventureland) We think this is the best way to enjoy a Dole Whip, but this a good spot for all things Dole Whip.
> - **Crème Brûlée Croissant** (Gaston's Tavern, Fantasyland) A chilled croissant, stuffed with vanilla cream. The menu here does change, but lately everything has been solid.
> - **Rapunzel Sundae** (Storybook Treats, Fantasyland) The combination of wild-berry and lemon Dole Whip is delicious, and the addition of fresh fruit is great. Keep an eye on the rotating cones here; there is almost always something good.

Columbia Harbour House (91%/Average) is the most well-rounded counter-service restaurant in the Magic Kingdom. Its menu focuses on seafood, with the tasty lobster roll, grilled salmon, and grilled shrimp all worth ordering, plus solid options for kids, vegans, and vegetarians. Secret bonus: If you go upstairs, you'll usually have almost the whole space to yourself! **Casey's Corner** (93%/Above Average), on Main Street, U.S.A., serves ballpark-style hot dogs and fries. It's one of the rare Disney restaurants to have improved its food quality over the past few years. **Liberty Square Market** (92%/Above Average) also serves tasty hot dogs, plus pretzels and other snacks. If you can make a meal of a waffle with some toppings, then your best bet is easily **Sleepy Hollow** (95%/Above Average), with limited seating but a gorgeous view of Cinderella Castle for those who succeed in finding seats.

> **AUTHORS' FAVORITE MAGIC KINGDOM COUNTER-SERVICE RESTAURANTS**
> - **Sleepy Hollow** Liberty Square   • **Columbia Harbour House** Liberty Square

If these places don't do it for you, be prepared to make some compromises at the Magic Kingdom's other counter-service restaurants, all of which struggle to achieve average levels of quality. The best is probably **Pecos Bill Tall Tale Inn and Cafe** (78%/Much Below Average) in Frontierland; it got a menu refresh in late 2024 that should cause its scores to go up. Avoid **Cosmic Ray's Starlight Café** (75%/Do Not Visit) and **The Lunching Pad** (63%/Do Not Visit) in Tomorrowland and **Tortuga Tavern** (71%/Do Not Visit) in Adventureland.

EPCOT

EVER SINCE EPCOT OPENED, dining has been a core part of its identity. World Showcase has many more restaurants than attractions, and EPCOT has added bars, tapas-style eateries, and full-service restaurants faster than any other park. (See the table on the next page for a list of all the park's full-service restaurants.)

EPCOT almost always features food festival booths. Its annual **International Food & Wine Festival** runs from late August through mid-November; the **International Festival of the Holidays** begins a few days later. The **International Festival of the Arts** follows in January and lasts through late February, and then it's time for the **International Flower & Garden Festival** from March through May.

While it's not the same as sitting inside a well-themed World Showcase pavilion, the food booths have their pluses: There's a lot of variety,

TABLE-SERVICE RESTAURANTS IN EPCOT
WORLD NATURE AND WORLD DISCOVERY
• **Coral Reef Restaurant** The Seas with Nemo & Friends • **Garden Grill Restaurant** The Land • **Space 220** World Discovery
WORLD SHOWCASE
• **Akershus Royal Banquet Hall** Norway • **Biergarten Restaurant** Germany • **Chefs de France** France • **La Crêperie de Paris** France • **La Hacienda de San Angel** Mexico • **Le Cellier Steakhouse** Canada • **Monsieur Paul** France • **Nine Dragons Restaurant** China • **Rose & Crown Dining Room** United Kingdom • **San Angel Inn Restaurante** Mexico • **Shiki-Sai** Japan • **Spice Road Table** Morocco • **Takumi-Tei** Japan • **Teppan Edo** Japan • **Tutto Italia Ristorante** Italy • **Via Napoli Ristorante e Pizzeria** Italy

the food quality can be quite good, and it's generally faster than a full sit-down meal.

For the most part, EPCOT's restaurants serve decent food, although World Showcase spots can be timid when it comes to delivering authentic representations of their host nations' cuisine—the "spicy" items in China are nowhere close to their domestic intensity, for example. While it's true that the less adventurous diner can find steak and potatoes on virtually every menu, the same kitchens will happily serve up a more traditional preparation of any dish, if you ask. (We've had wonderful experiences by asking for our food to be prepared the way the chefs would make it for themselves.)

unofficial **TIP**
EPCOT has 19 table-service restaurants: 3 in Future World and 16 in World Showcase. With a couple of exceptions, these are among the best restaurants at Walt Disney World, in or out of the theme parks.

An EPCOT evening without dinner in the World Showcase is like a birthday without presents. Each pavilion except The American Adventure has a beautifully themed restaurant. To tour through and not eat at any of them would be silly. Still, some are better than others.

EPCOT restaurants that combine attractive ambience and well-prepared food with good value are **Teppan Edo** (96%/Much Above Average) and **Shiki-Sai: Sushi Izakaya** (100%/Exceptional) in Japan; **Via Napoli Ristorante e Pizzeria** in Italy (94%/Above Average); **Spice Road Table** in Morocco (98%/Exceptional); and **Garden Grill Restaurant** in The Land (96%/Much Above Average). Those that *don't* provide good value for the money include **San Angel Inn Restaurante** in Mexico (86%/Below Average); **Rose & Crown Dining Room** in the United Kingdom (88%/Below Average); **Chefs de France** in France (81%/Much Below Average); **Nine Dragons** in China (77%/Do Not Visit); and **Monsieur Paul** in France (83%/Much Below Average). For the record, Monsieur Paul is one of the most expensive and least satisfying fine dining options at Walt Disney World.

Les Halles Boulangerie–Patisserie in France (95%/Above Average) is one of the highest-rated counter-service restaurants in Walt Disney World. It sells pastries, sandwiches, and quiches. The bread and pastries are made on-site, and the sandwiches are as close to actual French street food as you'll get anywhere in EPCOT. Another favorite is the barbecue at **Regal Eagle Smokehouse** (95%/Above Average).

TOP EPCOT SNACKS
Courtesy of The Main St Dish *podcast*

- **Queso** (La Cava del Tequila, Mexico) There's no better complement to a snack than tequila! The salsa and guacamole are excellent too.
- **Pretzel Bread Pudding** (Sommerfest, Germany) An excellent combination of sweet and salty, this takes pretzel bread and turns it into the perfect dessert.
- **Liege Waffle** (Connections Eatery, World Celebration) A great sweet treat. The waffle itself is brioche and packed with butter, making it a smart choice for a snack or dessert.
- **Ice Cream Macaron** (L'Artisan des Glaces, France) You can't go wrong with any of the choices here. The Brioche Ice Cream Sandwich is quite popular.

Becky is a barbecue snob from St. Louis, and even she will admit that the barbecue here is good. Plus, there is plenty of seating.

AUTHORS' FAVORITE EPCOT COUNTER-SERVICE RESTAURANTS
- **Les Halles Boulangerie–Patisserie** France • **Katsura Grill** Japan
- **Regal Eagle Smokehouse** American Adventure

In addition to these, we recommend the United Kingdom's **Yorkshire County Fish Shop** (94%/Above Average) for fresh fish-and-chips or Japan's **Katsura Grill** (90%/Average) for quick Japanese food. The kids' meals here are a good value and enough food for an adult. **Connections Café and Eatery** (86%/Below Average) started strong when it first opened, but scores have since been trending down. Still, if you're not in World Showcase and there's not a festival going on, it may be your best nearby option.

EPCOT FESTIVALS As mentioned, EPCOT hosts four major festivals a year. Food and drinks are the main draw at all of them, no matter the season or theme. For each festival, EPCOT operates small, semipermanent themed booths around the park. The booths serve appetizer-size portions—and almost always beer and wine—that fit the stand's theme. These festivals give EPCOT's chefs a chance to experiment with new ingredients and flavor combinations. The food quality is generally very good, and sometimes amazing. Readers rate the food quality of the booths at the Flower & Garden and Food & Wine Festivals as above average. Many guest favorites return year after year.

Drinking Around the World (Showcase)

A popular adult pastime in EPCOT is to make a complete circuit of World Showcase, sampling the alcoholic drinks from each nation. Here's a list of the don't-miss places.

LA CAVA DEL TEQUILA, MEXICO (98%/Exceptional) Located inside the pyramid of the Mexico Pavilion, this is one of the best bars in Walt Disney World and one of the best tequila bars in the country. Its ever-changing menu includes more than 200 kinds of tequila and mezcal, several margaritas, and various light appetizers. On most weekends and during special events such as the Food & Wine Festival, Cinco de Mayo, and National Tequila Day (July 24), expect a significant wait to get a drink.

Most days, La Cava has a tequila expert on hand to explain the different types and provide tasting notes. (Ask for Hilda or Humberto, both from Tequila in Jalisco, Mexico.) If you happen to be in EPCOT during the fall Food & Wine Festival, sign up for a tequila tasting if they're offered. Done in small groups with flights of tequila, it will teach you how to truly appreciate this spirit.

ROSE & CROWN PUB, UNITED KINGDOM (90%/Average) It's a little brighter than many British pubs we've seen elsewhere, but Rose & Crown serves a wide variety of ales, lagers, stouts, and ciders alongside traditional English pub fare such as fish-and-chips and sausage rolls. If you're wanting something stronger, the pub has Scotch whiskies and Irish whiskeys. Service is cheerful and fast.

SAKE BARS, JAPAN (93%/Above Average) There are two sake bars in Japan: One is an outdoor kiosk on the walking path toward the back of the pavilion, and the other is a small counter tucked into the back of the first floor of the Mitsukoshi Department Store. Both have decent, affordable selections of sakes. We're still amazed these haven't turned into a waterside bar.

WEINKELLER, GERMANY (91%/Average) If you love sweet white wines, this is the place to be. Decorated with stone, dark wood, and heavy chandeliers, Weinkeller serves wines by the glass (around $9). Selections usually include a couple of Rieslings, a Liebfraumilch, dessert wines, and ice wines. We highly recommend trying the Mozart chocolate liqueur. It's pricey but worth every penny. The bar has no seating, but the wine pours are generous.

TUTTO GUSTO WINE CELLAR, ITALY (98%/Exceptional) Tucked away on the left side of the Italy Pavilion, this small bar looks like the inside of a small home (or cave). With a wide selection of Italian wines, cheeses, and meats, it's perfect for drinking and snacking around the world.

DISNEY'S ANIMAL KINGDOM

ALONG WITH EPCOT, Animal Kingdom has some of the best dining options of any Disney theme park. The food isn't particularly exotic, and a lot of it is counter service, but the quality is superior to that found in the Magic Kingdom and Disney's Hollywood Studios.

The park's *Avatar*-themed **Satu'li Canteen** (96%/Much Above Average) is Disney's answer to Chipotle's rice bowls—you pick a base of starch, grain, or lettuce and then add a protein and garnishes. The nearby **Pongu Pongu** (91%/Average) serves drinks inspired by *Avatar*, plus the best breakfast biscuits in the park. If you need a drink and a place to gather yourself before venturing into Flight of Passage's long wait, stop at the **Nomad Lounge** (96%/Much Above Average), which is on the way to Pandora from Discovery Island. The drinks here are well balanced and flavorful, and the lounge's décor is immersive. Becky's younger daughter swears by the chicken nuggets, which aren't on any menu but can be ordered by anyone. If you're willing to venture into the realm of "food carts," **Eight Spoon Café** (100%/Exceptional), with its mac and cheese selections, and **Mr. Kamal's** (100%/Exceptional), with hot snacks such as fries, lead the pack.

A California dad praises Satu'li Canteen:

DISNEY DINING SUGGESTIONS

TOP ANIMAL KINGDOM SNACKS
Courtesy of The Main St Dish *podcast*

- **Churros** (Nomad Lounge, Discovery Island) Perfectly fried and gluten-free, these are the best churros in Disney World.
- **Baked Mac and Cheese** (Eight Spoons Café, Discovery Island) We love that you get to pick your own adventure with the different types of mac and cheese. We suggest the pulled pork.
- **Pineapple Crisp Sundae** (Tamu Tamu, Africa) In addition to this dessert—essentially a pineapple streusel topped with ice cream—Tamu Tamu offers some other great sweet treats you might want to check out too.
- **Pongu Lumpia** (Pongu Pongu, Pandora) Pineapple and cream cheese fried to perfection in a lumpia wrapper. This is an excellent cheap snack.
- **Barbacoa Nachos** (The Smiling Crocodile, Discovery Island) In general, The Smiling Crocodile is one of our favorite hidden foodie gems in the park, and we can never say no to the tender beef on these nachos.

Our favorite place to eat was, by far, Satu'li Canteen. I would honestly make a special trip just to eat there. First, the food was crazy good. Yes, they basically make a bowl of food, and that's all they serve, but everything was so delicious I could mix and match my ingredients to create something new every time. Second, they make everything from scratch there on-site. I can't stress enough how important this was to us, especially considering that our son has special dietary needs.

Besides Satu'li Canteen, our two other favorite counter-service dining options in the park are **Flame Tree Barbecue** (95%/Above Average), serving house-made barbecue at waterfront dining pavilions with excellent views of flotillas and Everest, and **Harambe Market** (92%/ Above Average) in Africa, serving rice bowls with various meats, plant-based "sausages," and salads. Beware if you visit Harambe Market: The food has started trending spicier.

Our choices for sit-down restaurants in the park include **Yak & Yeti Restaurant** (94%/Above Average) in Asia, serving familiar Asian and Indian dishes, and **Tusker House Restaurant** (93%/Above Average) in Africa, where the buffet choices are much more interesting than most others at Disney. **Tiffins Restaurant** (92%/Above Average) is too expensive for us to recommend it to everyone during a regular park day. Always skip the **Rainforest Cafe** (71%/Do Not Visit), which is among the lowest-rated restaurants in all of Walt Disney World.

AUTHORS' FAVORITE ANIMAL KINGDOM COUNTER-SERVICE RESTAURANTS

- **Flame Tree Barbecue** Discovery Island
- **Harambe Market** Africa
- **Satu'li Canteen** Pandora

DISNEY'S HOLLYWOOD STUDIOS

DINING QUALITY AT THE STUDIOS has improved since the pandemic but remains spotty at best. Two solid counter-service restaurants are in Galaxy's Edge: **Docking Bay 7 Food and Cargo** (92%/Above Average) serves chicken, ribs, and a vegetarian kefta with unique sides, and **Ronto Roasters** (94%/Above Average) serves a limited menu of

TOP HOLLYWOOD STUDIOS SNACKS
Courtesy of The Main St Dish *podcast*

- **Bavarian Pretzel** (BaseLine Tap House, Grand Avenue) Grab the pretzel or the charcuterie board. Their tap list is long and they have great nonalcoholic drinks too. We love the soda on tap!
- **Enchanted Rose** (Fairfax Fare, Sunset Boulevard) This is easily a collective favorite dessert of the group. You can't go wrong with the combination of chocolate and cherries.
- **Totchos** (Woody's Lunch Box, Toy Story Land) It's everything you love about nachos but over potato barrels. The breakfast version is wonderful too.
- **Glimmer & Shimmer Blondie** (Catalina Eddie's, Sunset Boulevard) The combination of this cookie-like dessert with the salted-caramel buttercream is out of this world.
- **Morning Ronto Wrap** (Ronto Roasters, Galaxy's Edge) Is this a snack or a meal? We don't know, but we love it so much it has to make the list. And while we love the original version, too, the breakfast version is our favorite.
- **Outpost Popcorn Mix** (Kat Saka's Kettle, Galaxy's Edge) This sweet and spicy popcorn is the perfect snack to eat while walking around Galaxy's Edge.

sausage wraps. Over on Commissary Lane, **ABC Commissary** (94%/Above Average) has made a remarkable comeback after a few menu revamps. **Woody's Lunch Box** (90%/Average) in Toy Story Land has popular food, but its inadequate seating area impacts its scores. Elsewhere in the park, **Catalina Eddie's, Dockside Diner** (both 92%/Above Average), and **Backlot Express** (86%/Below Average) are all skippable due to their uninspiring menus. Avoid **Fairfax Fare** (77%/Much Below Average) and **Rosie's All-American Café** (68%/Do Not Visit) at all costs.

If you're looking for something to beat the heat, **BaseLine Tap House** (97%/Exceptional) on Grand Avenue is one of the highest-rated bars in Walt Disney World. It's small and mostly unthemed, but service is quick, and there's a decent selection of beers, plus a few snacks. If you sit outside, the people-watching is excellent.

Table-service dining is a long-running weakness at Hollywood Studios. One (expensive) option for a good meal is the upscale **Hollywood Brown Derby** (90%/Average), which serves well-prepared steaks, chicken, and fish. Our recommendation would be **50's Prime Time Café** (94%/Above Average), where you sit in Mom's 1950s kitchen and scarf down meat loaf while watching clips of classic sitcoms. **Hollywood & Vine** (90%/Average) features characters such as Minnie Mouse and friends at lunch and dinner; kids will love it, and the food has been improving, which is reflected in its improved score.

Overall, reader responses reflect that there are few restaurants in the Studios that combine good food, good service, an entertaining atmosphere, *and* reasonable prices; almost every place has at least one major flaw. Recent menu additions have not improved the food quality at **Sci-Fi Dine-In Theater** (81%/Much Below Average)—where you eat in little cars at a simulated drive-in movie—but you won't find a better-themed restaurant in the World. A newer table-service restaurant, **Roundup Rodeo BBQ** (89%/Average), opened in early 2023. It's not a quiet meal option, thanks to all the young *Toy Story* fans, but the food is plentiful and higher-quality than most other sit-down options in the park. Ratings would be higher without all that noise.

Oga's Cantina (84%/Below Average), reminiscent of the bar from *A New Hope,* serves exotic alcoholic and nonalcoholic cocktails. It's the only Galaxy's Edge restaurant that offers reservations, and because the experience hasn't been getting rave reviews, reservations are easier to come by. You can join the walk-up waiting list if you're nearby and it's still open. But be warned: This is the lowest-rated bar in Walt Disney World because it's always packed (90% of people have to stand), the drinks seem abnormal, and food is almost nonexistent.

AUTHORS' FAVORITE HOLLYWOOD STUDIOS COUNTER-SERVICE RESTAURANT

• **Docking Bay 7 Food and Cargo** Galaxy's Edge

Our general advice when it comes to the Studios is to eat a good breakfast before you get to the park. For lunch and dinner, try for a cheap counter-service meal and a table-service meal where you'll enjoy the theming.

FULL-SERVICE DINING FOR FAMILIES WITH YOUNG CHILDREN

DISNEY RESTAURANTS OFFER an excellent (though expensive) opportunity to introduce younger kids to the variety and excitement of food from different cultures. No matter how formal a restaurant appears, the staff is accustomed to fidgety, impatient, and loud children.

unofficial **TIP**
Look for the Disney Check icon on healthy menu items such as fresh fruit and low-fat milk.

Almost all Disney restaurants offer kids' menus, and all have booster seats and high chairs. Servers understand how tough it is for children to sit still for an extended period, and they'll serve your dinner much faster than in comparable restaurants elsewhere. Reader comments suggest that being served too quickly is more common than waiting too long.

A New York dad says timing is key when dining with younger kids:

> As a family with three girls all under the age of 10, we quickly discovered that no sit-down restaurant is worth dragging the family to after 8 p.m. We ended up with at least two children sleeping on the chairs after ordering chicken nuggets for the second time that day. I would rather eat at a quick-service restaurant if it gets my family in bed by 9 p.m.

Good Restaurants for Children

Be Our Guest and **Cinderella's Royal Table** are hot tickets in the **Magic Kingdom,** and reservations at both can be difficult to get. (The only character at Be Our Guest is the Beast, and he only walks around briefly.) Be Our Guest's quality is substandard, it's overpriced, and you shouldn't eat there unless you're a huge *Beauty and the Beast* fan. We think the most kid-friendly table-service fare in the park is served at **Liberty Tree Tavern** in Liberty Square.

In **EPCOT,** preschoolers most enjoy Biergarten Restaurant in Germany, Teppan Edo in Japan, and Coral Reef Restaurant at The Seas Pavilion in World Nature. **Biergarten** (93%/Above Average) combines a rollicking musical atmosphere with tasty, mostly familiar foods. A German oompah band entertains guests at both lunch and dinner. One of Becky's favorite Disney memories is watching her girls dancing to the band on the main floor. **Teppan Edo** (96%/Much Above Average) is on the upper floor of the Japan Pavilion. Children can watch their food being cooked in front of them, along with the "show" elements of hibachi. **Coral Reef** (88%/Below Average), with tables beside windows looking into The Seas' aquarium, offers a satisfying mealtime diversion for all ages. For those who don't eat fish, there are beef, chicken, and vegetarian options, and with a new chef in 2023, scores have been slowly but steadily improving.

The best table-service restaurants for kids in **Disney's Animal Kingdom** are **Yak & Yeti Restaurant** and **Tusker House**.

In **Disney's Hollywood Studios**, kids of all ages enjoy the atmosphere and entertainment at **Hollywood & Vine**, **Sci-Fi Dine-In Theater Restaurant**, and **50's Prime Time Café**.

NOISE AT RESTAURANTS

RESTAURANTS ARE NOISY all around the World. A Pennsylvania adult dining with one other adult shared this:

> We ate four times at Signature restaurants. The food was always good, and the check, with wine and tip, was always at least $150. However, the noise, especially at Le Cellier and Il Mulino, was overwhelming. WDW seems to have really skimped on the acoustics, even at Cítricos and the California Grill.

QUIET, ROMANTIC PLACES TO EAT

RESTAURANTS WITH GOOD FOOD and a couple-friendly ambience are rare in the parks. If you're being really picky, only the following satisfy both requirements: the expensive Japanese restaurant **Takumi Tei** in EPCOT and the small and seemingly secluded **Tiffins Restaurant** at Animal Kingdom.

unofficial **TIP**
The **California Grill** at the Contemporary Resort and **Topolino's Terrace** at the Riviera have the best views at Walt Disney World.

Victoria & Albert's at the Grand Floridian Resort & Spa is Disney's showcase gourmet restaurant; the current menu starts at $295 per person. But once you have one meal there, you'll immediately start saving up to go back. Other good choices for couples include **Jiko—The Cooking Place** in Animal Kingdom Lodge, along with **Cítricos** and **Narcoossee's** at the Grand Floridian.

Eating later in the evening and choosing one of the restaurants mentioned here will improve your chances for intimate dining; nevertheless, children—well behaved or otherwise—are everywhere at Walt Disney World, no matter when or where you eat.

WALT DISNEY WORLD DINNER THEATER

AS IS THE CASE with other Disney restaurant reservations, when you make a reservation for **Hoop-Dee-Doo Musical Revue** (the only dinner show currently offered), you'll receive a confirmation number, and your credit card will be charged the full amount unless you cancel your tickets at least 48 hours before your reservation time. Reservations can be made 60 days in advance; book online or call ☎ 407-939-3463.

It's worth noting that obtaining reservations for *Hoop-Dee-Doo* during busy periods can be a trick of the first order. If you want to see a show but can't get reservations:

1. Call ☎ 407-939-3463 at 9 a.m. each morning while at Disney World to make a same-day reservation. There are two to three performances each night, and for each night, only 3–24 people total will be admitted with same-day reservations.

2. Arrive at the show 45 minutes before showtime (late shows are your best bets) and put your name on the standby list. If someone with reservations fails to show, you may be admitted.

unofficial **TIP**
To make reservations for the *Hoop-Dee-Doo Musical Revue,* book online or call as soon as you know the dates of your visit. The earlier you call, the better selection of dates and times you'll have.

Disney offers tiered seating for *Hoop-Dee-Doo*. The best seats are in **Category 1**. Next comes **Category 2**, with seats off to the side or behind Category 1. Finally, **Category 3** seats are farther still to the side or back, or on another level from the stage. Good views can be had from almost all seats, so you can decide if sitting closer to the action is worth the extra bucks. Tables within the category are assigned based on when you check in, so arriving early is your best bet.

Hoop-Dee-Doo Musical Revue

⊕ 93% (Above Average)

Pioneer Hall, Fort Wilderness Campground; ☎ 407-939-3463

Showtimes Nightly, 4, 6:15, and 8:30 p.m. **Cost** Category 1, $78 ($45 children ages 3–9); Category 2, $74 ($41 child); Category 3, $70 ($40 child). Prices include tax and gratuity. **Duration** 2 hours.

- **DESCRIPTION** *Hoop-Dee-Doo* is the longest-running (and now only) dinner show at Walt Disney World and a nostalgic favorite for many families. If you've ever thought *Country Bear Musical Jamboree* would benefit from free-flowing barbecue, beer, and wine, this is the show for you. Audience participation includes sing-alongs, hand-clapping, and a finale where you may find yourself onstage. During the most focused eating times, the music continues (softly). The food itself is pretty good for an all-you-can-eat establishment.
- **MENU** All-you-can-eat barbecue ribs, fried chicken, salad, baked beans, and cornbread; unlimited beer, wine, sangria, and soft drinks. Vegetarian, vegan, and gluten-free options available.
- **COMMENTS** Think about transportation when planning your evening at Fort Wilderness; it'll take some time to get there and back. There is no parking at Pioneer Hall, which is accessible only by boat (either from Magic Kingdom or via the loop between Fort Wilderness, Wilderness Lodge, and the Contemporary). After the show, resort buses at the Pioneer Hall stop will take you back to your resort. The quickest and most convenient option may be to take a **Minnie Van** (page 345).

MORE READER COMMENTS ABOUT WALT DISNEY WORLD DINING

DINING IS A POPULAR TOPIC among *Unofficial Guide* readers. In addition to participating in our restaurant survey after their vacation, many readers share their thoughts. The following comments are a representative sample.

WALT DISNEY WORLD LOUNGES
Courtesy of The Main St Dish *podcast*

THE UNOFFICIAL GUIDE has always provided overviews of counter-service and table-service restaurants. But some of the best dining experiences we've had were at lounges. To bring more awareness to these often overlooked options, we asked Bethany, Bella, and Colin of *The Main St Dish* podcast for their recommendations.

LOCATION	RECOMMENDED LOUNGES
MAGIC KINGDOM	• **Pirate Tavern** A new addition in 2025 and the only lounge inside the Magic Kingdom. Step inside this well-themed pirate adventure and enjoy a little rum.
EPCOT	• **La Cava del Tequila** This tequila cave hidden in the pyramid of the Mexico Pavilion is a must-stop in EPCOT. It has an impressive tequila list, and the entire team here is incredibly knowledgeable and happy to make recommendations for you. La Cava can get crowded, so we recommend being there when it opens at 11 a.m. • **Geo-82** Another new addition in 2025, this lounge at Spaceship Earth features views of EPCOT, and the cocktail list is a nod to EPCOT past and present.
ANIMAL KINGDOM	• **Nomad Lounge** A wonderful spot to cool off, with indoor and outdoor lounge seating. The menu has unique cocktails, mocktails, great small plates, and rotating seasonal menu selections. We recommend trying the Hightower Rocks, Lamu Libation, and Jenn's Tattoo. It is also the home of one of the best hidden menu items in Disney: the kids' chicken nuggets—they're some of the best nuggets in the parks!
DISNEY'S HOLLYWOOD STUDIOS	• **BaseLine Tap House** This California-themed tap house is the perfect place to grab a beer and a light snack. There is plenty of seating outside, and it's a great place to people-watch. • **Tune-In Lounge** Flash back to the 1950s in this retro-themed lounge, where you can duck the crowds and grab some air-conditioning or a drink to go. Ask the bartenders about a Mozart Moment—if you love chocolate and sweet drinks, this one's for you.
RESORTS	• **Enchanted Rose** (Grand Floridian) Located on the second floor of the main lobby, this is a stunning lounge inspired by the live-action remake of *Beauty and the Beast*. The cocktails here are on the more expensive side, but the quality of all the drinks is outstanding.

A 13-year-old from Nebraska recommends not getting bent out of shape over one bad meal:

> *Honestly, when was the last time you came home from Disney World and said, "Gosh, my vacation really sucked because I ate at a bad restaurant?"*

Sanaa, in the Kidani Village section of Animal Kingdom Lodge, really impressed a Florida family:

> *We got reservations just to be able to drive ourselves and take our time walking the grounds. Best thing ever. The grounds were incredible! We went at 4:30, and there were lots of animals on the savanna. The restaurant was wonderful. My mom is 86 and not an adventurous eater, but she would love to go back and try other things. This restaurant and this resort were the biggest pleasant surprise for us.*

And a Canadian family attests to the authenticity of some more adventurous Disney cuisine at Tusker House:

> *Really good quality and variety of food. I travel quite a bit in Africa, and the flavours here were perfect and gave a great introduction to some of the continent's cuisine. Everything was also fresh [even*

though we went] just before park close. Character interactions were also great, as the restaurant wasn't too busy. We saw each character at least two or three times, sometimes with longer interactions.

COUNTER-SERVICE
Mini-Profiles

TO HELP YOU FIND TASTY FAST FOOD, we've provided profiles for the counter-service restaurants in each theme park and Disney Springs. Each one is rated for quality and value. All participate in the dining plan, except where noted, though participating restaurants are subject to change; check theugseries.com/wdwupdates for the latest updates. Mobile ordering (see page 213) is encouraged at most of these restaurants. Value ratings range from A to F, as follows:

A	Exceptional value; a real bargain
B	Good value
C	Fair value; you get exactly what you pay for
D	Somewhat overpriced
F	Extremely overpriced

See page 202 for how the reader-survey percentages break down.

THE MAGIC KINGDOM
Aloha Isle

QUALITY Excellent   **VALUE** B   **PORTION** Medium   **LOCATION** Adventureland
READER-SURVEY RESPONSES ☺ 98% (Much Above Average)

SELECTIONS Soft-serve, ice-cream floats, and pineapple juice.
COMMENTS Located next to *Walt Disney's Enchanted Tiki Room*. The pineapple Dole Whip soft-serve is a world-famous Disney theme park treat.

Auntie Gravity's Galactic Goodies

QUALITY Fair   **VALUE** D   **PORTION** Small–Medium   **LOCATION** Tomorrowland
READER-SURVEY RESPONSES ☺ 85% (Below Average)

SELECTIONS Soft-serve, floats, churros, and other dessert options.
COMMENTS You can find Auntie Gravity's near Star Traders in Tomorrowland. But you probably shouldn't, unless you're desperate for a treat and don't want to leave the area. You'll find better desserts elsewhere.

Casey's Corner

QUALITY Good   **VALUE** B−   **PORTION** Medium   **LOCATION** Main Street, U.S.A.
READER-SURVEY RESPONSES ☺ 93% (Above Average)

SELECTIONS Hot dogs, plant-based "sausage" dogs, corn dogs, corn dog nuggets, fries, and the Baseball Brownie.
COMMENTS Casey's offers the best hot dogs in Walt Disney World—which isn't saying all that much. The quality rivals that of a good ballpark frank. Many visitors find it to be a comforting classic on Main Street.

Cheshire Café

QUALITY Good   **VALUE** B   **PORTION** Medium   **LOCATION** Fantasyland
READER-SURVEY RESPONSES ☺ 91% (Average)

SELECTIONS Different snacks depending on the season, usually including the Cheshire Cat Tail, a pastry filled with sweet cream and chocolate chips.

COMMENTS There is rarely a line. Grab a snack while your family spins on the teacups at Mad Tea Party.

Columbia Harbour House

| QUALITY Good | VALUE B | PORTION Medium | LOCATION Liberty Square |

READER-SURVEY RESPONSES ⊕ 91% (Average)

SELECTIONS Eat light with the grilled salmon with rice, indulge with fried shrimp and fish, or splurge on the lobster roll. Other choices: fried chicken, grilled shrimp, plant-based "crab" cake sandwich, salads, and hush puppies. *For kids:* shrimp skewer, grilled salmon, and more.

COMMENTS Columbia Harbour House is one of the most consistent counter-service restaurants in the Magic Kingdom (and Becky's personal go-to). The upstairs seating is quieter and often downright peaceful.

Cosmic Ray's Starlight Café

| QUALITY Poor–Fair | VALUE C | PORTION Medium | LOCATION Tomorrowland |

READER-SURVEY RESPONSES ⊕ 75% (Do Not Visit)

SELECTIONS Burgers, hot dogs, Greek salad, chicken sandwich, chicken strips, plant-based burgers, and a seasonal dessert. Kosher choices available on request.

COMMENTS This is a crowded, high-volume restaurant where food quality and ambience are sacrificed in the name of just getting something to eat.

The Friar's Nook

| QUALITY Good | VALUE B | PORTION Medium | LOCATION Fantasyland |

READER-SURVEY RESPONSES ⊕ 94% (Above Average)

SELECTIONS Tots, hand pies, and mac and cheese. Also serves breakfast sandwiches and tots in the morning.

COMMENTS A good place for a hearty snack or light meal, but it can be difficult to find seating, which is all outdoors.

Gaston's Tavern

| QUALITY Good | VALUE B | PORTION Medium | LOCATION Fantasyland |

READER-SURVEY RESPONSES ⊕ 90% (Average)

SELECTIONS Ham-and-Gruyère tart, cinnamon rolls, the Grey Stuff, Crème Brûlée Croissant, and LeFou's Brew (frozen apple juice with toasted-marshmallow flavoring).

COMMENTS Very popular throughout the day, especially in the morning. The cinnamon rolls are roughly the size of a barge. Ask for extra icing!

Golden Oak Outpost *(seasonal)*

| QUALITY Fair | VALUE C | PORTION Medium | LOCATION Frontierland |

READER-SURVEY RESPONSES ⊕ 88% (Average)

SELECTIONS Shrimp gumbo, hot honey chicken, and beignets.

COMMENTS With the opening of Tiana's Bayou Adventure, Golden Oak Outpost started serving New Orleans–inspired fare. It's worth trying if you're a fan of the movie. We recommend eating *after* you ride.

Liberty Square Market

| QUALITY Fair | VALUE C | PORTION Medium | LOCATION Liberty Square |

READER-SURVEY RESPONSES ⊕ 92% (Above Average)

SELECTIONS Hot dogs, plus fruit, pretzels, and packaged drinks and snacks.

COMMENTS There's seating nearby, but none of it is covered. It's a good fallback on crowded days.

COST OF COUNTER-SERVICE FOOD	
BAGEL OR MUFFIN $5	HOT DOG $10–$14
BROWNIE $7	ICE CREAM/FROZEN NOVELTIES $6–$13
BURRITO BOWL $12	NACHOS WITH CHEESE $12
CAKE OR PIE $6–$9	PB&J SANDWICH $8 *(kids' meal)*–$11
CEREAL WITH MILK $5–$6	PIZZA *(personal)* $12
CHEESEBURGER WITH FRIES $13–$14	POPCORN $5.50
CHICKEN BREAST SANDWICH $13–$14	PRETZEL $8
CHICKEN NUGGETS WITH FRIES $11–$12	SALAD *(entrée)* $0–$12
CHILDREN'S MEAL *(various)* $8–$12	SALAD *(side)* $9–$12
CHIPS $4	SMOKED TURKEY LEG $12–$15
COOKIE $4–$8	SOUP/CHILI $5–$7
FRIED-FISH BASKET *(with fries)* $14–$16	SUB/DELI SANDWICH $12–$14
FRIES $5	TACO SALAD $11–$13
FRUIT *(whole)* $2–$4	VEGGIE BURGER $13–$14
FRUIT CUP/FRUIT SALAD $6	
COST OF COUNTER-SERVICE DRINKS	
BEER small $9 large $14	BOTTLED WATER $4 (one size)
COFFEE $4 (one size)	LATTE small $5 large $6
FRUIT JUICE small $5 large $7	HOT TEA AND COCOA $4 (one size)
MILK $2 (one size)	
FLOAT, MILKSHAKE, OR SUNDAE small $9 large $14	
SOFT DRINKS, ICED TEA, AND LEMONADE small $4 large $5	

Each person on a dining plan gets a free mug, refillable at any Disney resort. If you're not on a dining plan, a refillable souvenir mug costs $23 plus tax (free refills) at Disney resorts and around $14 plus tax at the water parks.

The Lunching Pad

QUALITY Poor **VALUE** D **PORTION** Small–Medium **LOCATION** Tomorrowland
READER-SURVEY RESPONSES ⊕ 63% (Do Not Visit)

SELECTIONS Hot dogs, pretzels, and specialty frozen drinks.
COMMENTS Unless you want a cream cheese pretzel, sprint away.

Main Street Bakery *(Starbucks)*

QUALITY Good **VALUE** B **PORTION** Medium **LOCATION** Main Street, U.S.A.
READER-SURVEY RESPONSES ⊕ 98% (Much Above Average)

SELECTIONS Coffees, pastries, and breakfast sandwiches.
COMMENTS Extremely busy throughout the day, but the lines move fast. Highly rated because people love their coffee.

Pecos Bill Tall Tale Inn and Cafe

QUALITY Fair **VALUE** C **PORTION** Medium–Large **LOCATION** Frontierland
READER-SURVEY RESPONSES ⊕ 78% (Much Below Average)

SELECTIONS Burger, grilled masa flatbread, Caesar salad, tamale, and create-your-own nacho and rice bowls.
COMMENTS A menu revamp in late 2024 has nudged satisfaction scores slightly upward. It's worth trying if you enjoy this type of food.

Pinocchio Village Haus

QUALITY Poor–Fair **VALUE** D **PORTION** Medium **LOCATION** Fantasyland
READER-SURVEY RESPONSES ⊕ 83% (Below Average)

SELECTIONS Flatbread pizzas, chicken strips, fries, and Caesar salad.
COMMENTS The only reason to eat here is if you can get a seat overlooking It's a Small World.

Sleepy Hollow

QUALITY Fair–Good **VALUE** B– **PORTION** Medium-Large **LOCATION** Liberty Square
READER-SURVEY RESPONSES ⊕ 95% (Above Average)

SELECTIONS Large Mickey waffles, funnel cakes, and corn dogs.
COMMENTS Getting a table with a view of Cinderella Castle is spectacular, but a menu change in 2024 switched the popular waffle sandwiches to Mickey waffles, and scores have gone down since then.

Tomorrowland Terrace Restaurant *(seasonal)*

QUALITY Fair **VALUE** C– **PORTION** Medium-Large **LOCATION** Tomorrowland
READER-SURVEY RESPONSES Not enough surveys to rate

SELECTIONS Varies.
COMMENTS Rarely open. You'll typically only find fireworks dessert parties happening here.

Tortuga Tavern *(seasonal)*

QUALITY Poor–Fair **VALUE** C **PORTION** Medium **LOCATION** Adventureland
READER-SURVEY RESPONSES ⊕ 71% (Do Not Visit)

SELECTIONS Sandwiches, hot dogs, and more.
COMMENTS The eating area is large and shaded. Disney changes up the menu here from time to time—but it's never high-quality.

EPCOT

L'Artisan des Glaces

QUALITY Excellent **VALUE** C **PORTION** Medium-Large **LOCATION** France
READER-SURVEY RESPONSES ⊕ 89% (Average) **NOT ON DISNEY DINING PLAN**

SELECTIONS Ice-cream flavors change but include classics, along with some more-sophisticated options and dairy-free sorbets. Adults over age 21 can enjoy two scoops in a martini glass, topped with Grand Marnier, rum, or whipped cream–flavored vodka.
COMMENTS This is some of the best ice cream at Disney World. Be fancy and get yours served in a macaron or brioche! We especially recommend grabbing ice cream here if you have a walk back to your Crescent Lake resort.

La Cantina de San Angel

QUALITY Good **VALUE** B **PORTION** Medium-Large **LOCATION** Mexico
READER-SURVEY RESPONSES ⊕ 89% (Average)

SELECTIONS Tacos with beef, chicken, or shrimp; fried cheese empanada; nachos; grilled chicken; guacamole; churros; and margaritas. *For kids:* Chicken tacos, empanadas, chicken tenders, or mac and cheese.
COMMENTS A popular spot for a quick meal, with 150 covered outdoor seats, some well shaded. When it's extra busy, the back of the dining room is opened for air-conditioned seating.

Connections Café and Connections Eatery

QUALITY Good **VALUE** C **PORTION** Medium-Large **LOCATION** World Celebration
READER-SURVEY RESPONSES ⊕ 86% (Below Average)

SELECTIONS Burgers, pizza, and salads, with plant-based options. And Baumkuchen (cake)!

COMMENTS Spacious, bright, and cheerful seating areas, with open-kitchen views into the pizza-making process. It's the most reliable, if not exciting, option if you're in World Celebration and need an easy meal.

Festival Favorites / Outdoor Kitchen—Florida Fresh

QUALITY Fair–Good	VALUE C	PORTION Small	LOCATION World Celebration
READER-SURVEY RESPONSES ✚ 92% (Above Average)			

SELECTIONS The menu changes depending on the current festival.

COMMENTS Supposedly, this has favorites from festivals present and past, but your experience will vary based on what's actually being offered.

Fife & Drum Tavern

QUALITY Fair	VALUE C	PORTION Medium	LOCATION The American Adventure
READER-SURVEY RESPONSES ✚ 80% (Much Below Average)			

SELECTIONS Turkey legs, hot dogs, popcorn, soft-serve, slushies, beer, alcoholic lemonade, and root beer floats.

COMMENTS Seating is available in and around the Regal Eagle Smokehouse, behind Fife & Drum.

Les Halles Boulangerie–Patisserie

QUALITY Excellent	VALUE B	PORTION Medium	LOCATION France
READER-SURVEY RESPONSES ✚ 95% (Above Average)			

SELECTIONS The display case is filled with goodies such as sandwiches (ham and cheese; Brie, cranberry, and apple), quiches, soups, bread, and delicate pastries. You will be tempted to buy almost everything you see.

COMMENTS Les Halles is consistently rated as one of the top counter-service restaurants in EPCOT. Breads and pastries are made on-site. Lines build up but generally move quickly. Split up your party between waiting in line to order and waiting for a table if you want any chance of finding a seat.

Katsura Grill

QUALITY Good	VALUE B	PORTION Medium	LOCATION Japan
READER-SURVEY RESPONSES ✚ 90% (Average)			

SELECTIONS Basic sushi; udon noodle bowls (vegetarian or shrimp tempura); pork ramen; chicken, beef, or shrimp teriyaki; chicken curry; edamame; miso soup; yuzu tea cheesecake; teriyaki kids' plate; Kirin beer, sake, plum wine.

COMMENTS The food is just average, but this might be the loveliest spot to escape the EPCOT crowds and eat a quick meal outside. Bonus tip: Kids' meals here make a great value if you're an adult looking for a quick and cheaper meal.

Kringla Bakeri og Kafe

QUALITY Good	VALUE B	PORTION Small	LOCATION Norway
READER-SURVEY RESPONSES ✚ 97% (Much Above Average)			

SELECTIONS Norwegian pastries and desserts, iced coffee, and imported beers and wines.

COMMENTS Limited menu. The School Bread (a sweet roll filled with custard and dipped in coconut) is popular. Outdoor seating only.

Lotus Blossom Café

QUALITY Fair	VALUE C	PORTION Medium	LOCATION China
READER-SURVEY RESPONSES ✚ 85% (Below Average)			

SELECTIONS Pork and vegetable egg rolls, pot stickers, orange chicken, chicken fried rice, Mongolian beef with rice, caramel-ginger or lychee ice cream, plum wine, and Tsingtao beer.

COMMENTS The menu rarely changes, and the food is a snooze. Opt for a nearby festival booth instead.

Pizza al Taglio

QUALITY Good	VALUE B	PORTION Medium	LOCATION Italy
READER-SURVEY RESPONSES ⊕ 91% (Average)			

SELECTIONS Pepperoni or margherita pizza, tiramisu, alcoholic beverages.

COMMENTS If you can't get a reservation at **Via Napoli,** this is a good fallback. But there are other, better-rated counter-service options nearby.

Refreshment Outpost

QUALITY Good	VALUE B−	PORTION Small-Medium	LOCATION Between Germany and China
READER-SURVEY RESPONSES Not enough surveys to rate			

SELECTIONS Typically festival offerings.

COMMENTS Refreshment Outpost has been making a name for itself with some great festival food offerings, but if a festival isn't operating, skip it.

Refreshment Port

QUALITY Good	VALUE B−	PORTION Medium	LOCATION Near Canada
READER-SURVEY RESPONSES ⊕ 86% (Below Average)			

SELECTIONS Soft-serve and additional festival-related fare.

COMMENTS Ratings are boosted by festival options. Another skip if there's not a festival running.

Regal Eagle Smokehouse: Craft Drafts & Barbecue

QUALITY Good-Excellent	VALUE A−	PORTION Large	LOCATION The American Adventure
READER-SURVEY RESPONSES ⊕ 95% (Above Average)			

SELECTIONS Regional barbecue specialties, including Memphis smoked ribs, Kansas City chicken, North Carolina chopped pork, and Texas brisket; burgers; salads; vegetarian options; beer, hard cider, wine, cocktails.

COMMENTS Regal Eagle serves decent barbecue (says the barbecue snob from the Midwest) in hearty portions. If you have eaters who are skeptical of other options in World Showcase, it's a reliable choice. But if you're a barbecue fan, **The Polite Pig** at Disney Springs (see page 240) is where you really need to go.

Sommerfest

QUALITY Fair	VALUE C	PORTION Medium	LOCATION Germany
READER-SURVEY RESPONSES ⊕ 86% (Above Average)			

SELECTIONS Bratwurst, pretzel bread pudding, jumbo pretzel, cold beer.

COMMENTS Tables are set up in the courtyard. Much of the food looks (and sounds) better than it tastes. You're better off making a reservation for **Biergarten Restaurant** (see page 248).

Sunshine Seasons

QUALITY Fair-Good	VALUE B	PORTION Medium	LOCATION The Land
READER-SURVEY RESPONSES ⊕ 85% (Below Average)			

SELECTIONS There are three areas: (1) wood-fired grills and rotisserie; (2) sandwiches and flatbreads; and (3) the soup-and-salad shop, with soups made daily. There are also grab-and-go sections.

COMMENTS Sunshine Seasons used to set the standard for good cafeteria-style fare, but it hasn't rebounded since the pandemic. If someone with pre-pandemic Disney experience is recommending it, ignore their advice.

Tangierine Café

QUALITY Fair–Good	VALUE B–	PORTION Medium	LOCATION Morocco
READER-SURVEY RESPONSES ⊕ 79% (Much Below Average)			

SELECTIONS Generally festival offerings, with some filler in between festivals.
COMMENTS In the 2025 edition, this location was rated above average. How the mighty have fallen. Skip it unless a festival is running.

Yorkshire County Fish Shop

QUALITY Good	VALUE A	PORTION Large	LOCATION United Kingdom
READER-SURVEY RESPONSES ⊕ 94% (Above Average)			

SELECTIONS Fish-and-chips, Bass Pale Ale draft, and Harp Lager.
COMMENTS There's usually a line for the crisp, hot fish-and-chips at this convenient fast-food window. The smell alone will draw you in. Outdoor seating overlooks the lagoon.

DISNEY'S ANIMAL KINGDOM

Creature Comforts (Starbucks)

QUALITY Good	VALUE C	PORTION Small–Medium	LOCATION Discovery Island near Africa
READER-SURVEY RESPONSES ⊕ 86% (Below Average)			

SELECTIONS Coffee drinks and teas; sandwiches and pastries.
COMMENTS The fare is largely the same as you'd find at any other Starbucks, plus the occasional Animal Kingdom–themed treat. This is the lowest-rated Starbucks equivalent this year.

Eight Spoon Café

QUALITY Good	VALUE B	PORTION Medium	LOCATION Discovery Island
READER-SURVEY RESPONSES ⊕ 100% (Exceptional)			

SELECTIONS Baked mac and cheese, plus other stereotypical Disney snacks, including churros.
COMMENTS Eight Spoon Café is "just" a food cart, but it has reliably great mac and cheese if that's your jam.

Flame Tree Barbecue

QUALITY Good	VALUE A–	PORTION Large	LOCATION Discovery Island
READER-SURVEY RESPONSES ⊕ 95% (Above Average)			

SELECTIONS St. Louis–style ribs; smoked half chicken; pulled-pork sandwich; mac and cheese with pulled pork; plant-based "sausage" sandwich; Safari Amber beer, frozen mango-raspberry coconut rum drink.
COMMENTS One of our favorites for lunch, mostly for the location. Keep walking down and toward the water. Few others will trek that far with a tray, and you'll be rewarded with beautiful views. Portions are large enough that a family of four can order two or three entrées and not finish all the food.

Harambe Market

QUALITY Good	VALUE B	PORTION Medium	LOCATION Africa
READER-SURVEY RESPONSES ⊕ 92% (Above Average)			

SELECTIONS Grilled chicken or shrimp served over rice and salad greens, salads, plant-based "sausage." Kids' selections include PB&J, chicken strips, and chicken or shrimp rice bowls.

COMMENTS Disney Imagineers modeled Harambe's marketplace setting after a typical real-life market in an African nation during the 1960s colonial era. It looks and feels authentic, but perhaps as part of the authenticity, the spice (heat) levels have been trending upward.

Kusafiri Coffee Shop and Bakery

QUALITY Good	VALUE B	PORTION Medium	LOCATION Africa
READER-SURVEY RESPONSES ⊕ 93% (Above Average)			NOT ON DISNEY DINING PLAN

SELECTIONS Previously, this location was open all day but now only serves breakfast, including a pistachio-honey croissant, sausage biscuits, and colossal cinnamon rolls.

COMMENTS The cinnamon roll is a favorite, but whenever we try them, they are always stale.

Mr. Kamal's

QUALITY Good	VALUE B	PORTION Medium	LOCATION Between Asia and Africa
READER-SURVEY RESPONSES ⊕ 100% (Exceptional)			

SELECTIONS Small snacks like dumplings and seasoned fries.

COMMENTS The fries have their own cult following.

Pizzafari

QUALITY Poor	VALUE D	PORTION Medium	LOCATION Discovery Island
READER-SURVEY RESPONSES ⊕ 78% (Much Below Average)			

SELECTIONS Chicken pastas, personal pizzas, Caesar salad. *For kids:* Mac and cheese, pastas, cheese pizza, or PB&J. Cupcakes for dessert.

COMMENTS The menu is astoundingly unimpressive. Walk elsewhere.

Pongu Pongu

QUALITY Good	VALUE B	PORTION Medium	LOCATION Discovery Island
READER-SURVEY RESPONSES ⊕ 91% (Average)			

SELECTIONS Stuffed pancakes, pineapple–cream cheese spring rolls, pretzels.

COMMENTS Breakfast is the time to be here.

Royal Anandapur Tea Company

QUALITY Good	VALUE B	PORTION Medium	LOCATION Asia	READER-SURVEY RESPONSES Not enough surveys to rate	NOT ON DISNEY DINING PLAN

SELECTIONS Hot and iced teas, hot chocolate, coffee and espresso drinks, fantastic frozen chai, pastries.

COMMENTS This is the kind of small, eclectic, Animal Kingdom–specific food stand that you wish other parks had. Around 10 loose teas from Asia and Africa can be ordered hot or iced.

Satu'li Canteen

QUALITY Good-Excellent	VALUE A-	PORTION Medium-Large	LOCATION Pandora
READER-SURVEY RESPONSES ⊕ 96% (Much Above Average)			

SELECTIONS The signature item is the customizable bowl. Start with a base of salad, red and sweet potato hash, rice and beans, or whole grains and rice. Add wood-grilled chicken, slow-roasted beef, chili-garlic shrimp, or chili-spiced fried tofu, and finish with a choice of sauces. The menu also offers steamed "pods": bao buns with a cheeseburger filling, served with root-vegetable chips and crunchy vegetable slaw.

COMMENTS The top counter-service spot in the park—and one of the best in all of the World.

Yak & Yeti Local Food Cafes

QUALITY Fair	VALUE B−	PORTION Large	LOCATION Asia
READER-SURVEY RESPONSES ⊕ 89% (Average)			

SELECTIONS Honey chicken with steamed rice, cheeseburger, teriyaki chicken salad, vegetarian tikka masala, Korean-style fried chicken sandwich with kimchi, sweet-and-sour tempura shrimp, egg rolls, and fried rice. Breakfast is American-style fare such as breakfast bowls and English muffin breakfast sandwiches. *For kids:* Chicken tenders, PB&J, or cheeseburger with carrot sticks and fresh fruit.

COMMENTS Good for filling up with quality food when you're in a hurry, but it doesn't offer mobile ordering! There is an expanded seating area behind the pickup windows.

DISNEY'S HOLLYWOOD STUDIOS
ABC Commissary

QUALITY Fair-Good	VALUE B−	PORTION Medium	LOCATION Commissary Lane
READER-SURVEY RESPONSES ⊕ 94% (Above Average)			

SELECTIONS Pork carnitas or shrimp tacos, Buffalo chicken grilled cheese, Mediterranean salad with or without chicken, chicken club sandwich, plant-based burger, beer. *For kids:* Chicken salad sandwich, chicken arugula salad, pork taco, or grilled ham and cheese.

COMMENTS The Buffalo chicken grilled cheese and the shrimp tacos are the standout menu items. Scores here have been increasing steadily for a couple of years.

Backlot Express

QUALITY Fair	VALUE C	PORTION Medium	LOCATION Echo Lake
READER-SURVEY RESPONSES ⊕ 83% (Below Average)			

SELECTIONS Bacon cheeseburger, chicken strips, Cuban sandwich, Southwest salad (with or without chicken), teriyaki chicken bowl, or barbecue pulled pork burger. *For kids:* Chicken strips or mac and cheese.

COMMENTS Fun props, some used in movies, decorate this spacious eatery where scores have been on the decline.

Catalina Eddie's

QUALITY Fair	VALUE C	PORTION Medium-Large	LOCATION Sunset Boulevard
READER-SURVEY RESPONSES ⊕ 92% (Above Average)			

SELECTIONS Pizza, Caesar salad, or meatball sub.

COMMENTS Something turned the scores around here in 2024–2025 from terrible to OK. We don't claim to know what it was.

Docking Bay 7 Food and Cargo

QUALITY Good	VALUE A−	PORTION Medium	LOCATION Galaxy's Edge
READER-SURVEY RESPONSES ⊕ 92% (Above Average)			

SELECTIONS Smoked Kaadu Ribs, named after the creature Jar Jar Binks rode in *Episode I* (but actually pork), are cut vertically for an alien appearance, then glazed with a sticky-sweet sauce and served with down-home blueberry corn muffins. Endorian Tip Yip (chicken) is roasted on a salad or compressed into cubes, deep-fried, and served with mac and cheese and roasted vegetables. There are plenty of other unique options too.

COMMENTS This is our go-to for quick service in Hollywood Studios. Most items here are above-average quality. The Tip Yip chicken is moist and flavorful, as are the vegetable kefta in the Felucian Garden Spread. The ribs, however, are difficult to eat. Also, note that the kids' menu isn't particularly kid-friendly: In keeping with the idea that you're on an alien planet, many of the foods come in unfamiliar shapes and colors.

Dockside Diner

QUALITY Fair **VALUE** D **PORTION** Small–Medium **LOCATION** Echo Lake
READER-SURVEY RESPONSES ⊕ 92% (Above Average)

SELECTIONS Hot dogs with over-the-top toppings. Lots of variations on hot dogs, plus some bacon mac and cheese.

COMMENTS Limited seating at nearby picnic tables.

Fairfax Fare

QUALITY Poor–Fair **VALUE** C+ **PORTION** Medium **LOCATION** Sunset Boulevard
READER-SURVEY RESPONSES ⊕ 77% (Much Below Average)

SELECTIONS Bunches of bowls that don't impress anyone who tries them.

COMMENTS Just don't eat on Sunset Boulevard. Walk somewhere else.

Milk Stand

QUALITY Fair **VALUE** D **PORTION** Small **LOCATION** Galaxy's Edge
READER-SURVEY RESPONSES ⊕ 97% (Much Above Average)

SELECTIONS Frozen nondairy drinks, with or without alcohol.

COMMENTS These plant-based beverages have the consistency of a smoothie. Green milk, as seen in *The Last Jedi,* has floral flavors, while the blue drink from *A New Hope* tastes of melon and pineapple. These "milks" are expensive, so split one if you can. We recommend avoiding the optional splash of booze. It's not worth the upcharge.

Oga's Cantina

QUALITY Fair **VALUE** D **PORTION** Small–Medium **LOCATION** Galaxy's Edge
READER-SURVEY RESPONSES ⊕ 84% (Below Average)

SELECTIONS Alcoholic and nonalcoholic cocktails; charcuterie board, flatbread, and pretzel roll.

COMMENTS This cantina will instantly remind fans of the Mos Eisley watering hole from *A New Hope*. A droid DJ (a recycled Captain Rex from the original Star Tours) spins an original '80s-style soundtrack. All of the signature cocktails and nonalcoholic beverages are unique and delightful.

Although it's technically neither counter service nor table service, Oga's does take reservations, which are available up to 60 days in advance. Most of the cantina is standing room only. That, plus the lack of food options, kept scores low in 2023 and 2024. Disney is trying to address this by adding more food options (but not more seating).

Ronto Roasters

QUALITY Good **VALUE** B **PORTION** Medium **LOCATION** Galaxy's Edge
READER-SURVEY RESPONSES ⊕ 94% (Above Average)

SELECTIONS The Ronto Wrap (pita bread filled with roasted pork, grilled pork sausage, and slaw), pork rinds, nonalcoholic fruit punch. Breakfast wraps are available too.

COMMENTS A disgruntled smelting droid named 8D-J8 does the cooking, turning alien meats on a rotating spit beneath a recycled podracing engine. The wraps are delicious and filling.

Rosie's All-American Cafe

QUALITY Poor **VALUE** D **PORTION** Medium **LOCATION** Sunset Boulevard
READER-SURVEY RESPONSES ⊕ 68% (Do Not Visit)

SELECTIONS Burgers, hot dogs, chicken nuggets, fries, plant-based "lobster" roll. *For kids:* Cheeseburger or chicken nuggets.

COMMENTS It's close enough to the Tower of Terror that you can hear the screams as you eat—an ominous soundtrack to what is likely a disappointing meal.

The Trolley Car Cafe *(Starbucks)*

QUALITY Good	VALUE C	PORTION Medium	LOCATION Hollywood Boulevard
READER-SURVEY RESPONSES ⊕ 97% (Much Above Average)			

SELECTIONS Coffee drinks and teas, breakfast sandwiches, and pastries.

COMMENTS The building is the real attraction: The pink-stucco Spanish Colonial exterior calls to mind Old Hollywood, and the industrial-style interior evokes a trolley-car switching station.

Woody's Lunch Box

QUALITY Good	VALUE B	PORTION Medium	LOCATION Toy Story Land
READER-SURVEY RESPONSES ⊕ 90% (Average)			

SELECTIONS *Breakfast:* Lunch Box Tarts (think gourmet toaster pastries); breakfast bowl with scrambled eggs, potato barrels, and country gravy. *Lunch and dinner:* Sandwiches (barbecue brisket, smoked turkey, grilled three-cheese), tomato-basil soup, "totchos" (potato barrels smothered with chili, queso, and corn chips).

COMMENTS Limited seating and shade. Be prepared to hover and pounce!

DISNEY SPRINGS

Amorette's Patisserie

QUALITY Excellent	VALUE B-	PORTION Small-Medium	LOCATION Town Center
READER-SURVEY RESPONSES ⊕ 93% (Above Average) NOT ON DISNEY DINING PLAN			

SELECTIONS Cakes and pastries made by talented Disney chefs, Disney-themed 11-layer dome cake, sandwiches, Champagne.

COMMENTS Don't miss Amorette's Petit Cake, a smaller portion of its signature cake with 11 layers of red velvet and chocolate cakes, cherry and chocolate mousses, raspberry jelly, and Italian buttercream.

Blaze Fast-Fire'd Pizza

QUALITY Good	VALUE A	PORTION Large	LOCATION Town Center
READER-SURVEY RESPONSES ⊕ 97% (Much Above Average)			

SELECTIONS Specialty and build-your-own 11-inch pizzas, with a selection of 40-plus fresh toppings and sauces; salads.

COMMENTS Each fast-fired pizza is prepared in around 3 minutes after you select your toppings. Ignore any long line—it moves quickly. The versatility of making your own pizza goes a long way with parties of varying tastes or dietary restrictions.

Chicken Guy!

QUALITY Fair	VALUE C	PORTION Medium-Large	LOCATION Town Center
READER-SURVEY RESPONSES ⊕ 77% (Much Below Average)			

SELECTIONS Fried chicken tenders, fries, mac and cheese.

COMMENTS *Guy* refers to the restaurant's creator, celebrity chef Guy Fieri. The only way to get adventurous here is with the sauces; there are dozens.

Cookes of Dublin

QUALITY Fair	VALUE B-	PORTION Medium-Large	LOCATION The Landing
READER-SURVEY RESPONSES ⊕ 95% (Above Average)			

SELECTIONS Fried chicken tenders, burgers, fish-and-chips, plus more adventurous options like chicken-and-mushroom pie or Hog in a Box (pulled pork, fried skin-on potatoes, stuffing, caramelized onions, and apple sauce). *For kids:* Fish, chicken nuggets, cheeseburger with "chips."

COMMENTS Wait times can be on the high side, but even the pickiest eaters can dine here. Still, if you're in the area and can get a table at **Raglan Road** (see page 271) next door, do that instead.

D-Luxe Burger

QUALITY Good	VALUE C	PORTION Medium	LOCATION Town Center
READER-SURVEY RESPONSES ⊕ 91% (Average)			

SELECTIONS Specialty burgers, hand-cut fries with a variety of dipping sauces (curry ketchup and garlic ranch are zesty and unique), gelato shakes (spiked and nonalcoholic).

COMMENTS The food takes a little longer than we'd like, but the specialty options are worth the wait, if not the price. Mobile ordering available.

Earl of Sandwich

QUALITY Good	VALUE B	PORTION Medium	LOCATION Marketplace
READER-SURVEY RESPONSES ⊕ 90% (Average)			

SELECTIONS Sandwiches, salads, wraps, soups, brownies, and cookies.

COMMENTS There's always a long line here, but it tends to move quickly. Thanks to quality ingredients and plenty of options, Earl of Sandwich has been well rated by readers for many years.

Eet by Maneet Chauhan

QUALITY Good–Excellent	VALUE B+	PORTION Medium–Large
LOCATION Marketplace	READER-SURVEY RESPONSES ⊕ 100% (Exceptional)	

SELECTIONS Naan, naan pizza, samosas, tandoori poutine, salads, bowls.

COMMENTS The menu here is always changing and growing—a good thing. This is a fascinating selection of Indian fusion cuisine. The flavors are all thought-through, and the naan is authentically made. This is also a great place if you're looking for dining with fewer kids because even the kids' menu is slightly more adventurous than normal.

Pepe by José Andrés

QUALITY Good	VALUE B	PORTION Small	LOCATION West Side	READER-SURVEY
RESPONSES Not enough surveys to rate		NOT ON DISNEY DINING PLAN		

SELECTIONS Spanish sandwiches such as bikinis (think an elevated grilled cheese), as well as gazpacho.

COMMENTS Pepe is the first permanent location of José Andrés's popular food truck in Disney Springs.

Pizza Ponte

QUALITY Good	VALUE B	PORTION Medium	LOCATION The Landing
READER-SURVEY RESPONSES Not enough surveys to rate			

SELECTIONS Sandwiches, pizza by the slice, and Italian desserts such as cannoli and tiramisu.

COMMENTS Pizza Ponte is above average, even for New York. The prices ($7–$8 per slice) are high, but the slices are large.

The Polite Pig

QUALITY Excellent	VALUE B	PORTION Medium	LOCATION Town Center
READER-SURVEY RESPONSES ⊕ 88% (Average)			

SELECTIONS Southern barbecue staples (pulled pork, ribs, smoked chicken), specialty veggie sides (barbecue cauliflower, grilled corn, whiskey-caramel Brussels sprouts), bourbon bar, cocktails, local beers on tap, homemade cakes and pies for dessert.

COMMENTS A hybrid fast-casual restaurant, The Polite Pig offers more than your standard quick service. Meat smoked on-site is the name of the game, but the side dishes are the real star. Split a few entrées (the pulled pork and ribs are our favorites) with sides; it's the best bang for your buck and offers a chance to try as many sides as possible.

Salt & Straw

QUALITY Excellent	VALUE B	PORTION Medium	LOCATION West Side
READER SURVEY RESPONSES ⊕ 100% (Exceptional)			

SELECTIONS Gourmet flavors made by people who really care about ice cream.

COMMENTS Along with familiar flavors based around chocolate and vanilla, some favorites include the strawberry-honey-balsamic with black pepper; the Arbequina olive oil; and the salted, malted chocolate chip cookie dough.

Starbucks

QUALITY Good	VALUE C	PORTION Small	LOCATION Marketplace
READER-SURVEY RESPONSES ⊕ 96% (Much Above Average)			

SELECTIONS Coffee drinks and teas; breakfast sandwiches and pastries.

COMMENTS Your typical Starbucks. Why the high rating? People love coffee.

FULL-SERVICE RESTAURANTS
In Depth

THE RESTAURANT PROFILES IN THIS SECTION allow you to quickly check the cuisine, location, star rating, cost range, quality rating, and value rating of every full-service restaurant at Walt Disney World. Reservations are strongly recommended.

The profiles, including the reader ratings, reflect menus and prices as we went to press. Dining plan information is based on the 2025 version of the plan and was up-to-date as of April 2025.

OVERALL RATING Ranging from one to five stars, this rating encompasses the entire dining experience: style, service, ambience, and food quality. Five stars is the highest rating attainable. Our star ratings don't necessarily correspond to those awarded by AAA, Mobil, Zagat, or other restaurant reviewers.

COST RANGE This tells you approximately how much you can expect to spend on a full-service entrée (not including appetizers, side dishes, soups and salads, desserts, drinks, and tips). Cost ranges are categorized as **inexpensive** (less than $25), **moderate** ($25–$35), or **expensive** ($36 and up). Keep in mind that these are Disney prices. A $24 entrée may not be considered inexpensive in the "real world," but it is at Disney.

QUALITY RATING Food quality is rated from one to five stars, five being the highest possible rating. The criteria are taste, freshness of

continued on page 246

WDW RESTAURANTS BY CUISINE

CUISINE	LOCATION	OVERALL RATING	COST	QUALITY RATING	VALUE RATING
AFRICAN					
BOMA—FLAVORS OF AFRICA	Animal Kingdom Lodge–Jambo House	★★★★	Exp	★★★★	★★★½
JIKO—THE COOKING PLACE	Animal Kingdom Lodge–Jambo House	★★★★	Exp	★★★★	★★★★
SANAA	Animal Kingdom Villas–Kidani Village	★★★★	Mod	★★★★	★★★★½
JUNGLE NAVIGATION CO. LTD. SKIPPER CANTEEN	Magic Kingdom	★★★½	Mod	★★★½	★★★
TUSKER HOUSE RESTAURANT	Animal Kingdom	★★★	Exp	★★★½	★★★
AMERICAN					
CÍTRICOS	Grand Floridian	★★★★	Exp	★★★★½	★★★½
CHEF ART SMITH'S HOMECOMIN'	Disney Springs	★★★½	Inexp	★★★★	★★★½
STORY BOOK DINING AT ARTIST POINT WITH SNOW WHITE	Wilderness Lodge	★★★½	Exp	★★★★	★★★½
THE HOLLYWOOD BROWN DERBY	DHS	★★★½	Exp	★★★★	★★½
TIFFINS RESTAURANT	Animal Kingdom	★★★½	Exp	★★★★	★★★
LIBERTY TREE TAVERN	Magic Kingdom	★★★½	Exp	★★★½	★★★½
GARDEN GRILL RESTAURANT	The Land, EPCOT	★★★½	Exp	★★★½	★★★½
HOLLYWOOD & VINE	DHS	★★★½	Exp	★★★½	★★★
CALIFORNIA GRILL	Contemporary	★★★½	Exp	★★★½	★★
GRAND FLORIDIAN CAFE	Grand Floridian	★★★	Mod	★★★½	★★★
TUSKER HOUSE RESTAURANT	Animal Kingdom	★★★	Exp	★★★½	★★★
WOLFGANG PUCK BAR & GRILL	Disney Springs	★★★	Mod	★★★½	★★★
THE EDISON	Disney Springs	★★★	Exp	★★★½	★★
ROUNDUP RODEO BBQ	Disney's Hollywood Studios	★★★	Exp	★★★	★★★½
WHISPERING CANYON CAFE	Wilderness Lodge	★★★	Exp	★★★	★★★½
ALE & COMPASS RESTAURANT	Yacht Club	★★★	Mod	★★★	★★★
BEACHES & CREAM SODA SHOP	Beach Club	★★★	Inexp	★★★	★★★
CAPE MAY CAFE	Beach Club	★★★	Exp	★★★	★★★
50'S PRIME TIME CAFÉ	DHS	★★★	Mod	★★★	★★★
HOUSE OF BLUES RESTAURANT & BAR	Disney Springs	★★★	Inexp	★★★	★★★
OLIVIA'S CAFE	Old Key West	★★★	Mod	★★★	★★★
THREE BRIDGES BAR & GRILL	Coronado Springs	★★★	Inexp	★★★	★★★
CITY WORKS EATERY AND POUR HOUSE	Disney Springs	★★★	Mod	★★★	★★½
1900 PARK FARE	Grand Floridian	★★★	Exp	★★★	★★½

WDW RESTAURANTS BY CUISINE

CUISINE	LOCATION	OVERALL RATING	COST	QUALITY RATING	VALUE RATING
AMERICAN (continued)					
CINDERELLA'S ROYAL TABLE	Magic Kingdom	★★★	Exp	★★★	★★
PADDLEFISH	Disney Springs	★★½	Exp	★★★	★★½
BOATWRIGHT'S DINING HALL	Port Orleans Riverside	★★½	Mod	★★½	★★½
THE CRYSTAL PALACE	Magic Kingdom	★★½	Exp	★★½	★★½
CHEF MICKEY'S	Contemporary	★★½	Exp	★★½	★★
SPLITSVILLE DINING ROOM	Disney Springs	★★½	Inexp	★★½	★★
BE OUR GUEST RESTAURANT	Magic Kingdom	★★	Exp	★★★	★★
THE PLAZA RESTAURANT	Magic Kingdom	★★	Inexp	★★½	★★½
GARDEN GROVE	Swan	★★	Inexp	★★½	★★
THE FOUNTAIN	Dolphin	★★	Inexp	★★	★★
SCI-FI DINE-IN THEATER RESTAURANT	DHS	★★	Inexp	★★	★★
SPACE 220	World Discovery, EPCOT	★★	Exp	★★½	★½
THE TURF CLUB BAR AND GRILL	Saratoga Springs	★★	Mod	★★½	★★
T-REX	Disney Springs	★★	Mod	★★	★★
RAINFOREST CAFE	Animal Kingdom and Disney Springs	★★	Mod	★½	★★
PLANET HOLLYWOOD	Disney Springs	★½	Mod	★	★½
MAYA GRILL	Coronado Springs	★	Mod	★	★★
BRITISH					
ROSE & CROWN DINING ROOM	UK, EPCOT	★★★	Mod	★★★½	★★½
BUFFET					
BOMA—FLAVORS OF AFRICA	Animal Kingdom Lodge–Jambo House	★★★★	Exp	★★★★	★★★½
HOLLYWOOD & VINE	DHS	★★★½	Exp	★★★½	★★★
BIERGARTEN RESTAURANT	Germany, EPCOT	★★★	Exp	★★★	★★★★
CAPE MAY CAFE	Beach Club	★★★	Exp	★★★	★★★
1900 PARK FARE	Grand Floridian	★★★	Exp	★★★	★★½
THE CRYSTAL PALACE	Magic Kingdom	★★½	Exp	★★½	★★½
CHEF MICKEY'S	Contemporary	★★½	Exp	★★½	★★
CAJUN					
BOATWRIGHT'S DINING HALL	Port Orleans Riverside	★★½	Mod	★★½	★★½
CHINESE					
NINE DRAGONS RESTAURANT	China, EPCOT	★★½	Mod	★★★	★★

continued on next page

WDW RESTAURANTS BY CUISINE (continued)

CUISINE	LOCATION	OVERALL RATING	COST	QUALITY RATING	VALUE RATING
FRENCH					
TOPOLINO'S TERRACE	Riviera	★★★½	Exp	★★★★	★★★
LA CRÊPERIE DE PARIS	France, EPCOT	★★★½	Inexp	★★★½	★★★½
CHEFS DE FRANCE	France, EPCOT	★★½	Exp	★★½	★★★
MONSIEUR PAUL	France, EPCOT	★★½	Exp	★★½	★½
BE OUR GUEST RESTAURANT	Magic Kingdom	★★	Exp	★★★	★★
GERMAN					
BIERGARTEN RESTAURANT	Germany, EPCOT	★★★	Exp	★★★	★★★★
GOURMET					
VICTORIA & ALBERT'S	Grand Floridian	★★★★★	Exp	★★★★★	★★★★
INDIAN					
SANAA	Animal Kingdom Villas–Kidani Village	★★★★	Mod	★★★★	★★★★½
IRISH					
RAGLAN ROAD IRISH PUB & RESTAURANT	Disney Springs	★★★★	Mod	★★★★	★★★★
ITALIAN					
TOPOLINO'S TERRACE	Riviera	★★★½	Exp	★★★★	★★★
VIA NAPOLI RISTORANTE E PIZZERIA	Italy, EPCOT	★★★½	Mod	★★★½	★★★
TRATTORIA AL FORNO	BoardWalk	★★★	Mod	★★★½	★★½
IL MULINO	Swan	★★★	Mod	★★★	★★½
TUTTO ITALIA RISTORANTE	Italy, EPCOT	★★★	Exp	★★★	★★½
TERRALINA CRAFTED ITALIAN	Disney Springs	★★	Mod	★★½	★★
MARIA & ENZO'S RISTORANTE	Disney Springs	★★	Exp	★★	★★
TONY'S TOWN SQUARE RESTAURANT	Magic Kingdom	★★	Mod	★★	★★
JAPANESE/SUSHI					
TAKUMI-TEI	Japan, EPCOT	★★★★½	Exp	★★★★★	★★★½
SHIKI-SAI	Japan, EPCOT	★★★★	Mod	★★★★	★★★★
MORIMOTO ASIA	Disney Springs	★★★★	Mod	★★★★	★★★
TEPPAN EDO	Japan, EPCOT	★★★½	Exp	★★★★	★★★
KIMONOS	Swan	★★★	Inexp	★★★½	★★★½
LATIN					
JUNGLE NAVIGATION CO. LTD. SKIPPER CANTEEN	Magic Kingdom	★★★½	Mod	★★★½	★★★
SEBASTIAN'S BISTRO	Caribbean Beach	★★★	Exp	★★★	★★★½
PARADISO 37	Disney Springs	★★	Exp	★★	★★
MEDITERRANEAN					
AMARE	Swan	★★★	Exp	★★★½	★★★

FULL-SERVICE RESTAURANTS IN DEPTH

WDW RESTAURANTS BY CUISINE (continued)

CUISINE	LOCATION	OVERALL RATING	COST	QUALITY RATING	VALUE RATING
MEXICAN					
ROSA MEXICANO	Dolphin	★★★½	Exp	★★★★	★★★½
LA HACIENDA DE SAN ANGEL	Mexico, EPCOT	★★★	Exp	★★★	★★★½
SAN ANGEL INN RESTAURANTE	Mexico, EPCOT	★★★	Mod	★★★	★★
FRONTERA COCINA	Disney Springs	★★½	Mod	★★★	★★½
MAYA GRILL	Coronado Springs	★	Mod	★	★★
MOROCCAN					
SPICE ROAD TABLE	Morocco, EPCOT	★★★★	Inexp	★★★★	★★★½
NORWEGIAN					
AKERSHUS ROYAL BANQUET HALL	Norway, EPCOT	★★★	Exp	★★★	★★★
PAN-ASIAN/POLYNESIAN					
MORIMOTO ASIA	Disney Springs	★★★★	Mod	★★★★	★★★
TIFFINS RESTAURANT	Animal Kingdom	★★★½	Exp	★★★★	★★★
JUNGLE NAVIGATION CO. LTD. SKIPPER CANTEEN	Magic Kingdom	★★★½	Mod	★★★½	★★★
KONA CAFE	Polynesian Village	★★★	Mod	★★★	★★★
YAK & YETI RESTAURANT	Animal Kingdom	★★★	Mod	★★★	★★★
'OHANA	Polynesian Village	★★★	Exp	★★★	★★½
SEAFOOD					
THE BOATHOUSE	Disney Springs	★★★½	Exp	★★★½	★★★
FLYING FISH	BoardWalk	★★★½	Exp	★★★½	★★★
NARCOOSSEE'S	Grand Floridian	★★★★	Exp	★★★★	★★★½
SEBASTIAN'S BISTRO	Caribbean Beach	★★★	Exp	★★★	★★★½
CORAL REEF RESTAURANT	The Seas, EPCOT	★★★	Mod	★★★	★★½
PADDLEFISH	Disney Springs	★★½	Exp	★★★	★★½
TODD ENGLISH'S BLUEZOO	Dolphin	★★½	Exp	★★★	★★½
SPANISH/TAPAS					
JALEO BY JOSÉ ANDRÉS	Disney Springs	★★★★	Mod	★★★★½	★★★½
THREE BRIDGES BAR & GRILL	Coronado Springs	★★★	Inexp	★★★	★★★
TOLEDO—TAPAS, STEAK & SEAFOOD	Coronado Springs	★★★	Exp	★★★	★★★
STEAK					
STEAKHOUSE 71	Contemporary	★★★½	Exp	★★★½	★★★½
LE CELLIER STEAKHOUSE	Canada, EPCOT	★★★½	Exp	★★★★½	★★★
SUMMER HOUSE ON THE LAKE	Disney Springs	★★★	Mod	★★★½	★★★
STK ORLANDO	Disney Springs	★★½	Exp	★★★½	★★
YACHTSMAN STEAKHOUSE	Yacht Club	★★½	Exp	★★★½	★★
WINE/SMALL PLATES					
WINE BAR GEORGE	Disney Springs	★★★★	Exp	★★★★	★★★½

continued from page 241

ingredients, preparation, presentation, and the creativity of the food served. Price is no consideration.

VALUE RATING If, on the other hand, you're looking for both quality *and* value, then you should check this rating, which is also expressed as stars.

PAYMENT All Walt Disney World restaurants take the following credit cards: American Express, Diners Club, Discover, Japan Credit Bureau, MasterCard, and Visa.

NEW IN 2025
The Cake Bake Shop
Disney's BoardWalk; ☎ 407-574-3040

SUMMARY AND COMMENTS The Cake Bake Shop operated two locations in Indiana before opening on Disney's BoardWalk. All owned by Gwendolyn Rogers, each location is known for its elegant décor, indulgent cakes, and upscale menu. While the atmosphere is beautifully designed and perfect for special occasions, early reviews have been mixed, with some praising the presentation and others finding the food overpriced for the quality. Many guests agree that it's a lovely spot for a treat, but whether it's worth the cost depends on your expectations.

Bourbon Steak by Michael Mina
Dolphin; ☎ 407-934-1362

SUMMARY AND COMMENTS Bourbon Steak by Michael Mina replaced Shula's Steakhouse in the summer of 2025. The restaurant is intended to bring a modern twist to the classic American steakhouse at the Walt Disney World Dolphin. It promises an upscale dining experience, with premium cuts of beef and seafood infused with global flavor. Shula's was a long-time WDW dining fixture (it had been open for 30 years), so we're eager to see if the new concept can live up to the tradition.

FULL-SERVICE RESTAURANT PROFILES
Akershus Royal Banquet Hall ★★★

NORWEGIAN	EXPENSIVE	QUALITY ★★★	VALUE ★★★
READER-SURVEY RESPONSES ⊕ 89% (Average)			

Norway, World Showcase, EPCOT; ☎ 407-939-3463

Reservations Required. **Dining Plan credits** 1 per person, per meal at breakfast; 2 per person, per meal at lunch and dinner. **When to go** Anytime. **Cost range** Breakfast $59 (child $38), lunch and dinner $69 (child $46). **Service** ★★★★. **Bar** Full service. **Character breakfast** 8:30 a.m.–12:10 p.m. **Character lunch** 12:15–4:40 p.m. **Character dinner** 5:25–8:05 p.m.

SETTING AND ATMOSPHERE The interior looks like a fairy-tale castle, with high ceilings, stone archways, purple carpets, and regal banners.

HOUSE SPECIALTIES Norwegian meatballs, grilled salmon, chicken and dumplings, lefse, mashed potatoes, green beans. *For kids:* Macaroni and cheese, corn dogs.

OTHER RECOMMENDATIONS Aquavit cocktails.

SUMMARY AND COMMENTS If your child loves the Disney princesses, this is a great spot. The kitchen focuses on getting family-style food out fast.

At almost $20 less per adult than what you'd pay at Cinderella's Royal Table, we'd opt for this princess meal every time.

Ale & Compass Restaurant ★★★

AMERICAN	MODERATE	QUALITY ★★★	VALUE ★★★
READER-SURVEY RESPONSES ⊕ 93% (Above Average)			

Yacht Club Resort; ☎ 407-939-3463

Reservations Recommended. **Dining Plan credits** 1 per person, per meal. **When to go** Anytime. **Cost range** Breakfast buffet $25, à la carte items for all meals $16–$39. **Service** ★★★½. **Bar** Full service. **Breakfast** Daily, 7:30–11 a.m. **Lunch** Daily, 11:45 a.m.–2 p.m. **Dinner** Daily, 5–9 p.m.

SETTING AND ATMOSPHERE The large dining room is polished and pretty in a generic way but with no real theming.

HOUSE SPECIALTIES The burger and 12-layer chocolate cake were favorites, but neither is on the menu anymore.

OTHER RECOMMENDATIONS Vegetarians have two full-fledged meal options: the Protein Bowl (with quinoa, vegan Italian "sausage," sweet potato, and Broccolini) and a pasta with mushrooms and other veggies. Breakfast selections include salted caramel–apple French toast, plus the usual eggs, bacon, pancakes, and waffles.

KIDS' MENU Grilled chicken, baked fish, pasta Bolognese, or cheeseburger, with many side and dessert options.

SUMMARY AND COMMENTS The breakfast buffet here is one of the best values on-property, and it's somehow still a pretty well-kept secret. For $28 you get access to the buffet, a nonalcoholic beverage, and an entrée from the menu. It's worth checking out if you're staying in the area or as a pre-opening reservation on an EPCOT day.

Amare ★★★

MEDITERRANEAN	EXPENSIVE	QUALITY ★★★½	VALUE ★★★
READER-SURVEY RESPONSES ⊕ 90% (Average)			

Swan Reserve; ☎ 407-934-1609

Reservations Recommended. **Dining Plan credits** Not accepted. **When to go** Anytime. **Cost range** Breakfast $16–$25; lunch and dinner $18–$67. **Service** ★★★. **Bar** Full service. **Parking** Valet ($44) or hotel lot ($36), both free with validation. **Breakfast** Daily, 7–11 a.m. **Lunch** Daily, 11:30 a.m.–2 p.m. **Dinner** Daily, 5–11 p.m.

SETTING AND ATMOSPHERE Although this is lobby dining, it's not as loud as you might expect. The white, tan, and blue décor keeps things feeling light and airy.

HOUSE SPECIALTIES The flatbreads are some of the best "pizzas" on-property and are not very well-known.

OTHER RECOMMENDATIONS For the Mediterranean experience, try the grilled souvlaki (meat skewers, plus tabbouleh, hummus, pita bread, and more). It's a great introduction to this cuisine if you've never had it before.

KIDS' MENU Two flatbreads, two pastas, chicken fingers, or burger. Only the last two come with fries.

SUMMARY AND COMMENTS Worth the walk (or boat ride) from EPCOT if it's a particularly busy day there. Reservations should be easy to come by.

Beaches & Cream Soda Shop ★★★½

AMERICAN	INEXPENSIVE	QUALITY ★★★½	VALUE ★★★
READER-SURVEY RESPONSES ⊕ 94% (Above Average)			

Beach Club Resort; ☎ 407-939-3463

Reservations Strongly recommended. **Dining Plan credits** 1 per person, per meal. **When to go** Lunch or dinner. **Cost range** $16–$22. **Service** ★★★. **Bar** Beer, wine, hard floats. **Hours** Daily, 11 a.m.–11 p.m.

SETTING AND ATMOSPHERE Retro soda-fountain décor and servers.
HOUSE SPECIALTIES Burgers and fries; grilled cheese and soup; hand-scooped ice cream, including the gargantuan $38 Kitchen Sink dessert, featuring five flavors of ice cream drowning in toppings.
OTHER RECOMMENDATIONS Root beer float, the No Way José sundae.
KIDS' MENU Grilled chicken or turkey sandwich, mac and cheese, hot dog, cheeseburger with fruits and veggies.
SUMMARY AND COMMENTS Beaches & Cream is always popular, and the seating area is small. Make reservations!

Be Our Guest Restaurant ★★

FRENCH/AMERICAN	EXPENSIVE	QUALITY ★★★	VALUE ★★
READER-SURVEY RESPONSES ⊕ 87% (Below Average)			

Fantasyland, Magic Kingdom; ☎ 407-939-3463

Reservations Strongly recommended. **Dining Plan credits** 2 per person, per meal. **When to go** Lunch or dinner. **Cost range** $72 (child $43). **Service** ★★★. **Bar** Beer, solid selection of French wines. **Lunch** Daily, 11 a.m.–2:55 p.m. **Dinner** Daily, 3–9 p.m.

SETTING AND ATMOSPHERE Be Our Guest re-creates Beast's Castle from *Beauty and the Beast* with three themed rooms: the Grand Ballroom, the mysterious West Wing, and the Castle Gallery. The rooms fill up, with a noise level to match the crowd (up to 550 seats).
HOUSE SPECIALTIES French onion soup, dry-aged Duroc pork chop, the Grey Stuff.
OTHER RECOMMENDATIONS Filet mignon with smashed potatoes, short rib boeuf bourguignon.
KIDS' MENU Pan-seared chicken breast or shrimp, chicken strips, steak, or mac and cheese, with appetizer, sides, and dessert.
SUMMARY AND COMMENTS Be Our Guest has been the most popular restaurant in the Magic Kingdom since it opened in 2012. Unfortunately, it's also regularly one of the worst-rated restaurants on-property. The menu is heavy and expensive, and it lacks enough choices to justify the cost. Food quality has trended slightly upward recently, as have reader scores. A common refrain among many reader comments is that Be Our Guest is "just OK," like this one from Tennessee:

This was actually fine—service was good, and it was fun to see The Beast. Also, the restaurant was beautiful, but the food was just OK for the price.

If you're looking for good food nearby, **Jungle Navigation Co. Ltd. Skipper Canteen** (see page 263) and **Liberty Tree Tavern** (see page 264) are better choices.

Biergarten Restaurant ★★★

GERMAN/BUFFET	EXPENSIVE	QUALITY ★★★	VALUE ★★★★
READER-SURVEY RESPONSES ⊕ 93% (Above Average)			

Germany, World Showcase, EPCOT; ☎ 407-939-3463

Reservations Recommended. **Dining Plan credits** 1 per person, per meal. **When to go** Lunch or dinner. **Cost range** $49 (child $28). **Service** ★★★½. **Bar** Full service with German wine and beer. **Lunch** Daily, noon–3:55 p.m. **Dinner** Daily, 4–8 p.m.

SETTING AND ATMOSPHERE Biergarten is a German restaurant set inside a nighttime town square. You're seated at big tables lined up in rows emanating from a central dance floor and stage. A lederhosen-clad oompah band plays and encourages diners to sing along. German dancers perform throughout the day as well.

HOUSE SPECIALTIES Schnitzel, traditional German sausages, and homemade spaetzle. *For kids:* Mac and cheese, frankfurters.

OTHER RECOMMENDATIONS Rotisserie chicken, braised red cabbage.

SUMMARY AND COMMENTS The buffet is stacked with an astonishing amount of good-quality food. There are plenty of places in Walt Disney World where you could pay more for less. (If you leave here hungry, it's your own fault.) The lively 25-minute show (one every hour) and noisy dining room are part of the fun, especially for families. Becky's kids adore dancing along with the band.

The Boathouse ★★★½

SEAFOOD	EXPENSIVE	QUALITY ★★★½	VALUE ★★★
READER-SURVEY RESPONSES ⊕ 95% (Much Above Average)			

The Landing, Disney Springs; ☎ 407-939-BOAT (2628)

Reservations Strongly recommended. **Dining Plan credits** 2 per person, per meal. **When to go** Lunch or dinner. **Cost range** $19–$72 (child $12). **Service** ★★★★. **Parking** Orange garage. **Bar** Full service, with a good wine selection. **Hours** Daily, 11 a.m.–11 p.m. (until 11:30 p.m. on Friday and Saturday).

SETTING AND ATMOSPHERE The first things you notice about The Boathouse, which is located on the waterfront, are the vintage American Amphicars (1960s-era amphibious cars) and the Italian water taxis floating next to the front door—the multimillion-dollar fleet features 19 rare boats from around the world. The airy restaurant seats up to 600 in nautically themed dining rooms (two private) and outdoors. There are three bars, including one built over the water.

HOUSE SPECIALTIES The menu changes daily, but there's seafood of every sort: a raw bar with fresh oysters, tuna, and wild-caught shrimp; lobster; fish and shellfish; and jumbo lump crab. There's also filet mignon, as well as a selection of desserts.

KIDS' MENU Salmon, popcorn shrimp, mac and cheese, burger, or chicken tenders, served with either red grapes or fries.

SUMMARY AND COMMENTS If you're not sure where to eat in Disney Springs, The Boathouse is a solid choice with an extensive menu. While seafood is the star, the steaks are top-notch as well.

A family of four recommends saving room for dessert:

Great service. Everything was delicious, from the bread to the giant chocolate cake. We took the cake and ate it for three days.

Boatwright's Dining Hall ★★½

AMERICAN/CAJUN	MODERATE	QUALITY ★★½	VALUE ★★½
READER-SURVEY RESPONSES ⊕ 97% (Much Above Average)			

Port Orleans Resort–Riverside; ☎ 407-939-3463

Reservations Recommended. **Dining Plan credits** 1 per person, per meal. **When to go** Early evening. **Cost range** $25–$37 (child $11–$14). **Service** ★★★★. **Bar** Beer and liquor only. **Hours** Daily, 5–9 p.m.

SETTING AND ATMOSPHERE Always busy and a tad noisy, Boatwright's features a New Orleans–inspired dining room with a large boat frame serving as a focal point overhead.

HOUSE SPECIALTIES The Mardi Gras pimento cheese fritters are the best appetizer. The best entrées are the shrimp and grits and the crispy Cajun chicken (it's not that hot).

OTHER RECOMMENDATIONS Roasted prime rib, served with mashed potatoes and Cajun butter.

KIDS' MENU Grilled chicken or fish, mac and cheese, cheeseburger, or pasta with marinara, with a very large selection of kid-friendly sides.

SUMMARY AND COMMENTS The high score here reflects two things: guests who are staying at Port Orleans and are pleased with a table-service option that hits above its weight class, and excellent service. But don't be too fooled—the kitchen struggles with consistency.

Boma—Flavors of Africa ★★★★

AFRICAN/BUFFET	EXPENSIVE	QUALITY ★★★★	VALUE ★★★½
READER-SURVEY RESPONSES ⊕ 96% (Much Above Average)			

Animal Kingdom Lodge & Villas–Jambo House; ☎ 407-939-3463

Reservations Strongly recommended. **Dining Plan credits** 1 per person, per meal. **When to go** Late breakfast or early dinner. **Cost range** Breakfast $39 (child $23), dinner $58 (child $34). **Service** ★★★½. **Bar** Beer and some cocktails. **Breakfast** Daily, 7:30–11:30 a.m. **Dinner** Daily, 5–9:30 p.m.

SETTING AND ATMOSPHERE Boma's huge dining room mimics an African marketplace, complete with thatched-roof ceilings. With so many tables and buffet dining stations, plus the massive open kitchen where guests can observe all the goings-on, the dining room is always loud.

HOUSE SPECIALTIES Boma's buffet takes guests on an adventure full of rich flavors. Dishes represent regional cuisines from across Africa. Daily rotating entrées include carved African spice-crusted beef sirloin, Durban chicken, and tamarind barbecue ribs. Side dishes include tabbouleh, couscous, peanut rice, and spiced green beans. Boma's signature dessert, the Zebra Dome—a thin layer of white cake supporting an orb of Amarula cream-liqueur mousse, smothered with white chocolate ganache and drizzled with dark chocolate—has a cult following.

OTHER RECOMMENDATIONS For breakfast, the seasonal bread pudding always shines; made-to-order omelets and carved meats satisfy those in search of more-American options.

SUMMARY AND COMMENTS Boma is consistently rated as one of the best restaurants in Walt Disney World, but in recent years wait times (even with reservations) have gone way up, and tales of empty or sparse food trays on the buffet have become more frequent. The food is as good as ever, but operational issues may affect your experience.

A family from New York confirms:

Lots of variety, big buffet, good gluten-free options. But the area around the host stand is a zoo—too many people, confusing lines, not nearly enough seats, lots of chaos. And reservations had been overbooked, running 20–30 minutes late.

California Grill ★★★½

AMERICAN	EXPENSIVE	QUALITY ★★★½	VALUE ★★
READER-SURVEY RESPONSES ⊕ 90% (Average)			

Contemporary Resort; ☎ 407-939-3463

Reservations Strongly recommended. **Dining Plan credits** 2 per person, per meal. **When to go** During evening fireworks. **Cost range** Dinner $89 (child $39). **Service** ★★★★½. **Bar** Full service, with a fantastic wine selection. **Dinner** Daily, 5–10 p.m.

SETTING AND ATMOSPHERE California Grill remains one of the most popular choices for Disney dining, both for its remarkable view from the 15th floor of the Contemporary Resort and for its bustling open kitchen. It can be crowded and noisy; book a table early or late for a quieter experience. If you don't have a reservation, ask for a seat at the sushi bar, where you can order appetizers but not entrées. This area actually rates significantly higher than the rest of the restaurant.

HOUSE SPECIALTIES For starters, try the sushi roll or the raviolo. Stick to steak or fish for your entrée.

KIDS' MENU Spectacular and almost infinitely customizable, this is where the restaurant shines. Order a few sides or just an entrée. Make a side your dessert or a dessert your side. Each kid is the master of their own destiny. The kids' steak may be better than the one from the adult menu.

ENTERTAINMENT AND AMENITIES Magic Kingdom fireworks are the star of the show; guests with dinner reservations can watch from the terrace.

SUMMARY AND COMMENTS California Grill uses its fixed-price menu to discourage large groups from splitting one pizza and staying 3 hours to watch the fireworks. But the expensive adult menu is a large collection of disappointment, which can't make up for the excellent kids' menu.

Cape May Cafe ★★★

AMERICAN/BUFFET	EXPENSIVE	QUALITY ★★★	VALUE ★★★
READER-SURVEY RESPONSES ⊕ 90% (Average)			

Beach Club Resort; ☎ 407-934-3358

Reservations Strongly recommended. **Dining Plan credits** 1 per person, per meal. **When to go** Breakfast or dinner. **Cost range** Breakfast $49 (child $33), dinner $49 (child $29). **Service** ★★★½. **Bar** Full service. **Character breakfast** Daily, 7:30–11:30 a.m. **Dinner** Daily, 5–9 p.m.

SETTING AND ATMOSPHERE Cape May Cafe features nautical New England décor in two dining rooms and lots of comfortable seating.

HOUSE SPECIALTIES The breakfast buffet includes made-to-order crepes and omelets, a carving station, and salted caramel "beach buns" for dessert. It might be the best character breakfast in Walt Disney World for the money (only **Hollywood & Vine** is cheaper; see page 260).

SUMMARY AND COMMENTS Breakfast is a character buffet with Minnie Mouse and friends, and dinner is a buffet without characters. None of the dinner entrées are memorable; stick to breakfast. A better nearby dinner option is **Ale & Compass Restaurant** (see page 247).

Le Cellier Steakhouse ★★★½

STEAK	EXPENSIVE	QUALITY ★★★★½	VALUE ★★★
READER-SURVEY RESPONSES ⊕ 94% (Above Average)			

Canada, World Showcase, EPCOT; ☎ 407-939-3463

Reservations Required. **Dining Plan credits** 2 per person, per meal. **When to go** Before 6 p.m. **Cost range** $36–$65 (child $14–$19). **Service** ★★★★. **Bar** Full service, with an excellent selection of Canadian wines. **Lunch** Daily, noon–3:55 p.m. **Dinner** Daily, 4–9 p.m.

SETTING AND ATMOSPHERE Walk past the Canada Pavilion's pretty gardens into this small, darkened dining room, intended to look and feel like a wine cellar. The heavy wooden tables have no linens, but the steaks make up for the lack of ambience. Service is "cheerful Canadian," meaning servers apologize to *you* if you spill something on *them*.

HOUSE SPECIALTIES Filet mignon with mushroom risotto, Canadian cheddar cheese soup.

OTHER RECOMMENDATIONS For sides, share the smoked Gouda mac and cheese, the loaded mashed potatoes, or the poutine. For dessert, try the maple crème brûlée.

KIDS' MENU Grilled chicken or steak, fish, grilled cheese, or mac and cheese, with an extensive selection of sides.

SUMMARY AND COMMENTS Le Cellier is very expensive, but the steaks are perfectly seasoned and cooked, with a beautiful char. Service is unrushed—a full dinner could take 2 hours, so plan accordingly.

Chef Art Smith's Homecomin' ★★★½

AMERICAN	INEXPENSIVE	QUALITY ★★★★	VALUE ★★★½
READER-SURVEY RESPONSES ⊕ 94% (Much Above Average)			

The Landing, Disney Springs; ☎ 407-560-0100

Reservations Strongly recommended. **Dining Plan credits** 1 per person, per meal. **When to go** Anytime. **Cost range** Brunch $19–$34 (child $12), lunch and dinner $15–$42 (child $10). **Service** ★★★★. **Bar** Full service. **Lunch** Daily, 11 a.m.–3:55 p.m. **Dinner** Daily, 4–11 p.m. **Brunch** Saturday and Sunday, 9:30 a.m.–1 p.m. (full menu available after 11 a.m.).

SETTING AND ATMOSPHERE Florida farm style with a reclaimed-wood-and-mason-jar vibe. Born and raised in Florida, Art Smith was formerly Oprah Winfrey's private chef and has appeared on *Top Chef Masters* and *Iron Chef America*.

HOUSE SPECIALTIES Fried chicken, optionally with iced house-made doughnuts. The Thigh High Chicken Biscuits appetizer may be one of the best food items on Disney property. The cocktails and desserts are fabulous.

OTHER RECOMMENDATIONS Beyond the fried chicken, the Art Burger is good; ask for the house-made pimento cheese instead of American. The barbecue pork doesn't meet our standards.

KIDS' MENU Fish sticks, chicken tenders, fried chicken sandwich, or cheeseburger, served with a veggie and starch.

SUMMARY AND COMMENTS If you can't get a table, try the bar.

Chef Mickey's ★★½

AMERICAN/BUFFET	EXPENSIVE	QUALITY ★★½	VALUE ★★★
READER-SURVEY RESPONSES ⊕ 85% (Below Average)			

Contemporary Resort; ☎ 407-939-3463

Reservations Required. **Dining Plan credits** 1 per person, per meal. **When to go** Breakfast. **Cost range** Breakfast $58 (child $37), dinner $69 (child $44). **Service** ★★★½. **Bar** Full service. **Character breakfast** Daily, 7:30 a.m.–12:30 p.m. **Character dinner** Daily, 5–9:30 p.m.

SETTING AND ATMOSPHERE This is what every parent imagines as their nightmare character meal. The big, open dining room with the monorail whizzing by overhead (inside the hotel) is a cacophony of children's and parents' voices. And everyone is hyped about seeing Mickey and his pals.

HOUSE SPECIALTIES Whatever has been set out fresh recently.

OTHER RECOMMENDATIONS The breakfast buffet offers standard options, such as eggs, Mickey waffles, and bacon.

ENTERTAINMENT AND AMENITIES Mickey doesn't meet you until after the meal—his "friends" roam the restaurant.

SUMMARY AND COMMENTS Both breakfast and dinner are buffets. Nothing on the dinner menu is as good as at EPCOT's **Garden Grill Restaurant** (see page 258) or the Magic Kingdom's **Liberty Tree Tavern** (see page 264), but the kids' choices will satisfy picky eaters.

This family from the United Kingdom captures why the restaurant remains popular (and crowded) despite the subpar food and high prices:

Terrible food and terribly expensive. The kids love the characters, and we go as a tradition, but no one likes the food. This time, the kids' selection was very limited, and there was no carving station—just precut, terribly processed ham.

Chefs de France ★★½

FRENCH	EXPENSIVE	QUALITY ★★½	VALUE ★★★
READER-SURVEY RESPONSES ⊕ 81% (Much Below Average)			

France, World Showcase, EPCOT; ☎ 407-827-8709

Reservations Strongly recommended. **Dining Plan credits** 1 per person, per meal. **When to go** Lunch or dinner. **Cost range** $27–$50 (child $12–$14), prix fixe meal $68. **Service** ★★★★. **Bar** Beer and cocktails, with a very good wine selection. **Lunch** Daily, noon–3 p.m. **Dinner** Daily, 4–8:55 p.m.

SETTING AND ATMOSPHERE The smells are delicious, with baguettes from the on-site bakery on every table. White cloth napkins and cushioned banquettes accentuate the classic bistro décor in the main dining room, and the tables by the window are great for people-watching on the World Showcase Promenade.

HOUSE SPECIALTIES Dishes inspired by French chefs Paul Bocuse, Gaston Lenôtre, and Roger Vergé. For a classic meal, order the French onion soup with Gruyère cheese for your appetizer and the boeuf bourguignon for your entrée.

OTHER RECOMMENDATIONS The prix fixe menu can be a good value if you enjoy wine and would order three courses anyway.

KIDS' MENU Grilled chicken, salmon, or French burger, each with only one side. Relatively poor selection.

SUMMARY AND COMMENTS The kitchen has struggled with the basics of food temperature and seasoning during our recent visits.

Cinderella's Royal Table ★★★

AMERICAN	EXPENSIVE	QUALITY ★★★	VALUE ★★
READER-SURVEY RESPONSES ⊕ 93% (Above Average)			

Cinderella Castle, Fantasyland, Magic Kingdom; ☎ 407-939-3463

Reservations Required; must prepay in full. **Dining Plan credits** 2 per person, per meal. **When to go** Early. **Cost range** Breakfast $74 (child $45), lunch and dinner $88 (child $52). **Service** ★★★. **Bar** Limited selection of wine and beer. **Character breakfast** Daily, 8–10:15 a.m. **Character lunch** Daily, 11 a.m.–2:55 p.m. **Character dinner** Daily, 3–10:30 p.m.

SETTING AND ATMOSPHERE A medieval banquet hall located in Cinderella Castle. While the food is generally good, it's more about the location. Cinderella makes an appearance at all three meals, with plenty of time for photos. Other princesses include some combination of Ariel, Aurora, Snow White, Jasmine, and Rapunzel.

HOUSE SPECIALTIES Lunch and dinner have the same entrée selections: lamb chops, filet mignon, catch of the day, grilled chicken, or a vegetarian dish. For starters, try the braised beef or the Castle Salad. Dessert is generally phoned-in.

KIDS' MENU Seared fish, grilled steak, chicken strips, or mac and cheese, each with two sides (out of four options), an appetizer, and dessert.

SUMMARY AND COMMENTS We think the food quality is better than average, despite the reader-survey ratings, and service is good, though rushed. For more on reserving a spot at the Royal Table, see page 208.

Cítricos ★★★★

AMERICAN	EXPENSIVE	QUALITY ★★★★½	VALUE ★★★½
READER-SURVEY RESPONSES ⊕ 89% (Average)			

Grand Floridian Resort & Spa; ☎ 407-939-3463

Reservations Required. **Dining Plan credits** 2 per person, per meal. **When to go** Dinner. **Cost range** $39–$62 (child $14–$19). **Service** ★★★★★. **Bar** Full service. **Dress** Dressy casual. **Dinner** Daily, 5–9:30 p.m.

SETTING AND ATMOSPHERE Cítricos has a *Mary Poppins* theme, which feels fancy and fun at the same time. The full-view show kitchen is on display.

HOUSE SPECIALTIES The guava-barbecued short ribs belong with rainbows and puppies in the pantheon of things everyone should love. Other standouts are the (seasonal) strawberry salad and the grilled porcelet chop.

OTHER RECOMMENDATIONS For your first course, try the pork belly or the duck breast.

KIDS' MENU Grilled chicken, steak, shrimp, pizza, mac and cheese, grilled cheese, or pasta with marinara, with a fair selection of sides.

SUMMARY AND COMMENTS This is an excellent choice for a nice dinner, with enough availability that you'll have a decent chance of getting in. The menu changes often, so ask your server for recommendations. If you can't get a reservation at **Victoria & Albert's** next door (see page 285), Cítricos is the next place we recommend. Chef Andres Mendoza and his team care deeply about providing an excellent dining experience.

City Works Eatery and Pour House ★★★

AMERICAN	MODERATE	QUALITY ★★★	VALUE ★★½
READER-SURVEY RESPONSES ⊕ 90% (Average)			

West Side, Disney Springs; ☎ 407-801-3730

Reservations Accepted. **Dining Plan credits** 1 per person, per meal. **When to go** Anytime. **Cost range** Brunch $12–$16, lunch and dinner $18–$40 (child $12). **Service** ★★★. **Bar** Full service, with a good wine selection. **Lunch** Daily, 11 a.m.–2:55 p.m. **Dinner** Daily, 3–11 p.m. (until 11:30 p.m. on Friday and Saturday).

SETTING AND ATMOSPHERE Indoor seating may be available; the outdoor seats can be hot in the Florida sun.

HOUSE SPECIALTIES "A solid beer selection for brew nerds," says one of our resident beer experts. The fish tacos are a favorite.

KIDS' MENU Mini burgers, pizza, chicken tenders, or instant mac and cheese, all served with fries or a fruit cup. Too expensive for what you get.

SUMMARY AND COMMENTS City Works is a small chain of sports bars with an extensive list of beer taps. Its location near Cirque du Soleil means crowds before and after shows. The food is standard for a sports bar.

Coral Reef Restaurant ★★★

SEAFOOD	MODERATE	QUALITY ★★★	VALUE ★★½
READER-SURVEY RESPONSES ⊕ 88% (Below Average)			

The Seas with Nemo & Friends, World Nature, EPCOT; ☎ 407-939-3463

Reservations Required. **Dining Plan credits** 1 per person, per meal. **When to go** Lunch. **Cost range** $28–$45 (child $13–$16). **Service** ★★★★. **Bar** Full service. **Lunch** Daily, 11:30 a.m.–3:30 p.m. **Dinner** Daily, 3:45–8:30 p.m.

SETTING AND ATMOSPHERE You can't beat the view in this dining room, which faces one of the world's largest saltwater aquariums. Tiered seating gives everyone a good view of the fish, scuba divers, and sometimes even Mickey. The entryway gives the impression that you're going under the sea; special light fixtures throw ripple patterns on the ceiling.

HOUSE SPECIALTIES Surf and turf (filet mignon and grilled shrimp) or grilled mahi-mahi, chocolate mousse bar dessert.

KIDS' MENU Mac and cheese or grilled chicken, fish, steak, or shrimp, each served with a decent selection of sides.

SUMMARY AND COMMENTS Not the best restaurant in EPCOT but a great escape from the Florida sun. Coral Reef got a new chef in 2023, and its scores have been steadily increasing ever since.

La Crêperie de Paris ★★★½

FRENCH	INEXPENSIVE	QUALITY ★★★½	VALUE ★★★½
READER-SURVEY RESPONSES ⊕ 91% (Average)			

France, World Showcase, EPCOT; ☎ 407-939-3463

Reservations Strongly recommended. **Dining Plan credits** 1 per person, per meal. **When to go** Anytime. **Cost range** 3-course prix fixe $40 or $19 per crepe (child prix fixe $17). **Service** ★★★★. **Bar** Full service. **Breakfast** Daily, 9–10:55 a.m. **Lunch** Daily, 11 a.m.–3:55 p.m. **Dinner** Daily, 4–8:50 p.m.

SETTING AND ATMOSPHERE Found on the walk back to Remy's Ratatouille Adventure, La Crêperie de Paris looks from the outside like a streetside Parisian café. There's little theming inside—you could be anywhere from a Canadian poutine place to a nice Wendy's.

HOUSE SPECIALTIES Try the chèvre, spinach, and walnut savory crepe (galette) for dinner, with the banana-filled crepe for dessert. The fixed-price meal used to be a relative bargain for Walt Disney World, but price increases now make it too expensive.

KIDS' MENU Combo of one galette and one sweet crepe. Very limited options.

SUMMARY AND COMMENTS Generous portions. Walk-up window available.

The Crystal Palace ★★½

AMERICAN/BUFFET	EXPENSIVE	QUALITY ★★½	VALUE ★★½
READER-SURVEY RESPONSES ⊕ 90% (Average)			

Main Street, U.S.A., Magic Kingdom; ☎ 407-939-3463

Reservations Required. **Dining Plan credits** 1 per person, per meal. **When to go** Lunch or dinner. **Cost range** Breakfast $52 (child $33), lunch and dinner $62 (child $42). **Service** ★★★. **Bar** Full service. **Character breakfast** Daily, 8–10:45 a.m. **Character lunch** Daily, 11 a.m.–2:55 p.m. **Character dinner** Daily, 3–9 p.m.

SETTING AND ATMOSPHERE In the daytime, The Crystal Palace surrounds you with cool sunlight and decorative plants. The restaurant's white steel supports, arched ceilings, and glass roof (especially the atrium) are tributes to its namesake, which was built to house London's 1851 Great Exhibition—the first world's fair—and was among the first structures to use plate glass in large quantities.

HOUSE SPECIALTIES Nothing stands out.

SUMMARY AND COMMENTS Pooh, Piglet, and friends are at all meals. The restaurant has trouble maintaining its food quality on the buffet. The fried chicken is often greasy, and the prime rib is usually tough and overcooked. The best of the bunch might be the Southern Fried Cauliflower, but nobody should have to pay $62 for albino broccoli.

Reader ratings for The Crystal Palace remain low. Near the same price point, we recommend **Garden Grill Restaurant** (see page 258) in EPCOT or **Liberty Tree Tavern** (see page 264) in the Magic Kingdom instead.

The Edison ★★★

AMERICAN	EXPENSIVE	QUALITY ★★★½	VALUE ★★
READER-SURVEY RESPONSES ⊕ 83% (Much Below Average)			

The Landing, Disney Springs; ☎ 407-560-WATT (9288)

Reservations Recommended. **Dining Plan credits** 1 per person, per meal. **When to go** Dinner. **Cost range** $19–$51 (child $17). **Service** ★★★. **Bar** Full service. **Hours** Sunday–Thursday, 11:30 a.m.–10:30 p.m. (until 11 p.m. on Friday and Saturday).

SETTING AND ATMOSPHERE With its steampunk aesthetic and an abundance of gear imagery, the place has a distinct industrial vibe. Clips of black-and-white movies are projected onto some of the walls.

HOUSE SPECIALTIES The entrées here are American comfort food: prime rib and burgers. The food is decent but not a good value. The DB "Clothesline" Candied Bacon is the signature appetizer: four pieces of heavily smoked candied bacon and a few sprigs of rosemary clipped to a suspended string with clothespins. It's photogenic, and that's about it. And you're paying over $4 per piece of bacon.

OTHER RECOMMENDATIONS Drinks are where The Edison shines. In addition to signature cocktails such as the Time Turner, made with Bacardi light rum, Campari, lime, pineapple, and orgeat (almond-flavored flower-water syrup), there are about 10 draft beers, along with bottled and canned beers and ciders; substantial wine offerings by the bottle and glass; a dozen vodkas; and almost as many varieties of gin, tequila, whiskey, and rum.

KIDS' MENU Burgers, chicken strips, or grilled cheese, all with appetizer and dessert but all too expensive, even before this year's $2 increase.

SUMMARY AND COMMENTS This is not in the first or second tier of restaurants we would recommend at Disney Springs. It's not bad for an after-dinner drink, but service is pretty terse if you don't order a full meal.

50's Prime Time Café ★★★

AMERICAN	MODERATE	QUALITY ★★★	VALUE ★★★
READER-SURVEY RESPONSES ⊕ 94% (Above Average)			

Echo Lake, Disney's Hollywood Studios; ☎ 407-939-3463

Reservations Strongly recommended. **Dining Plan credits** 1 per person, per meal. **When to go** Lunch or dinner. **Cost range** $20–$32 (child $13–$15). **Service** ★★★★. **Bar** Full service. **Lunch** Daily, 10:45 a.m.–3:55 p.m. **Dinner** Daily, 4–9 p.m.

SETTING AND ATMOSPHERE Dine in a 1950s kitchen complete with antique fridges, laminate tabletops, and sunburst clocks. Black-and-white TVs play vintage sitcom clips while you wait for your meal.

HOUSE SPECIALTIES Pot roast, fried chicken, and meat loaf, plus a sampler platter with some of each; PB&J milkshake and other retro fare. Desserts are a strong point, with warm apple crisp and a chocolate–peanut butter layer cake being the highlights. This is filling comfort food.

KIDS' MENU Salmon (our recommendation), sloppy Joe, grilled chicken, or chicken strips; a good selection of sides, but your kids might be put off by the "stained glass dessert." Servers describe it as a bowl of Jell-O, but it's mostly "whipped pineapple fluff."

SUMMARY AND COMMENTS The cast members makes this location worthwhile, admonishing you just like Mom did to "take your elbows off the table!" and making sure you eat your vegetables. If that sort of interaction makes you cringe, you might want to eat elsewhere. This Ontario couple loved the service and gives some examples of what you might experience:

The food was excellent, and the waitstaff were so much fun. From the "dads'" telling people they don't have to eat their vegetables to our waitress telling us we had to set the table ourselves, we had a blast. The decorating brought us back to our childhood. Service was fast, and we made it on time to our next show.

Flying Fish ★★★½

SEAFOOD	EXPENSIVE	QUALITY ★★★½	VALUE ★★★
READER-SURVEY RESPONSES ⊕ 92% (Above Average)			

BoardWalk; ☎ 407-939-3463

Reservations Strongly recommended. **Dining Plan credits** 2 per person, per meal. **When to go** Dinner. **Cost range** $40–$62 (child $14–$24). **Service** ★★★★. **Bar** Full service, with an extensive wine selection. **Dress** Dressy casual. **Dinner** Daily, 5–9:30 p.m.

SETTING AND ATMOSPHERE At the heart of the BoardWalk, Flying Fish gives diners an upscale modern seafood dinner enveloped by splashy blue-and-silver décor. The open kitchen and showcase bar entertain guests seated near the front of the bustling restaurant, with a quieter experience in the rear of the main dining room.

HOUSE SPECIALTIES The potato-wrapped red snapper has remained on the menu through several iterations of chefs and management. Bartenders craft specialty cocktails that pair with most meals, while a strong wine program complements every dish from start to finish.

OTHER RECOMMENDATIONS Plancha-seared scallops with savory grits shine on the seafood-dominant menu, though landlubbers will be perfectly content with the filet mignon. Soup and salad, rotating frequently throughout every season, are solid ways to start any meal here, and both highlight the freshest produce Florida has to offer.

KIDS' MENU Grilled chicken or steak, red snapper or "fish," or pasta with marinara; there are only a few sides to choose from, including the unexpected kid favorite . . . asparagus.

SUMMARY AND COMMENTS The kitchen can sometimes force a slower-paced meal here.

The Fountain ★★

AMERICAN	INEXPENSIVE	QUALITY ★★	VALUE ★★
READER-SURVEY RESPONSES ⊕ 91% (Average)			

Dolphin Resort; ☎ 407-934-1609

Reservations Not accepted. **Dining Plan credits** Not accepted. **When to go** Lunch or dinner. **Cost range** $18–$23 (child $14). **Service** ★★★. **Bar** Limited beer and wine. **Parking** Valet ($44) or hotel lot ($36), both free with validation. **Hours** Daily, 11 a.m.–11 p.m.

SETTING AND ATMOSPHERE Informal soda-shop ambience.

HOUSE SPECIALTIES Hot dogs and burgers (including veggie and turkey burgers), milkshakes (go for the PB&J), and ice cream.

OTHER RECOMMENDATIONS Generous salads, including seared salmon and chicken Caesar.

KIDS' MENU Burger, chicken tenders, hot dog, mac and cheese, or grilled ham and cheese, all relatively expensive.

SUMMARY AND COMMENTS The Fountain is one of the Dolphin's few casual-dining spots, so it can get busy.

Frontera Cocina ★★½

MEXICAN	MODERATE	QUALITY ★★★	VALUE ★★½
READER-SURVEY RESPONSES ⊕ 92% (Above Average)			

Town Center, Disney Springs; ☎ 407-939-3463

Reservations Strongly recommended. **Dining Plan credits** 1 per person, per meal. **When to go** Dinner. **Cost range** $24–$58 (children $10–$13). **Service** ★★★★. **Parking** Lime garage. **Bar** Full service. **Hours** Daily, 11 a.m.–11 p.m.

SETTING AND ATMOSPHERE The outside has muted beige walls, but the interior is sleek and modern, with exposed ductwork, bright pops of color from the chandelier and bar, and cozy dark-wood furnishings. The open kitchen and Wall of Fame shelves, packed with specialty liquors and wines, are bathed in sunlight from the large windows on nearly every wall, showcasing the springs and the patio.

HOUSE SPECIALTIES Tacos with carne asada or chipotle chicken, enchiladas, plantains, margaritas, and specialty tequila flights.

OTHER RECOMMENDATIONS Guacamole, coconut-lime cuatro leches cake.

KIDS' MENU Quesadilla, shredded chicken, or tacos with inflexible side choices. Not for picky eaters.

SUMMARY AND COMMENTS The menu often spotlights the flavors and ingredients of a particular region of Mexico. **Frontera Cocina To Go,** a walk-up window, serves two kinds of tacos, soft drinks, beer, and margaritas.

Garden Grill Restaurant ★★★½

AMERICAN	EXPENSIVE	QUALITY ★★★½	VALUE ★★★½
READER-SURVEY RESPONSES ⊕ 96% (Much Above Average)			

The Land, World Nature, EPCOT; ☎ 407-939-3463

Reservations Required. **Dining Plan credits** 1 per person, per meal. **When to go** Anytime. **Cost range** Breakfast $49 (child $33), lunch and dinner $62 (child $42). **Service** ★★★★. **Bar** Wine, beer, and mixed drinks. **Character breakfast** Daily, 8:30–10:30 a.m. **Character lunch** Daily, 11:30 a.m.–3:40 p.m. **Character dinner** Daily, 3:45–8 p.m.

SETTING AND ATMOSPHERE The all-you-can-eat Garden Grill stays busy, even though the dining room has grown rather dated. The floor revolves slowly as you peer down into scenes from **Living with the Land,** The Land Pavilion's ride-through attraction (see page 418). During your meal, you complete one revolution, past scenes of a desert, a rainforest, and a farm.

Bonus: Mickey, Chip 'n' Dale, and Pluto stop at each table for autographs and photos at every meal.

HOUSE SPECIALTIES Grilled steak—at breakfast and dinner—is a highlight. In general, breakfast gets much better ratings than dinner. Mickey waffles and cinnamon-roll bread are both anchors of the meal.

SUMMARY AND COMMENTS The food quality has been improving, and you won't beat the retro-EPCOT setting. A worthy character meal. This reader from Salt Lake City says Garden Grill is one of the calmer character meals:

A fantastic character dining experience. The restaurant rotates and gives you different views of The Land ride. The food was great, but what we liked the most was that it was quiet and not crowded. We got to really talk to each other and have time with each character.

Garden Grove ★★

AMERICAN	INEXPENSIVE	QUALITY ★★½	VALUE ★★
READER-SURVEY RESPONSES ⊕ 84% (Below Average)			

Swan Resort; ☎ 407-934-1609

Reservations Recommended. **Dining Plan credits** Not accepted. **When to go** Breakfast or brunch. **Cost range** $17–$23 (child $10). **Service** ★★★. **Parking** Valet ($44) or hotel lot ($36), both free with validation. **Bar** Full service. **Hours** Daily, 7–11:30 a.m.

SETTING AND ATMOSPHERE A spacious dining room features a 25-foot faux oak tree in the center.

HOUSE SPECIALTIES Familiar breakfast combinations, including waffles, French toast, and eggs.

KIDS' MENU Waffles, pancakes, or American-style breakfast (eggs, potatoes, toast, and choice of bacon or sausage).

SUMMARY AND COMMENTS Garden Grove isn't worth a special trip if you aren't staying at the Swan. But the room is pretty, and the food is plentiful, if not highly rated.

Grand Floridian Cafe ★★★

AMERICAN	MODERATE	QUALITY ★★★½	VALUE ★★★
READER-SURVEY RESPONSES ⊕ 90% (Average)			

Grand Floridian Resort & Spa; ☎ 407-939-3463

Reservations Recommended. **Dining Plan credits** 1 per person, per meal. **When to go** Anytime. **Cost range** Breakfast and lunch $13–$27 (child $11–$14), dinner $26–$39 (child $12–$16). **Service** ★★★★. **Bar** Full service. **Breakfast** Daily, 7:30–11 a.m. **Lunch** Daily, 11:05 a.m.–2 p.m. **Dinner** Daily, 5–9 p.m.

SETTING AND ATMOSPHERE Light and airy with lots of sunlight and views of the pool and courtyard.

HOUSE SPECIALTIES The breakfast/lunch menu is extensive, ranging from eggs Benedict and buttermilk pancakes to miso-glazed salmon. Try the Signature Burger (with Brie, bacon-pepper jam, and roasted garlic aioli) or the buttermilk-fried chicken (which is outstanding) served with a waffle drizzled with sriracha honey. Dinner options include that same fried chicken, a slow-braised pork shank, and vegetable curries.

OTHER RECOMMENDATIONS Any dessert the kitchen recommends.

KIDS' MENU *Breakfast:* Seven entrées, with a terrible side selection. *Lunch and dinner:* Seven entrées but only four sides.

SUMMARY AND COMMENTS A quick place to grab a tasty bite in a pleasantly themed room.

La Hacienda de San Angel ★★★

MEXICAN	EXPENSIVE	QUALITY ★★★	VALUE ★★★½
READER-SURVEY RESPONSES ⊕ 82% (Much Below Average)			

Mexico, World Showcase, EPCOT; ☎ 407-939-3463

Reservations Required. **Dining Plan credits** 1 per person, per meal. **When to go** Dinner. **Cost range** $30–$52 (child $12–$16). **Service** ★★★. **Bar** Full service. **Hours** Daily, 3–9 p.m.

SETTING AND ATMOSPHERE Right along the waterfront in Mexico, La Hacienda is a prime spot for watching fireworks through the tall windows. The interior has authentic touches of Mexico in its lighting and décor.

HOUSE SPECIALTIES Excellent guacamole; queso fundido; carne asada–style New York strip; and osso buco.

OTHER RECOMMENDATIONS The margaritas are the real deal—or just go for a flight of fine tequila.

KIDS' MENU Tacos, quesadilla, chicken tenders, grilled chicken, or mac and cheese, all with limited side options.

SUMMARY AND COMMENTS The menu quality here used to be incredible, but in the past year the quality has been unreliable and the service slow.

Hollywood & Vine ★★★½

AMERICAN/BUFFET	EXPENSIVE	QUALITY ★★★½	VALUE ★★★
READER-SURVEY RESPONSES ⊕ 90% (Average)			

Echo Lake, Disney's Hollywood Studios; ☎ 407-939-3463

Reservations Strongly recommended. **Dining Plan credits** 1 per person, per meal. **When to go** Breakfast, lunch, or dinner. **Cost range** Breakfast $49 (child $33), lunch and dinner $63 (child $42). **Service** ★★★½. **Bar** Full service. **Character breakfast** Daily, 8:30-10:30 a.m. **Character lunch** Daily, 11:30 a.m.–3:55 p.m. **Character dinner** Daily, 4-8 p.m.

SETTING AND ATMOSPHERE Just off Hollywood Boulevard, this 1940s-era diner has a sleek Art Deco design (think chrome and tile) that gets lost amid all the Disney-character frenzy. Breakfast includes characters from Disney Junior, such as Doc McStuffins and Fancy Nancy, while seasonal lunches and dinners feature Minnie, Mickey, Goofy, Pluto, and Donald (and sometimes Daisy), usually in holiday- or Hollywood-themed outfits.

HOUSE SPECIALTIES *Breakfast:* Bananas Foster French toast, eggs Benedict, chicken with Mickey waffles. *Dinner:* Buffet with flank steak, baked salmon, roasted chicken, crispy tofu, smoked ham, and vegetables. There's also a plant-based option, most recently a mushroom risotto.

SUMMARY AND COMMENTS The food here is on the upswing, and the characters provide some of the highest-energy interactions you'll find in any park. Don't let old reviews fool you—this is a great character meal, and it's easier to get reservations for than many others.

The Hollywood Brown Derby ★★★½

AMERICAN	EXPENSIVE	QUALITY ★★★★	VALUE ★★½
READER-SURVEY RESPONSES ⊕ 90% (Average)			

Hollywood Boulevard, Disney's Hollywood Studios; ☎ 407-939-3463

Reservations Strongly recommended. **Dining Plan credits** 2 per person, per meal. **When to go** Early evening. **Cost range** $28-$52 (child $9-$18). **Service** ★★★★. **Bar** Full service. **Lunch** Daily, 11 a.m.–3:55 p.m. **Dinner** Daily, 4-8 p.m.

SETTING AND ATMOSPHERE This is a replica of the Brown Derby on Vine Street in Hollywood (not the original hat-shaped one). The sunken dining room has a certain elegance, with dark woods, tuxedoed servers, curved booths, and white linens. Hundreds of black-and-white photos and caricatures line the walls. Ask for a seat on the second-level gallery; it's much quieter and affords good people-watching in the hectic main space.

HOUSE SPECIALTIES Cobb salad (named for Bob Cobb, owner of the original restaurant) and the famous grapefruit cake made from the original Brown Derby's recipe.

OTHER RECOMMENDATIONS The menu varies. The kitchen is unusually adept with pork and lamb—we'd recommend those if available.

KIDS' MENU Grilled chicken, fish, or steak; hot dog; or mac and cheese, all served with two sides from a good selection.

SUMMARY AND COMMENTS The Brown Derby is expensive, yes, but also the most relaxing restaurant you'll find inside Hollywood Studios. If you don't have reservations, the patio lounge opens at 11 a.m. and is first come, first served, with a menu of small plates and cocktails.

Drink choices are extensive and include various flights—martinis, margaritas, Champagnes, wines, Scotches, and Grand Marnier vintages—along with wine by the bottle and glass, beer, and classic cocktails.

House of Blues Restaurant & Bar ★★★

AMERICAN	INEXPENSIVE	QUALITY ★★★	VALUE ★★★
READER-SURVEY RESPONSES ⊕ 83% (Much Below Average)			

West Side, Disney Springs; ☎ 407-934-2583

Reservations Recommended. **Dining Plan credits** 1 per person, per meal. **When to go** Lunch, early dinner, or weekend brunch. **Cost range** Brunch $15–$19, lunch and dinner $17–$36 (child $10). **Service** ★★★½. **Parking** Orange garage. **Bar** Full service. **Brunch** Saturday–Sunday: 10 a.m.–1:55 p.m. **Lunch** Monday–Friday, 11:30 a.m.–3:55 p.m.; Saturday–Sunday, 2–3:55 p.m. **Dinner** Daily, 4–11 p.m. (until 11:30 p.m. Friday–Sunday).

SETTING AND ATMOSPHERE Adjacent to the Cirque du Soleil theater, House of Blues has a ramshackle look, but it's a solid stop for lunch or dinner before or after a show. A separate concert hall hosts great live music, along with a lively Sunday gospel brunch. A quick-service window (**The Smokehouse**), along with the outdoor bar and seating, draws passersby. The fabulous folk art in the restaurant is worth a look.

HOUSE SPECIALTIES Barbecue sandwiches (pulled pork and brisket), ribs, steaks, burgers, and shrimp and grits.

OTHER RECOMMENDATIONS Jambalaya and jalapeño cornbread.

KIDS' MENU Pizza, burger, hot dog, chicken tenders, or mac and cheese, all served with a side of fruit.

SUMMARY AND COMMENTS Meat-centric menu on Disney Springs' West Side in a fun and casual setting.

Il Mulino ★★★

ITALIAN	MODERATE	QUALITY ★★★	VALUE ★★½
READER-SURVEY RESPONSES ⊕ 94% (Above Average)			

Swan Resort; ☎ 407-939-3463

Reservations Recommended. **Dining Plan credits** Not accepted. **When to go** Dinner. **Cost range** $20–$71 (child $13–$17). **Service** ★★★. **Parking** Valet ($44) or hotel lot ($36), both free with validation. **Bar** Full service. **Dress** Dressy casual. **Hours** Daily, 5–11 p.m.

SETTING AND ATMOSPHERE A spin-off of the acclaimed Manhattan restaurant, Il Mulino takes an upscale-casual, downtown New York approach to Italian cuisine, with family-style platters for sharing. An open kitchen creates a bustle. You can request private dining in one of the smaller rooms.

HOUSE SPECIALTIES Try the spaghetti carbonara or the veal saltimbocca. The risottos are well made too.

OTHER RECOMMENDATIONS Charcuterie, mussels in white wine, pizzas, sautéed jumbo shrimp, rib eye with sautéed spinach.

KIDS' MENU Pizza, four pasta options, or chicken parmesan; no sides.

SUMMARY AND COMMENTS A predictable menu, with a little bit of everything you would expect in an Italian restaurant and nothing particularly adventurous. The kids' menu is comparatively overpriced.

Jaleo by José Andrés ★★★★

SPANISH/TAPAS	MODERATE	QUALITY ★★★½	VALUE ★★★★
READER-SURVEY RESPONSES ⊕ 97% (Much Above Average)			

West Side, Disney Springs; ☎ 407-939-3463

Reservations Strongly recommended. **Dining Plan credits** 2 per person, per meal. **When to go** Dinner. **Cost range** Tapas $11–$32 or tasting menu $100–$150 (child $10–$14). **Service** ★★★★. **Parking** Orange garage. **Bar** Full service, with emphasis on Spanish drinks and wines. **Hours** Daily, 11:30 a.m.–11 p.m.

SETTING AND ATMOSPHERE Jaleo's entrance has tile mosaics and large-scale photo murals of iconic Spanish scenes. Warm colors from lighting in the kitchen and dining areas bathe the restaurant, reflecting off metal accents. The highlight is the paella pit and accompanying view into the kitchen—every time one of the massive paella dishes has finished cooking, the chefs ring a bell and the entire restaurant joins in the celebration.

HOUSE SPECIALTIES The restaurant serves Spain's famed Jamón Ibérico. A selection of Spanish cheeses and traditional pan de tomate are both good first courses. Garlic shrimp and grilled chicken with garlic sauce burst with flavor, highlighting incredibly fresh produce and tons of herbs. Don't skip the patatas bravas—fried potatoes topped with spicy tomato sauce and aioli. The paella is decent but maybe not worth all the hoopla . . . or the price (it starts at $130).

OTHER RECOMMENDATIONS Drinks are on par with other Disney Springs restaurants in terms of pricing and quality. The wine menu is extensive.

KIDS' MENU Grilled steak or chicken, chicken fritters, or grilled cheese; very limited side selections. Leave the kids at home for this one.

SUMMARY AND COMMENTS This restaurant from celebrity chef José Andrés brings classic Spanish cuisine to Disney Springs. This is one of the most underrated restaurants at Walt Disney World.

Jiko—The Cooking Place ★★★★

AFRICAN/FUSION	EXPENSIVE	QUALITY ★★★★	VALUE ★★★★
READER-SURVEY RESPONSES ⊕ 98% (Exceptional)			

Animal Kingdom Lodge & Villas–Jambo House; ☎ 407-939-3463

Reservations Required. **Dining Plan credits** 2 per person, per meal. **When to go** Dinner. **Cost range** $41–$62 (child $11–$19). **Service** ★★★★★. **Bar** Full service, with South African wines. **Dress** Dressy casual. **Hours** Daily, 5–9:30 p.m.

SETTING AND ATMOSPHERE Bathed in a perpetual sunset, with metal birds soaring around, the main dining room is warm and inviting, accented by the central *jiko* ("cooking place" in Swahili), where chefs prepare many of the appetizers featured on the restaurant's seasonal menu in view of a few lucky diners. As you enter, take a peek at the bottles on display, which are just a sample of the massive wine selection—the largest collection of South African wines available in any North American restaurant.

HOUSE SPECIALTIES Guests flock to Jiko for several dishes, among them the braised wild-boar tenderloin appetizer, African spice–infused flatbread, seafood tagine, and oak-grilled filet mignon with South African red-wine sauce and bobotie mac and cheese. The seasonally updated malva (mallow) pudding dessert highlights traditional African flavors on the sweet spectrum.

FULL-SERVICE RESTAURANTS IN DEPTH

OTHER RECOMMENDATIONS Botswanan-style beef short ribs and Moroccan lamb shank bring on the spices, while seasonal soups start any meal off on the right foot. For those in search of vegan and vegetarian options, Jiko stands out as one of the few Disney Signature restaurants to offer dedicated options that are both satisfying and flavorful. A large selection of specialty teas and Kenyan press-pot coffee complement the excellent dessert selections.

KIDS' MENU Grilled chicken, fish, shrimp, or steak; cheese pizza; or mac and cheese, with many side options—but half of them are desserts!

SUMMARY AND COMMENTS Jiko is one of the true hidden gems of fine dining in Walt Disney World. It provides superb service in an unfussy atmosphere, welcoming guests for a meal packed with unique flavors. Solo diners or small parties may want to take advantage of the jiko's seating for both dinner and a show. Becky ate solo at the jiko, and it is one of her favorite Disney dining experiences to this day.

Jungle Navigation Co. Ltd. Skipper Canteen ★★★½

AFRICAN/LATIN/PAN-ASIAN	MODERATE	QUALITY ★★★½	VALUE ★★★
READER-SURVEY RESPONSES ⊕ 91% (Average)			

Adventureland, Magic Kingdom; ☎ 407-939-3463

Reservations Strongly recommended. **Dining Plan credits** 1 per person, per meal. **When to go** Lunch or dinner. **Cost range** $23–$41 (child $12–$15). **Service** ★★★★. **Bar** Limited selection of beer and wine. **Hours** Daily, 11 a.m.–9 p.m.

SETTING AND ATMOSPHERE Themed as the home of off-duty Jungle Cruise skippers, Skipper Canteen offers guests an oasis in the theme park, with three distinct dining rooms (and a boatload of corny jokes). The crew's mess hall features high ceilings, dark wooden fixtures, and souvenirs collected from the skippers' travels, all bathed in stained glass–tinted natural light. Behind a hidden bookcase (with amusing titles), guests can visit the secret meeting room of the Society of Explorers and Adventurers, filled with posh fixtures, maps, and a beautiful collection of butterflies. The Jungle Room has intimate seating near intricately carved wood bookshelves and colorful stained glass lamps.

HOUSE SPECIALTIES The menu features flavors from several world cuisines, with Asian influences in the char siu pork (a house favorite) and Korean barbecue–inspired crispy fried chicken. Latin flavors make their way into the grilled steak, as well as the house-made corn pancakes topped with pork and avocado cream. The Kungaloosh! (chocolate cake with caramelized bananas) will close out any meal with a smile—and is the only dessert worth ordering here.

OTHER RECOMMENDATIONS Plant-based dining is well represented here, with an emphasis on vegetables instead of meat substitutes.

KIDS' MENU Grilled steak, crispy or grilled chicken, coconut-curry pineapple tofu, or mac and cheese, with a large selection of unique and tasty sides.

SUMMARY AND COMMENTS Skipper Canteen has fresh flavors and fine service. The menu doesn't cater to simpler tastes, which means reservations are easy to get.

If you think adult beverages at Disney skimp on the alcohol, this Philadelphia couple says you'll be pleasantly surprised at Skipper Canteen:

The food was excellent for the price (for a theme park). Waitstaff are all like Jungle Cruise skippers—funny and personable. I had a Jungle Bird cocktail, which is a "classic" that actually rarely appears on menus, so I appreciated that. I think there was actually some liquor in it.

Kimonos ★★★

JAPANESE	INEXPENSIVE	QUALITY ★★★½	VALUE ★★★½
READER-SURVEY RESPONSES ⊕ 87% (Below Average)			

Swan Resort; ☎ 407-934-1792

Reservations Not accepted. **Dining Plan credits** Not accepted. **When to go** Dinner. **Cost range** Sushi rolls and appetizers à la carte $10–$21. **Service** ★★★★. **Parking** Valet ($44) or hotel lot ($36), both free with validation. **Bar** Full service. **Hours** Daily, 5:30–11:30 p.m.

SETTING AND ATMOSPHERE Sushi and nightly karaoke—what a combo! Go early if you want a relaxing experience with sushi and sake in the serene setting: dark teak tabletops and counters, tall pillars rising to bamboo rafters with rice-paper lanterns, and elegant kimonos that hang outstretched on the walls and between the dining sections. The chefs will greet you, and you'll be offered a hot towel to clean your hands.

HOUSE SPECIALTIES Both cooked and raw sushi and hot dishes. Classic rolls include California, tuna, and soft-shell crab; the Kimonos Roll features tuna, salmon, yellowtail, and wasabi mayo. Small plates include Wagyu beef skewers and shrimp tempura.

KIDS' MENU None.

SUMMARY AND COMMENTS The skill of the sushi artists is as much a joy to watch as is eating the wonderfully fresh creations. Excellent sake choices. Karaoke starts at 9:30 p.m.

Kona Cafe ★★★

PAN-ASIAN/POLYNESIAN	MODERATE	QUALITY ★★★	VALUE ★★★½
READER-SURVEY RESPONSES ⊕ 85% (Below Average)			

Polynesian Village Resort; ☎ 407-939-3463

Reservations Strongly recommended. **Dining Plan credits** 1 per person, per meal. **When to go** Anytime. **Cost range** Breakfast $15–$22 (child $7–$11), lunch $16–$33 (child $11–$13), dinner $16–$41 (child $11–$14). **Service** ★★★½. **Bar** Full service. **Breakfast** Daily, 7:30–11 a.m. **Lunch** Daily, 11:30 a.m.–2 p.m. **Dinner** Daily, 5–10 p.m.

SETTING AND ATMOSPHERE Open for three meals a day, Kona Cafe is a casual, open dining room in the heart of the Polynesian. Located right next to the monorail station, it's easy to get to from the Magic Kingdom by boat or monorail.

HOUSE SPECIALTIES *Breakfast:* Tonga Toast (French toast with bananas) is the most popular order. *Lunch*: Turkey banh mi, stir-fry, noodle bowls with pork belly or vegetables, and sushi rolls. *Dinner:* Sushi, tuna poke, Kona coffee–braised short rib.

OTHER RECOMMENDATIONS Kona coffee served in a press pot. The kids' sushi makes for a great small meal. Desserts have improved a lot in the past couple of years.

KIDS' MENU Sushi, chicken taco, cheeseburger, or mac and cheese, with a limited selection of sides.

SUMMARY AND COMMENTS If you can't get a reservation or you want a quicker option, you can order food from Kona Cafe to go via mobile ordering on the app. One of Becky's favorite Disney meal "hacks" is ordering the kids' sushi meal to go and enjoying it in the Polynesian lobby.

Liberty Tree Tavern ★★★½

AMERICAN	EXPENSIVE	QUALITY ★★★½	VALUE ★★★½
READER-SURVEY RESPONSES ⊕ 94% (Above Average)			

FULL-SERVICE RESTAURANTS IN DEPTH

Liberty Square, Magic Kingdom; ☎ 407-939-3463

Reservations Strongly recommended. **Dining Plan credits** 1 per person, per meal. **When to go** Lunch or dinner. **Cost range** $44 (child $24). **Service** ★★★★. **Bar** Limited selection of beer, wine, and hard cider. **Hours** Daily, 11 a.m.–8 p.m.

SETTING AND ATMOSPHERE With six rooms themed to key figures in early American history—Betsy Ross, Benjamin Franklin, Thomas Jefferson, John Paul Jones, Paul Revere, and George and Martha Washington—Liberty Tree Tavern feels like a quaint and cozy Colonial home. Appropriately creaky wooden staircases flank the busy central lobby.

HOUSE SPECIALTIES Most guests come to Liberty Tree for the All-You-Care-to-Enjoy Patriot's Platter, consisting of roasted turkey, carved pork roast, mashed potatoes, stuffing, seasonal vegetables, and house-made mac and cheese. Save room for the Ooey Gooey Toffee Cake.

OTHER RECOMMENDATIONS The Impossible Meatloaf, a plant-based dish served with mashed potatoes, seasonal vegetables, and mushroom gravy, is a tasty vegan option.

SUMMARY AND COMMENTS A solid standby for families in search of classic American fare, the tavern serves up high-quality food with good service at a quick pace. Liberty Tree Tavern regularly ranks as one of the top meals inside the Magic Kingdom, especially during the holiday season.

Maria & Enzo's Ristorante ★★

ITALIAN	EXPENSIVE	QUALITY ★★	VALUE ★★
READER-SURVEY RESPONSES ❍77% (Do Not Visit)			

The Landing, Disney Springs; ☎ 407-939-3463

Reservations Recommended. **Dining Plan credits** 1 per person, per meal. **When to go** Dinner. **Cost range** Brunch $23–$52, lunch $14–$23 (child $16), dinner $28–$52 (child $16). **Service** ★★★. **Parking** Orange garage. **Bar** Full service; extensive wine selection. **Brunch** Saturday–Sunday, 11:30 a.m.–3:30 p.m. **Lunch** Monday–Friday, 11:30 a.m.–3:30 p.m. **Dinner** Daily, 4–10 p.m.

SETTING AND ATMOSPHERE This trattoria is housed in an elegant Art Deco replica of a 1930s airline terminal, with servers clad in spiffy period flight-attendant uniforms. A smaller seating area called the First Class Lounge offers dining in a quieter setting.

HOUSE SPECIALTIES The extensive bar menu features aperitivi, prosecco cocktails, and a variety of seasonal specialty drinks. The dishes consist primarily of Italian classics.

KIDS' MENU Chicken tenders, cheese pizza, or spaghetti with meatballs; all come with vanilla ice cream for dessert.

SUMMARY AND COMMENTS Excellent setting, mediocre food, high prices.

Maya Grill ★

AMERICAN/MEXICAN	MODERATE	QUALITY ★	VALUE ★★
READER-SURVEY RESPONSES 81% (Much Below Average)			

Coronado Springs Resort; ☎ 407-939-3463

Reservations Recommended. **Dining Plan credits** 1 per person, per meal. **When to go** Never. **Cost range** $23–$42 (child $12). **Service** ★★★. **Bar** Full service. **Hours** Daily, 5–10 p.m.

SETTING AND ATMOSPHERE The dated dining room is intended to evoke the ancient world of the Maya, but the idea misses the mark. The kitchen is open to view—but so is the barren walkway outside.

HOUSE SPECIALTIES Tex-Mex and Nuevo Latino dinner fare, including a fajita skillet and slow-cooked pork with corn tortillas.

KIDS' MENU Tacos, quesadilla, grilled chicken, chicken tenders, or mac and cheese; no sides.

SUMMARY AND COMMENTS Maya Grill is owned by the same folks who run the restaurants at the Mexico Pavilion in EPCOT. Go to any of those instead.

Monsieur Paul ★★½

FRENCH	EXPENSIVE	QUALITY ★★★	VALUE ★★★
READER-SURVEY RESPONSES ⊕ 83% (Much Below Average)			

France, World Showcase, EPCOT; ☎ 407-939-3463

Reservations Required; a $100 no-show fee applies if you fail to cancel at least 72 hours before your meal. **Dining Plan credits** Not accepted. **When to go** Late dinner. **Cost range** Fixed-price menu $195. **Service** ★★★★½. **Bar** Full service. **Dress** Dressy casual (no swimwear). **Hours** Daily, 5:30–7:30 p.m.

SETTING AND ATMOSPHERE Light and modern, Monsieur Paul is tucked away at the France Pavilion, accessed by a stairway lined with photos of legendary chef Paul Bocuse, whose son, Jérôme, owns and runs both this restaurant and **Chefs de France** (see page 253), located on the first floor. Request a table at the windows to watch the world go by on the World Showcase Lagoon.

HOUSE SPECIALTIES Black-truffle soup, snapper in potato "scales."

KIDS' MENU None.

SUMMARY AND COMMENTS Disney has moved a number of fancy restaurants to fixed-price menus, and Monsieur Paul is a casualty. The food doesn't live up to the price. And few people want to get dressed up, pay $160 for theme park admission, and then pay another $250 per person (including tax and tip) for a heavy nine-course dinner. Even if you do, the food quality is too unpredictable for the price. Go to **Takumi-Tei** (see page 279) or **Victoria & Albert's** (see page 285) instead.

Morimoto Asia ★★★★

JAPANESE/PAN-ASIAN	MODERATE	QUALITY ★★★★	VALUE ★★★★
READER-SURVEY RESPONSES ⊕ 90% (Average)			

The Landing, Disney Springs; ☎ 407-939-6686

Reservations Recommended. **Dining Plan credits** 1 per person, per meal for lunch; 2 per person, per meal for dinner. **When to go** Lunch or dinner. **Cost range** $15–$62 (child $16). **Service** ★★★★. **Parking** Lime garage. **Bar** Wide range of wine, beer, sake, and cocktails. **Lunch** Daily, 11:30 a.m.–3:30 p.m. **Dinner** Daily, 4:30–10 p.m. (until 10:30 p.m. on Friday and Saturday).

SETTING AND ATMOSPHERE Innovative takes on Chinese, Japanese, and Korean dishes join a substantial sushi menu from the kitchen and upstairs sushi bar, where Iron Chef Masaharu Morimoto makes appearances. Fishing baskets and steel beads form the chandeliers, and a continuous white engineered-stone ribbon runs from the "secret" entrance to the Forbidden Lounge upstairs, creating the handrail, bar, and seating areas throughout the building and framing the glass-bottle lighting upstairs.

HOUSE SPECIALTIES Pork dim sum; 24-hour-marinated, house-carved Peking duck; orange chicken; Morimoto spare ribs; Korean buri bop; lo mein and ramen noodles; sushi rolls and sashimi.

KIDS' MENU Orange chicken, lo mein, ramen, or egg fried rice; all come with boba tea and ice cream/sorbet.

SUMMARY AND COMMENTS Chef Morimoto is famously hands-on with this restaurant, and it's not uncommon to see him in the kitchen or behind the sushi counter. The food is both better and more expensive than at most hometown Asian restaurants. If you're ordering the Peking duck for yourself and the waitstaff says it serves two, the proper response is "Challenge accepted."

Narcoossee's ★★★★

SEAFOOD	EXPENSIVE	QUALITY ★★★★	VALUE ★★★½
READER-SURVEY RESPONSES ⊕ 88% (Average)			

Grand Floridian Resort & Spa; ☎ 407-939-3463

Reservations Required. **Dining Plan credits** 2 per person, per meal. **When to go** Early evening. **Cost range** $36–$89 (child $16–$19). **Service** ★★★★★. **Bar** Full service. **Dress** Dressy casual. **Hours** Daily, 5–9:30 p.m.

SETTING AND ATMOSPHERE Situated on the Seven Seas Lagoon at the far end of the Grand Floridian Resort, Narcoossee's completed an extended refurbishment in 2023. The view of the Magic Kingdom from window seats is great, and the small dining area keeps things quieter than at most other Disney restaurants.

HOUSE SPECIALTIES Anything with seafood, almond-crusted cheesecake.

KIDS' MENU Grilled chicken or steak, seasonal fish, or chicken strips, all served with two sides from a moderate selection.

SUMMARY AND COMMENTS This is the perfect spot to dine on a sunny day, when you can see the Magic Kingdom. Also makes a great date night with a fireworks view. Hot take: We think Narcoossee's risotto is better than the more popular version over at **Le Cellier Steakhouse** (see page 251).

Nine Dragons Restaurant ★★½

CHINESE	MODERATE	QUALITY ★★★	VALUE ★★
READER-SURVEY RESPONSES 77% (Do Not Visit)			

China, World Showcase, EPCOT; ☎ 407-939-3463

Reservations Recommended. **Dining Plan credits** 1 per person, per meal. **When to go** Lunch or dinner. **Cost range** $25–$35 (child $11–$14). **Service** ★★★. **Bar** Full service. **Hours** Daily, noon–9 p.m.

SETTING AND ATMOSPHERE Efficient service and an attractive interior—subdued wood tones, colorful lanterns, beautiful backlit glass sculptures from China—create a respite from the bustle of World Showcase.

HOUSE SPECIALTIES Crispy duck bao buns, honey-sesame chicken, smoked duck fried rice.

OTHER RECOMMENDATIONS Stick to the appetizers and put the chili oil on everything. It's made in-house and should be sold as a souvenir.

KIDS' MENU Honey chicken nuggets with egg fried rice, sweet-and-sour shrimp with lo mein noodles, or the Deluxe (shrimp and crispy chicken served with egg fried rice and a side of carrots and broccoli).

SUMMARY AND COMMENTS Nine Dragons already had a reputation for high prices and mediocre food, and then its prices went up 17%–25% in 2024. There are much better values for more exciting food in World Showcase.

1900 Park Fare ★★★

AMERICAN/BUFFET	EXPENSIVE	QUALITY ★★★	VALUE ★★½
READER-SURVEY RESPONSES ⊕ 83% (Much Below Average)			

Grand Floridian Resort & Spa; ☎ 407-939-3463

Reservations Required. **Dining Plan credits** 1 per person, per meal. **When to go** Breakfast or dinner. **Cost range** Breakfast $58 (child $37), dinner $69 (child $44). **Service** ★★★. **Bar** Full service. **Breakfast** Daily, 8 a.m.–noon. **Dinner** Daily, 4–9 p.m.

SETTING AND ATMOSPHERE The interior of this newly refurbished restaurant features an old pipe organ and paintings of various Disney characters making a wish but is otherwise pretty unremarkable. Characters are supposed to include Tiana, Mirabel, Cinderella, and Aladdin, but in multiple visits, we've never seen Aladdin (Snow White greets in his place).

HOUSE SPECIALTIES *Breakfast:* Bread pudding and guava-and-cream-cheese Danish. *Dinner:* Tiana's gumbo and prime rib.

SUMMARY AND COMMENTS 1900 Park Fare reopened in April 2024 with the theme of "The Power of a Wish." Characters at breakfast and dinner host a "wishing ceremony" once an hour, which is unique—but the food is mediocre, especially for the price.

'Ohana ★★★

POLYNESIAN	EXPENSIVE	QUALITY ★★★	VALUE ★★½
READER-SURVEY RESPONSES ⊕ 82% (Much Below Average)			

Polynesian Village Resort; ☎ 407-939-3463

Reservations Strongly recommended. **Dining Plan credits** 1 per person, per meal. **When to go** Breakfast or dinner. **Cost range** Breakfast $53 (child $33), dinner $65 (child $42). **Service** ★★★. **Bar** Full service. **Character breakfast** Daily, 7:30 a.m.–12:15 p.m. **Dinner** Daily, 3:30–10 p.m.

SETTING AND ATMOSPHERE Columns of carved tiki gods support the raised thatched roof in the center of 'Ohana's main dining room, while the dining tables, arranged in rows, resemble long, segmented surfboards. Disney aims to squeeze as many families as possible into the space, so you'll be seated close to other tables no matter where you sit.

HOUSE SPECIALTIES The menu here is fixed—your only choice is between the regular meal and the plant-based meal. With that decided, the food starts arriving and doesn't stop until you've had enough. Breakfast, a character meal with Lilo and Stitch, starts with seasonal fruit and pineapple-coconut "breakfast bread." Standard breakfast skillets include scrambled eggs, sausage, ham, potatoes, Mickey-shaped waffles, and biscuits; plant-based options are available too. At dinner, starters include honey-glazed chicken wings, fried pork dumplings, mixed green salads, and 'Ohana Bread. The main course features teriyaki beef, peel-and-eat shrimp, grilled chicken, noodles, and stir-fried vegetables.

SUMMARY AND COMMENTS *'Ohana* means "family," and *family-style* certainly applies to the portions—it's an astounding amount of food that just keeps coming. That being said, the character breakfast is the most painfully slow meal I (Becky) have ever had on Disney property. The food came out quickly; in fact, my daughter and I were finished eating within 25 minutes of being seated. But the first character didn't show up until 55 minutes after we were seated, and it took another 20 minutes before the last character got to our table.

Olivia's Cafe ★★★

AMERICAN	MODERATE	QUALITY ★★★	VALUE ★★★
READER-SURVEY RESPONSES ⊕ 94% (Above Average)			

Old Key West Resort; ☎ 407-939-3463

Reservations Recommended. **Dining Plan credits** 1 per person, per meal. **When to go** Brunch. **Cost range** Brunch $11–$26 (child $9–$12), dinner $24–$39 (child $12–$14). **Service** ★★★★. **Bar** Full service. **Brunch** Daily, 7:30 a.m.–2 p.m. **Dinner** Daily, 5–9 p.m.

SETTING AND ATMOSPHERE Many Disney Vacation Club (DVC) members consider Olivia's their home restaurant, and their photos decorate the walls. The décor features pastels, mosaic-tile floors, potted palms, and tropical trees in the center of the room. Some outside seating overlooks the waterway. The tile, wood siding, and lack of tablecloths make for a noisy dining room.

HOUSE SPECIALTIES *Brunch:* Banana-bread French toast, omelets, pancakes. *Dinner:* Slow-cooked prime rib, shrimp and grits, fried chicken.

OTHER RECOMMENDATIONS Catch of the day, tofu and coconut curry, bananas Foster, Key lime pie.

KIDS' MENU Grilled chicken or fish, chicken tenders, or pasta with marinara, all with a choice of two sides from a limited selection.

SUMMARY AND COMMENTS Brunch might be worth a special trip here. Service is super friendly, and the kitchen turns out tasty casual fare.

Paddlefish ★★½

AMERICAN/SEAFOOD	EXPENSIVE	QUALITY ★★★	VALUE ★★½
READER-SURVEY RESPONSES ⊕ 80% (Much Below Average)			

The Landing, Disney Springs; ☎ 407-934-2628

Reservations Recommended. **Dining Plan credits** 2 per person, per meal. **When to go** Lunch or dinner. **Cost range** Lunch $15–$54 (child $8–$17), dinner $15–$70 (child $8–$17). **Service** ★★★½. **Parking** Lime garage. **Bar** Full service. **Lunch** Daily, noon–3:55 p.m. **Dinner** Daily, 4–11 p.m.

SETTING AND ATMOSPHERE Paddlefish has a modern aesthetic, making the stationary "steamship" seem more like a classy yacht than a classic paddleboat. The interior's sleek design doesn't distract from the views offered from the large picture windows at the sides and rear of the ship, overlooking the iconic paddle wheel. Outdoor seating on the first and third decks offers prime views of the area, but the true star of the restaurant is the rooftop bar, where you can enjoy a Florida sunset with your cocktail.

HOUSE SPECIALTIES The crab fries (hand-cut and perfectly fried) are a solid choice for an appetizer. Ahi poke, ceviche, and crab guacamole will cool you down on hot summer days. That said, we don't think the food is good enough to justify the high prices.

OTHER RECOMMENDATIONS You can't go wrong with the lobster roll or the crab cakes.

KIDS' MENU With an impressive 11 entrée options, everyone should be able to find something to eat.

SUMMARY AND COMMENTS Readers don't think much of Paddlefish, and we don't blame them. You're better off at **The Boathouse** (see page 249), **Chef Art Smith's Homecomin'** (page 252), or **Morimoto Asia** (page 266).

Paradiso 37 ★★

GLOBAL	EXPENSIVE	QUALITY ★★	VALUE ★★
READER-SURVEY RESPONSES ⊕ 70% (Do Not Visit)			

The Landing, Disney Springs; ☎ 407-934-3700

Reservations Recommended. **Dining Plan credits** 1 per person, per meal. **When to go** Just don't. **Cost range** $22–$39 (child $14). **Service** ★★★. **Parking** Lime garage. **Bar** Full service. **Hours** Daily, 11 a.m.–11 p.m. (until 11:30 p.m. on Friday and Saturday).

SETTING AND ATMOSPHERE Paradiso's outdoor seating features elevated terrace dining and a stage along the waterfront for live music. The open kitchen keeps things festive and casual. The *37* in the name refers to the number of North, South, and Central American countries represented on the menu.
HOUSE SPECIALTIES Argentinean skirt steak; Caribbean salmon; burgers; and the P37 Swirl, a margarita–sangria combo.
OTHER RECOMMENDATIONS Baja fish tacos.
KIDS' MENU Chicken tenders, cheeseburger, pizza, or double dog (hot dog *and* mini corn dogs), all served with fries.
SUMMARY AND COMMENTS Readers rate this as one of the worst restaurants in Walt Disney World. It clearly does amazing bar business to remain in Disney Springs.

Planet Hollywood ★½

AMERICAN	MODERATE	QUALITY ★	VALUE ★½
READER-SURVEY RESPONSES ⊕ 58% (Do Not Visit)			

Town Center, Disney Springs; ☎ 407-827-7827

Reservations Recommended. **Dining Plan credits** 1 per person, per meal. **When to go** Lunch or dinner. **Cost range** $18–$50 (child $10). **Service** ★★★. **Parking** Orange garage. **Bar** Full service. **Hours** Daily, 11:30 a.m.–11 p.m. (until 11:30 p.m. on Friday and Saturday).

SETTING AND ATMOSPHERE The main dining room is exceptionally loud, but an outdoor patio offers seating with a view of Disney Springs in a much quieter atmosphere.
HOUSE SPECIALTIES Food much like what you'd find at your neighborhood chain restaurant makes up much of the menu. Thanks to celebrity chef Guy Fieri, over-the-top burgers reign supreme. L.A. Lasagna, St. Louis–style barbecue ribs served on a mini picnic table, and the High Roller appetizer sampler served on a Ferris wheel round out the highlights.
KIDS MENU Cheese pizza, mac and cheese, chicken tenders, or spaghetti with meatballs; all come with dessert.
SUMMARY AND COMMENTS With higher-quality food just a few steps away at the counter-service **Blaze Fast-Fire'd Pizza** (see page 239) and **D-Luxe Burger** (see page 240) and the full-service **Chef Art Smith's Homecomin'** (see page 252), Planet Hollywood isn't worth your time or money.

The Plaza Restaurant ★★

AMERICAN	INEXPENSIVE	QUALITY ★★½	VALUE ★★½
READER-SURVEY RESPONSES ⊕ 80% (Much Below Average)			

Main Street, U.S.A., Magic Kingdom; ☎ 407-939-3463

Reservations Strongly recommended. **Dining Plan credits** 1 per person, per meal. **When to go** Lunch or dinner. **Cost range** $17–$26 (child $11–$13). **Service** ★★★★. **Bar** Wine and beer only. **Hours** Daily, 11 a.m.–9 p.m.

SETTING AND ATMOSPHERE The Plaza, a quaint and cozy spot tucked away on a side street at the end of Main Street as you head to Tomorrowland, embraces Art Nouveau touches. It's an air-conditioned heaven on a sweltering Florida day.
HOUSE SPECIALTIES Bacon cheeseburger, the Plaza Restaurant Sundae.
OTHER RECOMMENDATIONS The chicken sandwich.
KIDS' MENU Cheeseburger, mac and cheese, turkey sandwich, or PB&J, all served with two sides from a small selection.
SUMMARY AND COMMENTS The Plaza isn't fine dining, but it was one of the first restaurants in the Magic Kingdom when the park opened in 1971. Go

and enjoy an old-timey indulgence, like a hot-fudge sundae. It's a small space, so reservations are important.

Raglan Road Irish Pub & Restaurant ★★★★

IRISH	MODERATE	QUALITY ★★★★	VALUE ★★★★
READER-SURVEY RESPONSES ⊕ 100% (Exceptional)			

The Landing, Disney Springs; ☎ 407-938-0300

Reservations Strongly recommended. **Dining Plan credits** 1 per person, per meal. **When to go** Weeknights. **Cost range** Brunch $18–$30 (child $8–$12), lunch and dinner $23–$40 (child $9–$12). **Service** ★★★½. **Parking** Lime garage. **Bar** Irish whiskeys and beers. **Brunch** Saturday–Sunday, 10 a.m.–3 p.m. **Lunch** Monday–Friday, 11 a.m.–3 p.m. **Dinner** Daily, 3:05–11 p.m.

SETTING AND ATMOSPHERE Many of the elements of this pub, including the four bars, were handcrafted from hardwoods in Ireland. The venue is huge by Irish-pub standards, but the snugs (small, private cubbyholes) and dark wood paneling preserve the feel of the traditional pub. The pentagonal main room sits beneath an impressive dome. In the middle of the room is a high platform for the Celtic dancers. A modest bandstand is situated along the wall in front of a large pseudo-hearth. Branching from this cavernous domed center room are cozy dining areas and snugs.

HOUSE SPECIALTIES Branch out and try the Worth the Wait beef sandwich (made with slow-braised beef, garlic aioli, mushrooms, onions, and cheddar) or the Gnocchi Now if you're feeling autumn-ish.

Brunch options include the Now You're Talkin' Chicken Sandwich (buttermilk fried chicken breast with hot sauce and scallions), a vegan shepherd's pie, the Full Irish breakfast (Cheshire heritage pork Irish banger, bacon, black-and-white pudding, roasted tomato, mushrooms, fried eggs, and double-cooked chips), and Irish coffee.

KIDS' MENU Grilled chicken, fried chicken or fish, or mac and cheese, each served with salad, "chips" (fries), or a vegetable medley.

ENTERTAINMENT AND AMENITIES The real draw here is the Celtic music. A talented band plays daily. Celtic dancers fill the stage, visit side rooms, and dance on the aforementioned table to some of the numbers.

SUMMARY AND COMMENTS A night at Raglan Road is a joyous and uplifting experience. If you're traveling with kids, they'll almost certainly be inspired to dance. A quick fish-and-chips can be had around the corner at **Cookes of Dublin** (see page 239) if you're in a hurry.

Rainforest Cafe ★★

AMERICAN	MODERATE	QUALITY ★½	VALUE ★★
READER-SURVEY RESPONSES ⊕ 71% (Do Not Visit)			

Disney's Animal Kingdom; ☎ 407-938-9100
Marketplace, Disney Springs; ☎ 407-827-8500

Reservations Recommended. **Dining Plan credits** 1 per person, per meal. **When to go** After the lunch rush, late afternoon, or before dinner hour. **Cost range** Breakfast $13–$27 (child $10–$12), lunch and dinner $20–$50 (child $12). **Service** ★★★. **Bar** Full service. **Hours** *Animal Kingdom:* Daily, 8:30 a.m.–7:30 p.m. *Disney Springs Marketplace:* Daily, 11 a.m.–11 p.m. (until 11:30 p.m. on Friday and Saturday).

SETTING AND ATMOSPHERE Families flock to this familiar restaurant—a national chain owned by Landry's—for big plates of food served in a noisy dining room with lots to keep the kids entertained. The dining room looks like a jungle, complete with animatronic elephants, bats, and monkeys—but they're not "Disney quality." There's occasional thunder and rainfall. At the Disney Springs location, look for the giant volcano that can be seen and heard all over the Marketplace as it erupts (the smoke is nonpolluting, in accordance with the restaurant's conservation theme).

HOUSE SPECIALTIES Spinach-and-artichoke dip, Caribbean coconut shrimp, burgers, brownie volcano with ice cream and sparklers.

KIDS' MENU With 13 options, the problem will be deciding.

SUMMARY AND COMMENTS If you're willing to pay to avoid the long wait, stop by the day before and buy a Landry's Select Club membership for $25 (you get a $25 Welcome Reward back for joining). Present your card on the day you want to dine, and you'll be seated much faster. But really, go to a Rainforest Café on other trips. Not at Disney.

Rosa Mexicano ★★★½

MEXICAN	EXPENSIVE	QUALITY ★★★★	VALUE ★★★½
READER-SURVEY RESPONSES ⊕ 89% (Average)			

Dolphin Resort; ☎ 407-934-4152

Reservations Recommended. **Dining Plan credits** Not accepted. **When to go** Dinner. **Cost range** $19–$89 (child $11–$12). **Service** ★★★. **Parking** Valet ($44) or hotel lot ($36), both free with validation. **Bar** Full service, with emphasis on margaritas. **Hours** Daily, 5–11 p.m.

SETTING AND ATMOSPHERE Lots of windows let the sunlight into a dining room decorated in neutrals and whites, accented with teal. The lack of soft surfaces could make this a loud location, but it's rarely crowded enough to make a big difference.

HOUSE SPECIALTIES Guacamole, tacos, and margaritas, especially the agave margaritas.

KIDS' MENU Burgers, chicken fingers, quesadilla, or mac and cheese, with specified sides.

SUMMARY AND COMMENTS This is in the running for the best Mexican restaurant on-property. If Mexico is too crowded in EPCOT, make the quick hike over to the Dolphin for your margaritas instead.

Rose & Crown Dining Room ★★★

BRITISH	MODERATE	QUALITY ★★★½	VALUE ★★½
READER-SURVEY RESPONSES ⊕ 84% (Below Average)			

United Kingdom, World Showcase, EPCOT; ☎ 407-939-3463

Reservations Strongly recommended. **Dining Plan credits** 1 per person, per meal. **When to go** Dinner. **Cost range** $25–$31 (child $16). **Service** ★★★★. **Bar** Full service, with beers on tap. **Hours** Daily, 4–9 p.m.

SETTING AND ATMOSPHERE Pub in the front, dining room in the back. The pub hops with activity from open to close and has the look and feel of a traditional English watering hole: a large, cozy bar with rich wood appointments, beamed ceilings, and hardwood flooring. The adjoining dining room is rustic and simple.

HOUSE SPECIALTIES Fish-and-chips, bangers and mash, and shepherd's pie (the vegetarian version is delicious too), washed down with Bass ale.

OTHER RECOMMENDATIONS The Scotch egg (a hard-boiled egg with a deep-fried sausage coating) and the sticky toffee pudding for dessert.

KIDS' MENU Grilled chicken with brown rice and carrots, or fish-and-chips.

SUMMARY AND COMMENTS At dinnertime, Rose & Crown is packed with folks staking out tables for the fireworks. If you're just after fish-and-chips, try the adjacent walk-up window, **Yorkshire County Fish Shop** (page 235).

Roundup Rodeo BBQ ★★★

BARBECUE	EXPENSIVE	QUALITY ★★★	VALUE ★★★½
READER-SURVEY RESPONSES ⊕ 89% (Average)			

Toy Story Land, Disney's Hollywood Studios; ☎ 407-939-3463

Reservations Strongly recommended. **Dining Plan credits** 1 per person, per meal. **When to go** Lunch or dinner. **Cost range** $49 (child $27). **Service** ★★★★½. **Bar** Full service. **Lunch** Daily, 10:45 a.m.–3:55 p.m. **Dinner** Daily, 4–9 p.m.

SETTING AND ATMOSPHERE Like the rest of Toy Story Land, you've been shrunk to toy size, and you're invited to dine in this rodeo setup that Andy made for his toys. Servers (some more than others) will refer to you as toys, you'll get to ride toy horses to your table, and more.

HOUSE SPECIALTIES Cheddar biscuits with sweet pepper jelly, salmon (by request only, but for no extra cost).

OTHER RECOMMENDATIONS Almost everything on the menu plays it safe to appeal to as many people as possible.

KIDS' MENU The same as the adults' menu, except kids have their own specialty cupcake dessert option!

SUMMARY AND COMMENTS Meats are of middling quality at best. The Slinky Dooooooooooog's Mac & Cheese, with spring-shaped pasta and Goldfish crackers on top, is clever, and the street corn and tots have bolder flavors than anything else on the table. Still, you'll forgive the boring food when the servers yell that Andy is coming and the entire restaurant freezes. Pure we're-all-in-this-together fun.

Sanaa ★★★★

AFRICAN/INDIAN	MODERATE	QUALITY ★★★★	VALUE ★★★★½
READER-SURVEY RESPONSES ⊕ 94% (Above Average)			

Animal Kingdom Lodge & Villas–Kidani Village; ☎ 407-939-3463

Reservations Strongly recommended. **Dining Plan credits** 1 per person, per meal. **When to go** Lunch or dinner. **Cost range** Lunch $21–$36 (child $11–$15), dinner $24–$37 (child $11–$14). **Service** ★★★★. **Bar** Full service. **Quick-service breakfast** Daily, 7:30–11 a.m. (reservations not necessary). **Lunch** Daily, 11:30 a.m.–3 p.m. **Dinner** Daily, 5–9:30 p.m.

SETTING AND ATMOSPHERE Sanaa's casual dining room is inspired by African outdoor markets, with baskets, beads, and art on the walls. It's a cozy space, with 9-foot-tall windows that look out on the resort's savanna—giraffes, zebras, and other animals wander right outside as you dine.

HOUSE SPECIALTIES The most famous dish here is the Indian-style bread service (naan, onion kulcha, and paneer paratha) served with an impressive array of sauces.

OTHER RECOMMENDATIONS Butter chicken, the burger (available at lunch only), African triple-chocolate mousse. Sanaa also offers a quick-service breakfast, with hot foods such as eggs, waffles, and bacon, as well as a limited array of grab-and-go cold foods.

KIDS' MENU Fish, butter chicken, cheese pizza, or cheeseburger, all served with two sides. My kids ask to come here mostly because of the Timon Grubs dessert, a creamy treat with gummy worms, graham cracker bugs, and chocolate rocks—the stuff kids' dreams are made of. Kids enjoy their time here so much that we've used it to convince them to visit Indian restaurants at home too.

SUMMARY AND COMMENTS Sanaa is a favorite of cast members and locals alike—the flavors are addicting. It's not as upscale as **Jiko,** the resort's fine-dining restaurant (see page 262), offering instead a casual take on African–Indian fusion cuisine. It was so good that it may have converted one member of a Virginia family into a Disney foodie:

We were very impressed with the food variety, pricing, and quality here. Husband commented, "You proved me wrong. I thought there was no good food at Disney." Delightful service as well, and our kids loved seeing the savanna during dinner. It set a high standard for the rest of our trip.

San Angel Inn Restaurante ★★★

MEXICAN	MODERATE	QUALITY ★★★	VALUE ★★
READER-SURVEY RESPONSES ⊕ 86% (Below Average)			

Mexico, World Showcase, EPCOT; ☎ 407-939-3463

Reservations Strongly recommended. **Dining Plan credits** 1 per person, per meal. **When to go** Lunch or dinner. **Cost range** $18–$54 (child $12–$16). **Service** ★★★. **Bar** Full service. **Hours** Daily, 11:30 a.m.–9 p.m.

SETTING AND ATMOSPHERE Step inside the Mexico Pavilion, navigate the busy marketplace, and end up at San Angel Inn, which overlooks a starry sky and the Gran Fiesta Tour boat ride. Its décor is inspired by the original San Angel Inn in Mexico City and is incredibly atmospheric—it really does feel like you're dining in an outdoor Mexican square.

HOUSE SPECIALTIES For appetizers try the queso fundido (melted cheese with flour tortillas).

OTHER RECOMMENDATIONS Rib eye tacos should please almost anyone. Vegetarians can try the huarache vegetariano—fried corn masa with pinto beans, grilled queso fresco, and salsa verde. The sweet-corn ice cream is fun.

KIDS' MENU Tacos, quesadilla, chicken tenders, grilled chicken, or mac and cheese, all with limited side options.

SUMMARY AND COMMENTS The prices are steep (which negatively affects reader ratings), but the menu goes beyond the typical tacos, offering regional dishes that are difficult to find in the States. The dining room is a cool respite from the theme park, but you might need a flashlight to read the menu.

Sci-Fi Dine-In Theater Restaurant ★★

AMERICAN	INEXPENSIVE	QUALITY ★★	VALUE ★★
READER-SURVEY RESPONSES ⊕ 81% (Much Below Average)			

Commissary Lane, Disney's Hollywood Studios; ☎ 407-939-3463

Reservations Strongly recommended. **Dining Plan credits** 1 per person, per meal. **When to go** Lunch or dinner. **Cost range** $20–$26 (child $13–$14). **Service** ★★★. **Bar** Full service. **Hours** Daily, 10:30 a.m.–9 p.m. (until 9:30 p.m. on Friday and Saturday).

SETTING AND ATMOSPHERE Walk into a set that resembles a drive-in from the 1950s, with faux classic cars instead of tables. Hop in, order, and watch campy black-and-white video clips. It's a blast. It's the most immersive and well-themed restaurant at Walt Disney World.

HOUSE SPECIALTIES The milkshakes are expensive but could be worth it. Burgers are also expensive and only mediocre on a good day.

KIDS' MENU Burgers, chicken skewer or bites, mini corn dogs, or mac and cheese, all served with two sides from a small selection.

ENTERTAINMENT AND AMENITIES Clips of cartoons and vintage horror and sci-fi movies, such as *Attack of the 50 Foot Woman, Robot Monster,* and *The Blob.*

SUMMARY AND COMMENTS The kitsch is fun, but the food remains solidly below average. Stick with simple fare like one of the burgers. Or just fill up on an appetizer and dessert or a milkshake. You're here for the theme, not the food. Slow service seems to be an emerging theme, according to multiple reviews, including this one from a family from Canada:

> Service was cheerful but slow. We arrived at 5:20 for a 5:40 reservation and were seated close to 6. We ordered burgers and dessert and weren't finished until 7:45.

Sebastian's Bistro ★★★

LATIN/SEAFOOD	EXPENSIVE	QUALITY ★★★	VALUE ★★★½
READER-SURVEY RESPONSES ⊕ 96% (Much Above Average)			

Caribbean Beach Resort; ☎ 407-939-3463

Reservations Recommended. **Dining Plan credits** 1 per person, per meal. **When to go** Dinner. **Cost range** $39 (child $21). **Service** ★★★½. **Bar** Full service. **Hours** Daily, 4:30–9:30 p.m.

SETTING AND ATMOSPHERE Sebastian's is remarkably understated for a Disney restaurant. White walls and tables are offset by blue-and-white chairs in two rooms with vaulted ceilings and plenty of windows to let in the sunlight.

HOUSE SPECIALTIES This family-style menu includes warm pull-apart rolls (with guava butter and caramelized onion jam), oven-roasted chicken, slow-cooked mojo pork, chili-rubbed beef, baked fish, cilantro rice and beans, seasonal vegetables, candied plantains, and coconut-pineapple bread pudding with caramel sauce and vanilla ice cream. There's also a plant-based menu option.

SUMMARY AND COMMENTS The pull-apart rolls alone are probably adding 10 points to the reader ratings. We'd still opt for the walk over to the dining options at the Riviera, but the scores don't lie. This is one of the best-value all-you-care-to-eat options on-property.

Shiki-Sai: Sushi Izakaya ★★★★

JAPANESE	MODERATE	QUALITY ★★★★	VALUE ★★★★
READER-SURVEY RESPONSES ⊕ 100% (Exceptional)			

Japan, EPCOT; ☎ 407-939-5277

Reservations Strongly recommended. **Dining Plan credits** 1 per person, per meal. **When to go** Dinner. **Cost range** $14–$38 (child $18–$20). **Service** ★★★★½. **Bar** Full service. **Lunch** Daily, noon–3:55 p.m. **Dinner** Daily, 4–9 p.m.

SETTING AND ATMOSPHERE The ambience is elegant and very Japanese, inspired by Japanese seasonal festivals, with warm lighting and traditional décor. In the center, you'll find an open sushi bar where you can watch dishes being prepared.

HOUSE SPECIALTIES Sushi—all of the sushi. Also takoyaki (octopus fritters), okonomiyaki (savory Japanese pancake), grilled Wagyu gyoza (pan-fried dumplings), and ishiyaki beef rice (beef and rice cooked tableside in a hot stone bowl).

OTHER RECOMMENDATIONS A robust sake menu.

KIDS' MENU Temaki sushi set (create-your-own sushi) or a bento box.

SUMMARY AND COMMENTS This is the most recent addition to an already-impressive slate of restaurants in the Japan Pavilion. Be prepared for a slow meal focused on culture and customs, with high-quality food. It won't be fast, but it'll be great.

Space 220 ★★

AMERICAN	EXPENSIVE	QUALITY ★★½	VALUE ★½
READER-SURVEY RESPONSES ⊕ 84% (Below Average)			

World Discovery, EPCOT; ☎ 407-939-3463

Reservations Strongly recommended. **Dining Plan credits** Not accepted. **When to go** Lunch. **Cost range** Lunch $55 (child $29), dinner $79 (child $35). **Service** ★★½. **Bar** Full service, with a fair wine selection. **Lunch** Daily, 11:30 a.m.–3:30 p.m. **Dinner** Daily, 4–9 p.m.

SETTING AND ATMOSPHERE The idea here is that you're transported from EPCOT to a space station orbit, where you dine in front of large windows (computer screens) that show the earth, moon, and stars and various passersby while you dine. Your journey includes a ride on a "space elevator" to and from the station. Otherwise, the dining room is pretty bland.

HOUSE SPECIALTIES The house specialty is disappointment. Used liberally. In everything.

SUMMARY AND COMMENTS A hassle to get into, overpriced for what you get, and in need of new ideas. There's no possible way that a four-person dinner here is worth $320 before tax and tip. If you want to experience the atmosphere without taking out a second mortgage, try to get (even more competitive) reservations at the lounge, where you can order individual items instead of the prix fixe menu. And the view is arguably better.

I (Becky) went to Space 220 two different times in the past year to try to figure out why visitors keep it so busy. Both times, our service was slow (once, I had to go tell the welcome cast that we hadn't been served 20 minutes after being seated), our orders had to be redone twice, and the bills were still astronomically high. I won't be back.

Spice Road Table ★★★★

MOROCCAN	INEXPENSIVE	QUALITY ★★★★	VALUE ★★★½
READER-SURVEY RESPONSES ⊕ 98% (Exceptional)			

Morocco, World Showcase, EPCOT; ☎ 407-939-3463

Reservations Recommended. **Dining Plan credits** 1 per person, per meal. **When to go** During nightly fireworks. **Cost range** Small plates $8–$15. **Service** ★★★★. **Bar** Full service, with extensive wine and cocktail lists. **Lunch** Daily, 11:30 a.m.–3:30 p.m. **Dinner** Daily, 3:45–9 p.m.

SETTING AND ATMOSPHERE Spice Road Table is situated directly along World Showcase Lagoon at the front of the Morocco Pavilion, making it perfect for watching fireworks. The covered patio features excellent dining in open air when the weather cooperates, with colorful pops of modern Moroccan décor inside too.

HOUSE SPECIALTIES The spiced shrimp and hummus fries.

OTHER RECOMMENDATIONS The lamb kefta with tzatziki offers a bit of punch and spice. Spiced chicken may sound simple, but the accompanying sauces and sides elevate the otherwise pedestrian dish.

KIDS' MENU None.

SUMMARY AND COMMENTS Food quality and service are both good. The appetizers and desserts pair excellently with the extensive wine and cocktail offerings. The service is attentive, and the casual atmosphere is relaxing. Spice Road Table has some of the most flavorful food found in World Showcase, if you're looking for something authentic and different from normal theme park fare.

FULL-SERVICE RESTAURANTS IN DEPTH 277

Splitsville Dining Room ★★½

AMERICAN	INEXPENSIVE	QUALITY ★★½	VALUE ★★
READER-SURVEY RESPONSES ⊕ 82% (Much Below Average)			

West Side, Disney Springs; ☎ 407-938-7467

Reservations Strongly recommended. **Dining Plan credits** Not accepted. **When to go** Lunch or dinner. **Cost range** $14–$42 (child $10). **Service** ★★½. **Parking** Orange garage. **Bar** Full service. **Hours** Monday–Thursday, 11 a.m.–10 p.m.; Friday–Sunday, 10:30 a.m.–11 p.m.

- **SETTING AND ATMOSPHERE** Part of a chain of combination restaurants and bowling alleys, Splitsville is loud, as you might expect, but there's plenty to see and room for rambunctious kids to roam while you wait for your food. Décor is vaguely midcentury modern, with Sputnik lamps and other space-age touches.
- **HOUSE SPECIALTIES** The sushi is regularly the best thing on the menu.
- **KIDS' MENU** Burgers, chicken tenders, cheese pizza, hot dog, mac and cheese, or grilled cheese, most served with either applesauce, fries, or carrots.
- **SUMMARY AND COMMENTS** The menu is more spread out than a 7/10 split: burgers, pizza, seafood, Asian, and Mexican are all represented, along with assorted bar food. Quality and satisfaction started out strong here but have been trending downward for years.

Steakhouse 71 ★★★½

STEAK	EXPENSIVE	QUALITY ★★★½	VALUE ★★★½
READER-SURVEY RESPONSES ⊕ 95% (Much Above Average)			

Contemporary Resort; ☎ 407-939-3463

Reservations Recommended. **Dining Plan credits** 1 per person, per meal. **When to go** Anytime. **Cost range** Breakfast $14–$21 (child $11), lunch $17–$28 (child $13–$15), dinner $27–$42 (child $14–$16). **Service** ★★★★. **Bar** Full service. **Breakfast** Daily, 7:30–11 a.m. **Lunch** Daily, 11:30 a.m.–2 p.m. **Dinner** Daily, 5–9 p.m.

- **SETTING AND ATMOSPHERE** A midcentury modern vibe with bold colors and sleek design. The murals in the back of the dining room are artistic perfection. Also check out all the photos in the hallway and waiting area.
- **HOUSE SPECIALTIES** *Breakfast:* Seasonal pancakes are the most popular order. *Dinner:* For appetizers, the Fork & Knife Caesar Salad or the chef's Bacon & Eggs—maple-lacquered pork belly with smoky cheese grits and a poached egg. For mains, pick a cut of meat that sounds appealing. Plant-forward folks should absolutely try Chef Nik's vegan take on Beef Wellington, which may be the best thing on the menu.
- **KIDS' MENU** *Breakfast:* Oatmeal, scrambled egg, or Mickey-shaped waffles, all served with two sides (including fruit, potatoes, and meats). *Lunch and dinner:* Grilled steak, chicken breast, baked fish, or cheeseburger, all served with two sides from a decent selection.
- **SUMMARY AND COMMENTS** Steakhouse 71 is designed to appeal to everyone, so it isn't very adventurous, but it is reliably good.

STK Orlando ★★½

STEAK	EXPENSIVE	QUALITY ★★★½	VALUE ★★
READER-SURVEY RESPONSES ⊕ 77% (Do Not Visit)			

The Landing, Disney Springs; ☎ 407-917-7440

Reservations Strongly recommended. **Dining Plan credits** Not accepted. **When to go** Weekend brunch and dinner. **Cost range** Brunch $10–$160, lunch $10–$112, dinner

$49–$160 **Parking** Orange garage. **Service** ★★★. **Bar** Full service. **Brunch** Saturday-Sunday, 11 a.m.–3 p.m. **Lunch** Monday–Friday, 11 a.m.–3 p.m. **Dinner** Daily, 4–10 p.m. (until 11 p.m. on Friday and Saturday).

SETTING AND ATMOSPHERE The turreted brick exterior couldn't be more different from the inside. The lower level houses a bar and seating area with a Las Vegas ultralounge feel, complete with a DJ and *lots* of noise. The quieter, less-glitzy upstairs has both indoor and outdoor seating.

HOUSE SPECIALTIES Steaks, ranging from a $49 filet mignon to a $160 34-ounce dry-aged tomahawk. Sides include mac and cheese, sweet-corn pudding, and Parmesan-truffle fries; all cost at least $19 extra.

KIDS' MENU None.

SUMMARY AND COMMENTS Since it opened, STK has been rated as one of the worst dining experiences in Disney World. The steaks are good but overpriced, and the restaurant is too loud. Instead, we recommend **The Boathouse** (see page 249), **Chef Art Smith's Homecomin'** (see page 252), **Jaleo by José Andrés** (see page 262), **Morimoto Asia** (see page 266), or **Wine Bar George** (see page 286), all in Disney Springs. If you're dedicated to eating at STK, go for lunch and get the $10 burger.

Story Book Dining at Artist Point with Snow White ★★★½

AMERICAN	EXPENSIVE	QUALITY ★★★★	VALUE ★★★½
READER SURVEY RESPONSES	⊕ 92% (Above Average)		

Wilderness Lodge, Boulder Ridge Villas, and Copper Creek Villas & Cabins; ☎ 407-939-3463

Reservations Recommended. **Dining Plan credits** 2 per person, per meal. **When to go** Dinner. **Cost range** $67 (child $41). **Service** ★★★½. **Bar** Full service. **Character dinner** Daily, 4–9:15 p.m.

SETTING AND ATMOSPHERE When Artist Point transformed from quiet Signature dining to loud character meals, the only décor change was the addition of many "enchanted" branches and leaves to the existing rustic décor. The branches sometimes dance and will twinkle after dark.

HOUSE SPECIALTIES The mushroom bisque appetizer is a holdover from the "old" Artist Point and is glorious. Entrées include prime rib, pork shank, roast chicken, a fish dish, and a vegetarian gnocchi dish. The pork shank is one of the best pork dishes I've ever eaten.

KIDS' MENU Grilled chicken or fish, prime rib, or chicken strips, all served with two sides from a decent selection.

ENTERTAINMENT AND AMENITIES The Evil Queen presides in the center of the restaurant with a decidedly chilly demeanor. Snow White, Grumpy, and Dopey frolic through the dining room, interacting with guests.

SUMMARY AND COMMENTS While the experience is loud and the character interactions short, the food here is some of the best you'll find at any character meal on-property. This is a character meal for food lovers, not necessarily for those who want a lot of quality character time.

Summer House on the Lake ★★★

STEAK	MODERATE	QUALITY ★★★½	VALUE ★★★
READER-SURVEY RESPONSES	⊕ 85% (Below Average)		

West Side, Disney Springs; ☎ 407-598-8645

Reservations Strongly recommended. **Dining Plan credits** Not accepted. **When to go** Dinner or weekend brunch. **Cost range** Brunch $16–$40, lunch $18–$40, dinner $18–$56 (child $10). **Parking** Orange garage. **Service** ★★★. **Bar** Full service.

Brunch Saturday–Sunday, 9 a.m.–2 p.m. **Lunch** Monday–Friday, 11 a.m.–3:55 p.m. **Dinner** Monday–Friday, 4–11 p.m. (until 11:30 p.m. on Friday); Saturday–Sunday, 2:05–11 p.m.

SETTING AND ATMOSPHERE Light, airy décor with a mix of modern and rustic touches gives Summer House a breezy coastal feel. Large windows and natural wood accents perfectly complement the waterfront location.

HOUSE SPECIALTIES Signature guacamole, fresh tacos (like carne asada and crispy fish), and great seafood.

KIDS' MENU Grilled cheese, chicken fingers, breakfast for dinner, pasta with turkey meatballs, mac and cheese, quesadilla, cheeseburger, and cheese pizza. Plenty of entrée options but very few side choices.

SUMMARY AND COMMENTS The location is a bit of a hike compared to a lot of the table-service restaurants in Disney Springs if you're arriving via bus. But the view is great, and the food is pretty reliable. Even more popular is the Cookie Bar, with grab-and-go desserts and drinks.

Takumi-Tei ★★★★½

JAPANESE	EXPENSIVE	QUALITY ★★★★★	VALUE ★★★½
READER-SURVEY RESPONSES ⊕ 100% (Exceptional)			

Japan, World Showcase, EPCOT; ☎ 407-939-3463

Reservations Strongly recommended. **Dining Plan credits** Not accepted. **When to go** Dinner. **Cost range** Prix fixe menu $250 (child $100). **Service** ★★★★★. **Bar** Full service. **Hours** Daily, 4:30–7:30 p.m.

SETTING AND ATMOSPHERE In keeping with the restaurant's name, which means "house of the artisan," the décor celebrates five natural elements revered by Japanese craftsmen: water, wood, earth, stone, and washi (paper). The private dining room, home to traditional kaiseki dining, features a custom waterfall that looks like it's flowing straight into the dining table.

HOUSE SPECIALTIES The fixed-price menu rotates seasonally to reflect the freshest and most seasonal produce at the chef's disposal. A-5 Wagyu beef—the most prized in the world—anchors the main-course menu and makes for a meal unlike any other.

OTHER RECOMMENDATIONS Sashimi and nigiri with the freshest fish you'll ever taste; specialty desserts tailor-made for Instagramming.

KIDS' MENU Multicourse menu including soba, sushi, entrées, and appetizers plus dessert.

SUMMARY AND COMMENTS Filtering classical Japanese cookery through an upscale modern lens, Takumi-Tei treats diners to an indulgent retreat from the hustle and bustle of the theme park. Ever since the restaurant implemented a multistep confirmation process that forces people to acknowledge this is an expensive prix fixe meal (not to be confused with **Teppan Edo**), scores have gone from much below average to perfect. It's not very popular—during our most recent meal, every dining room was a "private" dining room because there weren't that many parties dining. But it's worth the splurge. The only exception is that the plant-based menu used to be $150 and is now the same price as the regular menu, which includes Wagyu and very high-quality seafood. Don't get us wrong, the menu is still fantastic, but we don't see how they can charge the same price for tofu, eggplant, and vegetables, no matter how well prepared.

Teppan Edo ★★★½

JAPANESE	EXPENSIVE	QUALITY ★★★★	VALUE ★★★
READER-SURVEY RESPONSES ⊕ 96% (Much Above Average)			

Japan, World Showcase, EPCOT; ☎ 407-939-3463

Reservations Strongly recommended. **Dining Plan credits** 1 per person, per meal. **When to go** Lunch or dinner. **Cost range** $28–$120 (child $18–$26). **Service** ★★★★★. **Bar** Full service. **Hours** Daily, noon–9 p.m.

SETTING AND ATMOSPHERE Six Japanese dining rooms with grills on tables and entertaining chefs chopping, slicing, and dicing.

HOUSE SPECIALTIES Chicken, shrimp, beef, scallops, and Asian vegetables stir-fried on a teppanyaki grill by a knife-juggling chef.

KIDS' MENU Steak, shrimp, salmon, chicken breast, or vegetables and tofu, all served with udon noodles, salad, and seasonal vegetables.

SUMMARY AND COMMENTS A popular dining option for families, Teppan Edo has been one of the highest-rated restaurants in EPCOT for four years. The food quality is comparable to what you'd get at your hometown hibachi place. You'll get plenty to eat, plus entertainment. The only drawback is the pricing. A menu restructure in 2024 made some entrée options available only as enhancements to other purchases. But if you avoid the $31 upcharge for a single scallop, you can still eat happy.

Terralina Crafted Italian ★★

ITALIAN	MODERATE	QUALITY ★★½	VALUE ★★
READER-SURVEY RESPONSES ⊕ 71% (Do Not Visit)			

The Landing, Disney Springs; ☎ 407-934-8888

Reservations Recommended. **Dining Plan credits** Not accepted. **When to go** Lunch or dinner. **Cost range** Lunch and dinner $17–$46 (child $8–$13), brunch $16–$24. **Service** ★★½. **Parking** Lime garage. **Bar** Full service. **Lunch and dinner** Daily, 11:30 a.m.–11 p.m. **Brunch** Saturday–Sunday, 11:30 a.m.–3 p.m.

SETTING AND ATMOSPHERE "Italian Lake District" is the theme, with stonework, exposed wood beams, and warm colors. The waiting area has a fireplace and leather chairs.

HOUSE SPECIALTIES Mozzarella-stuffed rice ball appetizer, gnocchi with pork ragù and shaved Parmesan, eggplant Parmesan.

KIDS' MENU Kids have an astounding 12 entrées to choose from!

SUMMARY AND COMMENTS If you're in the mood for really good Italian, you won't find it here. This location has scored in the "Do Not Visit" range for many years.

Three Bridges Bar & Grill at Villa del Lago ★★★

AMERICAN/SPANISH	INEXPENSIVE	QUALITY ★★★	VALUE ★★½
READER-SURVEY RESPONSES ⊕ 96% (Much Above Average)			

Coronado Springs Resort; ☎ 407-939-3463

Reservations Not accepted. **Dining Plan credits** 1 per person, per meal. **When to go** Dinner. **Cost range** $18–$29 (child $11–$13). **Service** ★★★★. **Bar** Full service. **Hours** Daily, 4:30 p.m.–midnight.

SETTING AND ATMOSPHERE This bar and grill floats in the middle of picturesque Lago Dorado, reflecting sunsets nightly at the intersection of Coronado Springs' three commuter bridges and offering grand views of the complex's Gran Destino Tower. Three Bridges is a happening spot even in the late afternoon.

HOUSE SPECIALTIES Queso with chorizo, a unique house burger, fresh tacos (with made-from-scratch tortillas). Portions aren't large but are enough to satisfy anyone looking to split a few snacks or grab a light meal. The location is known for its sangria and even hosts Sangria University.

OTHER RECOMMENDATIONS Filling salads and poke bowls are good main-dish choices if you're seeking out healthier options.

KIDS' MENU Burger, grilled chicken, shrimp, chicken quesadilla, or Impossible tacos, all served with two sides from a small selection.

SUMMARY AND COMMENTS Taking waterside dining to the next level, Three Bridges unites traditional bar fare with Spanish flair. Dishes are well executed, and drinks are delightful at this beautiful island retreat.

Tiffins Restaurant ★★★½

AMERICAN/PAN-ASIAN	EXPENSIVE	QUALITY ★★★★	VALUE ★★★
READER-SURVEY RESPONSES ⊕ 92% (Above Average)			

Discovery Island, Animal Kingdom; ☎ 407-939-3463

Reservations Strongly recommended. **Dining Plan credits** 2 per person, per meal. **When to go** Lunch or dinner. **Cost range** $28–$69 (child $15–$19). **Service** ★★★★. **Bar** Full service. **Hours** Daily, 11:30 a.m.–6 p.m.

SETTING AND ATMOSPHERE Tiffins is found on a walking path to the land of Pandora. Inside are three relatively small, quiet dining rooms. The décor is said to be inspired by the travel adventures of the Imagineers who built Animal Kingdom. You'll see artifacts from Asia and Africa lining the walls of one room and giant butterflies in another. The main dining room's centerpiece is carved-wood sculptures.

HOUSE SPECIALTIES Charred octopus and pineapple-glazed pork belly appetizers. For entrées, try the tamarind-braised short rib or the signature burger—the cheapest entrée on the menu.

OTHER RECOMMENDATIONS Skip the bread service and desserts.

KIDS' MENU Grilled steak, teriyaki chicken thigh, grilled shrimp, or Impossible meatballs, each served with two sides from a small selection. Overpriced for the portions.

SUMMARY AND COMMENTS Despite the above-average reader ratings, we think the food here is trending toward overpriced and not as good as it used to be. The **Nomad Lounge** next door (page 228) is the better option.

Todd English's Bluezoo ★★½

SEAFOOD	EXPENSIVE	QUALITY ★★★	VALUE ★★½
READER-SURVEY RESPONSES ⊕ 78% (Much Below Average)			

Dolphin Resort; ☎ 407-934-1609

Reservations Recommended. **Dining Plan credits** Not accepted. **When to go** Dinner. **Cost range** $31–$95 (child $10–$12). **Service** ★★★. **Parking** Valet ($44) or hotel lot ($36), both free with validation. **Bar** Full service. **Dress** Dressy casual. **Hours** Daily, 5–11 p.m.

SETTING AND ATMOSPHERE The name is courtesy of celebrity chef Todd English's son, who as a youngster saw an under-the-sea movie and said it looked like a "blue zoo." There is an open kitchen and a circular rotisserie that makes the fish being grilled on it seem to dance on the coals.

HOUSE SPECIALTIES Nightly fish selection (from the rotisserie), Angus filet.

OTHER RECOMMENDATIONS New England–style clam chowder with salt-cured bacon, teppan-seared jumbo sea scallops.

KIDS' MENU Burger, cheese pizza, grilled chicken, fish-and-chips, or pasta, all served with predetermined sides.

SUMMARY AND COMMENTS You could fashion a good meal from just the appetizers and desserts, which are above average. But even that will be a pretty pricey meal.

Toledo—Tapas, Steak & Seafood ★★★

SPANISH	EXPENSIVE	QUALITY ★★★	VALUE ★★★
READER-SURVEY RESPONSES ⊕ 89% (Average)			

Gran Destino Tower, Coronado Springs Resort; ☎ 407-939-3463

Reservations Recommended. **Dining Plan credits** 1 per person, per meal. **When to go** Dinner. **Cost range** $31–$57 (child $13–$16). **Service** ★★★★. **Bar** Full service. **Hours** Wednesday–Sunday, 5–10 p.m.

SETTING AND ATMOSPHERE High atop Gran Destino Tower, Toledo envelops diners in a Cubist cloud heaven, complete with color-changing ceiling and trees reaching to the sky right beside several tables. A showcase bar anchors one side of the restaurant, while an open tapas kitchen greets guests at the far end of the dining room. The real attraction, though, is the massive wall of windows, offering views of some of Walt Disney World's most popular attractions and nighttime spectaculars.

HOUSE SPECIALTIES None. Everything is unreliable—it can be great, and it can be terrible.

OTHER RECOMMENDATIONS Stick to the less expensive small plates and save your money for somewhere else. If you do want to go all out, the Chef's Signature Dinner for Two is actually a good deal for everything that is included.

KIDS' MENU Fish, shrimp, grilled steak or chicken breast, or meatballs, all served with two sides from a rather large selection.

SUMMARY AND COMMENTS Jaleo by José Andrés (see page 262) has better food for less money. Toledo caters to resort guests and conventioneers stuck at the resort. We're baffled that it made it into the *Michelin Guide*. It can be a spectacular meal. But chances are just as good that it will be a mediocre or disappointing one.

Tony's Town Square Restaurant ★★

ITALIAN	MODERATE	QUALITY ★★	VALUE ★★
READER-SURVEY RESPONSES ⊕ 81% (Much Below Average)			

Main Street, U.S.A., Magic Kingdom; ☎ 407-939-3463

Reservations Strongly recommended. **Dining Plan credits** 1 per person, per meal. **When to go** Late lunch or early dinner. **Cost range** $26–$35 (child $12–$13). **Service** ★★★. **Bar** Limited selection of beer and wine. **Hours** Daily, 11:30 a.m.–9 p.m.

SETTING AND ATMOSPHERE Just inside the Magic Kingdom entrance on Main Street, Tony's Town Square is a rite of passage for Disney fans—who wouldn't want a plate of spaghetti in the restaurant that commemorates *Lady and the Tramp*? The food isn't great, but the dining room is filled with natural light from windows and skylights, and the porch is wonderful for watching the action outside.

HOUSE SPECIALTIES Spaghetti with meatballs (or Impossible meatballs), fettuccine Alfredo, chicken parmigiana. But mostly the garlic bread.

KIDS' MENU Spaghetti with turkey meatball, grilled chicken, or mac and cheese, all served with two sides from a kid-friendly selection.

SUMMARY AND COMMENTS Though it's consistently rated as one of the worst restaurants in the Magic Kingdom, Tony's does a decent job with simple pasta (multigrain and gluten-free options available).

Topolino's Terrace—Flavors of the Riviera ★★★½

FRENCH/ITALIAN	EXPENSIVE	QUALITY ★★★★	VALUE ★★★
READER-SURVEY RESPONSES ⊕ 97% (Much Above Average)			

Riviera Resort; ☎ 407-939-3463

Reservations Strongly recommended. **Dining Plan credits** 1 per person, per meal for breakfast; 2 per person, per meal for dinner. **When to go** Breakfast or dinner. **Cost range** Breakfast $52 (child $33); dinner $38–$62 (child $12–$19). **Service** ★★★★. **Bar** Full service. **Character breakfast** Daily, 7:30 a.m.–12:15 p.m. **Dinner** Daily, 5–9:30 p.m.

SETTING AND ATMOSPHERE This rooftop restaurant at the Riviera has a fantastic view of EPCOT and Disney's Hollywood Studios, especially at night when those parks run their fireworks spectaculars. Inside you'll find burgundy-and-cream carpets and dark wood tables and accents. In keeping with Disney's recent decorative trends, there's absolutely nothing here that's overtly tied to the Riviera.

HOUSE SPECIALTIES *Breakfast:* Sour cream waffle with roasted apples and orange-maple syrup; steak and eggs. *Dinner:* Sole meunière, braised beef cheeks, filet mignon.

KIDS' MENU *Breakfast:* Waffle dippers, scrambled egg, or fruit and yogurt, all with sides. *Dinner:* Grilled steak or chicken, or rigatoni, all served with two sides from a limited selection.

SUMMARY AND COMMENTS This is one of the most difficult reservations to get in Walt Disney World. There are seemingly no bad choices on the menu, and the service is excellent. Breakfast features a parade of Disney characters, including Mickey, Minnie, Donald, and Daisy. Breakfast has become a worse value, with no multi-entrée ordering and a significantly higher price than two years ago.

Trattoria al Forno ★★★

ITALIAN	MODERATE	QUALITY ★★★½	VALUE ★★½
READER-SURVEY RESPONSES ⊕ 93% (Above Average)			

BoardWalk; ☎ 407-939-3463

Reservations Strongly recommended. **Dining Plan credits** 1 per person, per meal. **When to go** Breakfast or dinner. **Cost range** Breakfast $13–$21 (child $7–$11), dinner $21–$41 (child $14–$17). **Service** ★★★★. **Bar** Full service, with all Italian wines. **Breakfast** Daily, 7:30–11:30 a.m. **Dinner** Daily, 5–10 p.m.

SETTING AND ATMOSPHERE The space contains three dining areas, a private room, and an open kitchen for watching the action. Our favorite spots are the informal dining room, right in front of the kitchen, or at a booth at the back.

HOUSE SPECIALTIES *Breakfast:* Oven-roasted egg over polenta with fennel sausage; pancakes; steak and eggs; breakfast pizza (scrambled eggs, bacon, ham, sausage, bell peppers, and cheese). *Dinner:* Lasagna al forno, truffle gnocchi.

KIDS' MENU Breakfast and dinner both feature four or five entrée options and a bunch of sides that should be manageable for all eaters.

SUMMARY AND COMMENTS The kitchen makes its own mozzarella and fresh pasta daily. The wines represent Italy's major regions, with over 60 offerings by the bottle and more than 25 by the glass. The breakfast is one of the best on Disney property, even without the characters that used to appear here. However, the quality of the dinner dishes is highly variable and therefore unreliable.

T-Rex ★★

AMERICAN	MODERATE	QUALITY ★★	VALUE ★★
READER-SURVEY RESPONSES ⊕ 77% (Do Not Visit)			

Marketplace, Disney Springs; ☎ 407-828-8739

Reservations Strongly recommended. **Dining Plan credits** 1 per person, per meal. **When to go** Lunch or dinner. **Cost range** $20–$44 (child $12). **Service** ★★½. **Parking** Orange garage. **Bar** Full service. **Hours** Daily, 11 a.m.–11 p.m.

SETTING AND ATMOSPHERE Sensory overload in a cavernous dining room with life-size robotic dinosaurs, giant fish tanks, bubbling geysers, waterfalls, fossils in the bathrooms, and crystals in the walls. It's unbelievably loud.
HOUSE SPECIALTY Megasaurus Burger.
KIDS' MENU Extensive.
SUMMARY AND COMMENTS Expect a wait unless there's an empty seat at the bar. Nobody's here just for the ordinary, overpriced food—it's nonstop "eatertainment," with kid-friendly food served in huge portions.

The Turf Club Bar and Grill ★★

AMERICAN	MODERATE	QUALITY ★★½	VALUE ★★
READER-SURVEY RESPONSES ⊕ 90% (Average)			

Saratoga Springs Resort & Spa; ☎ 407-939-3463

Reservations Accepted. **Dining Plan credits** 1 per person, per meal. **When to go** Dinner. **Cost range** $23–$39 (child $12–$14). **Service** ★★★. **Bar** Full service. **Hours** Wednesday–Sunday, 4:30–9 p.m.

SETTING AND ATMOSPHERE When the weather is nice, ask for an outdoor table; you can spot golfers on the adjacent Lake Buena Vista Golf Course and look across the way to Disney Springs. The dining room is equestrian themed.
HOUSE SPECIALTY Slow-roasted prime rib.
OTHER RECOMMENDATIONS Turf Club burger.
KIDS' MENU Chicken strips, prime rib, salmon, cheeseburger, or pasta with marinara, all served with two sides from a small selection.
SUMMARY AND COMMENTS Rarely crowded, but you'll find much better food nearby at Disney Springs.

Tusker House Restaurant ★★★

AFRICAN/AMERICAN	EXPENSIVE	QUALITY ★★★½	VALUE ★★★
READER-SURVEY RESPONSES ⊕ 93% (Above Average)			

Africa, Animal Kingdom; ☎ 407-939-3463

Reservations Required. **Dining Plan credits** 1 per person, per meal. **When to go** Anytime. **Cost range** Breakfast $49 (child $33), lunch and dinner $64 (child $42). **Service** ★★★. **Bar** Full-service bar next door. **Character breakfast** Daily, 8–10:30 a.m. **Character lunch** Daily, 11 a.m.–3:30 p.m. **Character dinner** Daily, 3:35–6 p.m.

SETTING AND ATMOSPHERE Character meals feature Mickey, Donald, Daisy, and Goofy. The setting—inside the Harambe Village square—is pretty plain, especially after dark. The food, however, is surprisingly good, with spices and taste combinations you won't find at other character-dining spots.
HOUSE SPECIALTIES Tandoori chicken, berbere-marinated pork, green curry shrimp, braised beef tagine, doro wat (Ethiopian chicken stew), and what Becky's daughter claims is the best salmon in all of Walt Disney World.
SUMMARY AND COMMENTS Tusker House appeals not just to kids but also to grown-ups who appreciate more-interesting dishes.

Tutto Italia Ristorante ★★★

ITALIAN	EXPENSIVE	QUALITY ★★★	VALUE ★★½
READER-SURVEY RESPONSES ⊕ 93% (Above Average)			

Italy, World Showcase, EPCOT; ☎ 407-939-3463

Reservations Strongly recommended. **Dining Plan credits** 1 per person, per meal. **When to go** Midafternoon. **Cost range** $26–$52 (child $11). **Service** ★★★. **Bar** Full service, with all Italian wines. **Hours** Daily, 12:30–9 p.m.

SETTING AND ATMOSPHERE Tutto Italia feels like a big restaurant in Rome or Milan, with murals of a piazza along the wall behind upholstered banquettes. It can get noisy—if the weather is nice, request an outside table.

HOUSE SPECIALTIES All of the food items are pretty reliably meh. Treat yourself to some interesting beverages instead.

OTHER RECOMMENDATIONS Stick to the least expensive menu items.

KIDS' MENU Spaghetti, chicken tenders, mozzarella sticks, or pizza.

SUMMARY AND COMMENTS This *should* be one of the best Italian restaurants in Orlando, but it's not. Everything that happens inside Tutto Italia—from the cooking to the service—feels like it's done on autopilot. The food quality can't support the prices: $34 for chicken parm is nearly double what you'd pay in many neighborhood Italian joints. Everything here should be done better.

Via Napoli Ristorante e Pizzeria ★★★½

ITALIAN	MODERATE	QUALITY ★★★½	VALUE ★★★
READER-SURVEY RESPONSES ⊕ 94% (Above Average)			

Italy, World Showcase, EPCOT; ☎ 407-939-3463

Reservations Strongly recommended. **Dining Plan credits** 1 per person, per meal. **When to go** Lunch or dinner. **Cost range** Entrées $27–$49, individual pizzas $21–$26, pizzas to share (serves 2–5) $36–$60. **Service** ★★★. **Bar** Beer and wine only. **Hours** Daily, 11:30 a.m.–9 p.m.

SETTING AND ATMOSPHERE Three big pizza ovens, named after the three active Italian volcanoes—Etna, Vesuvio, and Stromboli—are the stars of the show in this loud, cavernous dining room.

HOUSE SPECIALTIES This is some of the best pizza in Walt Disney World. Our favorites include the Carciofi (artichokes, fontina, and truffle oil) and Quattro Formaggi (four cheese).

KIDS' MENU Margherita pizza, chicken tenders, or spaghetti with meatball. Share pizza with them instead.

SUMMARY AND COMMENTS The main dining room is loud, but at least you won't feel out of place when your kids are loud and running around while waiting for their pizza.

Victoria & Albert's ★★★★★

GOURMET	EXPENSIVE	QUALITY ★★★★★	VALUE ★★★★
READER-SURVEY RESPONSES ⊕ 92% (Above Average)			

Grand Floridian Resort & Spa; ☎ 407-939-3463

Reservations Required; you must confirm special dietary needs before your seating. A $100 no-show fee applies if you fail to cancel at least 5 days before your meal; if you cancel less than 24 hours before, you'll be charged the full price. **Dining Plan credits** Not accepted. **When to go** Dinner. **Cost range** Main dining room $295, Queen Victoria's Room $375, Chef's Table $425 (all menus fixed price; tax and gratuities extra). Optional wine pairings start at $155, zero-proof beverage pairings start at $115. **Service** ★★★★★. **Parking** Valet (free). **Wine selection** Hundreds on the menu, thousands more in the cellar. **Dress** Semi-formal or formal attire only. **Hours** Open Tuesday–Saturday. Main dining room: 5:30–8:05 p.m. Queen Victoria's Room:

5:30–7 p.m. Chef's Table: One seating at 5:30 p.m. (Seating times may vary.) *Note:* No children under age 10 admitted except at Chef's Table.

SETTING AND ATMOSPHERE With just 14 tables in the main dining room, Queen Victoria's Room (with seating for up to eight) and the eight-seat Chef's Table, this is the top dining experience at Walt Disney World. A consecutive winner of AAA's Five Diamond Award since 2000—the only restaurant in Central Florida so honored—Victoria & Albert's is lavish and expensive, with Frette linens, Riedel crystal, Christofle silver, and a harpist playing every night.

HOUSE SPECIALTIES The menu changes regularly but always includes the finest ingredients prepared in the most spectacular ways. It will help you enjoy foods you've always dreamed of eating and make you fall in love with ingredients you didn't even know existed. Pace yourself throughout the meal because the desserts are always divine.

SUMMARY AND COMMENTS The team prepares modern American cuisine with the best of the best from around the world. The main dining room and Queen Victoria's Room are whisper-quiet, but the Chef's Table is convivial and relaxed.

Reopened in the fall of 2022 with a single, fixed-price menu and its usual excellent food and service, V&A made the *Michelin Guide* for the first time in 2023 and earned its first Michelin star in 2024. As long as you are OK with the price, you will never regret a meal here.

Whispering Canyon Cafe ★★★

AMERICAN	EXPENSIVE	QUALITY ★★★	VALUE ★★★½
READER-SURVEY RESPONSES ⊕ 94% (Above Average)			

Wilderness Lodge, Boulder Ridge Villas, and Copper Creek Villas & Cabins; ☎ 407-939-3463

Reservations Strongly recommended. **Dining Plan credits** 1 per person, per meal. **When to go** Anytime. **Cost range** Breakfast and lunch $11–$26 (child $6–$13), dinner $24–$40 (child $10–$17). **Service** ★★★★. **Bar** Full service. **Breakfast** Daily, 7:30–11:25 a.m. **Lunch** Daily, 11:30 a.m.–2 p.m. **Dinner** Daily, 5–10 p.m.

SETTING AND ATMOSPHERE A big, open dining room just off the lobby of Wilderness Lodge, with whimsical Wild West décor.

HOUSE SPECIALTIES For breakfast, the all-you-can-eat skillet offers bacon, sausage, scrambled eggs, waffles, and buttermilk biscuits and gravy. For lunch and dinner, a big skillet loaded with barbecue pulled pork or ribs, roasted chicken, mashed potatoes, green beans, and corn is a crowd-pleaser. Three other skillet options are also available at dinner.

KIDS' MENU One egg, Mickey waffles, oatmeal, cheeseburger, chicken tenders, grilled chicken, or mac and cheese, all served with two sides from a large selection.

SUMMARY AND COMMENTS The all-you-can-eat skillets give hungry folks their money's worth. Make sure you ask for ketchup!

Wine Bar George ★★★★

WINE/SMALL PLATES	EXPENSIVE	QUALITY ★★★★	VALUE ★★★½
READER-SURVEY RESPONSES ⊕ 94% (Above Average)			

The Landing, Disney Springs; ☎ 407-490-1800

Reservations Accepted. **Dining Plan credits** Not accepted. **When to go** Anytime. **Cost range** Brunch $18–$30, lunch $17–$23, dinner $32–$52 (child $10). Small plates $8–$18. **Parking** Lime garage. **Service** ★★★★½. **Bar** Full service. **Wine selection**

Wide-ranging—more than 140 wines in all—with a focus on affordability. **Brunch** Saturday–Sunday, 10:30 a.m.–2 p.m. **Lunch** Monday–Friday, 11:30 a.m.–2:55 p.m. **Dinner** Daily, 3–11 p.m. (until 11:30 p.m. on Friday and Saturday).

SETTING AND ATMOSPHERE Décor is spare and industrial: exposed air vents, concrete floors, brick walls, and lots of windows. The focus of the ground floor is the central bar, with an elevated wine rack and seating for around 18 people; a dozen 6-person high-tops and four 4-person tables are also available. It's noisy here even before you add alcohol, but the second floor is much quieter, and it has outdoor as well as indoor seating.

HOUSE SPECIALTIES Tapas-style small bites made for sharing—we like the saganaki (cheese set on fire!). Entrées are limited—try the family-style skirt steak with roasted potatoes and seasonal vegetables.

OTHER RECOMMENDATIONS Many of the wines are available by the ounce, the glass, and the bottle, letting you create your own inexpensive wine-flight theme.

KIDS' MENU Chicken tenders, mac and cheese, meatballs, or hot dog, all served with apple juice and fresh fruit.

SUMMARY AND COMMENTS Owner and namesake George Miliotes is one of just 279 Master Sommeliers in the world. Miliotes is also committed to making great wines affordable: The markups here are generally more reasonable compared to those at other Disney restaurants.

The Basket, a counter-service window beneath the second-story terrace, serves European-style sandwiches, cheese, olives, hummus, charcuterie, cookies, and wines on tap—served to-go by the glass.

Wolfgang Puck Bar & Grill ★★★

AMERICAN	MODERATE	QUALITY ★★★½	VALUE ★★★
READER-SURVEY RESPONSES ⊕ 95% (Much Above Average)			

Town Center, Disney Springs; ☎ 407-939-3463

Reservations Recommended. **Dining Plan credits** Not accepted. **When to go** Anytime. **Cost range** Brunch $18–$47, lunch and dinner $18–$65 (child $11–$14). **Parking** Orange garage. **Service** ★★★. **Bar** Full service. **Brunch** Saturday–Sunday, 10 a.m.–3 p.m. **Lunch** Monday–Friday, 11 a.m.–4 p.m. **Dinner** Monday–Friday, 4:05–10 p.m. (until 11 p.m. on Friday); Saturday–Sunday, 3:05–11 p.m.

SETTING AND ATMOSPHERE The décor melds the sleek style of the surrounding garage and over-the-top retail locations with the Florida-waterfront look of the rest of Town Center. As you enter, an open kitchen draws the eye, while exposed wood beams and a copper-accented pizza oven bring warmth to the restaurant's 250-seat interior, with an indoor bar offset from the main dining room. A slight outdoor seating area abuts one side of the restaurant's exterior, with the other side dedicated to a grab-and-go dessert and gelato window.

HOUSE SPECIALTIES The pizza is always good. For dinner, the chicken Wiener schnitzel and roasted half chicken are reliable.

OTHER RECOMMENDATIONS Nothing here is bad, but the meats and pizzas are better than the pastas.

KIDS' MENU Chicken strips, grilled chicken, spaghetti, cheeseburger, or pizza, all served with predetermined sides.

SUMMARY AND COMMENTS Not the flashiest restaurant, but it has good food at decent prices (for Disney). It's also often easier to get into than other places in Disney Springs.

Yachtsman Steakhouse ★★½

STEAK	EXPENSIVE	QUALITY ★★★½	VALUE ★★
READER-SURVEY RESPONSES ⊕ 83% (Much Below Average)			

Yacht Club Resort; ☎ 407-939-3463

Reservations Strongly recommended. **Dining Plan credits** 2 per person, per meal. **When to go** Dinner. **Cost range** $38–$68 (child $12–$17). **Service** ★★★½. **Bar** Full service. **Dress** Dressy casual. **Hours** Daily, 5–9:30 p.m.

SETTING AND ATMOSPHERE Wooden beams, white linens, and a view of the Yacht Club's sandy lagoon make Yachtsman feel light and airy rather than dark and masculine like the typical steakhouse. Beef is the star, of course, but there are other options on the menu.

HOUSE SPECIALTIES Bread service with roasted sweet garlic.

KIDS' MENU Grilled chicken, steak, baked fish, or pasta with marinara, all served with two sides from a decent selection.

SUMMARY AND COMMENTS We're consistently disappointed by Yachtsman, and the ratings prove that other visitors are as well. The kitchen struggles with the basics of flavor and temperature, and the prices are simply too high for the quality of the food being served.

Yak & Yeti Restaurant ★★★

PAN-ASIAN	MODERATE	QUALITY ★★★	VALUE ★★★
READER-SURVEY RESPONSES ⊕ 94% (Above Average)			

Asia, Animal Kingdom; ☎ 407-939-3463

Reservations Strongly recommended. **Dining Plan credits** 1 per person, per meal. **When to go** Dinner. **Cost range** $21–$49 (child $12). **Service** ★★★½. **Bar** Full service. **Hours** Daily, 10:30 a.m.–5:50 p.m.

SETTING AND ATMOSPHERE A rustic two-story Nepalese inn—with seating for hundreds. Windows on the second floor overlook the Asia section of the theme park.

HOUSE SPECIALTIES Lo mein bowls, coconut shrimp, chicken tikka masala.

OTHER RECOMMENDATIONS Try the Korean fried chicken tenders or the firecracker shrimp.

KIDS' MENU Kids have eight different entrée options—the most of any in-park restaurant. Each is served with two sides from a plentiful selection.

SUMMARY AND COMMENTS The food isn't groundbreaking, but Yak & Yeti is one of the highest-rated sit-down restaurants in a theme park. The early closing time used to be a problem, but now that the entire park almost always closes early, it's not as big of a deal.

PART 7
WALT DISNEY WORLD *with* KIDS

KEY QUESTIONS ANSWERED IN THIS CHAPTER

- How important will naps and rest be during our trip? *(page 292)*
- What do kids like best in Walt Disney World? *(page 296)*
- Will we need a stroller? *(page 299)*
- Which rides are scary? *(page 304)*
- How do we take turns riding something our child won't be riding? *(page 307)*
- Which rides have height requirements? *(page 308)*
- Where can we meet the Disney characters? *(page 312)*

MANAGING *the* MAGIC

IT'S SAFE TO SAY that most of the *Guide,* and especially this chapter, is based on real-world experience: what we and our readers have learned through extensive firsthand experience and by making our own mistakes in Walt Disney World. Prepare the best you can and don't beat yourself up when something goes wrong. That's the key to Disney vacation magic.

The reality of a family vacation, especially at Disney, and particularly if you chase perfection, can be closer to agony than to ecstasy. An Ohio mother who took her 5-year-old one summer recalls:

> I felt so happy and excited before we went, but when I look back, I think I should have had my head examined. The first day we went to the Magic Kingdom, it was packed. By 11 in the morning, we had walked so far and stood in so many lines that we were all exhausted. Kristy cried about going on anything that looked or even sounded scary and was frightened by all of the Disney characters (they're so big!) except Minnie and Snow White.
>
> We got hungry about the same time as everyone else, but the lines for food were too long and my husband said we'd have to wait. By 1 in the afternoon, we were just plugging along, not seeing anything we were really interested in, but picking rides because the lines were short or because they were air-conditioned. At around 2:30, we finally got something to eat, but by then we were so hot and tired

that it felt like we had worked in the yard all day. At the end, we were so P.O.'d and uncomfortable that we weren't having any fun.

This family's experience is not unusual. Most young children are as picky about rides as they are about what they eat (and where they are willing to use the bathroom, but I digress), and many preschoolers are intimidated by the Disney characters. Few people (of any age) are mentally or physically equipped to march around all day in a crowd of 60,000-plus people in the Florida heat and humidity. In fact, most preschoolers say the thing they liked best about their Disney trip is the hotel swimming pool! And it's not hard to imagine why—it's the one place the whole family feels like they can relax and have fun without worrying about waiting in lines, planning, or money. Plus, it's unstructured playtime during a bunch of planned days, hours, and minutes.

> *unofficial* **TIP**
> When considering a trip to Walt Disney World, think about whether your kids are prepared to enjoy what can be a very fun but exhausting trip.

Still, with some planning, appropriate responses when things inevitably go wrong, and a sense of humor, you'll be sending us comments like this one from a Virginia mom:

I thought I knew how magical Disney was. And then I brought my son for the first time. Nothing will ever beat seeing everything through his eyes on that first trip.

REALITY TESTING: WHOSE DREAM IS IT?

ASK YOURSELF A VERY IMPORTANT QUESTION about your vacation to Walt Disney World. Whose dream are you trying to make come true: yours or your child's? Either answer is OK—my (Becky's) older daughter doesn't remember her first trip, but I do, and those are some of my favorite Disney memories. But it's important to keep the answer in mind as you're planning your trip.

Kids have an uncanny ability to feed off their parents' emotions. When you ask, "Would you like to go to Disney World?" your child will respond more to your enthusiasm than to any idea of what Disney World is actually like. The younger the child, the more this holds true. From many preschoolers, you could get the same excited reaction by asking, "Would you like to ride through the desert on an ox?"

Follow up that first important question with a few others. For example, will your child have sufficient endurance and patience to cope with long lines, long days, and large crowds? Do they usually wilt in the heat or power through if they're having fun? Are they anxious or afraid in new situations? Do they need to stick to a specific schedule to avoid melting down? None of the answers to these questions are deal-breakers, but they are worth considering during your planning and preparation.

RECOMMENDATIONS FOR MAKING THE DREAM COME TRUE

WHEN YOU'RE PLANNING a Walt Disney World vacation with young children, consider the following:

AGE Although Disney World's bright colors and overall activity excite all children, and specific attractions delight toddlers and preschoolers, some entertainment and attractions are meant for older kids and adults. Every member of our family enjoyed every park at Walt Disney World when they were as young as 18 months old. But if this is a once-in-a-lifetime trip or your kids aren't used to long days and traveling, then you should take that into account when timing your vacation. Readers regularly debate how old a child should be or the ideal age to go to Disney World. But really, you need to know your kids and how to make a vacation successful for them.

A Georgia mother of two toddlers emphasizes the importance of maintaining your kids' regular schedule:

> *The first day, we tried your suggestion about an early start, so we woke the kids (ages 4 and 2) and hurried them to get going. Bad idea. This put them off-schedule for naps and meals for the rest of the day.*

A Pennsylvania mom with two young kids recounts her experience:

> *Eighteen months is the absolute worst age to bring a child to Disney. They have no concept of waiting in lines, can't stand the heat, will not sit in a stroller, only want to be carried, and only want to go up and down the stairs outside of the attraction you want to ride. Expect lots of meltdowns, and good luck with the baby swap when they have to go to someone else. (Mom didn't get to do much.)*

WHEN TO VISIT Avoid the exceedingly hot summer months, especially if you have preschoolers or your family isn't used to being outdoors in the heat. These times tend to be less crowded, but it's not worth melting a couple of hours into the day. Go in November (except Thanksgiving), early December, late January, or February (except Mardi Gras and Presidents' Day). If your children can't afford to miss school, try late August, before school starts, when crowds and hotel rates are lower. But keep in mind that special events, attraction downtime, and other factors can still combine to make any time of year feel crowded.

If you have children of varying ages and they're good students, you can consider taking them out of school and visiting during the cooler, less congested offseason. Most readers who have tried this at various times agree. A New Hampshire parent writes:

> *I took my grade-school children out of school for a few days to go during a slow time and highly recommend it. We communicated with the teachers about a month before traveling to seek their preference for whether classwork and homework should be completed before, during, or after our trip. It's so much more enjoyable to be at Disney when your children can experience rides, attractions, and all that is Disney rather than standing in line.*

There's another side to this story, and we've received some well-considered letters from parents and teachers who don't think taking kids out of school is such a hot idea. A California teacher offers a compelling analogy:

> *There are a precious 180 days for us as teachers to instruct our students, and there are 185 days during the year for Disney World. I've*

seen countless students struggle to catch up the rest of the year due to a week of vacation. The analogy I use with my students' parents is that it's like walking out of a movie after watching the first 5 minutes, then returning for the last 5 minutes and trying to figure out what happened.

But a teacher from New York sees things differently:

As a teacher and a parent, I disagree that it's horrible for a parent to take a child out for a vacation. If a parent takes the time to let us know that a child is going to be out, we help them get ready for upcoming homework the best we can. If the child is a good student, why shouldn't they go have a wonderful experience with their family?

Only you and your teacher know your kid and how missing some days of school might affect them. If possible, ask your child's teacher for a list of topics they'll be covering while you're away. Have your child study these on the plane or in the car, while waiting for meals, or at night before bed. You can even provide the teacher with all of the "bonus" education your child received from touring the World Showcase, seeing animatronics in action, and more. We try to give teachers a couple of weeks' advance notice so that if they choose to send work home, it's not a mad scramble of extra effort for them a day or two before we leave.

BUILD NAPS AND REST INTO YOUR ITINERARY By a wide margin, the thing most parents say they learned during their first Disney visit was the importance of daily breaks and naps or, more generically, vacationing at a pace the whole family can maintain through the entire trip.

unofficial **TIP**
If you want to return to the hotel during the day for rest, prioritize a resort with easy transportation or rent a car. See page 41 for more on the logistics of naptime.

Why? The parks are huge and require a lot of walking, and crowds can make them even more difficult to navigate, so it's inevitable that someone is going to run out of energy. And when that someone is too young to be expected to keep a good handle on their emotions when they're exhausted, things tend to happen—ugly things. Pushing the tired or cranky beyond their capacity will spoil the day for them *and* you. Go back to your hotel midday to rest and relax, and then return to the park (or hop to another) in the late afternoon or early evening. If a midday break sounds like a waste of time, plan for an entire rest day after two full days in the parks so everyone can catch up on sleep and downtime.

Regarding naps, this mom doesn't mince words:

Take the book's advice—get out of the park and take the nap, take the nap, TAKE THE NAP!

A mom from Illinois wishes her family had taken a rest day:

With small children, two days on, one day off is helpful. We did three park days in a row, with travel days on either end, and our third day was a waste for the 5-year-old—she was tired and sick of walking, and she and I ended up only doing a few rides while everyone else went off and had fun. If I'd thought through that, we would have made one of the travel days a park day and had a pool day in the middle.

Be prepared for someone (or everyone) to get tired and irritable. When it happens, mentally pause and trust your instincts: What would be the best decision for the long-term sustainability of the day and the vacation—another ride, an ice-cream break, or going back to the hotel room for a nap?

WHERE TO STAY If you're going to take midday breaks, you'll be making two trips per day to and from the theme parks, so you'll want to book lodging that's within a 20-minute drive. This doesn't necessarily mean you have to stay inside Disney World. Because the World is so spread out, some off-site hotels are very close to the parks (see our Hotel Information Table, pages 194–199, showing commuting times from Disney and non-Disney hotels).

If you want to stay in Walt Disney World, we recommend the **Crescent Lake, Skyliner,** and **monorail** resorts—in that order. Crescent Lake resorts provide walking access to EPCOT (great for parents looking for a high-quality bite or drinks later at night) and Skyliner or walking access to Hollywood Studios—no cars or buses to deal with for two parks. Other Skyliner resorts may not be walkable to any parks, but they get you quick access to EPCOT and Hollywood Studios—that's a win. Bonus: There are Moderate (**Caribbean Beach**) and Value (**Pop Century** and **Art of Animation**) resorts with Skyliner access, so there should be budget-friendly options for everyone. Monorail-loop resorts have walking, boat, and/or monorail access to the Magic Kingdom, but the resort loop can get *very* bogged down during busy seasons (for example, a 90-minute wait during the week before Christmas), and you have to transfer to get a monorail to EPCOT. These still avoid cars and buses for two parks, but the transportation is much less convenient. And prices are much higher.

BUILDING ENDURANCE Although most kids are active, their normal play usually doesn't condition them for all of the walking required to tour a Disney park. Start family walks four to six weeks before your trip to get in shape. A mother from Pennsylvania reports:

> *We had our 6-year-old begin walking with us a bit every day one month before leaving. When we arrived at Disney World, her little legs could carry her, and she had a lot of stamina.*

From a Delaware mom:

> *You recommended walking for six weeks prior to the trip, but we began months in advance, just because. My husband lost 10 pounds, my daughter never once complained, and we met a lot of neighbors!*

At the very least, run a little test—say, a trip to your local zoo or park—and walk a total of at least 6 miles together to establish your family's baseline level of fitness. Many find out the hard way that they're not as physically prepared as they think.

If your kids need incentives to "train" and build up that walking endurance, Becky recommends a set contribution to their souvenir budget for every mile walked in the weeks leading up to your trip. This doesn't have to be a large cost to the parents either—50 cents per mile does wonders as a motivator for her girls. Be prepared to average something closer to 10 miles during each park day. Fortunately for kids, 10 miles with incentives like a new ride or a favorite character is usually easier than 6 miles through your neighborhood or a local park.

SETTING LIMITS AND MAKING PLANS To avoid arguments and disappointments, set expectations for each day and get everybody on the same page. Communicate, communicate, communicate. It's amazing what a difference that just knowing the plan can make for a kid's attitude and reactions. Include the following:

1. Wake-up time and breakfast plans
2. When to leave for the park and what to take with you
3. A policy for splitting up the group or for staying together, and what to do if the group gets separated or someone is lost (see page 302)
4. What you want to see, including backup plans in case an attraction is closed or too crowded
5. A snack policy: Are you bringing your own? Do the kids have a budget or set number they can expect throughout the day?
6. How long you plan to tour and what time you'll return to your hotel to rest (if applicable)
7. When you'll return to the park and how late you'll stay
8. Meal plans
9. A policy for buying souvenirs, including who pays (kids or parents)
10. Bedtimes

BE FLEXIBLE Any day at Disney World includes surprises, so be prepared to adjust your plan. Trust your own judgement.

MAINTAINING SOME SEMBLANCE OF ORDER

DISCIPLINE AND ORDER are more difficult to maintain when traveling because everyone is in a new place, dealing with new situations, and out of their normal routine. For kids, it's hard to contain the excitement and anticipation that bubble to the surface in the form of hyperactivity (especially nerve-wracking for parents in large crowds where little limbs are flying), nervous energy, and (sometimes) acting out. Being confined in a car, plane, or hotel room only adds to the stress. Crowds, overstimulation, heat, and miles of walking, combined with inadequate rest, can lead to meltdowns even for kids who are normally very well behaved. This all happens to nearly every family that visits Disney World.

Remember that line about kids reading their parents' emotions well? That applies here too. It's amazing how easily they can pick up on the importance of this "big" trip and how they want it to go well—for themselves and for you. An incident that would result in only a pouty lip at home might escalate to sobbing or screaming at Disney World. Before your trip, it's important to discuss the ground rules with your children and to explore their needs and expectations as well.

No one wants to discipline their kids at the most magical place on earth, but the most important thing you can do is to remain consistent. Behaviors that aren't allowed at home need to stay on the no-no list on vacation. If kids get a warning before a consequence at home, they should get one at Disney too.

I (Becky) regularly have to remind myself that I'm the adult, and I'm the one expected to handle problems calmly, even when I'm tired. My kids are still kids. They are going to make mistakes, and then they're going to make mistakes when reacting to and handling their mistakes. It's my job to offer an example—and not be the parent yelling and creating a scene in the parks because I lost my temper.

Active Listening and Communication

Whining, tantrums, defiance, and holding up the group aren't just things your kids do to drive you nuts; they're also methods your kids use to communicate with you. A fit may *seem* to be about the ice cream you refused to buy because you ate lunch 30 minutes ago, but there's almost always something deeper just beneath the surface. Frequently, the root cause is simply a need for attention. Put the phone down (even if you have a ride reservation to make), get physically to their level, and listen. Make memories together. Spend time connecting.

Dealing with Negative Behaviors

Handling discipline during any stressful situation requires thought and preparation, so keep the following in mind when your world blows up as you try to rope-drop Slinky Dog Dash and you worry your whole day is going to be ruined:

unofficial **TIP**
Teaching your kids to tell you clearly what they want or need will help make the trip more enjoyable for everyone.

1. BE THE ADULT. Most kids are experts at knowing how to push their parents' buttons. If you take the bait and respond with a tantrum of your own, you're no longer the adult in the room; worse, you suggest by your example that ranting and raving is acceptable behavior. No matter what happens, take a deep breath and remind yourself, "I'm the adult here." Unironically, I find that watching episodes of *Bluey* on repeat helps me to ask myself, "What would Chilli do?" in the middle of stressful situations.

2. FREEZE THE ACTION. Instead of responding to your kids' behavior at a comparable maturity level, what you need to do is freeze the action. This usually means initiating a cool-down period where no one can talk about the problem for a short while. Find a place, preferably one that's private, to sit your child down, and take some deep breaths until you've both cooled off. If necessary, this can even happen in line for a ride. Just keep shuffling along and do a mini pause in the midst of the chaos.

3. TAKE A SHORT BREAK FROM THE GROUP. Let the rest of the family go eat or explore without you, and arrange to meet up later. In addition to letting the others get on with their day, this relieves the child of the pressure of being the focus of attention—and the object of the rest of the family's frustration. This step comes with an important caveat. If feeling like they're missing out on an exciting adventure makes things even more heated, then calmly give them the option of continuing with the group *if they're willing to talk calmly* about what is happening. Otherwise, the natural consequence is missing out for a bit.

4. REVIEW THE SITUATION AND TAKE ACTION. If you've made your expectations clear, stated the consequences of not meeting those expectations, and issued a warning, then review the situation with the child and follow through with the discipline warranted.

KIDS' FAVORITE MAGIC KINGDOM ATTRACTIONS *(2023–present)*		
RANK	PRESCHOOL	GRADE SCHOOL
1	Meet Mickey at Town Square Theater	Big Thunder Mountain Railroad
2	Bibbidi Bobbidi Boutique	Bibbidi Bobbidi Boutique
3	Dumbo the Flying Elephant	Evening fireworks
4	Christmas parade	Seven Dwarfs Mine Train
5	Meet Princess Tiana at Fairytale Hall	Meet Mickey at Town Square Theater
6	Pete's Silly Sideshow character greetings	Halloween parade
7	Prince Charming Regal Carrousel	Tron Lightcycle/Run
8	Adventure Friends Cavalcade	*Mickey's PhilharMagic*
9	Meet Ariel at Her Grotto	Meet Cinderella at Fairytale Hall
10	Festival of Fantasy Parade	Meet Princess Tiana at Fairytale Hall

5. BREAK THE CYCLE. Tantrums, of course, aren't always one-off events—kids often learn through experience that acting out will get them what they want. By scolding, admonishing, threatening, or negotiating, you actually continue the cycle and likely prolong the behavior, especially on vacation when your kid knows you want to avoid embarrassment and move on as quickly as possible.

To break the cycle, you must learn to speak calmly and not react with your own escalating voice. If you don't think you're capable of maintaining that calm manner, or it's not working, then you need to take a break and disengage. A private place is ideal for a break, but it's not absolutely necessary. You can carve out space almost anywhere: on a bench, in your car, in a restroom, or even on a sidewalk.

WHAT KIDS LIKE BEST IN WALT DISNEY WORLD

WHEN IT COMES TO DISNEY WORLD, what kids want is often different from what parents want: Kids consistently name their hotel's pool as one of their favorite activities, for example. Likewise, children prefer vastly different attractions than adults in Disney's theme parks.

While looking at our reader-survey responses for this, however, we noticed something else: Kids prefer almost any character greeting, parade, or fireworks show to any ride in Walt Disney World.

The table above lists the 10 most popular attractions in the Magic Kingdom for preschool and grade-school kids from 2023 to the present. The only two rides that appeared in the top 10 for preschoolers are **Dumbo the Flying Elephant** and **Prince Charming Regal Carrousel.** In fact, 15 of the top 20 attractions were parades, fireworks, or character greetings (the third, fourth, and fifth rides were **Under the Sea: Journey of the Little Mermaid, The Magic Carpets of Aladdin,** and **Mad Tea Party**).

Grade-school kids enjoy Disney's thrill rides more, but 5 of their 10 favorite attractions were also parades, fireworks, and character greetings. While the touring plans in this edition include character greetings and parades, keep these survey results in mind if you don't expect to use a touring plan. Each theme park chapter contains an updated list of age-group favorites too. (For more on the Disney characters, see page 310.)

ABOUT THE *UNOFFICIAL GUIDE* TOURING PLANS

CHILDREN HAVE A SPECIAL SKILL for wreaking havoc on a schedule. If you're following a touring plan or other strategy, here's what to expect regarding some common sources of interruptions:

1. CHARACTER GREETINGS CAN SLOW DOWN YOUR PLANS. Lines at character greetings can be as long as those for major attractions. And because none of them offer LLMP, you can't just pay to skip the line. Be very thoughtful about when and how you work character greetings into your day.

2. OUR TOURING PLANS CALL FOR VISITING ATTRACTIONS IN A CERTAIN ORDER, OFTEN SKIPPING ATTRACTIONS ALONG THE WAY. Typically, kids don't like to skip *anything* they want to do if they're walking by and it catches their eye. Some can be persuaded to skip attractions if you explain your plans in advance, but the siren call of a cool-looking ride may be too much for your kids. Plan in advance for how you think your child will react. Becky regularly detours her family onto a longer walking path to avoid an attraction she absolutely does not want to participate in—looking at you, Tomorrowland Speedway.

3. IF YOU'RE USING A STROLLER, YOU WON'T BE ABLE TO TAKE IT INTO ATTRACTIONS OR ONTO RIDES. It takes time to park and retrieve a stroller outside each attraction. Also, cast members will often move and rearrange strollers to make space, which adds to the time it takes to find yours later. Make sure to have a very visible name tag or some other way to pick out your stroller in the sea of similar-looking child-conveyance devices.

Magic Kingdom visitors can use the **Walt Disney World Railroad** to save on walking. The railroad, however, permits only folded strollers on board. If you're renting a Disney stroller, allow time to remove your stuff from it before boarding and allow time at your destination to get another stroller. Read more stroller advice on page 299.

OTHER CONSIDERATIONS FOR KIDS

OVERHEATING, SUNBURN, AND DEHYDRATION are the most common problems that younger children have at Walt Disney World. Carry and use sunscreen. Apply it on children in strollers, even if the stroller has a canopy. To avoid overheating, stop for rest regularly—find a spot in the shade or take advantage of the air-conditioning at a restaurant or show. Carry bottles of water—we recommend bringing your own from home to save money. Refill them with cups of ice water from any counter-service dining location.

BLISTERS AND SORE FEET are the next most common problem at Walt Disney World. In addition to wearing comfortable, broken-in shoes, bring along blister bandages if you or your children are susceptible to blisters. These bandages (also available at First Aid in more shapes than you can imagine) offer excellent protection, stick well, and won't sweat off. Remember that a preschooler may not say anything about a blister until it has already formed, so keep an eye on things during the day. See page 359 for more on blister prevention. As soon as one of my kids mentions something about a foot or toe hurting, we *immediately* stop to check out and address the situation. Even if it halts a very quick walk to Rise of the Resistance at the beginning of the day. Don't mess with foot issues.

GLASSES AND SUNGLASSES If your kids (or you) wear them, attach a strap or cord to the frames so the glasses will stay on during rides. Check Lost and Found (see page 358) if they go missing.

THINGS YOU FORGOT OR RAN OUT OF The theme parks and Disney Springs sell raingear, diapers, baby formula, sunburn treatments, and almost anything else you could have forgotten. The water parks sell towels and disposable waterproof cameras. If you don't see something you need, ask if it's in stock. Also keep in mind that Walmart, Target, and other retailers are often only a 10-minute drive or rideshare away, and Amazon, Instacart, and other services will deliver directly to your resort.

RUNNING OUT OF STEAM Battling heat, humidity, and crowds at Walt Disney World quickly contributes to exhaustion, especially with kids in the mix. Limiting calorie consumption to mealtimes just won't cut it. This is like a marathon where you need an almost constant intake of fluids, electrolytes, and calories. Becky's kids don't normally get sports drinks at home—she saves them for things like recovering from immunizations and calls them "medicine drinks." But most dining locations at Disney offer Powerade, so that bright-blue beverage full of electrolytes is a delightful treat that they gulp down happily, fueling their day. Keep close tabs on everyone's "hangry" levels and provide snacks accordingly.

WILD THINGS Alligators can be found in almost all bodies of fresh water in Florida, including those at Disney World, such as Seven Seas Lagoon and Bay Lake. Though attacks are very rare, adults and especially kids may become targets while swimming, wading, or sitting near the water's edge. Alligators are most active in the late afternoon and evening. If you happen to see one, put as much space between you and it as possible and keep kids close by. (In case you're wondering, alligators can run 11 mph but only for a short distance.)

BABY CARE AND FIRST AID

IN EACH OF THE MAJOR THEME PARKS, **First Aid** and the **Baby Care Center** are located next to each other. In the **Magic Kingdom,** they're at the end of Main Street on the left, by Casey's Corner and The Crystal Palace. In **EPCOT,** they're on the World Showcase side of Odyssey Center. In **Animal Kingdom,** they're in Discovery Island, on the left just before you cross the bridge to Africa, near Creature Comforts. In **Hollywood Studios,** they're at Guest Relations inside the main entrance.

Everything necessary for changing diapers, preparing formula, and warming bottles and food is available at the Baby Care Centers. A small shop at each center sells diapers, wipes, baby food, and other things you may need. Rockers and special chairs for nursing mothers are provided. Dads are welcome, too, and can use most services; in addition, many of the men's restrooms in the major parks have changing stations.

If your baby is on formula, this Wisconsin mom has a handy tip:

We got hot water from food vendors and mixed the formula as needed. It eliminated having to keep bottles cold and then warm them up.

Infants and toddlers are allowed at any attraction that doesn't have minimum height or age restrictions. Prioritize attractions like boat rides, theater shows, and walk-throughs if you don't want to deal with wrangling yourself and the baby into and out of ride vehicles.

NURSING Let us state unequivocally that nursing mothers are free to feed their babies whenever and wherever in Walt Disney World they choose. If you are comfortable feeding your baby in line, on Main Street while waiting for a parade, or in a souvenir shop, no one around you gets to judge. They can leave if they're uncomfortable. And plenty of moms have done it before you.

FIRST AID If your child or you need minor medical attention, go to a **First Aid** center. Staffed by registered nurses, the centers treat everything from paper cuts to allergic reactions in addition to sunburns and blisters. Basic over-the-counter meds are often available free in small quantities too.

STROLLERS

THE NEED FOR STROLLERS at Walt Disney World is a hot topic among families with kids. Some parents, in fact, don't realize just how important strollers are until they take their first trip to the World.

Walt Disney World Stroller Policy

The size limit for strollers in the theme parks is **31 inches wide by 52 inches long.** Stroller wagons, both pull and push models, are prohibited. Don't try to skirt the rules.

Strollers for Older Kids

It's not just the parents of babies and toddlers who rent strollers in the parks: Many parents tell us that they use them with kids who are well past needing them at home. If that seems odd, consider that a typical day in the parks requires at least a few miles of walking, which most kids don't do regularly (see "Building Endurance," page 293). But you have to consider the trade-offs. Kids in strollers may be more exhausting for parents as you push them around the park and do extra walking to park and pick up the stroller. But kids without strollers and lacking physical endurance can be an emotional drain on parents or an even bigger physical drain when they demand to be carried to the next attraction. Everyone has different opinions, and you need to decide what works best for your family.

We recommend the following method:

UNDER AGE 4 We would argue that anyone under the age of 4 needs a stroller (or parents blessed with an abundance of stamina and a baby sling or hip carrier). The littlest legs just can't do the miles of walking required in a Disney park day.

AGES 4–6 This is the transitional phase when you need to figure out what will work best for your kids. At these ages, we would start just bringing an umbrella stroller and taking it with us on a particularly busy day or leaving it in the room if we thought we could take it easy and not need it for a day.

AGE 6 AND UP At this point, the calculation was easy for us as parents. Once we stopped needing the umbrella stroller, we began traveling without a stroller altogether. Our youngest actually went without a stroller as young as age 4, but that was with weeks of "Disney walks" at home in preparation.

Stroller Options

You have three options for using a stroller in Walt Disney World: renting from Disney, bringing or buying your own, or renting from a third party. Let's discuss the pros and cons of each option.

RENTING A STROLLER You can rent a Disney stroller at all four WDW theme parks and at Disney Springs, and improved stroller models were introduced in 2021. To see what these strollers look like, Google "rental strollers at Walt Disney World." A single stroller rents for $15 per day with no deposit or $13 per day for a multiday rental; double strollers cost $31 per day with no deposit or $27 per day for a multiday rental. Note that stroller rentals at Disney Springs require a $100 credit card deposit. Strollers are welcome at Blizzard Beach and Typhoon Lagoon, but no rentals are available.

With multiday rentals, you can skip the rental line completely after your first visit—simply head over to the stroller pickup area, present your receipt, and you'll be wheeling out of there in no time. If you rent a stroller in the Magic Kingdom and decide to go to EPCOT, Animal Kingdom, or Hollywood Studios, just turn in your Magic Kingdom stroller and present your receipt at the next park. You'll be issued another stroller at no additional charge.

Note that you can rent a stroller in advance; this allows you to bypass the payment line and go straight to the pickup line. Disney resort guests can pay ahead at the resort's gift shop; keep your receipt.

Pick up strollers at the **Magic Kingdom** entrance; at **EPCOT**'s main and International Gateway entrances; and at **Oscar's Super Service,** just inside the entrance of **Disney's Hollywood Studios.** In **Animal Kingdom,** they're at **Garden Gate Gifts,** to the right just inside the entrance. Returning a stroller is a breeze—you can ditch it anywhere in the park when you get ready to leave.

Disney's strollers are too large and uncomfortable for infants and potentially small toddlers. If you want to rent one, bring blankets or towels for padding. On the plus side, because the strollers are large, they also provide a convenient place to stow water and snacks.

BRINGING OR BUYING A STROLLER Only collapsible strollers are permitted on monorails, the Walt Disney World Railroad, parking trams, and buses. Many Disney gift shops and stores like Walmart and Target sell umbrella strollers that you can use for the duration of the trip—potentially saving you money compared to renting every day.

THIRD-PARTY RENTAL Because Disney's stroller rentals are generally expensive and uncomfortable (especially in the heat), a few Orlando rental companies have sprung up that undercut Disney's prices, provide more comfortable strollers, and deliver them to your hotel or offer pickup and drop-off at the Orlando airport. Most of the larger companies offer the same stroller models (the Baby Jogger City Mini Single, for example), so the primary differences between the companies are price and service.

Regarding service, Disney no longer allows stroller companies to drop off and pick up at a Disney hotel without the guest being physically present. Guests must meet the delivery driver for all stroller and scooter rentals.

Kingdom Strollers (☎ 407-271-5301; kingdomstrollers.com) is well liked for its easy-to-use website, along with its stroller selection and condition and its overall customer service. The strollers it offers are much easier to use than Disney's plastic model, have more storage, and have an easier-to-use braking system. A rental of one to three nights costs $60; four to seven nights is $80. That's a five-day break-even point for choosing Kingdom Strollers over Disney's strollers.

Orlando Stroller Rentals (☎ 800-281-0884; orlandostrollerrentals.com), offers similar prices ($60 for one to three nights and $80 for four to seven nights) and an excellent website that allows you to easily compare the features of the different strollers.

Scooterbug Rentals (☎ 800-726-8284; scooterbug.com/orlando) is the only rental company that officially partners with Walt Disney World to allow for drop-off and pickup of strollers from the bell services desk at your resort. All other companies have to meet you in the lobby or in a parking lot for you to receive and return your stroller. So if you're looking for flexibility, along with better stroller selection than Disney has, this is your best bet. A City Mini will cost $64 for up to three nights, and five nights costs $80. Unlike other services, they offer an even cheaper option: a Britax Pathway Single that is just $38 for up to three nights.

STROLLER WARS Sometimes your stroller will seem to disappear while you're enjoying a ride or watching a show. Cast members frequently rearrange strollers to tidy up, clear a walkway, or make space for more parking. Don't assume that your stroller has been stolen because it isn't where you left it. It may be a few feet away—or perhaps more than a few feet away.

Sometimes, however, strollers are taken by mistake or ripped off by people too lazy to rent their own. Don't be alarmed if your Disney rental disappears: You won't have to buy it, and you'll be issued a new one at no charge.

unofficial **TIP**
Do not try to lock your stroller to a fence, post, or anything else.

In either case, it's a good idea to have some sort of very visible identifier on your stroller so you can pick it out in a sea of strollers from far away. I (Becky) have two strategies. The first is something bright (I sewed a personalized fabric name sign for theirs) so it's easy to spot during the day. The second is a strand of battery-powered "fairy lights" for a stroller that really stands out at night.

LOST CHILDREN

ALTHOUGH IT'S EASY to lose a child in the theme parks, it usually isn't a serious problem: Cast members are trained in handling the situation. If a cast member encounters a lost child, they will take the child immediately to the park's **Baby Care Center** (see page 298 for locations in each theme park). If you lose a child, let a cast member know, and then check at the Baby Care Center and at **Guest Relations,** where lost-children logs are kept. Paging isn't used except in an emergency, but a bulletin can be issued throughout the park(s) via internal communications.

unofficial **TIP**
Children under age 14 must be accompanied by someone age 14 or older when entering Disney World's theme parks and water parks.

One great way to try to avoid separation is to come up with a family "call." This shouldn't be "Mom" or "Dad." It should be some sort of unique noise or random word that can be yelled at the top of the kid's lungs in the middle of a crowded store, restaurant, or attraction where separations might occur. Your lost kid yelling "Mom" won't stand out in the cacophony of the crowd. But as a parent, if you start yelling "AVOCADO" as loud as you can in the middle of a store, chances are everyone around you will get quiet and your kid will be able to follow your voice. Momentary embarrassment is infinitely better than the stress of losing a kid.

You could sew a label onto each child's shirt with their name, your name, your hotel, and your phone number. You can also purchase custom iron-on labels or write the information on a strip of masking tape so your kid doesn't have to try to remember all that information.

An easier and trendier option is a **temporary tattoo** with the child's name and your phone number. Unlike labels, ID bracelets, or wristbands, the tattoos can't fall off or get lost. You can purchase customized tattoos online from **SafetyTat** (safetytat.com). Tattoos are available for children with nut allergies, asthma, diabetes, autism, or other medical conditions. Or you can purchase a **temporary tattoo marker,** such as **Bic BodyMark,** available from Amazon and at retailers such as CVS, Walmart, and Target. Cast members recommend the temporary tattoo method and are trained to look for phone numbers.

Another way to keep track of your family is to buy each person a Disney "uniform," such as matching brightly and distinctively colored T-shirts. An Arizona family tried this with great success:

We all got the same shirts (bright red) so that we could easily spot each other in case of separation (VERY easy to do). It was a lifesaver when our 18-month-old decided to get out of the stroller and wander off. No matter what precautions you may try, it seems there are always opportunities to lose a child, but the recognizable shirts helped tremendously.

HOW KIDS GET LOST

CHILDREN GET SEPARATED from their parents every day at Disney World under several predictable circumstances:

1. PREOCCUPIED SOLO PARENT The party's only adult is preoccupied with something like buying refreshments, booking a ride reservation, or using the restroom. It's remarkably easy for a child to disappear into a crowd in just a second or two.

2. THE HIDDEN EXIT Sometimes parents wait on the sidelines while two or more children experience a ride together. Parents expect the kids to exit in one place, but they pop out elsewhere. Exits from some attractions are distant from entrances. Know exactly where your children will emerge before you send them to ride (or play) by themselves.

3. AFTER THE SHOW At the end of many shows and rides, a cast member announces, "Check for personal belongings and take small children by the hand." This is because when dozens, if not hundreds, of people leave an attraction simultaneously, it's easy for parents to lose their children in the shuffle unless they have direct contact. If you are attending a show where children are seated separately (like **Turtle Talk with Crush**) give your kids instructions to either wait in place for you or just stay still until most of the crowds have already left.

4. RESTROOMS WITH MULTIPLE EXITS If you can't find a companion- or family-accessible restroom, make sure there's only one exit. One restroom in the Magic Kingdom, on a passageway between Frontierland and Adventureland, is notorious for disorienting visitors. Children and adults alike have walked in from the Adventureland side and walked out into Frontierland (and vice versa). Adults realize quickly that something is wrong, but kids sometimes fail to recognize the problem. Designate an easy-to-remember meeting spot and provide clear instructions: "I'll meet you by this flagpole. If you get out first, stay right here." Have your child repeat the directions back to you.

5. PARADES There are many parades and shows at which the audience stands. Children tend to jockey for a better view. By moving a little this way and that, the child quickly puts distance between you and them before either of you notices.

6. MASS MOVEMENTS Be on guard when huge crowds disperse after a fireworks presentation or parade, or at park closing. With thousands of people in an area at once, it's easy to get separated from a child or others in your party. Use extra caution after the evening fireworks or any other day-ending event. Make a plan for where to meet in case you get separated.

7. ANIMAL KINGDOM EXPLORATION It's especially easy to lose a child in this theme park, particularly in **The Oasis,** on the **Maharajah Jungle Trek,** and on the **Gorilla Falls Exploration Trail:** Mom and Dad will stop to observe an animal; Junior stays close for a minute or so, and then, losing patience, wanders to the exhibit's other side or to a different exhibit. In the multipath Oasis, locating a lost child can be maddening, as a Florida mother describes:

> *Manny wandered off in the paths that lead to the jungle village while we were looking at a bird. It reminded me of losing somebody in the supermarket, when you run back and forth looking down each aisle but can't find the person you're looking for because they're running around too. I was nutso before we even got to the first ride.*

KIDS *and* SCARY STUFF

DISNEY RIDES AND SHOWS are adventures with universal themes: good and evil, life and death, beauty and ugliness, heroes and villains. As you make your way through the attractions at Walt Disney World, you'll experience not just the spinning and bouncing of midway rides but also emotionally powerful entertainment that is sometimes too much for the littlest members of your family.

unofficial **TIP**
Every kid has different fright triggers. Research the attractions before you visit so that you'll know which ones you need to skip and which ones will likely be fine.

The endings are happy ones, but given Disney's gift for special effects, these adventures often intimidate and occasionally scare young children. There are attractions with menacing witches, burning towns, skeletons, and ghouls popping out of their graves—most done with humor, provided you're old enough to understand the joke.

Most children take Disney's more intense moments in stride, and others are easily comforted by an arm around the shoulder or a squeeze of the hand. Parents who know that their children tend to become upset should take it slow and easy, starting with fun adventures like the **Jungle Cruise,** gauging reactions, and discussing with the kids how they feel about what they've seen. Figure out what your child will and will not enjoy and try to identify coping mechanisms that could help them handle and enjoy more attractions. For example, Becky's younger kid can ride just about anything as long as she covers her own ears so she's not surprised by loud noises. But they also mix in a bunch of her more "soothing" favorites like **It's a Small World** and **Living with the Land** so she gets some relaxation.

Sometimes kids will try to rise above their anxiety in an effort to please their parents or siblings. This doesn't mean they weren't afraid or even that they enjoyed the attraction. If your child leaves a ride in apparently good shape, ask if they'd like to go on it again—not necessarily now, but sometime. Their response should tell you all you need to know. That same little kid, after riding **Guardians of the Galaxy: Cosmic Rewind** for the first (and only time) was asked if she enjoyed the ride. Her response: "I'm proud of myself for trying, but I don't want to do it again." A fair reaction.

Evaluating children's capacity to handle the visual and tactile effects of Walt Disney World requires patience and understanding. If your child balks at or is frightened by a ride, respond compassionately: Make clear that it's all right to be scared and that you won't think any less of your child for not wanting to ride.

What you definitely *don't* want to do is add to a child's fear and distress by coercing, belittling, or guilt-tripping. And don't let older siblings apply that pressure either.

THE FRIGHT FACTOR

WHILE EACH KID IS DIFFERENT, the following attraction elements, alone or combined, could push their buttons and indicate that a certain attraction isn't age appropriate for them:

SMALL-CHILD FRIGHT-POTENTIAL TABLE

THIS QUICK REFERENCE identifies attractions to be wary of if you have kids under age 7. Younger children are more likely to be frightened than older ones. Attractions not listed aren't typically frightening.

THE MAGIC KINGDOM

ADVENTURELAND

- **JUNGLE CRUISE** Moderately intense; some dark areas. This is a good test attraction to see how your kids handle the fright factor.
- **PIRATES OF THE CARIBBEAN** Slightly intimidating queuing area; intense boat ride with some scary (though humorously presented) sights and a short, unexpected drop.
- **SWISS FAMILY TREEHOUSE** Anyone who's afraid of heights may want to skip it.
- **WALT DISNEY'S ENCHANTED TIKI ROOM** A thunderstorm, the loud volume level, and simulated explosions frighten some preschoolers.

FRONTIERLAND

- **BIG THUNDER MOUNTAIN RAILROAD*** This is a moderate roller coaster, but it does have tight turns and some "threat" of explosion.
- **TIANA'S BAYOU ADVENTURE*** Visually intimidating from the outside, the ride ends in a 52-foot plunge down a steep chute.

LIBERTY SQUARE

- **THE HAUNTED MANSION** Intense attraction with humorously presented ghostly sights. The name, as well as the sounds and sights, can be scary, but the ride itself is gentle.

FANTASYLAND

- **THE MANY ADVENTURES OF WINNIE THE POOH** Heffalumps and Woozles frighten a few preschoolers.
- **SEVEN DWARFS MINE TRAIN*** May frighten some preschoolers—especially catching sight of the villain.
- **UNDER THE SEA: JOURNEY OF THE LITTLE MERMAID** Animatronic Ursula frightens some preschoolers.

TOMORROWLAND

- **ASTRO ORBITER** Could scare anyone afraid of heights.
- **BUZZ LIGHTYEAR'S SPACE RANGER SPIN** Villain and (bright, goofy) aliens may frighten some preschoolers.
- **MONSTERS, INC. LAUGH FLOOR** May frighten some preschoolers.
- **SPACE MOUNTAIN*** Very intense roller coaster in the dark; one of the Magic Kingdom's wildest rides and a scary coaster by any standard.
- **TRON LIGHTCYCLE/RUN*** Intense indoor/outdoor coaster.

EPCOT

FUTURE WORLD

- **GUARDIANS OF THE GALAXY: COSMIC REWIND*** Intense spinning coaster in the dark.
- **JOURNEY INTO IMAGINATION WITH FIGMENT** Loud noises and unexpected flashing lights startle younger children.
- **MISSION: SPACE*** Extremely intense space-simulation ride that has been known to cause some anxiety for guests of all ages.
- **THE SEAS WITH NEMO & FRIENDS** Sharks and fish-chasing scenes may scare preschoolers not familiar with the movie's storyline.
- **TEST TRACK*** Intense thrill ride that may frighten guests of any age.

* Rider Switch option provided *(see page 307)*

continued on next page

SMALL-CHILD FRIGHT-POTENTIAL TABLE (continued)

EPCOT (continued)

WORLD SHOWCASE
- **FROZEN EVER AFTER*** Small drop at the end could scare little ones.
- **REMY'S RATATOUILLE ADVENTURE** Chase scenes may frighten some preschoolers.

DISNEY'S ANIMAL KINGDOM

ASIA
- **EXPEDITION EVEREST*** The ride, especially the yeti, can frighten guests of all ages.
- **KALI RIVER RAPIDS*** Potentially frightening and certainly wet for guests of all ages.
- **MAHARAJAH JUNGLE TREK** Some children may balk at the bat exhibit.

PANDORA—THE WORLD OF AVATAR
- **AVATAR FLIGHT OF PASSAGE*** May frighten kids age 7 and younger, those with claustrophobia or a fear of heights, or those who are prone to motion sickness.
- **NA'VI RIVER JOURNEY*** Dark boat ride with imposing animatronic figures that frightens some preschoolers.

DISNEY'S HOLLYWOOD STUDIOS

SUNSET BOULEVARD
- *FANTASMIC!* Terrifies some preschoolers thanks to featured villains.
- **ROCK 'N' ROLLER COASTER*** The wildest coaster at Hollywood Studios. May frighten guests of any age.
- **THE TWILIGHT ZONE TOWER OF TERROR*** Visually intimidating to young kids; contains intense and realistic special effects. The plummeting elevator at the end frightens many adults as well as kids.

ECHO LAKE
- **STAR TOURS—THE ADVENTURES CONTINUE*** Less intense than Rise of the Resistance, but depending on scenes during the ride, may be scary for younger kids.

HOLLYWOOD BOULEVARD
- **MICKEY & MINNIE'S RUNAWAY RAILWAY** Track ride with wild twists and turns but an otherwise safe storyline. May scare kids age 6 and under.

TOY STORY LAND
- **SLINKY DOG DASH*** Mild first roller coaster for most kids. May frighten preschoolers.

STAR WARS: GALAXY'S EDGE
- *MILLENNIUM FALCON:* **SMUGGLERS RUN*** Intense visual effects and movement.
- **STAR WARS: RISE OF THE RESISTANCE** Intense visual effects and movement.

* Rider Switch option provided *(see page 307)*

THE NAME It's only natural that younger children will be apprehensive about something called, say, **The Haunted Mansion** or **The Twilight Zone Tower of Terror.** If you think your kid will enjoy the attraction but bristle at the name, feel free to call it something else.

THE VISUAL IMPACT OF THE RIDE FROM OUTSIDE Big Thunder Mountain Railroad, Tiana's Bayou Adventure, and the **Tower of Terror** look frightening enough to give adults second thoughts, and they scare away many little kids. A Utah grandma reports the following:

> *At 5 years old, my granddaughter was willing to go on almost everything. The problem was with the preliminary introductions to The Haunted Mansion and the Tower of Terror. Walking through and learning the stories before the actual rides were what frightened*

her and made her opt out without going in. The rides themselves wouldn't have been bad—she loved Splash Mountain [now Tiana's Bayou Adventure] and Big Thunder Mountain Railroad, but she could SEE those before entering.

THE VISUAL IMPACT OF THE INDOOR-QUEUING AREA The caves at **Pirates of the Caribbean** and the dungeons and "stretch rooms" of **The Haunted Mansion** can frighten kids.

THE INTENSITY Some attractions overwhelm with sights, sounds, movements, and even smells. **Journey into Imagination with Figment** is a cute exploration of the senses . . . until you get to the smell room. At that point, any scent-sensitive kids are turned off for good.

THE VISUAL IMPACT OF THE ATTRACTION Sights in various attractions range from falling boulders to waltzing ghosts. What one child calmly watches may scare the pants off another who's the same age.

THE DARKNESS Many attractions operate indoors in the dark, which can be scary. A child who gets frightened on one dark ride (such as **The Haunted Mansion**) may be unwilling to try others.

THE PHYSICAL EXPERIENCE Some rides are wild enough to cause motion sickness, wrench backs, and discombobulate guests of any age. **Space Mountain,** we're looking at you.

HEIGHT REQUIREMENTS

A NUMBER OF ATTRACTIONS require children to meet minimum height or age requirements (see table on page 308 for a list of height requirements). All rides, regardless of height requirements, state that children under age 7 must have someone age 14 or older ride with them. That means kids under age 7 can't use the single-rider line. If you have children who don't meet the posted requirements, you have several options, including Rider Switch (see below). If your group is headed to an attraction where some family members will not meet the height requirement, consider doing something nearby instead of just waiting at the exit. Take a look at the posted wait time and plan to busy yourself for that amount of time.

WAITING-*in*-LINE STRATEGIES *for* YOUNG CHILDREN

KIDS STAY HAPPIER THROUGH THE DAY if you limit the time they spend *bored* in lines. Arriving early and using a touring plan are two ways to greatly reduce waiting. Here are other ways to reduce stress or boredom in lines for kids:

1. RIDER SWITCH (AKA SWITCHING OFF OR BABY/CHILD SWAP) Some of Disney's best rides have height and/or age requirements. Couples with children too small or too young might either skip these attractions or take turns riding. Neither option is ideal: One is an unnecessary sacrifice, and the other is a tremendous waste of time. Disney's solution is a system called Rider Switch. There must be two or more adults in your party for this to work. Here's how to do it:

ATTRACTION HEIGHT RESTRICTIONS

THE MAGIC KINGDOM
The Barnstormer* 35" minimum

Big Thunder Mountain Railroad* 40" minimum

Seven Dwarfs Mine Train* 38" minimum

Space Mountain* 44" minimum

Tiana's Bayou Adventure* 40" minimum

Tomorrowland Speedway* 32" minimum to ride, 54" to drive unassisted

Tron Lightcycle/Run* 48" minimum

EPCOT
Guardians of the Galaxy: Cosmic Rewind* 42" minimum

Mission: Space* 40" minimum (Green); 44" minimum (Orange)

Soarin' Around the World* 40" minimum

Test Track* 40" minimum

DISNEY'S ANIMAL KINGDOM
Avatar Flight of Passage* 44" minimum

Expedition Everest* 44" minimum

Kali River Rapids* 38" minimum

DISNEY'S HOLLYWOOD STUDIOS
Alien Swirling Saucers* 32" minimum

Millennium Falcon:* Smugglers Run 38" minimum

Rock 'n' Roller Coaster* 48" minimum

Slinky Dog Dash* 38" minimum

Star Tours—The Adventures Continue* 40" minimum

Star Wars: Rise of the Resistance 40" minimum

The Twilight Zone Tower of Terror* 40" minimum

DISNEY SPRINGS
Marketplace Carousel 42" minimum

BLIZZARD BEACH WATER PARK
Downhill Double Dipper 48" minimum

Ski lift 32" minimum

Slush Gusher* 48" minimum

Summit Plummet 48" minimum

T-Bar zip line *(in Ski Patrol Training Camp)* 60" maximum

Tike's Peak children's area 48" maximum

TYPHOON LAGOON WATER PARK
Bay Slides 60" minimum

Crush 'n' Gusher 48" minimum

Humunga Kowabunga 48" minimum

Ketchakiddee Creek 48" maximum

Wave Pool *Adult supervision required*

* Rider Switch option provided *(see page 307)*

WAITING-IN-LINE STRATEGIES FOR YOUNG CHILDREN

ATTRACTIONS OFFERING RIDER SWITCH
MAGIC KINGDOM
• The Barnstormer • Big Thunder Mountain Railroad • Seven Dwarfs Mine Train • Space Mountain • Tiana's Bayou Adventure
EPCOT
• Frozen Ever After • Guardians of the Galaxy: Cosmic Rewind • Mission: Space • Soarin' Around the World • Test Track
DISNEY'S ANIMAL KINGDOM
• Avatar Flight of Passage • Expedition Everest • Kali River Rapids • Na'vi River Journey
DISNEY'S HOLLYWOOD STUDIOS
• Alien Swirling Saucers • *Millennium Falcon:* Smugglers Run • Rock 'n' Roller Coaster • Slinky Dog Dash • Star Tours—The Adventures Continue • The Twilight Zone Tower of Terror

1. When you approach the queue, tell the first cast member you see that you want to use Rider Switch.
2. The cast member will ask who is riding first and who is riding second—that is, the adults who will be supervising the nonriding child (up to three can ride second).
3. The first group will enter the queue.
4. The cast member will scan the MagicBands or tickets of the group riding second—along with any repeat riders—who then wait or do other attractions with the nonriding child.
5. When the first group returns, they take over watching the nonriding child while the second group goes to the Alternate Access line—usually the Lightning Lane.
6. The cast member will scan the second group's MagicBands or tickets again, after which the group enters the Alternate Access line.
7. Both groups reunite after the second group finishes the ride.

Rider Switch passes—digital entitlements scanned into your MagicBand or ticket—must be used on the day they're issued. Guests may hold only one Rider Switch pass at a time; one must be redeemed before another one can be issued.

Cast members administering Rider Switch are very accommodating and will typically let you self-select who is in the first and second group, within reason (don't plan on a 17-member party getting to ride Tron twice because the 18th person sits out with a nonriding child). But if you're a family of four and your older child wants to ride in the first *and* second groups, this will almost always be allowed.

2. LINE GAMES Anticipate that children will get restless in line, and plan activities to reduce the stress and boredom. In the morning, have waiting children discuss what they want to see and do during the day. Later, watch for and count Disney characters (or hidden Mickeys) or play simple games such as 20 Questions. Games requiring pen and paper are impractical in a fast-moving line, but you could pack a small notebook and a few crayons for places like theater shows or table-service meals.

3. PHONE FUN If games and coloring are likely to induce eye rolls, load some age-appropriate games on your phone. Many Disney games exist (even educational ones), and these can be a special vacation "treat" so that your kids don't expect to keep playing at home.

4. LAST-MINUTE COLD FEET If your young child gets cold feet while waiting to board a ride where Rider Switch isn't offered (this happens frequently in **Pirates of the Caribbean**'s dungeon waiting area), just alert an attendant and they will either 1) find a space for half of the party to wait while the other half rides, and then let you switch before you exit or 2) show you to the exit—whichever you prefer.

The DISNEY CHARACTERS

ONE OF MY (BECKY'S) CLEAREST MEMORIES is from my oldest daughter's first trip to Walt Disney World, when she was 18 months old and, like most children of that era, obsessed with *Frozen*. She had a set of small *Frozen* figurines at home and carried the little Kristoff (or, as she called him, "Bah-Boff") around *everywhere*. So of course we rode Frozen Ever After and then immediately lined up to spend time with Anna and Elsa.

That park day ended up being two days before Hurricane Irma swung through Orlando, so the parks were ghost towns and we didn't have to wait long. We got up to Anna, who started chattering away. Was my kid impressed or in awe that she was meeting one of the characters from her favorite movie? No. I looked at her face and saw pure skepticism. She fixed Anna in an intense glare only a 1-year-old can pull off and authoritatively asked, "Bah-Boff?" Once I translated that she was inquiring where Kristoff was, and Anna explained that he was off harvesting ice, big kid was done. We could move on. Bah-Boff wasn't here.

The automatically captured pictures of that meet and greet are some of my favorites to this day. One proudly hangs on our wall, partially because it was a memorable first character interaction but also because it was a great early insight into the opinionated personality that this kid has grown more into every year.

My memorable experience (and thousands of similar ones) is repeated every day throughout Walt Disney World by cast members determined to embody the Disney characters they're dressed as. We receive hundreds of reader comments telling us how much these cast members enhanced their theme park experience. This email from a Wisconsin mom is representative:

> *I can't say enough about the characters and how they react to the children and just people in general. They are highly trained in people skills and just add an extra dimension to the park.*

As we've mentioned, meeting the Disney characters is one of the highest-rated activities among all age groups who visit Walt Disney World. To those who love them, the characters in Disney's films and TV shows are as real as family or friends; never mind that they were drawn by an animator or generated by a computer.

By extension, the theme park personifications of the Disney characters are just as real: It's not a guy in a mouse costume but Mickey himself; she's not a cast member in a sequined fish tail but Ariel, Princess of Atlantica. Meeting a Disney character is an encounter with a real celebrity, a memory to be treasured.

MEETING THE CHARACTERS

DISNEY MAKES ITS MOST POPULAR CHARACTERS available in dedicated meet-and-greet venues in each theme park (see the table on pages 312 for the locations of specific characters) and at Disney Deluxe resorts that host character meals (see "Character Meals," page 313). Gone are the days of characters spontaneously wandering in parks. If you see one walking through the park, they are likely walking with a purpose and aren't stopping for interactions.

Some characters who don't have dedicated spaces appear only in parades or stage shows, and still others appear only in a location consistent with their starring role. Anastasia and Drizella, for example, are sometimes found near Cinderella Castle in Fantasyland, while Stitch regularly pops up in Tomorrowland. Characters may visit the Disney resorts and water parks and occasionally appear at Disney Springs.

A New York dad was surprised at how much time his family was willing to spend meeting characters:

The characters are now available practically all day long at different locations, according to a fixed schedule, which our son was old enough to read. We spent more time standing in line for autographs than we did for the most popular rides!

PREPARING YOUR CHILDREN TO MEET CHARACTERS There are two kinds of Disney characters: **fur characters,** whose costumes include face-covering headpieces (including animal characters and humanlike characters such as Captain Hook), and **face characters,** who wear no mask or headpiece, such as the Disney princesses and princes, Mary Poppins, and the like.

Only face characters speak. Because cast members can't easily speak in those face-covering headpieces, it's better for them to be silent. Nonetheless, fur characters are warm and responsive, and they communicate effectively with gestures. Most of the fur characters are quite large; a few, like Sully from *Monsters, Inc.,* are huge. Small children usually don't expect this, and preschoolers especially can be intimidated by them.

On first encounter, rather than thrusting your child at the character, allow the little one to deal with this big thing from whatever distance feels safe. If two adults are present, one should stay near the youngster while the other approaches the character and demonstrates that it's safe and friendly.

Be aware that some character costumes make it hard for the cast member inside to see well. (Eyeholes may be placed in the mouth of the costume or even on the neck or chest.) Children who approach the character from the back or side might not be noticed, even if the child touches the character. Kids should approach a character from the front, but occasionally not even this works—Donald and Daisy, for example, have to peer around their bills. If a character appears to be ignoring your child, the character's handler will get its attention.

It's OK for your child to touch, pat, or hug (but not hit, punch, or use The Force on) the character. Understanding the unpredictability of children, characters will keep their feet still, particularly refraining from moving backward or sideways.

CHARACTER-GREETING VENUES

MAGIC KINGDOM

MICKEY AND HIS POSSE

- **Mickey** Town Square Theater
- **Minnie, Daisy, Donald, and Goofy** Pete's Silly Sideshow

DISNEY ROYALTY *(Princesses, Princes, Suitors, and Such)*

- **Aladdin and Jasmine** Adventureland • **Ariel** Ariel's Grotto • **Belle** *Enchanted Tales with Belle* • **Cinderella, Elena of Avalor, Rapunzel, and Tiana** Princess Fairytale Hall • **Fairy Godmother, Evil Stepmother, and/or Anastasia and Drizella** Fantasyland near Cinderella's Castle • **Gaston** Fountain outside Gaston's Tavern • **Snow White** Next to City Hall

OTHER CHARACTERS

- **Alice and Mad Hatter** Mad Tea Party • **Captain Jack Sparrow** Adventureland • **Country Bears** Frontierland • **Mirabel** Fairytale Garden • **Peter Pan** Fantasyland next to Peter Pan's Flight • **Pooh and Tigger** Fantasyland by The Many Adventures of Winnie the Pooh • **Stitch** Tomorrowland

EPCOT

MICKEY AND HIS POSSE

- **Minnie, Mickey, and Goofy** CommuniCore Hall • **Donald** Mexico

DISNEY ROYALTY

- **Anna and Elsa** Norway • **Asha** International Gateway • **Aurora** France gazebo
- **Belle** France • **Jasmine** Morocco • **Mulan** China • **Snow White** Germany

OTHER CHARACTERS

- **Alice** United Kingdom • **Winnie the Pooh** United Kingdom
- **Joy and Figment** Inside the Imagination! Pavilion

DISNEY'S ANIMAL KINGDOM

MICKEY AND HIS POSSE

- **Mickey and Minnie** Adventurers Outpost on Discovery Island

DISNEY ROYALTY

- **Moana** Discovery Island at Character Landing

OTHER CHARACTERS

- **Kevin** (*Up*) Discovery Island • **Russell and Dug** Wilderness Explorers

DISNEY'S HOLLYWOOD STUDIOS

MICKEY AND HIS POSSE

- **Minnie and Sorcerer Mickey** *Red Carpet Dreams* on Commissary Lane
- **Chip 'n' Dale and Daisy** Outside Animation Courtyard • **Donald** Near Echo Lake
- **Pluto** Animation Courtyard

DISNEY JUNIOR STARS

- **Doc McStuffins, Fancy Nancy, and Vampirina** Animation Courtyard

OTHER CHARACTERS

- **Buzz, Jessie, Woody, and Green Army Men** Toy Story Land • **Chewbacca, Darth Vader, and BB-8** Star Wars Launch Bay • **Edna Mode, Frozone, the Incredibles, and Sully** Pixar Place • **Olaf** Celebrity Spotlight in Echo Lake • **Stormtroopers, Kylo Ren, Rey, Grogu, R2D2, and more from** *Star Wars* Galaxy's Edge

Characters are subject to change.

Most characters will pose for pictures or sign autographs, but note that costumes can make it difficult to wield a normal pen. Some can't sign autographs at all, but they are always glad to pose for photos.

During these meet and greets, characters often engage in dialogue appropriate to their storylines, which catches many people by surprise. Characters in the parks will also know about the park's attractions that involve them, as this Canadian mom found out:

> *Immediately after watching Mickey's PhilharMagic, my daughter was so worried about Donald smashing through a wall [on film as part of the show] that we had to drop what we were going to do and stand in line just so she could kiss Donald and make sure he was OK. Fortunately, Donald knew what she was talking about and played along with the doctoring.*

CHARACTER MEALS

DISNEY CHARACTERS APPEAR at meals served in table-service restaurants at the theme parks and Deluxe resorts, among other locations. For more information, see page 311. At press time, character-dining experiences were available only at the following locations:

- **AKERSHUS ROYAL BANQUET HALL** Norway, World Showcase, EPCOT (see page 246)
- **CAPE MAY CAFE** Beach Club Resort (see page 251)
- **CHEF MICKEY'S** Contemporary Resort (see page 252)
- **CINDERELLA'S ROYAL TABLE** Magic Kingdom (see page 253)
- **THE CRYSTAL PALACE** Magic Kingdom (see page 255)
- **GARDEN GRILL RESTAURANT** EPCOT (see page 258)
- **HOLLYWOOD & VINE** Disney's Hollywood Studios (see page 260)
- **1900 PARK FARE** Grand Floridian Resort (see page 267)
- **'OHANA** Polynesian Village Resort (see page 268)
- **RAVELLO** Four Seasons Orlando (see pages 211)
- **STORY BOOK DINING AT ARTIST POINT** Wilderness Lodge Resort (see page 278)
- **TOPOLINO'S TERRACE—FLAVORS OF THE RIVIERA** Riviera Resort (see page 282)
- **TUSKER HOUSE RESTAURANT** Animal Kingdom (see page 284)

CHILDCARE

IN-ROOM BABYSITTING Kid's Nite Out (☎ 877-761-3580; kidsniteout.com) provides in-room and in-park childcare in the Walt Disney World area. Base hourly rates (4-hour minimum) are $45 for one child and $3 per hour for each additional child, plus a $15 travel fee. Sitters are security-checked, bonded, and trained in CPR. See the website for additional services and fees.

unofficial **TIP**
Childcare is unavailable at Walt Disney World resort hotels.

SPECIAL KIDS' PROGRAMS

FREE ACTIVITIES

MANY DISNEY DELUXE AND DVC RESORTS offer a continuous slate of free kids' activities from early morning through the evening, from storytelling and cookie decorating to hands-on activities themed to the resort. (Many of these activities are outdoors, too.) These programs offer an inexpensive alternative to the theme parks on your first or last day of travel, or whenever parents need a quiet break by the pool.

BIRTHDAYS *and* SPECIAL OCCASIONS

WHEN YOU CHECK IN TO A HOTEL or restaurant, Disney cast members will generally ask if you're celebrating something special, such as a birthday or anniversary. Don't expect anything to happen, but if you get a birthday or celebration button from your resort or the park, cast members will regularly comment as you pass. And if you note the special occasion when checking in for a table-service reservation, you may even be given a special dessert.

PART 8

TIPS *for* VARIED CIRCUMSTANCES

KEY QUESTIONS ANSWERED IN THIS CHAPTER

- How does Disney accommodate people with disabilities? *(see below)*
- What is Disney's Disability Access Service? *(see page 316)*
- Can I use a wheelchair or scooter in the parks and resorts? *(page 318)*
- How do Disney restaurants handle dietary restrictions? *(page 319)*
- What should older guests know about visiting Disney World? *(page 323)*
- Can I get married in Walt Disney World? *(page 325)*

WALT DISNEY WORLD *for* GUESTS *with* DISABILITIES

DISNEY WORLD IS EXCEPTIONALLY ACCOMMODATING for guests with physical and cognitive disabilities. If you have a disability, Disney is well prepared to meet your needs.

DISNEY RESORTS

WHEN BOOKING YOUR ROOM, inform the reservation agent of any particular accommodations you'll need. The following equipment, services, and facilities are available at most Disney resorts (note that not all resorts offer all items, so check before you book).

- Accessible vanities
- Bed and bathroom rails
- Braille on signs and elevators
- Closed-captioned TVs
- Double peepholes in doors
- Handheld showerheads
- Knock and phone alerts
- Lowered beds
- Phone amplifiers
- Portable commodes
- Refrigerators
- Roll-in showers
- Rubber bed padding
- Shower benches
- Strobe-light smoke detectors
- TTYs
- Wheelchairs for temporary use
- Widened bathroom doors

SERVICE ANIMALS

DISNEY ALLOWS SERVICE DOGS AND MINIATURE HORSES in most locations in Disney resorts and theme parks, although they may not be allowed on certain rides. Visit disneyworld.disney.go.com/guest-services/service-animals for more information.

IN THE THEME PARKS

EACH THEME PARK OFFERS a free booklet describing services and accommodations for guests with disabilities. Find it at theugseries.com/disabilities-guide. You can also get one when you enter the parks, at resort front desks, and at wheelchair-rental locations in the parks. For specific requests, call ☎ 407-560-2547 (voice). When the recorded menu comes up, press 1. Limit your questions and requests to those regarding your disability; address other questions to ☎ 407-824-4321 or 407-827-5141 (TTY).

DISNEY'S DISABILITY ACCESS SERVICE (DAS)

WE GET MANY COMMENTS from readers whose traveling companion or child requires special assistance but who is not visibly disabled. Autism spectrum disorder, for example, can make it very difficult or impossible for someone to wait in line for more than a few minutes or in queues surrounded by a crowd. A trip to Disney World can nonetheless be a positive and rewarding vacation for guests with autism. And while any Disney vacation requires planning, a little extra effort to accommodate the affected person will pay large dividends.

Disney's Disability Access Service (**DAS**) is designed to accommodate guests with developmental disabilities such as autism. **Amy Schinner,** a member of the TouringPlans team, explains how it works:

- DAS lets you to make a reservation at the attraction, then join the Lightning Lane at your arrival time, allowing you to spend most of your wait time in a more comfortable space. In May 2024, the policy was overhauled, and the Guest Services team is not involved with DAS unless you have a technical problem while using the My Disney Experience app. You can only request DAS using video chat. We strongly suggest doing this 30 days before your trip (see theugseries.com/wdw-das). There will be iPads dedicated to video chat in the park. There will not be an opportunity to speak to a cast member in person.

- DAS is valid for as many park days as your ticket, and the service carries over to each subsequent park you visit. If you have an Annual Pass, you will need to renew DAS every 240 days. The process is explained below. For clarity, we'll refer to the person signing up for DAS as the enrollee. *Note:* Guests whose disability requires only a wheelchair or mobility vehicle do not need (or qualify for) DAS.

PREPARATION Before you sign up, make sure you have all your My Disney Experience (MDE) information, including an email address, mailing address, and phone number for each guest in your party. DAS works for parties of up to four people. If you have more than four immediate family members, ask about them when you request DAS.

SIGNING UP FOR DAS During your video chat, you'll be asked to present identification and describe the enrollee's limitations. You don't

QUIET SPOTS IN WALT DISNEY WORLD

WITH AN INCREASE IN CONSTRUCTION and crowds expected in 2026, we anticipate that many families will be looking for a small, quiet escape in the middle of their park day. If a member of your party needs a moment to rest their ears, eyes, or legs, **Steven from D•Introverts** (dintroverts.com and @dintroverts on Instagram) has just the spots for you. For more locations, visit disneyworld.disney.go.com/guest-services/neurodivergent (click on "Take a Break").

MAGIC KINGDOM
- **TOMORROWLAND** Between Space Mountain and Rockettower Plaza Stage restrooms A tucked-away area in the shade with benches and fans
- **LIBERTY SQUARE** Behind Ye Olde Christmas Shoppe Another shaded area with picnic tables and benches

EPCOT
- **WORLD SHOWCASE** Between the France and United Kingdom Pavilions by the water A large island with views of World Showcase Lagoon
- **IMAGINATION! PAVILION** By the exit of Disney & Pixar Short Film Festival A low-traffic area with benches and nearby water fountains

ANIMAL KINGDOM
- **ASIA** Pathway behind Caravan Road kiosk A "hidden" side path with tables and chairs under a gazebo
- **DISCOVERY ISLAND** Trails around the Tree of Life A network of trails with views of wildlife and the Tree of Life

DISNEY'S HOLLYWOOD STUDIOS
- **SUNSET BOULEVARD** To the right of The Hollywood Brown Derby Lounge A cozy corner with patio tables and chairs under umbrellas
- **ECHO LAKE** To the right of Indiana Jones Adventure Outpost A spot off the beaten path with standing tables and benches

---

have to share a diagnosis; Disney simply needs to know how the disability affects the enrollee in the parks. The goal is to determine the right level of assistance, not to make you prove that the enrollee qualifies. The enrollee must be present during this call. Be as detailed as possible in describing limitations. For instance, if your child has autism spectrum disorder and has trouble waiting in long lines or has sensory issues such as sensitivity to noise, let the cast member know each of these things specifically.

Finally, you must check a box that says you agree to Disney's DAS rules. While this seems like a formality, no video chat or any other assistance will happen until you accept those terms and conditions.

USING DAS ON THE DAY OF YOUR VISIT DAS is navigated using the MDE app. You can request return times for any attraction or character-greeting venue with a queue. Tap the hamburger menu (three stacked lines) on the app, tap "DAS," scroll to the attraction, tap the standby time, then tap the DAS time. Then click each participating guest, tap "Continue," then "Confirm," and finally "View My Day." Every guest who is linked to the enrollee will have access to the DAS times on their app and is able to request or modify return times.

The return time will be the current posted wait time minus 10 minutes. If, say, you tap on Seven Dwarfs Mine Train at 12:20 p.m. and the standby time is 40 minutes, your return time will be 30 minutes later, at 12:50 p.m. You may return at the specified time or anytime thereafter.

The enrollee's MagicBand will be scanned first; the scanner will turn blue initially, a cast member will confirm it's the right person, and the rest of the group will get green lights when they scan in. The whole group will use the Lightning Lane.

You can hold one DAS return time at a time. However, you can use Lightning Lane Multi Pass (LLMP) where offered, Lightning Lane Single Pass (LLSP), boarding groups, and DAS at the same time.

WHAT HAPPENS IF I'M LATE FOR THE RETURN WINDOW? A DAS return time is open-ended; you may not be early, but it remains available until the park closes.

For more information on facilities and services available to guests with cognitive disabilities, download Disney's guide to planning a trip at theugseries.com/wdw-cognitive-guide.

For a ride-by-ride chart of the sights, sounds, smells, and experiences you'll encounter on each ride, see Disney's guide to its attractions at theugseries.com/wdw-cognitive-matrix.

WHEELCHAIRS AND ELECTRIC VEHICLES

GUESTS MAY RENT WHEELCHAIRS or three-wheeled electric conveyance vehicles (ECVs), aka scooters. These give guests with limited mobility tremendous freedom. If you are in a park and need assistance with these devices, go to Guest Relations.

At the theme parks, wheelchairs rent for $12 per day (or $10 per day for length-of-stay rentals), while ECVs cost $65 per day, plus a $20 refundable deposit (length-of-stay rentals are not available for ECVs); see Parts 11–14 for rental locations in the theme parks. At the water parks and Disney Springs, the daily rates are the same as at the theme parks, but a $100 refundable deposit is required for both wheelchairs and ECVs.

Your rental deposit slip is good for a replacement wheelchair in any theme park or water park or at Disney Springs on the same day. You can rent a chair in the Magic Kingdom in the morning, return it, go to another location, present your deposit slip, and get another chair at no additional charge.

Apple Scooter (☎ 321-726-6837, applescooter.com) rents scooters with a wide variety of options and is typically the least expensive choice for rentals of three-plus days. **Buena Vista Scooters** (☎ 407-331-9147, buenavistascooters.com) also rents scooters with many options, but some are much more expensive. Both companies include free delivery to and pickup from your Disney resort. You'll need to be present for delivery and pickup. If you would rather not have to be present, your only option is **ScooterBug Orlando** (☎ 800-726-8284, scooterbug.com/orlando). Prices are slightly higher for the convenience.

All Disney parking lots have close-up spots for visitors with disabilities. Request directions when you pay your parking fee. Most (but not all) rides, shows, restrooms, and restaurants accommodate wheelchairs, as do monorails and buses, as outlined below.

Even if an attraction doesn't accommodate wheelchairs or ECVs, nonambulatory guests may ride if they can transfer from their wheelchair to the ride vehicle. Disney staff aren't trained or permitted to assist with transfers—guests must be able to board the ride unassisted or have a member of their party assist them. Members of the guest's party may ride with the guest.

Because the waiting areas of some attractions won't accommodate wheelchairs, nonambulatory guests and their parties should ask a cast member for boarding instructions as soon as they arrive at an attraction entrance.

Much of the Disney transportation system is accessible. Monorails can be accessed by ramp or elevator, the Skyliner has special gondolas for wheelchairs and scooters, and all bus routes are served by vehicles with wheelchair lifts, though unusually wide or long wheelchairs (or motorized chairs) may not fit the lift. Accommodations for wheelchairs are iffier on boats.

A large number of Disney hotel guests use scooters. This affects commuting times by bus, as each Disney bus can accommodate only two or three scooters or wheelchairs. A Minnesota woman touring with her parents shared her experience:

> I was stunned by the number of scooters this year. My parents each had one, and several times they had to wait to find a bus that had available space for scooters or wheelchairs. If people needing a scooter can make it to the bus stop on foot, they'd be better off waiting until they get to the park and renting a scooter there.

Food and merchandise locations at theme parks, Disney Springs, and hotels are generally accessible, but some fast-food queues and shop aisles are too narrow for wheelchairs. At these locations, ask a cast member or member of your party for assistance.

DIETARY RESTRICTIONS AND ALLERGIES

WALT DISNEY WORLD is one of the best places to eat for people with food allergies. The restaurants are very accommodating. **Bob Jacobs,** an author for the TouringPlans blog, shares his experience and things he's learned while navigating dietary restrictions at the World with members of his family:

unofficial **TIP**
Be aware that there is a charge for canceling a meal with kosher or other special requests, to cover the extra cost of ordering the individual meal components.

- Make your needs known when booking your visit. Follow up with an email to the **Special Dietary Requests** team (special.diets@disneyworld.com). Based on the information you provide, they may send a link asking you to fill out the Special Dietary Request Form to be sent back no sooner than 14 days before your visit.

- After you send back the completed form, Disney will share it with the restaurants you've indicated. If their culinary teams have any questions about the information you've sent, they'll reach out to you before your visit. When you arrive at a restaurant, tell a food-and-beverage cast member about your special dietary requests, and they can assist you. We have found that even quick-service culinary staff members are happy to discuss available options with you.

- With more than 200 dining locations, it would be impossible to share experiences at each. But at the following full-service restaurants, the head chef has come to the table to discuss our needs and then prepared an off-menu meal free of allergens: **Biergarten Restaurant,**

Chefs de France, Tutto Italia Ristorante, and Narcoossee's. We've also received excellent care at Kona Cafe, Rose & Crown Dining Room, and Le Cellier Steakhouse.

- Quick-service spots that have been especially accommodating include Captain Cooks (at the Polynesian), Columbia Harbour House, Cosmic Ray's Starlight Café, Gasparilla Island Grill (at the Grand Floridian), D-Luxe Burger, and Docking Bay 7 Food and Cargo. At each, a member of the culinary team has spoken with us directly before preparing our meal.

There are a couple of caveats worth mentioning:

1. While restaurants make reasonable efforts to accommodate dietary requests, they can't guarantee that they will be able to meet every request. Buffets may be susceptible to cross-contact due to their self-service approach. If there is a concern about cross-contact, you can speak to a special diets–trained cast member about having your meal prepared and delivered to you separately. (We have done that at the Biergarten buffet in the Germany Pavilion.)
2. Allergy-friendly offerings rely on supplier ingredient labels, so Disney can't guarantee the accuracy of the contents of each food item. And since there are no separate allergy-friendly kitchens, Disney can't guarantee that a menu item is completely free of allergens.

TREATMENT FOR ALLERGIC REACTIONS

GUESTS KNOWN TO EXPERIENCE life-threatening allergic reactions should always travel with their own supplies. However, in case of emergency, Disney has epinephrine injectors (**EpiPens**) at **First Aid** and other locations throughout the parks (check your park guide maps for locations). Nurses and first responders are trained in EpiPen use.

VISUALLY IMPAIRED, DEAF, OR HARD-OF-HEARING GUESTS

GUEST RELATIONS PROVIDES FREE **assistive-technology devices** ($25 refundable deposit, depending on the device). Visually impaired guests can customize the given information (such as architectural details, restroom locations, and descriptions of attractions and restaurants) through an interactive audio menu that is guided by a GPS in the device. Amplified audio and closed-captioning for attractions can be loaded into the same device. **Braille guidebooks** are available from Guest Relations at all parks ($25 refundable deposit), and **Braille menus** are available at some theme park restaurants. Some rides provide **closed-captioning;** many theater attractions provide **reflective captioning.**

Disney provides **sign language interpretations** of live shows at the theme parks on designated days of the week:

- MAGIC KINGDOM Mondays and Thursdays
- EPCOT Fridays
- DISNEY'S ANIMAL KINGDOM Tuesdays and Saturdays
- DISNEY'S HOLLYWOOD STUDIOS Sundays and Wednesdays

Get confirmation of the interpreted-performance schedule a minimum of one week in advance by calling Disney World information at ☎ 407-824-4321 (voice) or 407-827-5141 (TTY). You'll be contacted before your visit with a schedule of the interpreted performances.

WALT DISNEY WORLD *for* PREGNANT GUESTS

WHEN IT COMES TO VISITING DISNEY WORLD while pregnant, there are certainly attractions and experiences that are off-limits (more on that below), but since this is a vacation destination designed for families with little children, there is still plenty to do if you want to fill up a relaxing or exciting trip.

MAGIC KINGDOM You'll want to avoid any roller coasters like **Seven Dwarfs Mine Train, Tron Lightcycle/Run, Big Thunder Mountain Railroad,** and **Space Mountain. Tomorrowland Speedway** is also out, thanks to potential rear-ending by not-so-skilled drivers. Another one to avoid is **Tiana's Bayou Adventure** with its big drops and splashing stops. Spinners like Dumbo, Astro Orbiter, and The Magic Carpets of Aladdin are OK, but **Mad Tea Party** is too much spinning force.

ANIMAL KINGDOM The big roller coaster to avoid here is **Expedition Everest.** The positioning of the ride vehicle is difficult on **Avatar Flight of Passage.** And depending on your risk level, you may also want to skip **Kilimanjaro Safaris,** which can get very bumpy depending on the path taken by your truck.

EPCOT Mission: Space is a spinner with too much force. **Guardians of the Galaxy: Cosmic Rewind,** while smooth, is still a roller coaster and is therefore out. At press time, we don't know much about the new version of **Test Track,** but it's safe to assume it'll be jerky and include sudden stops, making it one to skip. Remy's Ratatouille Adventure, Frozen Ever After, and Soarin' Around the World should all be OK.

HOLLYWOOD STUDIOS *Millennium Falcon:* **Smugglers Run** and **Star Wars: Rise of the Resistance** are both out for their jerky motions and small drops. **Slinky Dog Dash** and **Rock 'n' Roller Coaster** are both out since they're roller coasters, and **Tower of Terror**'s drops make it a no-go. **Alien Swirling Saucers** has too much spinning force, and **Star Tours** is restricted because it's a simulator. Mickey & Minnie's Runaway Railway is probably doable—there's one scene where the ride vehicle shakes from side to side while you're doing the mambo (we're not making this up, we swear).

WATER PARKS Don't go on any of the slides, but enjoy the lazy rivers and wave pools (be careful with the big waves at Typhoon Lagoon).

MORE TIPS FOR MOMS-TO-BE

IN ADDITION TO THE TIPS BELOW, you should also discuss your Disney World plans with your OB-GYN before your trip.

1. **Drink plenty of water.** Staying hydrated is important for all Disney visitors, but when you're pregnant, it's the number one priority. You'll be hot. You'll be tired. You'll be sweaty. Replenish all that fluid!
2. **Eat frequently.** You burn a lot of calories as you tour the parks. Thankfully, there is no shortage of food. Snack regularly to keep your energy up. If you have gestational diabetes, focus on quick-service locations with protein-centered menus.
3. **Have a drink.** Not the alcoholic kind. Several Disney lounges and restaurants have robust mocktail programs. I recommend **Nomad Lounge,** where you can get a zero-proof version of any drink on the menu.

4. **Dress comfortably.** Feet do weird things during pregnancy, so make sure you do some practice walks in the shoes you'll be wearing in the parks. And focus on comfort over cuteness for your other clothing.
5. **Rest up.** Now is not the time for rope-drop-to-park-close touring. Sleep in, take afternoon breaks, or do whatever your body needs. You'll be avoiding most of the headliners with long waits anyway, so you can be more relaxed on your park days.

A New Jersey woman advises:

Moms-to-be should be really mindful of the temperature, staying hydrated, and having realistic expectations for how much you'll be able to do. We averaged 5–7 miles of walking per day during our trip, which may have been a bit too much for me (I was six months pregnant at the time). Once the temperatures started approaching 90°F, I found it difficult to catch my breath, and my feet began to swell. A midday nap or swim break was 100% required—I tried to skip it on a few days, and I was miserable as a result. I was most frustrated at EPCOT, where most of the headliner attractions are restricted for pregnant guests.

WALT DISNEY WORLD *for* LARGER GUESTS

WHEN YOU'RE SPENDING A SMALL FORTUNE on your vacation, you don't want to worry about whether you'll have trouble fitting into the ride vehicles. Fortunately, Disney realizes that its guests come in all shapes and sizes and is quite accommodating.

Deb Wills and **Debra Martin Koma**, authors of the 2005 guidebook *PassPorter's Walt Disney World for Your Special Needs*, offer the following suggestions.

- You'll be on your feet for hours at a time, so wear comfortable, broken-in shoes. If you feel a blister starting to form, take care of it quickly. (Each theme park has a **First Aid** center with bandages and other necessities.)
- If you're prone to chafing, consider bringing an antifriction product designed to control or eliminate rubbing (such as **Body Glide**).
- In restaurants, look for chairs without arms. Check with a dining host if you don't see one.
- Request a hotel room with a king-size bed. The good sleep you'll get will be worth it.
- Attractions have different kinds of vehicles and seating. Some have bench seats, while others have individual seats; some have overhead harnesses, while others have seat belts or lap bars. Visit theugseries.com/allears-ride-gallery to learn what type of seating or vehicle each attraction has before your trip so you know what to expect.
  If the attraction has a seat belt, pull it all the way out before you sit down, to make it easier to strap yourself in. Note that some attractions have seat-belt extenders—ask a cast member about these.
- Several attractions offer a sample ride vehicle for you to try before you get in line. These can be found at **Tron Lightcycle/Run** in the Magic Kingdom, **Test Track** in EPCOT, **Avatar Flight of Passage** and **Expedition Everest** in Animal Kingdom, and **Star Wars: Rise of the Resistance** and

Rock 'n' Roller Coaster in Disney's Hollywood Studios. Ask a cast member if the test seats aren't immediately visible.

Sometimes it isn't size in general but your particular build that can present a problem when it comes to ride vehicles. For example, Tron's leg restraints don't accommodate all guests with large calves, regardless of torso size.

A Connecticut reader relates her experience in Animal Kingdom:

Since I was a very young girl, I've dreamed of riding on a dragon, so I was extremely excited about the chance to experience Avatar Flight of Passage in Pandora. Unfortunately, though I was able to mount the ride's motorcycle-like seat without difficulty, the safety braces that came up behind would not lock due to my particular dimensions. The cast member in charge of checking the safeties was very kind and did try to coach me into a better fit, but in the end I had to get out and leave the ride as my husband and son looked on. I was absolutely mortified, though I was graciously offered two additional ride reservations as compensation.

Fast-forward to the next day at Disney's Hollywood Studios. I was determined not to repeat the experience, so when the time came to ride the Rock 'n' Roller Coaster, I asked if there were sample seats and restraints I could try before entering the line. I was ushered backstage by a cast member and was able to try out the exact seating configuration with success.

WALT DISNEY WORLD *for* OLDER GUESTS

OLDER VISITORS HAVE MANY OF THE SAME PROBLEMS and concerns as all Disney visitors. ("Is Space Mountain too rough? How much walking will I have to do? Why isn't Figment featured in more rides?") Pressure to endure the frantic pace set by their younger family members can cause older adults to concentrate on simply surviving Disney World rather than enjoying it. Instead, they should set their own pace or send the younger folks to tour separately. A reader in Alabama writes:

Being a senior is not for wussies, particularly at Disney World. Things that used to be easy take a lot of effort, and sometimes your brain has to wait for your body to catch up. Half the time, your grandchildren treat you like a crumbling ruin; then they turn around and trick you into getting on a roller coaster in the dark. Seniors must be alert and not trust anyone—not their children, not the Disney people, and especially not their grandchildren! Don't follow along blindly like a lamb to the slaughter. He who hesitates is launched!

Most older people we talk to enjoy Disney World much more when they tour with other people their age. But if you're considering visiting with your grandchildren, we recommend establishing limits, maintaining control of your own schedule and boundaries, and setting a comfortable pace. You could even take the grandkids to a local theme park, fair, or zoo before you extend the Walt Disney World invitation to see what you're getting yourself into.

When it comes to attractions, personal taste should trump age. Remember that even thrill rides like Rise of the Resistance are more about theme and visual effects than speed or extreme motion. Don't let age deter you from any attraction that seems interesting. The attraction profiles in Parts 11–14 will help you make informed decisions.

GETTING AROUND

YOU MAY LIKE TO WALK, but a 7-hour visit to a theme park can include up to 10 miles on foot. Consider renting a wheelchair or scooter (see page 318) if you're not up for that distance.

LOOK OUT FOR STROLLERS! Given the number of wheeled vehicles, pedestrians, and tight spaces, mishaps are inevitable. In response to a few incidents involving strollers taking up too much space or running into other guests, Disney limits stroller sizes to **31 inches wide by 52 inches long.**

TIMING YOUR VISIT

RETIREES SHOULD MAKE THE MOST of their flexible schedules and go to Walt Disney World in the fall or spring (excluding holiday weeks), when the weather is nicest and the crowds are comparatively thinner. Crowds and weather are also generally reasonable from late January through early February. See page 31 for more information.

LODGING

IF YOU CAN AFFORD IT, STAY ON-PROPERTY. Rooms are among the area's nicest, and transportation to any Disney destination is always available at no additional cost.

Walt Disney World hotels are spread out—it's easy to avoid stairs, but it's often a long way to your room from parking lots or bus stops. Resorts typically reserve some rooms close to restaurants and transportation for guests who can't do much walking. Just submit a room request or inquire about availability when you check in. They also provide golf carts to pick up and deliver guests to their rooms. Service can vary dramatically depending on the time of day and number of guests requesting carts. At check-in time, for example, the wait for a ride can be as long as 40 minutes.

If you enjoy watching birds and animals, try **Animal Kingdom Lodge & Villas.** For golf, try **Saratoga Springs Resort & Spa.** RVers will find pleasant surroundings at **The Campsites at Disney's Fort Wilderness Resort.**

TRANSPORTATION

ROADS IN DISNEY WORLD CAN BE DAUNTING. Armed with a decent sense of direction and a great sense of humor, however, even the most timid driver can get around. Plus, you don't have to be very specific to use a mapping app on your smartphone—if you want to go to EPCOT, for example, entering "EPCOT" or "EPCOT parking" will get the job done.

Parking for guests with disabilities is available near each theme park's entrance; toll plaza attendants will provide a dashboard ticket and direct you to the reserved spaces. Disney requires that you be officially recognized as disabled to use these, but temporarily disabled persons are also permitted access.

DINING

EAT BREAKFAST AT YOUR HOTEL RESTAURANT or have juice and pastries in your room. Bring your own snacks into the park, and supplement them with fresh or dried fruit, fruit juice, and soft drinks purchased from vendors. To avoid the crowds, make Advance Dining Reservations for lunch before noon. Then you can have an early dinner and be out of the restaurants, ready for evening touring and fireworks, before the main crowd even thinks about dinner.

WALT DISNEY WORLD *for* COUPLES

WEDDINGS, COMMITMENT CEREMONIES, AND VOW RENEWALS

SO MANY COUPLES TIE THE KNOT, get engaged, or honeymoon at Disney World that Disney has a department dedicated to helping arrange the day or vacation of your dreams.

Disney's Fairy Tale Weddings & Honeymoons (☎ 321-939-4610; disneyweddings.com) offers a range of in-park ceremony venues and services—including photographers, videographers, musicians, and floral designers—for any size or type of gathering. Have a fairy-tale wedding in front of Cinderella Castle or an intimate beach gathering at Crescent Cove. You can even request fireworks or Disney characters at your event, for an extra charge.

You are responsible for obtaining an officiant and a marriage certificate. Disney maintains a list of officiants to choose from, or you can bring your own (if you bring your own, the officiant counts as one of your guests).

LEGALITIES

TO GET MARRIED IN THE WORLD, you'll need to obtain a marriage license ($86), issued at any Florida county courthouse. Florida residents must complete a 4-hour premarital counseling session if they want to marry less than three days after applying for their license; completing the course reduces the license fee to $61. There is no waiting period for residents of other states.

All weddings must take place within 60 days of getting the marriage license. Both parties must present valid identification, along with their Social Security numbers. Finally, if you're widowed or divorced, you must also present a certified copy of the deceased spouse's death certificate or your divorce decree.

unofficial **TIP**
Contact Disney as soon as you have a date in mind—popular dates may not be available on short notice. If you wish to hold your ceremony inside a theme park, you're restricted to very early in the morning or late at night, when the park is closed to guests.

HONEYMOONS AND HONEYMOON REGISTRIES

HONEYMOON PACKAGES are really just regular Walt Disney World vacation packages, although you may purchase add-ons such as flowers and in-room gifts to make your trip more special.

Some couples who spend their honeymoon at Walt Disney World decide to create a registry that allows friends and family to give them tours, spa packages, special dinners, and the like. For more information on Disney honeymoon registries, visit disney.honeymoonwishes.com.

CELEBRATE . . . EVERYTHING!

DISNEY WORLD IS ALL ABOUT CELEBRATING—marriages, birthdays, anniversaries, the works—but only if you let somebody know. A Missouri newlywed offers this advice:

> If you're celebrating, ask for Celebration Buttons when you check in to your hotel or at any park's Guest Relations, then WEAR THEM! Cast members regularly congratulated us, and I'm relatively certain we were seated at better tables for dinner based on our buttons.

TIPS FOR VISITORS WHO NEED "ADULT TIME"

AS WE'VE NOTED, WALT DISNEY WORLD is a great destination for adults traveling without kids, whether they're traveling solo, as a couple, or with a group of friends. The self-contained Disney bubble, with its easy transportation; security; and variety of dining, drinking, and entertainment options, makes it a fabulous place to vacation without children (don't tell ours!).

Naturally, anyone who visits the most magical place on earth should be prepared to see children—lots of them. It would be naive to think otherwise. But that doesn't mean you need to be around the little ones every minute of your vacation. Here are some tips for getting some adults-only time.

- **Dine late.** Most families will try to eat dinner before 8 p.m. Have a late lunch and try for a reservation closer to the last seating at your restaurant. The exceptions to this are **California Grill** and **Topolino's Terrace,** where many people (families or not) will try to time their meals around the fireworks in the Magic Kingdom, EPCOT, and Disney's Hollywood Studios.
- **Dine at Victoria & Albert's.** Located at Disney's Grand Floridian Resort & Spa, Victoria & Albert's is the only on-property restaurant that bans guests under age 10 (except at the Chef's Table). Pricey? Yes. Worth it? You bet.
- **Go to the spa.** Senses Spa, also at the Grand Floridian, is profiled on page 514.
- **Linger in World Showcase.** We could spend hours poring over the details of the World Showcase pavilions. Once you wander past popular attractions or restaurants, you can usually find some quieter space.
- **Really take in the trails of Animal Kingdom.** The animal trails in Asia, Africa, and Discovery Island are peaceful and beautiful.
- **Stay up late.** Take a tip from Tom Bricker of the Disney Tourist Blog, and don't leave the park until well past closing. There's something magical about having all of Main Street or Sunset Boulevard to yourself with the lights and background music still playing. Don't miss the last bus to your resort, though, if you didn't drive.

TIPS FOR GOING SOLO

TRAVELING BY YOURSELF doesn't mean you can't have a great time at Disney World. **Deb Wills,** creator of the all-things-Disney website AllEars.net, offers this advice for making the most of your trip.

- One of the best parts about traveling solo is that you can be your own boss. Sleep in, have leisurely morning coffee on the balcony, relax by the pool . . . or not. If you'd rather get up and go early, who's to stop you?
- Put some spontaneity into your day. If you're taking Disney transportation, get on the first park bus that arrives.
- Get on the resort monorail at the Magic Kingdom and visit each of the resorts it stops at on its route. Each has its own theme and character, with lots to see and explore.
- Did you know you can walk through the queues and view the preshows of the thrill rides even if you don't ride? Wander through at your own pace, then tell the cast member before boarding that you don't wish to ride. You'll be shown to a nearby exit.
- If you *do* want to experience the thrill rides, take advantage of the **single-rider lines** (when available) for **Rise of the Resistance, Rock 'n' Roller Coaster, Expedition Everest,** *Millennium Falcon:* **Smugglers Run,** and **Test Track.** They can cut your wait time significantly.
- If you encounter folks taking photos of each other, ask if they'd like to be in one photo, then offer to snap the picture. This is a great way to meet people.
- Get your favorite Disney snack, find a bench, and people-watch. You'll be amazed at what you see: a honeymooning couple wearing bride-and-groom mouse ears, toddlers seeing Mickey and the characters for the first time, grandparents smiling indulgently as their grandchildren smear ice cream all over their faces. If you're missing the smiles of your own children, buy a couple of balloons and give them away. You'll make the recipients very, very happy.
- Learn how some of the magic is created. Take a **behind-the-scenes tour** (see Part 16) or one of the Deluxe hotel tours.
- Visit **Animal Kingdom Lodge** and relax at an animal-viewing area. Find an animal keeper; they'll gladly discuss care of the wild animals at the resort.
- Don't hesitate to strike up conversations with cast members or guests in line with you. International cast members in EPCOT's World Showcase will be happy to share stories about their homelands.
- Enjoy a leisurely shopping adventure around the World. Some stores, such as **Arribas Brothers** in Disney Springs and **Mitsukoshi Department Store** in the Japan Pavilion in EPCOT, have really neat displays and exhibits.
- Go to a restaurant you've always wanted to try but your picky eater has always declined. You don't have to order a full meal; try several appetizers or, better yet, just dessert.
- Special fun can be had at a character meal (no waiting in long lines). Which one has characters you love? Make an early or late reservation for fewer people and more character time. **Garden Grill Restaurant** in The Land, for example, is a hidden gem!
- Check the calendar for special events. EPCOT's annual **Flower & Garden Festival** has lots of eye candy that you can enjoy at your own pace.
- Use common sense about your personal security. I feel very comfortable and safe traveling alone at Walt Disney World and have done so many times, but I still don't do things that I wouldn't do at home (like announce to anyone listening that I'm traveling solo). If you aren't comfortable walking to your room alone, ask at the front desk for a security escort. Use extra caution in the parking lots at night, just as you would at home.

- **Take a tour.** Many Walt Disney World tours have an age limit for how young a guest can be to experience them.
- **Spend the morning at the pool.** Most families hit the parks in the morning and return to their hotel around lunch. Do the opposite and you'll often have the pool to yourself.
- **See page 106** for a list of the quietest rooms at Walt Disney World, or use the TouringPlans.com hotel room finder (touringplans.com/walt-disney-world/room-finder) to scope out the quietest rooms at any Disney resort.

ROMANTIC GETAWAYS

NOT ALL DISNEY RESORTS lend themselves to a couple's getaway: Some are too family-oriented, while others swarm with conventioneers. For romantic (though expensive) lodging, we recommend **Animal Kingdom Lodge & Villas**, **Bay Lake Tower** at the Contemporary, **Grand Floridian Resort & Spa** and its **Villas**, **Polynesian Village Resort** and **Polynesian Villas**, **Riviera Resort**, **Wilderness Lodge & Villas**, and the **Yacht Club Resort**.

The Alligator Bayou section at **Port Orleans Riverside**, a Disney Moderate resort, also has secluded rooms. And **Port Orleans French Quarter** typically has fewer families than other Moderate resorts.

WALT DISNEY WORLD *for* SINGLES

DISNEY WORLD IS GREAT FOR SINGLES. Safety and comfort are unsurpassed, especially for women traveling alone. Parking lots are well lit and constantly patrolled. And if you're looking for a place to relax without being hit on, the bars, lounges, and nightclubs are among the most laid-back and friendly you're likely to find. Between the BoardWalk and Disney Springs, nightlife abounds; virtually every type of entertainment is available at a reasonable price. If you overimbibe and you're a Disney resort guest, Disney buses will return you safely to your hotel.

See "Tips for Going Solo," page 327, for more ways to enjoy Walt Disney World on your own.

ODDS *and* ENDS

FRIENDS OF BILL W. For information on **Alcoholics Anonymous** meetings in the area, visit osceolacountyintergroup.org. For information on **Al-Anon** and **Alateen** meetings, visit al-anonorlando.org.

LOOSE ICE AND DRY ICE are prohibited in coolers inside the theme parks and water parks. Reusable ice packs are permitted.

SMOKING All Walt Disney World theme parks and water parks, along with the ESPN Wide World of Sports Complex, are smoke-free—*smoking is allowed only outside of the park entrances.* Disney resort guests may smoke only in designated areas; smoking in your room or on your balcony is prohibited.

For a full list of places where smoking is permitted, see disneyworld.disney.go.com/guest-services/designated-smoking-areas.

PART 9
ARRIVING *and* GETTING AROUND

KEY QUESTIONS ANSWERED IN THIS CHAPTER

- How do I get from the airport to Walt Disney World? *(see below)*
- Which rental-car companies rate highest with readers? *(page 332)*
- How does the Walt Disney World transportation system work? *(page 337)*
- How hard is it to drive around Walt Disney World? *(page 346)*
- When should I leave Walt Disney World for the airport? *(page 353)*

GETTING *to* WALT DISNEY WORLD

FROM ORLANDO INTERNATIONAL AIRPORT (MCO)

YOU HAVE SEVERAL OPTIONS for getting from MCO to Disney World. Because most readers stay at a Disney hotel, this section covers the Mears Connect bus service first, followed by town car services, ride-sharing apps, and car rentals. Driving directions are also included, in case you prefer navigating via book instead of map or app.

Bus Service

Disney's complimentary **Magical Express** bus service was discontinued in 2022. Fortunately, there are several alternatives to consider.

Behind the scenes, Disney's Magical Express was operated by Mears Transportation, which still runs taxi, town car, and shuttle services throughout Central Florida. Shortly after Disney announced the end of Magical Express, Mears launched a similar bus service, called **Mears Connect** (☎ 407-422-4561; mearsconnect.com), that runs between MCO and hotels in the Walt Disney World area.

Mears Connect offers two service levels: Standard and Express. **Standard** operates much like Magical Express, with shared bus service between the airport and Disney's hotels; the Disney Springs and Bonnet Creek hotels; and the Four Seasons, Shades of Green, Swan, Swan Reserve, and Dolphin. Pricing is $32 per adult and $26 per child,

MCO-TO-DISNEY RESORT TRANSPORTATION OPTIONS
MEARS CONNECT (BUS)
ROUND-TRIP PRICE • *Standard:* $32/adult, $26/child plus small gratuity • *Express:* $500 for up to 4 adults **PROS** • Cheapest option for 1 or 2 people • Mears Transportation ran Magical Express for years, so they know what they're doing • Child seats available **CONS** • Standard has the longest transportation time of any option and may make other stops before yours • Express service is wildly expensive
ORLANDO MAGICAL RIDES (TOWN CAR)
ROUND-TRIP PRICE • $250 plus gratuity for up to 6 adults **PROS** • Likely the fastest way to get to your resort • Direct service to your resort • Child seats available • Driver will meet at baggage claim and assist with luggage **CONS** • More expensive than other options
RIDE-SHARING APP (LYFT, UBER)
ROUND-TRIP PRICE • $80–$160 plus gratuity for up to 3 adults **PROS** • Possibly the cheapest option for fewer than 4 people • Direct service to resort **CONS** • Price varies considerably based on demand • May be hard to find cars with child seats • Car quality ranges from basic to luxurious

round-trip; one-way fares are half that. The bus may make multiple stops at other hotels before reaching yours, which can add time to your trip. It's best for solo travelers or couples who don't mind the wait and are looking for the cheapest transportation option.

The **Express** option takes you (and possibly other groups) directly to your hotel without other stops. The one-way cost is $250 for up to four people and $55 for each additional passenger. Other transportation options offer similar convenience for lower prices.

Fewer people seem to be using Mears Connect each year. This creates a downward spiral: With fewer passengers, buses take longer to fill or may take less-efficient routes, making more stops. Longer waits and additional stops frustrate guests, prompting them to choose alternative services. As demand drops, the problem worsens.

Town Car Service

If you're looking for a stress-free transportation option without the uncertainty of app-based rides or shared buses, a town car service might be your best choice. **Orlando Magical Rides** (☎ 407-856-6811; orlando magicalrides.com) offers town car, van, and SUV service between MCO (as well as the Sanford, Tampa, and Melbourne airports) and Disney World–area hotels. The company also provides transfers to and from Port Canaveral for Disney cruises. Child seats and boosters are available upon request. One-way trips start at $125 for a 6-person luxury SUV or van, and just $170 for an 11-person transit van. Other similar services are easy to find online, but Becky likes Orlando Magical Rides because it's run by former cast members, and her family consistently has exceptional experiences with them.

One advantage of a town car is that your driver will meet you at baggage claim with a placard displaying your name and will assist with your luggage. Another advantage is that town car services offer fixed pricing (not the surge pricing used by app-based options). You'll know the cost of your trip up front—no surprises. And you'll go straight to your hotel. For groups of five or more, the convenience and direct service often make town cars a cost-effective, hassle-free option.

Ride-Sharing Apps

We strongly recommend **Lyft** and **Uber** over taxis in the Orlando area. They're often much less expensive, and while you can't choose the exact car you'll get, it's rare that we find ourselves thinking a taxi would've been cleaner or more comfortable.

For rides originating at the airport, the pickup location is on MCO's second level, near baggage claim and the area where passengers are picked up by family and friends. Prices vary greatly depending on the number of people in your party, the kind of car you request, and the time of day. A one-way trip in a basic vehicle for up to three people in low crowds runs around $40, plus gratuity. The same ride could be $80 or more, depending on surges in demand. Likewise, a vehicle with room for five costs around $55 midday but more during peak times. Fancy cars, such as Uber Black or Lyft Premier, cost $80–$90 one-way.

Taxis

Taxis carry four to eight passengers, depending on vehicle type. Rates vary according to distance. If your hotel is in the World, your fare from the airport will be about $70–$82, plus tip. For the US 192 Maingate area, it will cost about $55. For International Drive or downtown Orlando, expect to pay in the neighborhood of $50–$70.

Mears provides local cab service, shuttle service, and an exclusive partnership with Uber called **Uber Taxi**. Using the Uber app, customers can book Mears taxis just as they would regular Uber rides. Mears says Uber Taxi is intended to offer the convenience of Uber to customers who prefer and trust a traditional taxi service over a rideshare.

Renting a Car

Readers staying in Walt Disney World often ask if they'll need a car. If your plans don't include regular visits to destinations outside Disney World or restaurants at other resorts, then the answer is generally no; Disney's extensive transportation system can get you almost anywhere on-property.

Fortunately for those who want or need a car, Orlando is one of the most affordable car-rental markets in the country. On average, rentals cost around $49 per day. At press time, the lowest price we could find for a weekly rental for mid-2025 was $42 per day at the airport.

My (Becky's) rule of thumb: If the cost of a rental car is within about $100 of what I'd pay for airport transfers, I'll opt for the rental. If you're traveling with young kids who are already tired from standing in lines all day, skipping "another line" for a bus can be well worth the extra cost and the short walk to your car. Plus, a car makes visiting restaurants at other resorts much easier, saving time and hassle.

A mom from Virginia has a slightly different logic:

If we're staying at [a hotel served by] the Skyliner, then I don't rent a car. I can get to two parks and many resorts easily. But if I'm anywhere else—yes, including the monorail loop—then I rent a car so

READER RATINGS FOR ORLANDO CAR-RENTAL COMPANIES

RENTAL COMPANY	PICKUP EFFICIENCY	CONDITION OF CAR	CLEANLINESS OF CAR	RETURN EFFICIENCY	OVERALL RATING	SURVEY RANK
NATIONAL	94	95	94	94	94	1
ALAMO	91	94	90	93	92	2 (tie)
ENTERPRISE	89	94	91	93	92	2 (tie)
TURO (car share)	89	91	86	92	90	4
HERTZ	83	92	88	90	88	5
AVERAGE	83	92	88	90	88	NA
SIXT	77	89	89	91	87	6
AVIS	77	91	85	88	85	7
BUDGET	74	91	85	86	84	8
DOLLAR	60	90	85	90	81	9
FOX	61	78	83	88	78	10
THRIFTY	55	88	81	82	77	11

Note: Agencies not shown did not get enough survey responses to analyze.

that we can get to parks and resorts quicker than relying on Disney transportation.

PLAN TO RENT A CAR IF

1. Your hotel is outside Walt Disney World.
2. Your hotel is in the World but you want to eat off-property or at other WDW resorts regularly.
3. You plan to return to your hotel during the day for naps or swimming.
4. You plan to visit other area theme parks or water parks.

unofficial **TIP**
MCO's terminal C houses an intermodal facility that includes commuter and intercity rail stations, plus rental car, taxi, shuttle, and public bus operations.

At **MCO,** most car-rental counters are on **level 1** of the main terminal. Courtesy shuttles to off-site rental locations are also available from level 1.

Orlando is the largest rental-car market in the world. At last count, 36 companies vie for your business. Ten—**Alamo, Avis, Budget, Dollar, Enterprise, Hertz, National, Payless, Sixt,** and **Thrifty**—have counters at terminals A, B, and C. **Fox** and 25 other companies have locations near the airport and provide courtesy shuttles outside the Arrivals level at all terminals. We recommend renting from one of the on-site companies for the following reasons:

1. You can complete your paperwork while waiting for your checked luggage to arrive at baggage claim.
2. It's just a short walk to the parking garage to pick up your car.
3. The extra time and effort required to use an off-site shuttle often isn't worth the money saved, especially if you're traveling with kids.

If you rent on-site, you'll return your car to the garage adjacent to the terminal where your airline is located. (If you return it to the wrong garage, you'll have the added hassle of hauling your luggage from one side of the airport to the other to reach your check-in area). Most rental companies charge about $5–$8 per gallon to refill the gas tank if you return it less than full. If you plan to drive a lot, either prepay for a fill-up so you can return the car empty or be sure to fill up on your way back to the airport. If you're just driving to or from the airport, with maybe a couple of other short trips around WDW property, you may not need to fill up at all.

HOW ORLANDO RENTAL-CAR COMPANIES STACK UP When it comes to renting a car, most *Unofficial Guide* readers value the following, as reflected in the table on the opposite page:

1. Quick, courteous, and efficient service during pickup
2. A nice, well-maintained, late-model vehicle
3. A vehicle that is clean and odor-free
4. Quick, courteous, and efficient service during return
5. An efficient shuttle between the rental agency and airport (if applicable)

The table shows how readers rate the Orlando operations of various rental car companies on scale of 0 (worst) to 100 (best). We strongly recommend renting from one of these companies. Reader feedback helps keep this data fresh. To participate in our survey, visit touringplans.com/walt-disney-world/survey.

For the 14th time in 15 years, **National** ranked as the top rental company in Orlando. If you prioritize excellent service and car condition as much as getting a good deal, National is a great choice. **Alamo,** the only other winner in the last 15 years, consistently ranks second and holds that position again this year. **Turo** is relatively new to the list—it's a car-sharing service (like Airbnb for vehicles) that lets you pick up and drop off the cars at the airport, making it a convenient alternative to traditional rental companies. If you use Turo, let us know your experience.

Most rental companies deliver reliable cars and decent service. If budget is a top priority, we're comfortable recommending any company in the top five that has the lowest price. In general, cars from budget-focused companies tend to have higher miles and fewer amenities, such as backup cameras and satellite navigation.

Readers complain most about the hassle of off-site shuttles and the paperwork involved in picking up cars at the off-site locations. At **Fox,** be prepared for the staff to assume you're going to steal the car; the voluminous paperwork must be to help the bounty hunters find you. Also, the pace is slow at **Sixt,** even if the line is short—we suspect most of their customers are visiting from outside the United States and the staff needs time to review differences in rental policies, insurance coverage, electronic tolls, and the like. Both companies' employees are fantastic at what they do.

INSURANCE AND FEES Before renting a car, make sure you understand what your auto insurance does and doesn't cover. If you have a question about your coverage, call your agent. Do the same with the credit card company you'll use for the rental fee: Many credit cards provide secondary coverage, which often picks up deductibles and other charges that your auto-insurance policy doesn't.

A 6%–7% sales tax, a $9-per-day airport-facility surcharge, and a vehicle-license-recovery fee of 10% will be added to your rental car bill. Some companies, including Alamo, add fees for tire and battery wear, plus other cryptic fees.

RENTAL-CAR DISCOUNT TIPS A great resource for finding deals is **AutoSlash** (autoslash.com), which does two things very well:

1. It applies every discount you're eligible for, saving you time and money.
2. If you've already reserved a car, tell AutoSlash the details, and it'll search continuously for a lower rate. If one turns up, you'll be sent a link to rebook.

AutoSlash frequently finds multiple low-price deals. In those cases, compare the car type, rental company, and price for every option and use our table on page 332 to choose the best fit.

My (Becky's) personal go-to Orlando-area car-rental company is **Alamo**. By joining their free Alamo Insiders club, you get benefits like free cancellation and occasional discounts. I'll usually book the car for the dates I need, then periodically check back to see if the rate has dropped. If it has, I cancel and rebook at the lower price. Alamo also offers the convenience of skipping the counter, and their cars are parked closest to the garage entrance, making pickup fast and easy.

TOLLS If you're flying into Orlando and plan on driving extensively, consider picking up a **Visitor Toll Pass** (visitortollpass.com) when you arrive at the airport. You'll pick up a small Toll Pass device from a vending machine at terminal A on level 1 and link it to your credit card. The Toll Pass hangs from your rearview mirror, pays tolls automatically, and allows you to use the electronic toll and express lanes throughout Florida. If the Visitor Toll Pass program isn't working, you can pick up a regular toll transponder at most grocery stores and drugstores, such as Publix and CVS. Otherwise, go old school and be prepared for about $3 in tolls each way to/from Walt Disney World.

Driving on I-4

Regardless of how you navigate to Orlando, you'll almost certainly drive on I-4. It's a route that requires careful attention, as it's almost always under construction. A four-year project that started in 2023 is adding lanes and interchanges between Exit 58 (Champions Gate) and Exit 67 (Osceola Parkway), affecting travel to Walt Disney World and surrounding areas.

WDW EXITS OFF I-4 East to west (in the direction of Orlando to Tampa), five exits serve Walt Disney World:

Exit 68 (FL 535/Lake Buena Vista) is best for Disney Springs and the Disney Springs Resort Area. It also serves non-Disney hotels with a Lake Buena Vista address. However, it leads to roads with lots of traffic and traffic signals near I-4. Avoid this exit unless you're headed to Disney Springs.

Exit 67 (FL 536/EPCOT/Disney Springs) delivers you to a four-lane expressway into the heart of Disney World. It's the fastest and most convenient way for westbound travelers to access almost all Disney destinations *except* Animal Kingdom and the ESPN Wide World of Sports Complex. Expect road construction through 2027.

Exit 65 (Osceola Parkway) is the best exit for westbound travelers to access Disney's Animal Kingdom, Animal Kingdom Lodge, Pop Century Resort, Art of Animation Resort, the All-Star Resorts, and the ESPN Wide World of Sports Complex. Construction also impacts this exit.

GETTING TO WALT DISNEY WORLD 335

I-4 & Walt Disney World Area

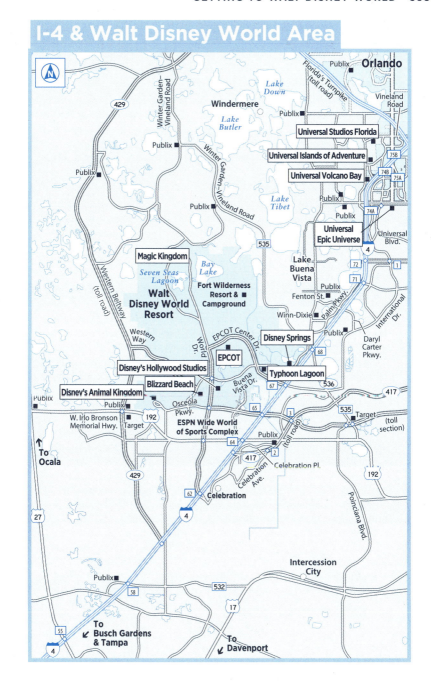

Exit 64 (US 192/Magic Kingdom) is the best route for eastbound travelers to access all Disney destinations. If eastbound traffic is heavy, get off at **Exit 62** instead. Construction also impacts this exit.

Exit 62 (Disney World/Celebration) is the first Disney exit you'll encounter heading east. This four-lane, controlled-access highway connects to the Walt Disney World Maingate. Construction also affects this exit.

I-4 DELAYS Traffic on I-4 can be unpredictable and congested, especially around major attractions. If you're heading east, expect jams near the FL 535 exit and around Universal Orlando. Traffic generally improves after these areas. If you're heading west, congestion often eases after passing the US 192 interchange. Delays can still occur near major Disney exits. Lots of drivers in this area are confused about where they're going. If you're staying near International Drive, choose a hotel closer to its southern end for easier commutes.

AVOIDING THE I-4 BLUES Many mapping apps will automatically reroute you around construction and traffic delays. But if you want to study in advance for possible detours, some are provided below.

To stay updated on road conditions and construction, check out these resources: The **I-4 Exit Guide** (i4exitguide.com/i-4-traffic) has traffic updates, and the **FDOT Interactive Project Map** (data.fdot.gov/road/projects) shows all active construction projects in Florida. Information about Orlando and its tourist areas can be found at **Central Florida Roads** (cflroads.com). For current conditions and other info about area toll roads, visit the **Central Florida Expressway Authority**'s website (cfxway.com).

Traveling southwest on I-4, you may be directed to bypass central Orlando via FL 417/Central Florida GreeneWay (a toll road). From this road, take Exit 3 and go west on West Osceola Parkway, which leads directly into Walt Disney World.

From MCO, exit the airport on Jeff Fuqua Boulevard and proceed south to the FL 417/Central Florida GreeneWay toll road. Turn right up the ramp and take FL 417 northwest. Take Exit 3 onto West Osceola Parkway and follow it to Walt Disney World.

From Sanford International Airport, take East Airport Boulevard west to the FL 417/Central Florida GreeneWay toll road and bypass Orlando to the east, taking Exit 3 onto West Osceola Parkway and continuing to Walt Disney World.

From Miami, Fort Lauderdale, and southeastern Florida, head north on Florida's Turnpike to Exit 249/Osceola Parkway West and follow the signs to Walt Disney World.

From Tampa and southwest Florida, take I-75 northbound to I-4; then drive east on I-4, take Exit 64/US 192 West and follow the signs.

ALTERNATIVE AIRPORTS

A SHORT DISTANCE northeast of Orlando is **Sanford International Airport** (**SFB;** orlandosanfordairport.com). Small, convenient, and easily accessible, it's low-hassle compared with the huge MCO and its mile-long security-checkpoint lines.

Carriers that serve Sanford include **Allegiant Air** and **Sun Country.** An Uber or Lyft from Sanford to Disney property will run you $70–$150 or more one-way.

A reader from Virginia who frequently uses Sanford writes:

The 45-minute drive to WDW is more than made up for by avoiding the chaos at Orlando International, and it's stress-free.

You could also fly into **Tampa International Airport** (**TPA**), but it's a 77-mile drive from there to the Magic Kingdom—about an hour and 15 minutes. My (Becky's) family has only used this option once, when a Tampa flight was many hundreds of dollars less expensive than one at MCO. I would do it again to save that much money, but otherwise Orlando is just more convenient.

HOW *to* TRAVEL *around the* WORLD

NAVIGATING AROUND WALT DISNEY WORLD can be frustrating and overwhelming because of the sheer number—and occasional unpredictability—of transportation options available, including cars, boats, monorails, and elevated gondolas.

Between any two points in Walt Disney World, there's almost always a free transportation option available. Some of the free options are slow enough, however, that paying for an alternative option often makes more sense. We'll walk you through those options right after some orientation.

FINDING YOUR WAY

WALT DISNEY WORLD IS HUGE—about the size of Boston. As with any big city, it's easy to get lost here. The easiest way to orient yourself is to think in terms of five major clusters:

1. **The Magic Kingdom area** encompasses all hotels and theme parks around Seven Seas Lagoon. This includes the Magic Kingdom; hotels connected by the monorail; Shades of Green resort; and the Palm, Magnolia, and Oak Trail Golf Courses.
2. **The Bay Lake area** includes developments on and around Bay Lake: Wilderness Lodge & Villas, Fort Wilderness campground, and the Four Seasons Resort Orlando and its Tranquilo Golf Club.
3. **The EPCOT area** contains EPCOT and its resort hotels, Disney's Hollywood Studios, the BoardWalk, ESPN Wide World of Sports, Pop Century Resort, Art of Animation Resort, Caribbean Beach Resort, and Riviera Resort.
4. **The Disney Springs area** includes Disney Springs; Typhoon Lagoon water park; Lake Buena Vista Golf Course; the Disney Springs Resort Area; and the Port Orleans, Saratoga Springs, and Old Key West resorts.
5. **The Animal Kingdom area** includes Disney's Animal Kingdom, Animal Kingdom Lodge & Villas, the All-Star Resorts, Coronado Springs Resort, and Blizzard Beach water park.

The following section covers how to get around Walt Disney World using the Disney transportation system. Tips for using non-Disney hotel shuttles and for driving yourself begin on page 346.

THE DISNEY TRANSPORTATION SYSTEM (DTS)

THE DISNEY TRANSPORTATION SYSTEM is large, diverse, and generally efficient, but it sometimes it gets overwhelmed, particularly at park opening and closing. If you could always be assured of getting on a bus, boat, monorail, or gondola at these critical times, we'd advise you to leave your car at home. In reality, delays are unavoidable when huge crowds want to go somewhere at once. In addition, some destinations are served directly, while many others require time-consuming transfers. Finally, it's sometimes difficult to figure out how Disney's various methods of transportation interconnect.

The DTS is a "hub and spoke" system. Hubs are located at the **Transportation and Ticket Center** (**TTC**), **Disney Springs,** and all four major **theme parks** (from about an hour before official opening time to 1 hour after closing). With some exceptions, direct service is available from Disney resorts to the major theme parks and Disney Springs, as well as between parks.

unofficial **TIP**
If a hotel offers boat or monorail service, its bus service will be limited—you'll have to transfer at a hub for many destinations.

If you're staying at a Magic Kingdom resort that's served by the monorail (the **Contemporary** and **Bay Lake Tower,** the **Grand Floridian Resort & Villas,** or the **Polynesian Village Resort & Villas** and its new **Island Tower**), you'll be able to commute efficiently to the Magic Kingdom. If you want to visit EPCOT, you must take the monorail to the TTC and transfer to the EPCOT monorail. (Guests at the Polynesian can eliminate the transfer by walking 5–10 minutes to the TTC and catching the direct monorail to EPCOT.) Direct buses will deliver you to Animal Kingdom or Hollywood Studios. **Wilderness Lodge** is another Magic Kingdom area resort, but it only offers boat service to Magic Kingdom. All other parks can be reached by direct bus link.

If you're staying at an EPCOT resort (**BoardWalk Inn & Villas, Dolphin, Swan, Swan Reserve, Yacht & Beach Club Resorts**), you can walk or take a boat to EPCOT's International Gateway entrance. You can also walk, take a boat, or ride the Skyliner to Hollywood Studios. Direct buses link the EPCOT resorts to the Magic Kingdom and Disney's Animal Kingdom, but there is no direct bus to EPCOT's main entrance or Disney's Hollywood Studios. Note that the Swan, Swan Reserve, and Dolphin use Mears Transportation, not Disney, for bus service—if you're headed to the Magic Kingdom, Mears will drop you off at the TTC, while Disney buses will drop you off at the park entrance. To get around this inconvenience, you can just walk over to the Yacht Club bus stop when you want to go to the Magic Kingdom.

Other Skyliner resorts (**Caribbean Beach, Pop Century, Art of Animation and Riviera Resort**) can access EPCOT and Hollywood Studios via Skyliner. Buses to those parks are generally offered only if the Skyliner is down or during very busy times of year.

Saratoga Springs, Port Orleans, Coronado Springs, Old Key West, Animal Kingdom Lodge & Villas, and the **All-Star Resorts** offer direct buses to all four theme parks. The rub is that you may have to walk a long way to bus stops or stop for more than half a dozen additional pickups before actually heading for the park(s). **Shades of Green** runs frequent shuttles from the resort to the TTC, where guests can transfer to their final destinations.

Hotels of the **Disney Springs Resort Area** (**DSRA**) provide shuttle service through an independent company. These shuttles are rated poorly by guests at these hotels—the service is substandard. Before you book a hotel, in this area, check its shuttle details and schedule.

Guests staying at **Fort Wilderness Resort & Campground** must use its internal buses or rented golf carts to reach boat landings or the bus stops at Settlement Depot and Reception Outpost. From these points, guests can travel directly by boat to the Magic Kingdom or by bus to other destinations. Other than going to the Magic Kingdom, the best way for Fort Wilderness guests to commute is in their own car.

Commuting Times by Car vs. the DTS

To help you assess your transportation options, we've developed a table comparing the approximate commuting times from the Disney resorts to various Disney World destinations, using the DTS or your own car (see pages 340–341). The table represents more than half a million data points collected and includes bus, monorail, and boat options. The Skyliner system has its own table (see page 344).

DISNEY TRANSPORTATION The times in the "Disney System" columns represent average-case and worst-case scenarios. For example, if you want to go from the All-Star Resorts to the Magic Kingdom, the table indicates the times as "33 (50)." The first number, 33, indicates how many minutes your commute will take on an average day. It assumes that buses arrive every 20 minutes (see "Walt Disney World Bus Service," page 339) that your average wait is half of that, that there are no major traffic delays, and that everything else is as usual. It represents the average time we observed during our research. For planning purposes, the number in parentheses (50) indicates the maximum trip time—the longest it should take for the next bus to show up, load, and deliver you to your destination. Use this number to plan for contingencies. (*Example:* The bus is pulling away as you arrive at the stop, and you must wait around 20 minutes for the next one. Once en route, the bus hits every red light on the way to the Magic Kingdom.)

Bus schedules are also adjusted based on demand and fuel costs. By far the biggest influence on your travel time between two points is the amount of time you have to wait for your bus to arrive. Once you hop on your bus, the travel time is pretty consistent—barring any unusual traffic problems—but your time waiting for the bus can vary greatly. Typically, buses are supposed to run every 20 minutes. The data indicates they run ever-so-slightly more often: about every 19 minutes. Also, the maximum bus travel time between any two destinations is regularly 50 minutes. And somewhat surprisingly, service at the Value and Moderate resorts is about the same as at Deluxe resorts.

Walt Disney World Bus Service

Each Disney bus has an illuminated panel above its windshield that flashes the bus's destination. Theme parks also have designated waiting areas for each Disney destination. To catch the bus to Old Key West Resort from Disney's Hollywood Studios, for example, go to the bus stop and wait in the area designated for passengers going to that resort.

continued on page 342

COMMUTING TIMES BY CAR VS. THE

Average MAXIMUM time in minutes from	to MAGIC KINGDOM		to EPCOT		to DHS	
	CAR	DTS	CAR	DTS	CAR	DTS
ALL-STAR RESORTS	37 (47)	33 (50)	18 (23)	27 (50)	16 (20)	29 (49)
ANIMAL KINGDOM	37 (48)	26 (44)	16 (17)	38 (49)	16 (17)	24 (34)
ANIMAL KINGDOM LODGE & VILLAS	39 (50)	32 (44)	19 (21)	32 (45)	18 (19)	34 (50)
ART OF ANIMATION RESORT	40 (51)	33 (49)	23 (28)	27 (50)	20 (24)	34 (50)
BEACH CLUB RESORT & VILLAS	36 (46)	32 (49)	16 (21)	29 (36*)	14 (18)	29 (41*)
BLIZZARD BEACH	36 (46)	28 (39)	18 (23)	—	18 (22)	39 (54)
BOARDWALK INN & VILLAS	36 (46)	30 (46)	16 (21)	29 (46*)	14 (18)	23 (49*)
CARIBBEAN BEACH AND RIVIERA	37 (47)	31 (49)	18 (23)	18-24 (12)	15 (19)	11-20 (7)
CONTEMPORARY/ BAY LAKE TOWER	—	—	21 (26)	36 (49)	23 (27)	31 (49)
CORONADO SPRINGS	37 (47)	39 (44)	18 (23)	39 (45)	16 (20)	31 (44)
DHS	36 (46)	25 (35)	19 (24)	25 (35)	—	—
DISNEY SPRINGS	Bus service only back to your Disney resort					
DISNEY SPRINGS RESORT AREA	41 (51)	69 (91)	21 (26)	47 (62)	20 (24)	45 (60)
DOLPHIN	35 (45)	33 (65)	15 (20)	16 (44*)	15 (19)	16 (42*)
EPCOT	36 (46)	26 (37)	—	—	19 (23)	21 (30)
FORT WILDERNESS	37 (47)	28 (50)	18 (23)	34 (51*)	19 (23)	34 (50)
GRAND FLORIDIAN RESORT & VILLAS	—	—	18 (23)	38 (50*)	20 (24)	33 (50)
MAGIC KINGDOM	—	—	26 (39)	33 (45)	22 (29)	24 (34)
OLD KEY WEST	36 (46)	29 (50)	18 (23)	30 (50)	18 (22)	30 (50)
POLYNESIAN VILLAGE	—	—	17 (22)	33 (43**)	19 (23)	31 (50)
POP CENTURY	40 (51)	32 (50)	23 (28)	31-45 (18)	20 (24)	22-35 (12)
PORT ORLEANS FRENCH QUARTER	37 (47)	32 (50)	19 (24)	29 (50)	19 (23)	32 (50)
PORT ORLEANS RIVERSIDE	38 (48)	34 (50)	20 (25)	29 (50)	20 (24)	32 (50)
RIVIERA	37 (47)	32 (50)	18 (23)	18 (10)	15 (19)	20-29 (11)
SARATOGA SPRINGS	38 (48)	28 (49)	18 (23)	31 (47)	20 (24)	31 (47)
SHADES OF GREEN	28 (36)	35 (49)	18 (23)	33 (45)	20 (24)	20 (28)
SWAN/SWAN RESERVE	35 (45)	24 (61)	15 (20)	18 (42*)	15 (19)	14 (33*)
TREEHOUSE VILLAS AT SARATOGA SPRINGS	37 (47)	28 (49)	18 (23)	31 (47)	19 (23)	31 (47)
TYPHOON LAGOON	37 (47)	41 (56)	18 (23)	51 (70)	15 (19)	62 (85)
WILDERNESS LODGE	—	24 (63)	20 (25)	27 (50)	22 (26)	30 (50)
YACHT CLUB	36 (46)	33 (65)	16 (21)	16 (40*)	14 (18)	15 (35*)

Note: Before 4 p.m., all transportation between the theme parks and Disney Springs requires a transfer at a nearby resort. After 4 p.m., buses run directly from the theme parks to Disney Springs. There are no buses from Disney Springs directly to the theme parks.

† Driving time vs. time on DTS. Driving times include time in your car, stops to pay tolls, time to park, and any transfers on Disney trams and monorails.

COMMUTING TIMES BY CAR VS. THE DTS

DISNEY TRANSPORTATION SYSTEM†

to ANIMAL KINGDOM		to TYPHOON LAGOON		to DISNEY SPRINGS		to BLIZZARD BEACH	
CAR	DTS	CAR	DTS	CAR	DTS	CAR	DTS
11 (12)	26 (49)	12 (13)	27 (63)	13 (14)	31 (50)	6 (7)	26 (46)
—	—	17 (19)	65 (83)	19 (21)	—	10 (13)	41 (50)
9 (10)	26 (50)	19 (21)	26 (67)	22 (24)	33 (50)	11 (14)	23 (50)
14 (16)	29 (50)	12 (14)	19 (59)	15 (16)	22 (49)	10 (12)	29 (50)
17 (18)	31 (49)	9 (10)	23 (59)	10 (11)	32 (50)	12 (13)	22 (60)
10 (13)	—	13 (14)	80 (103)	14 (15)	—	—	—
17 (18)	33 (50)	9 (10)	25 (59)	10 (11)	31 (49)	12 (13)	22 (58)
17 (18)	32 (50)	6 (7)	23 (59)	7 (8)	31 (40)	12 (13)	25 (61)
20 (21)	35 (50)	17 (18)	27 (63)	16 (17)	34 (49)	15 (16)	25 (62)
11 (12)	32 (49)	12 (13)	6 (54)	13 (14)	28 (49)	6 (7)	30 (46)
16 (17)	20 (30)	8 (9)	77 (99)	9 (10)	—	11 (12)	56 (71)
Bus service only back to your Disney resort							
21 (22)	48 (64)	9 (10)	26 (29)	6 (7)	—	16 (17)	66 (81)
16 (17)	36 (60)	10 (11)	21 (61)	11 (12)	25 (62)	11 (12)	22 (57)
16 (17)	33 (48)	12 (13)	50 (62)	13 (14)	—	11 (12)	51 (65)
29 (25)	35 (50)	10 (11)	26 (62)	11 (12)	33 (50)	19 (20)	30 (60)
18 (19)	34 (50)	15 (16)	26 (67)	16 (17)	33 (50)	13 (14)	24 (61)
17 (18)	45 (63)	23 (31)	59 (75)	27 (36)	—	12 (13)	61 (77)
19 (20)	28 (50)	8 (9)	20 (57)	9 (10)	32 (49)	14 (15)	20 (56)
17 (18)	32 (50)	14 (15)	25 (63)	15 (16)	32 (50)	12 (13)	18 (57)
14 (16)	30 (49)	12 (14)	23 (57)	15 (16)	32 (50)	10 (12)	20 (61)
19 (20)	28 (50)	9 (10)	20 (55)	10 (11)	29 (50)	14 (15)	23 (60)
20 (21)	30 (71)	10 (11)	19 (56)	11 (12)	31 (46)	15 (16)	24 (64)
15 (18)	29 (50)	5 (7)	24 (60)	7 (8)	28 (50)	10 (12)	25 (60)
21 (22)	28 (50)	9 (10)	23 (61)	6 (7)	36 (50)	16 (17)	24 (63)
18 (19)	22 (33)	15 (16)	59 (75)	18 (20)	57 (83)	13 (14)	50 (64)
16 (17)	35 (60)	10 (11)	21 (60)	11 (12)	24 (60)	11 (12)	21 (56)
17 (19)	28 (50)	9 (10)	22 (59)	6 (7)	36 (60)	13 (14)	24 (59)
20 (21)	28 (40)	—	—	8 (9)	—	15 (16)	55 (70)
20 (21)	32 (50)	17 (18)	28 (64)	18 (19)	33 (50)	15 (16)	24 (60)
17 (18)	31 (46)	8 (10)	24 (58)	10 (12)	31 (40)	12 (13)	21 (57)

* This hotel is within walking distance of EPCOT; time given is for boat transportation to the International Gateway (EPCOT's rear entrance).
** By foot to Transportation and Ticket Center and then by EPCOT monorail

continued from page 339

At the resorts, go to any bus stop and wait for the bus displaying your destination on the illuminated panel; the **My Disney Experience** app (see page 23) displays the approximate arrival time of the next bus to your destination. Directions to Disney destinations are available at check-in or at your resort's Guest Relations desk. Guest Relations can also answer questions about the transportation system.

Service from resorts to major theme parks is fairly direct. You may have intermediate stops, but you won't have to transfer. Service to the water parks and other Disney resorts almost always requires transfers or extra stops.

To travel between your Disney resort and **Blizzard Beach,** you must transfer at the Animal Kingdom. Traveling between your Disney resort and **Typhoon Lagoon** will probably also require a stop (and possibly a bus transfer) at Disney Springs; if you're unlucky, this round-trip journey could take 2–3 hours. Ask the staff at your resort if direct bus service to the water parks is available; if not, use Uber or Lyft.

unofficial **TIP**
If your Disney resort doesn't have direct bus service to the water parks, use Uber or Lyft instead.

The fastest way to commute among resorts by bus is to take a bus from your resort to one of the major theme parks and then transfer to a bus destined for your resort. This works, of course, only when the parks are open—actually, from 1 hour before the park opens for Early Theme Park Entry (ETPE) until 1 hour after closing. (Disney buses stop taking passengers *to* the theme parks when they close, but they'll take passengers *from* the parks for an hour afterward.) If the park is open late for Extended Evening Theme Park Hours, buses will continue to run for an hour after the end of that.

If the parks have already closed, then you'll have to transfer at **Disney Springs**—where Disney hopes you'll spend some extra cash during your "layover." If the theme park buses are running, though, you should head to the park closest to your resort and then transfer to the bus going to the resort you want to visit. Traffic is always worse around Disney Springs, which makes your overall trip longer.

Despite what Disney's official schedule says, bus service to the parks begins about 90 minutes before official park opening, which is 60 minutes before ETPE (that is, buses will start running around **7:30 a.m.** on days when ETPE is at 8:30 a.m. and official park opening is 9 a.m.). Buses to all four theme parks deliver you to the park entrance (except those from the Swan, Dolphin, and Swan Reserve, which deliver you to the TTC instead of the Magic Kingdom).

To be on time for ETPE, catch direct buses to the parks 60–90 minutes before official park opening. If you must transfer to reach your park, such as at Fort Wilderness, allow an additional 15–20 minutes.

Although bus service seems to have gotten more regular and predictable in the past couple of years, a reader who stayed at Port Orleans reports:

The DTS was wildly erratic, but we were lucky more often than not. For every time we had to wait half an hour at the bus stop, there were two or three times with no wait at all.

Rather than waiting at the bus stop, pull up upcoming bus arrivals in the MDE app while you're still in your room, then head to the stop a few minutes before your bus gets there.

If you're staying at a resort with multiple bus stops, the bus may be full or standing room only before it gets to your stop. It may be worth it to walk to the "first" bus pickup points for these resorts:

- **CARIBBEAN BEACH** Martinique
- **CORONADO SPRINGS** Gran Destino
- **OLD KEY WEST** Peninsular Road
- **PORT ORLEANS RIVERSIDE** West Depot
- **SARATOGA SPRINGS** The Grandstand

Walt Disney World Monorail Service

Picture the monorail system as three loops, with the TTC as the central hub. **Loop A** is an express route that runs counterclockwise, connecting the Magic Kingdom with the TTC. **Loop B** runs clockwise alongside Loop A, making all stops, with service to (in order) the TTC, Polynesian Village & Villas, Grand Floridian Resort & Villas, the Magic Kingdom, Contemporary Resort and Bay Lake Tower, and back to the TTC. The long **Loop C** dips southeast, connecting the TTC with EPCOT.

Loop B—the resort loop—usually starts running an hour or so before official park opening. If you're staying at one of these resorts, board the monorail at these times for an 8:30 a.m. Early Entry day:

- **FROM CONTEMPORARY RESORT AND BAY LAKE TOWER** 7:45–8 a.m.
- **FROM POLYNESIAN VILLAGE & VILLAS** 7:50–8:05 a.m.
- **FROM GRAND FLORIDIAN RESORT & VILLAS** 8–8:10 a.m.

If you're a day guest, monorail service from the TTC usually starts around 8 a.m. when Early Entry starts at 8:30. For an earlier or less crowded ride, consider walking from the TTC to the Polynesian Village Resort and boarding there instead.

If you have a Park Hopper ticket, you might think that means you can flit among the parks, but it's not that simple. For example, you can't go directly from the Magic Kingdom to EPCOT—you must catch the express monorail (Loop A) from the Magic Kingdom to the TTC and then transfer to the EPCOT monorail (Loop C). When lines are short, this trip typically takes 30–40 minutes. However, if you're leaving the Magic Kingdom in the late afternoon (a common time for EPCOT dinner plans), you may encounter long lines. It's not unusual to have a total travel time of up to an hour to reach EPCOT.

Disney may change the monorail's operating hours to allow for daytime inspection of the track and vehicles. Rain and lightning, which happen frequently in Orlando, will also stop the monorails, as this Michigan reader found out:

> *It would have helped to know that monorails shut down during thunderstorms and lightning. We got stuck at EPCOT trying to get back to our Magic Kingdom hotel at the end of the night due to a thunderstorm. There were thousands of people drenched, with nowhere to go, for hours. Had we known there was no bus service back, we would not have gambled with even a slight chance of rain.*

When the monorail is closed, Disney is supposed to provide bus or boat transportation to get you where you're going. But as the reader

WALT DISNEY WORLD BOAT ROUTES (ROUND-TRIP)
Magic Kingdom → Fort Wilderness → Magic Kingdom
Magic Kingdom → Grand Floridian Resort & Villas → Polynesian Village → Magic Kingdom
Fort Wilderness Campground → Wilderness Lodge → Contemporary Resort → Fort Wilderness *Note:* Walk or take the monorail from the Contemporary to the Magic Kingdom.
EPCOT → Boardwalk Inn & Villas → Beach Club → Yacht Club → Swan → Dolphin → EPCOT
Disney's Hollywood Studios → Boardwalk Inn & Villas → Beach Club Resort & Villas → Yacht Club → Swan → Dolphin → Disney's Hollywood Studios
Disney Springs → Saratoga Springs → Old Key West → Disney Springs
Disney Springs → Port Orleans French Quarter → Port Orleans Riverside → Disney Springs

above notes, that doesn't always happen. In that case, your best bet is a ride-sharing app or taxi. If you're going to book an expensive monorail resort, first call the resort and ask about monorail maintenance or construction that might affect its operating hours during your stay.

Walt Disney World Boat Service

Boats are a popular transportation option between some theme parks and resorts, as a reader from Iowa writes:

We stayed at Port Orleans French Quarter in December and took the ferry to Disney Springs several times. We also did a self-guided resort Christmas-decorations tour and had fun taking different boats around the Magic Kingdom and EPCOT resorts. These ferries were a much more pleasant option than buses for most legs of that tour.

The table above shows the routes served by boats. Note that most routes stop at several resorts and service may be suspended during thunderstorms or because of low water levels. Wheelchairs and scooters are permitted; strollers must be folded before you board and stowed while you're on the boat. Most routes run from about 45 minutes before park opening to 45 minutes after park closing.

Disney Skyliner

This elevated gondola connects the **Art of Animation** (**AOA**), **Pop Century, Caribbean Beach,** and **Riviera Resorts** with **Disney's Hollywood Studios** and **EPCOT's International Gateway.** The Skyliner routes are shown on our Walt Disney World overview map on pages 12–13 and on the maps for the resorts listed above (see Part 5). Each gondola holds about 10 guests, and unless the line is short you'll likely be sharing your cabin with another group. **Caribbean Beach Resort** serves as the hub for all Skyliner routes.

An initial concern with the Skyliner was that the gondolas lacked air-conditioning. However, their 17-mph speed and excellent ventilation keep passengers cool even on the hottest days.

One minor inconvenience is that all riders have to get off the gondolas at the Caribbean Beach hub, then transfer to another line to

SKYLINER TRAVEL TIMES (IN MINUTES)					
	POP CENTURY/ ART OF ANIMATION	CARIBBEAN BEACH	EPCOT	HOLLYWOOD STUDIOS	RIVIERA RESORT
POP CENTURY/ ART OF ANIMATION	–	9-18 (4)	31-45 (18)	22-35 (12)	16-32 (10)
CARIBBEAN BEACH RESORT	9-18 (4)	–	18-24 (12)	11-20 (7)	7-12 (4)
EPCOT	31-45 (18)	18-24 (12)	–	35-44 (19)	18 (10)
HOLLYWOOD STUDIOS	22-35 (12)	11-20 (7)	35-44 (19)	–	20-29 (11)
RIVIERA RESORT	16-32 (10)	7-12 (4)	18 (10)	20-29 (11)	–

reach their final destination. The only direct routes to theme parks are from Caribbean Beach to Hollywood Studios (and back) or Riviera to EPCOT (and back). The transfer process should be manageable for anyone and familiar if you've changed trains in a city subway system.

The table above shows typical point-to-point travel times between any two Skyliner stations. The first pair of numbers is the average trip time assuming normal crowds, and the number in parentheses is the trip time assuming no crowds.

For example, the time to get from the Pop Century/AOA station to EPCOT reads "31–45 (18)." Thus, you should expect the trip to EPCOT to take 31–45 minutes from the time you arrive at the Pop/AOA station. The actual time in transit will be about 18 minutes, and the rest of the time will be spent in line. During off-peak hours and seasons, your times could be much shorter.

RIDE-SHARING SERVICES

BOTH LYFT AND UBER are cheaper than taxis when commuting within the World. For example, on a recent trip from the Contemporary to Art of Animation—directly after fireworks at the Magic Kingdom that were at capacity—we paid $12 (plus tip) for two adults and two children. Lyft prices tend to run a little higher than Uber, but you'll need to have Lyft downloaded if you want to try a Minnie Van (see below) during your stay.

MINNIE VANS Disney's own ride-sharing service operates through the Lyft app. Driven by Disney cast members, these red-and-white polka-dot vehicles provide service exclusively within Walt Disney World and cannot be used to travel off-property.

Minnie Vans are certainly stylish, and interactions with the drivers are great. But they cost about three times as much as a standard Lyft ride. Availability can also be an issue due to the limited number of vehicles. For instance, on a recent visit to Fort Wilderness, Becky's family was unable to get a Minnie Van on three separate attempts to reach the Magic Kingdom on a rainy morning.

However, when it works, a Minnie Van is a great option, especially for trips to the Magic Kingdom, as it drops you off closer to the entrance than any other vehicle service.

DRIVING TO AND AROUND WALT DISNEY WORLD

THE VAST MAJORITY of *Unofficial Guide* readers rely on GPS to get around Orlando, whether through a smartphone app, an in-car system, or a dedicated device. Most modern GPS systems and apps recognize location names like Magic Kingdom or Pop Century, making navigation straightforward. If you have an older unit or are unsure about an address, such as for grocery delivery or a specific destination, use the addresses in the table below for the theme parks, water parks, and Disney Springs and the addresses in Part 5 for resorts.

If you're driving without GPS, print out directions to Walt Disney World from **Google Maps** (maps.google.com) before you leave home; then, once you're in Orlando, use the overview maps in Part 1 (see pages 10–13) and in this chapter to find your way around. For an even more low-tech approach, the rental-car companies have free maps available (we like **Alamo Rent a Car**'s Walt Disney World road map, also available at the front desk or concierge desk of any Disney resort). Once you're inside the World, Disney's road signs are generally clear and easy to follow even without a map.

GPS Names and Addresses for the Theme Parks

Google Maps gives correct directions for the addresses and/or names shown in the table below. Disney's road signs also direct you to parking as you get close. If you ever get lost, follow the signs to any theme park parking lot or pull into the nearest Disney resort and ask for directions.

Driving to and from the Theme Parks

1. PARKING LOT LOCATIONS The **Animal Kingdom, EPCOT,** and **DHS** lots are adjacent to each park's entrance; the **Magic Kingdom** lot is adjacent to the TTC. From the TTC, take a ferry or monorail to the park's entrance. You can usually see if the line for the ferry or the monorail is shorter.

THEME PARK GPS NAMES AND ADDRESSES		
DESTINATION PARKING LOT	**NAME TO LOOK FOR IN GPS**	**ADDRESS**
MAGIC KINGDOM	"Magic Kingdom Park" or "Magic Kingdom Toll Plaza" works better than the address.	3450 World Dr. Winter Garden, FL 34787
EPCOT	"EPCOT" (but not "EPCOT Parking Lot")	200 EPCOT Center Dr. Lake Buena Vista, FL 32830
ANIMAL KINGDOM	"Animal Kingdom" or "Disney's Animal Kingdom Theme Park"	2901 Osceola Pkwy. Lake Buena Vista, FL 32380
DHS	Try "Disney's Hollywood Studios-South Studio Drive" before using the address.	351 S. Studio Dr. Lake Buena Vista, FL 32830
BLIZZARD BEACH	"Blizzard Beach" should get you close, but the address works better.	1534 Blizzard Beach Dr. Lake Buena Vista, FL 32830
TYPHOON LAGOON	"Typhoon Lagoon" should work better than the address.	1145 E. Buena Vista Dr. Lake Buena Vista, FL 32830
DISNEY SPRINGS	"Disney Springs" should give a list of all parking lots to choose from.	1530 E. Buena Vista Dr. Lake Buena Vista, FL 32830

2. PAYING TO PARK Disney resort guests and Annual Pass holders park free; all others pay. If you paid to park and you move your car later that day, show your receipt and you won't have to pay again at the new lot. The daily parking rate for motorcycles and standard cars is $30; a preferred-parking option, with spots closer to the park entrances, costs $45–$55 per day.

3. REMEMBERING WHERE YOUR CAR IS PARKED Jot down, text, or take a picture of the section and row where you've parked. If you're driving a rental, note the make, model, and license plate number. You can also save the location in the MDE app, which has a new section for this purpose.

4. FACTORING IN TIME TO PARK AND GET TO THE PARK ENTRANCE At the **Magic Kingdom,** it'll take 35–50 minutes to get from the parking gate to the TTC; go through the security screening; board a monorail, ferry, or bus; and reach the park entrance. At **EPCOT, Hollywood Studios,** and **Animal Kingdom,** allow about 15–20 minutes to pay, park, walk, or ride to the entrance and get through the security screening.

5. COMMUTING FROM PARK TO PARK Using Disney transportation, allow 45–60 minutes one-way, entrance to entrance. If you plan to park-hop, you could leave your car in the lot of the park where you'll finish the day and use Disney transportation throughout the day.

6. LEAVING THE PARK AT THE END OF THE DAY If you stay at a park until closing, expect the parking-lot trams, monorails, Skyliner, and ferries to be mobbed. If the wait for a tram looks too long, walk to your car or walk to the first stop on the tram route and wait there for a tram. When someone gets off, you can get on.

7. DINNER AND A QUICK EXIT One way to beat closing crowds in the Magic Kingdom is to arrange reservations for dinner at the **Contemporary Resort.** When you leave the Magic Kingdom for dinner, move your car from the TTC lot to the Contemporary lot. After dinner, walk (8–10 minutes) or take the monorail back to the Magic Kingdom. When the park closes and everyone else is fighting to board the monorail or ferry, you can stroll back to the Contemporary, claim your car, and be on your way. Use the same strategy in EPCOT by arranging a reservation at an EPCOT resort. When the park closes after the fireworks, exit via the International Gateway and walk to the resort where you parked.

8. CAR TROUBLE Parking lots have security patrols; if you have a dead battery or minor automotive problem, they can help. For more-serious trouble, go to the **Car Care Center** (☎ 407-824-0976), near the Magic Kingdom parking lot. Prices for most services are comparable to those you might find in your hometown. The facility stays busy, so expect to leave your car unless the fix is simple. Hours are Monday–Friday, 8 a.m.–6 p.m.; Saturday, 8 a.m.–5 p.m.; and Sunday, 9 a.m.–5 p.m.

9. SCORING A GREAT PARKING SPOT If you arrive at a park after noon or move your car from park to park, check for available parking spaces close to the park entrance; these will have been vacated by early risers who've already left. Instead of following signs or being directed by staff to a distant space, drive straight to the front and start hunting, or use the approach of this Pennsylvania couple:

> *After leaving EPCOT for lunch, we returned to find a fullish parking lot. We were unhappy because we had left a third-row parking spot. My husband told the attendant that we had left just an hour ago and that there were lots of spaces up front. Without a word of protest, he waved us to the front and we got our same spot back!*

Speeders Beware

Orange County law enforcement's jurisdiction extends to Disney World's roads. Many readers have written to us surprised after receiving citations, assuming they'd be let off with a warning at worst. Remember, it's a speed limit, not a speed suggestion—even when other cars are zipping around.

Sneak Routes

If you have a GPS that will route you around traffic delays, use that. If not, try these sneak routes we've discovered:

US 192 (IRLO BRONSON MEMORIAL HIGHWAY) Traffic on US 192 runs east–west south of Walt Disney World. The road is divided into east and west sections—west is from I-4 to Kissimmee, and east is from I-4 east to US 27. Traffic is bad both ways. If your hotel is along the west section, you can bypass most of the traffic by driving north on **International Drive** or **Poinciana Boulevard** (a right turn if you're driving on US 192 in the direction of I-4) and accessing **Osceola Parkway,** a four-lane toll road that dead-ends in Disney World. If your hotel is on the east side, take US 192 to **Sherberth Road** at mile marker 5 and turn north to enter the World near Animal Kingdom.

DISNEY SPRINGS The 3-mile stretch of **Buena Vista Drive** from Coronado Springs Resort to Disney Springs has 15 traffic signals—about one every 1,000 feet—making it a major traffic bottleneck from late afternoon through late evening. And it's not just around Disney Springs: Buena Vista Drive is one of Walt Disney World's most important roads, connecting the hotels of the Disney Springs Resort Area (DSRA), EPCOT, Disney's Hollywood Studios, the Magic Kingdom, Disney's Animal Kingdom, and Typhoon Lagoon.

The good news is that if you're coming by car from I-4 or on foot from the DSRA, it's easy to get to Disney Springs. Westbound **I-4** offers three exits to Disney Springs, including a direct exit to its parking garages—take **Exit 67** for EPCOT/Disney Springs. Guests staying at a DSRA hotel will find convenient pedestrian bridges linking Disney Springs to Hotel Plaza Boulevard and Buena Vista Drive.

Coming from the theme parks, you can bypass the mess by taking **I-4** or by looping around on **Bonnet Creek Parkway** and **Disney Vacation Club Way.** If you're going back to an EPCOT or Magic Kingdom resort from Disney Springs, it may be faster to take I-4 West and follow the signs back to Disney property.

I-4 Expect heavy traffic and possible westbound delays from about 7 to 9:30 a.m.; eastbound toward Orlando, expect heavy traffic from 4 to 7 p.m. If you want to avoid I-4 altogether, check out the I-4 Sneak Routes map, on page 351.

HOW TO TRAVEL AROUND THE WORLD 349

US 192–Kissimmee Resort Area Sneak Routes

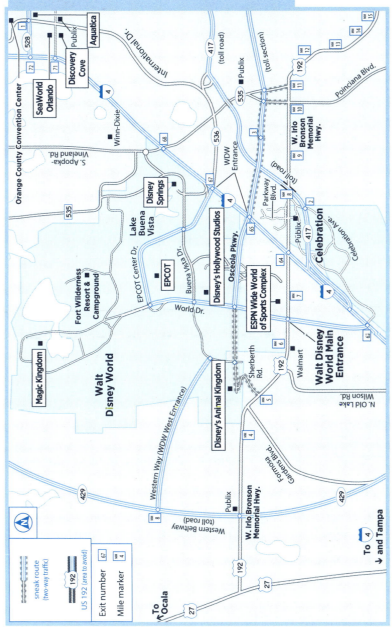

Disney Springs Sneak Routes

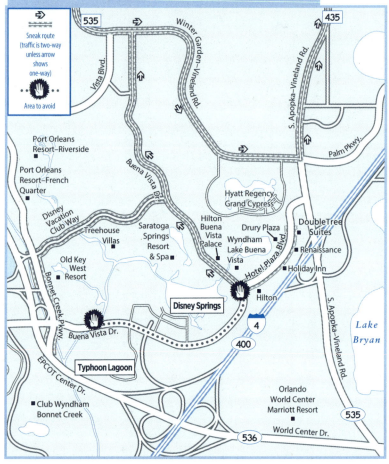

INTERNATIONAL DRIVE The I-Drive area is by far the most difficult to navigate without long traffic delays. Most hotels on I-Drive are between **Kirkman Road** to the north and **FL 417 (Central Florida GreeneWay)** to the south. Between Kirkman Road and FL 417, three major roads cross I-Drive: From north to south on I-Drive (in the direction of Disney World), the first is **Universal Boulevard**. Next is **Sand Lake Road (FL 482)**, pretty squarely in the middle of the hotel district. Finally, the **Beachline Expressway (FL 528)** connects I-4 and the airport.

The southern third of I-Drive can be accessed via **Central Florida Parkway,** which connects I-4 and Palm Parkway with the SeaWorld area of I-Drive, and by **Daryl Carter Parkway,** which connects Palm Parkway with the Orlando Vineland Premium Outlets.

The main goal here is to access I-4 westbound without getting on Sand Lake Road. If your hotel is north of Sand Lake, access **Kirkman Road** by going north on I-Drive (in the opposite direction of the heaviest traffic) to Kirkman Road and turning left, or by cutting over

HOW TO TRAVEL AROUND THE WORLD 351

I-4 Sneak Routes

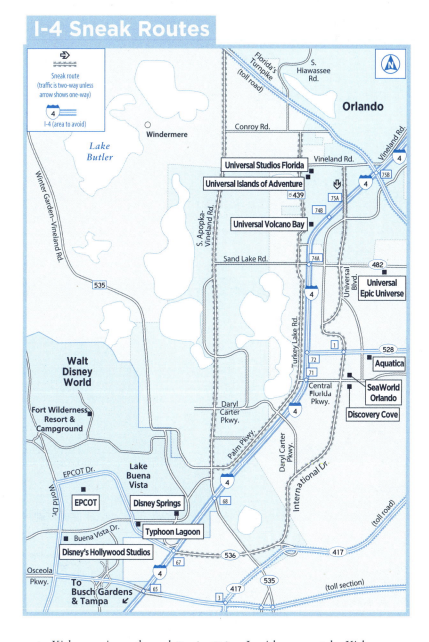

to Kirkman via eastbound **Carrier Drive.** In either case, take Kirkman north over I-4 and make a U-turn at the first traffic signal (at the entrance to Universal Orlando). This puts you directly onto a westbound I-4 ramp. You can also go north on **Universal Boulevard,** which parallels I-Drive to the east; after you cross I-4 onto Universal property, stay left and follow the signs through two left turns to I-4. The signs are small, so stay alert.

I-Drive Area Sneak Routes

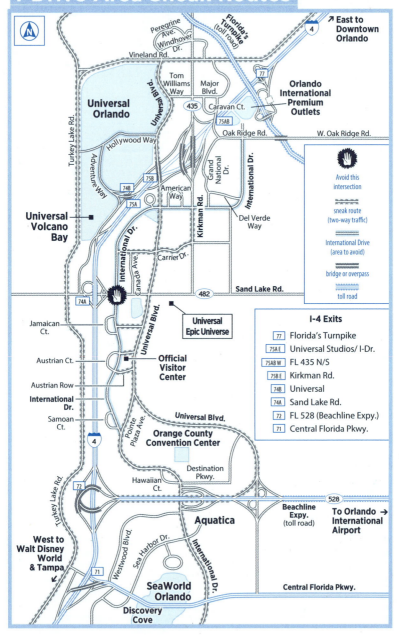

If your hotel is south of Sand Lake Road but north of Austrian Court, use **Austrian Row** to cut over to Universal Boulevard. Turn right (south) on Universal and continue until you intersect the **Beachline Expressway (FL 528)**; then take the Beachline west to I-4 (no toll).

TAKING A SHUTTLE BUS FROM YOUR OFF-SITE HOTEL

MANY INDEPENDENT HOTELS near Disney World provide trams and buses. They're fairly hassle-free, depositing you near theme park entrances and saving you parking fees. The problem is that they might not get you there as early as you desire (a critical consideration if you take our touring advice) or be available quickly when you wish to return to your lodging. Some shuttles go directly to Walt Disney World, while others stop at other hotels en route. This can be a problem if your hotel is the second or third stop on the route. During periods of high demand, buses frequently fill up at the first stop, leaving little or no room for passengers at subsequent stops. Before booking, it's smart to ask how many hotels are on the route and the sequence of the stops.

The different hotels are often so close together that you can easily walk to the first hotel on the route and board there. Similarly, if there's a large hotel nearby, it might have its own bus service that's more efficient; you can use that instead of the service provided by your hotel. Most out-of-the-World shuttles work on a fixed schedule instead of arriving and departing somewhat randomly like the Disney buses do. Knowing exactly when a bus will depart makes it easier to plan your day.

A family from Washington shared their experience:

We stayed at a hotel off-site and it was fine, but I think next time we'll stay in the World. The shuttles weren't all that convenient or frequent, so we ended up taking taxis more than we anticipated.

At park closing or during a hard rain, more people will be waiting for the shuttle than it can hold, and some will be left behind. Most shuttles return for stranded guests, but those guests might have to wait 20 minutes to over an hour.

If you're depending on non-Disney shuttles, leave the park at least 45 minutes before closing. If you stay until closing and don't want the hassle of the shuttle, take Uber or Lyft. If you're leaving the Magic Kingdom at closing, it's easier to walk or take the monorail to a hotel and hail a ride from there rather than at the TTC.

unofficial **TIP**
If you want to go from resort to resort or almost anywhere else, you'll have to transfer at a bus hub.

DEPARTING FROM ORLANDO INTERNATIONAL AIRPORT (MCO)

IF YOU'RE USING **Mears Connect** (see page 329), your bus will depart your hotel 3–4 hours before your flight, depending on how busy the airport is expected to be.

DRIVING Plan on leaving for the airport 2–3 hours before your flight, depending on whether you have to return a rental car, the route you take, and whether you have TSA PreCheck for security lines.

It takes about 35 minutes and around $3 in small bills and quarters to drive from Walt Disney World to MCO along the FL 417 or FL 528 toll roads. The same trip on I-4, FL 482 East, and Jeff Fuqua Boulevard is free but averages 50–60 minutes or even longer with traffic.

If you're returning a rental car, allow an extra 10 minutes to complete that process for on-site car rental companies; allow an extra 60 minutes to return a car to an off-site company and catch the airport shuttle to the terminal.

MCO handled more than 57 million passengers in 2024. It's not unusual to see the security-checkpoint lines snaking out of the terminal and into the main shopping corridor and food court, or for baggage drop-off areas to be an unmanageable tangle of humanity. Many passengers have reported missing their flight even when they arrived at the airport 90 minutes before departure. System improvements have alleviated some of the congestion. Most waits to clear security now average 20 minutes or less, compared with 55 minutes or longer before the improvements.

Waits in the **TSA PreCheck** lines are almost always 5 minutes or less. If you fly frequently, PreCheck (tsa.gov/precheck) is good for five years and costs $78 per person. We don't fly without it, and it's especially helpful at MCO.

ELECTRIC-VEHICLE CHARGING

CHARGING STATIONS are not incredibly easy to find or use within the World, but they do exist.

- **ANIMAL KINGDOM PARKING LOT (4 spots)** All located in medical parking. Ask an attendant if spaces are open.
- **CORONADO SPRINGS RESORT (6 spots)** In the parking lot adjacent to Gran Destino Tower
- **DISNEY'S FORT WILDERNESS RESORT** Campsites have 110V outlets plus 30-amp RV outlets
- **DISNEY'S HOLLYWOOD STUDIOS PARKING LOT (4 spots)** At the front of the Mickey lot
- **DISNEY'S RIVIERA RESORT (2 spots)** West parking lot
- **DISNEY SPRINGS GRAPEFRUIT GARAGE (3 spots)** Level 3
- **DISNEY SPRINGS LIME GARAGE (3 spots)** Top level
- **DISNEY SPRINGS ORANGE GARAGE (3 spots)** Level 5
- **DISNEY SPRINGS WATERMELON LOT (4 spots)** Near Cirque du Soleil
- **DISNEY'S WILDERNESS LODGE (2 spots)** Halfway down the first row, near the taxi stand
- **EPCOT PARKING LOT (4 spots)** At the front of the Journey lot
- **SHADES OF GREEN (1 generic charger plus 2 Tesla Destination Chargers)** Valet parking only
- **TRANSPORTATION AND TICKET CENTER (5 spots)** Four spaces at the front of the Zurg lot and 1 in medical parking

Check **PlugShare** (plugshare.com) for the locations of other chargers near Walt Disney World.

PART 10

BARE NECESSITIES

KEY QUESTIONS ANSWERED IN THIS CHAPTER

- Where can I charge my phone in the parks? *(page 356)*
- Where can I get raingear? *(page 356)*
- Where can I get medical attention or prescription refills? *(page 358)*
- How do I send comments or feedback to Disney? *(page 360)*
- How do I buy the photos taken of me and my family? *(page 360)*

MONEY, *Etc.*

CREDIT CARDS, MOBILE PAYMENTS, AND DISNEY GIFT CARDS

CREDIT CARDS ACCEPTED throughout Disney World are **American Express, Diners Club, Discover, Japan Credit Bureau, MasterCard,** and **Visa.** Most shops and restaurants also accept **Apple Pay** and **Google Pay.** However, some do not, so it's wise to carry a backup payment method. **Disney Gift Cards** can be used at most Disney-owned stores and restaurants and for recreational activities, tickets, and parking (visit disney giftcard.com).

If you're staying at a Disney-owned resort, a **MagicBand** or Key to the World (KTTW) Card (see page 73) or your room key can be linked to the credit card you'll put on file for incidental hotel charges. This lets you use your MagicBand, KTTW Card, or room key as you would a credit card at most Disney-owned stores and restaurants on-property. This is useful if you're covering the expenses of others in your group, such as teens or young adults who don't have their own credit cards or don't want to carry cash.

BANKING SERVICES

AT THE THEME PARKS, banking services are limited to ATMs, which are marked on park maps and are plentiful throughout Walt Disney World. You'll also find ATMs at all Disney resorts and throughout Disney Springs. All ATMs are provided by Chase.

CURRENCY EXCHANGE

YOU CAN EXCHANGE FOREIGN CURRENCY at **Guest Relations** in each theme park and at the **Welcome Center** at Disney Springs. (See the "Services" sidebars and park maps in Parts 11–14 and the Disney Springs map in Part 17 for locations.) All Disney resorts can do currency exchange at their front desks as well.

IN-PARK ISSUES

CELL PHONES

BRING YOUR CHARGING CABLE and an external battery pack to the parks. You will likely use your phone a lot in the parks, for everything from finding your way around to taking pictures, checking wait times, using mobile ordering, and making ride reservations. You'll probably want to increase your screen's brightness, too, for easier reading in the glaring Florida sun. All of that will drain your battery faster than normal. We're fans of **Anker** batteries as an external backup, but **FuelRods** are also easy to use and exchange in the parks. The table below shows where you can charge your phone in the parks.

Keep in mind that Wi-Fi in the parks can get overwhelmed on busy days, making it harder to check wait times, make ride reservations, and join virtual queues (if offered). And cell service is often weak or nonexistent inside large show buildings. A Georgia woman confirms:

> *I found the Wi-Fi horrible in all the parks. Dropped out continually, drained my battery, and wasn't strong enough to run Disney's own app. Very disappointing.*

CHARGING LOCATIONS IN THE THEME PARKS
MAGIC KINGDOM At the tent near the exit of **Pete's Silly Sideshow** and in the courtyard outside of the *Tangled* **restrooms.** Another sneaky option with plenty of outlets is the shared dining room between **Tortuga Tavern** and **Pecos Bill.** The second floor at **Columbia Harbour House** has outlets too.
EPCOT In **Connections Café and Eatery,** the longer white tables have wireless charging spots. Several seating areas in **World Celebration Gardens** have charging stations with multiple ports. You can also find outlets in the seating areas by the exit of **Soarin'.**
ANIMAL KINGDOM Your options are slim here, but you can find a few outlets or charging stations near the seating area at **Flame Tree Barbecue** or in **Nomad Lounge.**
DISNEY'S HOLLYWOOD STUDIOS At the exit from **The Twilight Zone Tower of Terror** or near the Djarik table in the **Galaxy's Edge** marketplace. If you want to get away from the crowds, head to **Star Wars Launch Bay** and find an outlet there.

RAIN

RAIN IS INEVITABLE in Orlando. If it doesn't rain during your vacation, you are one of a lucky few. It serves you well to prepare for rain because you absolutely should go to the parks even in bad weather. Not only are the crowds lighter, but most of the attractions and waiting areas are also covered, and rain showers, especially during warmer months, are short. Because most people will get scared back to their resorts, lines will be shorter during rainy periods.

Ponchos and umbrellas both cost about $13 in the parks. Ponchos sold at Walt Disney World are made of semi-opaque clear plastic, which makes it tricky to pick out someone in your party on a rainy day. You can buy less expensive and more colorful ponchos to bring with you to help set your family apart in a plastic-covered sea of humanity. And you should pack an umbrella that is rated well for wind and rain, rather than buying one in the parks. The umbrella Becky always uses is a Repel windproof umbrella. It consistently serves her well and has endured several years of frequent use.

Our friends over at the *Dis-List Podcast* share their top three ways of dealing with rain at Disney:

1. Bring your own ponchos or rain jackets.
2. Bring extra footwear just for walking in the rain, like Crocs or slides.
3. Avoid it all together. Rope-drop and leave before the afternoon rains come, or sleep in and show up later to enjoy a cooler, less crowded park after the rain.

A park pro from Kentucky recommends a good rainy-day spot:

When it rains at EPCOT, head to The Land Pavilion to wait it out. It has food, drinks, plenty of seating, and three attractions. We were there for 2–3 hours during one of those monsoons that leave 6 inches of water on the walkways. We sat there with beer and food, and we could watch the kids enter and exit the ride queues.

HEAT

HEAT AND HUMIDITY ARE PAR FOR THE COURSE in Orlando—even more than rain. I can't count the number of times I've seen medical evacuations from the park in July, August, and September because visitors aren't prepared for the heat or dehydration. *Don't let that be you.*

Temperatures and humidity are both high in Florida for about 10 months of the year and are extremely high for about 4 of those months. Don't take the weather lightly because it will affect your touring day and your trip as a whole. Our normal recommendations about taking full days off during a weeklong trip or midday breaks every day still apply, but you'll want to ramp up your preparation and strategy on the hottest days.

PLACES TO ESCAPE THE RAIN OR HEAT

The following indoor attractions have a longer duration, whether because of their indoor queues or the ride itself. Attractions with asterisks (*) have outdoor queues, so you'll need to decide how long you're willing to wait outside to take advantage of the indoor area.

THE MAGIC KINGDOM • *Country Bear Musical Jamboree* • It's a Small World • *Mickey's PhilharMagic* • Monsters, Inc. Laugh Floor • Pirates of the Caribbean • Space Mountain • Walt Disney's Carousel of Progress • Walt Disney's Enchanted Tiki Room

EPCOT • Frozen Ever After (some outdoor queue overflow) • Guardians of the Galaxy: Cosmic Rewind • Living with the Land • Mission: Space • Remy's Ratatouille Adventure (some outdoor queue overflow) • The Seas Main Tanks and Exhibits • Soarin' Around the World • Spaceship Earth*

ANIMAL KINGDOM • Avatar Flight of Passage (some outdoor queue overflow) • *Festival of the Lion King* • Finding Nemo: The Big Blue . . . and Beyond! • Na'vi River Journey*

DISNEY'S HOLLYWOOD STUDIOS • *For the First Time in Forever: A Frozen Sing-Along Celebration* • Disney Junior Play and Dance! • Millennium Falcon: Smugglers Run • Star Tours—The Adventures Continue • Star Wars: Rise of the Resistance (some outdoor queue overflow) • The Twilight Zone Tower of Terror*

If the high temperature is 85°F or higher, make it a point to sprinkle in indoor attractions or long shows throughout the day. Place more of an emphasis on doing indoor meals or snacks. You can even plan ahead so that your long walks through the park go through as many air-conditioned buildings as possible (shops along Main Street in the Magic Kingdom, as well as the front of the park and Sunset Boulevard in Hollywood Studios are especially good for this).

Above all, hydrate, hydrate, hydrate. All counter-service and table-service restaurants will give you free ice water, but you should also pack water bottles (plural) in your park bag for the day. You'll be sweating more than you'd think is humanly possible, so consider packing some electrolyte powder (such as Liquid IV) to mix into that ice water once or twice a day.

Finally, be sure to pack neck fans or handheld fans to use in the park. Any air movement will feel glorious and can make the difference between powering through in the park or collapsing in a heap.

LOST AND FOUND

IF YOU LOSE (OR FIND) something in one of the theme parks, go to **Guest Relations.** See the "Services" sidebar and park map in each theme park chapter (Parts 11–14) for locations. If you discover that you've lost something 24 hours or more after you've left the parks, call ☎ 407-824-4245. The central Lost and Found is on the east side of the Transportation and Ticket Center. You can also report lost items at disneyworld.com/lostandfound.

It's rare for readers to send us tips about Lost and Found, but a mom from Indiana sent one:

> *If you lose something on a ride and it has medication in it, Disney cast members will shut down the ride for 45 seconds to try to retrieve it. If they can't find it or it didn't contain meds, you have to come back to Lost and Found for it at the end of the day.*

LOST MAGICBANDS AND TICKETS Duplicates can be made, usually at no cost, at Guest Relations at any theme park or resort. A replacement fee may be charged, depending on your situation.

LOST CARS Don't forget where you parked—snap a picture with your smartphone or camera or save the location in the MDE app, which has a new section for this purpose.

MEDICAL MATTERS

HEADACHE RELIEF Over-the-counter medications and other sundries are sold at the **Emporium** on Main Street, U.S.A., in the Magic Kingdom (behind the counter—you have to ask); at most retail shops in EPCOT's Future World and World Showcase, Disney's Hollywood Studios, and Disney's Animal Kingdom; and at each Disney resort's gift shop.

ILLNESSES REQUIRING MEDICAL ATTENTION For the locations of the **First Aid** centers in the theme parks, see the "Services" sidebar and park map in each theme park chapter (Parts 11–14). Guests who use First Aid are generally very positive about it. This North Carolina reader's experience is representative:

We visited First Aid a time or two in the parks (my wife needed her blood pressure checked because she was worried about the heat and her pregnancy). We found trained medical staff, no wait, and all the friendliness and knowledge you would expect from Disney.

Off-property, there's an **Advent Health Centra Care** walk-in clinic at 12500 S. Apopka–Vineland Road (☎ 407-934-CARE [2273]; open 24 hours), as well as two other locations near WDW (see page 38).

A North Carolina family had a good experience at **Buena Vista Urgent Care** (8200 World Center Drive, Suite D; ☎ 407-465-1110):

We started day one needing medical care for our son, who has asthma and had developed croup. We found great care at Buena Vista Urgent Care. We waited 20 minutes and then were off to the parks.

The Medical Concierge (☎ 407-648-5252; themedicalconcierge.com) has board-certified physicians on call 24-7 to make in-person visits to your hotel room. Walk-in clinics are also available.

DENTAL NEEDS Call **Celebration Dental Group** (☎ 407-566-2222) or ask The Medical Concierge (see above) for a referral.

PRESCRIPTIONS Three drugstores located nearby are **CVS** (8242 World Center Drive; ☎ 407-239-1442), **Walgreens** (12100 S. Apopka–Vineland Road; ☎ 407-238-0600), and **Turner Drugs** (1530 Celebration Blvd., Suite 105A; ☎ 407-828-8125; turnerdrug.com).

PREVENT BLISTERS IN FIVE EASY STEPS

1. PREPARE You can easily cover 5–12 miles a day at the parks, so get your feet and legs into shape before you leave home. Start with short walks around the neighborhood. Increase your distance gradually until you can do 6 miles in a day. Give kids an incentive to join you by adding to their souvenir fund for every half mile they walk.

2. PAY ATTENTION During your training program, your feet will tell you if you're wearing the right shoes. Choose well-constructed, broken-in running or hiking shoes. If you feel a hot spot coming on, a blister isn't far behind. If you develop a hot spot in the same place every time you walk, cover it with a blister bandage (such as Johnson & Johnson) or cushion before you set out.

Don't wear sandals, flip-flops, or slip-ons in the theme parks. Even if your feet don't blister, they'll get stepped on by other guests or run over by strollers.

3. SOCK IT UP Good socks are as important as good shoes. When you walk, your feet sweat, and the moisture increases friction. To avoid that, wear socks made from material such as Smartwool or CoolMax, which wicks perspiration away from your feet (Smartwool socks come in varying thicknesses). To further fight moisture, you can dust your feet with antifungal powder.

4. DON'T BE A HERO Take care of foot problems the minute you notice them. Carry a small foot-emergency kit or stop by **First Aid** (see page 298) as soon as you notice a hot spot forming.

5. CHECK THE KIDS Children might not say anything about blisters forming until it's too late. Stop several times a day and check their feet. If you find a blister, either treat it using the kit you're carrying or stop by First Aid.

LODGING A COMPLAINT WITH DISNEY

COMPLAINING ABOUT A LEAKY FAUCET or not having enough towels is pretty straightforward, and you'll usually find cast members to be highly responsive. But for a complaint that goes beyond an on-site manager's ability to resolve, don't expect much—if anything.

Disney's unresponsiveness in fielding complaints is one of our readers' foremost gripes. A Rhode Island dad's remarks are typical:

> *It's all warm fuzzies and big smiles until you have a problem—then everybody plays hide-and-seek. The only thing you know for sure is it's never the responsibility of the Disney person you're talking to.*

Disney prefers to receive formal complaints in writing. Address your letter to **Walt Disney World Guest Communications** at PO Box 10040, Lake Buena Vista, FL 32830, or email wdw.guest.communications@disneyworld.com. Be aware, though, that by the time you get home and draft a letter, it's often too late to correct the problem. And although Disney would have you believe they're an empathetic lot, they generally won't make things right for you after the fact. You *may* receive an acknowledgment ("we're sorry you *felt* inconvenienced"), but don't count on them actually offering to fix anything—even if you decide to take it up with Bob Iger himself.

SERVICES

PHOTOPASS AND MEMORY MAKER

DISNEY EMPLOYS roaming photographers to take photos of guests as part of its **PhotoPass** service. Use the **My Disney Experience** (**MDE**) app to find the locations of these photographers on the day of your visit.

unofficial **TIP**
If you're the trip planner and picture taker of your group, it's often worth it to purchase Memory Maker so that you're sure to receive a few pictures of your entire party.

PhotoPass images can be purchased at disneyphotopass.com. Prices range from $19 (plus tax and shipping) for two 4-by-6-inch prints or one 5-by-7-inch print to $21 for an 8-by-10-inch print. You can also buy personalized photo products such as mugs and smartphone cases.

Photographs are also sold in a package called **Memory Maker** (see disneyworld.disney.go.com/memory-maker) that includes not only PhotoPass pictures but also photos and videos taken by automated cameras on theme park rides (for the full list, see the table on the opposite page) and at character greeting locations. Memory Maker costs $185 when purchased at least three days before your trip or $210 when purchased in the park. If you're planning to spend just one day in a park, you can buy a **Memory Maker One Day Entitlement** ($75), available exclusively through the MDE app. Disney Annual Pass holders can download photos at no charge if they purchase the PhotoPass supplement.

Because PhotoPass and Memory Maker are linked to your MDE account (see page 23), you can also see the photos of friends and family you've linked to there. Here's how to get started:

1. Find a PhotoPass photographer to take your first picture. Photographers roam throughout the theme parks and water parks, including near park entrances and around iconic attractions such as the Tower of Terror.
2. The photographer will scan your MagicBand, KTTW Card, or phone. This links your pictures to your MDE account. Onboard ride-photo systems should automatically detect your MagicBand and link the photos to your account.
3. Visit the MDE website within 45 days of your trip to view and download your photos.

ATTRACTIONS WHERE PHOTOS ARE AUTOMATICALLY LINKED TO YOUR MDE ACCOUNT
THE MAGIC KINGDOM • Big Thunder Mountain Railroad • Buzz Lightyear's Space Ranger Spin • *Enchanted Tales with Belle* • Pirates of the Caribbean • Seven Dwarfs Mine Train • Space Mountain • Tiana's Bayou Adventure • Tron Lightcycle/Run
EPCOT • Guardians of the Galaxy: Cosmic Rewind • Frozen Ever After • Test Track
ANIMAL KINGDOM • Expedition Everest
DISNEY'S HOLLYWOOD STUDIOS • Rock 'n' Roller Coaster • Slinky Dog Dash • The Twilight Zone Tower of Terror

You can download Memory Maker photos as many times as you want, subject to a few restrictions: First, if you purchase Memory Maker at the advance-purchase price less than three days before your trip, note that photos taken within three days of the date of purchase are not included and must be bought separately. Next, each photo expires 45 days from the date it was taken, so you'll need to download them promptly once you return home (you can apply for a one-time 15-day extension).

Because any two families can share a Memory Maker package via MDE (thanks to that friends-and-family piece), if you're traveling with another family, it's easy to have one family purchase Memory Maker and then split the cost.

We get a lot of reader comments about PhotoPass and Memory Maker, most of them positive. From an Ohio mom:

The PhotoPass option is awesome and so easy. Everywhere we went, we would find Disney photographers, and we got a lot of great pictures, which is nice since usually when you are on vacation you have part of your family missing as he/she is taking the photo.

A Maryland dad got an unexpected disappointment:

I advance-purchased Memory Maker largely because we were planning several character meals, under the apparently incorrect assumption that photographers would be there. There was no sign of any photographer at any of the four character meals we did.

Disney used to offer a lot more photographers or automated photos at character meals, but now it's a rarity. Don't assume they will be part of your package. The exception is at **Ravello**'s character breakfast (at the **Four Seasons Resort Orlando**), where character photos are included with your meal—no Memory Maker purchase required.

In addition to the in-park photographers, there is now a PhotoPass station at **Disney Springs.** There are no characters, but if you want a photographer to take a few snaps of your family, stop by. This can be a quick alternative to a formal posed photo session, and as a bonus, the pictures will be included in your existing photo package.

PET CARE

ACROSS FROM THE PORT ORLEANS RESORTS, **Best Friends Pet Care** accommodates up to 270 dogs in its Doggy Village, which has standard and luxury suites, some with private outdoor patios and play yards; the Kitty City pavilion houses up to 24 cats in two- and four-story cat condos. There's also a separate area just for birds and "pocket pets" such as hamsters. Encompassing more than 17,000 square feet of air-conditioned indoor space plus 10,000 square feet of covered outdoor runs and play areas, the resort is open to both on-site and off-site guests. This location comes highly recommended from many pet parents who are frequent Disney visitors. The staff will even email you photos of your pets during their stay. For more information, call ☎ 877-4-WDW-PETS (877-493-9738) or visit bestfriendspetcare.com. (*Note:* You must provide written proof of your pet's current vaccinations from a veterinarian, either at check-in or by fax at 203-840-5207.)

In addition, dogs are welcome at four hotels on Disney property: **Art of Animation, Port Orleans Riverside, Fort Wilderness Resort & Campground,** and **Yacht Club.** Additional fees of $50–$75 per night apply, along with a host of human- and animal-conduct rules; inquire when making your hotel reservation. This policy was met with skepticism by some when it debuted, but we haven't seen a single complaint regarding dogs at Disney hotels in all the reader surveys we've received since the policy was enacted many years ago.

WHERE CAN I FIND . . .

RELIGIOUS SERVICES? There are currently no regular religious services offered on-property, although they may be offered on holidays such as Easter or Christmas. Check with the front desk at your resort for potential service times and locations.

A PLACE TO PUT ALL THESE PACKAGES? Lockers are located in each theme park (see the "Services" sidebars and park maps in Parts 11–14). At the theme parks, the cost is $10 per day for small lockers and $12 per day for large lockers. At the water parks, lockers cost $10 for small and $15 for large. Jumbo lockers, in EPCOT and the Magic Kingdom only, cost $15 per day. All lockers are now keyless.

If you live in the United States, most merchandise locations will ship any items you purchase to you via standard ground shipping. We're told that the maximum shipping cost is $40, so it might pay to stock up on souvenirs.

GROCERY DELIVERY? If you don't have a car or don't want to take time to shop, you have a couple of options. Amazon Prime members can use **Amazon Pantry** to order prepackaged items—from boxed cereals and snacks to coffee, sunscreen, aspirin, and diapers—at very competitive prices and have them delivered to their resort.

If you're looking for local shopping, services such as **Garden Grocer, Instacart, Vacation Grocery Delivery,** and **Walmart+** deliver to Disney resorts. Unless you order alcohol, most are able to drop off the order at bell services even if you are not present. Deliveries that include alcoholic beverages generally require ID at delivery.

WINE, BEER, AND LIQUOR? In Florida, wine and beer are sold in grocery stores; for the stronger stuff, you'll have to go to a state-licensed liquor store. The best range of booze in the Disney area is sold at **ABC Fine Wine & Spirits** (11951 S. Apopka–Vineland Road; ☎ 407-239-0775), less than a mile north of the Crossroads shopping center. You could also try **Publix Liquors** in the Water Tower Shoppes (29 Blake Blvd., Celebration; ☎ 321-939-3109).

PART 11

The
MAGIC KINGDOM

KEY QUESTIONS ANSWERED IN THIS CHAPTER

- How do I get to the Magic Kingdom? *(see below)*
- How does park opening (rope drop) work? *(page opposite page)*
- What are the don't-miss rides? *(page 368)*
- What's the best way to use Lightning Lane Multi Pass and Lightning Lane Single Pass in the Magic Kingdom? *(page 370)*
- Where are the best spots for watching parades and fireworks? *(page 396)*
- What's the easiest way to leave the park at the end of the day? *(page 397)*
- Is "Always go left (or right)" a good strategy for avoiding crowds? *(page 399)*
- How do I incorporate special events into my touring plans? *(pages 402–403)*

OVERVIEW

OPENED IN 1971, the Magic Kingdom is Walt Disney World's original theme park and remains its crown jewel. Built by many of the same visionaries who created Disneyland nearly 20 years earlier, it is the embodiment of Disney's storytelling magic. When most people think of Disney World, the Magic Kingdom is what comes to mind—Cinderella Castle calling dreamers of all ages, or the timeless thrills of Pirates of the Caribbean and The Haunted Mansion. For more than 50 years, these iconic attractions have set the benchmark for theme park design, blending cutting-edge technology with unforgettable storytelling to create a park that defines the Disney experience.

ARRIVING

FROM INSIDE WALT DISNEY WORLD Guests staying at **Disney's Contemporary Resort** or **Bay Lake Tower** have one of the most convenient options: a short 10-minute walk directly to the park entrance. These resorts, along with the **Grand Floridian** and **Polynesian Village** (and their DVC counterparts), also offer monorail and boat service. Walking from the Grand Floridian takes 15–20 minutes; walking from the Polynesian is possible but less convenient due to the distance.

Guests at **Wilderness Lodge, Copper Creek Villas & Cabins, Boulder Ridge Villas,** or **Fort Wilderness Resort and Campground** can travel by boat or bus. Keep in mind that monorails and boats don't operate during lightning storms. If a storm hits, Disney provides buses as a backup option.

If you're staying at any of Disney's other resorts, the primary mode of transportation to the Magic Kingdom is by bus. Buses deliver you directly to the park entrance—a clear advantage over driving.

DRIVING Driving to the Magic Kingdom requires parking at the **Transportation and Ticket Center** (**TTC**), followed by additional steps to reach the park itself. After parking, you'll either board a tram or walk to the TTC, where you'll clear security and then take a monorail or ferry to the park entrance. This process can take more than an hour on busy days, so it's important to budget extra time. On quieter days, the entire process may take as little as 15–20 minutes.

One other important parking note: The TTC is the fourth-largest parking lot in the world, with 11,000 spots. This, coupled with being in an unfamiliar rental vehicle, can make finding your car especially difficult. Take a picture of your license plate and your row name/number before you catch a tram or walk. You can also record your location in the MDE app using the Car Locator feature.

For those looking to save time, ride-sharing apps like Uber or Lyft can be an effective option. You can request to be dropped off at the **Contemporary** or **Grand Floridian** and walk from there to the park. Be aware, though, that security at these resorts may ask for proof of a hotel or dining reservation. At the end of the day—especially after fireworks, when Disney transportation gets crowded—walking to the Contemporary or Grand Floridian and hailing a ride can save a significant amount of time. While this option isn't free—more like $12–$20 depending on where you're staying—it can be worth avoiding an hourlong wait for a bus, ferry, or monorail.

If driving is unavoidable and you're bringing a stroller, a New Jersey family recommends the **ferry**, which starts operating 30–90 minutes before official park opening:

> *The ferry to the Magic Kingdom is a must if you're using a stroller. You can drive the stroller right onto the ferry and then just head to the back to be the first ones off when it docks.*

MAGIC KINGDOM OPENING PROCEDURES (ROPE DROP)

AS MENTIONED IN PART 3, arriving early is key to minimizing wait times and making the most of your day at the parks. Guests who arrive at the Magic Kingdom **30–60 minutes before official opening** will experience the shortest lines for popular attractions.

continued on page 368

The Magic Kingdom

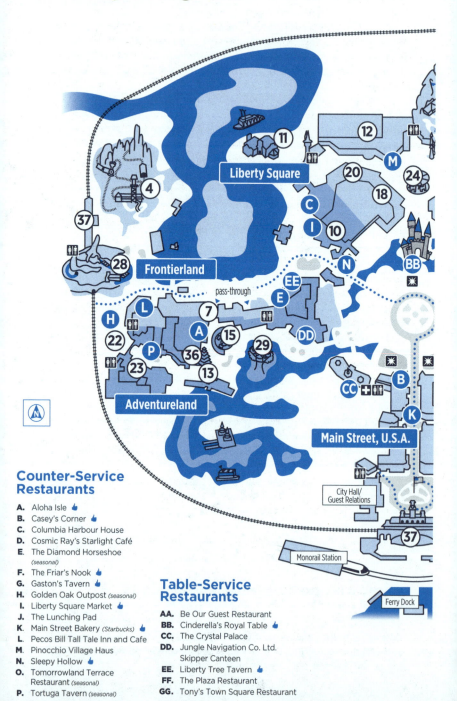

Counter-Service Restaurants

- **A.** Aloha Isle 👍
- **B.** Casey's Corner 👍
- **C.** Columbia Harbour House
- **D.** Cosmic Ray's Starlight Café
- **E.** The Diamond Horseshoe *(seasonal)*
- **F.** The Friar's Nook 👍
- **G.** Gaston's Tavern 👍
- **H.** Golden Oak Outpost *(seasonal)*
- **I.** Liberty Square Market 👍
- **J.** The Lunching Pad
- **K.** Main Street Bakery *(Starbucks)* 👍
- **L.** Pecos Bill Tall Tale Inn and Cafe
- **M.** Pinocchio Village Haus
- **N.** Sleepy Hollow 👍
- **O.** Tomorrowland Terrace Restaurant *(seasonal)*
- **P.** Tortuga Tavern *(seasonal)*

Table-Service Restaurants

- **AA.** Be Our Guest Restaurant
- **BB.** Cinderella's Royal Table 👍
- **CC.** The Crystal Palace
- **DD.** Jungle Navigation Co. Ltd. Skipper Canteen
- **EE.** Liberty Tree Tavern 👍
- **FF.** The Plaza Restaurant
- **GG.** Tony's Town Square Restaurant

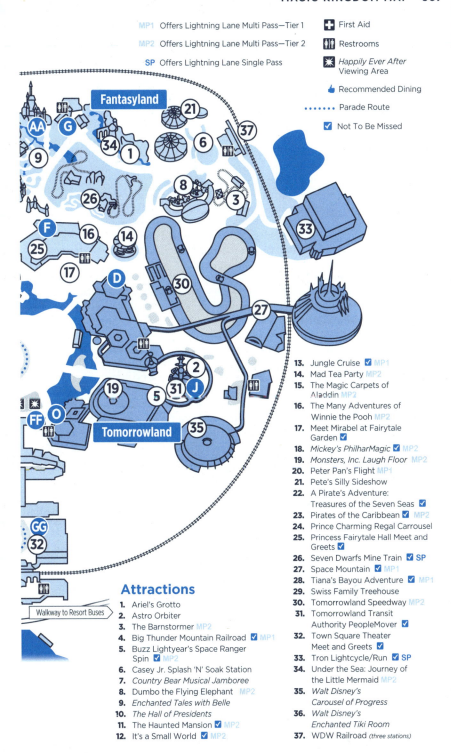

continued from page 365

On-site guests who want to take advantage of Early Theme Park Entry (see page 34) should arrive at the park entrance 60 minutes before official opening (that is, 30 minutes before Early Entry) on all days. Off-site guests who aren't eligible for Early Theme Park Entry should arrive 30 minutes before official opening on all days.

Once in the park, you'll find most of the rides in Fantasyland and Tomorrowland operating during Early Entry, while rides in Adventureland, Frontierland, and Liberty Square will open at the park's official opening time.

> *unofficial* **TIP**
> Rope drop refers to cast members using a length of rope to hold back crowds until the park opens. After the rope is dropped—or rewound, to be precise—crowds race-walk to their first rides.

If you need last-minute essentials such as sunscreen, rain ponchos, or pain relievers, Main Street's larger shops, such as the **Emporium**, will be open when you're admitted into the park. **Main Street Bakery** (**Starbucks**) will also be open for coffee and breakfast items.

Upon entering the park, most guests head straight for one of the headliners: **Seven Dwarfs Mine Train** in Fantasyland attracts families, and Tomorrowland's **Space Mountain** draws some of the secondary crowds. **Tiana's Bayou Adventure,** in Frontierland, is another big draw in this park for families with older children, along with many teens and adults. When **Tron Lightcycle/Run** (in Tomorrowland) is open during Early Entry, it will be the biggest rope-drop draw in the park. At press time, both Tron and Tiana's opened at official park opening.

If you have young children, we recommend heading immediately to **Peter Pan's Flight** to get that quick attraction out of the way with minimal wait. This popular attraction tends to build long lines quickly, so knocking it out first thing will save you time later.

GETTING ORIENTED

IN THE MAGIC KINGDOM, **stroller, wheelchair, scooter, and locker rentals** are on the right, just past the gates. Once you go under the train tracks, **City Hall** is on your left. It serves as the center for **Guest Relations,** lost and found, and guided tours.

Be sure to pick up a **guide map** at the park entrance or at City Hall. It shows all attractions, shops, and dining spots; provides information

NOT TO BE MISSED IN THE MAGIC KINGDOM
ADVENTURELAND • Jungle Cruise • Pirates of the Caribbean
FANTASYLAND • Character greetings • It's a Small World • Seven Dwarfs Mine Train
FRONTIERLAND • Big Thunder Mountain Railroad • Tiana's Bayou Adventure
LIBERTY SQUARE • The Haunted Mansion
MAIN STREET, U.S.A. • Meet Mickey at Town Square Theater
PARADES AND FIREWORKS • Festival of Fantasy afternoon parade • *Happily Ever After* fireworks show • Starlight evening parade
TOMORROWLAND • Buzz Lightyear's Space Ranger Spin • Space Mountain • Tron Lightcycle/Run

MAGIC KINGDOM SERVICES

MOST PARK SERVICES are centered on Main Street, U.S.A., including:

ATMs Underneath the Main Street railroad station

Baby Care Center Next to The Crystal Palace, left around the Central Plaza (toward Adventureland)

Cell Phone Charging Space Mountain exit, behind Big Top Treats in Storybook Circus, and benches outside of *Tangled*-themed restrooms. You can also drop your phone at City Hall with cord for charging.

First Aid Next to The Crystal Palace, left around the Central Plaza (toward Adventureland)

Live Entertainment and Parade Information In the *Times Guide*, available at City Hall/Guest Relations, at the railroad-station end of Main Street

Lost and Found City Hall/Guest Relations

Lost Persons City Hall/Guest Relations

Storage Lockers Inside the tapstiles, to the right as you face the train station

Walt Disney World and Local Attraction Information City Hall/Guest Relations

Wheelchair, ECV, and Stroller Rentals Inside the tapstiles, to the right as you face the train station

---

about first aid, baby care, and assistance for guests with disabilities; and provides tips for good photos. It also lists times for the day's special events, live entertainment, parades, and concerts; plus, it tells you when and where to find Disney characters. It's a great backup if your phone battery is low or your **My Disney Experience** (**MDE**) app (see page 23) is misbehaving.

The guide map is supplemented by a daily entertainment schedule, the **Times Guide.** The *Times Guide* also contains information on Disney-character appearances and what Disney calls **Special Hours,** or operating hours for attractions and restaurants that open late or close early. The MDE app also contains this information, but—in a rare triumph of analog over digital—it's faster to use the *Times Guide.*

At the end of Main Street, U.S.A., is the **Central Plaza.** From here, paths branch out into the Magic Kingdom's five themed lands: (clockwise from left) **Adventureland, Frontierland, Liberty Square, Fantasyland,** and **Tomorrowland.**

Cinderella Castle, at the entrance to Fantasyland, is the Magic Kingdom's visual anchor and an excellent meeting place if your group decides to split up or gets separated.

unofficial **TIP**
Because Cinderella Castle is so large, designate a specific meeting spot, such as the entrance to Cinderella's Royal Table restaurant at the rear of the castle.

FAVORITE ATTRACTIONS BY AGE GROUP

THERE ARE ALMOST 80 INDIVIDUAL ATTRACTIONS (rides, shows, and other entertainment) in the Magic Kingdom. The table on the next page lists the 10 most popular attractions by age group.

Parades and fireworks appear in the top 10 for every age group. Character greetings are especially popular with preschool and grade-school children, and meeting Mickey Mouse ranked in the top 20 park experiences for every age group.

These top attractions form the core of our Magic Kingdom touring plans. If you're looking for step-by-step instructions on where to go and when, start with these (see page 551). Many of the attractions offer Lightning Lane to reduce waits in line (see next section).

PART 11 MAGIC KINGDOM

MAGIC KINGDOM MOST POPULAR ATTRACTIONS BY AGE GROUP					
PRESCHOOL	**GRADE SCHOOL**	**TEENS**	**YOUNG ADULTS**	**OVER 30**	**OVER 65**
Meet Princess Tiana at Fairytale Hall	Big Thunder Mountain Railroad	Tron Lightcycle/ Run	Big Thunder Mountain Railroad	Big Thunder Mountain Railroad	The Dapper Dans barbershop quartet
Dumbo the Flying Elephant	Meet Mickey at Town Square Theater	Big Thunder Mountain Railroad	*Happily Ever After* fireworks	*Happily Ever After* fireworks	The Haunted Mansion
Meet Cinderella at Fairytale Hall	Seven Dwarfs Mine Train	Space Mountain	Tron Lightcycle/ Run	The Dapper Dans barbershop quartet	*Happily Ever After* fireworks
Bibbidi Bobbidi Boutique	*Happily Ever After* fireworks	*Happily Ever After* fireworks	The Haunted Mansion	The Haunted Mansion	Pirates of the Caribbean
Meet Mickey at Town Square Theater	Bibbidi Bobbidi Boutique	The Haunted Mansion	Halloween/ Christmas parades	Tomorrowland Transit Authority PeopleMover	Tomorrowland Transit Authority PeopleMover
Meet Ariel at Her Grotto	Meet Cinderella at Fairytale Hall	Pirates of the Caribbean	Pirates of the Caribbean	Pirates of the Caribbean	*Mickey's PhilharMagic*
Prince Charming Regal Carrousel	Meet Princess Tiana at Fairytale Hall	Seven Dwarfs Mine Train	The Dapper Dans barbershop quartet	Casey's Corner Pianist	Walt Disney World Railroad
Mickey's Magical Friendship Faire	*Mickey's PhilharMagic*	Tomorrowland Transit Authority PeopleMover	Casey's Corner Pianist	Tron Lightcycle/ Run	Casey's Corner Pianist
The Magic Carpets of Aladdin	Tron Lightcycle/Run	Tiana's Bayou Adventure	Walt Disney World Railroad	*Mickey's PhilharMagic*	Seven Dwarfs Mine Train
Meet Meet Daisy at Pete's Silly Sideshow	Disney Adventure Friends Cavalcade	*Mickey's PhilharMagic*	Tomorrowland Transit Authority PeopleMover	Walt Disney World Railroad	Peter Pan's Flight

ATTRACTION RATINGS The attractions profiled in this book have two sets of ratings: an overall rating next to the attraction's name, which reflects the authors' opinions, and reader ratings broken down by age group. Both use a five-star scale, with five stars being best.

Appeal by Age ratings are rounded to the nearest half star. To help put them in context, we also provide a label, such as Above Average, showing how that attraction stacks up to others in the park. Labels are assigned using the attraction's average number of reader ratings and incorporate a 95% confidence interval (sort of like a margin of error), similar to our restaurant ratings (see page 202). As with restaurants, authors' ratings for attractions don't always match readers'.

Based on the 120,000 attraction ratings we received over the past year, the average reader ratings for all Magic Kingdom attractions by age group are as follows:

PRESCHOOL	GRADE SCHOOL	TEENS	YOUNG ADULTS	OVER 30	OVER 65
4.3 stars	4.3 stars	4.2 stars	4.3 stars	4.2 stars	4.3 stars

LLMP, LLSP, AND THE TOURING PLANS

NOTE: See page 53 for detailed information and strategy suggestions for LLMP and LLSP. The big questions addressed in this section are:

GETTING ORIENTED

LLMP AND LLSP SELECTIONS IN THE MAGIC KINGDOM
ADVENTURELAND • Jungle Cruise *(Tier 1)* • The Magic Carpets of Aladdin *(Tier 2)* • Pirates of the Caribbean *(Tier 2)*
FANTASYLAND • The Barnstormer *(Tier 2)* • Dumbo the Flying Elephant *(Tier 2)* • It's a Small World *(Tier 2)* • Mad Tea Party *(Tier 2)* • The Many Adventures of Winnie the Pooh *(Tier 2)* • Mickey's PhilharMagic *(Tier 2)* • Peter Pan's Flight *(Tier 1)* • Seven Dwarfs Mine Train (**LLSP**) • Under the Sea—Journey of the Little Mermaid *(Tier 2)*
FRONTIERLAND • Big Thunder Mountain Railroad *(Tier 1)* • Tiana's Bayou Adventure *(Tier 1)*
LIBERTY SQUARE • The Haunted Mansion *(Tier 2)*
TOMORROWLAND • Buzz Lightyear's Space Ranger Spin *(Tier 2)* • Monsters, Inc. Laugh Floor *(Tier 2)* • Space Mountain *(Tier 1)* • Tomorrowland Speedway *(Tier 2)* • Tron Lightcycle/Run (**LLSP**)

1. Are LLMP and LLSP worth paying for in the Magic Kingdom?
2. If they're worth the cost, which attractions benefit most?
3. How can you avoid paying for LLSP?
4. How do LLMP and LLSP work with the touring plans?

Are LLMP and LLSP Worth Paying For in the Magic Kingdom?

The Magic Kingdom is the easiest park to recommend using LLMP for. It's also the most expensive. We think LLMP is worth the cost here if you meet any of these criteria:

- You'll arrive at the park after Early Theme Park Entry begins (that is, you won't be at the park as soon as it opens). This includes off-site guests who aren't eligible for Early Theme Park Entry and on-site guests who want to sleep in.
- You won't be using a touring plan.
- You're visiting at a time of year when crowds are moderate to high.

	ESTIMATED TIME SAVINGS USING LLMP BY CROWD LEVEL		
CROWD LEVEL	**TYPICAL USE** (3-4 RESERVATIONS PER DAY)	**OPTIMISTIC USE** (5-7 RESERVATIONS PER DAY)	**PERFECT USE** (8+ RESERVATIONS PER DAY)
LOW	40 minutes	60 minutes	80 minutes
MEDIUM	50 minutes	80 minutes	125 minutes
HIGH	75 minutes	110 minutes	175 minutes

The other consideration with LLMP is the number of LLMP ride reservations you'll be able to get in a given day. Above, we break down how much time we think you can save using LLMP, based on data models showing how to optimize the number of time-saving reservations throughout the day.

The **Typical Use** scenario assumes you'll be able to obtain reservations for roughly three or four attractions in your touring plan, provided you haven't already experienced those rides, the reservations don't conflict with any meals or breaks you've already planned, and the standby lines are long enough to justify obtaining the reservation. The **Optimistic Use** scenario assumes all the preceding *and* that LLMP reservations are available at almost exactly the pace at which you'll visit the attractions, plus you'll get another reservation or two. The **Perfect Use** scenario assumes you're able to get LLMP reservations,

MAGIC KINGDOM ATTRACTIONS THAT BENEFIT MOST FROM LLMP AND LLSP
(Highest Priority to Lowest)

ATTRACTION	AVG. TIME IN LINE SAVED (IN MINUTES)	ATTRACTION	AVG. TIME IN LINE SAVED (IN MINUTES)
TRON LIGHTCYCLE/RUN (LLSP)	40	UNDER THE SEA—JOURNEY OF THE LITTLE MERMAID	20
SEVEN DWARFS MINE TRAIN (LLSP)	30	PIRATES OF THE CARIBBEAN	20
JUNGLE CRUISE	27	BUZZ LIGHTYEAR'S SPACE RANGER SPIN	19
TIANA'S BAYOU ADVENTURE	26	THE MAGIC CARPETS OF ALADDIN	18
PETER PAN'S FLIGHT	25	TOMORROWLAND SPEEDWAY	16
SPACE MOUNTAIN	20	IT'S A SMALL WORLD	14
BIG THUNDER MOUNTAIN RAILROAD	17	THE BARNSTORMER	12
THE HAUNTED MANSION	15	MAD TEA PARTY	11
THE MANY ADVENTURES OF WINNIE THE POOH	13	DUMBO THE FLYING ELEPHANT	10

Mickey's PhilharMagic and *Monsters, Inc. Laugh Floor* don't show any significant time savings with LLMP.

one by one, with a nearly immediate return time, for every eligible ride on your touring plan. We think that's exceedingly unlikely; we mention it here to show the upper limit on what might be possible. Finally, remember that attractions that offer LLSP are not part of LLMP; there's a separate cost to use Lightning Lane at those attractions.

Which Attractions Benefit Most from LLMP and LLSP?

For LLMP, the table above shows the attractions that might benefit most, based on the data we've collected from touring plan users in 2024 and 2025. The chart does *not* assume the use of a touring plan.

Whether LLSPs will be worth the cost will depend on what Disney is charging for them and how that lines up with your personal time-versus-money spectrum.

When Do LLMP and LLSP Reservations Run Out in the Magic Kingdom?

The table on the next page shows the approximate time (or day) at which the Magic Kingdom's attractions run out of LLMP or LLSP capacity, by crowd level. Use this table in conjunction with the "Attractions That Benefit Most" table, above, to determine which reservations to get first.

How Can You Avoid Paying for LLSP?

There are a few strategies to avoid paying for LLSP. Several of them involve additional cost:

1. Stay at a Disney resort, use Early Theme Park Entry over multiple days, and head to each attraction as soon as the park opens or right before it closes. For popular attractions, such as Seven Dwarfs Mine Train, this is likely to be the strategy recommended by the touring plan software.

GETTING ORIENTED

ATTRACTION	LOW ATTENDANCE	MODERATE ATTENDANCE	HIGH ATTENDANCE
THE BARNSTORMER	Park close	Park close	9 p.m.
BIG THUNDER MOUNTAIN RAILROAD	7 p.m.	3 p.m.	Noon
BUZZ LIGHTYEAR'S SPACE RANGER SPIN	Park close	2 p.m.	11 a.m.
DUMBO THE FLYING ELEPHANT	Park close	Park close	Park close
THE HAUNTED MANSION	2 p.m.	10 a.m.	2 days early
IT'S A SMALL WORLD	Park close	Park close	3 p.m.
JUNGLE CRUISE	8 p.m.	Noon	10 a.m.
MAD TEA PARTY	Park close	Park close	4 p.m.
THE MAGIC CARPETS OF ALADDIN	Park close	Park close	3 p.m.
THE MANY ADVENTURES OF WINNIE THE POOH	2 p.m.	Noon	1 day early
MICKEY'S PHILHARMAGIC	Park close	Park close	Park close
MONSTERS, INC. LAUGH FLOOR	Park close	Park close	Park close
PETER PAN'S FLIGHT	1 p.m.	11 a.m.	1 day early
PIRATES OF THE CARIBBEAN	Park close	9 p.m.	Noon
SEVEN DWARFS MINE TRAIN (LLSP)	1 day early	2 days early	5 days early
SPACE MOUNTAIN	8 p.m.	3 p.m.	11 a.m.
TIANA'S BAYOU ADVENTURE	2 days early	2 days early	3 days early
TOMORROWLAND SPEEDWAY	9 p.m.	7 p.m.	1 p.m.
TRON LIGHTCYCLE/RUN (LLSP)	3 days early	5 days early	7 days early
UNDER THE SEA—JOURNEY OF THE LITTLE MERMAID	Park close	8 p.m.	5 p.m.

LOW ATTENDANCE Crowd levels 1-3 on the TouringPlans.com crowd calendar
MODERATE ATTENDANCE Crowd levels 4-7 **HIGH ATTENDANCE** Crowd levels 8-10

2. Stay at a Disney Deluxe or DVC resort and visit the attractions during Extended Evening Theme Park Hours.
3. Visit the attraction during an After Hours event or the Halloween or Christmas party.
4. Visit the attraction in the last 30 minutes the park is open. Your actual wait will be significantly lower than the time posted at the entrance.

How Do LLMP and LLSP Work with the Touring Plans?

FOR LLSP Before you begin, obtain a LLSP return time using the MDE app. Next:

If you're using one of the touring plans from this book, follow the plan step-by-step until it's time to use your reservation. Suspend the touring plan while riding the attraction, then pick up the plan where you left off. If the plan recommends visiting the attraction before or after your return time, skip that step.

If you're using the **Lines** app, enter the reservation return time into the software. The software will organize your plan so that you return to the attraction at your designated return time.

FOR LLMP If you're using one of the touring plans in this book, keep track of the next two or three steps in your plan as you go through the park. Get the first available reservation for any of those three attractions, and fit that return-time window into the plan.

For example, suppose the next three steps in your touring plan are Jungle Cruise, Pirates of the Caribbean, and Big Thunder Mountain Railroad. Upon checking LLMP for the next available return time for those three attractions, you find that they are 10:45 a.m. for Big Thunder Mountain, 11 a.m. for Jungle Cruise, and 11:30 a.m. for Pirates. In this case, you'd select Big Thunder Mountain because it's the next available return time from among the three. Once in line for Big Thunder, check LLMP availability for the next three attractions in your plan. If none of the next three steps in your plan participate in LLMP, then get a reservation for the next attraction in your plan that does participate.

DINING IN THE MAGIC KINGDOM

HERE'S A QUICK RECAP of readers' highest-rated restaurants in the Magic Kingdom. Restaurants not shown are rated as average or below. See Part 6 for details.

HIGHEST-RATED MAGIC KINGDOM RESTAURANTS	
COUNTER SERVICE	
• **Aloha Isle** (⊕ 98%/MAA), Adventureland	• **Liberty Square Market** (⊕ 92%/AA), Liberty Square
• **Casey's Corner** (⊕ 93%/AA), Main Street, U.S.A.	• **Main Street Bakery** (⊕ 98%/MAA), Main Street, U.S.A.
• **The Friar's Nook** (⊕ 94%/AA), Fantasyland	• **Sleepy Hollow** (⊕ 95%/AA), Liberty Square
TABLE SERVICE	
• **Cinderella's Royal Table** (⊕ 93%/AA), Fantasyland	• **Liberty Tree Tavern** (⊕ 94%/AA), Liberty Square

E = Exceptional   **MAA** = Much Above Average   **AA** = Above Average

MAIN STREET, U.S.A.

YOU'LL BEGIN AND END YOUR DAY on Main Street, which opens about an hour before and closes about an hour after the rest of the park. A Disneyfied version of a turn-of-the-20th-century small-town American thoroughfare, it's lined with shops, character-greeting venues, places to eat, **City Hall,** and a fire station displaying an old fire engine. In the morning, **vintage vehicles** transport visitors along the street. You'll regularly hear live music throughout the day, from **The Dapper Dans,** the **Casey's Corner Pianist,** and the **Main Street Philharmonic** to marching bands from around the country.

The circular area around the **Central Plaza** is a paved, landscaped viewing spot for the large crowds that watch the **parades** and **evening fireworks.** To disperse heavy crowds during these events, the areas behind the shops on either side of Main Street can become **pedestrian walkways** on which guests can exit and enter the park. The walkway most frequently used during parades and fireworks runs from just past **Tony's Town Square Restaurant** to the Tomorrowland side of **The Plaza Restaurant.** The other walkway runs from near

MAIN STREET, U.S.A.

First Aid, next to The Crystal Palace, to the Main Street fire station (**Engine Co. 71**), near City Hall.

The **Walt Disney World Railroad** stops at Main Street Station; get on to tour the park or ride to Frontierland or Fantasyland. It's not faster than walking, but it's easier on the feet.

KEY TO ABBREVIATIONS In the attraction profiles that follow, each Appeal by Age rating is accompanied by a category label in parentheses (see page 370). **E** means **Exceptional,** **MAA** means **Much Above Average,** **AA** means **Above Average,** **A** means **Average,** **BA** means **Below Average,** and **MBA** means **Much Below Average.**

Cinderella Castle ★★★★

YOUNG ADULTS ★★★★★ (E) **ALL OTHER AGE GROUPS** ★★★★½ (MAA)

What it is The big castle in the middle of the park. **Scope and scale** Diversion. **When to go** Anytime. **Duration** Minimal. **ECV/wheelchair access** May remain in wheelchair. **Participates in LLMP** No. **Early Theme Park Entry** No. **Extended Evening Hours** Yes.

DESCRIPTION AND COMMENTS It's one of the top-rated attractions in the whole park. Admire it from any angle throughout the day. Make sure to walk through and enjoy the mosaics when the entrance isn't closed for a stage show. Our favorite spot for taking family photos with a castle background is on the bridge/walkway near Sleepy Hollow.

Main Street Musical Acts ★★★½

PRESCHOOL ★★★★ (A) **GRADE SCHOOL** ★★★★ (BA) **TEENS** ★★★★ (A)
YOUNG ADULTS ★★★★½ (MAA) **OVER 30** ★★★★½ (AA) **OVER 65** ★★★★½ (A)

What it is Various live entertainment along Main Street. **Scope and scale** Diversion. **When to go** Check for showtimes. **Duration** 5–20 minutes. **ECV/wheelchair access** May remain in wheelchair. **Participates in LLMP** No. **Early Theme Park Entry** No. **Extended Evening Hours** No.

DESCRIPTION AND COMMENTS Many talented performers entertain the crowds along Main Street throughout the day, including the **Casey's Corner Pianist, The Dapper Dans** (a barbershop quartet), and the **Main Street Philharmonic** (a marching band).

TOURING TIPS If stage shows are for the kids, these musical acts are clearly for the adults. At least for us, a Magic Kingdom day isn't complete until we've heard The Dapper Dans singing somewhere along Main Street. It's the type of atmospheric addition that is classic Disney.

Main Street Stage Shows ★★★½

PRESCHOOL ★★★★½ (AA) **GRADE SCHOOL** ★★★★½ (A) **TEENS** ★★★½ (MBA)
YOUNG ADULTS ★★★★ (BA) **OVER 30** ★★★★ (BA) **OVER 65** ★★★½ (BA)

What it is Entertainment on the main stage in front of Cinderella Castle. **Scope and scale** Minor attraction. **When to go** Check for showtimes. **Duration** 5–20 minutes. **ECV/wheelchair access** May remain in wheelchair. **Participates in LLMP** No. **Early Theme Park Entry** No. **Extended Evening Hours** No.

DESCRIPTION AND COMMENTS Multiple shows throughout the day, including **Let the Magic Begin** at park opening, and **Mickey's Magical Friendship Faire** sporadically throughout the day.

TOURING TIPS These shows are for the kids. The sheer number of characters onstage is impressive. But even if you don't plan on attending, be aware of the showtimes because you won't be able to walk through Cinderella Castle during the shows.

Main Street Vehicles ★★★

PRESCHOOL ★★★★ (A) **GRADE SCHOOL** ★★★★ (BA) **TEENS** ★★★½ (BA)
YOUNG ADULTS ★★★★ (BA) **OVER 30** ★★★★ (A) **OVER 65** ★★★★½ (AA)

What it is Vehicles driving up and down Main Street. **Scope and scale** Diversion. **When to go** Midmorning. **Duration** 2–5 minutes. **Probable waiting time** 5–10 minutes. **Queue speed** Slow. **ECV/wheelchair access** Must transfer. **Participates in LLMP** No. **Early Theme Park Entry** No. **Extended Evening Hours** No.

DESCRIPTION AND COMMENTS These vintage vehicles take you on a one-way trip down Main Street. Choose from a horse-drawn trolley, an omnibus, a jitney, or a fire engine.

TOURING TIPS Fun and saves footsteps but not worth a wait. Not available during parades.

Meet Mickey at Town Square Theater ★★★★

PRESCHOOL ★★★★½ (MAA) **GRADE SCHOOL** ★★★★½ (MAA) **TEENS** ★★★★ (A)
YOUNG ADULTS ★★★★½ (AA) **OVER 30** ★★★★½ (AA) **OVER 65** ★★★★½ (AA)

What it is Character greeting. **Scope and scale** Minor attraction. **When to go** Early or late. **Duration** 2 minutes. **Probable waiting time** Varies. **Queue speed** Slow. **ECV/wheelchair access** May remain in wheelchair. **Participates in LLMP** No. **Early Theme Park Entry** No. **Extended Evening Hours** No.

DESCRIPTION AND COMMENTS Children and teenagers alike rate character greetings among the highest of any Disney attractions, and there's no bigger celebrity than Mickey Mouse. Meet Mickey throughout the day at Town Square Theater on Main Street, to your right as you enter the park.

TOURING TIPS Lines tend to die down after dinner, but if you want fresh-looking family pictures, you may want to go near park opening.

Walt Disney World Railroad ★★★

PRESCHOOL ★★★★½ (AA) **GRADE SCHOOL** ★★★★ (A) **TEENS** ★★★★ (A)
YOUNG ADULTS ★★★★½ (AA) **OVER 30** ★★★★½ (AA) **OVER 65** ★★★★½ (AA)

What it is Scenic railroad ride around the park. **Scope and scale** Minor attraction. **When to go** Anytime. **Comment** Main Street is usually the least congested station. **Duration** 20 minutes for round-trip. **Loading speed** Moderate. **ECV/wheelchair access** At the Frontierland and Fantasyland stations; must transfer from ECV to provided wheelchair. **Participates in LLMP** No. **Early Theme Park Entry** No. **Extended Evening Hours** No.

DESCRIPTION AND COMMENTS View the Magic Kingdom from aboard a steam-powered locomotive, with stops in Frontierland and Fantasyland. The most scenic portion is between the Frontierland and Fantasyland stations. If you're in Frontierland and headed out of the park, it's a nice way to end your visit.

TOURING TIPS Save the railroad until after you have seen the major attractions. On busy days, lines form at the Frontierland station but rarely at the Main Street station. Only folded strollers are permitted on the train, so you can't board with your Disney stroller (but you can get a replacement if you keep your stroller name card and receipt with you).

A dad from New Jersey points out that all stations are not equal:

> Tell your readers that if they ride the railroad, they should go to the Main Street station. We tried to get on [at another station], and it was a zoo—there were people shoving past other people and rolling over other people with strollers and wheelchairs. The Main Street station is much more organized, efficient, and relaxing because of the extra cast members working there.

Finally, note that the railroad shuts down immediately before and during parades and fireworks; check your park map or *Times Guide* for times. This is not the time to get in line.

ADVENTURELAND

WITH A TROPICAL ISLAND ATMOSPHERE, Adventureland is the first land to the left of Main Street, U.S.A. Many of its attractions are theme park classics and are among the oldest in the park, so crowds don't usually build here until late morning.

Jungle Cruise ★★★½

PRESCHOOL ★★★★ (A)	GRADE SCHOOL ★★★★ (A)	TEENS ★★★★ (A)
YOUNG ADULTS ★★★★½ (AA)	OVER 30 ★★★★½ (AA)	OVER 65 ★★★★½ (AA)

What it is Outdoor comedic boat ride. **Scope and scale** Major attraction. **When to go** Early or late. **Duration** 8–9 minutes. **Loading speed** Moderate. **ECV/wheelchair access** May remain in ECV/wheelchair and wait for specially configured boats. **Participates in LLMP** Yes. **Early Theme Park Entry** No. **Extended Evening Hours** No.

DESCRIPTION AND COMMENTS On this outdoor group boat ride through tropical waterways, you'll pass through forest and jungle filled with animatronic animals and people.

Jungle Cruise was the park's signature ride when it opened at Disneyland. This now seems silly since you can go on a safari in Animal Kingdom and see the real thing. But the skippers do the cheesiest, most groan-inducing stand-up you've ever heard. If you dig that sort of thing (or just want to admire the excellent animatronics), it's glorious.

This is one of the rare attractions where a pause in operations may be a good thing. That's when the skippers can go (more) off-script and run through a bunch of jokes that don't feel as stale or predictable.

TOURING TIPS The ride is creepier at night, if that's your thing.

The Magic Carpets of Aladdin ★★

PRESCHOOL ★★★★½ (MAA)	GRADE SCHOOL ★★★★ (A)	TEENS ★★★½ (BA)
YOUNG ADULTS ★★★½ (BA)	OVER 30 ★★★½ (MBA)	OVER 65 ★★★½ (BA)

What it is Themed spinner ride. **Scope and scale** Minor attraction. **When to go** Before noon or after dark. **Duration** 1½ minutes. **Loading speed** Slow. **ECV/wheelchair access** Must transfer from ECV to provided wheelchair. **Participates in LLMP** Yes. **Early Theme Park Entry** No. **Extended Evening Hours** Yes.

DESCRIPTION AND COMMENTS This ride is like **Dumbo,** with magic carpets instead of elephants. A spitting camel sprays jets of water on riders. Riders can maneuver their carpets up and down and tilt; the front seat controls height, while the back seat controls tilt.

TOURING TIPS This ride has great eye appeal but an extremely slow loading time—slower than Dumbo because there is only one spinner. That means its line moves surprisingly slow. The whole queue is visible, so you'll be able to tell if you're in for a long wait.

A Pirate's Adventure: Treasure of the Seven Seas ★★½

| PRESCHOOL ★★★★ (A) | GRADE SCHOOL ★★★★ (A) | TEENS ★★★★½ (BA) |
| YOUNG ADULTS ★★★½ (BA) | OVER 30 ★★★★ (BA) | OVER 65 ★★★ (MBA) |

What it is Interactive game. **Scope and scale** Diversion. **When to go** Afternoon. **Duration** About 20 minutes to play the entire game. **ECV/wheelchair access** May remain in ECV/wheelchair. **Participates in LLMP** No. **Early Theme Park Entry** No. **Extended Evening Hours** No.

DESCRIPTION AND COMMENTS A Pirate's Adventure features interactive areas with physical props and narrations that lead guests through a quest to help Captain Jack Sparrow find lost treasure, all within Adventureland.

You begin your journey at The Crow's Nest, where your group of up to six people chooses a leader. The leader's MagicBand (or KTTW Card) activates a video screen that assigns the group to one of five missions. Your group is given a map and sent off to the first location.

Once at the location, the leader of the party touches their MagicBand to the symbol at the station, and the animation begins. Each adventure has four or five stops throughout Adventureland; each stop contains 30–45 seconds of activity. No strategy or action is required: Simply watch what unfolds on the screen, get your next destination, and head off.

A Rhode Island mom writes:

My youngest had never done this before, so he was overly excited about it. As a parent, I like it because it's a way to do something interactive in the park. It's not just waiting in line.

TOURING TIPS This is a good way to spend time on a busy afternoon if you want to avoid lines, but it's not a must-do.

Pirates of the Caribbean ★★★★

| PRESCHOOL ★★★★ (A) | GRADE SCHOOL ★★★★½ (AA) | TEENS ★★★★½ (AA) |
| YOUNG ADULTS ★★★★½ (MAA) | OVER 30 ★★★★½ (MAA) | OVER 65 ★★★★½ (MAA) |

What it is Indoor boat ride. **Scope and scale** Headliner. **When to go** Anytime. **Duration** About 7½ minutes. **Loading speed** Fast. **ECV/wheelchair access** Must transfer from ECV to provided wheelchair and then from wheelchair to the ride vehicle. **Participates in LLMP** Yes. **Early Theme Park Entry** No. **Extended Evening Hours** Yes.

DESCRIPTION AND COMMENTS Originally opened in Disneyland in 1967, this cruise through a series of scenes depicting a pirate raid on an island settlement is one of the most influential theme park attractions ever created. The Magic Kingdom's version retains the elaborate queuing area, grand scale, and detailed sets that have awed audiences since the ride's debut.

As one of the theme park's most popular rides, Pirates is scrutinized and revised often. The successful *Pirates of the Caribbean* movies led to the addition of animatronic figures of Captain Jack Sparrow and Captain Barbossa. These additions, however, make the ride's story confusing. Why did the raid stop for a chicken auction? Why is Jack randomly appearing and hiding in the middle of all of this? Still, if you don't attempt to find a storyline, the sets are fun.

TOURING TIPS Pirates moves large crowds in a hurry. There are some dark scenes that could scare younger children. And you might get wet.

Swiss Family Treehouse ★★

| PRESCHOOL ★★★★ (BA) | GRADE SCHOOL ★★★½ (MBA) | TEENS ★★★ (MBA) |
| YOUNG ADULTS ★★★★ (MBA) | OVER 30 ★★★½ (MBA) | OVER 65 ★★★½ (BA) |

What it is Outdoor walk-through treehouse. **Scope and scale** Diversion. **When to go** Anytime. **Duration** 8–10 minutes. **Probable waiting time** None. **ECV/wheelchair access** Must be ambulatory. **Participates in LLMP** No. **Early Theme Park Entry** No. **Extended Evening Hours** Yes.

DESCRIPTION AND COMMENTS An immense replica of the Swiss Family Robinson's treetop home. It's the queen of all treehouses.

TOURING TIPS This self-guided walk-through tour involves a lot of stairs but no ropes, ladders, or anything too crazy. Folks who must pay attention to every small detail or people stopping to rest sometimes create bottlenecks that slow things down, as the walkways are generally too narrow for passing.

Walt Disney's Enchanted Tiki Room ★★★

PRESCHOOL ★★★★½ (AA)	GRADE SCHOOL ★★★★ (BA)	TEENS ★★★½ (BA)
YOUNG ADULTS ★★★★ (A)	OVER 30 ★★★★ (A)	OVER 65 ★★★★½ (AA)

What it is Audio-Animatronic musical show. **Scope and scale** Minor attraction. **When to go** Afternoon. **Duration** 15½ minutes. **Probable waiting time** Less than one show. **ECV/wheelchair access** May remain in ECV/wheelchair. **Participates in LLMP** No. **Early Theme Park Entry** No. **Extended Evening Hours** Yes.

DESCRIPTION AND COMMENTS This show, conceived by Walt Disney himself, stars four singing, wisecracking mechanical parrots: José, Fritz, Michael, and Pierre (aka the Tiki Birds). The quartet performs songs arranged in styles from the 1940s to the 1960s, accompanied by dozens of other birds, plants, and tikis that come to life all around you.

The show was an engineering marvel when it opened in Disneyland in 1963, and it remains a favorite of many fans of classic Disney, including us, who enjoy the music and direct link back to Walt. But most kids today don't get it and may be bored.

TOURING TIPS Go in the late afternoon, when you will most appreciate the air-conditioning.

If you have young kids, be prepared for a dark and stormy scene that may startle some.

FRONTIERLAND

FRONTIERLAND'S THEME is mostly 19th-century America, with pioneer roots. Before the introduction of Tiana's Bayou Adventure, if you started at Big Thunder Mountain Railroad and walked toward The Haunted Mansion in Liberty Square, you'd also be walking back in time: The different rides and buildings represent distinct eras in US history, from the settling of the frontier through the California gold rush to the early-19th-century South. Just treat that beautiful bayou as a nice break from history. And geography.

A note for 2026: Significant construction has been announced for this area, including the filling in of the Rivers of America and the closure of Tom Sawyer Island. This is all to make way for a new land, themed to the *Cars* film franchise. Expect to see and hear construction from anywhere in Frontierland throughout the year.

Big Thunder Mountain Railroad ★★★★

PRESCHOOL ★★★★ (A)	GRADE SCHOOL ★★★★½ (MAA)	TEENS ★★★★½ (MAA)
YOUNG ADULTS ★★★★½ (MAA)	OVER 30 ★★★★½ (MAA)	OVER 65 ★★★★½ (AA)

What it is Western-themed roller coaster. **Scope and scale** Headliner. **When to go** Early or late. **Comments** Must be 40" tall to ride; Rider Switch option provided (see page 307). **Duration** About 3½ minutes. **Loading speed** Moderate-fast. **ECV/wheelchair access** Must transfer to the ride vehicle. **Participates in LLMP** Yes. **Early Theme Park Entry** No. **Extended Evening Hours** No.

DESCRIPTION AND COMMENTS Not only is Big Thunder Mountain well themed, but it also has a moderately long duration for a WDW coaster. It doesn't leave you wanting more, unlike some of the other coasters in the park. On this attraction, you're on a runaway mine train careening through a gold rush frontier town. Big Thunder contains first-rate examples of Disney Imagineering at work, such as caverns, an earthquake, and swinging opossums. Seats in the back offer the best experience.

In terms of intensity, we put this coaster right in the middle of the scary scale—rather than big hills, drops, and upside-down parts, it has tight turns. Because of these, it rates higher on the motion-sickness scale than you might expect. But because it's outdoors and kids can see most of the ride, it's a much better introduction to "real" roller coasters for first-timers than Space Mountain.

The ride closed in January 2025 for a major refurbishment expected to last for at least a year. The entire track is being replaced, and some "little extra bits of magic" are promised.

TOURING TIPS Nearby **Tiana's Bayou Adventure** (see page 381) affects traffic flow to Big Thunder—guests who ride one usually ride both. This translates to large crowds in Frontierland all day and longer waits for Big Thunder. A good one-day schedule might be Big Thunder and Tiana's in the morning, Space Mountain and Seven Dwarfs Mine Train in the evening, and Tron if you spot a drop in the posted wait time.

Country Bear Musical Jamboree ★★★½

PRESCHOOL ★★★★½ (AA)　**GRADE SCHOOL** ★★★★ (BA)　**TEENS** ★★★½ (BA)
YOUNG ADULTS ★★★★ (BA)　**OVER 30** ★★★★ (A)　**OVER 65** ★★★★ (A)

What it is Corny Audio-Animatronic hoedown. **Scope and scale** Minor attraction. **When to go** Anytime. **Duration** 11 minutes. **Probable waiting time** Less than one show. **ECV/wheelchair access** May remain in wheelchair. **Participates in LLMP** No. **Early Theme Park Entry** No. **Extended Evening Hours** Yes.

DESCRIPTION AND COMMENTS A charming cast of animatronic bears sings and stomps through a series of Disney songs. It's an air-conditioned refuge on hot days, and the revamp from custom songs to Disney classics has resulted in higher ratings for almost every age group. While the reimagining of this classic show made many longtime fans anxious, the ratings speak for themselves. A mom from Alabama agrees:

> *I cannot stress enough how much we enjoyed the* Country Bear Musical Jamboree. *It's like the greatest Chuck E. Cheese show you've ever seen—with much nicer, less greasy seats. We laughed, we sang along, we clapped, and the kids asked if we could watch the next show too. Kids love singing animal animatronics, and so do adults who grew up in the '90s! Plus, almost zero wait time, cool AC, and a show that doesn't drag on too long—just the perfect amount of time and indoor entertainment.*

TOURING TIPS On hot and rainy days, the *Country Bear Musical Jamboree* draws crowds looking for an air-conditioned indoor haven. It's more popular now than it was before 2024, but you still probably won't have to wait more than one show.

Tiana's Bayou Adventure ★★★★

| PRESCHOOL ★★★★ (BA) | GRADE SCHOOL ★★★★½ (AA) | TEENS ★★★★½ (AA) |
| YOUNG ADULTS ★★★★½ (AA) | OVER 30 ★★★★½ (AA) | OVER 65 ★★★★ (A) |

What it is Water-flume adventure. **Scope and scale** Headliner. **When to go** As early or late as possible. **Comments** Must be 40" tall to ride; Rider Switch option provided (see page 307). **Duration** About 10 minutes. **Loading speed** Moderate. **ECV/wheelchair access** Must transfer to the ride vehicle; transfer device available. **Participates in LLMP** Yes. **Early Theme Park Entry** No. **Extended Evening Hours** Yes.

DESCRIPTION AND COMMENTS Tiana's Bayou Adventure is a welcome rethemeing of Frontierland's Splash Mountain. The new story follows Tiana as she looks for musicians to play at her restaurant. The revamped ride keeps Splash Mountain's architecture, including its pacing, small drops, and big drop near the end. But the new version has some stunning animatronics and a great jazzy soundtrack.

From a thematic perspective, the Disneyland version is straightforward: Tiana's is adjacent to The Haunted Mansion in New Orleans Square, where Tiana's post-1927 New Orleans story fits in just fine. But at Walt Disney World, Frontierland is solidly in the 1800s. If you ask any cast members, including those who lead **Keys to the Kingdom** or **VIP** tours (see pages 494 and 496), none of them can explain how Tiana's fits in with the area.

TOURING TIPS If you ride in the front seat, you'll almost certainly get wet; riders elsewhere get at least splashed. Be prepared—on a cool day, bring a poncho or a plastic garbage bag with holes in the bottom and sides for your head and arms. Or store a change of clothes in a rental locker.

Leave your camera or phone with a nonriding member of your group, or put it in a ziplock bag. Find a way to waterproof your shoes, or store a second pair in your locker for after the ride.

Walt Disney World Railroad

DESCRIPTION AND COMMENTS The railroad stops in Frontierland on its park tour. See page 376 for additional details.

TOURING TIPS It's a pleasant, feet-saving link to Main Street and Fantasyland, but the Frontierland station is more congested than the others.

LIBERTY SQUARE

LIBERTY SQUARE re-creates the United States at the time of the Revolutionary War. The **Liberty Tree,** a live oak more than 150 years old and selected by Walt Disney himself, lends dignity and grace to the patriotic setting.

The Hall of Presidents ★★½

| PRESCHOOL ★★★ (MBA) | GRADE SCHOOL ★★★½ (MBA) | TEENS ★★★½ (MBA) |
| YOUNG ADULTS ★★★★ (BA) | OVER 30 ★★★★ (BA) | OVER 65 ★★★★½ (AA) |

What it is Audio-Animatronic historical presentation. **Scope and scale** Minor attraction. **When to go** Anytime. **Duration** Almost 23 minutes. **Probable waiting time** Less than one show. **ECV/wheelchair access** May remain in wheelchair. **Participates in LLMP** No. **Early Theme Park Entry** No. **Extended Evening Hours** No.

DESCRIPTION AND COMMENTS *The Hall of Presidents* combines a widescreen theater presentation of key highlights and milestones in the political history of the United States with a short stage show featuring life-size animatronic replicas of every US president. Their physical resemblances and costumes are masterful.

Abraham Lincoln and George Washington have speaking roles, and the current president recites the oath of office.

The current version of the show reiterates many of the same social and political points as *The American Adventure* in EPCOT, so it's probably not worthwhile to see both. Of the two, *The American Adventure* is better.

Many visitors comment that they appreciate this spot more for the cool, dark space it provides for naps or snacking than for the show itself.

TOURING TIPS In the last decade or so, it's become commonplace for some members of the audience to cheer or jeer as the current president and his contemporaries are named. Skip *The Hall of Presidents* if you'd rather not be reminded of politics on vacation.

The Haunted Mansion ★★★★

PRESCHOOL ★★★½ (BA)   **GRADE SCHOOL** ★★★★½ (AA)   **TEENS** ★★★★½ (MAA)
YOUNG ADULTS ★★★★½ (MAA)   **OVER 30** ★★★★½ (MAA)   **OVER 65** ★★★★½ (MAA)

What it is Haunted-house dark ride. **Scope and scale** Major attraction. **When to go** Early or late. **Duration** 7 minutes. **Loading speed** Fast. **ECV/wheelchair access** Must transfer to the ride vehicle. **Participates in LLMP** Yes. **Early Theme Park Entry** No. **Extended Evening Hours** Yes.

DESCRIPTION AND COMMENTS The Haunted Mansion—which opened with the rest of the World in 1971—proves that top-notch special effects don't always require 21st-century technology. "Doom Buggies" on a conveyor belt transport you through the house and graveyard. The effects range from generally spooky to totally laughable and aren't scary for most age groups. That said, there are enough jump-scare moments and creepy sound effects, especially at the beginning of the ride, to draw lower ratings from preschoolers.

Interactive elements in the outdoor queue occupy guests when lines are long. These include an interactive musical monument and a ship captain's tomb that squirts water.

TOURING TIPS When admitted to the mansion, you'll first enter a foyer with a fireplace and then be guided quickly into a second, wood-paneled preshow room with four paintings above you. Keep close to the wall, find the wall panel with a small red light at about eye level, and stand with your back to that panel while you watch the preshow.

FANTASYLAND

FANTASYLAND IS THE HEART of the Magic Kingdom. Spread out like a village festival behind and beneath the towers of **Cinderella Castle,** the land is divided into several distinct sections. Directly behind Cinderella Castle and set upon a snowcapped mountain is **Beast's Castle,** part of a *Beauty and the Beast*–themed area. Most of this section holds dining and shopping, such as **Be Our Guest Restaurant, Gaston's Tavern,** and a gift shop. The far-right corner of Fantasyland is called **Storybook Circus** as an homage to the *Dumbo* films and includes **Dumbo the Flying Elephant, The Barnstormer,** some character greeting spots, and the train station. A covered seating area with plush chairs, electrical outlets, and USB phone chargers is located behind **Big Top Souvenirs.**

The middle of Fantasyland holds the headliner, **Seven Dwarfs Mine Train,** and a secondary attraction, **Under the Sea—Journey of the Little Mermaid.** The placement of these two attractions allows good traffic flow either to the left (toward Beast's Castle) for dining, to the right for attractions geared to smaller children, or back to the original part of Fantasyland for Disney classics such as **It's a Small World, Peter Pan's Flight,** and **The Many Adventures of Winnie the Pooh.**

The original section, behind Cinderella Castle, holds **Princess Fairytale Hall,** *Mickey's PhilharMagic,* and the restored antique **Prince Charming Regal Carrousel.** Finally, the *Tangled*-themed restrooms and outdoor seating are a can't-miss section. We're not kidding—people have photo shoots in this restroom area.

Ariel's Grotto ★★★

PRESCHOOL ★★★★½ (MAA)	GRADE SCHOOL ★★★★½ (AA)	TEENS ★★★½ (BA)
YOUNG ADULTS ★★★★ (A)	OVER 30 ★★★★ (BA)	OVER 65 ★★★½ (BA)

What it is Character-greeting venue. **Scope and scale** Minor attraction. **When to go** Early or late. **Duration of experience** A minute. **Probable waiting time** Varies. **Queue speed** Slow. **ECV/wheelchair access** May remain in wheelchair. **Participates in LLMP** No. **Early Theme Park Entry** No. **Extended Evening Hours** No.

DESCRIPTION AND COMMENTS This is Ariel's home turf, next to her signature ride (see page 389). She greets guests from a seashell throne. The line here is slower than at many other meet and greets, so be prepared for a wait. Kids love this attraction, but others in their party rate it poorly, generally because the long wait catches them by surprise.

TOURING TIPS The greeting area is set up almost as if to encourage guests to linger, which keeps the line long—and the queue isn't air-conditioned.

The Barnstormer ★★

PRESCHOOL ★★★★ (A)	GRADE SCHOOL ★★★★ (BA)	TEENS ★★★½ (BA)
YOUNG ADULTS ★★★½ (MBA)	OVER 30 ★★★ (MBA)	OVER 65 ★★★ (MBA)

What it is Small roller coaster. **Scope and scale** Minor attraction. **When to go** Early or late. **Comment** Must be 35" tall to ride. **Duration of ride** 53 seconds. **Loading speed** Slow. **ECV/wheelchair access** Must transfer to the ride vehicle. **Participates in LLMP** Yes. **Early Theme Park Entry** Yes. **Extended Evening Hours** Yes.

DESCRIPTION AND COMMENTS The Barnstormer is a dinky (read: jerky) little coaster with a zippy ride lasting only 53 seconds, 32 of which are spent starting and stopping. Actual time zooming around the track: 21 seconds. It's a good introduction to roller coasters for the littlest kids but should be avoided by all others.

TOURING TIPS The cars are too small for most adults and tend to give taller people whiplash. If The Barnstormer is high on your children's must-do list, try to ride within the first 2 hours Fantasyland is open, before any sort of line forms.

Casey Jr. Splash 'N' Soak Station ★★½

PRESCHOOL ★★★★ (A)	GRADE SCHOOL ★★★★ (BA)	TEENS ★★★ (MBA)
YOUNG ADULTS ★★★½ (MBA)	OVER 30 ★★★ (MBA)	OVER 65 ★★½ (MBA)

What it is Elaborate water-play area. **Scope and scale** Diversion. **When to go** When it's hot. **ECV/wheelchair access** May remain in wheelchair. **Participates in LLMP** No. **Early Theme Park Entry** No. **Extended Evening Hours** No.

DESCRIPTION AND COMMENTS Casey Jr., the circus train from *Dumbo*, plays host to an absolutely drenching play area in the Storybook Circus area. Cars full of captive circus beasts spray water on kids and parents. So. Much. Water.

TOURING TIPS Bring a change of clothes and a big towel. Note that it doesn't run during cooler weather.

A mom from Kansas suggests another way to handle this attraction:

Casey Jr. is like a bright lamp, and toddlers are like moths. I almost wish we had skipped [Storybook Circus] just so I didn't have to keep dragging my child away from this spot that would leave him soggy for the rest of the day.

Dumbo the Flying Elephant ★★★

PRESCHOOL ★★★★½ (MAA) **GRADE SCHOOL** ★★★★½ (A) **TEENS** ★★★½ (BA)
YOUNG ADULTS ★★★★ (BA) **OVER 30** ★★★★ (BA) **OVER 65** ★★★★ (BA)

What it is Disneyfied spinner ride. **Scope and scale** Minor attraction. **When to go** Early or late. **Duration of ride** 1½ minutes. **Loading speed** Slow-ish. **ECV/wheelchair access** Must transfer to the ride vehicle. **Participates in LLMP** Yes. **Early Theme Park Entry** Yes. **Extended Evening Hours** Yes.

DESCRIPTION AND COMMENTS A sweet ride based on the classic movie. Parents and kids sit in small elephants mounted on long metal arms that spin around a central axis. Controls inside each vehicle allow you to go higher off the ground. Dumbo is the favorite Magic Kingdom attraction of many very young children.

TOURING TIPS If Dumbo is essential, ride after dinner; not only are the crowds smaller at night, but the lighting and effects also make the ride much prettier. There is a covered play area mid-queue. You'll often be able to walk right past, but you can take advantage of the space if your little ones need some unstructured play.

Enchanted Tales with Belle ★★★★

PRESCHOOL ★★★★½ (AA) **GRADE SCHOOL** ★★★★½ (AA) **TEENS** ★★★ (MBA)
YOUNG ADULTS ★★★½ (BA) **OVER 30** ★★★★ (A) **OVER 65** ★★★★ (A)

What it is Interactive live character show. **Scope and scale** Minor attraction. **When to go** Early or late. **Duration of presentation** Approximately 20 minutes. **Queue speed** Slow. **ECV/wheelchair access** Must transfer from ECV to provided wheelchair. **Participates in LLMP** No. **Early Theme Park Entry** No. **Extended Evening Hours** No.

DESCRIPTION AND COMMENTS This multiscene *Beauty and the Beast* experience begins in the cottage and workshop of Belle's father, Maurice, which happens to feature a magic mirror.

No spoilers here, but you'll eventually enter a room with The Wardrobe. Once there, cast members explain that you're here to reenact the story of *Beauty and the Beast* for Belle on her birthday. Guests are chosen to act out key parts in the play.

Next, everyone walks into the library and takes a seat, and cast members introduce Belle. The play is acted out within a few minutes, and all of the actors get a chance to take photos with Belle and get a bookmark as a gift.

During our visits, only guests who chose to act in the play got to take photos with Belle. Those photos are accessed with a separate Memory

Maker card. If you have a small child who is too shy to take part, cast members will usually allow them to take a picture with Belle if you ask nicely.

Enchanted Tales with Belle is the most interactive character encounter in Walt Disney World. For those who get to act in the play, it's also a chance to interact with Belle in a way that isn't possible at other meet and greets. Even parties without kids can have an enjoyable time, as this man from Ontario attests:

We don't have kids, but we had a great time. The experience is lighthearted, and the cast are so good at making it fun for everyone. My partner was selected to be a "guard" in the play, and it made my week since we had decided we wouldn't be doing any character greetings but he got roped into one. The Lumière animatronic and the "magic mirror" were amazing.

TOURING TIPS Because the line moves slowly, see *Enchanted Tales* early in the morning or try to visit during the last 2 hours the attraction is open.

It's a Small World ★★★½

| PRESCHOOL ★★★★½ (AA) | GRADE SCHOOL ★★★★ (BA) | TEENS ★★★½ (BA) |
| YOUNG ADULTS ★★★★ (BA) | OVER 30 ★★★★ (BA) | OVER 65 ★★★★½ (AA) |

What it is World harmony–themed indoor boat ride. **Scope and scale** Major attraction. **When to go** Early or late. **Duration of ride** About 11 minutes. **Loading speed** Fast. **ECV/wheelchair access** Must transfer from ECV to provided wheelchair. **Participates in LLMP** Yes. **Early Theme Park Entry** Yes. **Extended Evening Hours** Yes.

DESCRIPTION AND COMMENTS Happy and upbeat to an almost unsettling degree, It's a Small World is guaranteed to leave you humming its song for the rest of the day. Small boats carry you on a tour around the world, with singing and dancing dolls showcasing the dress and culture of each nation represented. One of Disney's oldest entertainment offerings, Small World first unleashed its mind-numbing theme song and unbearable cuteness at the 1964 New York World's Fair; the original exhibit was moved to Disneyland afterward, and a duplicate was created for Disney World when it opened in 1971. Almost everyone enjoys It's a Small World. It stands as a monument to a bygone age of entertainment.

But you'll want to keep in mind that it's hard for Disney to maintain this giant showcase. It's been many years since its last refurbishment, and issues are starting to stick out more. This Oregon family certainly noticed:

The ride is run-down. Electrical plugs are clearly visible for some of the moving decorations, some of the group animatronics are worse for wear and do not move in a synchronized manner with their peers. Lots of paneling is clearly worn and simply painted over. Burned-out bulbs and dirty carpets are obvious.

Still, it's not all bad news if you can focus on the experience rather than the details, like this mom from Mississippi:

My 2-year-old loved it. My 10-year-old found the music too repetitive. I loved it because I got to sit for 15 minutes. And I loved it because I have memories of riding it as a child. And I love it because of the message it teaches. Makes me tear up as I ride through.

Mad Tea Party ★★½

| PRESCHOOL ★★★★½ (AA) | GRADE SCHOOL ★★★★½ (AA) | TEENS ★★★★ (A) |
| YOUNG ADULTS ★★★★ (A) | OVER 30 ★★★★ (MA) | OVER 65 ★★★½ (BA) |

What it is Spinning ride. **Scope and scale** Minor attraction. **When to go** Anytime. **Comment** The teacup spins faster when you turn the wheel in the center. We're not sure if that's a good thing or not. **Duration of ride** 1½ minutes. **Loading speed** Slow. **ECV/wheelchair access** Must transfer to the ride vehicle; transfer device available. **Participates in LLMP** Yes. **Early Theme Park Entry** Yes. **Extended Evening Hours** Yes.

DESCRIPTION AND COMMENTS Riders whirl around in big teacups. *Alice in Wonderland*'s Mad Hatter provides the theme. Kids like to lure adults onto the teacups and then turn the wheel in the middle—making the cup spin faster—until the adults are plastered helplessly against the sides and on the verge of tossing their tacos.

TOURING TIPS Mad Tea Party is notoriously slow-loading, especially if someone before you lost their lunch.

The Many Adventures of Winnie the Pooh ★★★½

| PRESCHOOL ★★★★½ (AA) | GRADE SCHOOL ★★★★ (A) | TEENS ★★★★ (A) |
| YOUNG ADULTS ★★★★ (A) | OVER 30 ★★★★ (A) | OVER 65 ★★★★ (A) |

What it is Indoor track ride. **Scope and scale** Minor attraction. **When to go** Early or late. **Duration of ride** About 4 minutes. **Loading speed** Moderate. **ECV/wheelchair access** Must transfer from ECV to provided wheelchair. **Participates in LLMP** Yes. **Early Theme Park Entry** Yes. **Extended Evening Hours** Yes.

DESCRIPTION AND COMMENTS Ride a Hunny Pot through the pages of a huge picture book into the Hundred Acre Wood, where you encounter all the familiar faces as they contend with a blustery day. There's even a dream sequence with Heffalumps and Woozles.

This is another attraction where LLMP sometimes slows the standby line to a crawl. If the Lightning Lane looks backed up, your standby wait will move at a snail's pace.

An Indiana mom loved Pooh's interactive queue:

The queue for The Many Adventures of Winnie the Pooh was amazing! There were so many things for little kids to do and, consequently, fewer meltdowns! I wish there were more queues like that.

TOURING TIPS Sunny, happy, and upbeat, Pooh is a good choice if you have small children or if you've ever wanted to bounce like Tigger. Be aware that they may fall in love with the characters and you'll have a hard time peeling them away from the gift shop.

Meet Mirabel at Fairytale Garden ★★★½

RATINGS NOT COLLECTED

What it is Character greeting. **Scope and scale** Minor attraction. **When to go** Early or late. **Duration of experience** About 3 minutes. **Queue speed** Slow. **ECV/wheelchair access** May remain in wheelchair. **Participates in LLMP** No. **Early Theme Park Entry** No. **Extended Evening Hours** No.

DESCRIPTION AND COMMENTS Mirabel, of *Encanto* fame, takes over this spot from Merida (who occasionally wanders Fantasyland instead). You'll find the **Fairytale Garden** in front of Cinderella Castle on the Tomorrowland side, between the castle and **Cosmic Ray's Starlight Café**.

TOURING TIPS This meet and greet tends to be exceedingly popular, so expect long lines. If meeting Mirabel is a must for your child, try to get in line about 15 minutes before her character location opens for the day.

Mickey's PhilharMagic ★★★½

PRESCHOOL ★★★★½ (AA)   **GRADE SCHOOL** ★★★★½ (AA)   **TEENS** ★★★★ (AA)
YOUNG ADULTS ★★★★½ (AA)   **OVER 30** ★★★★½ (AA)   **OVER 65** ★★★★½ (MAA)

What it is 3D movie. **Scope and scale** Minor attraction. **When to go** Anytime. **Duration of presentation** About 12 minutes. **Probable waiting time** Less than one show. **ECV/wheelchair access** May remain in wheelchair. **Participates in LLMP** Yes. **Early Theme Park Entry** Yes. **Extended Evening Hours** Yes.

DESCRIPTION AND COMMENTS Mickey's PhilharMagic is a 3D film with a fun collection of Disney characters, mixing Mickey and Donald with Simba and Ariel, as well as Jasmine, Aladdin, and characters from Coco.

Presented in a theater large enough to accommodate a 150-foot-wide screen—huge by 3D standards—the movie is augmented by a variety of special effects built into the theater. The plot involves Donald attempting to take charge of Mickey's symphony, with disastrous results.

Mickey's PhilharMagic is sure to leave you grinning. And where other Disney 3D movies are loud, in-your-face affairs, this one is softer and cuddlier. Things pop out of the screen, but they're not scary. Even young children are rarely frightened, as evidenced by the high ratings across the board.

TOURING TIPS Provides a nice midday air-conditioning break.

Peter Pan's Flight ★★★★

PRESCHOOL ★★★★½ (AA)   **GRADE SCHOOL** ★★★★½ (A)   **TEENS** ★★★★ (A)
YOUNG ADULTS ★★★★ (A)   **OVER 30** ★★★★ (A)   **OVER 65** ★★★★½ (AA)

What it is Indoor flying track ride. **Scope and scale** Major attraction. **When to go** First or last 30 minutes the park is open. **Duration of ride** About 3 minutes. **Loading speed** Moderate-slow. **ECV/wheelchair access** Must be ambulatory. **Participates in LLMP** Yes. **Early Theme Park Entry** Yes. **Extended Evening Hours** Yes.

DESCRIPTION AND COMMENTS Peter Pan's Flight combines beloved characters, beautiful effects, and charming music. The ride begins in the Darling family's house before embarking on a relaxing trip in a "flying pirate ship" over old London and then to Neverland. Nothing here will frighten young children.

A themed queue has air-conditioning and features a walk through the Darlings' home, where you'll see various rooms, play a few games, and get sprinkled with a bit of (virtual) pixie dust.

Peter Pan's Flight had a scene refresh in 2024, which redeemed it in the eyes of many commenters, including this group from New York:

We really loved the new scene with Tiger Lily and her grandma. We used to avoid this ride because the awful racial stereotyping of the native characters felt very dehumanizing and disturbing to me as a person of color. But the new scene is so cute—the figures now just look cartoonish in the same way as the other characters, instead of caricatures.

TOURING TIPS Count on long lines all day. Fortunately, the queue is out of direct sun and rain and has tons of art and interactive games to help pass the time. Ride in the first 30 minutes the park is open, during a parade, or just before the park closes. Peter Pan's Flight is one of the most helpful LLMP reservations you can get in the Magic Kingdom. Because its Lightning Lane is so popular, even a deceptively short-looking standby line will take eight forevers to load. That's been scientifically measured.

Pete's Silly Sideshow ★★★★

PRESCHOOL ★★★★½ (AA) **GRADE SCHOOL** ★★★½ (AA) **TEENS** ★★½ (BA)
YOUNG ADULTS ★★★ (BA) **OVER 30** ★★★ (BA) **OVER 65** ★★½ (BA)

What it is Character-greeting venue. **Scope and scale** Minor attraction. **When to go** Early or late. **Duration of experience** 3 minutes per character. **Queue speed** Slow. **ECV/wheelchair access** May remain in wheelchair. **Participates in LLMP** No. **Early Theme Park Entry** No. **Extended Evening Hours** No.

DESCRIPTION AND COMMENTS Pete's Silly Sideshow is a circus-themed character-greeting area. The characters' costumes are unique to this location. Characters include Goofy as The Great Goofini, Donald Duck as The Astounding Donaldo, Daisy Duck as Madame Daisy Fortuna, and Minnie Mouse as Minnie Magnifique.

TOURING TIPS The queue is indoors and air-conditioned. There's one queue for Goofy and Donald and a second queue for Minnie and Daisy; you can meet two characters at once, but you have to line up twice to meet all four. If you or your kids feel like character greetings are awkward, you'll appreciate the unique backdrops and costumes that make for easy conversation and interactions here. We find that the characters here take more time with each party, which makes for great interactions . . . and longer lines.

Prince Charming Regal Carrousel ★★★

PRESCHOOL ★★★★½ (MAA) **GRADE SCHOOL** ★★★½ (A) **TEENS** ★★½ (BA)
YOUNG ADULTS ★★★★ (A) **OVER 30** ★★★★ (BA) **OVER 65** ★★★★ (BA)

What it is Merry-go-round. **Scope and scale** Minor attraction. **When to go** Anytime. **Duration of ride** About 2 minutes. **Loading speed** Slow. **ECV/wheelchair access** Must transfer from ECV to provided wheelchair. **Participates in LLMP** No. **Early Theme Park Entry** Yes. **Extended Evening Hours** Yes.

DESCRIPTION AND COMMENTS One of the most elaborate and beautiful merry-go-rounds you'll ever have the pleasure of seeing, especially when its lights are on.

TOURING TIPS Unless young children in your party insist on riding, appreciate the carousel from the sidelines—it loads and unloads very slowly.

Princess Fairytale Hall ★★★½

PRESCHOOL ★★★★½ (MAA) **GRADE SCHOOL** ★★★★½ (MAA) **TEENS** ★★★★ (A)
YOUNG ADULTS ★★★★ (A) **OVER 30** ★★★★ (A) **OVER 65** ★★★★ (BA)

What it is Character-greeting venue. **Scope and scale** Minor attraction. **When to go** Early or late. **Duration of experience** 6-7 minutes. **Queue speed** Slow. **ECV/wheelchair access** May remain in wheelchair. **Participates in LLMP** No. **Early Theme Park Entry** No. **Extended Evening Hours** No.

DESCRIPTION AND COMMENTS Fairytale Hall is Princess Central in the Magic Kingdom. Inside are two greeting venues, each holding a small reception area for two princesses. Thus, there are four princesses meeting and greeting at any time, and you can see two of them at once. Signs outside tell you which line leads to which princess pair. Tiana leads one side, usually paired with Rapunzel. Cinderella and Elena of Avalor (a Disney Channel character) are the usual pair on the other. Around 5-10 guests at a time are admitted to each greeting area, where there's plenty of time for small talk and a photo with each princess.

TOURING TIPS These lines can be substantial, especially if new princesses are introduced. If your kids love princesses, get Fairytale Hall out of the way early. The two queues are identical and almost always move at similar speeds, so if you're going standby, you'll be able to see which pair of princesses has a shorter wait, regardless of what the posted wait says.

Seven Dwarfs Mine Train ★★★★

PRESCHOOL ★★★★ (A) GRADE SCHOOL ★★★★½ (MAA) TEENS ★★★★½ (AA)
YOUNG ADULTS ★★★★½ (MAA) OVER 30 ★★★★½ (AA) OVER 65 ★★★★½ (AA)

What it is Themed roller coaster. **Scope and scale** Super-headliner. **When to go** As soon as the park opens. **Comment** Must be 38" tall to ride. **Duration of ride** About 2 minutes. **Loading speed** Fast. **ECV/wheelchair access** Must transfer to the ride vehicle. **Participates in LLMP** No (it offers LLSP). **Early Theme Park Entry** Yes. **Extended Evening Hours** Yes.

DESCRIPTION AND COMMENTS Seven Dwarfs Mine Train is geared to older grade-school kids who've been on amusement park rides before. There are no upside-down sections and no massive hills or steep drops. It's a curvy track with steep turns, and your ride vehicle's seats swing side-to-side as you go through the turns. An elaborate (but short) indoor section shows the dwarfs' underground mining operation.

The exterior design includes waterfalls, forests, and landscaping. The swinging effect is more noticeable the farther back you're seated in the train. The duration is almost jarringly short, so take that into consideration when deciding how long you're willing to wait.

A family from Michigan sums up what's great about this ride:

My whole family loves this ride. My 6-year-old is a little tentative about rides, but it goes fast and your stomach doesn't drop, so even he likes it! My 4-year-old is short but tall enough to ride this, so he gets excited. My 9-year-old still enjoys it, too, although he prefers more thrilling roller coasters, so it's an overall win for the family.

One of Becky's all-time favorite WDW memories is riding Seven Dwarfs for the first time, with a train full of adults singing "Heigh Ho" together as they got pulled up the hill in the mine. Still, this is a deceptively short coaster. Decide how long you'll be OK waiting for a ride that lasts less than 2 minutes.

TOURING TIPS If you have children who might be interested in riding this but not Space Mountain, head for Seven Dwarfs as soon as the park opens. Depending on how they handle this ride, try **Big Thunder Mountain Railroad** or **Tiana's Bayou Adventure** next. Keep in mind that Seven Dwarfs Mine Train is one of the most unreliable attractions at rope drop, so you'll also need to have a backup plan.

Under the Sea—Journey of the Little Mermaid ★★★

PRESCHOOL ★★★★½ (MAA) GRADE SCHOOL ★★★★½ (A) TEENS ★★★★ (A)
YOUNG ADULTS ★★★★ (A) OVER 30 ★★★★ (A) OVER 65 ★★★★ (A)

What it is Story-retelling dark ride. **Scope and scale** Minor attraction. **When to go** Early or late. **Duration of ride** About 5½ minutes. **Loading speed** Fast. **ECV/wheelchair access** Must transfer from ECV to provided wheelchair. **Participates in LLMP** Yes. **Early Theme Park Entry** Yes. **Extended Evening Hours** Yes.

DESCRIPTION AND COMMENTS Under the Sea takes riders through almost a dozen scenes retelling the story of *The Little Mermaid* with animatronics, video effects, and a vibrant set. Guests board a clamshell-shaped ride vehicle running along a continuously moving track (similar to The Haunted

Mansion's), then descend "underwater" past Ariel's grotto to King Triton's undersea kingdom. Ursula is the most impressive animatronic.

The attraction's exterior is attractive, with detailed rockwork and water elements. Our favorite effect is a hidden Mickey, created by the alignment of the sun's shadow and the rockwork, that appears only at **noon on November 18,** Mickey's birthday.

This ride isn't Disney's most ambitious, but it's cute. Most of the effects are simple and unimaginative, and almost the whole second half of the story is crammed into a few small scenes at the end, as if the budget ran out before the ride could be finished properly.

TOURING TIPS Under the Sea is one of several attractions that used to almost always be a walk-on but gets weirdly long wait times with LLMP, thanks to plenty of visitors grabbing immediately available return times and backing up the Lightning Lane.

Walt Disney World Railroad

DESCRIPTION AND COMMENTS The railroad stops in Fantasyland on its circuit of the park. See the description under Main Street, U.S.A. (page 376), for additional details.

TOURING TIPS Pleasant, feet-saving link to Main Street and Frontierland.

TOMORROWLAND

AT VARIOUS POINTS IN ITS HISTORY, Tomorrowland's attractions presented life's possibilities, ranging from present-day adventures (such as the 1970s ride If You Had Wings, which simulated around-the-world travel) to those imagining the distant future (such as Mission to Mars, which ran from 1975 to 1992). The problem that Disney repeatedly ran up against was that the future came faster and looked different than it had predicted, which made this land constantly feel outdated.

Today, Tomorrowland's theme makes the least sense of any land at any Disney World park. Its current attractions are based on gas-powered race cars, rocket travel (two rides), a look back at 20th-century technology, aliens and lasers, a comedy show with monsters, and a motorcycle race inside a computer. It's less a vision of the future and more a collection of attractions that don't fit anywhere else.

Astro Orbiter ★★

| PRESCHOOL ★★★★ (A) | GRADE SCHOOL ★★★★ (BA) | TEENS ★★★½ (MBA) |
| YOUNG ADULTS ★★★½ (BA) | OVER 30 ★★★ (MBA) | OVER 65 ★★★ (MBA) |

What it is Retro rocket spinner. **Scope and scale** Minor attraction. **When to go** Before 11 a.m. or just before park closing. **Duration of ride** 1½ minutes. **Loading speed** Painfully slow. **ECV/wheelchair access** Must transfer to the ride vehicle. **Participates in LLMP** No. **Early Theme Park Entry** Yes. **Extended Evening Hours** Yes.

DESCRIPTION AND COMMENTS Though visually appealing, this carnival ride with little rocket ships flying in circles is slow-loading. The best thing about it is the nice view while you're aloft.

TOURING TIPS Easily skippable. If you ride with preschoolers, seat them first. The Astro Orbiter flies higher and faster than Dumbo and frightens some young children. Even if you are capable of riding stable spinners, consider the combination of spinning and heights before deciding to ride.

Buzz Lightyear's Space Ranger Spin ★★★★

| PRESCHOOL ★★★★½ (AA) | GRADE SCHOOL ★★★★½ (A) | TEENS ★★★★ (A) |
| YOUNG ADULTS ★★★★ (A) | OVER 30 ★★★★ (A) | OVER 65 ★★★★½ (AA) |

What it is Space-themed indoor blaster ride. **Scope and scale** Minor attraction. **When to go** First or last hour the park is open. **Duration of ride** About 4½ minutes. **Loading speed** Fast. **ECV/wheelchair access** Must transfer from ECV to provided wheelchair. **Participates in LLMP** Yes. **Early Theme Park Entry** Yes. **Extended Evening Hours** Yes.

DESCRIPTION AND COMMENTS At press time, Disney had announced a major refurbishment of this attraction, which will take place in late 2025, potentially extending into 2026. It's definitely needed, as shown by many reader comments like this one from Wisconsin:

This ride feels very antiquated, especially in comparison to the very similar Toy Story–themed gallery shooter in Hollywood Studios. The laser dots are so small you have no idea where you are aiming, making the shooting portion feel very arbitrary. My younger child couldn't figure out at all what he should even be doing, whereas he had no problem in Hollywood Studios.

Thankfully, Disney took many opinions like this one into account and has totally redesigned the aiming technology. New ride vehicles will feature handheld, always-on lasers that come in two colors per ride vehicle. Analog score displays will also be replaced with video monitors in each vehicle. All of these changes are meant to help riders of all ages have a more enjoyable and engaging experience.

We expect most of the story to stay the same, so hopefully many more guests will get to become Galactic Heroes as they successfully battle Zurg after the refurbishment.

TOURING TIPS The standby queue, like a few others in the Magic Kingdom, gets remarkably slowed down by the prioritization of Lightning Lane riders. If the line is out the door and not moving, you will have at least a 20-minute wait from that point.

Most folks spend their first ride learning how to use the equipment and figuring out how the targets work. Hopefully, most of this learning curve is removed with the newly implemented technology. But we still bet that on your next ride, you'll be surprised by how much better you do because you know where to look and aim in advance.

If targets and scores stay similar to the older version of the attraction, the first room's mechanical claw and red robot, plus the top of the volcano in the second room, contain high-value targets, so aim for those. You'll be a Galactic Hero in no time.

Monsters, Inc. Laugh Floor ★★★

| PRESCHOOL ★★★★ (A) | GRADE SCHOOL ★★★★½ (AA) | TEENS ★★★★ (A) |
| YOUNG ADULTS ★★★★½ (AA) | OVER 30 ★★★★ (A) | OVER 65 ★★★★½ (AA) |

What it is Interactive animated comedy show. **Scope and scale** Minor attraction. **When to go** Anytime. **Duration of presentation** About 15 minutes. **ECV/wheelchair access** May remain in wheelchair. **Participates in LLMP** Yes. **Early Theme Park Entry** No. **Extended Evening Hours** Yes.

DESCRIPTION AND COMMENTS In the movie *Monsters, Inc.*, monsters discover that kids' laughter works even better than kids' screams as an energy source. In this attraction, they've set up a comedy club to capture as many laughs as possible.

Mike Wazowski, the one-eyed green monster, emcees the club's three comedy acts. Each act consists of an animated monster trying out various bad jokes. Using technological wizardry, behind-the-scenes cast members voice the characters and often interact with audience members during the skits. Disney experiments with new routines and jokes, so the show rarely feels stale. If you enjoy entertainment where the whole crowd is laughing together, you will enjoy the *Laugh Floor*.

A family from Ohio were happy they stopped in:

We hadn't heard anything about this attraction and had assumed that it was a show or short film. We had no idea it was improv with audience interaction and were blown away by how funny and clever it was.

TOURING TIPS The theater holds several hundred people, so there's no need to rush here first thing in the morning.

Space Mountain ★★★★

| PRESCHOOL ★★★ (MBA) | GRADE SCHOOL ★★★★½ (A) | TEENS ★★★★½ (MAA) |
| YOUNG ADULTS ★★★★½ (AA) | OVER 30 ★★★★ (A) | OVER 65 ★★★½ (BA) |

What it is Dark roller coaster. **Scope and scale** Super-headliner. **When to go** At park opening or the last hour before closing. Must be 44" tall to ride; Rider Switch option provided (see page 307). **Duration of ride** Almost 3 minutes. **Loading speed** Moderate–fast. **ECV/wheelchair access** Must transfer from ECV to provided wheelchair then to the ride vehicle. **Participates in LLMP** Yes. **Early Theme Park Entry** Yes. **Extended Evening Hours** Yes.

DESCRIPTION AND COMMENTS Space Mountain has long been one of the Magic Kingdom's most popular attractions. This ride is one of the fastest, darkest, and wildest in the Magic Kingdom: It's zippier than Big Thunder Mountain Railroad but slower than Tron next door, Rock 'n' Roller Coaster in Hollywood Studios, or Expedition Everest in Animal Kingdom. Even though the premise is that you're flying through space, there are no long drops or swooping hills—only quick, unexpected turns and small drops. The coaster is a classic midway ride design called a Wild Mouse; Disney just added a space theme and put it in the dark.

People who can handle a fairly wild coaster will take Space Mountain in stride. What sets it apart is the darkness. Half the fun is not knowing where the car will go next.

TOURING TIPS Most guests head to Seven Dwarfs Mine Train first, then visit Space Mountain. If Tron isn't open during Early Entry, one of the best Magic Kingdom Early Entry strategies is to head straight for Space Mountain and then immediately get in line for Tron.

Seats are one behind another, as opposed to side by side, which means that parents can't sit next to their kids who might get scared. We recommend sitting behind them and reaching forward to hold their shoulder if they need some help being brave.

Tomorrowland Speedway ★★

| PRESCHOOL ★★★★½ (AA) | GRADE SCHOOL ★★★★½ (A) | TEENS ★★★½ (BA) |
| YOUNG ADULTS ★★★½ (MBA) | OVER 30 ★★★ (MBA) | OVER 65 ★★★ (MBA) |

What it is Drive-'em-yourself minicars. **Scope and scale** Minor attraction. **When to go** Not in the hot sun. **Comment** Must be 54" tall to drive unassisted, 32" to ride with a person age 14 or older. **Duration of ride** About 4¼ minutes. **Loading speed** Slow.

ECV/wheelchair access Must transfer to the ride vehicle; transfer device available. **Participates in LLMP** Yes. **Early Theme Park Entry** Yes. **Extended Evening Hours** Yes.

DESCRIPTION AND COMMENTS A mini raceway with gas-powered cars that poke along at about 7 miles per hour on a guide rail, leaving drivers little to do. Any small child that passes will want to drive, so some families (including Becky's) try to bypass the area entirely.

TOURING TIPS This ride is visually appealing (except for the puffs of fumes), and the 9-and-under set loves it. If your child is too short to drive, let them steer the car while you work the pedal.

In a world where large, generally unpopular attractions are getting the ax, it's a wonder that this still exists.

Tomorrowland Transit Authority PeopleMover ★★★½

PRESCHOOL ★★★★½ (AA) **GRADE SCHOOL** ★★★★½ (AA) **TEENS** ★★★★½ (AA)
YOUNG ADULTS ★★★★½ (MAA) **OVER 30** ★★★★½ (MAA) **OVER 65** ★★★★½ (MAA)

What it is Scenic tour of Tomorrowland. **Scope and scale** Minor attraction. **When to go** Anytime. **Duration of ride** 10 minutes. **Loading speed** Fast. **ECV/wheelchair access** Must be ambulatory. **Participates in LLMP** No. **Early Theme Park Entry** Yes. **Extended Evening Hours** Yes.

DESCRIPTION AND COMMENTS An early prototype of a linear induction–powered mass-transit system carries riders on a leisurely tour of Tomorrowland, including a peek inside Space Mountain.

A family from Georgia shares a perspective similar to Becky's:

The PeopleMover is one we recommend to every family that asks us for Disney advice. The line moves quickly, it offers a great overview of the land, and it has unbeatable views at night.

TOURING TIPS This is a great choice during busier times of day or to keep littles entertained while others experience Tron or Space Mountain.

Tron Lightcycle/Run ★★★★

PRESCHOOL ★★½ (MBA) **GRADE SCHOOL** ★★★★½ (AA) **TEENS** ★★★★★ (E)
YOUNG ADULTS ★★★★½ (MAA) **OVER 30** ★★★★½ (MAA) **OVER 65** ★★★★ (BA)

What it is High-speed indoor-outdoor roller coaster. **Scope and scale** Super-headliner. **When to go** At park opening or just before the park closes. **Comments** Must be 48" tall to ride. Seating arrangement may prove uncomfortable for some. **Duration of ride** 1 minute. **Loading speed** Fast. **ECV/wheelchair access** Must transfer from wheelchair to the ride vehicle. **Participates in LLMP** No (it offers LLSP). **Early Theme Park Entry** No. **Extended Evening Hours** Yes.

DESCRIPTION AND COMMENTS Riders sit as if on a motorcycle while they rocket through dark scenes with neon lighting. The ride vehicles are set up as 14 semidetached "lightcycles," with seven rows of two cycles each. Riders must lift one leg up and over to board and must lean forward slightly to hold onto the cycle's handlebars. They are then launched from zero to super speed in no time into the first set of turns.

The ride is incredibly smooth, and thanks to the unique positioning, it really feels like you're flying around the track. But maybe you fly a little too fast because those 60 seconds of ride time are over very quickly.

Tron is most like Hollywood Studios' Rock 'n' Roller Coaster, which has a similar launch. Tron is by far the most intense coaster in the Magic

Kingdom, but it doesn't have any loops or inversions. If Seven Dwarfs Mine Train or Space Mountain gives you pause, skip Tron.

Tron has safety restraints that may not fit every body type. Disney has two solutions for this: (1) a more traditional, seated car at the end of the motorcycle-like train of ride vehicles and (2) a test vehicle with test restraints, located just before you enter the ride's main building. Ask a cast member if you'd like to try one or the other. (See page 322 for more tips for larger guests.)

TOURING TIPS Tron is one of the Magic Kingdom's hottest rides. Expect LLSP reservations to sell out days in advance. Standby lines here will be longer than at any other attraction in the Magic Kingdom, making LLSP a worthwhile purchase unless you can get in line right at park opening or are willing to stay late and jump in line just before park closing.

This attraction is even more impressive at night.

Walt Disney's Carousel of Progress ★★★

| PRESCHOOL ★★★½ (BA) | GRADE SCHOOL ★★★★ (BA) | TEENS ★★★★ (A) |
| YOUNG ADULTS ★★★★ (A) | OVER 30 ★★★★ (A) | OVER 65 ★★★★½ (AA) |

What it is Audio-Animatronic theater show. **Scope and scale** Minor attraction. **When to go** Afternoon. **Duration of presentation** 21 minutes. **Probable waiting time** Less than 10 minutes. **ECV/wheelchair access** May remain in wheelchair. **Participates in LLMP** No. **Early Theme Park Entry** Yes. **Extended Evening Hours** No.

DESCRIPTION AND COMMENTS *Carousel of Progress* is a four-act play offering a nostalgic look at how electricity and technology changed the lives of an animatronic family. General Electric sponsored the first version of the show for the 1964 World's Fair in New York. The first scene is set in 1901; the second, around 1927; and the third, in the late 1940s. The fourth scene is allegedly contemporary, but your mileage may vary.

Carousel of Progress is the only attraction in the park that displays Walt's optimistic vision of a better future through technology. If you're interested in the man behind the mouse, this show is a must-see.

TOURING TIPS The show handles big crowds effectively and is a good choice during busier times of day.

MAGIC KINGDOM ENTERTAINMENT

LIVE ENTERTAINMENT

FOR SPECIFIC EVENTS on the day you visit, check the schedule in the MDE app or in the *Times Guide*, available at Guest Relations.

CHARACTER CAVALCADES In addition to the main parade, Disney runs a small one- or two-float cavalcade on some days, usually in the afternoon. The cavalcade, called **Disney Adventure Friends,** is more of a random smattering of characters, from Miguel (of *Coco*), Baloo, and Mirabel to Stitch and Mary Poppins. This small cavalcade actually rates slightly higher than Festival of Fantasy parade across several age groups, likely because of the large array of characters and the ability to watch without lining up early.

FESTIVAL OF FANTASY PARADE The Magic Kingdom's afternoon parade typically runs once a day (maybe twice during busy seasons). Multiple floats and troupes of dancers, along with a multitude of Disney characters, make their way from Frontierland through Liberty Square, and then around the central hub and down Main Street. The parade start time listed in the MDE app is when the parade will start in Frontierland. If you're watching from Main Street, expect another 20-plus-minute wait. Still, it's worth watching to see the big Maleficent rolling along.

unofficial **TIP**
If you're short on time, keep in mind that it's impossible to see all of the Magic Kingdom's feature attractions and live performances. Prioritize!

FLAG RETREAT Taking place at 5 p.m. daily at **Town Square** (the Walt Disney World Railroad end of Main Street), this ceremony honoring veterans is sometimes performed with large college marching bands and sometimes with a smaller Disney band or **The Dapper Dans.**

DISNEY STARLIGHT PARADE At press time, Disney had announced that a new nighttime parade would debut in the Magic Kingdom in the summer of 2025. The parade will feature lighted performers and floats and follow the same route as Festival of Fantasy. Expect this to be the biggest draw of the day, with crowds lining the parade route at least an hour in advance.

FIREWORKS SHOWS AND OTHER NIGHTTIME ENTERTAINMENT

LIKE ITS PARADES, the Magic Kingdom's dazzling nighttime spectaculars are highly rated and not to be missed.

BAY LAKE AND SEVEN SEAS LAGOON ELECTRICAL WATER PAGEANT ★★★★ Usually performed at nightfall (8:50 at the Polynesian Village Resort, 9 at the Grand Floridian Resort, and 10:15 at the Contemporary Resort) on Seven Seas Lagoon and Bay Lake, this is a classic Disney nighttime spectacular, but you must leave the Magic Kingdom to view it. The pageant is a stunning electric-light show set to nifty electronic music. This was meant to be a one-night show on opening day of the Magic Kingdom in 1971, but it's been running ever since.

HAPPILY EVER AFTER FIREWORKS SHOW ★★★★ This multisensory show of fireworks, music, and video projections is one of the highest-rated attractions in Disney World across all age groups. The show is about princesses and romance but also includes messages about work and determination as part of a path to . . . happily ever after. Images projected onto the castle include snippets from the usual suspects of *Frozen* and *Cinderella*, as well as *Hunchback of Notre Dame; Monsters, Inc.; Cars;* and *Wreck-It Ralph*, among others. *Happily Ever After*'s fireworks can be enjoyed from outside the park. However, due to the strong integration of the castle projections into the performance, you'll be missing a substantial portion of the show if you're not viewing from the central hub or Main Street area inside the park.

Paid Fireworks Viewing Opportunities

FIREWORKS DESSERT PARTIES Disney reserves the **Plaza Gardens** and **Tomorrowland Terrace** restaurant for three fireworks-viewing parties:

1. **Happily Ever After Pre-Party** ($99–$109/adult, $59/child) begins approximately 90 minutes before the show. You'll be served unlimited desserts, beer, wine, and sodas until just before the fireworks begin, when you'll be escorted to a special, standing-room-only viewing spot.

2. **Happily Ever After Fireworks Dessert Parties (Seats & Sweets)** ($119–$129/adult, $69/child) run before, during, and after the show inside Tomorrowland Terrace. Note that the view of the castle is blocked at many seats, and the sound quality is poor in the all-concrete echo chamber of the restaurant. The big advantage here is that you get actual seats for the show.

3. **Happily Ever After Post-Party** (99–$109/adult, $59 per child) gives you a special, standing-room-only viewing location before the fireworks begin. After the fireworks, you'll be admitted to Tomorrowland Terrace for desserts, beer, wine, and sodas, for the next hour.

Reservations can be made 60 days in advance online or by calling ☎ 407-WDW-DINE (939-3463). Even the reserved viewing area can get crowded, though. And if you are participating in the pre-party, chances are all of the postparty attendees will already be in the reserved spot before you walk over. Still, we think the dessert party can be "worth it"—only during party season on nonparty nights. Even on low-crowd days, the Magic Kingdom becomes a madhouse for *Happily Ever After* from August through the end of the year. If it's important to you to watch and you don't want to claim a spot hours in advance, a dessert party can be a worthwhile purchase.

A Missouri reader who went to the dessert party declared it meh:

> *We did the fireworks dessert party at Tomorrowland Terrace against my better judgment. While the vantage point was pretty good and the desserts were tasty, it was definitely not worth the price.*

FIREWORKS CRUISE For a different view, you can watch the fireworks from Seven Seas Lagoon aboard a pontoon boat. The cost is $449 (plus tax) for up to 10 people. Bottled sodas, water, and a selection of sweet and savory snacks are provided; sandwiches and other more substantial food items may be arranged through reservations. Your Disney captain will take you for a little cruise and then position the boat in a perfect place to watch the fireworks. (A major indirect benefit of the charter is that you can enjoy the fireworks without fighting the mob afterward.) If you have a larger group and the projections on the castle aren't important to you (see tip, opposite page), this is an even better deal than the dessert party.

Because this is a private charter, only your group will be aboard. Life jackets are provided, but wearing them is at your discretion. To reserve a charter, call ☎ 407-WDW-PLAY (939-7529) at exactly 7 a.m. Eastern time about 180 days before the day you want to cruise.

VIEWING AND EXIT STRATEGIES FOR PARADES AND FIREWORKS

Vantage Points for Parades

Magic Kingdom parades begin in **Frontierland** by Tiana's Bayou Adventure and follow the waterfront through **Liberty Square**. From there, they cross the Liberty Square Bridge to the **Central Plaza**, circle it, then head down **Main Street**. A quick trip around **Town Square** follows before they head off-stage behind the Main Street fire station.

Because most spectators pack Main Street and the Central Plaza, we recommend watching the parades from **Liberty Square** or **Frontierland** instead. Great spots that are often overlooked are:

1. **Sleepy Hollow, immediately to your right as you cross the bridge into Liberty Square.** If you arrive early, buy refreshments and claim a table closest to the rail. You'll have a perfect view of the parade as it crosses Liberty Square Bridge.
2. **Pathway on the Liberty Square side of the moat from Sleepy Hollow to Cinderella Castle.** Any point along the way offers an unobstructed view as the parade crosses Liberty Square Bridge.
3. **Covered walkway between Liberty Tree Tavern and The Diamond Horseshoe.** This elevated vantage point is perfect (particularly on rainy days) and usually goes unnoticed until just before the parade starts.
4. **Elevated platforms in front of Frontier Trading Post and the building with the sign reading FRONTIER MERCANTILE.** These spots usually get picked off 10–12 minutes before parade time.
5. **Benches on the perimeter of the Central Plaza, between the entrances to Liberty Square and Adventureland,** offer a comfortable resting place and an unobstructed (though somewhat distant) view of the parade as it crosses Liberty Square Bridge.
6. **Liberty Square and Frontierland dockside areas.** Spots here usually go early.
7. **The porch of Tony's Town Square Restaurant,** on Main Street, provides an elevated viewing platform and an easy exit path when the fireworks are over.

Vantage Points for Fireworks

The best viewing spots for the fireworks show are **between the Central Plaza and the castle,** offering up-close views of the castle projections. The next-best spots are in **Plaza Gardens East and West** nearest the castle. The gardens are specifically constructed for fireworks viewing. We prefer Plaza Gardens East (the Tomorrowland side) because the configuration of light/audio poles is slightly less obtrusive.

If those spots are taken, your next-best alternatives are on Main Street, where you'll get to see the (smaller) projections closer. Watching from the train-station end of Main Street is the easiest way to leave the park quickly, but you won't recognize most of the castle's images.

If we're staying in the park and trying to avoid the crowds on Main Street, our two favorite spots to see just the fireworks are:

1. **Fantasyland between Seven Dwarfs Mine Train and *Enchanted Tales with Belle.*** Some of the minor fireworks above the castle will be behind you, but all of the major effects will be right in front of you.
2. **Bridge between the Central Plaza and Tomorrowland.** A few trees block some of the castle, but if Tinker Bell does her flight from the castle, she'll fly directly over this area.

Leaving the Park Before or During Fireworks

If you're trying to exit the park just before or during the fireworks, you'll need to walk down the passageways behind the east and west sides of Main Street to get out, or use the Tomorrowland Main Street passageways (see next page) if they're open. (If you're facing the train station, with Cinderella Castle behind you, east is on your left.)

Leaving the Park After Fireworks

With armies of guests leaving the park after fireworks, the Disney Transportation System gets overwhelmed, causing long waits for the ferry, monorail, or buses. An Oklahoma dad offers this advice:

Never, never leave the Magic Kingdom just after the evening fireworks. Go for another ride—no lines!

Congestion persists from the end of the fireworks until closing time. If you're parked at the Transportation and Ticket Center (TTC) and are intent on beating the crowd, view the fireworks from the Town Square end of Main Street, leaving the park as soon as the show ends and hustling to your transportation as quickly as possible.

MAIN STREET PASSAGEWAYS The Magic Kingdom has two pedestrian walkways behind the shops on either side of Main Street, specifically for guests who want to get in or out of the park without walking down the middle of the street. If you're on the Tomorrowland side, look for a passageway that runs from between **The Plaza Restaurant** and **Tomorrowland Terrace**, back behind the east side of Main Street, to **Tony's Town Square Restaurant** near the park exit. If you're on the Adventureland side, the passageway runs from **First Aid** to the **Main Street fire station** near the park exit. These passageways aren't used every night, so there's no guarantee they'll be available.

If the passageways aren't open and you're on the Tomorrowland side, cut through Tomorrowland Terrace, and then work your way down Main Street until you're past Main Street Bakery (Starbucks) and have crossed a small cul-de-sac. Bear left into the side door of that corner shop. Work your way from shop to shop until you reach Town Square—easy because people will be outside watching the fireworks. At Town Square, bear left to reach the train station and park exit.

unofficial **TIP**
Instead of walking outside, you can cut through the Main Street shops—they have interior doors that let you pass from one shop to the next.

This also works if you're on the Adventureland side of the park. You can make your way through **Casey's Corner** to Main Street and then work your way through the shops, and when you pop out of the **Emporium** at Town Square, you can bolt for the exit.

If your car is parked at the TTC lot, you could line up for the **ferry;** one will depart about every 8–10 minutes. You could even leave before the fireworks and try to catch the ferry that will be crossing Seven Seas Lagoon while the fireworks show is in progress. The best vantage point is on the top deck to the right of the pilothouse as you face the Magic Kingdom—the sight of fireworks silhouetting the castle and reflecting off the lagoon is unforgettable.

While there's no guarantee that a ferry will load and depart within 3 or 4 minutes of the fireworks, your chances are about 50–50 of timing it just right. If you're in the front of the line for the ferry and don't want to board the boat that's loading, stop at the gate and let people pass you. You'll be the first to board the next boat.

Strollers, wheelchairs, and ECVs make navigating crowds more difficult. If you have one, or if you're staying at a Disney resort that is not served by the monorail, and you have to depend on Disney transportation, watch the fireworks, and then enjoy the attractions or a rapidly emptying park until the crowds disperse. Then catch the Disney bus or boat back to your hotel.

One supersneaky crowd-beating option is to take the **walking path over to the Contemporary Resort** instead of battling the crowds for a spot on a bus, ferry, or monorail. Request an Uber or Lyft from the Contemporary and quickly be on your way. My (Becky's) family uses this option, and even with smaller legs in the party, it's usually a 10- to 12-minute walk to the Contemporary, an immediate pickup, and a quick ride to our resort—for as little as $12! Since it's already after bedtime if we've stayed for fireworks, this is *well* worth not hearing an hour of complaining as we wait for Disney transportation, and I consider it a good investment in better sleep for everyone.

MAGIC KINGDOM HARD-TICKET EVENTS

THE MAGIC KINGDOM HOSTS several **holiday-themed events** after the park closes from mid-August through December. Celebrating Halloween and Christmas, they require separate paid admission and almost always sell out. Space doesn't permit us to cover them with more than a brief mention (see "The Walt Disney World Calendar," page 32). That said, ride wait times during these events are as low as they can be, making them a plausible alternative to, say, paying for a second day (and another hotel night) to finish seeing the Magic Kingdom.

TRAFFIC PATTERNS *in* *the* MAGIC KINGDOM

1. WHICH SECTIONS OF THE PARK AND WHICH ATTRACTIONS DO GUESTS VISIT FIRST? When the park opens, guest traffic is heaviest going to Fantasyland and Tomorrowland, then Frontierland (at official park opening). **Seven Dwarfs Mine Train** pulls people to Fantasyland, at the back of the park, while **Space Mountain** and **Tron Lightcycle/Run** pull a few to Tomorrowland, on the right (east) side. **Tiana's Bayou Adventure** and **Big Thunder Mountain Railroad** draw large crowds to Frontierland, on the left (west) side.

unofficial **TIP**
As the park fills up, visitors head for the top attractions before lines get long. This, more than anything else, determines morning traffic patterns.

2. HOW LONG DOES IT TAKE FOR THE PARK TO FILL UP? HOW ARE VISITORS DISPERSED IN THE PARK? A surge of early birds arrives before or around Early Entry, but they are quickly dispersed throughout the empty park. After this initial wave is absorbed, there's a lull lasting about an hour after opening. Then the park is inundated for about 2 hours, peaking between 10 a.m. and noon. Arrivals continue in a steady but diminishing stream until around 2 p.m. Lines are typically longest between 1 and 2 p.m., indicating more arrivals than departures into the early afternoon. For touring purposes, long lines start to develop between 10 and 11:30 a.m.

From late morning until early afternoon, guests are evenly distributed among all the lands. However, guests concentrate in **Fantasyland, Liberty Square,** and **Frontierland** in late afternoon, with a decrease of visitors in Adventureland and Tomorrowland. Adventureland's **Jungle Cruise** and Tomorrowland's **Space Mountain** and **Tron Lightcycle/Run** continue to be crowded, but most other attractions in those lands are readily accessible.

3. HOW DO MOST VISITORS TOUR THE PARK? Many **first-time visitors** are guided by friends or relatives familiar with the Magic Kingdom;

these groups may or may not follow an orderly sequence. First-timers without guidance, who tend to be more orderly in their touring, also tend to be drawn to Cinderella Castle upon entering the park and thus begin their day in Fantasyland. **Repeat visitors** usually head straight to their favorite attractions.

4. WILL GOING LEFT (OR RIGHT) HELP AVOID CROWDS? Some claim that most people turn right into Tomorrowland and tour the Magic Kingdom counterclockwise. The claim is baseless. Neither do most people turn left and start in Adventureland.

Here's why: Magic Kingdom headliner attractions are intentionally located at opposite points around the park to distribute crowds evenly: **Space Mountain** and **Tron** on the east side, **Tiana's Bayou Adventure** and **Big Thunder Mountain Railroad** on the west, **Seven Dwarfs Mine Train** to the north, and so on.

If, therefore, you were to start touring by heading left, you'd have low crowds in Adventureland and moderate crowds in Frontierland—but by the time you got to Fantasyland and Tomorrowland, you'd run into the largest crowds of the day. A similar scenario would await you if you started by bearing right into Tomorrowland: packed crowds in the rest of the lands you visit.

Avoiding the biggest crowds in the Magic Kingdom requires:

- Knowing which attractions to visit and when.
- Knowing how to make the best use of LLMP and LLSP (if you're willing to pay for them).
- Being willing to cross the park to save time.

5. HOW DO DAILY EVENTS, SUCH AS PARADES AND LIVE SHOWS, AFFECT TRAFFIC PATTERNS? Parades pull large numbers of guests away from attractions and provide a window of opportunity for experiencing the more popular attractions with less of a wait. (Character cavalcades don't have this effect.) Castle Stage shows also attract crowds but barely affect lines because they're offered more regularly throughout the day.

6. WHAT ARE THE TRAFFIC PATTERNS NEAR AND AT CLOSING TIME? On almost all days, in busy times and off-season, departures outnumber arrivals beginning in midafternoon. Many visitors leave in late afternoon as dinnertime approaches.

There is a *big* exception to this rule, and it happens during party season: On the relatively rare nights when the park doesn't close early for a party, guests flock into the park later in the day, with increasing crowds around dinner and leading up to fireworks, so some of the longest waits of the day will happen in the evening instead of midday.

Because Main Street and transportation services remain open after the other lands close, crowds at closing mainly congregate on Main Street and at the monorail-, ferry-, and bus-boarding areas. In the hour before closing, the other lands are normally not crowded.

To get a complete view of actual traffic patterns while you're in the park, pull up the MDE app on a couple of days before your travel, at different points during the day. You can see current wait times at every attraction in any park and get an idea of when things get crowded or start emptying out.

MAGIC KINGDOM TOURING PLANS

OUR STEP-BY-STEP TOURING PLANS, starting on page 551, have been carefully field-tested to help you experience *as much as possible* in one day while minimizing time spent in lines. They're designed to help you avoid crowds and bottlenecks, especially on days of moderate to heavy attendance. You should understand, however, that there's more to see in the Magic Kingdom than can be experienced in one day.

unofficial **TIP**
Don't worry that other people will be following the touring plans, rendering them useless. Less than 4% of people in the park will have been exposed to this info.

On days with lighter attendance (see "Selecting the Time of Year for Your Visit," page 29), our plans save you time but aren't as critical to successful touring as they are on busier days.

Each Magic Kingdom touring plan has two versions: one for Disney resort guests and one for off-site guests. Disney resort guests can take advantage of Early Theme Park Entry to significantly reduce wait times, while off-site guests will need a different strategy to compensate for the thousands of guests who will already be in the park when they enter. Even with an optimal plan, off-site guests who are not eligible for Early Entry may face an additional hour or more in line per day.

The touring plans work without requiring LLMP or LLSP. If you choose to use one or both, simply input your reservation times into TouringPlans.com's free touring plan software to automatically adjust your itinerary (see page 26 for details).

CHOOSING THE APPROPRIATE TOURING PLAN

THIS BOOK FEATURES FOUR Magic Kingdom touring plans:

1. ONE-DAY TOURING PLAN FOR ADULTS (see pages 551–552) This plan is for adults without young children who have just a single day to visit but want to see as much as possible. It assumes a willingness to experience all major rides (including roller coasters) and shows. It does not assume the use of LLMP or LLSP.

This plan includes the attractions we think best represent the Magic Kingdom, from its newest roller coasters to those created by Walt Disney himself. It requires a lot of walking and some backtracking to avoid lines. Extra walking and morning hustling will spare you hours of standing in line. How far you get depends on how quickly you move from ride to ride, how many times you rest or eat, how quickly the park fills, and what time the park closes. Yes, it's a beast, but it gives you maximum bang for your buck.

2. ONE-DAY TOURING PLAN FOR PARENTS WITH SMALL CHILDREN (see pages 553–554) This plan is for parents with children younger than age 8 and assumes you'll take periodic stops for rest, restrooms, and refreshments. A compromise that blends the highest-rated attractions for younger children with those of older siblings and adults, it includes many children's rides in Fantasyland, along with the evening fireworks, but omits the more-intense attractions that may frighten young children

unofficial **TIP**
Rider Switch allows adults to enjoy the more adventurous attractions while keeping the group together.

or are off-limits because of height requirements. The plan has a slower pace, with some free time throughout the day.

You could also use the **One-Day Touring Plan for Adults** and take advantage of **Rider Switch** on rides with height requirements (see page 307 for more on Rider Switch).

3. DUMBO-OR-DIE-IN-A-DAY TOURING PLAN FOR PARENTS WITH SMALL CHILDREN (see pages 555–556) This plan is designed for parents who are happy to self-sacrificially stand around, sweat, wipe noses, pay for stuff, and watch the kids enjoy themselves. It assumes frequent stops for rest, restrooms, and refreshments and will provide a youngster with about as perfect a day as possible in the Magic Kingdom. Families using this plan should review the Magic Kingdom attractions in our **Small-Child Fright-Potential Table** on pages 305–306.

4. TWO-DAY TOURING PLAN FOR ADULTS (see pages 557–558) If you have two days (or two mornings) in the Magic Kingdom, this plan is *by far* the most relaxed and efficient way to experience all the major rides and shows with the least time waiting in lines. It takes advantage of early morning, when lines are short and the park hasn't filled up with guests. Each day, you should complete the structured part of the plan by about 4 p.m., which leaves plenty of time for live entertainment or a break at your hotel while deciding what to do at night. The plan works well year-round and eliminates much of the extra walking required by the one-day plans. It's perfect for guests who want to sample both the attractions and the atmosphere of the park.

"Not a Touring Plan" Strategies

For the type-B reader, these strategies (described on page 548) avoid detailed step-by-step plans for saving every last minute in line. To paraphrase one of our favorite movies, they're more guidelines than actual rules. Use them to avoid the longest waits in line while having maximum flexibility to see whatever interests you in a particular part of the park.

For the Magic Kingdom, these strategies include advice for adults and parents with one day in the park, for anyone with two days, and for anyone with an afternoon and a full day to tour.

Two-Day Touring Plan for Families with Small Children

If you have young children and are looking for a two-day itinerary, combine the **One-Day Touring Plan for Parents with Small Children** with the second day of the **Two-Day Touring Plan**.

Alternate Two-Day Touring Plan: Sleep In on Day Two

Many visitors enjoy an early start in the Magic Kingdom on one day, followed by a second day with a lazy sleep-in morning, resuming touring in the afternoon and/or evening. If this appeals to you, use the **One-Day Touring Plan for Adults** or the **One-Day Touring Plan for Parents with Small Children** on your early day. Stick to the plan for as long as it feels comfortable (many folks leave after the afternoon parade). On the second day, pick up where you left off. Customize the rest of the plan to

MAGIC KINGDOM TOURING PLANS

incorporate parades, fireworks, and other live performances according to your preferences.

TOURING PLAN COMPANIONS

WE'VE CONSOLIDATED A GREAT DEAL of information about the theme parks in the Touring Plan Companions, which start on page 569, just after the touring plans. Like the touring plans, the companions are designed to be clipped out and taken with you to the parks. They recap key information: the best times to visit each attraction, the authors' ratings, attraction height requirements and fright potential, and quick-reference info on dining and places to take a break.

THE SINGLE-DAY TOURING CONUNDRUM

TOURING THE MAGIC KINGDOM in a single day is complicated by two facts:

1. The park's average day is shorter than it was before the pandemic.
2. The premier attractions are at opposite ends of the park.

Tiana's Bayou Adventure and **Big Thunder Mountain Railroad** are in Frontierland, **Space Mountain** and **Tron** are in **Tomorrowland,** and **Seven Dwarfs Mine Train** is in **Fantasyland.** It's virtually impossible to ride all five without encountering lines at any of them.

If, for example, you hit Tron and Space Mountain right as the park opens, you won't have too bad of a wait, but by the time you get to Fantasyland, the line for Seven Dwarfs Mine Train will already be substantial. Likewise, you can ride Seven Dwarfs without a problem first thing in the morning, but by the time you get to Tomorrowland, Space Mountain and Tron will already have fair-size lines. See the **One-Day Touring Plans for Adults** on pages 551–552 for our recommendations about how to hit all the headliners.

PRELIMINARY INSTRUCTIONS FOR USING THE TOURING PLANS

BECOME FAMILIAR WITH THE MAGIC KINGDOM'S **opening procedures** (see page 365). On days of moderate to heavy attendance, follow your chosen touring plan exactly, deviating from it only as follows:

1. **When you're not interested in an attraction in the plan.** Simply skip it and proceed to the next attraction.
2. **When you encounter a very long line at an attraction.** In this case, skip to the next attraction and try again later.

Before You Go

1. At 7 a.m. either 7 or 3 days before your vacation starts, make LLMP or LLSP purchases and reservations if you want to use them.
2. Check disneyworld.disney.go.com or the MDE app the day before you go to verify official opening time.
3. Review the park-opening procedures and reread the plan you've chosen so you know what you're likely to encounter.

PART 12

EPCOT

KEY QUESTIONS ANSWERED IN THIS CHAPTER

- How do I get to EPCOT? *(opposite page)*
- What are the don't-miss rides? *(opposite page)*
- How does park opening (rope drop) work? *(page 408)*
- What's the best way to use LLMP and LLSP in EPCOT? *(page 409)*
- Where are the best spots for watching fireworks? *(page 431)*
- What's the easiest way to leave the park at the end of the day? *(page 432)*

OVERVIEW

WALT DISNEY'S ORIGINAL 1960s-era vision for EPCOT was a groundbreaking concept for future urban living. The acronym stood for "Experimental Prototype Community of Tomorrow," and Walt envisioned a city featuring self-driving electric cars, prefabricated solar-powered homes, and a network of electronic information services (welcome to the future), all centered under a massive, air-conditioned dome.

After Walt's death in 1966, company leaders considered his ambitious plans too risky to pursue. When EPCOT Center opened 16 years later, it became a theme park with two distinct themes: **Future World,** which offered a semi-educational glimpse into technology and innovation, and **World Showcase,** a permanent world's fair celebrating global culture and traditions—another of Walt's passions.

IS EPCOT WORTH VISITING NOW?

EPCOT HAS EXPERIENCED something of a renaissance, having undergone a multitude of changes in the past few years. Two new headliners opened: **Remy's Ratatouille Adventure,** a family-friendly ride through a French kitchen, opened in the France Pavilion in 2021, and the **Guardians of the Galaxy: Cosmic Rewind** roller coaster opened in 2022. **Journey of Water, Inspired by Moana** (an interactive walk-through) and a new fireworks show, ***Luminous,*** both debuted in late 2023. In addition to new attractions, a lot of atmospheric changes were made between Spaceship Earth and World Showcase.

> **NOT TO BE MISSED IN EPCOT**
>
> **FUTURE WORLD** • Guardians of the Galaxy: Cosmic Rewind • Living with the Land • The Seas Main Tank and Exhibits • Soarin' Around the World • Spaceship Earth • Test Track • *Turtle Talk with Crush*
>
> **WORLD SHOWCASE** • Frozen Ever After • Japan and Mexico Pavilions • Remy's Ratatouille Adventure • Voices of Liberty

EPCOT LANDS

THE FRONT HALF OF EPCOT is subdivided into three lands. **World Discovery** covers the east side (left if you enter from the main entrance) and includes the Test Track, Mission: Space, and Guardians of the Galaxy Pavilions. **World Nature** is on the west (right) side and includes The Land Pavilion and The Seas with Nemo & Friends Pavilion. The central part, including Spaceship Earth and the Imagination! Pavilion, is known as **World Celebration**. The **World Showcase** is the back half of the park.

We'll use the older term "Future World" to generally refer to the front half of the park (everything but World Showcase), and we'll use the new land names when discussing the specific lands.

ARRIVING

ENTRANCES EPCOT has two entrances. The larger one (the **main entrance**) is in Future World, at the front of the park, and it's the one you'll use if you arrive by car, bus, or monorail. The **International Gateway** (**IG**) entrance is in the rear of the park, between France and United Kingdom in the World Showcase. The main (Future World) entrance can handle more people and is closer to headliner rides such as Guardians of the Galaxy, Soarin' Around the World, and Test Track, while the IG entrance will put you closer to Remy's Ratatouille Adventure, which is important if you're touring with small children.

ARRIVING FROM INSIDE WALT DISNEY WORLD If you're staying at an EPCOT resort, it will take you about 10–20 minutes to walk the mile or so from your hotel to the IG. **Boat service** is also available from the EPCOT resorts to the IG. If you're staying at Disney's Caribbean Beach, Riviera, Pop Century, and Art of Animation Resorts, you can take a 10- to 20-minute ride (20–40 minutes with crowds) on the **Skyliner** (see page 344). Add another 5–8 minutes to walk to Future World from the IG if that's your final destination.

> *un*official **TIP**
> Arriving at EPCOT 30–60 minutes before official opening ensures the shortest possible waits for rides.

DRIVING Arriving by car is easy and direct (see page 346 for GPS names and addresses). EPCOT has its own parking lot, and you can take a tram or walk from the parking lot to the front gate. Monorail service connects EPCOT with the Magic Kingdom (transfer required), the Magic Kingdom resorts (transfer required), and the Transportation and Ticket Center.

continued on page 408

EPCOT

Attractions

1. *The American Adventure*
2. *Awesome Planet*
3. *Canada Far and Wide*
4. *¡Celebración Encanto!*
5. *Club Cool*
6. *Disney & Pixar Short Film Festival* MP2
7. *Frozen Ever After* ☑ MP1
8. *Gran Fiesta Tour Starring the Three Caballeros*
9. *Guardians of the Galaxy: Cosmic Rewind* ☑ SP
10. *Impressions de France/Beauty and the Beast Sing-Along*
11. *Journey into Imagination with Figment* MP2
12. *Journey of Water, Inspired by Moana*
13. *Living with the Land* ☑ MP2
14. *Meet Anna and Elsa at Royal Sommerhus*
15. *Meet Mickey & Friends*
16. *Mission: Space* MP2
17. *Reflections of China*
18. *Remy's Ratatouille Adventure* ☑ MP1
19. *The Seas Main Tank and Exhibits* ☑
20. *The Seas with Nemo & Friends* MP2
21. *Soarin' Around the World* ☑ MP1
22. *Spaceship Earth* ☑ MP2
23. *Test Track* ☑ (likely MP1 and possibly LLSP when it reopens)
24. *Turtle Talk with Crush* MP2

MP1 Offers Lightning Lane Multi Pass—Tier 1
MP2 Offers Lightning Lane Multi Pass—Tier 2
SP Offers Lightning Lane Single Pass
☑ Not To Be Missed
👍 Recommended Dining
✚ First Aid
✹ Fireworks Top Viewing Spot
🚻 Restrooms

EPCOT MAP

Counter-Service Restaurants

- **A.** L'Artisan des Glaces
- **B.** La Cantina de San Angel
- **C.** Connections Cafe and Eatery
- **D.** La Crêperie de Paris
- **E.** Festival Favorites / Outdoor Kitchen—Florida Fresh
- **F.** Fife & Drum Tavern
- **G.** Les Halles Boulangerie-Pâtisserie
- **H.** Katsura Grill
- **I.** Kringla Bakeri og Kafe
- **J.** Lotus Blossom Café
- **K.** Pizza al Taglio
- **L.** Refreshment Outpost
- **M.** Refreshment Port
- **N.** Regal Eagle Smokehouse
- **O.** Sommerfest
- **P.** Sunshine Seasons
- **Q.** Tangierine Café
- **R.** Yorkshire County Fish Shop

Table-Service Restaurants

- **AA.** Akershus Royal Banquet Hall
- **BB.** Biergarten Restaurant
- **CC.** Le Cellier Steakhouse
- **DD.** Chefs de France
- **EE.** Coral Reef Restaurant
- **FF.** La Crêperie de Paris
- **GG.** Garden Grill Restaurant
- **HH.** La Hacienda de San Angel
- **II.** Monsieur Paul
- **JJ.** Nine Dragons Restaurant
- **KK.** Rose & Crown Dining Room
- **LL.** San Angel Inn Restaurante
- **MM.** Shiki-Sai
- **NN.** Space 220
- **OO.** Spice Road Table
- **PP.** Takumi-Tei
- **QQ.** Teppan Edo
- **RR.** Tutto Italia Ristorante
- **SS.** Via Napoli Ristorante e Pizzeria

EPCOT SERVICES

EPCOT'S SERVICE FACILITIES, most located in Future World, include:

ATMs Outside the main entrance, on the Future World bridge, and in World Showcase at The American Adventure Pavilion and International Gateway entrance

Baby Care Center On the World Showcase side of the Odyssey Center (by the Mexico Pavilion)

Cell Phone Charging Outlets available in The Seas with Nemo & Friends Pavilion, upstairs near the women's restroom; in The Land Pavilion, upstairs near Garden Grill; and in the outdoor seating areas in World Celebration Gardens

Dining Reservations At Guest Relations, to the left of Spaceship Earth, or through the My Disney Experience app

First Aid On the World Showcase side of the Odyssey Center, next to the Baby Care Center

Live-Entertainment Information In the *Times Guide*, available at Guest Relations

Lost and Found At the main entrance at the gift shop or Guest Relations

Lost Persons At Guest Relations and the Baby Care Center

Walt Disney World and Local Attraction Information At Guest Relations

Wheelchair, ECV, and Stroller Rentals Inside the main entrance and to the left, toward the rear of the Entrance Plaza; also at the International Gateway entrance

continued from page 405

If you're not at a Skyliner or EPCOT resort but you want to start your day at the IG, it's possible to park at Disney's Hollywood Studios and take the Skyliner to EPCOT. You won't be among the first to queue at the IG, but you'll be there long before anyone walking to Remy (for example) from the main entrance.

EPCOT OPENING PROCEDURES (ROPE DROP)

FUTURE WORLD AND WORLD SHOWCASE both typically open at 9 a.m. and close at 9 p.m. On-site guests who want to take advantage of Early Theme Park Entry (see page 34) should arrive 60–75 minutes before official opening (that is, 30–45 minutes before Early Entry) on all days. Off-site guests who aren't eligible for Early Theme Park Entry should arrive 30 minutes before official opening on all days.

WHICH EPCOT ENTRANCE SHOULD YOU USE? The IG entrance is about 10 minutes closer to the family-friendly **Remy's Ratatouille Adventure**, located in World Showcase's France Pavilion, than the Future World entrance is, and that's a huge head start. But if the rat ride isn't a priority, then enter at Future World instead for easier access to **Soarin' Around the World, Test Track,** and **Guardians of the Galaxy: Cosmic Rewind**. If you're heading for **Frozen Ever After**, both entrances are about equidistant.

LLMP AND LLSP SELECTIONS IN EPCOT

FUTURE WORLD • Disney and Pixar Short Film Festival *(Tier 2)* • Guardians of the Galaxy: Cosmic Rewind *(LLSP)* • Journey into Imagination with Figment *(Tier 2)* • Living with the Land *(Tier 2)* • Mission: Space *(Tier 2)* • The Seas with Nemo & Friends *(Tier 2)* • Soarin' Around the World *(Tier 1)* • Spaceship Earth *(Tier 2)* • Test Track *(likely Tier 1 and possibly LLSP when it reopens)* • Turtle Talk with Crush *(Tier 2)*

WORLD SHOWCASE • Frozen Ever After *(Tier 1)* • Remy's Ratatouille Adventure *(Tier 1)*

GETTING ORIENTED

EPCOT'S THEMED AREAS are markedly different: World Showcase features the landmarks, cuisine, and culture of almost a dozen nations and is meant to be a sort of permanent World's Fair. Future World is in flux: Its older attractions examine where mankind has come from and where it's going, while its newer attractions are themed to various Disney characters.

EPCOT is visually open, unlike the very visually siloed Magic Kingdom. And while it might seem odd to see a Japanese pagoda and the Eiffel Tower on the same horizon, getting around is fairly simple.

The park's architectural anchor is **Spaceship Earth,** a shiny 180-foot geosphere that's visible from almost everywhere in the park. Like Cinderella Castle in the Magic Kingdom, Spaceship Earth can help you keep track of where you are in EPCOT. But it's in a high-traffic area, and it's not centrally located, so it's not a good meeting place.

Instead, try to meet inside CommuniCore Hall or on the bridge between Future World and World Showcase. Both are centrally located but may be busy at any time during the day.

FAVORITE ATTRACTIONS BY AGE GROUP

EPCOT'S LINEUP INCLUDES more than 50 attractions, shows, live performers, and festival and seasonal entertainment. The table on the next page shows the park's 10 most popular attractions by age group. EPCOT's live entertainers are popular across all age groups. Those should be part of your day in EPCOT when they're available and convenient. The average reader ratings for all EPCOT attractions by age group are as follows, based on the 45,000 attraction ratings we received over the past 13 months:

PRESCHOOL	GRADE SCHOOL	TEENS	YOUNG ADULTS	OVER 30	OVER 65
4.1 stars	4.2 stars	4.1 stars	4.2 stars	4.1 stars	4.2 stars

RIDER SWITCH IN EPCOT At all Disney parks, select attractions allow one parent to ride while the other stays with a nonriding child. The parents then switch roles so that the other can ride using the Alternate Access line (Lightning Lane). See page 307 for complete details.

In EPCOT, however, there are potentially longer waits in that line than in other parks because there are fewer attractions where using Lightning Lane is worth it, and those queues back up farther. Be prepared to have a wait on the second leg of Rider Switch.

LLMP, LLSP, AND THE TOURING PLANS

NOTE: See page 53 for detailed information and strategy suggestions for LLMP and LLSP. The big questions addressed in this section are:

1. Is LLMP worth paying for in EPCOT?
2. If it's worth the cost, which attractions benefit most from LLMP or LLSP?
3. How can you avoid paying for LLSP?
4. How do LLMP and LLSP work with the touring plans?

EPCOT MOST POPULAR ATTRACTIONS BY AGE GROUP					
PRESCHOOL	**GRADE SCHOOL**	**TEENS**	**YOUNG ADULTS**	**OVER 30**	**OVER 65**
Journey of Water, Inspired by Moana	Meet Anna and Elsa at Royal Sommerhus	Guardians of the Galaxy: Cosmic Rewind	Guardians of the Galaxy: Cosmic Rewind	Guardians of the Galaxy: Cosmic Rewind	Soarin' Around the World
The Seas Main Tanks and Exhibits	Guardians of the Galaxy: Cosmic Rewind	Test Track	Mexico Pavilion	Voices of Liberty	Living with the Land
Meet Anna and Elsa at Royal Sommerhus	Test Track	Soarin' Around the World	Voices of Liberty	Soarin' Around the World	Remy's Ratatouille Adventure
Frozen Ever After	Remy's Ratatouille Adventure	Club Cool	Japan Pavilion	Japan Pavilion	Voices of Liberty
The Seas with Nemo & Friends	Soarin' Around the World	Remy's Ratatouille Adventure	France Pavilion	Mariachi Cobre	Friendship Boats
Remy's Ratatouille Adventure	Journey of Water, Inspired by Moana	Japan Pavilion	Soarin' Around the World	Mexico Pavilion	JAMMitors
Gran Fiesta Tour	*Turtle Talk with Crush*	Mexico Pavilion	Germany Pavilion	Remy's Ratatouille Adventure	*Luminous*
Turtle Talk with Crush	The Seas Main Tanks and Exhibits	France Pavilion	United Kingdom Pavilion	JAMMitors	Japan Pavilion
Journey into Imagination with Figment	Club Cool	The Seas Main Tanks and Exhibits	JAMMitors	Living with the Land	Guardians of the Galaxy: Cosmic Rewind
Soarin' Around the World	Frozen Ever After	Journey of Water, Inspired by Moana	Test Track	France Pavilion	Japan Pavilion

Are LLMP and LLSP Worth Paying For in EPCOT?

LLSP, potentially. LLMP, almost certainly not. Why? Several reasons:

1. A LLSP for Guardians of the Galaxy will save you a large amount of time, and it frees you up to visit other attractions during Early Entry or other morning hours.
2. Three attractions on LLMP can potentially save you significant time compared to standby. But under all crowd conditions, you will likely be able to use only one or two of them. Instead, avoid those one or two waits by taking advantage of Early Entry.
3. Can't do Early Entry? That's the one situation in which you may want to consider LLMP at EPCOT.

Regardless of the time of year you visit, arriving during Early Entry (or even at opening) should allow you to see at least one of EPCOT's headliner attractions without significant waits. Using LLMP saves a decent amount of time at only three attractions. All others are a wash. And a bunch of people are competing for return times at those three attractions, which means they book up quickly. The table on the opposite page (top) shows how much time we estimate you'll be able to save using LLMP, at various crowd and LLMP usage levels (see page 371 for an explanation of the usage levels):

ESTIMATED TIME SAVINGS USING LLMP BY CROWD LEVEL			
CROWD LEVEL	TYPICAL USE (3-4 RESERVATIONS PER DAY)	OPTIMISTIC USE (5-6 RESERVATIONS PER DAY)	PERFECT USE (7+ RESERVATIONS PER DAY)
LOW	40 minutes	55 minutes	70 minutes
MODERATE	60 minutes	75 minutes	100 minutes
HIGH	75 minutes	115 minutes	145 minutes

Which EPCOT Attractions Benefit Most from LLMP and LLSP?

The table below shows the attractions that might benefit most from using LLMP, based on current wait times and historical LLMP wait times. Regarding LLSP, we think Guardians of the Galaxy: Cosmic Rewind has much higher value now that it operates a standby queue with high average wait times, rather than a controlled virtual queue.

EPCOT ATTRACTIONS THAT BENEFIT MOST FROM LLMP AND LLSP (Highest Priority to Lowest)			
ATTRACTION	AVG. TIME IN LINE SAVED (IN MINUTES)	ATTRACTION	AVG. TIME IN LINE SAVED (IN MINUTES)
GUARDIANS OF THE GALAXY: COSMIC REWIND	47	MISSION: SPACE (Orange/Green)	10/4
REMY'S RATATOUILLE ADVENTURE	40	LIVING WITH THE LAND	9
FROZEN EVER AFTER	35	SPACESHIP EARTH	9
TEST TRACK*	32	JOURNEY INTO IMAGINATION WITH FIGMENT	6
SOARIN' AROUND THE WORLD	13	TURTLE TALK WITH CRUSH	1
THE SEAS WITH NEMO & FRIENDS	12	DISNEY & PIXAR SHORT FILM FESTIVAL	0

* Test Track will likely be much more popular after its 2024-2025 refurbishment, so time savings should go up significantly.

When Do LLMP and LLSP Reservations Run Out in EPCOT?

The table on the next page shows the approximate time at which EPCOT attractions run out of LLMP or LLSP capacity, by crowd level. Use this table along with the "Which Attractions Benefit Most" table, above, to determine which reservations to get first.

How Can You Avoid Paying for LLSP?

At EPCOT, you have to arrive before Early Entry and queue up for Guardians of the Galaxy: Cosmic Rewind—ideally from the main entrance. This means that if you also want to ride Remy's Ratatouille Adventure or Frozen Ever After, those will already have longer waits by the time you arrive.

How Do LLMP and LLSP Work with the Touring Plans?

See our advice on page 373.

WHEN LLMP AND LLSP RESERVATIONS RUN OUT BY ATTENDANCE LEVEL*

ATTRACTION	LOW ATTENDANCE	MODERATE ATTENDANCE	HIGH ATTENDANCE
DISNEY & PIXAR SHORT FILM FESTIVAL	Park close	Park close	Park close
FROZEN EVER AFTER	10 a.m.	7 a.m.	3 days early
GUARDIANS OF THE GALAXY: COSMIC REWIND (LLSP)*	7 a.m.	1 day early	4 days early
JOURNEY INTO IMAGINATION WITH FIGMENT	Park close	Park close	Park close
LIVING WITH THE LAND	Park close	Park close	8 p.m.
MISSION: SPACE	Park close	2 p.m.	2 days early
REMY'S RATATOUILLE ADVENTURE	9 a.m.	2 days early	6 days early
THE SEAS WITH NEMO AND FRIENDS	Park close	Park close	Park close
SOARIN' AROUND THE WORLD	Park close	Park close	7 p.m.
SPACESHIP EARTH	Park close	Park close	6 p.m.
TEST TRACK**	10 a.m.	8 a.m.	2 days early
TURTLE TALK WITH CRUSH	Park close	Park close	6 p.m.

* Guardians of the Galaxy data based on virtual queue–era information. Reservations should run out even earlier with standby being offered.

** Test Track data based on preclosure information. Reservations should run out much earlier when it reopens.

DINING IN EPCOT

BELOW IS A RECAP of readers' highest-rated restaurants in EPCOT. Restaurants not listed are rated average or below. See Part 6 for details.

HIGHEST-RATED EPCOT RESTAURANTS

COUNTER SERVICE	TABLE SERVICE
Kringla Bakeri og Kafe (● 97%/MAA) Norway, World Showcase	**Shiki-Sai: Sushi Izakaya** (L, D) (● 100%/E) Japan, World Showcase
Les Halles Boulangerie-Pâtisserie (● 95%/AA) France, World Showcase	**Takumi-Tei** (D) (● 100%/E) Japan, World Showcase
Regal Eagle Smokehouse (● 95%/AA) The American Adventure, World Showcase	**Spice Road Table** (L, D) (● 98%/E) Morocco, World Showcase
Yorkshire County Fish Shop (● 94%/AA) United Kingdom, World Showcase	**Garden Grill** (B, L, D) (● 96%/MAA) The Land, World Nature
Festival Favorites (● 92%/AA) World Celebration	**Teppan Edo** (L, D) (● 96%/MAA) Japan, World Showcase
Sommerfest (● 86%/AA) Germany, World Showcase	**Le Cellier** (L, D) (● 94%/AA) Canada, World Showcase
	Via Napoli Ristorante e Pizzeria (L, D) (● 94%/AA) Italy, World Showcase
	Biergarten Restaurant (L, D) (● 93%/AA) Germany, World Showcase
	Tutto Italia Ristorante (L, D) (● 93%/AA) Italy, World Showcase

E = Exceptional   **MAA** = Much Above Average   **AA** = Above Average

FUTURE WORLD

IMMENSE, GLEAMING FUTURISTIC STRUCTURES define the first themed area just beyond EPCOT's main entrance. Broad walkways are punctuated with advertisements or decorations for the current festival. Front and center is the **Spaceship Earth** geosphere. Pavilions in **World Discovery** (to the left as you enter from the main entrance) are dedicated to technological achievements (or Marvel characters); those in **World Nature** (to the right) celebrate human imagination and the natural world. The pavilions and their attractions are described on the following pages.

KEY TO ABBREVIATIONS In the attraction profiles that follow, each star rating is accompanied by a category label in parentheses. **E** means **Exceptional, MAA** means **Much Above Average, AA** means **Above Average, A** means **Average, BA** means **Below Average,** and **MBA** means **Much Below Average.** See page 370 for more on Appeal by Age ratings.

WORLD DISCOVERY

Guardians of the Galaxy: Cosmic Rewind ★★★★★

| **PRESCHOOL** ★★★½ (BA) | **GRADE SCHOOL** ★★★★½ (MAA) | **TEENS** ★★★★★ (E) |
| **YOUNG ADULTS** ★★★★★ (E) | **OVER 30** ★★★★★ (E) | **OVER 65** ★★★★½ (AA) |

What it is Massive indoor roller coaster. **Scope and scale** Super-headliner. **When to go** When your boarding group is called. **Comments** Must be 42″ tall to ride. **ECV/wheelchair access** Must transfer to the ride vehicle. **Participates in LLMP** No (it offers LLSP). **Early Theme Park Entry** Yes. **Extended Evening Hours** Yes.

DESCRIPTION AND COMMENTS Guardians of the Galaxy: Cosmic Rewind is one of the highest-rated attractions in Walt Disney World. In fact, despite low ratings from motion-sick riders, it still ranks as the third-best attraction in the World. The premise of the ride is that it's EPCOT's newest technology showcase . . . except you have to get out into space to view the new tech.

You'll start your interplanetary voyage at the Guardians of the Galaxy building near EPCOT's main entrance, in World Discovery. Once inside, the preshow area consists of walkways curved around displays that explain the history and culture of the planet Xandar and introduce the *Guardians of the Galaxy* cast for those who haven't seen the movies. The queue incorporates several holding areas—small preshow rooms through which guests are "pulsed" in regular intervals. The theory is that by switching you from lines to rooms to lines again, you'll feel better about the wait than if you were just in one long, uninterrupted line. Eventually, you make it to the final preshow room, where the ride's actual plot is revealed. In this case, a villain steals some very important equipment. You're tasked with joining the Guardians of the Galaxy to get it back.

From this last preshow, you enter the ride's loading area, a large room with two identical loading platforms to the left and right. The ride begins with a backward launch. Then, at the exact moment you're supposed to enter deep space, your vehicle turns around to face forward. This might be the best effect in the entire ride. Disney has programmed the ride vehicle to spin and tilt down just a bit as you enter a massive room that's pitch black other than some simulated stars and planets. It feels like you're floating in space—a real wow moment.

Much of the rest of the ride continues that feeling of soaring through space, with a rock-and-roll soundtrack (songs include "I Ran" by A Flock of Seagulls; "September" by Earth, Wind, and Fire; and "One Way or Another" by Blondie). The ride doesn't ever go upside down.

TOURING TIPS Guardians of the Galaxy is one of EPCOT's three thrill rides. Disney calls it a "family thrill ride." In practice, it's about as intense as **Space Mountain** or **Expedition Everest**—with the addition of spinning cars, which ups the motion sickness factor.

A woman from Maryland captures how the ride can be a different experience depending on your susceptibility to motion sickness:

Mind-boggling! I screamed throughout and had the best time. But I'm glad hubby decided to sit this one out because it would have been too intense for him. It's way more than a roller coaster—you are spun and don't know which way you'll go next, all at top speed.

Mission: Space ★★★½

| PRESCHOOL ★★★½ (BA) | GRADE SCHOOL ★★★★ (BA) | TEENS ★★★½ (BA) |
| YOUNG ADULTS ★★★½ (BA) | OVER 30 ★★★½ (MBA) | OVER 65 ★★★½ (MBA) |

Motion Sickness

What it is Space-flight simulator ride. **Scope and scale** Major attraction. **When to go** Anytime. **Comments** Orange version not recommended for pregnant guests or anyone prone to motion sickness or claustrophobia; must be 40" tall to ride the Green (nonspinning) version and 44" to ride the Orange version. **Duration** About 5 minutes plus preshow. **Loading speed** Moderate. **ECV/wheelchair access** Must transfer to the ride vehicle. **Participates in LLMP** Yes. **Early Theme Park Entry** Yes. **Extended Evening Hours** Yes.

DESCRIPTION AND COMMENTS Mission: Space is a centrifuge-based space simulator that spins riders around a central axis to simulate the g-forces of rocket liftoff and, eventually, a moment of weightlessness. There is also a tamer, nonspinning version.

Even before you walk into the building, you're asked whether you want your ride with or without spin. Choose the spinning version and you're on the **Orange** team; the **Green** team trains on the nonspinning side.

The Orange version is a journey to Mars. The Green version, in which you orbit Earth, is comparatively smooth and mild enough for first-time astronauts—Becky's child rode it at age 4. This Texas reader says you don't give up much by choosing the Green option:

I am 65 and have ridden the Orange version a number of times. On our latest trip, we went on the Orange version again and felt a little uncomfortable. My wife suggested we try the Green version, which I mistakenly believed was some sort of boring mission-control exercise where we would sit behind a computer. The Green version gave us a great experience, including the feeling of liftoff and zero gravity, without the nausea.

In both versions, guests are strapped into space capsules for a simulated flight. Each capsule accommodates a crew consisting of a group commander, a pilot, a navigator, and an engineer, with a guest in each role. The buttons you push (or don't push) have no effect on the outcome of the flight.

The capsules are small (if you have any sort of claustrophobia, you *will* be uncomfortable), and both ride versions are amazingly realistic. The nonspinning (Green) version doesn't subject your body to g-forces, but it does bounce and toss you around in a manner roughly comparable to other Disney motion simulators.

TOURING TIPS Supposedly, the posted wait time for the Orange version is always higher than the Green one to give those on the fence about riding a nudge toward trying the tamer version.

Your bladder will be shaken up and squished on this ride—hit the restroom before you ride.

There is a play area at the exit where younger kids can play while older family members ride. Becky's kids enjoy playing here during Rider Switch for any of the attractions on this side of the park.

TEST TRACK PAVILION

SPONSORED BY CHEVROLET, this pavilion consists of the **Test Track** ride and some postshow multimedia presentations and interactive exhibits. At press time, it was still closed for a major refurbishment that will reimagine the entire pavilion.

Test Track ★★★★

PRESCHOOL ★★★★ (BA)	GRADE SCHOOL ★★★★½ (MAA)	TEENS ★★★★½ (MAA)
YOUNG ADULTS ★★★★½ (AA)	OVER 30 ★★★★½ (AA)	OVER 65 ★★★★ (A)

What it is Automotive simulator ride. **Scope and scale** Super-headliner. **When to go** The first 30 minutes the park is open or just before closing, or use the single-rider line. **Comment** Must be 40" to ride. **Duration** About 4 minutes. **Loading speed** Moderate-fast. **ECV/wheelchair access** Must transfer to the ride vehicle. **Participates in LLMP** Probably, upon reopening **Early Theme Park Entry** Yes. **Extended Evening Hours** Yes.

DESCRIPTION AND COMMENTS Test Track began a lengthy refurbishment in June 2024. Disney is calling it a "reimagining" that draws inspiration from the original EPCOT attraction, World of Motion. When it reopens in late summer 2025, it may be available only via LLSP instead of LLMP. If it participates in LLMP, it will be the top option at EPCOT.

TOURING TIPS We expect the attraction to still offer a **single-rider line,** especially in the opening months. This will be the best way to ride if you're willing and able to split up your party.

WORLD CELEBRATION

¡Celebración Encanto! ★★★

PRESCHOOL ★★★★½ (AA)	GRADE SCHOOL ★★★★ (BA)	TEENS ★★★½ (BA)
YOUNG ADULTS ★★★ (MBA)	OVER 30 ★★★★ (BA)	OVER 65 ★★★★ (A)

DESCRIPTION AND COMMENTS An *Encanto*-themed sing- and dance-along show hosted on the CommuniCore Plaza Stage multiple times daily. The energy is infectious even if you are just walking past. Enjoy the music while you walk, but only make time for the full show if you have big *Encanto* fans in your party.

Club Cool ★★½

PRESCHOOL ★★★★½ (AA)	GRADE SCHOOL ★★★★½ (AA)	TEENS ★★★★½ (AA)
YOUNG ADULTS ★★★★½ (AA)	OVER 30 ★★★★ (A)	OVER 65 ★★★★ (A)

DESCRIPTION AND COMMENTS Attached to the Creations Shop in the center of Future World, this Coca-Cola–sponsored retail space and soda fountain provides free, unlimited samples of soft drinks from around the world. Some of the flavors will taste strange to Americans (such as cola from China that my daughter and many others describe as carbonated barbecue sauce). Perhaps because it's free and refreshing on a hot day, some age groups rate Club Cool higher than most EPCOT attractions.

A Texas teen recommends it:

Club Cool is a refreshing escape from the Florida heat! It's a fun and free way to sample unique Coca-Cola flavors from around the world. Some are delightful surprises, while others are an adventurous taste bud challenge. It's a must-try for soda lovers.

TOURING TIPS Club Cool can get crowded, so you may have to wait a bit before dispensing your drink during busier times. But don't worry—people don't usually spend a lot of time inside. Don't come in expecting to fill a Big Gulp–size cup of free soda—the cups hold just an ounce or two at a time. Watch out for sticky floors! And please be sure to clean up after yourself. There are plenty of trash cans.

Meet Beloved Disney Pals at Mickey & Friends ★★★½

PRESCHOOL ★★★★ (E)   **GRADE SCHOOL** ★★★★½ (MAA)   **TEENS** ★★★★ (A)
YOUNG ADULTS ★★★★½ (MAA)   **OVER 30** ★★★★½ (MAA)   **OVER 65** ★★★★★ (E)

What it is Meet-and-greet with Mickey and two friends. **Scope and scale** Minor attraction. **When to go** Early or late. **Duration** Varies. **ECV/wheelchair access** May remain in wheelchair. **Participates in LLMP** No. **Early Theme Park Entry** No. **Extended Evening Hours** No.

DESCRIPTION AND COMMENTS Opened in 2024, this is Disney's newest Mickey greeting location. The spaces are bright and colorful, and you get three characters for the "price" of one—that is, you'll wait in one line and meet three characters in different spaces. Typically, Mickey is joined by Minnie and Goofy, but exact characters are not guaranteed.

TOURING TIPS Wait times for Mickey and his friends are longer here than almost anywhere else. The wait climbs quickly and stays elevated throughout the day. If meeting him here is a priority, get in line before 10 a.m. or in the evening before *Luminous*.

Spaceship Earth ★★★★

PRESCHOOL ★★★★ (BA)   **GRADE SCHOOL** ★★★★ (BA)   **TEENS** ★★★★½ (A)
YOUNG ADULTS ★★★★ (A)   **OVER 30** ★★★★ (A)   **OVER 65** ★★★★½ (AA)

What it is Educational dark ride. **Scope and scale** Headliner. **When to go** Midday. **Duration** About 16 minutes. **Loading speed** Fast. **ECV/wheelchair access** Must transfer to provided wheelchair, then to the ride vehicle. **Participates in LLMP** Yes. **Early Theme Park Entry** Yes. **Extended Evening Hours** Yes.

DESCRIPTION AND COMMENTS EPCOT's signature landmark, Spaceship Earth spirals through an 18-story geosphere, taking visitors past animatronic scenes depicting humankind's developments in communications, from cave painting to printing to television and computer networks. The ride is a remarkably efficient use of the geosphere's interior.

Interactive screens (if they're working) in the vehicles let you customize the ending animated video. A postshow area with interactive exhibits rounds out the attraction.

TOURING TIPS Because it's located near EPCOT's main entrance, Spaceship Earth attracts arriving guests soon after the park opens. Your time is better spent on other Future World attractions, such as **Soarin' Around the World** or **Test Track**. Wait times usually fall after 4 p.m., so you could see it on the way out of the park.

Spaceship Earth has regular pauses and slowdowns. Be prepared for lots of stops throughout the dark attraction.

IMAGINATION! PAVILION

THIS MULTI-ATTRACTION PAVILION is located just south of World Nature. Outside are an "upside-down" waterfall and a fountain that "hops" over the heads of unsuspecting passersby.

Disney & Pixar Short Film Festival ★★

| PRESCHOOL ★★★★½ (AA) | GRADE SCHOOL ★★★★ (A) | TEENS ★★★★½ (AA) |
| YOUNG ADULTS ★★★★ (A) | OVER 30 ★★★★ (A) | OVER 65 ★★★★ (A) |

What it is Short films from Disney and Pixar. **Scope and scale** Diversion. **When to go** Anytime. **Duration** About 20 minutes. **Probable waiting time** Less than one show. **ECV/wheelchair access** May remain in wheelchair. **Participates in LLMP** Yes. **Early Theme Park Entry** No. **Extended Evening Hours** No.

DESCRIPTION AND COMMENTS This theater screens three 3D shorts (Pixar's *Feast* and *Piper* and Disney's *Get a Horse*), all of which can be easily found online, and the lineup hasn't changed for many years. The only reason to go here is to get out of the sun (or rain) and sit in the AC for a few minutes.

TOURING TIPS The shorts are cute, but watch them at home unless you need a place to cool down.

Journey into Imagination with Figment ★★½

| PRESCHOOL ★★★★½ (AA) | GRADE SCHOOL ★★★★ (BA) | TEENS ★★½ (BA) |
| YOUNG ADULTS ★★★½ (BA) | OVER 30 ★★★½ (MBA) | OVER 65 ★★★★ (MBA) |

What it is Fantasy dark ride. **Scope and scale** Minor attraction. **When to go** Anytime. **Duration** About 6 minutes. **Loading speed** Moderately fast. **ECV/wheelchair access** May remain in wheelchair. **Participates in LLMP** Yes. **Early Theme Park Entry** No. **Extended Evening Hours** No.

DESCRIPTION AND COMMENTS The story takes you on a tour of a fictitious research lab dedicated to studying human imagination. Sometimes you're a passive observer and sometimes you're a test subject. You'll encounter optical illusions, a room that defies gravity, and other brain teasers. Along the way, Figment (a purple dragon) makes surprise appearances. After the ride, you can visit an interactive-exhibit area with fun meet and greets.

Reader responses to Figment and company are pretty consistent—and negative. It's one of the lowest-rated attractions in EPCOT. Either you'll dislike the concept in general or, like this Texas family, you'll expect more:

A once great attraction that desperately needs a refurb. The only reason this isn't rated lower is because our family loves Figment (and he deserves so much better than this ride).

TOURING TIPS You can do any of the meet and greets without the ride if you'd like. Scent-sensitive souls beware: You will get skunked on the ride.

WORLD NATURE

JOURNEY OF WATER, INSPIRED BY MOANA ★★★★

| PRESCHOOL ★★★★★ (E) | GRADE SCHOOL ★★★★½ (AA) | TEENS ★★★★ (AA) |
| YOUNG ADULTS ★★★★½ (AA) | OVER 30 ★★★★ (A) | OVER 65 ★★★★ (A) |

BUILT TO SIMULATE THE LUSH LANDSCAPES of waterfalls and streams, this walk-through exhibit sits on the walk from the center of Future World to The Seas with Nemo & Friends Pavilion and can be toured at any time. The attraction offers some of the best nuanced Imagineering in any of Disney World's theme parks. With no frightening aspects and no hours-long lines, it offers interactive elements that guests of any age can enjoy. A mom from New Hampshire captures our feelings well:

> Perfect addition for EPCOT—informative and entertaining. Literally every person we saw walked out with a smile. Beautiful design and fun interactivity.

Journey of Water takes about 10 minutes to tour (unless your kids fall in love with the interactive portions, in which case it can take *much* longer) and is accessible for guests using wheelchairs or scooters. It does not participate in LLMP, Early Entry, or Extended Evening Hours.

THE LAND PAVILION

THIS HUGE, ENVIRONMENT-THEMED PAVILION contains three attractions and two restaurants. Strollers aren't allowed inside, and the stroller-parking area is a decent walk away, so those with babies might want to bring a carrier.

Awesome Planet ★★

| PRESCHOOL ★★★ (MBA) | GRADE SCHOOL ★★★½ (MBA) | TEENS ★★★½ (BA) |
| YOUNG ADULTS ★★★★ (BA) | OVER 30 ★★★½ (BA) | OVER 65 ★★★★ (BA) |

What it is Indoor film about the environment. **Scope and scale** Diversion. **When to go** Anytime. **Comments** The film is on the pavilion's upper level. **Duration** About 15 minutes. **Probable waiting time** Less than one show. **ECV/wheelchair access** May remain in wheelchair. **Participates in LLMP** No. **Early Theme Park Entry** No. **Extended Evening Hours** No.

DESCRIPTION AND COMMENTS *Awesome Planet* is a short film that reviews the planet's animals and biomes. The script has narrator Ty Burrell mimicking his role as real estate agent Phil Dunphy from the ABC/Disney TV show *Modern Family*. The film's premise is that you're looking for a planet to buy and Phil is walking you through the benefits of Earth—at this point an outdated gimmick.

TOURING TIPS The theater is large enough to accommodate everyone who wants to see the film, at any time of year. We suspect that most people who go into the theater only do so because they feel sorry for the lonely cast member standing outside.

Living with the Land ★★★★

| PRESCHOOL ★★★★ (A) | GRADE SCHOOL ★★★★ (BA) | TEENS ★★★★ (A) |
| YOUNG ADULTS ★★★★½ (AA) | OVER 30 ★★★★½ (AA) | OVER 65 ★★★★½ (MAA) |

What it is Indoor boat ride showcasing farming and some agricultural history. **Scope and scale** Minor attraction. **When to go** Anytime. **Duration** About 14 minutes. **Loading speed** Moderate. **ECV/wheelchair access** Must transfer from ECV to provided wheelchair. **Participates in LLMP** Yes. **Early Theme Park Entry** No. **Extended Evening Hours** No.

DESCRIPTION AND COMMENTS The boat ride takes you through simulated rainforest and farm environments, and then a futuristic greenhouse where real crops are grown using the latest agricultural technologies. The greenhouse exhibits change constantly: Along with familiar fruits and grains such as tomatoes, corn, and rice, recent plantings include Mickey-shaped pumpkins, hot peppers, Malabar nuts, pandan, caimito, and amaranth. This produce is used in restaurants throughout Walt Disney World.

Don't assume that Living with the Land will be too dry and educational. A woman from Texas writes:

I had a bad attitude about Living with the Land—I just didn't think I was up for a movie about wheat farming. Wow, was I surprised!

TOURING TIPS If you have an interest in the agricultural techniques being demonstrated, take the **Behind the Seeds at EPCOT** tour (see page 495).

During **Festival of the Holidays,** Living with the Land is decked out with lights and decorations for **Glimmering Greenhouses.** As a result, the attraction frequently has some of the longest wait times in the park after dark during this time of year.

If you or someone in your party especially loves Living with the Land, check out the small desk near the exit. It sells Mickey's Mini Garden tubes, which hold a plant tissue culture (generated from the cells of a parent plant) that you can easily grow at home. Even Becky, who has no green thumb, was able to keep her souvenir alive . . . after forgetting about it for two months. It's an affordable and long-lasting souvenir.

Soarin' Around the World ★★★★½

PRESCHOOL ★★★★ (A)   GRADE SCHOOL ★★★★½ (MAA)   TEENS ★★★★½ (MAA)
YOUNG ADULTS ★★★★½ (MAA)   OVER 30 ★★★★½ (MAA)   OVER 65 ★★★★½ (MAA)

What it is Flight simulator ride. **Scope and scale** Super-headliner. **When to go** First 2 hours the park is open or after 4 p.m. **Comments** Must be 40" tall to ride; Rider Switch option provided (see page 307). **Duration** 5½ minutes. **Loading speed** Moderate. **ECV/wheelchair access** Must transfer to the ride vehicle. **Participates in LLMP** Yes. **Early Theme Park Entry** Yes. **Extended Evening Hours** Yes.

DESCRIPTION AND COMMENTS Soarin' Around the World is a ride for all ages, as exhilarating as being a hawk in the sky and as mellow as swinging in a hammock. If you have ever experienced flying dreams, that's how Soarin' feels.

Once you enter the main theater, you're secured in a seat hanging from a "hang glider." Then the rows of seats swing into position, making you feel as if the floor has dropped away, and you're suspended with your legs dangling. You embark on a simulated hang-glider tour, with images projected all around you and with the flight simulator moving in sync with the movie. Special effects include wind, sound, and even smell. The ride itself is exciting but perfectly smooth.

The film travels the globe, from the Matterhorn and an Arctic glacier to the Taj Mahal and the Great Wall of China. The visuals are stunningly sharp thanks to laser IMAX projectors, but computer-animated animals are regularly distracting. Soarin' is a must for anyone who meets the height requirement, thanks to its smooth glide and stunning visuals.

A Maine dad gives it a hearty thumbs-up:

Soarin' is amazing! Even if the "trip around the world" doesn't make a lot of sense, it's still stunning.

TOURING TIPS A late 2024 fix finally helped tall, skinny buildings not appear comically bent or tilted, and it updated the final scene to match current EPCOT, not the one from the early 2000s. The best views are from row B1.

With three theaters operating, Soarin' Around the World can almost always keep up with its crowds. But if a special event, like a limited-time showing of the original Soarin', happens or if any theater breaks down, then lines get long quickly and can stay that way all day.

THE SEAS WITH NEMO & FRIENDS PAVILION

FEATURING CHARACTERS from Disney/Pixar's *Finding Nemo* and *Finding Dory*, The Seas encompasses what was once one of America's largest aquariums, a ride that tunnels through the aquarium, an interactive animated show, and walk-through exhibits. The tank alone makes the pavilion a must-visit.

The Seas Main Tank and Exhibits ★★★½

PRESCHOOL ★★★★½ (MAA) **GRADE SCHOOL** ★★★★½ (AA) **TEENS** ★★★★ (AA)
YOUNG ADULTS ★★★★½ (AA) **OVER 30** ★★★★ (A) **OVER 65** ★★★★½ (AA)

What it is A huge saltwater aquarium, plus exhibits. **Scope and scale** Major attraction. **When to go** When you need a break from the elements. **ECV/wheelchair access** May remain in wheelchair. **Participates in LLMP** No. **Early Theme Park Entry** Yes. **Extended Evening Hours** Yes.

DESCRIPTION AND COMMENTS The Seas is among Future World's most ambitious offerings, housed in a 200-foot-diameter, 27-foot-deep tank containing fish, marine mammals, and crustaceans. Visitors can watch the activity through 8-inch-thick windows below the surface (including some at **Coral Reef Restaurant**; see page 254).

The aquarium is home to reef species, including sharks, rays, sea turtles, manatees (occasionally), and many fish. The aquarium used to house dolphins, but they were moved to another Florida facility in late 2024.

TOURING TIPS If you see a cast member standing near the tank's windows, ask them what kind of fish you're looking at and whether they have names. Kids enjoy an interactive booklet with stickers that they can fill out while touring the tanks.

The Seas with Nemo & Friends ★★★

PRESCHOOL ★★★★½ (AA) **GRADE SCHOOL** ★★★★ (BA) **TEENS** ★★★½ (BA)
YOUNG ADULTS ★★★★ (MBA) **OVER 30** ★★★½ (BA) **OVER 65** ★★★★ (BA)

What it is Omnimover (ride vehicles on a track) through the aquarium building. **Scope and scale** Minor attraction. **When to go** Anytime. **Duration** 4 minutes. **Loading speed** Fast. **ECV/wheelchair access** Must transfer to the ride vehicle. **Participates in LLMP** Yes. **Early Theme Park Entry** Yes. **Extended Evening Hours** Yes.

DESCRIPTION AND COMMENTS This ride features characters from *Finding Nemo* and deposits you at the heart of the pavilion, where you'll find the exhibits, the interactive animated show *Turtle Talk with Crush,* and viewing platforms for the main aquarium.

You'll be ushered to the loading area and seated in a "clamobile" for your journey through the aquarium. The attraction features technology that makes it seem like the animated characters are swimming with live fish. It quickly retells the basic plot of *Finding Nemo.* Unlike the film, however, the ride ends with a musical finale that might be even more catchy than "It's a Small World." If you have small kids who are unfamiliar with the film, the anglerfish and shark scenes may be scary.

TOURING TIPS The ride is a fun way to enter the tanks, but if the wait is too long, it's not a necessary experience—you can head straight for the exhibits by going through the pavilion's exit, around back, and to the left of the main entrance. Due to a combination of LLMP and increasing pauses and downtime, the line regularly gets longer than it should be. I recommend bailing out any time the posted wait is 25 minutes or more. It'll be lower later if you really want to ride.

Turtle Talk with Crush ★★★★

PRESCHOOL ★★★★½ (AA)   **GRADE SCHOOL** ★★★★½ (AA)   **TEENS** ★★★★ (A)
YOUNG ADULTS ★★★★ (A)   **OVER 30** ★★★★ (A)   **OVER 65** ★★★★★ (AA)

What it is Interactive animated show. **Scope and scale** Minor attraction. **When to go** Anytime. **Duration** 15 minutes. **Probable waiting time** One or two shows. **ECV/wheelchair access** May remain in wheelchair. **Participates in LLMP** Yes. **Early Theme Park Entry** No. **Extended Evening Hours** No.

DESCRIPTION AND COMMENTS *Turtle Talk with Crush* is a theater show starring the 153-year-old surfer-dude turtle from *Finding Nemo* and characters from *Finding Dory*. The on-screen Crush has (often humorous) conversations with guests in the audience. Real-time computer graphics are used to accurately move Crush's mouth as he forms words.

A mom from Colorado has a crush on *Turtle Talk:*

Turtle Talk with Crush i*s a must-see. Our 4-year-old was picked out of the crowd by Crush, and we were just amazed by the technology. It was adorable and enjoyed by everyone from Grammy and Papa to the 4-year-old!*

TOURING TIPS It's unusual to wait more than one or two shows to get in. If you find long lines at park opening, try back after 3 p.m., when more of the crowd has moved on to World Showcase.

WORLD SHOWCASE

WORLD SHOWCASE IS AN ONGOING WORLD'S FAIR encircling a 40-acre lagoon. Eleven national pavilions line the 1.2-mile promenade, showcasing the cuisine, culture, history, and architecture of their respective countries. Each pavilion features landmarks and charming street scenes designed to transport you to the heart of the host nation.

Some of the most stunning gardens in the United States can be found here, especially in the pavilions for **Germany, Japan, France, the United Kingdom, Canada,** and to a lesser extent **China.** Many are tucked away, so keep an eye out for these hidden gems.

World Showcase also boasts top-rated live entertainment that appeals to all ages. Performances by musicians, dancers, and other acts bring the pavilions to life. Standout shows are highlighted starting on page 430. Check the *Times Guide* for schedules and details.

For kids, the **Kidcot Fun Stops,** one in each pavilion, add an extra layer of fun. These stations, staffed by friendly cast members, provide postcards, informational cards, or stamps representing each country. Visiting all the pavilions becomes a scavenger hunt, complete with a bonus card as a reward for collecting every country's offering. It's an engaging way to spark curiosity and excitement for exploring the world.

Drinking Around the World (see page 221), an adult version of passport-stamp collecting, is enthusiastically endorsed by a woman from Louisiana:

> *We drank a beer and posed for photos in each country at EPCOT—Dad was the designated driver—and it quickly became hilarious, as were the progression-of-drunkenness photos that followed.*

There's another side to Drinking Around the World, as this reader from New York points out:

> *I had not been to EPCOT since 2018, and I was wholly unprepared for the HERDS OF DRUNK PEOPLE circling World Showcase in the evening. I counted at least five groups of 10+ people, in matching shirts that said stuff like "Let's Get Sheet-Faced," behaving very irresponsibly, acting out, and generally causing misery for people around them.*

For this reason, we recommend avoiding EPCOT on the opening weekends of all the park's festivals and trying to avoid World Showcase with kids after dark on all weekends.

World Showcase also offers some of the most diverse and interesting shopping in Walt Disney World. See Part 17 for details.

DuckTales World Showcase Adventure ★★½

| PRESCHOOL ★★★ (MBA) | GRADE SCHOOL ★★★★ (A) | TEENS ★★★½ (MBA) |
| YOUNG ADULTS ★★★ (MBA) | OVER 30 ★★★★ (A) | OVER 65 ★★ (MBA) |

What it is Interactive scavenger hunt. **Scope and scale** Diversion. **When to go** Anytime. **Duration** Allow 30 minutes per adventure. **Probable waiting time** None. **ECV/Wheelchair access** May remain in wheelchair. **Participates in LLMP** No. **Early Theme Park Entry** No. **Extended Evening Hours** No.

DESCRIPTION AND COMMENTS In DuckTales World Showcase Adventure, you help Scrooge McDuck find valuable artifacts located in and around select World Showcase pavilions. DuckTales requires a smartphone and the **Play Disney Parks app** to play; download it before you leave home.

Once you arrive at a pavilion, you'll be assigned a "mission" to find an artifact. Your phone provides clues to help solve a set of simple puzzles to find the artifacts.

Playing the game is free, and there are more than 35 possible "missions." Unfortunately, this activity is one of the worst-rated attractions in any park. The sweet spot may be if you're a family with at least one parent and at least one grade-schooler. Preschoolers are too young, and everyone else would rather spend their time on something else.

Friendship Boats ★★

| PRESCHOOL ★★★★ (A) | GRADE SCHOOL ★★★★ (BA) | TEENS ★★★★ (AA) |
| YOUNG ADULTS ★★★★ (A) | OVER 30 ★★★★ (A) | OVER 65 ★★★★½ (MAA) |

What it is Boat transportation across the lagoon. **Scope and scale** Diversion. **When to go** Anytime. **Probable waiting time** 15 minutes or less. **ECV/Wheelchair access** May remain in wheelchair. **Participates in LLMP** No. **Early Theme Park Entry** No. **Extended Evening Hours** No.

DESCRIPTION AND COMMENTS Friendship boats operate in the World Showcase Lagoon from about an hour after park opening until about an hour before the nightly fireworks. These are an efficient way to get to the other side of the lagoon. Boats connect launches in Canada and Morocco and (separately) launches in Mexico and Germany. The views from the middle of the lagoon can be great, and adults over age 65 rate this as one of their top 10 attractions in the World. EPCOT already requires more steps in a day than any other park, so a boat bypass is popular.

WORLD SHOWCASE PAVILIONS

MOVING CLOCKWISE AROUND World Showcase Promenade, these are the nations represented and their attractions.

For World Showcase, we list Appeal by Age ratings not just for the attractions but for the pavilions themselves. In addition to rides and films, they offer peaceful gardens; unique architecture; interesting places to eat, drink, and rest; stellar live entertainment; and more. Not every pavilion has a dedicated attraction.

MEXICO PAVILION

PRESCHOOL ★★★★ (A)	GRADE SCHOOL ★★★★½ (AA)	TEENS ★★★★½ (AA)
YOUNG ADULTS ★★★★½ (MAA)	OVER 30 ★★★★½ (AA)	OVER 65 ★★★★½ (AA)

PRE-COLUMBIAN PYRAMIDS dominate Mexico's architecture. One pyramid forms the pavilion's facade; the other overlooks the restaurant and plaza alongside the **Gran Fiesta Tour** indoor boat ride.

Readers rate Mexico as one of the best pavilions in World Showcase. The village scene inside the pavilion is beautiful and exquisitely detailed. A retail shop occupies most of the inner pavilion, including Mexico's **Kidcot Fun Stop,** on the left side of the plaza. On the opposite side of the main floor is **La Cava del Tequila,** a bar serving more than 200 tequilas, as well as cocktails, Mexican beer, wine, and mezcal.

The pyramids contain many authentic and valuable artifacts. Take the time to stop and see these treasures.

Gran Fiesta Tour Starring the Three Caballeros ★★½

PRESCHOOL ★★★★½ (AA)	GRADE SCHOOL ★★★★ (BA)	TEENS ★★★★ (A)
YOUNG ADULTS ★★★★ (BA)	OVER 30 ★★★★ (BA)	OVER 65 ★★★★ (A)

What it is Scenic indoor boat ride. **Scope and scale** Minor attraction. **When to go** Anytime. **Duration** About 7 minutes. **Loading speed** Moderate. **ECV/wheelchair access** Must transfer from ECV to provided wheelchair. **Participates in LLMP** No. **Early Theme Park Entry** No. **Extended Evening Hours** Yes.

DESCRIPTION AND COMMENTS This ride incorporates animated versions of Donald Duck, José Carioca, and Panchito Pistoles from Disney's 1944 animated musical film *The Three Caballeros.*

The storyline has the caballeros scheduled to perform at a fiesta when Donald suddenly goes missing; large video screens show him enjoying Mexico's sights and sounds while José and Panchito try to track him down. Everyone is reunited in time for a rousing concert near the end of the ride.

TOURING TIPS More of the ride's visuals seem to be on the left side of the boat, so have small children sit nearer the left to keep their attention, and listen for Donald's humorous monologue as you wait to disembark.

If the line is still contained within the center of the pavilion, you shouldn't wait more than 5 minutes, no matter what the MDE app tells you. There's no Lightning Lane slowing the standby queue down.

NORWAY PAVILION

PRESCHOOL ★★★★ (A)	GRADE SCHOOL ★★★★ (A)	TEENS ★★★★ (A)
YOUNG ADULTS ★★★★ (AA)	OVER 30 ★★★★ (A)	OVER 65 ★★★★ (A)

THIS PAVILION CAPTURES both everything we love about EPCOT and everything we dislike about how corporate Disney is handling the parks today. Parts of the pavilion—those based on the actual country of Norway—are complex, beautiful, and diverse. Highlights include replicas of Oslo's 14th-century **Akershus Castle**, a miniature version of a **stave church** built in 1212 in Gol (go inside—the doors open!), and other buildings that accurately represent traditional Scandinavian architecture. Oh, and you must try a spritz of Laila perfume in the gift shop.

However, when Disney released 2013's *Frozen*, set in the mythical Scandinavian-ish kingdom of Arendelle, the fate of the Norway Pavilion was set. In an unprecedented (and, we hope, never repeated) move, Disney replaced the main attraction in the Norway Pavilion with **Frozen Ever After**, a boat ride about a fictional place in an animated movie.

Nothing against *Frozen*—it is one of the best Disney movies ever made and deserves to be celebrated in the parks. We just wish it wasn't a shot at the very heart of EPCOT's original purpose.

Frozen Ever After ★★★★

PRESCHOOL ★★★★½ (AA)　**GRADE SCHOOL** ★★★★½ (AA)　**TEENS** ★★★★ (A)
YOUNG ADULTS ★★★★ (A)　**OVER 30** ★★★★ (A)　**OVER 65** ★★★★½ (AA)

What it is Indoor boat ride. **Scope and scale** Headliner. **When to go** At park opening or after 7 p.m. **Duration** Almost 5 minutes. **Loading speed** Moderately fast. **ECV/wheelchair access** Must transfer to the ride vehicle. **Participates in LLMP** Yes. **Early Theme Park Entry** Yes. **Extended Evening Hours** Yes.

DESCRIPTION AND COMMENTS The premise of this boat ride through Arendelle is that you've arrived in time for the Winter in Summer celebration, in which Elsa will use her magical powers to make it snow during the hottest part of the year. Nearly every character from the film is represented, along with many of the film's songs.

Be aware that there's a short, mild section where you're propelled backward for a few seconds, followed by a short downhill and small splash that most kids should take in stride. The ride's detailed sets are augmented with digital projection mapping and more than a dozen animatronics sporting somewhat jarring video-screen faces. These were state-of-the-art when the ride debuted but haven't aged well.

TOURING TIPS The opening of Cosmic Rewind, Remy's Ratatouille Adventure, and Test Track has diverted a large portion of the park-opening crowd away from Frozen Ever After. If you have young kids, we recommend starting the day at the International Gateway, heading to Remy first and then to Frozen to start your day. Just be sure to arrive during Early Entry, if possible. As soon as the Lightning Lane is open, the standby line slows to a crawl for the rest of the day..

Meet Anna and Elsa at Royal Sommerhus ★★★★

PRESCHOOL ★★★★½ (MAA)　**GRADE SCHOOL** ★★★★½ (MAA)　**TEENS** ★★★★ (A)
YOUNG ADULTS ★★★★½ (AA)　**OVER 30** ★★★★ (A)　**OVER 65** ★★★★ (BA)

What it is Character greeting. **Scope and scale** Minor attraction. **When to go** At park opening, at lunch or dinner, or in the last hour the park is open. **Duration** Varies. **Probable waiting time** 15–25 minutes. **ECV/wheelchair access** May remain in wheelchair. **Participates in LLMP** No. **Early Theme Park Entry** No. **Extended Evening Hours** No.

- **DESCRIPTION AND COMMENTS** Royal Sommerhus is a character-greeting venue for Anna and Elsa. They both meet in their *Frozen 2* outfits, in case that matters to the kids in your group. In a nod to its host pavilion, the meet and greet features traditional Norwegian architecture and crafts. The queue winds through a home where Anna and Elsa spent time as children and is filled with many details that are fun to find as you wait.
- **TOURING TIPS** During times of peak crowds, Royal Sommerhus has multiple rooms with multiple Annas and Elsas receiving guests. If you're visiting World Showcase in the afternoon, waits tend to be shortest around lunchtime, 4 p.m., and 6–7 p.m.

CHINA PAVILION

| PRESCHOOL ★★★ (MBA) | GRADE SCHOOL ★★★★ (BA) | TEENS ★★★★ (BA) |
| YOUNG ADULTS ★★★★ (A) | OVER 30 ★★★★ (A) | OVER 65 ★★★★½ (AA) |

A HALF-SIZE REPLICA of the **Temple of Heaven** in Beijing identifies this pavilion. Gardens and reflecting ponds simulate those found in Suzhou, and an art gallery features a lotus-blossom gate and formal saddle roofline. There are also exhibits on Chinese history and culture.

Reflections of China ★★½

| PRESCHOOL ★★½ (MBA) | GRADE SCHOOL ★★★½ (MBA) | TEENS ★★★½ (MBA) |
| YOUNG ADULTS ★★★★ (A) | OVER 30 ★★★★ (BA) | OVER 65 ★★★★ (A) |

What it is Film about the Chinese people and culture. **Scope and scale** Diversion. **When to go** Anytime. **Comment** Audience stands throughout performance. **Duration** About 14 minutes. **Probable waiting time** Less than one show. **ECV/wheelchair access** May remain in wheelchair. **Participates in LLMP** No. **Early Theme Park Entry** No. **Extended Evening Hours** No.

- **DESCRIPTION AND COMMENTS** Pass through the Hall of Prayer for Good Harvest to view this Circle-Vision 360° film. Warm and appealing (albeit politically sanitized), it's a brilliant introduction to the people and natural beauty of China. The film's relatively low marks (including the authors' rating) are due to the theater's lack of seats, not its cinematic quality. My kids even enjoyed this one when they were 5 and 3, so don't feel like you have to skip it for the littles.
- **TOURING TIPS** *Reflections of China* can usually be enjoyed anytime without much waiting.

GERMANY PAVILION

| PRESCHOOL ★★★½ (MBA) | GRADE SCHOOL ★★★★ (BA) | TEENS ★★★★ (A) |
| YOUNG ADULTS ★★★★½ (MAA) | OVER 30 ★★★★ (AA) | OVER 65 ★★★★½ (AA) |

GERMANY'S *PLATZ* (PLAZA), dominated by a clock tower and a fountain depicting St. George's victory over the dragon, is encircled by buildings in traditional architectural styles. The main attraction is **Biergarten Restaurant** (see page 248), which serves hearty German food and beer. Yodeling, folk dancing, and oompah-band music are part of the festivities there, courtesy of the band **Oktoberfest Musikanten.**

The biggest draw here may be **Karamell-Küche** ("Caramel Kitchen"), offering small caramel-covered sweets, including apples and cupcakes. The large and elaborate model railroad, just beyond the restrooms as you walk from Germany toward Italy, is a treasure, with enough detail to keep you discovering something new for hours. The display changes periodically thanks to the attention of very dedicated cast members.

ITALY PAVILION

PRESCHOOL ★★★½ (MBA) **GRADE SCHOOL** ★★★★ (BA) **TEENS** ★★★★ (BA)
YOUNG ADULTS ★★★★ (A) **OVER 30** ★★★★ (A) **OVER 65** ★★★★ (A)

THE ENTRANCE TO ITALY is marked by an 83-foot-tall campanile (bell tower) modeled after the tower in St. Mark's Square in Venice. Left of the campanile is a replica of the 14th-century Doge's Palace, also in the famous square. The pavilion has a waterfront on World Showcase Lagoon where gondolas are tied to striped moorings. Walk over the bridge to this spot for some excellent photos with Spaceship Earth in the background across the lagoon.

The streets and courtyards in Italy are among the most realistic in World Showcase. **Via Napoli** (see page 285) has some of the best pizza in the World, and **Tutto Gusto Wine Cellar** (see page 222) serves small plates along with libations. This pavilion is all about eating, drinking, and shopping—there's no film or ride.

THE AMERICAN ADVENTURE PAVILION

PRESCHOOL ★★★ (MBA) **GRADE SCHOOL** ★★★½ (MBA) **TEENS** ★★★ (MBA)
YOUNG ADULTS ★★★★ (BA) **OVER 30** ★★★★ (BA) **OVER 65** ★★★★ (A)

THE AMERICAN ADVENTURE (UNITED STATES) PAVILION consists of a decent barbecue place (**Regal Eagle Smokehouse**; see page 234), a preshow gallery of rotating exhibits on American history (the **American Heritage Gallery**), and a patriotic presentation called *The American Adventure.* The wildly talented and popular singing group **Voices of Liberty** performs American and Disney classics either inside the pavilion or at the **America Gardens Theatre** stage opposite the pavilion. Teens and adults rate the performances highly, and my kids were in awe of the group even at young ages.

The American Adventure ★★★½

PRESCHOOL ★★★½ (BA) **GRADE SCHOOL** ★★★ (MBA) **TEENS** ★★★★½ (MBA)
YOUNG ADULTS ★★★★ (BA) **OVER 30** ★★★★ (A) **OVER 65** ★★★★ (A)

What it is Mixed-media and Audio-Animatronic US history presentation. **Scope and scale** Minor attraction. **When to go** Anytime. **Duration** About 29 minutes. **Probable waiting time** Less than one show. **ECV/wheelchair access** May remain in wheelchair. **Participates in LLMP** No. **Early Theme Park Entry** No. **Extended Evening Hours** No.

DESCRIPTION AND COMMENTS *The American Adventure* demonstrates how good Disney theater presentations can be. Housed in an imposing brick structure reminiscent of Colonial Philadelphia, the 29-minute show is a stirring, albeit sanitized, rendition of American history, narrated by an animatronic Mark Twain, who carries a burning cigar, and Ben Franklin. Behind a stage almost half the size of a football field is a 72-foot screen on which videos and images are interwoven with onstage action.

The American Adventure's scale is both its strength and its weakness: It takes a lot of time and money to mount a presentation this big, which explains why the stage scenes have not been updated since the show opened more than 40 years ago. In the meantime, our understanding of America's history has evolved, but the show hasn't kept pace: Topics such as racism, gender equality, labor relations, and the environment are treated as solved problems instead of the ongoing challenges they are.

It's past time for this attraction to be updated. This pavilion would do well to focus on our country's natural beauty; the unique benefits we have as a nation of people from diverse backgrounds; and the challenges we face as we work to appreciate, embrace, and empower those different voices.

TOURING TIPS *The American Adventure* is still Disney's best patriotic attraction, and because of the theater's large capacity, it's highly unusual not to be admitted to the next performance. But don't bring the kids unless they need a half-hour-long nap.

JAPAN PAVILION

PRESCHOOL ★★★★ (A)   **GRADE SCHOOL** ★★★★½ (AA)   **TEENS** ★★★★½ (AA)
YOUNG ADULTS ★★★★½ (MAA)   **OVER 30** ★★★★½ (AA)   **OVER 65** ★★★★½ (AA)

A FIVE-STORY, BLUE-ROOFED PAGODA, inspired by an eighth-century shrine in Nara, sets this pavilion apart. A hill garden behind it features waterfalls, rocks, flowers, lanterns, paths, and rustic bridges. On the right as you face the entrance, a building inspired by the ceremonial and coronation hall at Kyoto's Imperial Palace contains restaurants and a branch of Japan's **Mitsukoshi** department store (see page 507), in business since 1673. Through the center entrance and to the left, **Bijutsukan Gallery** exhibits colorful displays on Japanese pop culture.

Matsuriza demonstrates the art of Japanese drumming in popular shows multiple times a day, and this pavilion is home to one of the most impressive slates of dining options anywhere in the World. The second floor of the Japan Pavilion is also a decent viewing spot for EPCOT's fireworks show.

MOROCCO PAVILION

PRESCHOOL ★★★½ (MBA)   **GRADE SCHOOL** ★★★½ (BA)   **TEENS** ★★★½ (BA)
YOUNG ADULTS ★★★★ (BA)   **OVER 30** ★★★★ (BA)   **OVER 65** ★★★★ (A)

A BUSTLING MARKET, WINDING STREETS, stuccoed archways, and lofty minarets re-create the romance and intrigue of Marrakesh and Casablanca. Unfortunately, the pavilion is a shell of its former self since the nation stopped sponsoring the area after the pandemic. Disney has taken over and turned one restaurant into a festival booth and another into a lounge, and has replaced stunning original artisan mosaics with what looks like a rush job made from tiles bought at IKEA. What remains are some stores, a Kidcot Fun Stop, the aforementioned lounge, and **Spice Road Table** (see page 276) along the lagoon.

What is one thing the Morocco Pavilion is still good for? A Minnesota mother discovered the secret—it's peace and quiet:

We found an awesome resting place in Morocco—an empty, air-conditioned gallery with padded benches. No one came in during the 15 minutes that we rested, which was quite a difference from the rest of the park. Look for the red doors on your left when you enter.

FRANCE PAVILION

PRESCHOOL ★★★★ (A)   **GRADE SCHOOL** ★★★★ (A)   **TEENS** ★★★★ (AA)
YOUNG ADULTS ★★★★½ (MAA)   **OVER 30** ★★★★½ (AA)   **OVER 65** ★★★★½ (AA)

A REPLICA OF THE EIFFEL TOWER is, *naturellement*, this pavilion's centerpiece. The restaurants, along with the bakery and ice-cream shop, are very popular. The pavilion hosts two films: the **Beauty and the Beast Sing-Along**, which plays in the same theater as **Impressions de France**.

Along with Norway, this is the pavilion where the use of so many characters bugs us the most. But at least the two featured films actually take place in France, not a fictional country (as is the case in Norway).

Beauty and the Beast Sing-Along ★★

| **PRESCHOOL** ★★★★ (A) | **GRADE SCHOOL** ★★★½ (MBA) | **TEENS** ★★★½ (BA) |
| **YOUNG ADULTS** ★★★½ (BA) | **OVER 30** ★★★½ (MBA) | **OVER 65** ★★★½ (BA) |

What it is Film retelling of the story. **Scope and scale** Diversion. **When to go** 10 a.m.–6:30 p.m. **Duration** About 15 minutes. **Probable waiting time** Less than one show. **ECV/wheelchair access** May remain in wheelchair. **Participates in LLMP** No. **Early Theme Park Entry** No. **Extended Evening Hours** No.

DESCRIPTION AND COMMENTS This is the third current Walt Disney World attraction to tell the *Beauty and the Beast* story, along with the Magic Kingdom's **Enchanted Tales with Belle** (see page 384) and Disney's Hollywood Studios' **Beauty and the Beast—Live on Stage** (see page 466). It's also the lowest-rated version.

For this show, Disney's script writers threw a twist into the original *Beauty* story—supposedly, LeFou, Gaston's sidekick during the film, was secretly working behind the scenes the whole time to bring Belle and Beast together. This might be confusing to kids (and discerning adults) because it doesn't fit with LeFou's behavior in the movie.

What's even more confusing is that Mrs. Potts starts the film by saying that this is the true story of Beauty and the Beast, leaving viewers wondering whether everything they thought they knew was wrong or if the trusty teapot is lying.

Sadly, Disney doesn't take advantage of the full screen capacity in this theater—the entire film plays on just one of the five screens.

TOURING TIPS Stop by anytime, if you or your kids like sing-alongs.

Impressions de France ★★★½

| **PRESCHOOL** ★★ (MBA) | **GRADE SCHOOL** ★★★ (MBA) | **TEENS** ★★★ (BA) |
| **YOUNG ADULTS** ★★★½ (BA) | **OVER 30** ★★★★ (A) | **OVER 65** ★★★★ (A) |

What it is Film essay on France and its people. **Scope and scale** Diversion. **When to go** 9–9:30 a.m. or 7–8:45 p.m. **Duration** About 18 minutes. **Probable waiting time** Less than one show. **ECV/wheelchair access** May remain in wheelchair. **Participates in LLMP** No. **Early Theme Park Entry** Yes. **Extended Evening Hours** No.

DESCRIPTION AND COMMENTS *Impressions de France* is an 18-minute movie with beautiful scenery, beautiful music, and beautiful towns, all projected over 200 degrees onto five screens. Unlike at China and Canada, the audience sits to view the film.

Almost every age group rates this film better than the *Beauty and the Beast Sing-Along*, which occupies the same theater most of the day. We're all for starting a petition to give *Impressions de France* more of the schedule—Becky plays the soundtrack regularly at home when she needs a pick-me-up. This Wisconsin woman seems to agree:

I could watch this ALL DAY. This piece of French cinema is unmatched in all of Walt Disney World. It's a MUST for my vacation—the score is beautiful, the imagery is both nostalgic and thought-provoking, and I simply cannot

WORLD SHOWCASE

get enough. My family refers to it as "French Soarin'" but I refer to it as incroyable!

While we think this is the best film in World Showcase, it was outdated way before the Notre Dame fire in the spring of 2019. Disney definitely needs to update the film.

TOURING TIPS Usually begins on the half hour.

Remy's Ratatouille Adventure ★★★★

PRESCHOOL ★★★★½ (AA) **GRADE SCHOOL** ★★★★½ (MAA) **TEENS** ★★★★½ (AA)
YOUNG ADULTS ★★★★½ (AA) **OVER 30** ★★★★½ (AA) **OVER 65** ★★★★½ (MAA)

What it is Indoor dark ride. **Scope and scale** Major attraction. **When to go** As soon as the park opens. **Duration** About 4½ minutes. **Loading speed** Moderate. **ECV/wheelchair access** Must transfer to the ride vehicle. **Participates in LLMP** Yes. **Early Theme Park Entry** Yes. **Extended Evening Hours** Yes.

DESCRIPTION AND COMMENTS On this ride, you're shrunk to the size of a rat and whisked through Paris for a retelling of the *Ratatouille* film's story. The storytelling combines 3D films on room-size screens with large, detailed ride-through sets that include water and heat effects. A couple of frenetic scenes, such as one in which Remy is chased with a cleaver, may frighten small children.

TOURING TIPS Remy is the first all-new major attraction in World Showcase since 1988. It's family-friendly, with good theming and a lead character who's as lovable and cute as any rodent could hope to be.

Because it's located in a far corner of the park, Remy is difficult to work into any touring plan that doesn't start at the International Gateway during Early Entry. From anywhere else, it's a hike. If you head here directly from the main entrance, even during Early Entry, there will likely be a 45-minute wait when you arrive, even on the least crowded days, because every IG visitor is lined up before you are even released into Future World.

Your best bet to experience Remy without paying for Lightning Lane is to arrive at the International Gateway entrance about an hour before opening. If you have small children, head next to Frozen Ever After in Norway, about 0.5 mile either way around World Showcase. After experiencing Frozen Ever After, you'll have completed two of the park's five big rides, with Guardians of the Galaxy, Test Track, and Soarin' Around the World remaining.

If you're willing to split up your party, the new **single-rider line,** which opened in late 2024, is undoubtedly the best way to experience the attraction with a reliably low wait. It's often faster than the Lightning Lane.

UNITED KINGDOM PAVILION

PRESCHOOL ★★★ (A) **GRADE SCHOOL** ★★★★ (A) **TEENS** ★★★★ (A)
YOUNG ADULTS ★★★★½ (AA) **OVER 30** ★★★★½ (AA) **OVER 65** ★★★★ (A)

A HODGEPODGE OF PERIOD ARCHITECTURE attempts to depict Britain's urban and rural sides. One street has a thatched-roof cottage, a four-story Tudor building, a pre-Georgian plaster building, a formal Palladian facade, and a city square with a Hyde Park bandstand (whew!). The pavilion consists mostly of shops. The **Rose & Crown Pub** and **Rose & Crown Dining Room** (see page 272) offer dining on the water side of the promenade. For fish and chips to go, try **Yorkshire County Fish Shop** (see page 235). Reservations aren't required for the Rose & Crown Pub, making it a nice place to stop for a beer.

There are no attractions here. We recommend visiting when the bands play in the pavilion, generally between 3 and 8 p.m. daily.

CANADA PAVILION

| PRESCHOOL ★★★½ (MBA) | GRADE SCHOOL ★★★½ (MBA) | TEENS ★★★½ (BA) |
| YOUNG ADULTS ★★★★ (A) | OVER 30 ★★★★ (BA) | OVER 65 ★★★★ (A) |

THE DIVERSITY OF CANADA—cultural, natural, and architectural—is reflected in this large, impressive pavilion. Totem poles embellish a native village at the foot of a replica of a magnificent château-style hotel. **Le Cellier Steakhouse** (see page 251) is on Canada's lower level. Make sure to experience the gorgeous gardens on the path to the restaurant. It'll feel like you stepped out of EPCOT and into Vancouver (other than the heat).

Canada Far and Wide ★★★

| PRESCHOOL ★★★½ (BA) | GRADE SCHOOL ★★★½ (MBA) | TEENS ★★★½ (MBA) |
| YOUNG ADULTS ★★★½ (MBA) | OVER 30 ★★★★ (BA) | OVER 65 ★★★★ (A) |

What it is Film essay on Canada and its people. **Scope and scale** Diversion. **When to go** Anytime. **Comment** Audience stands for the show. **Duration** About 14 minutes. **Probable waiting time** Less than one show. **ECV/wheelchair access** May remain in wheelchair. **Participates in LLMP** No. **Early Theme Park Entry** No. **Extended Evening Hours** No.

DESCRIPTION AND COMMENTS *Canada Far and Wide* combines all the visual majesty you'd want in a 360-degree film, with a fast, modern script that works its way from one end of the country to the other. Montreal, Calgary, and Vancouver get their own segments. The film has additional clips of Canada's capital, Ottawa, and specifically mentions its three territories—Yukon, Northwest Territories, and Nunavut—and highlights their Indigenous peoples and cultures. Comments accompanying low ratings generally mention the lack of seating, not the content of the film.

EPCOT ENTERTAINMENT

LIVE ENTERTAINMENT IN EPCOT is incredibly diverse. In World Showcase, it reflects the nations represented. Future World provides a perfect setting for new and experimental entertainment. Offerings on the day you visit can be found in the EPCOT guide map, often supplemented by a *Times Guide*. WDW live-entertainment expert Steve Soares usually posts EPCOT's performance schedule about a week in advance at wdwent.com. Here are some of the venues, performers, and performances you'll encounter:

AMERICA GARDENS THEATRE This large amphitheater, near The American Adventure Pavilion, faces World Showcase Lagoon. It hosts pop and oldies musical acts throughout much of the year, EPCOT's popular **Candlelight Processional** for the Christmas holidays, and sometimes **Voices of Liberty.** The special concerts hosted here are some of the best-rated entertainment acts in the park.

AROUND WORLD SHOWCASE Scheduled performances take place in and around the pavilions. Acts include a strolling mariachi group in Mexico (**Mariachi Cobre**); a juggler in Italy (**Sergio**); an a cappella group (**Voices of Liberty**) at The American Adventure Pavilion; traditional songs, drums, and dances (**Matsuriza**) in Japan; more traditional music in Morocco and the UK pub; and a band in Canada. Performances occur about every half hour somewhere around the lagoon.

FUTURE WORLD The **JAMMitors,** a crew of drumming janitors, work near the main entrance and around the rest of Future World, according to the daily entertainment schedule.

Luminous ★★★★

| PRESCHOOL ★★★★ (A) | GRADE SCHOOL ★★★★ (A) | TEENS ★★★★ (AA) |
| YOUNG ADULTS ★★★★ (A) | OVER 30 ★★★★ (A) | OVER 65 ★★★★½ (AA) |

DESCRIPTION AND COMMENTS *Luminous* is Disney's attempt at a new classic nighttime show at EPCOT, following the ill-fated *Harmonious*. But it's the lowest-rated nighttime entertainment at Walt Disney World by far.

Luminous tells the story of various stages of life, set to music—some original, but mostly songs from Disney and Pixar films. The show doesn't skimp on pyrotechnics or light and water features. But telling the story of a life obviously involves a lot of growing, learning, and heartbreak. All of these are captured in songs like "You'll Be in My Heart" from *Tarzan,* "When She Loved Me" from *Toy Story 2,* "Remember Me" from *Coco,* and "So Close" from *Enchanted.* If you're familiar with those movies and their soundtracks, you know those are all slow numbers—good for tugging at the heartstrings, not great for a rousing fireworks spectacular. We prefer the light-and-music shows at Spaceship Earth after dark for a better balance of emotional and uplifting vibes.

TOURING TIPS Fireworks dining packages let you see the show at the **Rose & Crown Dining Room** in the United Kingdom ($89 per adult, $39 per child) or **Spice Road Table** in Morocco ($79 per adult, $29 per child). Check-in starts 45 minutes before the show begins, meaning your meal should end around the same time the show ends. Otherwise, you can get a decent view of the show from anywhere around the lagoon. Spots fill up on the northern end (between Canada and Mexico) and anywhere near the International Gateway long before they do on the southern or eastern sides.

VIEWING AND EXIT STRATEGIES FOR EPCOT'S FIREWORKS

AS NOTED ABOVE, EPCOT debuted a new fireworks show called *Luminous* in late 2023. One of *Harmonious*' many flaws was that it couldn't be viewed properly from anywhere except two spots around World Showcase Lagoon. In contrast, *Luminous* has at least decent views from all around the lagoon.

The best viewing location for fireworks is in **Showcase Plaza**—the area where Future World meets World Showcase—between the Disney Traders and Port of Entry shops.

The best place for viewing fireworks on the south side of World Showcase Lagoon is around Japan. Come early—at least 60 minutes before the show during busy seasons—and relax with a cold drink or a snack while you wait for the show.

La Hacienda de San Angel in Mexico, **Rose & Crown Pub** in the United Kingdom, and **Spice Road Table** in Morocco also offer lagoon views. The views at Spice Road Table are better than those at the other restaurants. If you want to combine dinner at these table-service locations with viewing the show, make a reservation for about 1 hour and 15 minutes before showtime. Report a few minutes early for your seating, and tell the host that you want a table outside where you can watch the show. Cast members will do their best to accommodate you (but Fireworks Dining Package guests get priority at Rose & Crown and Spice Road Table).

Because most guests run for the exits after the show and islands in the southern (American Adventure) half of the lagoon block the view from some places, the most popular spectator positions are along the **northern waterfront,** from Norway and Mexico to Canada and the UK. Although this half of the lagoon offers good views, you usually must claim a spot 60–90 minutes before the show begins.

If you're late finishing dinner or don't want to spend an hour or more standing by a rail, these viewing spots along the **southern perimeter** (moving counterclockwise from the United Kingdom to Germany) often go unnoticed until 10–30 minutes before showtime:

1. **International Gateway Island.** The pedestrian bridge across the canal near the IG spans an island that offers great viewing. It fills 30+ minutes before showtime.

2. **Second-floor (restaurant-level) deck of the Mitsukoshi building in Japan.** A Torii gate slightly blocks your sight line, but this covered deck offers a great vantage point, especially if the weather is iffy. If you find the wind blowing directly at you, the smoke from the fireworks won't be far behind. May be reserved by Disney for private viewings.

3. **Gondola landing at Italy.** An elaborate waterfront promenade offers decent viewing of all but the central barge. Claim a spot at least 30 minutes before showtime.

4. **Boat dock opposite Germany.** The dock generally fills 30 minutes before the show. This area may be exposed to more smoke from the fireworks because of EPCOT's prevailing winds.

5. **Waterfront promenade by Germany.** Views are good from the 90-foot-long walkway between Germany and China.

None of these locations are reservable (except by Disney), and the best spots get snapped up early on busy nights. Most nights, you can still find an acceptable vantage point 15–30 minutes before the show. Don't position yourself under a tree, an awning, or anything that blocks your overhead view.

Getting Out of EPCOT After the Fireworks

When the fireworks are over, everyone leaves at once, so it's important to not only decide how quickly you want to flee the park after the show but also to pick a vantage point that will help you exit efficiently.

The **Skyliner** connects EPCOT with Disney's Hollywood Studios as well as the **Caribbean Beach, Riviera, Pop Century,** and **Art of Animation Resorts.** EPCOT's station is just beyond the IG exit. Waits to board the Skyliner can be an hour or more on busy nights. Also, the Skyliner doesn't operate during thunderstorms or when lightning is in the area. To be among the first to board, watch the show from as close to the IG as possible, and leave when you see crowds starting to walk out, about 5 minutes before the show ends.

If you're staying at (or you parked at) one of the EPCOT resorts, watch the show from somewhere on the American Adventure half of the lagoon, then leave through the IG between France and the United Kingdom. You can walk or take a boat back to your hotel from the IG.

If you are staying at any other Disney resort and don't have a car, the fastest way home is to join the crowd exiting through the main entrance and catch a bus or the monorail.

If you've left a car in the EPCOT lot, find a viewing spot at the end of World Showcase Lagoon nearest Future World (and the exits). Leave as soon as the show wraps up, trying to exit ahead of the crowd (noting that thousands of people will be doing the same thing).

More groups get separated and more kids get lost following the evening fireworks than at any other time. In summer, you'll be walking in a throng of up to 30,000 people. If you're heading for the parking lot, pick a spot in the main-entrance area where you can meet back up if you get separated.

For those with a car, the hardest part is reaching the parking lot: Once you've made it there, you're in the clear. If you've paid close attention to where you parked, consider skipping the tram and walking. If you walk, watch your children closely and hang on to them—the parking lot can get dicey at this time of night with so many cars.

This Utah mom has an even quicker suggestion if you're willing to pay for transportation:

> *We watched the fireworks from the bridge at the International Gateway by the United Kingdom; then we just walked straight to the BoardWalk Inn and got a ride from Lyft. It took us 10 minutes from leaving the fireworks to getting to our ride to getting dropped off at our hotel.*

We have to say, though, if you don't have kids who need to immediately get back for bedtime, a slow post-park-closing stroll around World Showcase not only gives the transportation system time to get back to normal, but it's also just about the most spectacular way to spend a night at Walt Disney World. Within 20 minutes after the end of the fireworks, you'll have entire pavilions to yourself, still beautifully lit. Minute-for-minute, it's Becky's favorite way to spend time in any Disney park.

TRAFFIC PATTERNS *in* EPCOT

WITH REMY'S RATATOUILLE ADVENTURE, **Frozen Ever After, Guardians of the Galaxy: Cosmic Rewind,** and **Test Track** as the biggest rope-drop draws (and **Soarin' Around the World** as a very distant fifth), crowds head for two opposite ends of EPCOT when it opens. Frozen Ever After in Norway is the second stop for many of the guests who headed to Remy first, while guests who headed to Test Track and Cosmic Rewind then disperse among the other attractions in Future World, with Soarin' Around the World being the usual third choice.

EPCOT TOURING PLAN

TOURING EPCOT is much more strenuous than touring the other theme parks. EPCOT requires about twice as much walking and, unlike the Magic Kingdom, has no efficient in-park transportation—wherever you want to go, it's always quicker to walk.

Our **One-Day Touring Plan** (see pages 559–560) is for guests who are willing to experience all major rides and shows. It will help you avoid crowds on days of moderate to heavy attendance, but it can't shorten the distance you have to cover. On days of lighter attendance, the touring plan will still help you organize your day. The plan packs as much as possible into one long day and requires a lot of hustle and stamina. It has two versions: one for Disney resort guests and one for off-site guests. Because Early Entry means thousands of guests will already be in lines and on rides before off-site guests set foot in the park, the touring strategy for off-site guests is different. The plan does not assume the use of LLMP or LLSP. If you opt for either of these, you can use the free touring plan software to enter your return times.

The **One-Day Touring Plan for Families** (see pages 561–562) follows the same principles but focuses on a plan that keeps younger and older kids happy and engaged throughout the day.

Two-Day Touring Plan

To convert the One-Day Touring Plan to a two-day plan, see the attractions on the east side of the park on your first day, and those on the west side on the second. Alternatively, tour Future World's attractions on one day and World Showcase's on the other. The latter strategy has a couple of disadvantages: One is that Future World has three headliner attractions, while World Showcase has two; the second is that World Showcase has better restaurant choices for dinner.

"Not a Touring Plan" Touring Plans

For the type-B reader, these touring plans (starting on page 548) forgo detailed step-by-step strategies in favor of saving every last minute in line. For EPCOT, these strategies include advice for adults and parents with one day in the park, for anyone with two days, and for anyone with an afternoon and a full day to tour.

PRELIMINARY INSTRUCTIONS FOR USING THE TOURING PLANS

BECOME FAMILIAR WITH EPCOT'S **opening procedures** (see page 408). On days of moderate to heavy attendance, follow the touring plan exactly, deviating from it only as follows:

1. **When you're not interested in an attraction in the plan.** In this case, simply skip it and proceed to the next attraction.
2. **When you encounter a very long line at an attraction.** In this case, skip to the next attraction and try again later at the one with the line.

Before You Go

1. At 7 a.m. either seven (for on-site guests) or three (for off-site guests) days before your vacation starts, make LLMP or LLSP purchases and reservations if you want to use them.
2. Check disneyworld.disney.go.com or the MDE app the day before to verify official opening time.
3. Review the park-opening procedures and reread the touring plan you've chosen so you know what you're likely to encounter.

PART 13

DISNEY'S ANIMAL KINGDOM

KEY QUESTIONS ANSWERED IN THIS CHAPTER

- How do I get to Animal Kingdom? *(page 439)*
- How does park opening (rope drop) work? *(page 439)*
- What are the don't-miss rides? *(page 439)*
- What's the best way to use LLMP and LLSP in Animal Kingdom? *(page 443)*
- How do I ride Avatar Flight of Passage with a minimal wait in line? *(pages 454–455)*

OVERVIEW

WITH ITS LUSH VEGETATION, winding streams, meandering paths, and exotic settings, Animal Kingdom is Disney's most visually stunning park and a feast for the senses. The landscaping alone transports visitors to rainforests, savannas, and formal gardens, creating a soothing, mysterious, and exciting environment. Add to that its population of 1,700 animals, incredible replicas of African and Asian architecture, and a carefully curated selection of attractions, and you have a park unlike any other.

Animal Kingdom is currently divided into five lands (**Africa, Asia, Discovery Island, The Oasis,** and **Pandora—The World of Avatar**). DinoLand U.S.A. is closing to make way for the new **Tropical Americas** land, which won't open until at least 2027. While the park's sprawling 500 acres provide ample space for breathtaking views and immersive environments, it has

unofficial **TIP**
Disney's Animal Kingdom is four times the size of the Magic Kingdom and almost twice the size of EPCOT, but most of it is accessible only on guided tours or as part of attractions.

relatively few attractions: five rides, several walk-through trails and exhibits, three indoor theaters (two for live shows and one for a 4D film), two amphitheaters (only one of which currently hosts shows), and a Conservation Station accessible by train. With Tropical Americas and its *Indiana Jones* and *Encanto* attractions on the horizon, the

continued on page 438

Disney's Animal Kingdom

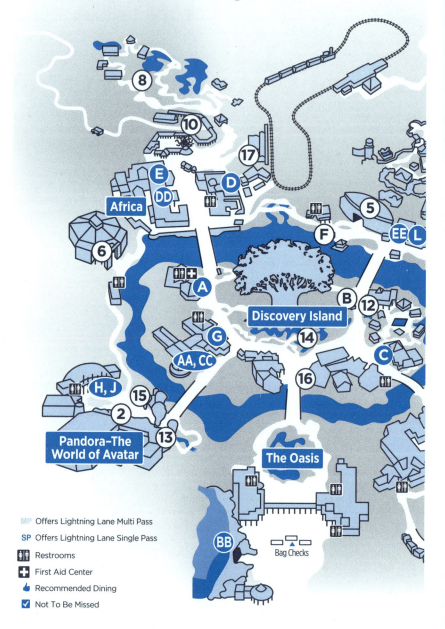

DISNEY'S ANIMAL KINGDOM MAP

Attractions

1. The Animation Experience at Conservation Station
2. Avatar Flight of Passage ☑ SP
3. Conservation Station and Affection Section
4. Expedition Everest ☑ MP
5. Feathered Friends in Flight! ☑ MP
6. Festival of the Lion King ☑ MP
7. Finding Nemo: The Big Blue . . . and Beyond! ☑ MP
8. Gorilla Falls Exploration Trail
9. Kali River Rapids MP
10. Kilimanjaro Safaris ☑ MP
11. Maharajah Jungle Trek
12. Meet Favorite Disney Pals at Adventurers Outpost
13. Na'vi River Journey ☑ MP
14. Tree of Life ☑ / Awakenings / Zootopia—Better Zoogether!
15. Valley of Mo'ara
16. Wilderness Explorers ☑
17. Wildlife Express Train

Table-Service Restaurants

- AA. Nomad Lounge
- BB. Rainforest Cafe
- CC. Tiffins 👍
- DD. Tusker House Restaurant 👍
- EE. Yak & Yeti Restaurant 👍

Counter-Service Restaurants

- A. Creature Comforts (Starbucks) 👍
- B. Eight Spoon Cafe 👍
- C. Flame Tree Barbecue 👍
- D. Harambe Market 👍
- E. Kusafiri Coffee Shop & Bakery
- F. Mr. Kamal's 👍
- G. Pizzafari
- H. Pongu Pongu
- I. Royal Anandapur Tea Company
- J. Satu'li Canteen 👍
- K. Thirsty River Bar & Trek Snacks
- L. Yak & Yeti Local Food Cafes

continued from page 435

ride count will increase to eight, helping to address the park's most common critique: a perceived lack of rides.

Once upon a time, Disney's idea of animals in theme parks was limited to cartoon characters and Audio-Animatronic figures (think Jungle Cruise). But there's nothing like competition to make Disney innovate and evolve. Since its opening in 1959, **Busch Gardens Tampa Bay** had been slowly building on a successful combination of natural-habitat zoological exhibits and thrill rides that by the 1990s had become immensely popular. In 1995, Disney announced its plans for Animal Kingdom, and the park opened in 1998 (that's significantly less time than it took to build Tron Lightcycle/Run, but we digress).

What sets Animal Kingdom apart is its sheer space and authenticity. There are sweeping vistas worthy of *National Geographic* or the Discovery Channel. Our favorite is when you're crossing the bridge from Discovery Island toward Africa: Look off to your right and find Everest looming over the waterway. It's perfection. And then there are the enclosures—natural in appearance, with few or no apparent barriers between you and the animals. The key word, of course, is *apparent*: That flimsy stand of bamboo separating you from a gorilla is actually a neatly disguised set of steel rods embedded in concrete.

Guest reviews of Animal Kingdom are often mixed. Visitors consistently praise the animal exhibits, intricate architecture, and lush landscaping. But some find the park's layout confusing and wish for more rides. Again, the ride-count issue should be addressed with the debut of Tropical Americas.

In spite of its weaknesses, Animal Kingdom works and is a favorite of many. It's a place where you can linger and explore—an experience that rewards those who are willing to slow down and savor its unique beauty. While Disney often trains guests to rush from attraction to attraction, Animal Kingdom invites a more thoughtful and relaxed approach, and that's what you'll need to embrace here.

A mother of three (ages 5, 7, and 9) from New York writes:

To enjoy Animal Kingdom, you must have the right attitude. It's an educational experience, not a thrill park. We spoke to a cast member who played games with the kids—my daughter found a drawer full of butterflies, and the boys located a hidden ostrich egg and lion skull.

We agree: Animal Kingdom's best features are its animals, nature trails, and cast members. The **Wilderness Explorers** scavenger hunt (see page 446) ties together all of the park's best elements, and it's part of our Animal Kingdom touring plan, described on page 457. It's a lot of fun to play, and you're sure to learn something along the way.

unofficial **TIP**
To beat the lines in Pandora, arrive well before opening or wait until the last hour the park is open.

Opened in 2017, **Pandora—The World of Avatar** is Animal Kingdom's newest land, themed to the James Cameron films. Pandora has two attractions: **Avatar Flight of Passage,** a state-of-the-art flight simulator, and **Na'vi River Journey,** a slow-moving boat ride through colorful forests and swamps. Readers rate Flight of Passage as one of the best attractions at any

NOT TO BE MISSED IN ANIMAL KINGDOM
AFRICA • *Festival of the Lion King* • *Kilimanjaro Safaris*
ASIA • *Expedition Everest* • *Feathered Friends in Flight!*
DISCOVERY ISLAND • *Wilderness Explorers* • *Zootopia: Better Zoogether*
FORMER DINOLAND AREA • *Finding Nemo: The Big Blue . . . and Beyond!*
PANDORA—THE WORLD OF AVATAR • *Avatar Flight of Passage*

theme park in the United States. Still, it has been hosting many thousands of visitors every day since it opened and is beginning to show some wear. We hope when Tropical Americas opens, Flight of Passage gets the refurbishment that it needs and deserves.

ARRIVING

FROM INSIDE WALT DISNEY WORLD, Disney buses are the only free option for getting to Animal Kingdom from on-property resorts, but service from many resorts can be slow.

DRIVING Animal Kingdom is in the southwest corner of Walt Disney World. From I-4, take **Exit 65** for Osceola Parkway. (For GPS address, see page 346.) **Animal Kingdom Lodge** is about a mile from the park on its west side; **Blizzard Beach** water park, **Coronado Springs Resort,** and the **All-Star Resorts** are also in the vicinity.

Animal Kingdom has its own vast parking lot with closer parking for guests with disabilities. Disney usually opens the parking lot about 60–75 minutes before official park opening. Once parked, you can walk or catch a tram to the entrance.

ANIMAL KINGDOM OPENING PROCEDURES (ROPE DROP)

ANIMAL KINGDOM is usually the first park to open in the morning and is always the first to close. Expect it to open at 8 a.m. daily, although it may open at 9 a.m. during slow times of year.

Disney resort guests eligible for Early Theme Park Entry should arrive at the entrance 60 minutes before official opening (30 minutes before Early Entry). Off-site guests who are not eligible for Early Entry should arrive 30 minutes before official opening. Once you're in the park, you'll usually find all of **Pandora,** along with **Expedition Everest,** already open.

Avatar Flight of Passage remains among the hottest tickets in all of Disney World. As a result, Animal Kingdom adjusts its opening procedures based on crowd levels, catching some guests by surprise. Here's what an Indiana reader experienced:

unofficial **TIP**
To confirm the official park-opening time, check online the night before you go. To stay abreast of ride closures, delays, and the like, also check the daily *Times Guide,* the MDE app, or the Lines app.

> We arrived at 7:20 expecting to be in the crowd for rope drop [for 7:30 a.m. Early Entry], but the crowd had already been admitted, and we immediately had a 90-minute wait—before 7:40 a.m.—for Avatar Flight of Passage.

ANIMAL KINGDOM SERVICES
MOST PARK SERVICES are inside the main entrance and on Discovery Island, including:
ATMs At the main entrance, by the tapstiles
Baby Care Center On Discovery Island
Cell Phone Charging Outlets available at Pizzafari, Tusker House, and Conservation Station
Entertainment Information In the *Times Guide*, available at Guest Relations
First Aid On Discovery Island
Guest Relations/Information Inside the main entrance, to the left
Lost and Found Inside the main entrance, to the left
Lost Persons Can be reported at Guest Relations and the Baby Care Center
Storage Lockers Inside the main entrance to the left
Wheelchair, ECV (Scooter), and Stroller Rentals Inside the main entrance, to the right

Because the park has relatively few attractions, most guests who arrive at park opening leave by midafternoon, leading to shorter waits later in the day. However, the low number of attractions also results in long waits in the middle of the day during busy holidays.

GETTING ORIENTED

AT THE ENTRANCE PLAZA, you'll find the security checkpoint and ticket kiosks just before the main entrance. Once you pass through the tapstiles, **wheelchair and stroller rentals** are to your right, and **Guest Relations** is to the left, along with **restrooms and lockers.** Beyond the entrance plaza, you enter **The Oasis,** a serene network of winding walkways surrounded by streams, waterfalls, and misty glades and a collection of what Disney calls "colorful and unusual animals."

Animal Kingdom is arranged somewhat like the Magic Kingdom, in a hub-and-spoke configuration. Similar to Main Street, U.S.A., The Oasis funnels visitors to **Discovery Island,** the heart of the park. Dominated by the 14-story hand-carved **Tree of Life,** Discovery Island serves as the park's central hub for dining and shopping. It also features a theater attraction in the Tree of Life, along with several short nature trails. From here, guests can venture out into themed lands: **Africa, Asia, Pandora—The World of Avatar,** and the area formerly known as DinoLand, which is currently transforming into **Tropical Americas.**

While you can experience most of Animal Kingdom in a single day, this is a park that rewards unhurried exploration. Take your time, soak in the incredible details, and enjoy the unique atmosphere.

LLMP AND LLSP SELECTIONS IN ANIMAL KINGDOM
AFRICA • Kilimanjaro Safaris • *Festival of the Lion King*
ASIA • Expedition Everest • *Feathered Friends in Flight!* • Kali River Rapids
DISCOVERY ISLAND • *Zootopia: Better Zoogether* (likely when it opens)
FORMER DINOLAND AREA • *Finding Nemo: The Big Blue . . . and Beyond!*
PANDORA—THE WORLD OF AVATAR • Avatar Flight of Passage (*LLSP*) • Na'vi River Journey

ANIMAL KINGDOM MOST POPULAR ATTRACTIONS BY AGE GROUP					
PRESCHOOL	**GRADE SCHOOL**	**TEENS**	**YOUNG ADULTS**	**OVER 30**	**OVER 65**
Kilimanjaro Safaris	Avatar Flight of Passage	Expedition Everest	Avatar Flight of Passage	Avatar Flight of Passage	Tam Tam Drummers of Harambe
Winged Encounters—The Kingdom Takes Flight	Kilimanjaro Safaris	Avatar Flight of Passage	Expedition Everest	Kilimanjaro Safaris	Winged Encounters—The Kingdom Takes Flight
Finding Nemo: The Big Blue . . . and Beyond	Tam Tam Drummers of Harambe	Kilimanjaro Safaris	Kilimanjaro Safaris	Expedition Everest	Festival of the Lion King
Festival of the Lion King	Wilderness Explorers	Meet Favorite Disney Pals at Adventurers Outpost	Festival of the Lion King	Festival of the Lion King	Kilimanjaro Safaris
Meet Favorite Disney Pals at Adventurers Outpost	Expedition Everest	Tam Tam Drummers of Harambe	Winged Encounters—The Kingdom Takes Flight	Tam Tam Drummers of Harambe	Avatar Flight of Passage
Feathered Friends in Flight!	Feathered Friends in Flight!	Valley of Mo'ara	Animation Experience at Conservation Station	Valley of Mo'ara	DiVine
Wilderness Explorers	Winged Encounters—The Kingdom Takes Flight	Winged Encounters—The Kingdom Takes Flight	Tam Tam Drummers of Harambe	Harambe Village Acrobats	Gorilla Falls Exploration Trail
Na'vi River Journey	Festival of the Lion King	Festival of the Lion King	Feathered Friends in Flight!	Feathered Friends in Flight!	Animation Experience at Conservation Station
Wildlife Express Train	Valley of Mo'ara	Feathered Friends in Flight!	Valley of Mo'ara	Winged Encounters—The Kingdom Takes Flight	Valley of Mo'ara
Gorilla Falls Exploration Trail	Meet Favorite Disney Pals at Adventurers Outpost	Animation Experience at Conservation Station	Discovery Island Trails	African Village Band	Finding Nemo: The Big Blue . . . and Beyond

*Two of preschoolers' top 10 attractions closed in early 2025: The Boneyard (first place) and Triceratop Spin

FAVORITE ATTRACTIONS BY AGE GROUP

ANIMAL KINGDOM HAS about two dozen rides, shows, performers, and seasonal entertainment. The table above shows the most popular attractions in the park by age group. Several age groups put **Avatar Flight of Passage** first. All age groups include **Kilimanjaro Safaris,** and all but preschoolers include **Expedition Everest** in their top attractions. Every age group's list of favorites includes at least one animal-centered attraction.

The average reader ratings for all Animal Kingdom attractions by age group are as follows, based on the 24,000 attraction ratings we received over the past year:

PRESCHOOL	GRADE SCHOOL	TEENS	YOUNG ADULTS	OVER 30	OVER 65
4.2 stars	4.4 stars	4.3 stars	4.4 stars	4.3 stars	4.4 stars

LLMP, LLSP, AND THE TOURING PLANS

NOTE: See page 53 for detailed information and strategy suggestions for LLMP and LLSP. The big questions addressed in this section are:

1. Is LLMP worth paying for in Animal Kingdom?
2. Which attractions benefit most from LLMP and LLSP?
3. How can you avoid paying for LLSP?
4. How do LLMP and LLSP work with the touring plans?

Is LLMP Worth Paying For in Animal Kingdom?

We think LLMP is rarely worth the cost at Animal Kingdom because of the limited options and the ability to avoid significant waits in other ways. That being said, you should at least consider purchasing it if you meet any of these criteria:

- You won't be at the park for Early Entry. This includes off-site guests who aren't eligible for Early Theme Park Entry and on-site guests who want to sleep in.
- You're visiting during a peak season and don't want to use a touring plan.
- You're starting the day at Animal Kingdom and then hopping to the Magic Kingdom or Disney's Hollywood Studios. You can buy LLMP for Animal Kingdom at a lower price, use one reservation at that park, and then start selecting attractions at your second park.

Regardless of the time of year you visit, arriving at park opening should allow you to see at least two headliner attractions without significant waits. Since only nine Animal Kingdom attractions (including *Zootopia: Better Zoogether!* when it opens) participate in LLMP or LLSP, it's unlikely you'd need more than three or four reservations per day. On days of heavy attendance, though, the lack of attractions means you'll be competing with lots of people, which pushes out return times and limits how many you can obtain. Below, we break down how much time we think you can save using LLMP with a touring plan, based on different assumptions about how many reservations it's possible to obtain in a day. See page 371 for an explanation of the different usage levels.

ESTIMATED TIME SAVINGS USING LLMP BY CROWD LEVEL			
CROWD LEVEL	TYPICAL USE (2 RESERVATIONS PER DAY)	OPTIMISTIC USE (3 RESERVATIONS PER DAY)	PERFECT USE (4 RESERVATIONS PER DAY)
LOW	20 minutes	35 minutes	45 minutes
MODERATE	40 minutes	60 minutes	75 minutes
HIGH	50 minutes	75 minutes	100 minutes

Which Attractions Benefit Most from LLMP and LLSP?

The table on the opposite page shows the attractions that benefit most from LLMP and LLSP, based on historical wait times over the past year.

For LLSP, we think **Avatar Flight of Passage** is worth the cost at almost any time of year, unless you can arrive at the park around 20 minutes before Early Entry or you're staying until the park closes.

LLMP is generally useful at only a handful of attractions, especially **Na'vi River Journey** and **Kilimanjaro Safaris**. These two should be your priorities if you're using LLMP here. But really, there is almost no

ANIMAL KINGDOM ATTRACTIONS THAT BENEFIT MOST FROM LLMP AND LLSP (Highest Priority to Lowest)	
ATTRACTION	AVERAGE TIME IN LINE SAVED (IN MINUTES)
AVATAR FLIGHT OF PASSAGE (LLSP)	48
KILIMANJARO SAFARIS	25
NA'VI RIVER JOURNEY	21
EXPEDITION EVEREST	14
KALI RIVER RAPIDS	10

Note: No time savings were observed using LLMP at the Animal Kingdom's live shows or The Animation Experience at Conservation Station. Depending on the popularity of *Zootopia: Better Zoogether,* it may also be a decent use of a LLMP reservation.

Time savings at Kali River Rapids varies significantly based on time of year and, specifically, on average temperature during the day.

reason to purchase LLMP for Animal Kingdom unless you're traveling at the busiest time of year.

When Do LLMP and LLSP Reservations Run Out in Animal Kingdom?

The table below shows the approximate time at which Animal Kingdom's attractions run out of LLMP or LLSP capacity, by crowd level. Use this table in conjunction with the "Attractions That Benefit Most" table, above, to determine which reservations to get first.

WHEN LLMP AND LLSP RESERVATIONS RUN OUT BY ATTENDANCE LEVEL*			
ATTRACTION	LOW ATTENDANCE	MODERATE ATTENDANCE	HIGH ATTENDANCE
AVATAR FLIGHT OF PASSAGE (LLSP)	11 a.m.	9 a.m.	4 days early
EXPEDITION EVEREST	Park close	Park close	Noon
FEATHERED FRIENDS IN FLIGHT!	Last showtime	Last showtime	Last showtime
FESTIVAL OF THE LION KING	Last showtime	Last showtime	Noon
FINDING NEMO—THE BIG BLUE . . . AND BEYOND!	Last showtime	Last showtime	Last showtime
KALI RIVER RAPIDS	Park close	Park close	2 p.m.
KILIMANJARO SAFARIS	Attraction close	Attraction close	10 a.m.
NA'VI RIVER JOURNEY	11 a.m.	8 a.m.	3 days early

* Flight of Passage typically drops more LLSP reservations at 45 minutes past every hour, in almost all crowd conditions. These sellout times ignore those drops. *Zootopia: Better Zoogether,* was not yet open at press time.

LOW ATTENDANCE Crowd levels 1–3 on the TouringPlans crowd calendar
MODERATE ATTENDANCE Crowd levels 4–7 **HIGH ATTENDANCE** Crowd levels 8–10

How Can You Avoid Paying for LLSP?

Animal Kingdom doesn't regularly participate in Extended Evening Theme Park Hours (it does just once a week when DHS and the Magic Kingdom are both in Christmas party season), so your best option to see Flight of Passage is to stay at a Disney resort and use Early Theme Park Entry. Head to Flight of Passage as soon as the park opens. Otherwise, wait until late in the evening, when most people have left.

444 PART 13 DISNEY'S ANIMAL KINGDOM

How Do LLMP and LLSP Work with the Touring Plans?

See our advice on page 373.

DINING IN ANIMAL KINGDOM

HERE'S A QUICK RECAP of Animal Kingdom's top restaurants, rated by readers, starting with the highest rated. Restaurants not listed are rated average or below. See Part 6 for details.

HIGHEST-RATED ANIMAL KINGDOM RESTAURANTS	
COUNTER SERVICE	**TABLE SERVICE**
Eight Spoon Cafe (⊕ 100%/E), Discovery island	**Yak & Yeti** (⊕ 94%/AA), Asia
Mr. Kamal's (⊕ 100%/E), Between Asia and Africa	**Tusker House Restaurant** (⊕ 93%/AA), Africa
Satu'li Canteen (⊕ 96%/MAA), Pandora	
Flame Tree Barbecue (⊕ 95%/AA), Discovery Island	**Tiffins** (⊕ 92%/AA), Discovery Island
Harambe Market (⊕ 92%/AA), Africa	

E = Exceptional **MAA** = Much Above Average **AA** = Above Average

The OASIS

WHILE THE OASIS SERVES THE SAME PURPOSE as the Magic Kingdom's Main Street—guiding guests to the park's central hub—it does so with a unique approach that sets the tone for your day. Designed as a "transitional experience," The Oasis immediately signals that this is not just another theme park to rush through.

Rather than a single broad thoroughfare leading you straight to the center, The Oasis has multiple meandering paths surrounded by greenery, streams, waterfalls, and grottoes. Unlike the direct routes of Main Street in the Magic Kingdom or Hollywood Boulevard in Disney's Hollywood Studios, The Oasis envelops you in a canopy of natural beauty, encouraging exploration. If (and only if) you slow down and look closely, you'll be rewarded with glimpses of animals tucked into the landscape. Disney is inviting you from the start to slow down and appreciate the environment at a different pace.

The zoological exhibits in The Oasis reflect those found throughout the park. Signs identify the animals, but keep in mind that spotting them often requires patience. With spacious habitats designed to give the animals plenty of places to roam or hide, you'll need to linger, watch carefully, and look for subtle movements to catch a glimpse.

The Oasis is a place to explore and appreciate—plan to spend some time here on your way into or out of the park. The Oasis stays open 30–60 minutes after the rest of Animal Kingdom, but some animals may go indoors sooner.

DISCOVERY ISLAND

DISCOVERY ISLAND COMBINES tropical greenery with Equatorial African–inspired architecture. Connected to the other lands by bridges, it's arranged like a village in a crescent around the base of the park's iconic **Tree of Life.** Towering 14 stories high, the tree is surrounded by pools, meadows, and gardens filled with exotic birds and animals. Inside the tree, *Zootopia—Better Zoogether!*, a new 4D theater attraction inspired by *Zootopia*, is set to open in winter 2025.

As you cross the bridge from The Oasis, you'll see the Tree of Life directly ahead, at 12 o'clock. The bridge to **Asia** is to the right at 2 o'clock, and the bridge to what will eventually be **Tropical Americas** is at roughly 4 o'clock. The bridge connecting The Oasis to Discovery Island is at 6 o'clock, the bridge to **Pandora—The World of Avatar** is at 8 o'clock, and the bridge to **Africa** is at 11 o'clock.

Discovery Island is also the park's central headquarters for shopping and services. Here you'll find **First Aid** and the **Baby Care Center**. **Island Mercantile, Riverside Depot,** and **Discovery Trading Company** are the go-to spots for Disney merchandise. Dining options here include plenty of counter-service snacks and meals, along with the upscale table-service restaurant **Tiffins**, for those looking to indulge in a more refined meal.

KEY TO ABBREVIATIONS In the attraction profiles that follow, each star rating is accompanied by a category label in parentheses (see page 370 for details). E means **Exceptional**, MAA means **Much Above Average**, AA means **Above Average**, A means **Average**, BA means **Below Average**, and MBA means **Much Below Average**.

Discovery Island Trails ★★★

| PRESCHOOL ★★★★ (A) | GRADE SCHOOL ★★★★ (BA) | TEENS ★★★★ (A) |
| YOUNG ADULTS ★★★★½ (AA) | OVER 30 ★★★★ (A) | OVER 65 ★★★★ (A) |

What it is Scenic walking trails. **Scope and scale** Diversion. **When to go** Anytime. **ECV/wheelchair access** May remain in wheelchair. **Participates in LLMP** No. **Early Theme Park Entry** Yes. **Extended Evening Hours** Yes.

DESCRIPTION AND COMMENTS A network of walking trails winds around and behind the tree, with about a dozen animal-viewing opportunities, from otters and tortoises to lemurs, storks, and porcupines. One end of the path begins just before the bridge from Discovery Island to Africa, on the right side of the walkway; the other is to the right of the entrance to the Tree of Life. In addition to the animals, you'll find verdant landscaping, waterfalls, and quiet spots for sitting and reflecting. Or play I Spy using all of the animals—both real and carved—as subjects. Pocahontas also meets sporadically throughout the day on the trail to the west of the Tree of Life.

Meet Favorite Disney Pals at Adventurers Outpost ★★★½

| PRESCHOOL ★★★★½ (MAA) | GRADE SCHOOL ★★★★½ (AA) | TEENS ★★★★½ (MAA) |
| YOUNG ADULTS ★★★★½ (MAA) | OVER 30 ★★★★ (A) | OVER 65 ★★★★ (BA) |

What it is Character-greeting venue. **Scope and scale** Minor attraction. **When to go** First thing in the morning or after 5 p.m. **Duration** Varies. **Probable waiting time** About 25 minutes. **Queue speed** Slow. **ECV/wheelchair access** May remain in wheelchair. **Participates in LLMP** No. **Early Theme Park Entry** No. **Extended Evening Hours** Yes.

DESCRIPTION AND COMMENTS This air-conditioned greeting location for Mickey and Minnie is decorated with photos and other memorabilia from the Mouses' world travels. The Outpost has two greeting rooms with two identical sets of characters in cute safari gear.

TREE OF LIFE

THE TREE OF LIFE IS A WORK OF ART—the most visually compelling structure in any Disney theme park. Although it's magnificent from afar, it's not until you get close that you can truly appreciate its rich detail. What appears from a distance to be ancient, gnarled bark is, in fact, hundreds of carvings depicting all manner of wildlife, integrated seamlessly into the tree's trunk, roots, and limbs. Our favorite place for discovering new creatures is walking up the exit path for the theater show.

Zootopia: Better Zoogether!

NOT YET OPEN AT PRESS TIME

DESCRIPTION AND COMMENTS At press time, Disney had announced a replacement for *It's Tough to Be a Bug!* in the theater below the Tree of Life. It will be themed to *Zootopia* and is scheduled to open in 2025. When it opens, it will be a popular draw for families.

Awakenings ★★★

| PRESCHOOL ★★★★½ (AA) | GRADE SCHOOL ★★★★½ (AA) | TEENS ★★★★½ (AA) |
| YOUNG ADULTS ★★★★ (A) | OVER 30 ★★★★½ (MAA) | OVER 65 ★★★★½ (MAA) |

What it is Nighttime projection show. **Scope and scale** Minor attraction. **When to go** After sunset. **Duration** 3 minutes. **ECV/wheelchair access** May remain in wheelchair. **Participates in LLMP** No. **Early Theme Park Entry** No. **Extended Evening Hours** Yes (when they're offered).

DESCRIPTION AND COMMENTS The Tree of Life also hosts *Awakenings,* a child-friendly nighttime show projected onto the tree's trunk and canopy. Shown several times a night (when the park is open after dark), *Awakenings* combines digital video projections with music and special effects. Several shows rotate; in each, special projection effects make it appear that some animals carved into the tree trunk have come alive. Other special effects happen in the leaves and branches. The park is now rarely open after dark, but if you're visiting in winter when the sun sets early, it's worth sticking around to see.

TOURING TIPS The best viewing spots are directly in front of the tree on Discovery Island, across from Island Mercantile.

Wilderness Explorers ★★★★

| PRESCHOOL ★★★★½ (AA) | GRADE SCHOOL ★★★★½ (MAA) | TEENS ★★★★ (A) |
| YOUNG ADULTS ★★★★ (A) | OVER 30 ★★★★½ (A) | OVER 65 ★★★★ (A) |

What it is Parkwide educational scavenger hunt. **Scope and scale** Diversion. **When to go** Sign up in the morning and complete activities throughout the day. **ECV/wheelchair access** May remain in wheelchair. **Participates in LLMP** No. **Early Theme Park Entry** No. **Extended Evening Hours** No.

DESCRIPTION AND COMMENTS Walt Disney World offers several interactive games in its theme parks. Wilderness Explorers is the best one—an educational and fun scavenger hunt based on Russell's Scout-like troop from the movie *Up.* Players earn "badges" (stickers) for completing predefined activities throughout the park. For example, to earn the Gorilla Badge, you might walk the Gorilla Falls Exploration Trail to observe how the primates behave, then mimic that behavior back to a cast member to show what you've seen.

Sign up near the bridge from The Oasis to Discovery Island or at other stations throughout the park as you come across them. You'll be given an instruction book and a map showing the park location where each badge can be earned.

Cast members have been specially trained for this game and can tailor the activities based on the age of the child playing: Small children might get an explanation about what deforestation means, for example, while older kids may have to figure out why tigers have stripes. It's tons of fun for kids and adults, and we participate every time we're in the park.

The program is a big hit with kids, as an Australian mom shares:

Wilderness Explorers was the highlight of my son's day. Much time is spent collecting badges, but it is well worth the investment of time!

TOURING TIPS Activities are spread throughout the park, so sign up early in the day and collect badges whenever you pass stations as you tour.

AFRICA

THE LARGEST OF ANIMAL KINGDOM'S LANDS, Africa is entered through **Harambe**, a Disneyfied take on a modern rural African town. Harambe features a bustling market equipped with modern cash registers; dining options that range from a buffet restaurant to bars, counter-service meals, and snacks; and a sense of architectural authenticity. Though idealized and better maintained than its real-life inspiration, Harambe feels more at home in Africa than the Magic Kingdom's Main Street would in small-town Missouri. Its understated design is part of its charm, offering a glimpse into what everyday life might be like in an African village.

Harambe serves as the gateway to Animal Kingdom's most ambitious environment: the African savanna habitat. Guests can explore the savanna on **Kilimanjaro Safaris**, located at the end of Harambe's main street near a striking baobab tree. Harambe is also the departure point for the train to **Rafiki's Planet Watch** and **Conservation Station** (the park's veterinary headquarters) and the home of *Festival of the Lion King*, a popular and long-running live show. A scenic walkway by the theater connects Africa with Pandora.

Festival of the Lion King ★★★★½

PRESCHOOL ★★★★½ (MAA) **GRADE SCHOOL** ★★★★½ (MAA) **TEENS** ★★★★½ (AA)
YOUNG ADULTS ★★★★½ (MAA) **OVER 30** ★★★★½ (MAA) **OVER 65** ★★★★★ (E)

What it is Theater-in-the-round stage show. **Scope and scale** Major attraction. **When to go** Earlier or later showtimes. **Duration** 30 minutes. **Comment** Arrive 20–30 minutes before showtime. **ECV/wheelchair access** May remain in wheelchair. **Participates in LLMP** Yes. **Early Theme Park Entry** No. **Extended Evening Hours** No.

DESCRIPTION AND COMMENTS Inspired by Disney's 1994 animated feature *The Lion King*, *Festival of the Lion King* is part stage show and part parade. Guests sit in four sets of bleachers surrounding the stage and are organized into cheering sections that are called on to make elephant, warthog, giraffe, and lion noises. (You won't be alone if you don't know what a giraffe sounds like.) There's a great deal of strutting around and a lot of singing and dancing. By my count, every tune from *The Lion King* is belted out—some more than once. Kids will adore being involved in the action, and parents might get teary-eyed watching them participate in the magic (not that we know from experience).

Unofficial Guide readers are almost unanimous in their praise of the show. This take from a California family is typical:

> The singers, the acrobats, and the dancers were all visually impressive and surprisingly moving. I choked up during the trapeze "dance" of "Can You Feel the Love Tonight?" and I don't even like that song!

TOURING TIPS *Festival of the Lion King* is a big draw, so try to see the first show in the morning or one of the last two at night. For midday performances, you'll need to queue up at least 20–30 minutes before showtime. The bleachers can make viewing difficult for shorter folks—if you have small children or short adults in your party, snag a seat higher up. Despite the attraction's popularity, using LLMP here doesn't actually save much time.

Gorilla Falls Exploration Trail ★★★★

PRESCHOOL ★★★★ (A)	GRADE SCHOOL ★★★★½ (A)	TEENS ★★★★ (A)
YOUNG ADULTS ★★★★ (A)	OVER 30 ★★★★½ (AA)	OVER 65 ★★★★½ (MAA)

What it is Walk-through zoological exhibit. **Scope and scale** Major attraction. **When to go** Before or after Kilimanjaro Safaris. **Duration** About 20–30 minutes. **ECV/wheelchair access** May remain in wheelchair. **Participates in LLMP** No. **Early Theme Park Entry** No. **Extended Evening Hours** No.

DESCRIPTION AND COMMENTS On this beautiful trail winding between the domain of two troops of lowland gorillas, it's hard to see what, if anything, separates you from the primates. Other highlights are a naked mole rat exhibit, a hippo pool with an underwater viewing area, and an exotic-bird aviary so craftily designed that you can barely tell you're in an enclosure.

TOURING TIPS The Gorilla Falls Exploration Trail is filled with people much of the time. Guests exiting Kilimanjaro Safaris can choose between returning to Harambe or walking the Gorilla Falls Exploration Trail. Many opt for the trail. Thus, when Kilimanjaro Safaris is operating at full capacity, it spews hundreds of guests onto the Exploration Trail every couple of minutes.

If Kilimanjaro Safaris closes early, Gorilla Falls probably does too. Be sure to check its operating hours.

Kilimanjaro Safaris ★★★★★

PRESCHOOL ★★★★★ (E)	GRADE SCHOOL ★★★★★ (E)	TEENS ★★★★½ (MAA)
YOUNG ADULTS ★★★★★ (E)	OVER 30 ★★★★★ (E)	OVER 65 ★★★★½ (MAA)

What it is Ride through a simulated African wildlife reservation. **Scope and scale** Super-headliner. **When to go** As soon as the park opens or after 3 p.m. **Duration** About 20 minutes. **Loading speed** Fast. **ECV/wheelchair access** Must transfer from ECV to provided wheelchair. **Participates in LLMP** Yes. **Early Theme Park Entry** No. **Extended Evening Hours** No.

DESCRIPTION AND COMMENTS As Animal Kingdom's premier zoological attraction, Kilimanjaro Safaris offers an exceptionally realistic, albeit brief, imitation of an actual African photo safari. It's one of the top-rated attractions not only in this park but in all four Disney World theme parks. Thirty-two guests at a time board tall, open vehicles to travel into a simulated African savanna habitat. Zebras, wildebeests, impalas, Thomson's gazelles, giraffes, and even rhinos roam seemingly free, while predators such as lions, as well as potentially dangerous large animals like hippos, are separated from both prey and guests by nearly invisible, natural-looking barriers. Although the animals have more than 100 acres of savanna, woodland, streams, and rocky hills to call home, careful placement of watering holes, forage, and salt licks ensures that they are hanging out by the road when safari vehicles roll by.

As on a real African safari, what animals you see, and how many, is pretty much a matter of luck. First thing in the morning, you'll generally see a lot of activity from the giraffes and antelopes. In the late afternoon, the rhinos are more active. Every safari is a different experience.

TOURING TIPS Kilimanjaro Safaris is one of Animal Kingdom's busiest attractions, along with the two Pandora attractions. From a touring standpoint, this is a good thing: By distributing guests evenly throughout the park, those other attractions make it unnecessary to run to Kilimanjaro Safaris first thing in the morning. You can do Pandora first, then Safaris, and still have lower waits and active animals.

Most animals appear on the left side of the safari truck (except on the open savanna section), so have kids—or photographers—sit on that side.

RAFIKI'S PLANET WATCH

NOT A TRUE "LAND" IN SCOPE OR SCALE, this section of Animal Kingdom, named for a beloved *Lion King* character, consists of the park's animal-care center (**Conservation Station**), a petting zoo, an animation class, and educational exhibits, all accessible from Harambe via the **Wildlife Express Train.**

The Animation Experience at Conservation Station ★★★½

PRESCHOOL ★★★★½ (BA)	GRADE SCHOOL ★★★★ (A)	TEENS ★★★★ (AA)
YOUNG ADULTS ★★★★½ (MAA)	OVER 30 ★★★★½ (AA)	OVER 65 ★★★★½ (MAA)

What it is Character-drawing class. **Scope and scale** Minor attraction. **When to go** Check *Times Guide*. **Duration** 30 minutes. **Comments** Accessible only by the Wildlife Express Train. **Participates in LLMP** No. **Early Theme Park Entry** No. **Extended Evening Hours** No.

DESCRIPTION AND COMMENTS This experience provides insight into the history of Disney animation and gives participants of any skill level a chance to draw Disney characters with the help of an instructor, using real-life animals as inspiration. When a 5-year-old, 35-year-old, and 65-year-old can all follow the same instruction and end up with a recognizable Disney character, you've got yourself a winning activity.

TOURING TIPS Board the train 45 minutes prior to the experience start time.

Conservation Station and Affection Section ★★★

PRESCHOOL ★★★★ (BA)	GRADE SCHOOL ★★★★ (BA)	TEENS ★★★★ (A)
YOUNG ADULTS ★★★★ (A)	OVER 30 ★★★½ (BA)	OVER 65 ★★★★ (BA)

What it is Behind-the-scenes educational exhibit and petting zoo. **Scope and scale** Minor attraction. **When to go** Morning. **Comments** Check *Times Guide* for hours. Accessible only by the Wildlife Express Train. **ECV/wheelchair access** May remain in wheelchair. **Participates in LLMP** No. **Early Theme Park Entry** No. **Extended Evening Hours** No.

DESCRIPTION AND COMMENTS Conservation Station is Animal Kingdom's veterinary and conservation headquarters. Here, guests can meet wildlife experts, learn about the behind-the-scenes operations of the park, and observe ongoing projects. If you want to see activity instead of empty rooms, you'll want to go pretty early in the morning.

While there are several permanent exhibits, including Affection Section (an animal-petting area), what you see at Conservation Station will largely depend on what's going on when you arrive.

A reader from England was amused by both the goings-on and the other guests:

The most memorable part of Animal Kingdom for me was watching a veterinary surgeon and his team at Conservation Station perform an operation on a rat snake that had inadvertently swallowed a golf ball, presumably believing it to be an egg. This operation caused at least one onlooker to pass out.

TOURING TIPS Because Conservation Station is so removed from the rest of the park, you won't see any of it unless you take the train. It's a great place to go in the middle of the afternoon if you're overwhelmed by crowds in other areas of the park.

Wildlife Express Train ★★

PRESCHOOL ★★★★ (A)	GRADE SCHOOL ★★★★ (BA)	TEENS ★★★★ (A)
YOUNG ADULTS ★★★★ (A)	OVER 30 ★★★★ (BA)	OVER 65 ★★★★ (A)

What it is Scenic railroad ride to Rafiki's Planet Watch. **Scope and scale** Minor attraction. **When to go** Anytime. **Comments** Last train departs at 4:30 p.m. **Duration** About 7 minutes one-way. **Loading speed** Moderate. **ECV/wheelchair access** May remain in wheelchair. **Participates in LLMP** No. **Early Theme Park Entry** No. **Extended Evening Hours** No.

DESCRIPTION AND COMMENTS This ride winds behind the African wildlife reserve as it connects Harambe to Rafiki's Planet Watch. En route, you see the barns for the animals that populate Kilimanjaro Safaris, and on the way back to Harambe, you see the backstage areas of Asia. None of the sights are especially stunning.

TOURING TIPS The train tends to get crowded only when people exit the Safaris and flood the loading area.

ASIA

CROSSING THE BRIDGE from Discovery Island, you enter Asia through the village of **Anandapur,** inspired by the architecture and ruins of India, Indonesia, Nepal, and Thailand. Situated near the bank of the Discovery River and surrounded by mature vegetation, Anandapur is home to some dining options, an animal trail, a gibbon exhibit, and Asia's two feature attractions: the **Kali River Rapids** raft ride and **Expedition Everest.** At 200 feet tall, Everest is the tallest mountain in Florida! "Across the street" from Everest is a large indoor theater that used to be part of DinoLand U.S.A. but is now homeless after the closure of that land.

Expedition Everest ★★★★½

PRESCHOOL ★★★½ (BA)	GRADE SCHOOL ★★★★½ (MAA)	TEENS ★★★★★ (E)
YOUNG ADULTS ★★★★★ (E)	OVER 30 ★★★★★ (E)	OVER 65 ★★★★½ (AA)

What it is High-speed roller coaster. **Scope and scale** Super-headliner. **When to go** Early or late. **Comments** Must be 44" tall to ride; Rider Switch option provided (see page 307); single-rider line available. **Duration** 4 minutes. **Loading speed** Moderate-fast. **ECV/wheelchair access** Must transfer to the ride vehicle. **Participates in LLMP** Yes. **Early Theme Park Entry** Yes. **Extended Evening Hours** Yes.

DESCRIPTION AND COMMENTS Expedition Everest is the only roller coaster in Animal Kingdom. Your journey begins in a heavily themed queue modeled after a Nepalese village; then you board an old train headed for the base camp of Mount Everest. Notes from previous expeditions are posted throughout the waiting area, some with cryptic observations regarding a mysterious creature who is said to guard the mountain.

This coaster consists of tight turns (some traveling backward), hills, and dips but no loops or inversions. As you climb the first two hills, you'll see some of the most spectacular panoramas in Disney World. You should be able to spot everything from Animal Kingdom Lodge to Spaceship Earth in EPCOT and the Tower of Terror in Disney's Hollywood Studios. The final drop and last few turns are among Disney's best coaster elements.

Disney bills Expedition Everest as a "family thrill ride"—more like Big Thunder Mountain Railroad than Rock 'n' Roller Coaster—but it's an exciting experience nonetheless. An Indiana family gives it a thumbs-up:

Expedition Everest is tremendous. It has enough surprises and runaway speed to make it one of the more enjoyable thrill rides in the whole Orlando area.

A Georgia teen successfully recruited Grandma to ride:

One of our favorites. Not too jerky for us older people, and the ride is one that I feel has a lot of variety in that you go fast, you go up, you have minor drops and big drops, and you go backwards. Great value!

And we also hit a milestone here: the first-ever comment about a Disney roller coaster being . . . too long?!

It wasn't as scary as I had expected, but it wasn't as great as others. It was kind of long.

TOURING TIPS Expedition Everest reaches a top speed of around 50 mph, about twice that of Space Mountain. Ask to be seated up front—the first few rows offer the best front-seat experience of any Disney coaster. If you're in Animal Kingdom after sunset, Everest feels like a totally different attraction—it's even more intense in the dark.

Feathered Friends in Flight! ★★★★

PRESCHOOL ★★★★½ (AA) **GRADE SCHOOL** ★★★★½ (MAA) **TEENS** ★★★★½ (AA)
YOUNG ADULTS ★★★★½ (MAA) **OVER 30** ★★★★½ (MAA) **OVER 65** ★★★★½ (MAA)

What it is Stadium show about birds. **Scope and scale** Minor attraction. **When to go** Anytime; check *Times Guide* for performance times. **Comment** Arrive 10 minutes before the show. **Duration** 30 minutes. **ECV/wheelchair access** May remain in wheelchair. **Participates in LLMP** Yes. **Early Theme Park Entry** No. **Extended Evening Hours** No.

DESCRIPTION AND COMMENTS Asia's amphitheater has presented a show featuring live birds for years. *Feathered Friends in Flight!* is the best version ever. The hosts are some of Disney's animal trainers, who explain different bird species' habitats and characteristics. The show is fast-paced, informative, and entertaining for everyone, with birds literally flying overhead. We consider it not to be missed. Keep in mind, though, that the birds get to choose whether and how they participate, so your mileage may vary.

Feathered Friends focuses on the birds' natural talents and characteristics, which far surpass any tricks they might have learned from humans (don't expect parrots riding bikes or cockatoos playing tiny pianos). A reader from Maryland appreciated the education and the humor:

Not only were the birds well trained, and it was cool seeing unusual birds fly over our heads so up close and personal, but also the two guys were an absolute stitch—so entertaining. I really didn't expect to love this show as much as I did.

TOURING TIPS *Feathered Friends* plays at the stadium near the bridge on the walkway into Asia. The stadium is covered, but it's not air-conditioned, so early-morning and late-afternoon performances are more comfortable. There is also a snack stand by the bridge that sells frozen drinks that are perfect for enjoying while you watch.

Kali River Rapids ★★★½

PRESCHOOL ★★★★ (A)	GRADE SCHOOL ★★★★½ (A)	TEENS ★★★★ (AA)
YOUNG ADULTS ★★★★ (A)	OVER 30 ★★★★ (BA)	OVER 65 ★★★★ (A)

Wet

What it is Whitewater raft ride. **Scope and scale** Major attraction. **When to go** Before 11 a.m. or the last hour the park is open. **Comments** You're likely to get wet; must be 38" tall to ride; Rider Switch option provided (see page 307). **Duration** About 5 minutes. **Loading speed** Moderate. **ECV/wheelchair access** Must transfer to the ride vehicle; transfer device available. **Participates in LLMP** Yes. **Early Theme Park Entry** No. **Extended Evening Hours** No.

DESCRIPTION AND COMMENTS Kali River Rapids takes you on an unguided trip down an artificial river in a circular rubber raft with a top-mounted platform that seats 12 people. The raft essentially floats free in the current and is washed downstream through rapids and waves. Because the river is fairly wide, with various waves, currents, eddies, and obstacles, each trip is different.

Disney's trademark attention to visual detail is on full display—Kali River Rapids flows through a dense rainforest and past waterfalls, temple ruins, and bamboo thickets, emerging into a cleared area where greedy loggers have ravaged the forest and finally drifting back under the tropical canopy as the river returns to Anandapur. Along the way, your raft runs a gauntlet of raging rapids, logjams, and other dangers. That said, you get only about 3½ minutes on the water, and it's not a thrill ride. Yes, you get wet, but the drops and rapids aren't scary.

TOURING TIPS Kali River Rapids is hugely popular on hot days. Plan accordingly! You won't get totally soaked, but you'll still get pretty wet. We recommend wearing shorts and sport sandals (such as Tevas) on the ride and/or putting anything you want to stay dry into a plastic bag.

Kali River Rapids offers free 2-hour locker rentals to the left of the attraction entrance, near the restrooms. You could store a change of dry clothes here or, alternatively, wear as little as the law and Disney will allow. If you're wearing closed shoes, prop up your feet above the bottom of the raft to keep them from getting completely soaked—slogging around in wet shoes is a surefire ticket to Blisterville.

Maharajah Jungle Trek ★★★★

PRESCHOOL ★★★★ (A)	GRADE SCHOOL ★★★★ (A)	TEENS ★★★★ (A)
YOUNG ADULTS ★★★★ (A)	OVER 30 ★★★★½ (AA)	OVER 65 ★★★★½ (AA)

What it is Walk-through zoological exhibit. **Scope and scale** Major attraction. **When to go** Anytime. **Duration** About 20–30 minutes. **ECV/wheelchair access** May remain in wheelchair. **Participates in LLMP** No. **Early Theme Park Entry** No. **Extended Evening Hours** No.

DESCRIPTION AND COMMENTS This walk resembles the **Gorilla Falls Exploration Trail** (see page 448) but with a Southeast Asian setting. Animals you might see range from Komodo dragons to large fruit bats. Ruins of the maharajah's palace provide the setting for Bengal tigers. Look for a plaster triptych just after the tiger exhibit that shows a parable about humans living in harmony with nature. The trek concludes with an aviary.

Labyrinthine, seemingly overgrown, and elaborately detailed, the ruins would be a compelling attraction even without the animals. Most readers, like this Washington, DC, couple, agree:

> The Maharajah Jungle Trek was absolutely amazing. We were able to see all the animals, which were awake by that time (9:30 a.m.), including the elusive tigers. The part with the birds was fabulous; you could spot hundreds, some of which were eating on the ground a mere 3 feet away from us.

TOURING TIPS The Maharajah Jungle Trek doesn't get as jammed up as the Gorilla Falls Exploration Trail and is a good choice for midday touring when most other attractions are crowded. The downside, of course, is that the exhibit showcases tigers, bats, and other creatures that might not be very active in the heat of the day. The tigers are notoriously difficult to spot.

Finding Nemo: The Big Blue . . . and Beyond! ★★★½

PRESCHOOL ★★★★½ (MAA) **GRADE SCHOOL** ★★★★½ (A) **TEENS** ★★★★ (A)
YOUNG ADULTS ★★★★½ (AA) **OVER 30** ★★★★½ (AA) **OVER 65** ★★★★½ (MAA)

What it is Live stage show. **Scope and scale** Major attraction. **When to go** Check *Times Guide* for showtimes. **Duration** About 24 minutes. **When to arrive** 30 minutes before showtime. **ECV/wheelchair access** May remain in wheelchair. **Participates in LLMP** Yes. **Early Theme Park Entry** No. **Extended Evening Hours** No.

DESCRIPTION AND COMMENTS Along with **Festival of the Lion King** (see page 447), *Finding Nemo* is arguably the most elaborate live show in any of the Disney World theme parks. Incorporating sophisticated digital backdrops of the undersea world, dancing, and special effects, it features onstage human performers retelling Nemo's story with colorful, larger-than-life puppets. To be fair, *puppets* doesn't adequately convey the size or detail of these props, many of which are as big as a car and require two people to manipulate.

TOURING TIPS Access to the theater is via a relatively narrow pedestrian path—if you arrive as the previous show is letting out, you'll feel like a salmon swimming upstream. This attraction is never a good use of LLMP.

PANDORA—*The World of Avatar*

DISNEY SIGNED DIRECTOR JAMES CAMERON to a theme park development deal in 2011 based on his 2009 blockbuster, *Avatar*. Six years later, **Avatar Flight of Passage** debuted as Pandora's headlining attraction, and it remains one of the highest-rated rides in any Disney or Universal theme park. But Pandora isn't just about the rides; its breathtaking setting, the **Valley of Mo'ara,** is an attraction in itself. Simply wandering through the alien landscape, with its floating mountains and colorful flora, is a highlight for guests of all ages.

Rather than directly integrating *Avatar*'s main characters or storylines, Disney set the land's narrative a generation after the events of the first film. In this version of Pandora, the Na'vi and humans have made peace, transforming the once exploited moon into an ecotourism destination and a hub for scientific research. How this fits with the ongoing *Avatar* sequels remains to be seen.

What Disney has created in Pandora is a world even more striking than nature itself. The colors are richer, the sounds more dynamic, and the landscape more surreal. Towering bioluminescent plants, cascading waterfalls, and impossibly floating mountains make Pandora one of the most visually stunning and immersive areas in any Disney park.

Avatar Flight of Passage ★★★★½

PRESCHOOL ★★★★ (A)   **GRADE SCHOOL ★★★★★ (E)**   **TEENS ★★★★★ (E)**
YOUNG ADULTS ★★★★★ (E)   **OVER 30 ★★★★★ (E)**   **OVER 65 ★★★★½ (MAA)**

What it is Flight simulator. **Scope and scale** Super-headliner. **When to go** As soon as the park opens or after 3 p.m. **Comments** One of Disney's most advanced rides; must be 44" to ride. **Duration** About 6 minutes. **Loading speed** Moderate. **ECV/wheelchair access** Must transfer from ECV to provided wheelchair, then to the ride vehicle; transfer device available. **Participates in LLMP** No (it offers LLSP). **Early Theme Park Entry** Yes. **Extended Evening Hours** Yes.

DESCRIPTION AND COMMENTS Flight of Passage is one of the most technologically advanced rides Disney has ever produced: a flight simulator in which you hop on the back of a Pandora banshee (a winged, dragonlike creature) for a flight through the moon's scenery.

The queue takes you from the base of Pandora, up into abandoned cave dwellings, and then to the research laboratory of the humans who have settled on Pandora and are studying the planet's wildlife. The lab's star exhibit is a Na'vi avatar that is floating gently in suspended animation, with occasional finger twitches or leg movements.

Once through the queue, you're brought to a 16-person chamber to prepare for your flight. Your preparation includes several quasi-scientific processes, mainly to help pass the time until your ride vehicles are ready. When it's time to ride, you enter a small room housing what looks like 16 stationary bicycles without pedals. You put on 3D goggles and mount the "bike," and restraints are deployed along your calves and lower back. The snugness of the restraints, coupled with the somewhat confined space, makes some claustrophobic guests exit before riding.

> *unofficial* **TIP**
> During summer and holidays, your best chance to avoid a long wait at Avatar Flight of Passage (without paying for LLSP) is to stay at a Disney resort and get to the Animal Kingdom entrance 1 hour before park opening.

During the ride, you soar over plains, through mountains, and across seas, all through an HD video projected onto a giant screen in front of you. As you fly, airbags at your legs inflate and deflate to simulate the banshee's breathing beneath you.

The technology at work here is like that used at EPCOT's **Soarin' Around the World,** with the individual "bikes" replacing the grouped seats. The video is clear and well synchronized with the ride vehicles, and we've heard few reports of motion sickness—unusual for screen-based motion simulators.

All that said, Flight of Passage is showing its age. After almost a decade in operation, the preshow screens have some images burnt in, the misting effects are unreliable (not that we're complaining), and your banshee's breathing may be more of a whack in the calf than a gentle inflation. We're hoping this excellent attraction gets the love and attention it needs soon.

The word *rave* hardly does justice to how Flight of Passage has been received. From an Indiana family of four:

> *Our favorite ride in all of Walt Disney World is Avatar Flight of Passage. The experience is magical. It really does feel like you're flying because of the wind, smells, and movement of the banshee. A lot of people compare it to Soarin', but after riding Flight of Passage first, Soarin' was a letdown.*

TOURING TIPS Ninety-five percent of people head straight for Flight of Passage first thing in the morning. The good news is that when the park opens by 8 a.m., most guests leave well before closing. Thus, lines for Flight of Passage drop considerably near closing. If you can't arrive before park opening or stay until closing, then purchasing LLSP is worth the cost. Flight of Passage is one of the best cost-per-minute-saved line-skipping options in the World.

Na'vi River Journey ★★★½

PRESCHOOL ★★★★½ (AA)	GRADE SCHOOL ★★★★ (BA)	TEENS ★★★★ (A)
YOUNG ADULTS ★★★★ (BA)	OVER 30 ★★★★ (BA)	OVER 65 ★★★★ (A)

What it is Boat ride. **Scope and scale** Major attraction. **When to go** Before 9:30 a.m. or in the last 2 hours before closing. **Duration** 5 minutes. **Loading speed** Moderate. **ECV/wheelchair access** Must transfer to the ride vehicle; transfer device available. **Participates in LLMP** Yes. **Early Theme Park Entry** Yes. **Extended Evening Hours** Yes.

DESCRIPTION AND COMMENTS Na'vi River Journey is a 4½-minute boat ride through the Pandora jungle. You begin by boarding a small hewn raft. Each raft has two rows of seats, so six people can fit in each boat.

Off you go into the nighttime jungle, past glowing plants and interplanetary animals. Disney has used traditional physical sets for the flora, coupled with video screens showing the movement of the fauna. These video screens are semitransparent, though. What's past them are more screens, with background scenes that also move. That means you're seeing action in the foreground and background simultaneously, all surrounded by densely packed landscaping.

The big star, however, is displayed in the ride's final scene: the Shaman of Songs, the most lifelike animatronic figure Disney has ever created. The shaman's arms move with astonishing grace—we don't know any real people who are that coordinated.

The main problem with Na'vi River Journey has to do with storytelling: You go into it not knowing anything about the character, and not enough story unfolds during the ride to get you excited about meeting the shaman. It's like Pirates of the Caribbean, with even prettier scenery but with absolutely no storyline.

TOURING TIPS It's not worth waiting longer than 30 minutes or standing in any unshaded part of the queue.

ANIMAL KINGDOM ENTERTAINMENT

ANIMAL ENCOUNTERS Throughout the day, Animal Kingdom cast members may conduct short, impromptu lessons on specific animals at the park. Look for a cast member in safari garb holding a bird, reptile, or small mammal. *Winged Encounters—The Kingdom Takes Flight* (★★★), a small interactive event featuring macaws and their handlers, takes place on Discovery Island in front of the Tree of Life. Guests can talk to the trainers and see the birds fly around the middle of the park.

CHARACTER ENCOUNTERS Other than Adventurers Outpost, Animal Kingdom is a little short on character greetings now that DinoLand

U.S.A. is closed (its Cretaceous Trail used to host several characters throughout the day). You'll still be able to find **Moana** across from Flame Tree Barbecue, and **Kevin** from *Up* roams Discovery Island and the bridge to Asia. **Pocahontas** typically meets on the Discovery Island trails west of the Tree of Life, and you may find **Russell and Dug** in the Wilderness Explorers clubhouse.

STREET PERFORMERS The park's most popular live performers are found in Africa, including the **Tam Tam Drummers of Harambe** (★★★½) and **Kora Tinga Tinga** (★★★½), a musician playing a harplike instrument. The **Harambe Village Acrobats** (★★★½) dance, vault, and climb through sets around the Dawa Bar. Over on Discovery Island, the **Viva Gaia Street Band** (★★★½) plays high-energy music across from Flame Tree Barbecue. Many of these musical acts have higher satisfaction scores than several of the big attractions in the park.

One of the most elusive and intriguing of these performers is a stilt walker named **DiVine** (★★★½). Bedecked in foliage and vines, she blends so completely with Animal Kingdom's vegetation that you don't notice her until she moves. We've seen guests standing less than a foot away gasp in amazement as DiVine brushes them with a leafy tendril. Occasionally found near the park entrance, DiVine is a fun find if you can spot her.

TRAFFIC PATTERNS *in* ANIMAL KINGDOM

THIS THEME PARK'S MAIN DRAWS are the **Pandora** attractions and **Kilimanjaro Safaris** in Africa, with **Expedition Everest** in Asia as a distant fourth.

During busy times of year, guests will start lining up outside the Animal Kingdom entrance 30 minutes to an hour before opening to be close to the front of the standby line for Flight of Passage. Plan on arriving 60 minutes before park opening.

Most rope-drop crowds head straight for Pandora at opening or to Kilimanjaro Safaris when it opens. Crowds don't peak at Expedition Everest until about an hour after park opening, and even later than that at Kali River Rapids. As the day wears on, guests who have already experienced the headliners turn their attention to other rides, animal exhibits, and shows, further distributing crowds across the entire park.

unofficial **TIP**
Wait times at the Pandora attractions often peak in the 2 hours after park opening. Less popular attractions generally don't get high traffic until 11 a.m.

Many guests who arrive at opening will leave by late afternoon, having completed their tour of the park. Wait times at the headliners historically dip as the afternoon wears on, usually bottoming out between 3 and 6 p.m. The main exception is Pandora's attractions as guests stay to see the "bioluminescent" landscaping if the park is open after sunset.

ANIMAL KINGDOM TOURING PLAN

OUR ANIMAL KINGDOM TOURING PLAN (see pages 563–564) assumes a willingness to experience all major rides and shows—if you have children under age 8, refer to the **Small-Child Fright-Potential Table** on pages 305–306. The plan has two versions: one for Disney resort guests and one for off-site guests; the former uses Early Theme Park Entry (see page 34) to minimize waits in line. Because Early Entry means thousands of guests will already be in lines and on rides before off-site guests even set foot in the park, the touring strategy for off-site guests must be different. The plan does not assume use of LLMP or LLSP. If you opt for either (or both) of these, just use our free touring plan software (see page 26) to enter your return times.

"Not a Touring Plan" Touring Plans

For the type-B reader, these "not" touring plans (see page 548) dispense with detailed step-by-step instructions designed for saving every last minute in line. For Animal Kingdom, these strategies include advice for adults and parents with one day to tour the park, arriving either at park opening or later in the morning.

PRELIMINARY INSTRUCTIONS FOR USING THE TOURING PLAN

BECOME FAMILIAR WITH Animal Kingdom's **opening procedures** (see page 439). On days of moderate to heavy attendance, follow the touring plan exactly, deviating from it only as follows:

1. **When you're not interested in an attraction in the plan.** In this case, simply skip it and proceed to the next attraction.
2. **When you encounter a very long line at an attraction.** In this case, skip to the next attraction and try again later.

Before You Go

1. At 7 a.m. either seven or three days before your vacation starts, make LLMP or LLSP purchases and reservations if you want to use them.
2. Check disneyworld.disney.go.com or the MDE app the day before to verify the opening time.
3. Review the park-opening procedures and reread the plan you've chosen so you know what you're likely to encounter.

PART 14

DISNEY'S HOLLYWOOD STUDIOS

KEY QUESTIONS ANSWERED IN THIS CHAPTER

- How do I get to Disney's Hollywood Studios? *(opposite page)*
- How does park opening (rope drop) work? *(opposite page)*
- What are the don't-miss rides? *(opposite page)*
- What's the best way to use LLMP and LLSP in the Studios? *(page 463)*
- How do I experience Star Wars: Rise of the Resistance with minimal waits in line? *(page 477)*

OVERVIEW

SEVERAL YEARS HAVE NOW PASSED since the opening of **Toy Story Land** (2018) and **Star Wars: Galaxy's Edge** (2019) and the launch of **Mickey & Minnie's Runaway Railway** (2020), and Disney's Hollywood Studios had reached something of an equilibrium as a park. But now a whole new land dedicated to *Monsters, Inc.* is on the way, and two new shows debuted in 2025.

Despite its progress, Hollywood Studios still experiences more downtime and has longer waits than any other WDW park. You could have the best day of your vacation with all of the thrill rides and shows, or you could leave in a huff of frustration.

WHO SHOULD SEE THE STUDIOS

SEVERAL OF THE STUDIOS' attractions are among Disney's best and most popular for older children, teens, and adults. **Star Wars: Rise of the Resistance** is one of the best rides (and certainly the most complicated) that Disney has made in decades, while **Mickey & Minnie's Runaway Railway** is so immersive, colorful, and full of Mickey's personality that it's impossible to leave it without a smile on your face.

Parents with small children may want to look through the attractions and entertainment before deciding to do a full day in this park. The Studios has relatively few child-friendly rides and entertainment options—but the immersive lands appeal to everyone. In fact, even preschoolers rate this park above any other.

ARRIVING

ARRIVING FROM INSIDE DISNEY WORLD If you're staying at an EPCOT resort, you can walk to Hollywood Studios in about 20–30 minutes, covering roughly a mile from your hotel to the park entrance. If you prefer not to walk, you have other options: **Boat service** is available from the EPCOT resorts, offering a scenic but leisurely ride, and the **Skyliner** provides a 15- to 20-minute aerial journey, connecting EPCOT's International Gateway with Hollywood Studios, as well as Disney's **Caribbean Beach, Riviera, Pop Century,** and **Art of Animation Resorts.** Guests staying at other Disney resorts can access the park via **bus transportation.**

DRIVING The Hollywood Studios parking lot is adjacent to the park (for GPS names and addresses, see page 346). The lot opens about an hour before official park opening, but anticipate traffic delays on busy mornings, as cars may line up to enter. Once parked, you can either walk or take a parking tram to the front entrance.

HOLLYWOOD STUDIOS OPENING PROCEDURES (ROPE DROP)

SOME RIDES BEGIN OPERATING as soon as guests are admitted into the park (**Rise of the Resistance** is the most frequent example), while others won't start operating until Early Theme Park Entry officially begins. Stage shows normally don't begin running until an hour or more after the rest of the park opens.

Disney resort guests wishing to use Early Entry should arrive at the Studios entrance 60 minutes before official opening on off-peak days and 90 minutes before official opening on days of high attendance. Off-site guests who are not eligible for Early Entry should arrive 30 minutes before official opening to be among the first in line when general admission begins.

HOW MUCH TIME TO ALLOCATE

TYPICALLY, YOU'LL NEED A FULL DAY to experience Hollywood Studios, but the exact time required depends on when you arrive, the time of year, and how interested you are in *Star Wars*. For those looking to maximize park time with shorter waits, **After Hours** events provide access to attractions at night with reduced crowds—these are separately ticketed events (see page 76).

NOT TO BE MISSED IN DISNEY'S HOLLYWOOD STUDIOS
ECHO LAKE • Star Tours—The Adventures Continue • Meet Olaf at Celebrity Spotlight • For the First Time in Forever: A Frozen Sing-Along Celebration
HOLLYWOOD AND SUNSET BOULEVARDS • *Fantasmic!* • Mickey & Minnie's Runaway Railway • Rock 'n' Roller Coaster • The Twilight Zone Tower of Terror
TOY STORY LAND • Slinky Dog Dash • Toy Story Mania!
STAR WARS: GALAXY'S EDGE • *Millennium Falcon:* Smugglers Run • Star Wars: Rise of the Resistance

continued on page 462

Disney's Hollywood Studios

MP1 Offers Lightning Lane Multi Pass—Tier 1
MP2 Offers Lightning Lane Multi Pass—Tier 2
SP Offers Lightning Lane Single Pass
☑ Not To Be Missed
👍 Recommended Dining

Restrooms
First Aid Center

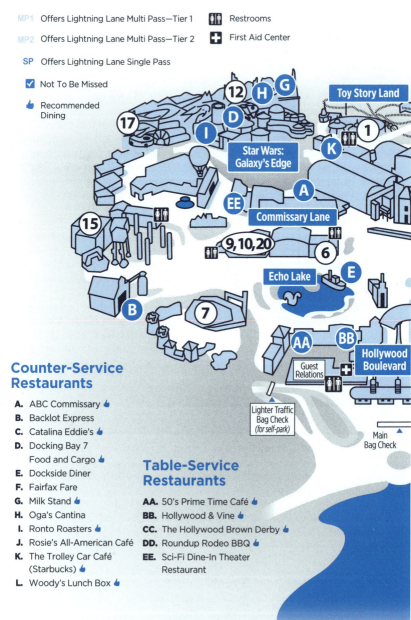

Counter-Service Restaurants

- **A.** ABC Commissary 👍
- **B.** Backlot Express
- **C.** Catalina Eddie's 👍
- **D.** Docking Bay 7 Food and Cargo 👍
- **E.** Dockside Diner
- **F.** Fairfax Fare
- **G.** Milk Stand 👍
- **H.** Oga's Cantina
- **I.** Ronto Roasters 👍
- **J.** Rosie's All-American Café
- **K.** The Trolley Car Café (Starbucks) 👍
- **L.** Woody's Lunch Box 👍

Table-Service Restaurants

- **AA.** 50's Prime Time Café 👍
- **BB.** Hollywood & Vine 👍
- **CC.** The Hollywood Brown Derby 👍
- **DD.** Roundup Rodeo BBQ 👍
- **EE.** Sci-Fi Dine-In Theater Restaurant

Attractions

1. *Alien Swirling Saucers* MP2
2. *Beauty and the Beast—Live on Stage* / Theater of the Stars MP2
3. *Disney Junior Play and Dance!* MP2
4. *Disney Villains: Unfairly Ever After* / Sunset Showcase Theater
5. *Fantasmic!* ☑
6. *For the First Time in Forever: A Frozen Sing-Along Celebration* MP2
7. *Indiana Jones Epic Stunt Spectacular!* MP2
8. *The Little Mermaid—A Musical Adventure*
9. Meet Disney Stars at *Red Carpet Dreams*
10. Meet Olaf at Celebrity Spotlight ☑
11. *Mickey & Minnie's Runaway Railway* ☑ MP1
12. *Millennium Falcon: Smugglers Run* ☑ MP1
13. *Rock 'n' Roller Coaster* ☑ MP1
14. *Slinky Dog Dash* ☑ MP1
15. *Star Tours—The Adventures Continue* ☑ MP2
16. Star Wars Launch Bay
17. *Star Wars: Rise of the Resistance* ☑ SP
18. *Toy Story Mania!* ☑ MP2
19. *The Twilight Zone Tower of Terror* ☑ MP2
20. *Vacation Fun* at Mickey Shorts Theater
21. *Walt Disney Presents*

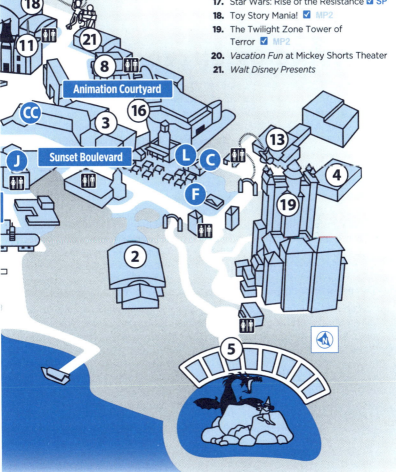

HOLLYWOOD STUDIOS SERVICES

MOST PARK SERVICES are on Hollywood Boulevard, including:

ATM Just inside the park, on the right

Baby Care Center At Guest Relations; baby food and other necessities also available at Oscar's Super Service, just inside the park, on the right

Cell Phone Charging Outlets in the Hollywood Brown Derby lobby, inside Backlot Express, and near the restrooms next to Toy Story Mania!

First Aid Center At Guest Relations

Guest Relations Just inside the park, on the left

Live Entertainment and Character Information In the *Times Guide*, available at Guest Relations

Lockers Just inside the park, on the right

Lost and Found At Guest Relations

Lost Persons Report at Guest Relations/Baby Care Center

Wheelchair, ECV (Scooter), and Stroller Rentals At Oscar's Super Service, just inside the park, on the right

continued from page 459

GETTING ORIENTED

ON YOUR LEFT AS YOU ENTER THE PARK, **Guest Relations** serves as the Studios' information center. Go there to pick up a park map or entertainment schedule (***Times Guide***); report lost persons; or access the **Baby Care Center, First Aid,** and **Lost and Found.** To the right of the entrance, **Oscar's Super Service** offers **locker, stroller, ECV,** and **wheelchair rentals.**

Like the Magic Kingdom, DHS begins with a main street. In this case, it's the **Hollywood Boulevard** of the 1930s and '40s. At the end of the street is a replica of the iconic **Grauman's Chinese Theatre,** home to **Mickey & Minnie's Runaway Railway.**

As you face the Chinese Theatre, two themed areas, **Sunset Boulevard** (closest to the park entrance) and **Animation Courtyard** (farther back) branch off Hollywood Boulevard to the right and offer shops, rides, and entertainment. Branching off to the left is **Echo Lake,** home to several dining and show venues, and the former **Grand Avenue,** which is being transformed into **Monstropolis.**

Behind the Chinese Theatre, **Toy Story Land** brings Pixar's beloved characters to life just beyond Animation Courtyard. **Star Wars: Galaxy's Edge** is in the upper-left corner of the park, accessible from Grand Avenue and Toy Story Land.

LLMP AND LLSP SELECTIONS IN DHS

ANIMATION COURTYARD • Disney Junior Play and Dance! (Tier 2)

ECHO LAKE • For the First Time in Forever—A Frozen Sing-Along Celebration (Tier 2) • Indiana Jones Epic Stunt Spectacular! (Tier 2) • Star Tours—The Adventures Continue (Tier 2)

GALAXY'S EDGE • *Millennium Falcon:* Smugglers Run (Tier 1) • Star Wars: Rise of the Resistance (*LLSP*)

HOLLYWOOD AND SUNSET BOULEVARDS • Beauty and the Beast—Live on Stage (Tier 2) • Mickey & Minnie's Runaway Railway (Tier 1) • Rock 'n' Roller Coaster (Tier 1) • The Twilight Zone Tower of Terror (Tier 2)

TOY STORY LAND • Alien Swirling Saucers (Tier 2) • Slinky Dog Dash (Tier 1) • Toy Story Mania! (Tier 2)

DISNEY'S HOLLYWOOD STUDIOS MOST POPULAR ATTRACTIONS BY AGE GROUP

PRESCHOOL	GRADE SCHOOL	TEENS	YOUNG ADULTS	OVER 30	OVER 65
Meet Olaf at Celebrity Spotlight	Droid Depot	Star Wars: Rise of the Resistance	The Twilight Zone Tower of Terror	Star Wars: Rise of the Resistance	Star Wars: Rise of the Resistance
Toy Story Mania!	Toy Story Mania!	The Twilight Zone Tower of Terror	Star Wars: Rise of the Resistance	Toy Story Mania!	Toy Story Mania!
Alien Swirling Saucers	*Fantasmic!*	Meet Chewbacca at Star Wars Launch Bay	Savi's Workshop	The Twilight Zone Tower of Terror	*Beauty and the Beast—Live on Stage*
For the First Time in Forever sing-along	Slinky Dog Dash	Toy Story Mania!	Toy Story Mania!	Mickey & Minnie's Runaway Railway	Mickey & Minnie's Runaway Railway
Mickey & Minnie's Runaway Railway	Mickey & Minnie's Runaway Railway	Rock 'n' Roller Coaster	*Fantasmic!*	Slinky Dog Dash	*For the First Time in Forever sing-along*
Disney Junior Play and Dance!	Star Wars: Rise of the Resistance	Savi's Workshop	Rock 'n' Roller Coaster	*Fantasmic!*	Slinky Dog Dash
Meet Disney Stars at *Red Carpet Dreams*	Savi's Workshop	*Fantasmic!*	Meet Chewbacca at Star Wars Launch Bay	Meet Chewbacca at Star Wars Launch Bay	The Twilight Zone Tower of Terror
Fantasmic!	Meet Chewbacca at Star Wars Launch Bay	Slinky Dog Dash	Encounter Darth Vader at Star Wars Launch Bay	Savi's Workshop	*Fantasmic!*
Beauty and the Beast—Live on Stage	Meet Olaf at Celebrity Spotlight	Droid Depot	Mickey & Minnie's Runaway Railway	*For the First Time in Forever sing-along*	Encounter Darth Vader at Star Wars Launch Bay
Green Army Drum Corps	*Millennium Falcon: Smugglers Run*	Mickey & Minnie's Runaway Railway	Green Army Drum Corps	Encounter Darth Vader at Star Wars Launch Bay	*Muppet* Vision 3D* (now closed)

FAVORITE ATTRACTIONS BY AGE GROUP

THE TABLE ABOVE SHOWS the 10 most popular attractions by age group. Below are the average ratings for DHS attractions, by age group, for the 30,000 attraction ratings we received in the past year:

PRESCHOOL	GRADE SCHOOL	TEENS	YOUNG ADULTS	OVER 30	OVER 65
4.3 stars	4.5 stars	4.4 stars	4.5 stars	4.4 stars	4.4 stars

LLMP, LLSP, AND THE TOURING PLANS

NOTE: See page 53 for detailed information and strategy suggestions for LLMP and LLSP. The big questions answered in this section are:

1. Is LLMP worth paying for in Disney's Hollywood Studios?
2. Which attractions benefit most from LLMP or LLSP?
3. How can you avoid paying for LLSP?
4. How do LLMP and LLSP work with the touring plans?

Is LLMP Worth Paying For in Disney's Hollywood Studios?

Along with the Magic Kingdom, the Studios can potentially be one of the best uses of LLMP, especially if you meet any of these criteria:

- You'll arrive at the park after Early Theme Park Entry begins. This includes off-site guests who aren't eligible for Early Entry and on-site guests who want to sleep in.
- You won't be using a touring plan.

Regardless of when you visit, arriving before park opening should allow you to see one or two of the Studios' headliners without significant waits. Since only 13 attractions participate in LLMP or LLSP (and several of those are shows), you'll be competing with lots of people for reservations, which pushes out return times and limits how many you can use in a day. In the table below, we break down how much time we think you can save using LLMP, based on algorithms that optimize the use of LLMP to various degrees, given what we know about sell-out times and standby waits avoided. See page 371 for more on the usage levels.

ESTIMATED TIME SAVINGS WITH LLMP BY CROWD LEVEL			
CROWD LEVEL	**TYPICAL USE**	**OPTIMISTIC USE**	**PERFECT USE**
LOW	45 minutes	65 minutes	80 minutes
MEDIUM	70 minutes	100 minutes	120 minutes
HIGH	90 minutes	120 minutes	180 minutes

Which Attractions Benefit Most from LLMP and LLSP?

For LLMP, the table below shows the attractions that might benefit most from using LLMP, based on current wait times and historical LLMP and LLSP data.

DHS ATTRACTIONS THAT BENEFIT MOST FROM LLMP AND LLSP *(Highest Priority to Lowest)*	
ATTRACTION	**AVERAGE TIME IN LINE SAVED (IN MINUTES)**
STAR WARS: RISE OF THE RESISTANCE (LLSP)	40
SLINKY DOG DASH	35
ROCK 'N' ROLLER COASTER	22
TOY STORY MANIA!	21
MICKEY & MINNIE'S RUNAWAY RAILWAY	20
MILLENNIUM FALCON: SMUGGLERS RUN	20
THE TWILIGHT ZONE TOWER OF TERROR	15
ALIEN SWIRLING SAUCERS	12
STAR TOURS—THE ADVENTURES CONTINUE	8

We have no evidence that LLMP reduces waits at shows.

When Do LLMP and LLSP Reservations Run Out in Hollywood Studios?

The table on the opposite page shows the approximate time at which the Studios' attractions run out of LLMP or LLSP capacity, by crowd level. Use this table along with the "Attractions That Benefit Most" table (opposite, top) to determine which reservations to get first.

WHEN LLMP AND LLSP RESERVATIONS RUN OUT BY ATTENDANCE LEVEL			
ATTRACTION	LOW ATTENDANCE	MODERATE ATTENDANCE	HIGH ATTENDANCE
ALIEN SWIRLING SAUCERS	8 p.m.	6 p.m.	11 a.m.
BEAUTY AND THE BEAST—LIVE ON STAGE	Last showtime	Last showtime	1:30 p.m.
DISNEY JUNIOR PLAY AND DANCE!	Last showtime	Last showtime	4 p.m.
FOR THE FIRST TIME IN FOREVER	Last showtime	Last showtime	2:30 p.m.
INDIANA JONES EPIC STUNT SPECTACULAR!	Last showtime	Last showtime	11 a.m.
MICKEY & MINNIE'S RUNAWAY RAILWAY	4 p.m.	1 p.m.	10:30 a.m.
MILLENNIUM FALCON: SMUGGLERS RUN	8 p.m.	3 p.m.	11 a.m.
ROCK 'N' ROLLER COASTER	3 p.m.	12:30 p.m.	10 a.m.
SLINKY DOG DASH	1 day early	2 days early	4 days early
STAR TOURS—THE ADVENTURES CONTINUE	Park close	Park close	2:30 p.m.
STAR WARS: RISE OF THE RESISTANCE (LLSP)	1 day early	3 days early	5 days early
TOY STORY MANIA!	9 a.m.	1 day early	3 days early
THE TWILIGHT ZONE TOWER OF TERROR	Noon	1 day early	2 days early

LOW ATTENDANCE Crowd levels 1–3 on the TouringPlans crowd calendar
MODERATE ATTENDANCE Crowd levels 4–7 **HIGH ATTENDANCE** Crowd levels 8–10

How Can You Avoid Paying for LLSP?

The easiest way to avoid paying for LLSP at Rise of the Resistance is to be at the park for Early Entry, then head for Rise as soon as you enter. Note that Rise of the Resistance averages over an hour of downtime daily. It frequently opens significantly earlier than any other attraction in the park. But ask a cast member if it's running because it is also broken down about half the time at park opening.

How do LLMP and LLSP Work with the Touring Plans?

See our advice on page 373.

DINING IN DISNEY'S HOLLYWOOD STUDIOS

ON THE NEXT PAGE IS A QUICK RECAP of the Studios' top restaurants, rated by readers from highest to lowest. Restaurants not listed are rated below average or lower. See Part 6 for details.

HOLLYWOOD *and* SUNSET BOULEVARDS

PALM-LINED **Hollywood Boulevard** transports you to the golden age of Tinseltown, re-creating the glitz and charm of classic Hollywood. Many of the Studios' service facilities are located along this bustling main street, interspersed with a mix of eateries and shops. The merchandise sold here includes everything from Disney trademark items to movie-related souvenirs.

HIGHEST-RATED HOLLYWOOD STUDIOS RESTAURANTS	
COUNTER SERVICE	**FULL SERVICE**
Milk Stand (E 97%/MAA), Galaxy's Edge	**50's Prime Time Café** (E 94%/AA), Echo Lake
The Trolley Car Cafe (Starbucks) (E 97%/MAA), Hollywood Boulevard	**Hollywood & Vine** (E 90%/A), Echo Lake
ABC Commissary (E 94%/AA), Commissary Lane	**The Hollywood Brown Derby** (E 90%/A), Hollywood Boulevard
Ronto Roasters (E 94%/AA), Galaxy's Edge	**Roundup Rodeo BBQ** (E 89%/A), Toy Story Land
Catalina Eddie's (E 92%/AA), Sunset Boulevard	
Docking Bay 7 Food and Cargo (E 92%/AA), Galaxy's Edge	
Dockside Diner (E 92%/AA), Echo Lake	
Woody's Lunch Box (E 90%/A), Toy Story Land	

E = Exceptional   **MAA** = Much Above Average   **AA** = Above Average

Branching off to the right, **Sunset Boulevard** continues the Old Hollywood theme in a 1940s-inspired setting that feels straight out of a classic film. It offers more options for dining, shopping, and live entertainment.

KEY TO ABBREVIATIONS In the attraction profiles that follow, each star rating is accompanied by a category label in parentheses (see page 370 for details). **E** means **Exceptional**, **MAA** means **Much Above Average**, **AA** means **Above Average**, **A** means **Average**, **BA** means **Below Average**, and **MBA** means **Much Below Average**.

Beauty and the Beast—Live on Stage / Theater of the Stars ★★★★

| PRESCHOOL ★★★★½ (AA) | GRADE SCHOOL ★★★★½ (AA) | TEENS ★★★★ (A) |
| YOUNG ADULTS ★★★★½ (AA) | OVER 30 ★★★★½ (AA) | OVER 65 ★★★★½ (MAA) |

What it is Live musical in an open-air theater. **Scope and scale** Major attraction. **When to go** Check *Times Guide* for showtimes; arrive 15 minutes in advance. **Duration** 25 minutes. **ECV/wheelchair access** May remain in wheelchair. **Participates in LLMP** Yes. **Early Theme Park Entry** No. **Extended Evening Hours** No.

DESCRIPTION AND COMMENTS This long-running show combines a shortened (but complete) retelling of the story with all of the major musical numbers, tons of characters, and beautiful sets. The theater affords a clear view from almost every seat. A canopy protects the audience from the Florida sun (or rain), but it still gets very hot in the summer.

TOURING TIPS *Beauty and the Beast* usually runs from midmorning to around 5 p.m. The show is popular, so arrive early for the best seats.

Disney Villains Unfairly Ever After / Sunset Showcase Theater

TOO NEW TO RATE

What it is Live villains show

DESCRIPTION AND COMMENTS This space used to house Lightning McQueen's Racing Academy, which closed in 2024. At press time, *Unfairly Ever After* was set to debut in summer 2025, but few other details were known.

Fantasmic! ★★★★½

ALL AGE GROUPS ★★★½ (MAA)

What it is Epic nighttime spectacular. **Scope and scale** Super-headliner. **When to go** Check *Times Guide* for schedule; if two shows are offered, the second will be less crowded. **Duration** 25 minutes. **ECV/wheelchair access** May remain in wheelchair. **Participates in LLMP** No. **Early Theme Park Entry** No. **Extended Evening Hours** No.

DESCRIPTION AND COMMENTS Off Sunset Boulevard by the Tower of Terror, this spectacular is staged on an island opposite the 6,900-seat Hollywood Hills Amphitheater. By far the largest theater facility Disney has ever created, it can accommodate an additional 3,000 standing guests for an audience of nearly 10,000.

Fantasmic! is one of the most innovative outdoor spectacles at any theme park. Starring Mickey Mouse as the Sorcerer's Apprentice, the production uses lasers, fireworks, lighting effects, music, and images projected on a shroud of mist in powerful combinations. The theme is simple: good versus evil. That "evil" part means there is some focus on villains and the mean things they do. If you have an especially sensitive younger child in your party, you may want to prepare them for what they will see.

Hang on to your kids after the show and tell them what to do should you get separated. The postshow crowd is particularly crushing.

TOURING TIPS While it's hard to imagine a 10,000-person amphitheater running out of space, that's exactly what happens almost every time the show is staged. If you attend the first (or only) performance of the night, arrive at least an hour in advance; if you opt for the second, arrive 45 minutes early.

A multigenerational family from Ontario, Canada, makes this suggestion for guests who are short on nature's upholstery:

Bring pillows or towels to sit on. We were sitting on those benches from 6 p.m. for the 7:30 show, and boy, did our rears hurt by the end!

Rain and wind sometimes cause *Fantasmic!* to be canceled; unfortunately, Disney usually doesn't make a final ruling about whether to proceed or cancel until just before showtime. On rainy or windy nights, keep touring the park until 10–20 minutes or so before showtime; then head to the stadium to see what happens.

FANTASMIC! DINING PACKAGE If you're planning to eat at any of the park's table-service restaurants during the day, you can obtain a voucher for the members of your dining party to enter *Fantasmic!* via a special entrance and sit in a reserved section. This saves you 30–90 minutes of waiting in the regular line to be admitted. If you know you're going to eat at one of these restaurants, the dining package can be a better way to see *Fantasmic!* than lining up in advance. Unfortunately, it was a much better deal back in 2024, before Disney increased the price of every package by at least $6.

Fixed-price menus are included in the package; prices listed below are the most recent available for adults and kids ages 3–9:

- **50'S PRIME TIME CAFÉ** Lunch and dinner $60 (child $23)
- **HOLLYWOOD & VINE** Breakfast $65 (child $39), lunch and dinner $81 (child $49)
- **THE HOLLYWOOD BROWN DERBY** Lunch and dinner $83 (child $31)
- **SCI-FI DINE-IN THEATER RESTAURANT** Lunch and dinner $57 (child $23)

Nonalcoholic drinks are included; tax, tips, and park admission are not. Prices may vary; call ☎ 407-WDW-DINE (939-3463) to confirm.

You'll receive your vouchers at the restaurant during your meal. Then, at least half an hour before the show, you'll report to the theater entrance. A cast member will collect your vouchers and point you to the reserved-seating section of the amphitheater. The reserved section is in the center of the stadium. You won't have assigned seats—it's first come, first served—so arrive early for the best choice. If the show is canceled, you'll get a voucher for another showing within five days.

We used the *Fantasmic!* dining package with a meal at 50's Prime Time Café in September 2023. The slight upcharge for the package earned us an extra 45 minutes in the parks, less time waiting in the amphitheater for the show to start, and third-row seats for the show despite arriving just barely 30 minutes before showtime.

Mickey & Minnie's Runaway Railway ★★★★

PRESCHOOL ★★★★½ (MAA) **GRADE SCHOOL** ★★★★½ (MAA) **TEENS** ★★★★½ (AA)
YOUNG ADULTS ★★★★½ (MAA) **OVER 30** ★★★★½ (MAA) **OVER 65** ★★★★½ (MAA)

What it is Indoor dark ride. **Scope and scale** Headliner. **When to go** Early or late. **Duration** 5 minutes. **Loading speed** Moderate. **ECV/wheelchair access** Must transfer to the ride vehicle. **Participates in LLMP** Yes. **Early Theme Park Entry** Yes. **Extended Evening Hours** Yes.

DESCRIPTION AND COMMENTS From 2013 through 2023, Disney produced new Mickey Mouse cartoons in which Mickey and Minnie sported a 1930s look, with "pie eyes," and embarked on wild adventures (with Goofy, Donald, and the rest of the gang) that always seemed to end up just fine.

Runaway Railway places you in the center of one of those cartoons. You careen, gently, through 10 large cartoon show scenes, from tropical islands to cities to out-of-control factories. In each scene, Mickey and Minnie attempt to save you from disaster, with mixed results.

In each scene, Disney uses a mix of traditional, three-dimensional painted sets and the latest in video projection technology to show movement and special effects. It's very well done, and there are so many things to see that it's impossible to catch everything in one or two rides. A couple from New York was pleasantly surprised:

> We had low expectations, but it made us feel like we were inside of a cartoon. There was so much to look at that I'm sure we missed a lot and would love to ride it again.

TOURING TIPS Runaway Railway is one of the Studios' rare all-ages hits, so expect long lines for most of the day.

Rock 'n' Roller Coaster ★★★★

PRESCHOOL NA **GRADE SCHOOL** ★★★★½ (A) **TEENS** ★★★★½ (MAA)
YOUNG ADULTS ★★★★½ (MAA) **OVER 30** ★★★★½ (AA) **OVER 65** ★★★★ (BA)

What it is Rock music–themed roller coaster. **Scope and scale** Headliner. **When to go** Early or late. **Comments** Must be 48" tall to ride; Rider Switch option provided (see page 307). **Duration** Almost 1½ minutes. **Loading speed** Moderate. **ECV/wheelchair access** Must transfer from ECV to provided wheelchair, then to the ride vehicle; transfer device available. **Participates in LLMP** Yes. **Early Theme Park Entry** Yes. **Extended Evening Hours** Yes.

DESCRIPTION AND COMMENTS Rock 'n' Roller Coaster is made for fans of high-speed thrill rides. Although the synchronized music adds measurably to the experience, the ride itself is what you're here for. Its loops, corkscrews, and drops make Space Mountain seem like

It's a Small World. What really makes this coaster great is that it's in the dark (like Space Mountain) and you are launched up the first hill like a jet off a carrier deck. By the time you crest the hill, you'll have gone from 0 to 57 mph in less than 3 seconds. When you enter the first loop, you'll be pulling almost 5 g's—two more than astronauts experienced at liftoff on a space shuttle.

In 2024, Disney announced a rethemeing of Rock 'n' Roller Coaster. Formerly Aerosmith-themed, it will now welcome the Muppets, who were displaced when *Muppet*Vision 3D* closed to make way for construction of Monstropolis. At press time, no timeline had been released.

Reader opinions of Rock 'n' Roller Coaster are predictably mixed, and colored by how the reader feels about roller coasters in general.

From an Australian couple:

My wife and I are definitely not roller-coaster people. However, we found Rock 'n' Roller Coaster quite exhilarating—and because it's dark, we didn't always realize that we were being thrown upside down. We rode it twice!

TOURING TIPS Rock 'n' Roller Coaster is not for everyone—skip it if Space Mountain or Big Thunder Mountain Railroad pushes your limits. This is a "real" roller coaster, and you should ride it only if you already know you enjoy intense thrill rides.

A single-rider queue is offered, but, oddly, it frequently has a longer wait than the standby line. Don't count on it as a time-saver. Plus, even when you exclude the lengthy planned downtime for refurbishment, this attraction still has a significant amount of unplanned downtime. That makes figuring out a good strategy for when to ride even trickier.

The Twilight Zone Tower of Terror ★★★★★

PRESCHOOL ★★★ (MBA) **GRADE SCHOOL** ★★★★ (A) **TEENS** ★★★★★ (E)
YOUNG ADULTS ★★★★★ (E) **OVER 30** ★★★★½ (MAA) **OVER 65** ★★★★½ (MAA)

What it is Indoor drop thrill ride. **Scope and scale** Super-headliner. **When to go** Early or late. **Comments** Must be 40" tall to ride; Rider Switch option provided (see page 307). **Duration** About 4 minutes plus preshow. **Loading speed** Moderate. **ECV/wheelchair access** Must transfer from ECV to provided wheelchair, then to the ride vehicle. **Participates in LLMP** Yes. **Early Theme Park Entry** Yes. **Extended Evening Hours** Yes.

DESCRIPTION AND COMMENTS The Tower of Terror is peak Imagineering—the perfect combination of story and thrill. The story is that you're touring a Hollywood hotel gone to ruin. The queue area immerses you immediately as you pass through the hotel's once opulent public rooms. From the lobby, you are escorted into the hotel's library, where *Twilight Zone* creator Rod Serling, speaking from an old black-and-white television, greets you and introduces the plot.

The Tower of Terror is a whopping 13 stories tall. The ride vehicle, one of the hotel's service elevators, takes guests to see the haunted hostelry. At about the fifth floor, things get pretty weird as you cross into the Twilight Zone—your elevator moves both horizontally and vertically. There are several lift-and-drop sequences that are selected randomly, keeping you guessing about when, how far, and how many times the elevator will fall.

An older guest from the United Kingdom loved the Tower of Terror:

I was thankful I had read your review of the Tower of Terror, or I certainly would have avoided it. As you say, it's so full of magnificent detail that it's worth riding even if you don't fancy the drops involved.

TOURING TIPS Newer attractions draw crowds away from Tower of Terror when the park opens. If you can't ride first thing in the morning, waits should be shorter in the last hour the park is open.

To save time once you're inside the queuing area, when you enter the library waiting room, stand in the far back corner across from the door where you entered and at the opposite end of the room from the TV. When the doors to the loading area open, you'll be the first admitted. Once you get into the second queueing area and the line splits, don't turn right. Continue straight for an almost-always shorter wait.

ECHO LAKE

THIS MINIATURE LAKE near the middle of the Studios, to the left of Hollywood Boulevard, pays homage to its California counterpart, which served as a backdrop for many early motion pictures.

For the First Time in Forever: A Frozen Sing-Along Celebration ★★★½

PRESCHOOL ★★★★½ (MAA)   **GRADE SCHOOL** ★★★★½ (AA)   **TEENS** ★★★★ (AA)
YOUNG ADULTS ★★★★½ (AA)   **OVER 30** ★★★★½ (MAA)   **OVER 65** ★★★★½ (MAA)

What it is Sing-along stage show retelling the story of *Frozen*. **Scope and scale** Minor attraction. **When to go** Check *Times Guide;* arrive 15 minutes before showtime. **Duration** 30 minutes. **ECV/wheelchair access** May remain in wheelchair. **Participates in LLMP** Yes. **Early Theme Park Entry** No. **Extended Evening Hours** No.

DESCRIPTION AND COMMENTS This musical recap of the iconic Disney hit *Frozen* includes songs from the movie and visits from Anna, Kristoff, and Elsa. Scenes from the movie, projected on a drive-in-size screen, provide continuity and bring those who haven't seen the film up to speed. Live performers, including two "royal historians," retell the story with corny humor.

Most of the show unfolds at a leisurely pace, but the ending is presented in a nanosecond. The finale features Anna and Elsa and another rousing rendition of "Let It Go." If you're a *Frozen* fan, it's pure magic when the snow falls. Even if you're not a fan, you'll enjoy the show's spirit as well as that of a theater full of enraptured kids. Yes, it's contagious.

Most readers really like the sing-along, including this mom from Texas:

I'm glad we didn't skip it, because it was a total hoot—my husband and I loved it, and it turned out to be the highlight of our DHS visit! When we got home, my husband and 9-year-old son, neither of whom had seen the movie before, watched Frozen *with my daughter.*

TOURING TIPS The indoor theater is one of Disney World's largest and most comfortable, with excellent sight lines from every seat.

Indiana Jones Epic Stunt Spectacular! ★★★½

PRESCHOOL ★★★★ (A)   **GRADE SCHOOL** ★★★★½ (A)   **TEENS** ★★★★ (A)
YOUNG ADULTS ★★★★ (A)   **OVER 30** ★★★★ (A)   **OVER 65** ★★★★½ (AA)

What it is Movie-stunt demonstration and action show. **Scope and scale** Major attraction. **When to go** Check *Times Guide;* arrive 20 minutes before showtime. **Duration** 30 minutes. **ECV/wheelchair access** May remain in wheelchair. **Participates in LLMP** Yes. **Early Theme Park Entry** No. **Extended Evening Hours** No.

DESCRIPTION AND COMMENTS Educational and entertaining, this popular production features professional stuntpeople who offer behind-the-scenes demonstrations of their craft. The sets, props, and special effects are very elaborate. It's one of the rare callbacks to when Hollywood Studios was dedicated to what actually went on behind the scenes of music, movies, and TV.

TOURING TIPS The Stunt Theater holds 2,000 people; capacity audiences are possible. The first performance is always the easiest to see. If the first show is at 11 a.m. or earlier, you can usually walk in, even if you arrive 5 minutes late. If you want to beat the crowd out of the stadium, sit on the far right (as you face the staging area) and near the top.

Meet Disney Stars at *Red Carpet Dreams* ★★★½

PRESCHOOL ★★★½ (AA)   **GRADE SCHOOL** ★★★½ (AA)   **TEENS** ★★★½ (AA)
YOUNG ADULTS ★★★½ (MAA)   **OVER 30** ★★★½ (AA)   **OVER 65** ★★★½ (AA)

What it is Character-greeting venue. **Scope and scale** Minor attraction. **When to go** First or last hour the park is open or during mealtimes. **Duration** About 2 minutes. **Queue speed** Slow. **ECV/wheelchair access** May remain in wheelchair. **Participates in LLMP** No. **Early Theme Park Entry** No. **Extended Evening Hours** No.

DESCRIPTION AND COMMENTS This is the venue for meeting Mickey and Minnie Mouse in Disney's Hollywood Studios. Minnie's greeting area is the set of her latest film, a musical blockbuster. Mickey is dressed as the Sorcerer's Apprentice from *Fantasia*.

TOURING TIPS The meet-and-greet entrance is found on Commissary Lane, across from the entrance to the ABC Commissary and the entrance to the Sci-Fi Dine-In Theater. Long lines form once the park is full but drop considerably during lunch and dinner.

Meet Olaf at Celebrity Spotlight ★★★½

PRESCHOOL ★★★★★ (E)   **GRADE SCHOOL** ★★★★½ (MAA)   **TEENS** ★★★★ (AA)
YOUNG ADULTS ★★★★ (MBA)   **OVER 30** ★★★★ (A)   **OVER 65** ★★★★ (A)

What it is Character-greeting venue. **Scope and scale** Diversion. **When to go** First or last hour the park is open or during mealtimes. **Duration** About 2 minutes. **Queue speed** Slow. **ECV/wheelchair access** May remain in wheelchair. **Participates in LLMP** No. **Early Theme Park Entry** No. **Extended Evening Hours** No.

DESCRIPTION AND COMMENTS Though this is a low-frills photo shoot, Olaf puts forth a ton of effort. And I hear he loves warm hugs. Younger kids are typically thrilled to meet him.

TOURING TIPS Wait times are lowest during lunch and after 4 p.m.

Star Tours—The Adventures Continue ★★★★

PRESCHOOL ★★★★ (A)   **GRADE SCHOOL** ★★★★½ (AA)   **TEENS** ★★★★½ (AA)
YOUNG ADULTS ★★★★ (A)   **OVER 30** ★★★★ (A)   **OVER 65** ★★★★ (A)

What it is Indoor space-flight-simulation ride. **Scope and scale** Minor attraction. **When to go** Lunchtime or after 4 p.m. **Comments** Pregnant guests and anyone with a weak stomach should not ride; must be 40″ tall to ride; Rider Switch option available (see page 307). **Duration** About 7 minutes. **Loading speed** Moderate. **ECV/wheelchair access** Must transfer from ECV to provided wheelchair, then to the ride vehicle. **Participates in LLMP** Yes. **Early Theme Park Entry** Yes. **Extended Evening Hours** Yes.

DESCRIPTION AND COMMENTS Based on the *Star Wars* saga, this was Disney's first modern simulator ride. Guests ride in a flight simulator, experiencing dips, turns, twists, and climbs. The ride film, projected in high-definition 3D, has more than 700 combinations of possible scenes, including ones from *Andor*, *Ahsoka*, and *The Mandalorian*.

You could ride Star Tours all day without seeing the same combination of scenes twice. This used to be a huge draw for *Star Wars* fans, but it now feels slightly out of place, detached from Galaxy's Edge.

Still, if you're a fan of the original films, a man from Iowa argues that this is the attraction for you:

Fantastic ride, and randomization makes going again and again worth it. It's a better Star Wars *ride for fans of the originals and prequels than the Galaxy's Edge stuff. Fun queue as well.*

I've tried for decades to be the (randomly selected) Rebel Spy, and I've never succeeded. May the odds be ever in your favor.

TOURING TIPS Most crowds skip over this attraction and head straight to Galaxy's Edge. Make sure you ride this one at least once if you're a *Star Wars* completionist!

Vacation Fun at Mickey Shorts Theater ★★★

| PRESCHOOL ★★★★½ (AA) | GRADE SCHOOL ★★★★½ (AA) | TEENS ★★★★ (AA) |
| YOUNG ADULTS ★★★★ (A) | OVER 30 ★★★★ (A) | OVER 65 ★★★★ (A) |

What it is Cartoon featuring Mickey Mouse. **Scope and scale** Diversion. **When to go** Anytime. **Duration** 10 minutes. **ECV/wheelchair access** May remain in wheelchair. **Participates in LLMP** No. **Early Theme Park Entry** No. **Extended Evening Hours** No.

DESCRIPTION AND COMMENTS The Mickey Shorts Theater shows a "new" (2020) 10-minute Mickey Mouse cartoon called *Vacation Fun,* which combines clips from several of the newest and best Mickey Mouse cartoons. If you loved Mickey & Minnie's Runaway Railway, this is your chance to see more of the new-style cartoons.

TOURING TIPS Even if you've seen some of the clips, the theater is large, comfortable, and air-conditioned—perfect for a short break on a hot day.

GRAND AVENUE

THIS AREA, including *Muppet*Vision 3D,* closed in 2025 to make way for **Monstropolis,** which won't open until at least 2027.

TOY STORY LAND

THIS 11-ACRE LAND opened in 2018. The concept is that you've been shrunk to the size of a toy and placed in Andy's backyard, where you get to play with other toys he's set up.

Toy Story Land's attractions are designed to appeal to young children. Because there are few other options for young kids in the park, you should expect long waits throughout the day for everything here.

Toy Story Land is one of two ways to access Galaxy's Edge, the other being **Grand Avenue.**

Alien Swirling Saucers ★★½

| PRESCHOOL ★★★★½ (MAA) | GRADE SCHOOL ★★★★½ (A) | TEENS ★★★½ (BA) |
| YOUNG ADULTS ★★★½ (MBA) | OVER 30 ★★★½ (BA) | OVER 65 ★★★½ (BA) |

What it is Spinning car ride. **Scope and scale** Minor attraction. **When to go** After 3 p.m. **Comment** Must be 32" tall to ride. **Duration** 3 minutes. **Loading speed** Painfully slow. **ECV/wheelchair access** Must transfer. **Participates in LLMP** Yes. **Early Theme Park Entry** Yes. **Extended Evening Hours** Yes.

DESCRIPTION AND COMMENTS Alien Swirling Saucers is themed around *Toy Story*'s Claw-obsessed aliens. Ride cars move, whiplike, in an elongated figure-eight around three circular tracks embedded in the ground. The ride experience is much milder than the Magic Kingdom's Mad Tea Party. Most age groups rate Saucers below average, but little kids *adore* it. On a day where she had full control of the schedule, my (Becky's) littlest kid and I took the Skyliner from EPCOT to Hollywood Studios just to ride Saucers before heading back to EPCOT again. It's got some sort of strange appeal.

TOURING TIPS For the shortest waits, ride during the first or last hour the park is open. We recommend skipping the Saucers if the posted wait is more than 20 minutes.

Slinky Dog Dash ★★★★

PRESCHOOL ★★★★½ (AA) **GRADE SCHOOL** ★★★★½ (MAA) **TEENS** ★★★★½ (MAA)
YOUNG ADULTS ★★★★½ (AA) **OVER 30** ★★★★½ (MAA) **OVER 65** ★★★★½ (MAA)

What it is Mild outdoor roller coaster. **Scope and scale** Headliner. **When to go** As soon as the park opens or just before closing. **Comment** Must be 38" tall to ride. **Duration** 2 minutes. **Loading speed** Moderate. **ECV/wheelchair access** Must transfer from ECV to provided wheelchair, then to the ride vehicle. **Participates in LLMP** Yes. **Early Theme Park Entry** Yes. **Extended Evening Hours** Yes.

DESCRIPTION AND COMMENTS Slinky Dog Dash is a long outdoor children's roller coaster designed to look as if Andy built it out of Tinkertoys. The trains are themed to *Toy Story*'s Slinky Dog. It's less intense than the Magic Kingdom's Seven Dwarfs Mine Train—lots of turns, dips, and hills but no loops or high-speed curves—and not nearly as rough as Big Thunder Mountain Railroad. For adults, it's more fun than you might expect, but not worth the very long waits it usually attracts. A family from Indiana thinks it strikes the perfect balance:

Slinky Dog is a fun coaster, but the Toy Story theming makes it great! Enough speed and dips to make it fun for an older crowd but also not too intimidating for young elementary kids.

TOURING TIPS Slinky Dog Dash gets crowded as soon as the park opens and stays that way all day. Visit at park opening or right before closing. It also experiences a significant amount of downtime, especially during summer rainstorm season.

Toy Story Mania! ★★★★½

PRESCHOOL ★★★★½ (MAA) **GRADE SCHOOL** ★★★★★ (E) **TEENS** ★★★★½ (MAA)
YOUNG ADULTS ★★★★½ (MAA) **OVER 30** ★★★★½ (MAA) **OVER 65** ★★★★½ (MAA)

What it is 3D ride through a shooting gallery. **Scope and scale** Major attraction. **When to go** Early or late. **Duration** About 6½ minutes. **Loading speed** Moderate-fast. **ECV/wheelchair access** Must transfer from ECV to provided wheelchair. **Participates in LLMP** Yes. **Early Theme Park Entry** Yes. **Extended Evening Hours** Yes.

DESCRIPTION AND COMMENTS Toy Story Mania! ushered in a new generation of Disney attraction: the virtual 3D dark ride. Conceptually, it's an interactive shooting gallery much like **Buzz Lightyear's Space Ranger Spin** (see page 391), but in Toy Story Mania!, your ride vehicle passes through a totally virtual midway, with booths offering games such as ring tossing and ball throwing. You use a cannon on your vehicle to play as you move from booth to booth. Throughout the ride, *Toy Story* characters cheer you on.

The ride begins with a training round, then continues through a number of "real" games in which you compete against your riding mate. There

are plenty of easy targets for small children to reach. If you're competitive, your elbow and shoulder will ache after one ride, but you'll want to ride again immediately anyway to improve your score.
- **TOURING TIPS** Toy Story Mania! is one of the most reliable rides in the park and is often the first spot guests go to when Slinky Dog Dash is down. If you find yourself behind a large crowd, come back in an hour or try LLMP.

ANIMATION COURTYARD

THIS AREA IS TO THE RIGHT of Mickey & Minnie's Runaway Railway in the middle of the park. It holds two large theaters used for live stage shows, a walk-through display of *Star Wars* movie props, and several character-greeting locations.

Disney Junior Play and Dance! ★★½

PRESCHOOL ★★★★½ (AA)	GRADE SCHOOL ★★★★½ (AA)	TEENS NA
YOUNG ADULTS ★★★★ (A)	OVER 30 ★★★½ (MBA)	OVER 65 ★★★★ (A)

What it is Live show for preschoolers. **Scope and scale** Minor attraction. **When to go** Check *Times Guide* for showtimes. **Comment** Audience sits on the floor; arrive 10–15 minutes before showtime. **Duration** 10 minutes. **ECV/wheelchair access** May remain in wheelchair. **Participates in LLMP** Yes. **Early Theme Park Entry** No. **Extended Evening Hours** No.

DESCRIPTION AND COMMENTS This high-energy music-and-video show features Disney Channel characters from *The Lion Guard*, *Doc McStuffins*, and *Vampirina*, along with Mickey Mouse and a DJ, who all rile up the kids. A simple narrative guides all the singing, dancing, and audience participation. The audience sits on the floor so that kids can spontaneously erupt into motion when the mood strikes (it does, and they do). Watching them live their best lives evokes those contagious feelings of Disney magic.

TOURING TIPS Staged in a huge building on the right side of the courtyard. Get here around 10 minutes before showtime, pick a spot on the floor, and relax until the action begins.

Star Wars Launch Bay Character Greetings ★★★½

PRESCHOOL ★★★★ (A)	GRADE SCHOOL ★★★★½ (AA)	TEENS ★★★★½ (MAA)
YOUNG ADULTS ★★★★½ (MAA)	OVER 30 ★★★★½ (AA)	OVER 65 ★★★★½ (AA)

What it is *Star Wars* character greetings. **Scope and scale** Minor attraction. **When to go** Anytime. **Comment** There are separate lines for each character greeting. **Probable waiting time** 20–30 minutes each for the character greetings. **ECV/wheelchair access** May remain in wheelchair. **Participates in LLMP** No. **Early Theme Park Entry** No. **Extended Evening Hours** No.

DESCRIPTION AND COMMENTS Launch Bay opened when the Studios needed more things for guests to do while new rides were being built; now it's essentially a walk-through commercial for the latest *Star Wars* films or shows. There are a few interesting models on display for the serious fan to admire, but the real draw is the character greetings.

Three characters hold court: Chewbacca, Darth Vader, and BB-8. Waits in line for Chewie and Vader usually run about 20–30 minutes. Chewie gives the best hugs of any character in any park. Prove me wrong.

The Little Mermaid—A Musical Adventure
TOO NEW TO RATE

What it is Live *Little Mermaid* show.

DESCRIPTION AND COMMENTS This space used to house *Voyage of the Little Mermaid*, which never reopened following the pandemic. Disney announced that a new version of the show would open in fall 2024, but that was pushed to summer 2025.

Walt Disney Presents ★★½

PRESCHOOL ★★★ (MBA)	GRADE SCHOOL ★★★½ (MBA)	TEENS ★★★★ (A)
YOUNG ADULTS ★★★★ (BA)	OVER 30 ★★★★ (AA)	OVER 65 ★★★★½ (AA)

What it is Disney-memorabilia collection and short film. **Scope and scale** Diversion. **When to go** Anytime. **Duration** Varies. **Probable waiting time** For the film, less than one show. **ECV/wheelchair access** May remain in wheelchair. **Participates in LLMP** No. **Early Theme Park Entry** No. **Extended Evening Hours** No.

DESCRIPTION AND COMMENTS *Walt Disney Presents* consists of an exhibit area showcasing Disney memorabilia and recordings, followed by a short film, sometimes about Walt Disney's life and achievements, narrated by Julie Andrews. (More often, the film is replaced by shorts about upcoming Disney or Pixar features). On display are various innovations in animation developed by Walt, along with models and plans for Disney World and other Disney theme parks.

TOURING TIPS Every minute spent among these extraordinary artifacts will enhance your visit, taking you back to a time when the creativity and vision that created Disney World were personified by one struggling entrepreneur.

STAR WARS: GALAXY'S EDGE

STAR WARS HAS SO MANY PASSIONATE FANS that it was only a matter of time before the movies became a real-life set in a theme park.

In 2015, Disney announced its plans for Galaxy's Edge, arguably the biggest bet made on its US theme parks since EPCOT in 1982. Two nearly identical 14-acre versions were built (the other at Disneyland); together they're rumored to have cost more than $2 billion. By way of comparison, Disney bought the whole *Star Wars* franchise for $4 billion, and building all of Animal Kingdom cost $1.5 billion when adjusted for inflation.

Disney's goal with Galaxy's Edge was to redefine the entire theme park experience. It put more money, technology, and storytelling effort into this one project than it had put into anything in a long time. Disney used the *Star Wars* alphabet of Aurebesh for signage. Disney cast members were provided background stories about their lives in Galaxy's Edge, and they used invented terminology and idioms in conversation with guests: "Hello!" became "Bright suns!" (or "Bright moons!" after dark). Even soda bottles got out-of-this-world redesigns and became collector items.

The expectations were impossible to live up to. **Millennium Falcon: Smugglers Run,** the first ride to open in Galaxy's Edge, got mixed reviews. The land itself, while looking reasonably like a *Star Wars* planet's outpost, doesn't include moving features like waterfalls to give visual interest, and guests didn't appreciate having to navigate the land's language when all they wanted was directions to the nearest bathroom. Most cast members have abandoned their stories and verbiage. And while **Star Wars: Rise of the Resistance** is one of the best rides Disney has built in decades, it has more operational delays and problems than almost any other Disney World ride. Still, its unsteady operation, coupled with its incredible popularity, means long lines throughout the day.

The biggest gamble was Disney's decision to place Galaxy's Edge at a very specific time in the *Star Wars* canon: during the third trilogy, between *The Last Jedi* and *Rise of Skywalker*. That means the land doesn't have any characters from the original trilogy, though Disney has added characters from the hit Disney+ series *The Mandalorian*. Disney thought this would make the land future-proof, able to host new stories and new characters that are written into subsequent films in the *Star Wars* franchise. The problem, of course, is that not only do those stories or characters not yet exist, but many *Star Wars* fans love the characters from the original three films most.

unofficial **TIP**
Costumes are prohibited at Galaxy's Edge for guests age 14 and up.

THE LAND Galaxy's Edge is in the village of Black Spire Outpost, on the planet of Batuu. Formerly a busy trading port and waypoint, it's now a dusty backwater filled with smugglers, bounty hunters, and those who make a living by not being recognized. As if that weren't enough, members of the Resistance and the First Order live in and around the town in an uneasy coexistence.

Galaxy's Edge has two access points: on **Grand Avenue** and in **Toy Story Land.** Entering through Grand Avenue puts you in the middle of the Resistance's encampment, while the side closest to Toy Story Land is controlled by the First Order.

GALAXY'S EDGE ATTRACTIONS

Millennium Falcon: **Smugglers Run** ★★★★

| PRESCHOOL ★★★★ (A) | GRADE SCHOOL ★★★★½ (AA) | TEENS ★★★★½ (AA) |
| YOUNG ADULTS ★★★★½ (AA) | OVER 30 ★★★★½ (AA) | OVER 65 ★★★★ (A) |

What it is Interactive simulator ride. **Scope and scale** Headliner. **When to go** Before 10 a.m. or after 6 p.m. **Comments** Must be 38" tall to ride; Rider Switch option available (see page 307). **Duration** 4½ minutes. **Loading speed** Moderate–fast. **ECV/wheelchair access** Must transfer to the ride vehicle. **Participates in LLMP** Yes. **Early Theme Park Entry** Yes. **Extended Evening Hours** Yes.

DESCRIPTION AND COMMENTS Smugglers Run lets guests fly Han Solo's *Millennium Falcon,* the "fastest hunk of junk in the galaxy." You'll see a life-size *Millennium Falcon* parked outside the spaceport.

You're recruited by Hondo Ohnaka, an animatronic pirate who has cut a deal with Chewbacca to use the *Falcon* for some sketchy transportation business. After Hondo explains the mission, you enter the *Falcon* through a bridge and are assigned to a flight crew of up to six people. While awaiting your turn, you can relax in the ship's instantly recognizable main hold, complete with a holographic chess board from the movies.

When the time arrives, your flight crew walks down the ship's curving corridors and appears to enter the *Falcon*'s one and only cockpit, thanks to a patented carousel system that keeps the small simulator cabins hidden from each other. Each rider is assigned their own station: pilots up front, two gunners in the middle, and a pair of engineers in the rear to repair the ship. Scenery is projected on an ultra-HD dome outside the windshield.

What separates this ride from other simulators (such as **Star Tours**) are the 200 functional buttons, switches, and levers found in the cockpit. Lighted rings illuminate certain controls to indicate when to use them. Another difference is that the video screen isn't attached to the ride vehicle. This allows for a more realistic display of the action and helps prevent motion sickness.

The problem with Smugglers Run has always been that the experience is much better for guests who get to be pilots. Seats for everyone else are far enough back that it's like watching a drive-in movie through a tunnel. But an enhancement announced for 2026 will include new tasks for non-pilots as well as multiple missions you could go on, which should go a long way to addressing these issues.

TOURING TIPS If you use the single-rider line, you'll usually have little to no wait. But you'll also almost always be in the back of the ride vehicle.

Star Wars: Rise of the Resistance ★★★★★

PRESCHOOL ★★★★ (A)　　**GRADE SCHOOL** ★★★★½ (MAA)　　**TEENS** ★★★★★ (E)
YOUNG ADULTS ★★★★★ (E)　　**OVER 30** ★★★★★ (E)　　**OVER 65** ★★★★★ (E)

What it is Next-generation dark ride. **Scope and scale** Super-headliner. **When to go** First thing or late at night. **Comments** Not to be missed; must be 40" tall to ride; Rider Switch option available (see page 307). **Duration** About 25 minutes with all preshows; about 5 minutes for ride. **Loading speed** Moderate-fast. **ECV/wheelchair access** Must transfer to the ride vehicle. **Participates in LLMP** No (it offers LLSP). **Early Theme Park Entry** Yes. **Extended Evening Hours** Yes.

DESCRIPTION AND COMMENTS This is easily the most epic indoor dark ride in Walt Disney World history. It is an innovative attempt to integrate at least four different ride experiences—trackless vehicles, a motion simulator, walk-through environments, and even an elevator drop—into Disney's longest and most complex attraction ever.

The adventure begins when BB-8 rolls into the first preshow room, accompanied by a hologram of Rey. Fifty guests at a time exit the briefing room to board a standing-room-only shuttlecraft piloted by Nien Nunb from *Return of the Jedi*. As the ship breaks orbit, you can feel the rumble and see Poe Dameron accompanying you in his X-Wing, until you get stuck in a tractor beam.

When the doors to your shuttlecraft reopen, you've been convincingly transported into an enormous hangar, complete with 50 Stormtroopers, TIE Fighters, and a 100-foot-wide bay window looking into outer space. Cast members clad as First Order officers brusquely herd captive guests into holding rooms to await their interrogation.

Before long, you're making a break for it in an eight-passenger (two four-seat rows) troop transport with an animatronic droid as your driver. The ride blends dozens of animatronic characters and enormous sets with video projections to create some of the most overwhelming environments ever seen in an indoor ride. One scene sends you between the legs of two towering AT-ATs while dodging laser fire from legions of Stormtroopers, while another puts you face-to-face with Kylo Ren. In the epic finale, you'll survive an escape pod's dramatic crash back to Batuu, a heart-stopping multistory plunge enhanced by digital projections.

TOURING TIPS We think Rise of the Resistance is one of the best rides Disney has produced in decades. It would be the best if all of its elements worked reliably. It's the most popular ride in the park and the most complex ride Disney has ever made. But its complexity makes it prone to breakdowns—last year, it didn't open with the rest of the park about half the time.

The best way to experience Rise without a long wait is to stay at a Disney resort, use Early Entry, and get in line as soon as the park opens. Alternatively, LLSP reservations will save you significant time on crowded days.

In 2025, Disney started offering a single-rider line at Rise of the Resistance. You'll have much shorter waits if you use it, but it skips the BB-8/Rey and transporter preshows, instead taking you directly into the large hangar scene.

Galaxy's Edge Shopping, Dining, and More

SHOPPING Galaxy's Edge boasts a labyrinth of shops selling unique in-universe merchandise; some of the shops are practically attractions themselves. To maintain the illusion that everything on offer was actually crafted by and for the Black Spire Outpost villagers, none of the items for sale bear the standard *Star Wars* or Disney logos.

At **Savi's Workshop** (★★★★), small groups are led by "Gatherers" through the process of building their own lightsabers, from picking a colorful kyber crystal to selecting customizable handles. The cost of this experience is around $266; reservations via Disney's website or app are strongly recommended, and you pay when you make the reservation. (A small number of same-day reservations might be available for spots starting 2 hours before reservation time.) Despite the steep price tag, it's one of the highest-rated pieces of entertainment in any Disney park. It makes the top 10 of several age groups (and the top 5 for young adults). It's not the final product that makes such an impact; it's the experience. If you want to build a lightsaber of your own, make reservations for Savi's up to 60 days in advance. You can also pair your saber with a screen-accurate Jedi tunic ensemble from **Black Spire Outfitters.**

At **Droid Depot** (★★★), you can pick robot parts from conveyor belts to build your own small R-series or BB-series droid (for around $120), which will then communicate with its counterparts around the land; preassembled droids are also available. Droid Depot is highly rated by many guests and is in the top 10 "attractions" in any WDW park for grade-schoolers. Reservations can be made 60 days in advance and are strongly recommended.

DINING When you get hungry, you'll find that just as much attention has gone into the food and drink at Galaxy's Edge as everything else; even the Coca-Cola sodas come in spherical bottles emblazoned in Aurebesh, the *Star Wars* alphabet. There's no table-service restaurant, but Galaxy's Edge has two of the highest-rated counter-service restaurants in the park: Rustle up galactic food-truck grub from **Docking Bay 7** or grab a sausage grilled under a podracer engine at **Ronto Roasters.** Wash it down with a cold glass of blue or green (nondairy) milk from the **Milk Stand. Oga's Cantina** pours exclusive adult drinks, from Spice Runner cider to Jet Juice cocktails; reservations are strongly recommended. See pages 237–238 for reviews of these four venues.

INTERACTIVITY IN GALAXY'S EDGE Perhaps the most intriguing elements of Galaxy's Edge are its experiments in live interaction, both digital and analog. Live performers, actor-controlled creature puppets, and roving droids can engage with guests. Characters include Rey, Chewbacca, Kylo Ren, and various Stormtroopers.

DISNEY'S HOLLYWOOD STUDIOS ENTERTAINMENT

IN ADDITION TO THE SHOWS and performances profiled earlier in this chapter, the Studios offers the following. Check your *Times Guide* for showtimes.

CHARACTER GREETINGS Chip 'n' Dale, Daisy, and **Donald** can often be found near Mickey & Minnie's Runaway Railway or Animation Courtyard, from around 10 a.m. to 5 p.m. **Toy Story characters** appear in Toy Story Land from around noon until dinnertime. **Sully** from *Monsters, Inc.* and many of the *Incredibles* **characters** (including Edna Mode, Frozone, and some of the famous family) meet in Pixar Place throughout most of the day. **Fancy Nancy, Vampirina, Doc McStuffins** and **Pluto** greet guests for most of the day in Animation Courtyard.

WONDERFUL WORLD OF ANIMATION This 12-minute nighttime projection show displayed on the front of Grauman's Chinese Theatre (home of Mickey & Minnie's Runaway Railway) shows classic clips from Disney and the studios it has acquired. It's not the best (or the second-, third- or fourth-best) projection show Disney has done, but it's a nice way to end the evening, if you're around, and can be a low-hassle substitute for seeing *Fantasmic!*

DISNEY'S HOLLYWOOD STUDIOS TOURING PLAN

OUR HOLLYWOOD STUDIOS TOURING PLAN (see pages 565–566) has two versions: one for Disney resort guests and one for off-site guests; the plan for on-site guests uses Early Theme Park Entry (see page 34) to minimize waits in line. Because Early Entry means thousands of guests will already be in lines and on rides before off-site guests set foot in the park, the touring strategy for off-site guests must be different.

The plan does *not* assume the use of LLMP or LLSP. If you opt for these, just use the free touring plan software to adjust the plan (see page 26).

PART 15

DISNEY'S WATER PARKS

KEY QUESTIONS ANSWERED IN THIS CHAPTER

- What are Disney's water parks, and how much do they cost? *(see below)*
- How do we get there, and when should we go? *(see below and opposite)*
- Which water park is best for my family? *(see opposite)*
- How do we prepare for a day at a water park? *(page 482)*
- Are there touring plans? *(page 493)*
- What attractions are offered at the water parks? *(pages 489 and 490)*

OVERVIEW

DISNEY OFFERS TWO WATER PARKS in Orlando: **Blizzard Beach** and **Typhoon Lagoon.** Both are much larger and more elaborately themed than the local or regional water parks you may have visited. Almost all the waterslides, wave pools, and lazy rivers at these parks are larger and longer than those at other water parks too.

COST One day of admission to either park costs around $79 for adults and $72 for children ages 3–9, including tax. Peak season is late May–late September. If you visit outside of that window, Disney offers a discount of around $10 per ticket—this is the "with blockout dates" ticket option.

Most visitors to Walt Disney World will spend only one day at a water park, if they choose to go to one at all. If you are planning on visiting only one theme park per day during your trip and then spending one day in a water park, buying separate water park admission is almost always cheaper than buying the **Park Hopper Plus** add-on (see page 67).

GETTING THERE Disney provides regular daily bus service between its resorts and its water parks. However, the bus service might route you through other hotels or Disney Springs, and when it does, it takes a long time to get there. If you're staying at a Disney resort and don't have a car, Uber or Lyft is the quickest way to go. If you do have a car, parking at the water parks is free.

WHEN TO GO

DISNEY TYPICALLY OPENS at least one of its water parks every day of the year. Even in winter, Orlando temperatures can range from the high 40s to the low 80s. When it's warmer out, these off-season months can make for a great water park experience, as an Ohio reader confirms:

unofficial **TIP**
A good time to visit the water parks is midafternoon or later in the day, when the weather has cleared after a storm.

> Going to Blizzard Beach in December was the best decision ever! They told us at the entrance that if the park didn't reach 100—yes, I said 100—people by noon, they would be closing. I guess they got to 101, because it stayed open but was virtually empty. There was no wait for anything all day! In June we waited in line for an hour for Summit Plummet, but in December it was just the amount of time it took to walk up the stairs. We had the enormous wave pool to ourselves. We did everything in the entire park and ate lunch in less than 3 hours. It was perfect. The weather was slightly chilly at 71°F and overcast with very light rain, but the water was heated, so we were fine.

The water parks may close if the daytime high temperatures are forecast to be below 60°F or so. If you're visiting when temperatures are low, check the operating hours in the MDE app before you visit.

AVOIDING LINES The best way to avoid standing in lines is to visit the water parks when they're least crowded. Because most visitors on any given day are tourists, not locals, the water parks tend to be less crowded on weekends, when many out-of-towners are traveling to or from Orlando. A visitor from New York shares her crowd-avoidance strategy:

> On our second trip to Typhoon Lagoon, we dispensed with the locker rental (having planned to stay for only the morning, when it was least crowded), and at park opening we just took right off for the Storm Slides before the masses arrived—it was perfect! We must have ridden the slides at least five times before any kind of line built up, and then we were also able to ride the tube and raft rides (Keelhaul and Mayday Falls) in a similar uncrowded, quick fashion because everyone else was busy getting their lockers.

When a water park reopens after inclement weather has passed, you'll almost have the whole place to yourself. And like the theme parks, if you stay until closing on any day, you'll be able to take advantage of the dwindling crowds as other visitors filter out.

WHICH WATER PARK TO VISIT?

UNOFFICIAL GUIDE READERS rate water park attractions, just as they rate the theme park attractions. The water park over at Universal (**Volcano Bay**) ranks first overall; you can read about it in *The Unofficial Guide to Universal Orlando*. Blizzard Beach and Typhoon Lagoon tie for second.

If you're looking for the best choice for a diverse group, Blizzard Beach is probably your best bet because it's rated first or second by every age group. That said, since 2020, Disney typically opens only

MOST POPULAR WATER PARKS BY AGE GROUP					
PRESCHOOL	GRADE SCHOOL	TEENS	YOUNG ADULTS	OVER 30	SENIORS
Blizzard Beach	Blizzard Beach	Volcano Bay	Volcano Bay	Volcano Bay	Typhoon Lagoon
Typhoon Lagoon	Typhoon Lagoon	Blizzard Beach	Blizzard Beach	Blizzard Beach	Blizzard Beach
Volcano Bay	Volcano Bay	Typhoon Lagoon	Typhoon Lagoon	Typhoon Lagoon	Volcano Bay

one water park per day (sometimes both may be open during the summer). If you're intent on visiting a specific water park, check Disney's website for its operating status before purchasing tickets.

PLANNING YOUR DAY

DISNEY WATER PARKS are almost as large and elaborate as the theme parks. You should be prepared for a lot of walking (and potentially stair climbing), sun, and jostling crowds. To have a great day and beat the crowds, consider the following:

1. GETTING INFORMATION Check disneyworld.disney.go.com or the MDE app the night before to verify when the park opens.

2. TO PICNIC OR NOT TO PICNIC Guests are permitted to take coolers into the parks, so decide whether you want to carry a picnic lunch. Alcoholic beverages, glass containers, and loose ice and dry ice are prohibited; reusable ice packs are permitted. Only one cooler per family is allowed. The in-park food is comparable to fast food, but the prices are high, and ratings are lower than those at other theme park dining locations.

3. GETTING STARTED Get up early and have breakfast. If you have a car, drive instead of taking a Disney bus. If you don't have a car, ask a cast member at your hotel if direct bus service to the water park is available. If it is, take the bus; if not, use Uber or Lyft instead. Either way, plan to arrive at the park 20 minutes before opening.

4. USING A GOOD TOURING PLAN The touring plans on pages 567 and 568 are designed to help you avoid crowds and bottlenecks at Disney's water parks. If you're attending on a day of moderate to heavy attendance (see the crowd calendar at **TouringPlans.com**), consider using one of these tested plans.

5. ATTIRE Wear your swimsuit under shorts and a T-shirt so you don't need to use lockers or dressing rooms. Be advised that it's surprisingly easy for those wearing two-piece swimsuits to accidentally lose one of the pieces on the slides. Also, the walking paths and beach sand get incredibly hot during the summer, so some form of foot protection is a must. Water shoes or sandals that strap to your feet are best. Shops in the parks sell sandals, water shoes, and other protective footwear that can be worn in and out of the water.

6. WHAT TO BRING You'll need a towel, sunscreen, and some form of payment for things like food. If you don't have towels, they can be rented for $2 each. Sunscreen is available in all park shops. Leave wallets and purses at your hotel (or lock them in your car's trunk if you must bring them). Carry your Disney resort ID (if you have one) and enough money for the day in a plastic bag or other waterproof container, or use your MagicBand to pay for things.

One reader cautions against keeping items in your pocket:

> Our family absolutely loved Summit Plummet, but it claimed all four of our park passes/room-key cards as its victims. My husband had the four cards in an exterior pocket of his swimsuit, secured closed by Velcro AND a snap. But after doing Summit Plummet and Slush Gusher twice apiece and Teamboat Springs once, he looked down, noticed the pocket flapping open, and found all four cards missing! So we had to cancel all the cards (they had charging privileges) and couldn't purchase any food or drinks while we were there (we didn't bring any cash because we'd planned to use our cards)!

MagicBands are a much more secure option at the water parks. Anything in your pockets, such as cash and keys, might come out.

Though nowhere is completely safe, we usually feel comfortable hiding our money in our cooler. Nobody disturbs our stuff, and our cash is much easier to reach than if we'd stashed it in a locker across the park. But if you're going to spend the day worrying about your belongings being stolen, just rent the locker.

A Canadian reader suggests the following option if you don't feel comfortable stashing your valuables in a locker, a cooler, or the like:

> As our admission was from an all-inclusive ticket [not a MagicBand], I was concerned about our passes being stolen or lost, yet I didn't want the hassle of a locker. I discovered that the gift shop sells water-resistant plastic boxes (with strings to go around your neck) in two sizes for around $5, with the smallest being just big enough for passes, credit cards, and a bit of money. I would've spent nearly as much on a locker rental, so I was able to enjoy the rest of the day with peace of mind.

A limited number of **wheelchairs** are available for rent for $12 per day with a $100 refundable deposit. Personal flotation devices (life jackets) can be rented for free with a refundable deposit.

7. WHAT NOT TO BRING Personal swim gear, such as fins, masks, and rafts, isn't allowed. The one exception is Coast Guard–approved personal flotation devices (like your toddler's swim vest), which you are allowed to bring if you've packed your own. Everything you need is provided or available to rent or purchase, including life jackets.

8. ADMISSION Buy your admission in advance or at least 45 minutes before official opening.

9. LOCKERS Keyless rental lockers are $10 per day for a standard and $15 per day for a large. Standard lockers are roomy enough for one person or a couple, but a family will generally need a large. You can access your locker freely all day, but not all lockers are conveniently located. Getting a locker is truly competitive. When the gates open, guests race to the rental desk. The rental procedure is somewhat slow;

SOGGY TIPS FROM A WATER-LOVING FAMILY

A New Hampshire family—who are evidently working on a PhD in Disney water parks—were kind enough to share their knowledge.

IF YOU'RE GOING TO THE WATER PARKS, **train on a stair-climber** prior to going, especially if you visit Blizzard Beach. For Runoff Rapids, you climb 125 stairs (yes, I counted). Imagine doing that three times in a row, trying to keep up with kids who want to go down the slide multiple times. In addition, there are at least (and here, I'm guessing) 300 stairs if you choose the Alpine Path instead of the chairlift to get to Summit Plummet. At Typhoon Lagoon, each slide, except Miss Adventure Falls, has about 60 steps, so at either park you have quite a bit of stairs to climb or go down.

We were at Blizzard Beach 15 minutes before park opening in late August, and we felt that this was plenty of time to beat the crowds. We noticed crowds building about an hour after opening. If you are there at park opening, **stash your things as quickly as possible while you take the chairlift to Summit Plummet.** We were first in line for the chairlift, and we were at the top with no lines. The chairlift is definitely faster if you are one of the first in line, and you won't get winded from walking the Alpine Path. However, if you arrive later in the day, the line for the chairlift builds, and you'll be left having to climb the Alpine Path—great if you're in shape, but not so much if you're not!

Check the closing time of the water parks if you plan on arriving in late afternoon. When Typhoon Lagoon closed at 8 p.m. and we arrived shortly after 2 p.m., lines tended to thin out by 4 p.m. However, when we tried that same tactic (arriving in the afternoon) when Typhoon Lagoon closed at 6 p.m., we noticed that the lines were still long, and it seemed like the crowd wasn't thinning at all. On those days, we wished that we had been there for park opening and left when crowds started to build.

We enjoyed the water parks, but **we only stayed about 3 hours max.** Though the water parks are big (as in spread out), there weren't enough attractions to keep us there the entire day. Yes, if you aren't among the first in line, you can waste a lot of time waiting. We recommend skipping the locker, if possible (also see No. 6 on page 482).

unofficial **TIP**
Both water parks fill early during hotter months. To stake out a nice sunning spot and to enjoy the slides without long waits, arrive at least 20 minutes before the official opening time (check hours the night before).

10. TUBES for bobbing on the waves, floating in the creeks, and riding the tube slides are available for free.

11. GETTING SETTLED Establish your base for the day. There are many beautiful sunning and lounging spots throughout both parks—arrive early and you can have your pick.

The breeze is best along the beaches of the wave pools at Blizzard Beach and Typhoon they have slides, but not as many as I expected a Disney park to have. When lines started to build, it became less fun to wait 15-plus minutes for a slide that takes less than 2 minutes to go down. Also, the less popular attractions, such as the lazy river, got really busy, and there were hardly any tubes to be found.

Some of the slides at Blizzard Beach, such as the **Downhill Double Dipper,** take *forever* in line because you're waiting for a tube to make it from the pool up the conveyor belt to the slide stairs. Once the tube finally arrives, you still have to wait for both parties to go down together and to exit the pool. This process takes a long time. If this slide is important to you, make it one of the first things you do. The toboggan rides can also take a while because there is no clear system of who can take the mat when it finally arrives at the top (two mat rides are at the top of the mat conveyor belt: **Toboggan Racers** and **Snow Stormers**).

Some of the slides aren't very comfortable. At Typhoon Lagoon, the **Humunga Kowabunga** should be called the Wedgie Maker. Also, if your family will be going to both water parks (like we did), I suggest **skipping Gangplank Falls at Typhoon Lagoon and doing Teamboat Springs at Blizzard Beach instead.** Not only is Teamboat Springs *a lot* longer than Gangplank Falls, but it's also more fun.

The wave pools at both parks are very different. At Typhoon Lagoon, it's "The Wave" pool—as in, there's only one HUGE wave that you can try to bodysurf (good luck with that!). At Blizzard Beach, it's more like "The Waves" pool, where waves are put out at a continual rate, at all times, like a gentle rocking motion, and there are tubes you can use. Typhoon Lagoon has no flotation devices of any kind because, well, they'd be dangerous to everyone involved.

If you have something electronic like a smartphone or tablet that you need to stay dry at the water parks, **buy a waterproof container BEFORE you go.** The water parks sell only water-resistant containers, and even though the one we bought didn't seem to leak, it would have given us more peace of mind to have a waterproof bag/container.

Lagoon. At Typhoon Lagoon, if there are children younger than age 6 in your party, choose an area to the left of Mount Mayday near the children's swimming area.

Also available are flat (nonadjustable) loungers and chairs (better for reading), picnic tables, a few hammocks, and shelters for guests who prefer shade. If you want more dedicated space, private cabanas are available by reservation for up to six guests. Named **Polar Patios** at Blizzard Beach and **Beachcomber Shacks** at Typhoon Lagoon, these come outfitted with lounge chairs, tables, towels, private lockers, a refillable drink mug, and an attendant who'll be available at all times. Cabanas run from around $225 to $500 (plus tax) depending on the season. Reserve at disneyworld.disney.go.com.

12. SLIDES Waterslides come in many shapes and sizes. Some are steep and vertical, and some are slower and winding. Some resemble corkscrews, while others imitate the pool-and-drop nature of whitewater streams. Depending on the slide, you might ride on a mat, tube, or raft. On body slides, you don't ride on anything but the water.

Though both parks are huge, with many slides, armies of guests overwhelm them during busy season. If your main reason for going to a water park is the slides and you hate long lines, be among the first guests to enter the park. Go directly to the slides and ride as many times as you can before the park gets crowded.

Some slides and rapids have height requirements (see the tables on pages 489 and 490). Riders for **Humunga Kowabunga** at Typhoon Lagoon and **Slush Gusher** and **Summit Plummet** at Blizzard Beach, for example, must be at least 4 feet tall. Guests who are pregnant or who have back problems or other health difficulties should not ride.

> *unofficial* **TIP**
> When lines for the slides become intolerable, head for the wave pool or the lazy river.

For maximum speed on a body slide, cross your legs at the ankles, and cross your arms over your chest. When you take off, arch your back so almost all your weight is on your shoulder blades and heels (the less contact with the surface, the less resistance). Steer by shifting most of your upper-body weight onto one shoulder blade. For top speed on turns, weight the shoulder blade on the outside of each curve. If you want to go slowly, distribute your weight equally, as if you were lying on your back in bed. For curving slides, maximize speed by hitting the entrance to each curve high and exiting the curve low. Physics!

13. LAZY RIVERS Each of the water parks offers a lazy river. These long, tranquil streams flow ever so slowly around the entire park, through caves, beneath waterfalls, past gardens, and under bridges, offering a relaxing alternative to touring on foot. Lazy rivers can be reached from several put-in and take-out points. There are never lines; just wade into the creek and plop into one of the inner tubes floating by. Ride the current all the way around or get out at any exit. It takes 30–35 minutes to float the full circuit.

14. BAD WEATHER Thunderstorms and rain showers are common in Florida. On summer afternoons, storms can occur daily. Water parks close during a storm. Most storms, however, are short-lived, allowing the parks to resume normal operations. If a storm is severe and prolonged, it can cause a logistic mess: Not only does the park close, but guests also compete aggressively for shelter, and Disney resort guests may have to vie for seats on the bus back to their hotels.

You should monitor the local weather forecast the day before you go, checking again in the morning before leaving for the water park. Scattered thunderstorms are no big deal, but daylong storms should be avoided.

15. ENDURANCE The water parks are large and require almost as much walking as the theme parks. Add to this wave surfing, swimming, and all the climbing required to reach the slides, and you'll be exhausted by the end of the day. Unless you spend your hours like a lizard on a rock, don't expect to return to the hotel with much energy. Consider something low-key for the evening. You'll probably want to fall asleep early.

16. LOST CHILDREN AND LOST ADULTS It's even easier to lose a child or become separated from your party in one of the water parks than it is in the theme parks. Upon arrival, pick a very specific place to meet in case you get separated. If you split up on purpose, set times for checking in. Lost-children stations are so out of the way that neither you nor your child will find them without help from a Disney cast member. Explain to your children how to recognize cast members (by their distinctive name tags) and how to ask for help.

BLIZZARD BEACH

AT BLIZZARD BEACH, the story is that an entrepreneur tried to open a ski resort in Florida during a particularly savage winter. Alas, the snow melted; the palm trees grew back; and all that remained of the ski resort was its alpine lodge, the ski lifts, and of course the mountain. You visit Blizzard Beach during the big thaw—icicles drip, and patches of snow remain. The melting snow has formed a lagoon (the wave pool), which is fed by gushing mountain streams. Plunging off the mountain are ski slopes and bobsled runs transformed into waterslides. In the ski resort's lodge area are shops; counter-service food; restrooms; and tube, towel, and locker rentals. Blizzard Beach has its own parking lot. Disney's **All-Star** and **Coronado Springs Resorts** are the closest resorts.

The park has 19 waterslides, and with slides on both the front and back of the mountain, it isn't always easy to find a path to where you want to go. As you enter Blizzard Beach, you face the mountain. To the left is the wave pool, **Melt-Away Bay,** with gentle, bobbing waves. Coming off the highest peak and splitting the area at the mountain's base are two long slides: **Slush Gusher** and **Summit Plummet.** On either side of the highest peak are tube, raft, and body slides. On the right, a **chairlift** carries you to the mountaintop (you can also walk up), where you can choose from Slush Gusher, Summit Plummet, or **Teamboat Springs.** For all other slides, the only way to reach the top is on foot. To the right of the mountain are the children's swimming areas, **Tike's Peak** and **Ski Patrol Training Camp.** The children's areas are creatively designed, nicely isolated, and—like the rest of the park—visually interesting. Tike's Peak features characters from Disney's *Frozen*. The lazy river, **Cross Country Creek,** circles the park, passing through the mountain.

For our money, the most exciting and interesting slides are Slush Gusher and Teamboat Springs (on the front right of the mountain) and Runoff Rapids (on the back side). Slush Gusher is a speed slide with hills; it's as exciting, but not as bone-jarring, as the more vertical Summit Plummet, Disney World's longest speed slide, which begins with a 120-foot free fall. On Teamboat Springs—a 1,200-foot-long

Blizzard Beach

Attractions

1. Chairlift
2. Cross Country Creek
3. Downhill Double Dipper
4. Melt-Away Bay
5. Runoff Rapids
6. Ski Patrol Training Camp
7. Slush Gusher
8. Snow Stormers
9. Summit Plummet
10. Teamboat Springs
11. Tike's Peak
12. Toboggan Racers

Restaurants

A. Avalunch
B. Cooling Hut
C. Frostbite Freddy's
D. Lottawatta Lodge
E. Polar Pub
F. Warming Hut

 Restrooms

water-bobsled run—you ride in a round raft that looks like a children's blow-up wading pool.

Runoff Rapids, accessible from a path that winds around the far-left bottom of the mountain, consists of three corkscrew tube slides, one of which is enclosed and dark. You'll go much faster on a multi-person tube than on a one-person tube (the same is true for Teamboat Springs). Beware if you pick the enclosed tube: Crashing through the pitch-dark tunnel isn't always a pleasant feeling.

The **Snow Stormers** mat slides, on the front of the mountain, are fun but not as fast or as interesting as Runoff Rapids or **Downhill**

BLIZZARD BEACH ATTRACTIONS

CHAIRLIFT UP MOUNT GUSHMORE Minimum height: 32". Great ride even if you go up just for the view. When the park is packed, use the singles line.

CROSS COUNTRY CREEK No height requirement. Lazy river circling the park; grab a tube.

DOWNHILL DOUBLE DIPPER Minimum height: 48". Side-by-side tube-racing slides. The tube zooms through water curtains and free falls, with riders reaching speeds of up to 25 mph. It's a lot of fun, but it's rough.

MELT-AWAY BAY No height requirement. Wave pool with gentle, bobbing waves. Great for younger swimmers.

RUNOFF RAPIDS No height requirement. Three corkscrew tube slides to choose from. The center slide is for solo raft rides; the other two slides offer one- or two-person tubes. The dark, enclosed tube gives you the feeling of being flushed down the john.

SKI PATROL TRAINING CAMP Maximum height: 60" for T-Bar (zip line). A place for preteens to train for the big rides.

SLUSH GUSHER Minimum height: 48". 90-foot double-humped slide. Cling to those swimsuit tops and hang on for your life.

SNOW STORMERS No height requirement. Consists of three mat-slide flumes; you go down on your belly.

SUMMIT PLUMMET Minimum height: 48". 120-foot free fall at 60 mph. Needless to say, this ride is very intense. Make sure your child knows what to expect; being over 48" tall doesn't guarantee an enjoyable experience. If you think you'd enjoy being washed out of a 12th-floor window during a heavy rain, then this slide is for you.

TEAMBOAT SPRINGS No height requirement. 1,200-foot group whitewater raft flume. Wonderful ride for the whole family.

TIKE'S PEAK Maximum height: 48". Kid-size version of Blizzard Beach. Recently rethemed to Disney's *Frozen* films. This is the place for little ones.

TOBOGGAN RACERS No height requirement. Eight-lane race course. You go down the flume on a mat. Less intense than Snow Stormers.

Double Dipper, on the far-left front. **Toboggan Racers,** at the front and center of the mountain, consists of eight parallel slides where riders are dispatched to race to the bottom. The ride itself is no big deal, and the time needed to get everybody lined up means you'll wait a long time to ride. The side-by-side slides of the hilly Downhill Double Dipper are a faster, more exciting race venue—competitors here can reach speeds of up to 25 miles per hour.

TYPHOON LAGOON

WITH ITS TYPHOON-AFTERMATH THEME, Typhoon Lagoon is comparable in size to Blizzard Beach. The park has 15 waterslides, some as long as 420 feet, and two streams. Most of the slides drop from the top of a 100-foot-tall artificial mountain (with a ship on top!). Guests enter the park through a misty rainforest and emerge in a ramshackle tropical town where concessions and services are situated. Rides have a sense of adventure, as swimmers encounter bat caves, lagoons and pools, spinning rocks, and formations of dinosaur bones.

Just like over at Blizzard Beach, if you're going primarily for the slides, you'll have just two early-morning hours to enjoy them before

TYPHOON LAGOON ATTRACTIONS

BAY SLIDES **Maximum height: 60".** Miniature two-slide version of Storm Slides designed for small children. The kids splash down into a far corner of the Surf Pool.

CASTAWAY CREEK **No height requirement.** Half-mile lazy river in a tropical setting with cool mists, waterfalls, and a tunnel through Mount Mayday. Wonderful!

CRUSH 'N' GUSHER **Minimum height: 48".** Water roller coaster where you can choose from three slides—Banana Blaster, Coconut Crusher, and Pineapple Plunger—ranging from 410 to 420 feet long. This thriller is not for the faint of heart. If your kids are new to water park rides, this is not the place to break them in, even if they're tall enough to ride.

GANGPLANK FALLS **No height requirement.** Whitewater raft flume in a four-person tube.

HUMUNGA KOWABUNGA **Minimum height: 48".** Speed slides that hit 30 mph. A five-story drop in the dark rattles even the most courageous rider. If you want to try this one, we recommend doing it in a one-piece swimsuit.

KEELHAUL FALLS **No height requirement.** Fast whitewater ride in a single-person tube.

KETCHAKIDDEE CREEK **Maximum height: 48".** Toddlers and preschoolers love this area reserved only for them.

MAYDAY FALLS **No height requirement.** Wild single-person tube ride. Hang on!

MISS ADVENTURE FALLS **No height requirement.** Gentle family raft ride down a well-themed slide.

STORM SLIDES **No height requirement.** Three body slides plunge down and through Mount Mayday.

SURF POOL **No height requirement.** World's largest inland surf facility, with waves up to 6 feet high. Adult supervision required. Surfing lessons may be offered (see page 492).

---

the waits become annoying. Try the slides early, and then explore the other areas and attractions for the rest of the day.

Typhoon Lagoon provides something for all ages. Activity pools for young children and families feature geysers, tame slides, bubble jets, and fountains. For the older and more adventurous are the enclosed **Humunga Kowabunga** speed slides; the corkscrew **Storm Slides;** and three whitewater raft rides: **Gangplank Falls, Keelhaul Falls,** and **Mayday Falls. Crush 'n' Gusher,** billed as a water roller coaster, consists of a series of flumes and spillways that course through an abandoned tropical fruit–processing plant. It features tubes that hold one or two people, and you can choose from three routes—Banana Blaster, Coconut Crusher, and Pineapple Plunger—ranging from 410 to 420 feet long. Only Crush 'n' Gusher and the Humunga Kowabunga speed slides (where you can hit 30 mph) have a minimum height requirement of 48 inches.

An Ontario, Canada, mom found Typhoon Lagoon more strenuous than she'd anticipated:

> *I wish I'd been prepared for the fact that we'd have to haul the tubes up the stairs of Crush 'n' Gusher. My daughter was not strong enough to carry hers, so I had to lug them up by myself. I was exhausted by the end of the day, and my arms ached for a couple of days afterward. Had I known that was the case, I would have started lifting weights several months before our trip in preparation!*

Those of you who don't want to train in advance will appreciate **Miss Adventure Falls,** near Crush 'n' Gusher. Riders hop into a circular

Typhoon Lagoon

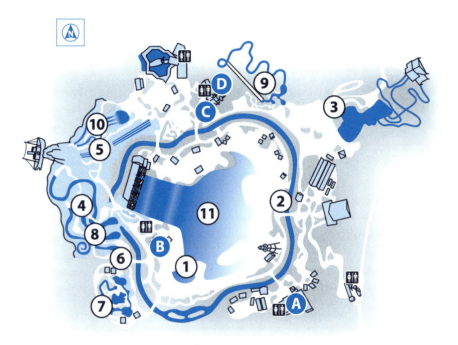

Attractions

1. Bay Slides
2. Castaway Creek
3. Crush 'n' Gusher
4. Gangplank Falls
5. Humunga Kowabunga
6. Keelhaul Falls
7. Ketchakiddee Creek
8. Mayday Falls
9. Miss Adventure Falls
10. Storm Slides
11. Surf Pool

Restaurants

A. Leaning Palms
B. Lowtide Lou's
C. Snack Shack
D. Typhoon Tilly's

 Restrooms

four-person raft at the bottom of the slide, then ride a conveyor belt up to the top in about a minute. Though the rafts hold four, the ride works just as well for singles and couples. The queuing area is inadequate, making for major jams on busy days. Because the attraction is suitable for all ages, expect big crowds and long waits unless you ride just after park opening.

Those looking for a more relaxing experience will also enjoy the meandering, 2,000-foot-long **Castaway Creek,** which floats tubers through hidden grottoes and rainforests.

SURF POOL

WHILE BLIZZARD BEACH has a wave pool, Typhoon Lagoon has a Surf Pool. Most people will encounter larger waves here than they have in the ocean. The surf machine puts out a wave about every 90 seconds (just about how long it takes to get back in position if you caught the previous wave). Perfectly formed and ideal for riding, each wave is about 5–6 feet from trough to crest. Before you join the fray, watch two or three waves from shore. Because each wave breaks in almost the same spot, you can get a feel for position and timing. Observing other surfers is also helpful.

The best way to ride the waves is to swim about three-fourths of the way to the wall at the wave-machine end of the pool. When the waves come, swim vigorously toward the beach and try to position yourself one-half to three-fourths of a body length below the breaking crest. The waves are so perfectly engineered that they'll either carry you forward or bypass you. Unlike ocean waves, though, they won't slam you down.

The best way to avoid collisions while surfing is to paddle out far enough that you'll be at the top of the wave as it breaks. This tactic eliminates the possibility of anyone landing on you from above and ensures maximum forward visibility. A corollary to this: The worst place to swim is where the wave actually breaks. You'll look up to see a 6-foot wall of water carrying eight dozen screaming surfers bearing down on you.

A Virginia mom was caught off-guard by the size and power of the waves:

> *I had forgotten how violent the Surf Pool is at Typhoon Lagoon. Thinking I'd be able to hold on to two young(ish) nephews is a mistake I made only once before getting them back to shallower water.*

A reader from New Jersey alerted us to another problem:

> *Typhoon Lagoon is a great family water park—our unexpected favorite. However, please tell your readers not to sit on the bottom of the wave pool—I got a horrible scratch/raspberry and saw about five others with similar injuries. The waves are stronger than they look.*

Either in the early morning before the park opens or in the evening after it closes (hours vary), Typhoon Lagoon gives experienced surfers the opportunity to participate in **Open Surf** or **Private Surf**. One hundred waves are sent out in sets of 25, and each surfer is guaranteed at least 10 rides over the 3-hour event. The cost for Open Surf is $270–$335 per person (including tax) for 3 hours. The price you pay is based on time of day and day of week. You must provide your own board. The cost for Private Surf starts at $1,450, which covers a party of 15 surfers. Maximum party size is 40. For details and to see if sessions are being offered, visit disneyworld.disney.go.com/recreation/surf-lessons.

AFTER HOURS EVENTS As we went to press, Disney was holding After Hours events at Typhoon Lagoon during summer months, from roughly mid-May through early September. Usually staged on

Saturday from 8 to 11 p.m., with ticket holders admitted into the park at 6 p.m., these events include access to all of the park's major rides and slides. Tickets cost $80 for adults and $75 for children.

WATER PARK TOURING PLANS

ONE-DAY TOURING PLANS for Typhoon Lagoon and Blizzard Beach can be found on pages 567 and 568, respectively. These plans are for parents with small children. Touring plans for adults are available at **TouringPlans.com**.

The plans presented in this book include all the slides, flumes, and rides appropriate for kids in both parks. They also include tips on which slides to try first if this is your child's first water park experience. For example, at Typhoon Lagoon, the family whitewater raft ride, Miss Adventure Falls, is a great first option. If your child enjoys that, then you can try Gangplank Falls and then Keelhaul Falls. If that seems a bit much, however, the touring plan recommends the Ketchakiddee Creek play area as an alternative.

PART 16

BEHIND-THE-SCENES *and* VIP TOURS

KEY QUESTIONS ANSWERED IN THIS CHAPTER

- How can I see the park's utilidor network? *(see below)*
- How can I interact with animals? *(page 496)*
- How can I get a VIP tour? *(page 496)*

IF YOU'RE INTERESTED IN THE MOUSE'S INNARDS—um, make that inner workings—several tours offer a glimpse of what goes on behind the scenes. Reservations must be guaranteed with a credit card, and you must cancel at least 48 hours in advance for a full refund. Many tours require that you also buy park admission; we note where it isn't mandatory. Prices do not include tax. Some tours are available only on certain days of the week (search for them online to confirm). For reservations and details, call ☎ 407-WDW-TOUR (939-8687).

BEHIND *the* SCENES *at the* MAGIC KINGDOM

AS ITS NAME SUGGESTS, **Disney's Keys to the Kingdom Tour** ($129–$149 per person) is a deep dive into the inner workings of the Magic Kingdom, offering a behind-the-scenes look at how the park operates. This 5-hour guided tour takes guests through areas typically off-limits to visitors, including the parade staging area, the underground utilidor tunnels, and even past the waste-processing system. Along the way, you'll usually get to experience a few attractions, like the Jungle Cruise. The program also includes lunch; guests must be at least 16 years old. Annual Pass holders and DVC members receive a discount.

This tour is also an ode to Roy Disney, who spearheaded the completion of the Magic Kingdom after the death of his brother Walt. I didn't think crying in the utilidors was on my bucket list, but I can definitely check it off now (along with every other person in my tour group) thanks to the moving stories shared about how Roy inspired everyone to bring his younger brother's vision to life.

For a different kind of exclusive experience, a private **Fireworks Cruise** (starts at $449 per sailing, depending on the date, for up to 10 guests) provides a 2-hour sailing on Seven Seas Lagoon, culminating in a prime viewing spot for *Happily Ever After*. On select nights, the Electrical Water Pageant is also visible from your boat. Each cruise is piloted by a Disney captain and departs from the marinas at the Contemporary, Grand Floridian, Polynesian, Wilderness Lodge, or Fort Wilderness. Soft drinks and snacks are provided, and for special occasions, banners and balloons can be requested at booking for no additional charge. Boats depart roughly 75 minutes before fireworks are scheduled to begin.

> *unofficial* **TIP**
> Many tours involve lots of walking, standing, and time spent outdoors, so check the forecast before you head out.

You won't be able to really see any projections on the castle from your vantage point on the lagoon, but this is still one of our favorite ways to watch the Magic Kingdom fireworks. If you have a larger group, the per-person cost isn't unreasonable, especially with snacks and drinks included. The view of the fireworks is unique, and you don't have to deal with any of the post-fireworks traffic in the Magic Kingdom. Plus, cruise captains are a wealth of stories and information about the lagoon and the surrounding resorts. It's a great way to learn some new things as you motor around the lake for scenic views until fireworks, instead of sitting in crowds around the castle for an hour.

BEHIND *the* SCENES *at* EPCOT

FOR THOSE INTERESTED IN AGRICULTURE and sustainability, **Behind the Seeds** ($39–$45 per guest, age 3 and up) offers a 1-hour guided tour inside the greenhouses and aquaculture labs of The Land Pavilion. The tour provides an up-close look at the innovative growing techniques used to cultivate food for EPCOT's restaurants. You walk in and around the environments that you can see from the boat during Living with the Land. If you're a fan of that attraction, this is a great way to experience it in a new way. Reservations are required and can be made online or at the lower level of The Land Pavilion near Soarin' Around the World. While this used to be considered one of Disney's best-value tours, the price has nearly doubled since 2017, making it less of a bargain than before.

For those who prefer exploring beneath the water, **DiveQuest** ($229–$249 per person, age 10 and up, with proof of scuba certification) at The Seas Pavilion offers certified divers a chance to swim in the park's massive 5.7-million-gallon saltwater aquarium. The 2-hour experience includes about 40 minutes of actual dive time. Participants share the water with more than 2,000 sea creatures, including sharks, rays, and sea turtles. The tour also provides a look at how Disney maintains one of the largest aquariums in North America. If you have nondivers in your group, they can watch from the 56 viewing windows in The Seas while the divers explore. Disney provides all the necessary equipment; the only personal gear allowed is a dive mask. Swimsuits are required, and wet suits are provided.

BEHIND *the* SCENES *at* DISNEY'S ANIMAL KINGDOM

FOR AN UNFORGETTABLE 3-hour adventure, the **Wild Africa Trek** ($219–$229 per person) takes small groups through hiking trails, rope bridges, and a private safari through the park's savanna. The tour includes a gourmet meal served in the middle of the savanna and comes with professional photos of your journey. Participants must be at least 8 years old, weigh between 45 and 300 pounds, and stand at least 4 feet tall to fit the required safety gear. The trek involves plenty of walking, and closed-toe shoes are mandatory. These rules are for good reason—you'll be walking on bridges directly above the hippo and alligator enclosures!

If hiking and bridges over predators sound too intense, consider **Savor the Savanna** ($189–$199 per person) instead. For this experience, you skip the ropes course and focus on the safari and an even finer dining experience.

For a nighttime twist, the **Starlight Safari** ($75–$89 per person, age 8 and up) offers a chance to explore the savannas of Animal Kingdom Lodge under the stars. Once exclusive to guests of the resort, it's now available to all Disney resort guests. The 1-hour tour provides night-vision devices to help spot animals in the dark.

If you prefer a closer look at specific animals, Up Close with Rhinos and Caring for the Giants provide intimate access to a couple of species. **Up Close with Rhinos** ($49 per person, age 4 and up) brings guests "backstage" to see white rhinos. This tour happens in the building where the rhinos are housed instead of "onstage" at the safari, so you are guaranteed time up close with these fascinating animals.

Caring for the Giants ($39 per person, age 4 and up) focuses on the park's elephant herd, with guests standing 80–100 feet away on a backstage platform while learning about their behavior and care. The elephants are onstage for this tour, so visibility and distance may vary. Still, tour guides here are very well trained in making the hour engaging, no matter how "cooperative" the elephants are or whether you're 4, 44, or 84.

VIP TOURS

WE CAN TELL by the book you're reading that you're smart, and probably hilarious to boot. If you're also flush with disposable income and looking to avoid every possible line at Walt Disney World while having most of your whims catered to, then a **private VIP tour** is what you want.

For $450–$900 per hour (depending on the season; 7 hours minimum), a Disney VIP host will pick you up at your resort (or meet you at the park of your choosing), precheck your admission tickets, and whisk you and up to nine of your friends through a private entrance to a Disney theme park. Once in the park, your VIP guide will ensure that you wait as little as possible for whatever attractions you want to see—usually by taking you through the Lightning Lane, even if you don't have reservations—and make sure you get prime spots for parades and fireworks. If you want to visit multiple parks, the VIP guide will drive you in a private car. (Valid theme park admission is required for each theme park visited on the tour and is not included in the price of the tour.)

Unofficial Guide readers rave about the guides, who do everything from entertain the kids to regale the adults with obscure theme park trivia. They also provide lots of snacks and can arrange meals.

VIP tours can be booked 3–90 days in advance by calling ☎ 407-560-4033. You must cancel at least 48 hours in advance to avoid a charge of 2 hours at the booked rate.

PART 17

DISNEY SPRINGS, SHOPPING, *and* NIGHTLIFE

KEY QUESTIONS ANSWERED IN THIS CHAPTER

- How do I get to Disney Springs? *(see below)*
- What are the best shops and experiences at Disney Springs? *(page 502)*
- Where are the best bars and nightclubs at Disney Springs? *(page 504)*
- Where is the best shopping in the Disney theme parks? *(page 505)*
- Where is the best shopping outside the theme parks? *(page 509)*
- Which are the best bars and nightclubs at the Disney resorts, and where can I find free concerts in Walt Disney World? *(page 510)*

A DISNEY WORLD VACATION isn't just theme parks and attractions. If you're looking for activities after the parks close, planning a non-park day, or simply in the mood to shop or catch live entertainment, this chapter has you covered with Disney Springs, a sprawling outdoor complex with restaurants, shopping, and theaters. With so much to do, there's little reason to venture off-property to spend your time or money (or so Disney hopes).

In this chapter, you'll find a guide to the offerings at Disney Springs; tips about some of the best shopping in the theme parks and Orlando; and a rundown of the nightlife options at Disney resorts and other locations around the World.

DISNEY SPRINGS

ARRIVING AT DISNEY SPRINGS

BY CAR Guests driving to Disney Springs will take Buena Vista Drive from Disney property, and Hotel Plaza Boulevard from the Disney Springs resorts and FL 535. I-4 westbound offers direct access to the complex via Exit 67.

There are three parking garages and four surface lots. The **Lime** garage serves The Landing, Town Center, and Marketplace areas of Disney Springs. The **Orange** garage is closest to the West Side, the AMC 24 movie theater, and Planet Hollywood. The third garage,

Grapefruit, sits across Buena Vista Drive from the Lime garage. It is connected to Disney Springs via a raised walkway. There is no charge to park in the garages.

An LED display on each level of the garages indicates how many open spaces there are on each level. Typically, the lower levels fill up first, with more open spaces available on each successive level up.

You'll ultimately want to navigate to Level 2, where all guests are funneled through security. If there are no spots on that level, park as close as possible to the center of the level where you find a spot and walk to Level 2, the security checkpoint. There's also "preferred" parking available in the Lemon and Mango surface lots for $20. We're not sure why you'd pay this much to park, but it's there if you can't find a spot and you're desperate.

BY DISNEY TRANSPORTATION All Disney resorts and theme parks offer **bus transportation** to Disney Springs; some bus routes are shared with **Typhoon Lagoon,** one of Disney's two water parks. The Disney bus area is centrally located between the Orange and Lime parking garages. **Saratoga Springs Resort, Old Key West Resort,** and the **Port Orleans Resorts** offer boat transportation to the Disney Springs dock at The Landing.

BY TAXI/RIDESHARE Drop-off and pickup are at the **Cirque du Soleil** theater on the far west side of Disney Springs and at the far east side of the Marketplace.

ON FOOT Saratoga Springs Resort has walking paths to Disney Springs, and guests staying at hotels in the **Disney Springs Resort Area** (see page 173) can walk to Disney Springs on walkways and pedestrian bridges to avoid traffic.

GETTING ORIENTED

DISNEY SPRINGS IS DIVIDED INTO FOUR AREAS, each with its own theme. **Marketplace,** on the east side of Disney Springs, is the most kid-friendly, with the **World of Disney** store and many activities for children. It has a small carousel and minitrain rides for a fee. A free splash area is great for cooling down, and free concerts take place in the amphitheater across from World of Disney.

The Landing is the waterfront section of Disney Springs. Open, winding paths offer sweeping views of the water and Saratoga Springs as you walk between the Marketplace and the West Side.

The third area is the Old Florida–style **Town Center,** which has most of the well-known retail stores in Disney Springs (**Uniqlo** and **Zara** are the largest). If you've ever found yourself at Pirates of the Caribbean and thought, "What this place needs is upscale shopping," you'll love this section. Town Center sits between The Landing and the parking lot.

On the **West Side,** a Disney-themed **Cirque du Soleil** production called *Drawn to Life* opened in 2021. **Jaleo by José Andrés** (see page 262), an **AMC** multiplex theater, the **Splitsville** bowling lanes, and **Starbucks** are some of the biggest draws here.

continued on page 502

Disney Springs

WEST SIDE Shopping
1. Bowes Signature Candles
2. Disney's Candy Cauldron
3. DisneyStyle
4. M&Ms Store
5. Pelé Soccer
6. Star Wars Galactic Outpost
7. Sunglass Hut
8. Super Hero Headquarters

WEST SIDE Dining
9. City Works Eatery & Pour House
10. Everglazed Donuts & Cold Brew
11. Food Trucks at Exposition Park
12. House of Blues Restaurant & Bar
13. The Front Porch/The Smokehouse at House of Blues
14. Jaleo/Pepe by José Andrés
15. McGuffins
16. Salt & Straw
17. Splitsville Dining Room
18. Starbucks
19. Summer House on the Lake

THE LANDING Shopping
20. Chapel Hats
21. **Group 1:** Oakley, Savannah Bee Company
22. Havaianas
23. OluKai

THE LANDING Dining
24. The Boathouse
25. Chef Art Smith's Homecomin'
26. The Edison
27. Enzo's Hideaway
28. Erin McKenna's Bakery NYC
29. The Ganachery
30. Gideon's Bakehouse
31. Jock Lindsey's Hangar Bar
32. Joffrey's Coffee & Tea
33. Maria & Enzo's Ristorante
34. Morimoto Asia
35. Morimoto Asia Street Food
36. Paddlefish
37. Paradiso 37
38. Pizza Ponte
39. Raglan Road/Cookes of Dublin
40. STK Orlando
41. Terralina Crafted Italian
42. Vivoli il Gelato
43. Wine Bar George/The Basket at Wine Bar George

TOWN CENTER Shopping
44. Coca-Cola Store
45. **Group 1:** American Threads, Johnston & Murphy, Tommy Bahama, Fit2Run, lululemon
46. **Group 2:** Columbia Sportswear, Free People, Johnny Was, Kate Spade New York, Lilly Pulitzer, Rothy's, Sperry, Sugarboo, Vera Bradley
47. **Group 3:** Coach, MAC Cosmetics, Jo Malone London
48. **Group 4:** Lacoste, Luxury of Time
49. **Group 5:** Lovepop, Ron Jon Surf Shop, Sephora, Shore, Stance, Superdry
50. **Group 6:** Levi's, Orlando Harley-Davidson

DISNEY SPRINGS MAP

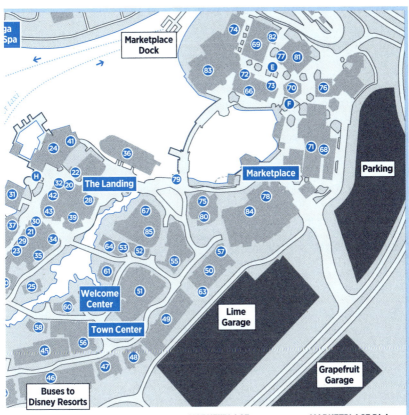

51. **Group 7:** Anthropologie, Disney Ever After, Everything but Water, Fabletics, Francesca's, Kendra Scott, L'Occitane en Provence, Pura Vida, Under Armour, UNOde50, Vineyard Vines
52. **Group 8:** Edward Beiner, Na Hoku
53. Pandora Jewelry
54. Sundries
55. Uniqlo
56. Zara

TOWN CENTER Dining
57. Amorette's Patisserie
58. Blaze Fast-Fire'd Pizza
59. Chicken Guy!
60. D-Luxe Burger
61. Frontera Cocina
62. Planet Hollywood/Stargazers Bar
63. The Polite Pig
64. Sprinkles
65. Wolfgang Puck Bar & Grill

MARKETPLACE Shopping
66. The Art Corner
67. Build-a-Dino/Dino Store
68. Disney PhotoPass Studio
69. Disney's Days of Christmas
70. Disney's Pin Traders
71. **Group 1:** Basin, Crystal Arts by Arribas Brothers, Ghirardelli Soda Fountain & Chocolate Shop, Marketplace Co-Op/D-Tech on Demand, Tren-D
72. Goofy's Candy Company,
73. Star Wars Trading Post
74. **Group 2:** The Art of Disney, Disney's Wonderful World of Memories
75. The Lego Store
76. Once Upon a Toy
77. The Spice & Tea Exchange
78. World of Disney

MARKETPLACE Dining
79. B.B. Wolf's Sausage Co.
80. The Daily Poutine
81. Earl of Sandwich
82. eet by Maneet Chauhan
83. Rainforest Cafe/Lava Lounge
84. Starbucks
85. T-Rex

Entertainment and Attractions
A. Aerophile
B. AMC Disney Springs 24 Dine-In Theatres
C. Cirque du Soleil
D. House of Blues
E. Marketplace Carousel
F. Marketplace Train Express
G. Splitsville Luxury Lanes
H. Vintage Amphicar & Italian Water Taxi Tours

continued from page 499

DISNEY SPRINGS SHOPPING AT A GLANCE
Marketplace

DISNEY'S DAYS OF CHRISTMAS This shop is sheer holiday magic, with hundreds of holiday decorations for sale. We especially like the ornament personalization—for a small fee, an artist will handwrite your name and a phrase or date. What better way to remember your Disney vacation than an ornament you put on your tree every year?

THE ART OF DISNEY Browse fine art, watch artists draw characters, or pick up some postcards as fun and cheap souvenirs.

BASIN If you want fancy soap, bath bombs, and other scented bath products, including a Disney-themed selection, this is the place to go.

CRYSTAL ARTS BY ARRIBAS BROTHERS Sparkly collectibles and works of art abound in this shop full of Arribas Brothers products. Avoid it if you have clumsy family members!

unofficial **TIP**
At **Ghirardelli Soda Fountain & Chocolate Shop**, near Basin and Crystal Arts, you can smell the chocolate when you walk in. Chocolate souvenirs abound, but go ahead and treat yourself to a "world famous" sundae topped with hot fudge made daily. The line for ice cream often winds out the door.

GOOFY'S CANDY CO. Interactive show kitchen with lots of sweets. Enjoy create-your-own pretzel rods, marshmallows, and candy apples.

THE LEGO STORE Inside you'll find an impressive selection of all the latest Lego sets, while the hands-on outdoor play area has bins of Legos that kids can get creative with. Photo ops with life-size Disney characters surround the shop, and you can design and create your own personalized minifigure to take home too.

MARKETPLACE CO-OP The Co-op has six pop-up-style retail experiences within one shop. Shops rotate depending on what is popular at the time.

ONCE UPON A TOY This is the place to find toy sets and a huge selection of plushies. We also appreciate that Once Upon a Toy is much less crowded than World of Disney. You're less likely to lose your kids (or partner) here.

STAR WARS TRADING POST Although *Star Wars* merchandise can be found in other stores, this is the largest consolidated collection anywhere on-property outside of Galaxy's Edge in Hollywood Studios. Shop here for collectibles and Galaxy's Edge merch specifically.

THE SPICE AND TEA EXCHANGE Flavored salts and sugars, teas, and spice mixes. You can also purchase wines and cookbooks.

TREN-D Women's apparel and accessories, plus exclusive items from cutting-edge designers.

WORLD OF DISNEY With the largest selection of Disney merchandise in the world, World of Disney can get oppressively crowded. It has a little bit of everything. If you can't find something to love here, you won't find it anywhere on-property.

Town Center

AMORETTE'S PATISSERIE Beautiful cakes and pastries, including Disney character–themed cakes, large and small, that you won't see anywhere else, plus sandwiches and beverages.

COCA-COLA STORE A fun visit, especially for fans of soda. The roof deck has a bar with Coke flights and views of Disney Springs.

JO MALONE Perfumes, candles, and other scented lifestyle items.

KATE SPADE NEW YORK What sets this location apart from the one at your local mall is that it often has Disney-themed bags and accessories only available here or online.

LILLY PULITZER Bright, fun prints synonymous with summertime.

PANDORA The jewelry retailer has an agreement with Walt Disney World that includes another shop on Main Street, U.S.A. Many Disney-exclusive charms sell out quickly.

SUPERDRY Fun casual wear for teens and young adults.

TOMMY BAHAMA One of the few shops at Disney Springs with a decent selection of casual menswear. It also has a nice selection of swimwear for both men and women.

UNIQLO Fast fashion and exclusive Disney apparel. Uniqlo is handy if you need to buy basics such as sweatshirts and T-shirts.

VERA BRADLEY The ubiquitous quilted bags with a fanatical following. You'll find both Disney-exclusive and mainline prints here.

Other shops in Town Center include **American Threads, Anthropologie, Coach, Columbia Sportswear, Fabletics, Francesca's, Free People, Johnny Was, Johnston & Murphy, Kendra Scott, Lacoste, Levi's, L'Occitane, Lovepop, Lululemon, Mac Cosmetics, Na Hoku, Harley-Davidson, Ron Jon Surf Shop, Rothy's, Sephora, Sperry, Sugarboo, Under Armour, Volcom,** and **Zara.**

The Landing

THE GANACHERY Exquisite handmade chocolates in gourmet flavor combinations. This Disney-run shop may be more pricey than you're expecting, but—coming from a chocolate connoisseur—it's worth it. Don't skip the Old Fashioned–flavored chocolate, if it's available. They card you for it for a reason.

GIDEON'S BAKEHOUSE This bakery and coffee shop serves cookies that weigh almost half a pound, admirably attempting to redefine the phrase *single serving*. Expect a line of at least 30 minutes for most of the day.

JOFFREY'S COFFEE & TEA COMPANY You can purchase leaves to take home or enjoy a hot or cold tea at the counter. Very pleasant and less hectic than Starbucks for your caffeine needs.

You'll also find kiosks selling everything from wind chimes to yo-yos as you walk through The Landing.

West Side

DISNEY'S CANDY CAULDRON Watch as treats are made in the open kitchen. Dipped candy apples (befitting the Snow White theme) are the house specialty. There's also a decent selection of bulk candies.

DISNEYSTYLE Packed full of the trendiest Disney apparel and accessories you'll find on the West Side. You'll find everything from T-shirts and trinkets to home décor items and gift baskets.

M&M'S A large store selling everyone's favorite melt-in-your-mouth chocolates in every flavor and color imaginable, along with clothing, mugs, and other merchandise.

PELÉ SOCCER A store for the soccer fans in your life. Find official club jerseys, balls, cleats, and more.

STAR WARS GALACTIC OUTPOST A large selection of *Star Wars* souvenirs, from T-shirts to Stormtrooper helmets. Focuses more on clothing and "fun" than the Marketplace's Star Wars Trading Post.

SUNGLASS HUT Got to sunny Florida and forgot your shades? This is the place to pick up a pair to save your retinas.

SUPER HERO HEADQUARTERS Guardians of the Galaxy: Cosmic Rewind is the only Marvel-themed ride at Walt Disney World and, oddly, it doesn't deposit you directly into the Marvel-themed gift shop. So if you're missing Marvel merch, head here instead.

BARS AND NIGHTLIFE AT DISNEY SPRINGS

DISNEY SPRINGS IS A POPULAR NIGHTTIME DESTINATION for visitors who aren't ready to go to sleep yet but don't want to burn park admission for just a few hours in the evening. You'll find street entertainment, including singers, musicians, and performance artists, spread throughout Disney Springs. There's even more entertainment at many of the restaurants, including bands and singers at **House of Blues** (see pages 261 and 511) and **Splitsville Dining Room** (see page 277) and music and Irish dancers at **Raglan Road Irish Pub & Restaurant** (see page 271).

Some of our favorite places to grab a drink are at Disney Springs. Raglan Road has multiple bars and a fantastic menu of appetizers. **Summer House on the Lake** (see page 278) offers a cookie bar with tea, coffee, and espresso drinks—an ideal combination—plus a martini bar. **Jaleo by José Andrés** (see page 262) and **Wine Bar George** (see page 286) have excellent drinks and tasty small-plate menus. **The Boathouse** (see page 249) and **Morimoto Asia** (see page 266) both have bars worth a visit. Reader ratings for **The Edison, Enzo's Hideaway,** and **STK Orlando** are so low that we don't recommend them.

TAKE IT ON THE RUN, BABY

FOR AN EVENING OF DRINKING AND STROLLING, Disney Springs has you covered. Starting with the **AmphiBar** outside the entrance to The Boathouse, several restaurants quickly figured out that there was a market for cocktails to go. Find Guinness outside **Raglan Road** and margaritas at **Frontera Cocina** and **Dockside Margaritas**.

MAGIC KINGDOM SHOPPING SAMPLER

I WANT...	FIND IT AT...
• One-stop shopping	• **The Emporium,** Main Street
• Candy, pastries, and fudge	• **Main Street Confectionery,** Main Street • **Big Top Souvenirs,** Fantasyland
• Disney art and collectibles	• **Main Street Cinema,** Main Street
• Holiday décor	• **Olde Christmas Shoppe,** Liberty Square
• Memory cards and batteries	• **Box Office Gifts,** Main Street
• Personalized mouse ears	• **Box Office Gifts,** Main Street • **Fantasy Faire,** Fantasyland
• Princess wear	• **The Emporium,** Main Street
• Tech gifts	• **Space Mountain Gift Shop,** Tomorrowland
• Women's jewelry, handbags, and accessories	• **Main Street Jewelers** (has a **Pandora** shop)

SHOPPING *in* WALT DISNEY WORLD *and* ORLANDO

SHOPPING AT DISNEY WORLD

EACH THEME PARK has at least one major retail store, several minor ones, and gift shops attached to most attractions. While we occasionally groan about how the merchandise selection at each store and park gets more and more similar every year, this does mean that if something catches your eye, you'll most likely see it again. Ditto for prices; pricing is consistent throughout the resorts—an item on sale in one location will be the same price at all locations.

See the following pages for a quick-reference guide to which theme park shops carry what you're looking for.

Magic Kingdom Shopping

BIBBIDI BOBBIDI BOUTIQUE Located in Cinderella Castle, this salon for kids ages 3–12 will give princess hopefuls a royal makeover. Packages range from $107 to above $500, plus tip. Photo packages, a Knight Package (for those who don't want to be princesses), and other add-ons are available for an extra charge.

Preschoolers and grade-schoolers rate this experience as much above average. But teens and up (aka, the folks footing the bill) rate it much below average.

Reservations can be made up to 60 days in advance (70 days for Disney resort guests); call 407-939-7895 for information or reservations. Allow 30 minutes–1 hour for the whole makeover.

EPCOT Shopping

Shopping is a big part of the **World Showcase** experience in this theme park, much more so than in the others. This is one of the rare times that most merchandise you see will be unique. With a selection that ranges from affordable trinkets to $99,000 pieces of art, the shops in World

EPCOT SHOPPING SAMPLER	
I WANT...	FIND IT AT...
• One-stop shopping	• **Creations Shop,** World Celebration
• Disney art and collectibles	• **The Art of Disney,** The American Adventure Pavilion
• Disney comics and books	• **ImageWorks,** Imagination! Pavilion
• Eco-friendly gifts	• **Outpost,** World Showcase
• Kitchen supplies and décor	• **Port of Entry,** World Showcase
• Marvel merchandise	• **Treasures of Xandar,** Guardians of the Galaxy
• Memory cards and batteries	• **Camera Center,** World Celebration
• Personalized mouse ears	• **Creations Shop,** World Celebration
• Princess wear	• **The Wandering Reindeer,** Norway Pavilion
• Tech gifts	• **Creations Shop and Camera Center,** World Celebration

Showcase have something for everyone. Becky's family has a whole shelf at home dedicated to unique World Showcase tchotchkes they find during their trips. Walking clockwise, you'll find the following:

★ **MEXICO** The most well-themed shopping experience in all of World Showcase, **Plaza de los Amigos** is a re-creation of a Mexican shopping village at dusk. You'll find all manner of sombreros, Día de los Muertos (Day of the Dead) items, Oaxacan carved wooden animals, and blankets. Along the side of the shopping area is **La Princesa de Cristal,** with crystal jewelry and trinkets, and another shop with leather items, women's dresses and blouses, and other accessories.

★ **NORWAY The Fjording** is a series of small shopping galleries with popular imports such as trolls (from $15) and wooden Christmas ornaments (from $5). Other hard-to-find imports include Scandinavian foods and candies, Laila perfume (Becky never passes by without a sample) and body lotion, and Helly Hansen and Dale of Norway clothing, including thick wool sweaters. You'll also find all things *Frozen* here.

★ **CHINA** This pavilion features one of our favorite shops, **House of Good Fortune,** which is more like a rambling department store than a shop. You'll find everything from darling handbags and silk fans, kimonos, and ties to cloisonné, jade sculptures, and antique furniture. And we always admire the handwoven pure-silk carpets.

Village Traders, a shop between China and Germany, sells beautiful, handmade African woodcarvings. You can also find these carvings in Animal Kingdom and Animal Kingdom Lodge, where an artisan is frequently working on them live. Another specialty here is bead jewelry, crafted in Uganda from repurposed Disney paper products such as old handout guides.

★ **GERMANY** Shops interconnect on both sides of the cobblestoned central plaza. From left to right, you'll first find **Karamell-Küche** which has take-home candies in addition to its wide array of snacks. If you can tear yourself away from that amazing smell, next you'll get to **Die Weihnachts Ecke,** where Christmas ornaments (pick up a pickle!) and handmade nutcrackers are on display year-round. Next is the

SHOPPING IN WALT DISNEY WORLD AND ORLANDO

DISNEY'S ANIMAL KINGDOM SHOPPING SAMPLER	
I WANT . . .	**FIND IT AT . . .**
• One-stop shopping	• **Discovery Trading Company,** Discovery Island
• African souvenirs	• **Mombasa Marketplace,** Harambe, Africa
• African wines, cookbooks, and Flame Tree Barbecue Sauce	• **Zuri's Sweets Shop,** Africa
• Memory cards and batteries	• **Island Mercantile,** Discovery Island
• My own shoulder-top banshee or glowing Pandora merch	• **Windtraders,** Pandora—The World of Avatar
• Personalized mouse ears	• **Island Mercantile,** Discovery Island

Weinkeller, with nearly 300 varieties of German wine and liqueur to sample or bring home. Becky recommends the Mozart chocolate liqueur. Farther on is **Kunstarbeit in Kristall,** which carries a fabulous collection of Swarovski crystal, including pins, glassware, and Arribas Brothers collectibles (check out the limited-edition $37,500 replica of Cinderella Castle or the $99,000 Spaceship Earth Beacon of Magic). Across the plaza, **Stein Haus** is stocked with limited-edition steins and glassware, as well as Biergarten gear. Prost! Tiny **Das Kaufhaus** stocks a nice selection of Adidas sportswear. Next door is **Volkskunst,** where the walls are covered with Schneider cuckoo clocks and the shelves are lined with German candies and souvenirs. On your way to the next pavilion, you'll find yet another shop, **Glaskunst,** featuring glass boots and steins, with options for personalization. Who knew Germans liked shopping so much?

★ **ITALY** At **Il Bel Cristallo,** you'll find sportswear, Bulgari and Emilio Pucci fragrances, Murano figurines, elaborate Venetian masks, wine by the bottle, and a small selection of Christmas decorations in the back room.

★ **JAPAN** An outpost of the country's 350-year-old **Mitsukoshi Department Store** stretches along one entire side of the Japan Pavilion. Kid-friendly merchandise (like Hello Kitty, Naruto, and Yu-Gi-Oh!) fills the front, with kimonos, slippers, handbags, and lots more at the back. Mitsukoshi's expanded culinary display includes a sake-tasting bar, along with chopsticks, pretty rice bowls, and a large variety of teas and teapots. The selection of products related to anime is great as well. Guests line up for an oyster that is guaranteed to have a pearl in its shell (pearls are polished for you by the salesperson). And there is an entire room dedicated to Japanese snacks, which can be a fun culinary adventure.

★ **MOROCCO** Several shops used to populate this pavilion, including Tangier Traders, The Brass Bazaar, and Casablanca Carpets. But as of 2025, your only option is **Souk-al-Magreb** (beside Spice Road Table), where you can find authentic Moroccan clothing, Morocco Pavilion souvenirs, and colorful lanterns.

★ **FRANCE** The courtyard at the France Pavilion has some *merveilleux* shopping opportunities. A dedicated Guerlain shop, **La Signature,** offers cosmetics and fragrances from the French house, along with makeup consultations. **Plume et Palette** has fragrances, cosmetics, and

DISNEY'S HOLLYWOOD STUDIOS SHOPPING SAMPLER

I WANT...	FIND IT AT...
• One-stop shopping	• **Mickey's of Hollywood,** Hollywood Boulevard
• Trendy clothing, accessories, jewelry, and bags	• **Keystone Clothiers,** Hollywood Boulevard
• MagicBands and other Disney gifts	• **The Darkroom,** Hollywood Boulevard
• Personalized mouse ears	• **Legends of Hollywood,** Sunset Boulevard
• Princess wear	• **Legends of Hollywood,** Sunset Boulevard
• *Star Wars* souvenirs	• **Black Spire Outfitters,** Galaxy's Edge • **Tatooine Traders,** Grand Avenue

women's accessories from Christian Dior, Givenchy, Kenzo, Le Tanneur, and Thierry Mugler, to name a few.

Find wines and kitchen goods, including a Champagne-tasting counter, at **Les Vins de Chefs de France** and **L'Esprit de la Provence,** which are connecting shops. And finally, at the back of the pavilion by Les Halles Boulangerie-Patisserie, **Souvenirs de France** sells a smattering of everything French, from berets and Eiffel Tower models to T-shirts and language books. You'll often find *Beauty and the Beast* souvenirs here too.

★ **UNITED KINGDOM** The **Toy Soldier** sells costumes, books, and items with a British rock-and-roll theme. You'll find plenty of Alice in Wonderland, Peter Pan, and Winnie the Pooh merchandise too. Stop at **The Crown & Crest** to look up your family name in the coat-of-arms book, and the shop will create your family's insignia in a beautiful frame of your choice. At the adjacent **Sportsman's Shoppe,** you'll find plenty of football (soccer) apparel, balls, and books.

Across the street, you'll find **The Queen's Table,** a gift shop with UK-themed clothing (and commemorative tartan), glassware, and more. The quaint **Lords and Ladies** offers lotions, soaps, scarves, jewelry, and perfume from the United Kingdom. **The Tea Caddy** stocks Twinings tea, biscuits (cookies), and candy.

★ **CANADA** There's not much shopping here, but **Northwest Mercantile** has a wide selection of merchandise, including NHL jerseys, T-shirts, sweatshirts, aprons, and pajamas, especially flannel.

Free Souvenirs from Walt Disney World

BIRTHDAY TREATS Be sure to mention any special occasions you're celebrating when you check in for your meal at a table-service restaurant. You may get a surprise dessert.

CELEBRATION BUTTONS Just married? Just graduated? Just happy to be nominated? There's a button for that. Get one when you check in to your hotel or from Guest Services.

KIDCOT FUN STOPS Kids love collecting and coloring the postcards from each EPCOT pavilion (see page 421).

STICKERS Cast members give out so many of these, we're afraid they might cause an adhesive shortage.

SHOPPING IN WALT DISNEY WORLD AND ORLANDO

TIPS FOR AVOIDING BUYER'S REMORSE

1. Know ahead of time how much things cost. You can browse many theme park items at disneystore.com.
2. Be specific. Disney collecting can spiral out of control if you don't narrow your focus. Pick a character or movie you love, and stick to that.
3. Don't buy merchandise with a date on it. That Walt Disney World 2026 T-shirt you buy to commemorate your vacation isn't going to look as fresh on January 1, 2027. There's a reason you see so much of this stuff at Disney outlets.
4. Buy lower-priced Disney souvenirs at local big-box stores, then hand them to your kids for that brand-new-thing thrill.
5. Don't fall for limited editions. If they make 2,000 of something, is it that rare?
6. Wait. Don't make your purchases until you've been to more than one shop.
7. Some of the best things in life are free. Consider the freebies at Walt Disney World (see opposite page) and skip the cash register.

TRANSPORTATION TRADING CARDS Did you know that monorail and bus drivers have trading cards to give out? Ask nicely, and be aware that supplies are often limited.

If you realize on your flight home that you forgot to buy mouse ears for the friend who watched your cats, don't worry. **ShopDisney** online (shopdisney.com) has a dedicated section of parks merchandise.

SHOPPING OUTSIDE DISNEY WORLD

Upscale Shopping

The Mall at Millenia (mallatmillenia.com) is anchored by **Bloomingdale's, Macy's,** and **Neiman Marcus.** You'll find designer boutiques, such as **Burberry, Chanel, Gucci, Hermès,** and **Louis Vuitton,** and the closest **Apple Store** to Walt Disney World. Millenia also has fast-fashion staples such as **H&M** and **Forever 21,** as well as the usual suspects, including **Gap, Victoria's Secret,** and **J.Crew.**

Midscale Shopping

The Florida Mall is home to **Dillard's, JCPenney, Macy's,** and **Sears.** Apart from the anchors and high-end designer shops, it has many of the same stores as The Mall at Millenia. Visit simon.com/mall/the-florida-mall. Also found at The Florida Mall is **Primark Orlando,** known for its low-priced clothing and accessories. Every Primark store has a good selection of Disney merchandise, and this one in particular has an entire floor dedicated to all things Disney.

Outlet Shopping

If you think the crowds at the parks are overwhelming, you'll want to avoid the two **Orlando Premium Outlets** at International Drive and Vineland Avenue (premiumoutlets.com/outlet/orlando-vineland). Tourists arrive here by the busload, and the experience will leave you questioning everything from consumer culture to your own judgment.

For the theme park visitor, the only redeeming aspect of these two malls is the **Disney Character Warehouse** (there are locations at both outlets). The Vineland location is about twice the size of the I-Drive location. To get an idea of what you might find there, check out Derek Burgan's past **"The Magic, The Memories, and Merch!"** entries on the **TouringPlans.com** blog.

Disney Shopping Outside of Walt Disney World

Forever Vintage, 30 minutes south of WDW, offers a wide array of Disney gear from the parks and resorts. You can also shop their inventory online at shopforevervintage.com. Becky loves using the site for unique or hard-to-find items, like the ceramic picnic-style plates used at Roundup Rodeo BBQ.

Fans seeking one-of-a-kind souvenirs, including costumes, props, and local art, should check out **TD Collectibles** (☎ 407-347-0670; tdcollectibles.net).

Orlando International Airport has three Disney shops, one at each terminal, for making purchases on the way home. The shops are fairly large and well themed for what they are; plus, they're run by Disney.

NIGHTLIFE *at* WALT DISNEY WORLD RESORTS

DISNEY'S BOARDWALK CURRENTLY OFFERS one adult-oriented venue, **Atlantic Dance Hall.** (**Jellyrolls,** a dueling-piano bar, closed in early 2025 to make way for a new concept.) The dance hall, for adults age 21 and up only, is regularly booked for private events, but on weekends it's generally open in the evenings, with free admission. The house DJ spins everything from '70s disco to top 40 and EDM.

unofficial **TIP**
Nightlife doesn't just mean stuff for the adults to do. There are plenty of kid-friendly activities after dark for the young ones. Check your resort's recreation schedule for campfires, movies on the beach or at the pool, and more.

At **Coronado Springs Resort,** you'll find **Rix Sports Bar & Grill.** It usually isn't busy unless there's a convention at the resort. Other Disney resort bars with live entertainment are **Scat Cat's Club** at **Port Orleans French Quarter** and **River Roost** at **Port Orleans Riverside.**

Inspired by the bar at the Disneyland Hotel in California, **Trader Sam's Grog Grotto** at the **Polynesian Village Resort** is a delight. If you've ever found yourself at *Walt Disney's Enchanted Tiki Room* and thought, "You know, booze would really make this better," then this is your place. But beware: There is typically a long wait to get in, especially on weekends.

Our favorite nightspot at Walt Disney World, **Top of the World** at the Contemporary Resort's **Bay Lake Tower,** is for Disney Vacation Club members and their guests. If you're a member or you can talk one into letting you in, try to stay after the Magic Kingdom fireworks—the view and setting are outstanding.

Free Concerts at Walt Disney World

CANDLELIGHT PROCESSIONAL During EPCOT's **International Festival of the Holidays,** celebrity narrators join a world-class orchestra and choir to retell the Christmas story. Depending on the narrator, these can be incredibly popular concerts. Many locals attend multiple times each year.

DISNEY ON BROADWAY During EPCOT's **International Festival of the Arts** in January and February, stars from well-known Disney musicals on Broadway perform in the America Gardens Theatre.

EAT TO THE BEAT For this concert series, classic and once-in-the-news acts accompany your trip around EPCOT's World Showcase during the fall **International Food & Wine Festival.** Featured artists tend to be from the 1980s and later.

GARDEN ROCKS Held during EPCOT's **International Flower & Garden Festival** in the spring, this series features acts from the 1960s onward.

House of Blues

Type of show Live concerts with an emphasis on rock and blues. **Tickets and information** ☎ 407-934-BLUE (2583); houseofblues.com/orlando. You can also purchase tickets in person at the box office Tuesday–Thursday, noon–7 p.m., and after noon on show days. **Nights of lowest attendance** Monday and Tuesday. **Usual showtimes** Between 7 and 9:30 p.m., depending on who's performing.

DESCRIPTION AND COMMENTS Developed by Blues Brother Dan Aykroyd, House of Blues consists of a restaurant and blues bar, as well as a concert hall. The restaurant is one of the few late-night dining options in Walt Disney World. Live music cranks up every night at 10:30 p.m. in the restaurant and blues bar, but even before then, the volume in the joint is usually above 110 decibels. The music hall next door features concerts by an eclectic array of musicians and groups. Genres have included gospel, blues, funk, ska, dance, salsa, rap, zydeco, hard rock, groove rock, and reggae.

TOURING TIPS Ticket prices vary from night to night according to the fame and drawing power of the featured band. They ranged from $29 to $135 in early 2025, with the better-known performers drawing higher prices. Shows are all ages unless otherwise indicated.

The music hall is set up like a nightclub, with tables and barstools for only about 150 people and standing room for a whopping 1,850. The tables and stools are first come, first served, with doors opening an hour before showtime on weekdays and 90 minutes before showtime on weekends. Arrive early if you want a seat.

PART 18

RECREATION *and* SPAS

KEY QUESTIONS ANSWERED IN THIS CHAPTER

- What is RunDisney, and how do I participate? *(see below)*
- What are the best places to relax on-property? *(page 514)*
- How can I get out onto the water while at Walt Disney World? *(page 516)*
- Where can I play minigolf with my family? *(page 516)*
- Can I learn any new skills while on vacation? *(page 517)*

MOST WALT DISNEY WORLD GUESTS never make it beyond the theme parks, water parks, and Disney Springs. Those who do, however, will be rewarded with an extraordinary selection of recreational opportunities. From guided fishing adventures and archery lessons to horseback or Segway riding, fitness center workouts, world-class massages, and minigolf, there is something for everyone.

RUN, DISNEY, RUN

RUNDISNEY EVENTS offer a completely different way to explore Walt Disney World, taking participants through the parks and along the resort's roadways in themed races held throughout the year. Runners and walkers alike can enjoy a high-energy course filled with Disney characters, live entertainment, and fun photo opportunities, with many participants dressing in costumes inspired by their favorite Disney characters. Every finisher earns a Disney-themed medal. Depending on the event, race options include a 5K, a 10K, a 10-miler, a half marathon, or a full marathon.

WALT DISNEY WORLD RUNDISNEY EVENTS

TYPICALLY, FOUR RUNDISNEY EVENTS are held at Walt Disney World every year:

WALT DISNEY WORLD MARATHON WEEKEND *(January 7–11, 2026)* This event offers a 5K, 10K, half marathon, and full marathon. Participants can also complete the Goofy's Race and a Half Challenge by finishing the half marathon and full marathon, or the Dopey Challenge by finishing all four races during the weekend.

DISNEY PRINCESS HALF MARATHON WEEKEND *(February 26–March 2, 2026)* This event offers a 5K, 10K, and half marathon. Participants can also complete the Disney Fairytale Challenge by finishing the 10K and half marathon.

SPRINGTIME SURPRISE WEEKEND *(April 16–19, 2026)* This newer event offers a 5K, 10K, and 10-miler. Participants can also complete the Springtime Surprise Challenge by finishing all three races.

DISNEY WINE & DINE HALF MARATHON *(typically held in late October or early November)* This event offers a 5K, 10K, and half marathon. Participants can also complete the Two Course Challenge by finishing the 10K and half marathon.

REGISTRATION

SIGNING UP FOR A RUNDISNEY EVENT is a competition in itself. It's not uncommon for a race to sell out the same day registration opens—and sometimes within the hour if it's a popular event or a new theme. Preparation is key if you want to secure a spot.

Before registration day, create an account on the RunDisney website. Save your payment information in advance so that you can get through the registration process quickly.

Once registration opens, "Register Now" buttons will appear below each race. Clicking any of them will place you into a virtual queue, where wait times can exceed an hour. Be patient and do not refresh or leave the page. When you reach the end of the countdown, you will be directed to the registration site. At this point, you can register for any of the races or challenges that haven't sold out, regardless of which "Register Now" button you clicked. To complete the process as efficiently as possible, be ready with your name, email address, phone number, mailing address, and emergency contact information.

COST

RUNDISNEY RACES ARE NOT A CHEAP WAY to experience the theme parks. Still, the unique entertainment offered along each course, the exclusive medals, and the opportunity to run with thousands of other Disney fans mean that events are still in high demand despite the cost. Prices for the 2025 season were as follows:

- **5K** $112–$114
- **10K** $155–$161
- **10-MILER** $221
- **HALF MARATHON** $224–$246
- **MARATHON** $242
- **CHALLENGE** $400 (Two-Course)–$688 (Dopey)

Your registration fee includes your race bib, your finisher medal, and a race shirt. After the race, you'll also receive a snack box and hydration. The fee doesn't include theme park admission, a resort stay, your race photos, or any merchandise.

RUNDISNEY EXPO

YOUR RUNDISNEY RACE WEEKEND kicks off at the RunDisney Expo at the ESPN Wide World of Sports Complex, where you'll pick up your required race bib. If you're staying at a Walt Disney World resort, complimentary bus transportation to the expo is available. Otherwise, you'll need to drive (parking is free) or use Uber, Lyft, or a Minnie Van. After getting your bib, you can pick up your race shirt and explore the expo, which offers a variety of running gear, themed merchandise, and exclusive souvenirs.

TREAT YOURSELF *in* WALT DISNEY WORLD

YOU'VE JUST COMPLETED another 30,000-step day in the theme parks, and after you get the kids into bed, you realize you barely have enough energy to crawl into bed yourself. Fortunately, there are plenty of ways to pamper yourself and your ailing body in the World.

SENSES SPA

LOCATED AT THE GRAND FLORIDIAN, Senses is easily the best spa in the Disney area, offering a luxurious escape from the hustle and bustle of the parks. It has all the bells and whistles (actually, that doesn't sound very relaxing—make that tranquil music and soft lighting) you could hope for. The elegant décor is tasteful, and everything from the seamless check-in process to the cozy lounge to your actual treatment exudes serenity, pampering, and relaxation.

You can book spa treatments online, but reservations don't integrate well with My Disney Experience, so make sure you save your confirmation and set a reminder. You're encouraged to check in 30–60 minutes before your treatment to allow time to unwind and enjoy the lounge, which is a major part of the experience.

Senses offers massages (solo or couples), facials, nail services, haircuts and styling, and makeup consultations. There is also a dedicated menu for kids and teens. Prices range from $55 for an express manicure to $310 for an 80-minute Grand Signature Massage.

Once you check in for your appointment, you'll be invited to choose a stone that will help set the tone for your experience. This small ritual determines elements like the lighting in your treatment room or the scent of the products used. But you can always request to change these anyway.

After you make your selection, you'll be guided to the gender-specific lounge, where first-time visitors receive a brief tour and an overview of the spa's amenities. The lounge includes locker rooms, well-appointed restrooms, plush lounge chairs with optional blankets and curtains, and a wet lounge. If you'd like to use the wet lounge, you'll need to bring a swimsuit—you'll have access to a sauna, a hot bath area, and heated tile loungers (a personal favorite of Becky's).

At your appointment time, an attendant will escort you to a private treatment room and then back to the lounge afterward. Once you're ready to leave, you'll complete your payment at the front desk.

While Senses Spa is undeniably a splurge, the experience is worth every penny, especially after long days of walking through the parks.

A massage here is the perfect way to melt away stress and recharge for the rest of your trip.

IN-ROOM OPTIONS

IF YOU'RE LOOKING FOR A MORE PRIVATE or perhaps more budget-friendly alternative to Disney's in-park spa experiences, a number of options have emerged in recent years. The **Ear for Each Other** Facebook group (facebook.com/groups/earforeachother) was created during the pandemic to support laid-off or furloughed cast members. Some of these cast members launched their own businesses that helped replace offerings that were suspended at Disney at the time (like in-room makeovers, Bibbidi Bobbidi Boutique–style experiences, or spa treatments). Even now that Disney services are available again, many guests continue to choose these independent providers for the flexibility, affordability, and exceptional customer service they provide. Whether you're looking for a customized princess makeover, an in-room massage, or other personal services, these small businesses provide a unique and often more personalized alternative to Disney's official options.

MASSAGES One such option that's directly comparable to Senses Spa is an in-room massage at your Walt Disney World resort. Denise from **Sol, A Wellness Company** (solwellnessllc.com) offers a variety of massage options, all in the comfort of your room. Times are flexible, and prices are reasonable. To compare: In 2024, a 50-minute massage at Senses Spa cost $180 plus tax and tip, while a 60-minute massage with Denise in a room at the Riviera was $130 plus tip. That's a savings of more than 25%. Of course, there are trade-offs. There's no spa lounge, and your room needs to have enough space for the heated massage table to be set up. But the convenience of skipping the trip to the Grand Floridian, avoiding crowds, and enjoying a treatment in total privacy makes the experience even more relaxing. For those who love to treat themselves while getting the best value, an in-room massage is a stress-free, budget-friendly way to unwind at Disney.

MAKEOVERS Whether for kids or adults, in-room makeovers offer a fun and personalized way to add a little extra magic to your Disney trip. These services gained popularity during the pandemic when Bibbidi Bobbidi Boutique and Harmony Barber Shop were closed, and they've remained a guest favorite for their convenience, flexibility, and unique offerings.

A search on Ear for Each Other for these services returns countless options. You can get haircuts (even first haircuts), extensions, hairstyling, makeup, and more. In 2022, Becky got her younger daughter's first haircut from **Selina Ashley,** one of the vendors on Ear for Each Other, in their room at Caribbean Beach. Both of her girls also got their hair curled (and glittered, of course) and a little princess makeup applied for a day at the Magic Kingdom that included lunch at the castle—an unforgettable experience for all.

In late 2024, they treated themselves to custom henna from another Ear for Each Other vendor, **@two4art** on Instagram. Each of them chose a design—artistic Mary Poppins accessories for Becky, Pinocchio for her younger daughter, and a capybara from *Encanto* for her older daughter—and the results were stunning. Not only did they receive tons of compliments in the parks, but the henna also became a unique take-home souvenir that lasted for over a week.

SPECIAL DELIVERIES If you've never indulged in chocolate or other sweet treats at Disney World, you're missing out, especially when there are vendors that deliver them directly to your resort. One of Becky's family's favorites is **A New Hope Confections** (anewhopeco.com), which makes some of the most delicious and beautifully crafted chocolate they've ever had—and from a family of chocolate aficionados, that's saying something. Jenna and Dean, the talented duo behind the company, are former Disney cast members who design, handcraft, and deliver their creations themselves. Once when Becky picked up her chocolates from bell services, Goofy and Donald, who were in the lobby greeting guests, came over to try to "steal" the chocolates—they're that good.

The WILDERNESS MUST *be* EXPLORED

MORE RECREATIONAL OPPORTUNITIES are offered at **Fort Wilderness** than at any other Walt Disney World resort. And you don't have to be staying there to participate. Some activities require reservations, while others can be arranged on-site upon arrival.

Tri-Circle-D Ranch (located just behind Pioneer Hall, which hosts the *Hoop-Dee-Doo Musical Revue*) is easily accessible by boat from the Magic Kingdom or Wilderness Lodge. This is where many of the horses and ponies that serve Walt Disney World spend their time when they're not working. You can visit the animals or even take a carriage ride or pony ride. The pony ride is a perfect, quick animal interaction for kids who meet the requirements (riders must be at least 3 years old, under 80 pounds, and no taller than 48 inches).

If you'd like to explore more of the resort, you can take a **Segway tour** ($90–$99 per person) or **rent bikes, canoes, or kayaks** to navigate the resort's scenic trails and waterways. Fort Wilderness even offers **archery lessons** ($49 per person), if you really want to feel like you're at summer camp. The fun doesn't stop there—**crafting sessions** and **gem panning** are also available, making Fort Wilderness an incredible destination for outdoor and hands-on activities.

BIG COMPETITION *at* MINIATURE GOLF

DECADES AGO, Disney execs noticed that families were venturing outside the WDW bubble to enjoy a little friendly competition on the minigolf courses. Their solution? Bringing the fun to Disney property. The result was **Fantasia Gardens and Fairways Miniature Golf,** an 11-acre complex that offers two 18-hole courses. The **Fantasia Gardens** course is an adventure-style course themed after Disney's animated film *Fantasia*. More about story than skill, it features whimsical obstacles and playful water features. The **Fantasia Fairways** course is a true test of skill for older children and adults. Complete with sand traps and water hazards, it's a very convincing miniature golf course in the truest sense. It's what we imagine would result from Ant-Man shrinking a real golf course. Both of the courses are beautifully landscaped, featuring fountains, statues, topiaries, and creative details that make for magical minigolf play.

Located on Epcot Resorts Boulevard, right by the Swan Reserve, Fantasia Gardens is easily accessible. To reach the course, you can either arrange your own transportation or take a bus or boat to the Swan, Dolphin, or Swan Reserve and walk over. The Fantasia Gardens course is open daily, 10 a.m.–10 p.m.; the Fantasia Fairways course closes an hour earlier. The cost to putt is $19 for adults and $12 for kids ages 3–9 (plus tax). It's expensive minigolf, but you can't put a price on defeating your loved ones at Disney.

Winter Summerland Miniature Golf offers another two-course property near Blizzard Beach water park. The **Winter Course** has a "blizzard in Florida" theme, and the **Summer Course** boasts a tropical-holiday theme. Both courses are easier than the Fantasia Gardens and Fairways courses, making them a good choice for families with young children. Daily operating hours for both courses are 10 a.m.–10 p.m., and the cost is the same at both.

SKILL UP!

LOOKING TO PICK UP A NEW TRICK OR TWO while on vacation? Walt Disney World offers plenty of ways to learn something fun and memorable in a hands-on class. It's a great way to bring a little Disney magic home with you.

Coronado Springs has two offerings you won't find at other resorts. First, you can enroll at **Sangria University** ($69–$79 per person, plus tax and tip; age 21 and up) at Three Bridges Bar and Grill. Offered on Saturdays and Sundays, the 2-hour afternoon class covers the history of sangria and reveals recipes for the restaurant's four house-made varieties. You'll get to taste them all, enjoy a light appetizer, and make your own glass of sangria from a selection of fruits and spirits.

Every Friday afternoon at Coronado Springs, **Colors of Coronado** ($45 per person, plus tax) invites guests to create their own Disney-themed painting on an 11-by-14-inch canvas. A local artist provides step-by-step guidance, and the featured design changes monthly. The class takes place at Toledo, where the views add to the relaxing atmosphere. It's a creative way to spend an afternoon at Disney.

Over at **Disney Springs,** you can try your hand at cake artistry with a **Cake Decorating Class** at **Amorette's Patisserie.** Typically offered once per day, in the morning, this 90-minute class allows you to create a Mickey Mouse or Minnie Mouse dome cake. (Mickey is offered Sunday, Tuesday, Thursday, and Saturday, and Minnie is offered Monday, Wednesday, and Friday. Each has different flavors, so make sure you book the one that sounds better to you.) The class sizes are small, so you'll get plenty of hands-on instruction as you learn professional decorating techniques. One reservation ($199, plus tax) gets you a table for up to two people (you'll pay the same price if you're solo) and complimentary beverages, including alcoholic options for those age 21 and older. While this class offers a fun introduction to cake decorating, it's important to know that the cakes come preassembled and iced. Participants pour glaze and add fondant decorations rather than building the cake from scratch. Still, it's a great way to create something beautiful and delicious to take back to your resort.

The Ear for Each Other Facebook group (see page 515• Where can I play minigolf with my family? (page 516)
) also has a bevy of options for upskilling while in your room or elsewhere at your Disney resort. There are plenty of options to explore, but one standout is a private **Jedi training session.** Before the pandemic, one of the most popular experiences at Disney's Hollywood Studios was Jedi Training Academy. Families rushed to sign up for this free show, where their children would learn the ways of The Force before battling a *Star Wars* villain. Although Disney hasn't brought back the show, former Jedi master **Justin Aldridge** continues to train young Padawans in private sessions at Disney resorts.

Becky's daughters had a lesson with him during their 2023 vacation at Animal Kingdom Lodge, where they practiced using the lightsabers they'd built at **Tatooine Traders** (Justin can provide lightsabers if you don't have your own). The session far exceeded expectations. Justin emphasized focus, control, and discipline as opposed to chaotic lightsaber swinging. He explains lightsaber colors; the Jedi philosophy of keeping the peace and fighting only as a last resort; and the importance of practicing any skill you want to hone—all lessons that apply in real life as much as they do in *Star Wars.*

At the time of our lesson, Justin charged $75 for one participant and $25 for each additional participant. The base lesson is 30 minutes, but Justin happily sticks around for more-advanced training or answering questions about the parks. Our session ended up being about 45 minutes. Families often comment that Jedi training with Justin was the highlight of their trip.

If you're more inclined toward art and animation, consider a **private drawing lesson** with **Jason Zucker,** a Disney animator who has created designs for pins, watches, and collectibles. If you love the Animation Academy offered at Animal Kingdom or on Disney Cruise Line but want something more personalized, this is the option for you. Jason offers both in-person and virtual animation classes, and you'll learn real drawing skills tailored to your experience level, rather than simply following along. He'll come to your Disney resort for a one-on-one or small group session, or you can book a virtual lesson after your vacation.

ACCOMMODATIONS INDEX

Note: Page numbers in **bold** indicate a resort's main entry.

Airbnb, 182
Alligator Bayou. *See* Port Orleans Resort—French Quarter and Port Orleans Resort—Riverside, Disney's
All-Star Resorts (Movies, Music, Sports), Disney's, **160-64**
   amenities/services and recreation, 93, 95, 96, 161-63
   as an author pick, 107
   contact information, 37
   costs, 61, 79, 91, 92, 94
   dining, 204
   information table, 194, 195
   lighting in, 105
   map, 12-13, 162
   noise, 99, 105, 106, 161, 163
   readers' report card, 108-9, 110
   room diagram, 104
   room quality/type, 89, 160-64
   room size, 99, 161
   theme, 96, 98, 161, 163-64
   transportation to/from, 14, 164, 338, 340-41, 439, 487
Animal Kingdom Lodge & Villas, Disney's, **154-57**
   amenities/services and recreation, 95, 96, 154-57
   as an author pick, 107
   costs, 85, 92, 94
   dining, 97, 155-57, 202, 212, 242-44, 250, 262-63, 271-72, 273-74, 284, 288
   information table, 194, 195
   map, 12-13, 155
   older guests, 324
   readers' report card, 108-9
   romantic getaways, 328
   room diagram, 100
   room quality/type, 83, 89, 90, 91, 154-57
   theme, 95, 98, 154, 156
   transportation to/from, 14, 156, 338, 340-41, 439
Animal Kingdom resorts, **153-69**. *See also* All-Star Resorts (Movies, Music, Sports), Disney's; Animal Kingdom Lodge & Villas, Disney's; Art of Animation Resort, Disney's; Coronado Springs Resort, Disney's; Pop Century Resort, Disney's
Art of Animation Resort, Disney's, **166-69**
   amenities/services and recreation, 93, 95, 96, 166-69
   as an author pick, 107
   costs, 92, 94
   dining, 204
   dog policies, 362
   information table, 195
   map, 12-13, 167
   noise, 99, 105, 168
   readers' report card, 108-9
   room diagram, 104
   room quality/type, 89, 166-67, 168-69
   room size, 99
   theme, 96, 98, 167
   transportation to/from, 93, 168, 293, 338, 340-41, 344, 345, 405, 459
Aventura Hotel, Universal's, **187,** 199

Bay Lake Tower. *See* Contemporary Resort & Bay Lake Tower, Disney's
Beach Club Resort and Beach Club Villas, Disney's, **129-32**
   amenities/services and recreation, 96, 129-32
   as an author pick, 107
   costs, 85, 92, 94
   dining, 97, 131, 216, 242, 243, 247-48, 251
   information table, 194, 195
   map, 12-13, 130
   noise, 106
   readers' report card, 108-9
   room diagram, 100, 101
   room quality/type, 89, 91, 131-32

See also the Restaurant Index on pages 525-528 and the Subject Index on pages 529-547.

ACCOMMODATIONS INDEX

Beach Club Resort and Beach Club Villas *(continued)*
  theme, 98, 129-30
  transportation to/from, 9, 32, 93, 131, 340-41, 344
BoardWalk Inn & Villas, Disney's, **133-36**
  amenities/services and recreation, 95, 96, 133-36
  contact information, 37
  costs, 85, 92, 94
  dining, 97, 244-45, 257, 283
  information table, 194
  location of, 16
  map, 12-13, 134
  noise, 106, 135, 136
  readers' report card, 108-9
  room diagram, 100, 101
  room quality/type, 89, 91, 135-36
  theme, 98, 133
  transportation to/from, 9, 32, 93, 133, 338, 340-41, 344
Bonnet Creek resorts, 93, **143-53**. *See also* Old Key West Resort, Disney's; Port Orleans Resort—French Quarter and Port Orleans Resort—Riverside, Disney's; Saratoga Springs Resort & Spa, Disney's; Treehouse Villas at Disney's Saratoga Springs Resort & Spa
Boulder Ridge Villas at Disney's Wilderness Lodge. *See* Wilderness Lodge, Boulder Ridge Villas, and Copper Creek Villas & Cabins, Disney's

Cabana Bay Beach Resort, Universal's, **187,** 199
camping. *See* Fort Wilderness Resort & Campground, Disney's
Caribbean Beach Resort, Disney's, **139-42**
  amenities/services and recreation, 95, 96, 139-42
  as an author pick, 107
  contact information, 37
  costs, 92, 94
  dining, 140, 204, 244-45, 275
  information table, 195
  map, 12-13, 141
  noise, 99, 105, 106
  readers' report card, 108-9
  room diagram, 104
  room quality/type, 89, 90, 140, 141-42
  theme, 98, 139-42
  transportation to/from, 93, 140, 142, 293, 338, 340-41, 343, 344, 345, 405, 459
Club Wyndham Bonnet Creek, 93
condominiums, vacation rental, 183-86
Contemporary Resort & Bay Lake Tower, Disney's, **123-26**
  amenities/services and recreation, 93, 95, 96, 123-26

contact information, 37
costs, 85, 92, 94
dining, 124, 202, 212, 216, 242-43, 245, 250-51, 252-53, 277, 347
information table, 194, 195
lighting in, 105
map, 12-13, 124
noise, 99, 105, 106
readers' report card, 108-9
romantic getaways, 328
room diagram, 100, 101
room quality/type, 89, 90, 91, 123-26
theme, 96, 97, 98, 123-24
transportation to/from, 8, 32, 93, 123, 338, 340-41, 344, 364-65, 495
Copper Creek Villas & Cabins at Disney's Wilderness Lodge. *See* Wilderness Lodge, Boulder Ridge Villas, and Copper Creek Villas & Cabins, Disney's
Coronado Springs Resort, Disney's, 15, **157-60**
  amenities/services and recreation, 95, 96, 157-60
  contact information, 37
  costs, 61, 92, 94, 158
  dining, 158, 204, 242-43, 245, 265-66, 280-81, 282
  information table, 195
  map, 12-13, 159
  readers' report card, 108-9
  room diagram, 103-4
  room quality/type, 89, 90, 157-60
  theme, 98, 158
  transportation to/from, 14, 158, 338, 340-41, 343, 439, 487

Disney Deluxe Villa (DDV) resorts. *See* Disney Vacation Club (DVC) resorts
Disney Springs Resort Area (DSRA), **173-78**. *See also* DoubleTree Suites by Hilton Orlando—Disney Springs Area; Drury Plaza Hotel Orlando; Hilton Orlando Buena Vista Palace; Hilton Orlando Lake Buena Vista—Disney Springs Area; Holiday Inn Orlando—Disney Springs Resort Area; Renaissance Orlando Resort and Spa; Wyndham Garden Lake Buena Vista
  amenities/services and recreation, 79, 80, 173-74
  costs, 174
  dining and reservations, 97, 202-3, 210, 239-41, 242-45, 249, 252, 254, 256, 258, 260-71, 277-80, 283-84, 286-87
  transportation to/from, 174, 338-39, 340-41, 344, 499
Disney Vacation Club (DVC) resorts, 79, 80, 85-87, 100-103.
Dockside Inn & Suites, at Universal's Endless Summer Resort, **188,** 199

See also the Restaurant Index on pages 525-528 and the Subject Index on pages 529-547.

Dolphin, Walt Disney World, **136–39**
  amenities/services and recreation, 79, 80, 95, 96, 136–38
  contact information, 37
  costs, 92, 94, 137
  dining and reservations, 97, 210, 212, 243, 244–45, 246, 257–58, 272, 281
  Early Theme Park Entry and, 34
  information table, 199
  map, 12–13, 138
  readers' report card, 108–9
  refurbishment, 137
  room quality/type, 89, 137, 139
  theme, 96, 97, 98
  transportation to/from, 9, 32, 91, 93, 136, 137, 338, 340–41, 344
DoubleTree Suites by Hilton Orlando—Disney Springs Area, 12–13, 97, **174–75,** 197. See also Disney Springs Resort Area (DSRA)
Drury Plaza Hotel Orlando, 97, **175,** 196. See also Disney Springs Resort Area (DSRA)

Endless Summer Resort, Universal's, **188,** 198, 199
EPCOT resorts, **129–43**. See also Beach Club Resort and Beach Club Villas, Disney's; BoardWalk Inn & Villas, Disney's; Dolphin, Walt Disney World; Swan, Walt Disney World; Swan Reserve, Walt Disney World; Yacht Club Resort, Disney's
Evermore Orlando Resort, **188,** 196
Flamingo Crossings, **192–93**
Florida Dream Homes, 186
Fort Wilderness Resort & Campground, Disney's, 85, 89, **169–73**
  amenities/services and recreation, 93, 95, 96, 169, 172
  attractions at, 516
  campsites, 169
  contact information, 37
  costs, 94, 169
  dining, 97, 204, 210
  dog policies, 362
  information table, 194
  map, 10–13, 170–71
  older guests, 324
  parking, 107
  readers' report card, 108–9, 110
  room and site quality/type, 91, 172–73
  room diagram, 103
  room size, 98, 99
  transportation to/from, 8–9, 91, 93, 172, 173, 339, 340–41, 344, 365, 495
Four Seasons Resort Orlando at Walt Disney World Resort, 12–13, 79, 80, 94–95, **188,** 196, 361
  dining, 217

Early Theme Park Entry and, 34, 79
French Quarter, Port Orleans Resort. See Port Orleans Resort—French Quarter and Port Orleans Resort—Riverside, Disney's

Gaylord Palms Resort & Convention Center, **190,** 197
Gran Destino Tower, **157–160**
  amenities/services and recreation, 96
  costs, 92, 94
  map, 12–13, 159
  noise, 99, 105
  room diagram, 103
  theme, 98
Grand Floridian Resort & Spa, Disney's, and The Villas at Disney's Grand Floridian Resort & Spa, **110–14**
  amenities/services and recreation, 95, 96, 110–13
  contact information, 37
  costs, 79, 85, 92, 94
  dining, 97, 202, 212, 217, 242–45, 254, 259, 267–68, 285–86
  information table, 194, 198
  map, 12–13, 112
  noise, 99, 105
  readers' report card, 108–9
  romantic getaways, 328
  room diagram, 100, 101
  room quality/type, 83, 89, 90, 91, 110–14
  room size, 98
  Senses Spa, 514–15
  theme, 98, 111
  transportation to/from, 8, 32, 91, 93, 338, 340–41, 343, 344, 364–65, 495
Hard Rock Hotel Orlando, **187,** 197
Helios Grand Hotel, Universal's, **188,** 198
Hilton Orlando Buena Vista Palace, 12–13, 97, **175–76,** 197. See also Disney Springs Resort Area (DSRA)
Hilton Orlando Lake Buena Vista—Disney Springs Resort Area, 97, **177,** 196. See also Disney Springs Resort Area (DSRA)
Holiday Inn Club Vacations at Orange Lake Resort, **190,** 196
Holiday Inn Orlando—Disney Springs Resort Area, 12–13, 97, **177**. See also Disney Springs Resort Area (DSRA)
Home2Suites by Hilton, **192,** 197
Homewood Suites by Hilton Orlando at Flamingo Crossings, **192,** 197

I-4 corridor and Lake Buena Vista resort area, 180, 181, **188–90**
International Drive (I-Drive) resort area, 180, 181, **187–88**
Irlo Bronson Memorial Highway (US 192) resort area, 180, 181, **190–91**

See also the Restaurant Index on pages 525–528 and the Subject Index on pages 529–547.

ACCOMMODATIONS INDEX

Jambo House. *See* Animal Kingdom Lodge & Villas, Disney's

Kidani Village. *See* Animal Kingdom Lodge & Villas, Disney's

Lake Buena Vista and I-4 corridor resort area, 180, 181, **188–90**
Loews Portofino Bay Hotel at Universal Orlando, **187,** 197
Loews Royal Pacific Resort at Universal Orlando, **187,** 196
Loews Sapphire Falls Resort at Universal Orlando, **187,** 196

Magic Kingdom resorts, **110–29**. *See also* Contemporary Resort & Bay Lake Tower, Disney's; Grand Floridian Resort & Spa, Disney's; Polynesian Village Resort, Villas & Bungalows, Disney's
Margaritaville Resort Orlando, **190,** 196
Marriott's Harbour Lake, 61, **188,** 197

Old Key West Resort, Disney's, **147–49**
  amenities/services and recreation, 95, 96, 147–49
  as an author pick, 107
  contact information, 37
  costs, 85, 94
  dining, 242, 268–69
  information table, 194
  map, 12–13, 148
  readers' report card, 108–9
  room diagram, 101
  room quality/type, 89, 91, 149
  room size, 98
  theme, 98, 149
  transportation to/from, 93, 149, 338, 340–41, 343, 344, 499

Polynesian Isles Resort (Diamond Resorts), **190,** 197
Polynesian Village Resort, Villas & Bungalows, Disney's, 15, **114–19**
  amenities/services and recreation, 93, 95, 96, 114–19
  contact information, 37
  costs, 85, 92, 94
  dining, 115, 117, 202, 217, 245, 264, 268
  information table, 194, 195
  lighting in, 105
  map, 12–13, 116
  noise, 99, 105, 117, 118
  readers' report card, 108–9
  remodeling/refurbishments, 115
  romantic getaways, 328
  room diagram, 100, 102, 103
  room quality/type, 89, 90, 91, 114–19
  room size, 98, 99
  theme, 95, 98, 115
  transportation to/from, 8, 91, 93, 117, 118, 119, 338, 340–41, 343, 344, 364–65, 495
Pop Century Resort, Disney's, **165–66**
  amenities/services and recreation, 93, 95, 96, 165–66
  as an author pick, 107
  contact information, 37
  costs, 79, 92, 94
  dining, 165–66, 204
  information table, 195
  map, 12–13, 167
  noise, 165
  readers' report card, 108–9
  room diagram, 104
  room quality/type, 89, 165–66
  theme, 96, 97, 98
  transportation to/from, 93, 166, 293, 338, 340–41, 344, 345, 405, 459
Portofino Bay Hotel at Universal Orlando, Loews, **187,** 197
Port Orleans Resort—French Quarter and Port Orleans Resort—Riverside, Disney's, **150–53**
  amenities/services and recreation, 95, 96, 150–53
  as an author pick, 107
  contact information, 37
  costs, 92, 94
  dining, 151, 152, 204, 243, 249–50
  dog policies, 362
  information table, 195, 196
  lighting in, 105
  map, 12–13, 150, 151
  noise, 99, 105, 106, 153
  readers' report card, 108–9
  refurbishment, 151, 152
  romantic getaways, 328
  room diagram, 104
  room quality/type, 89, 90, 150–53
  theme, 98, 150–53
  transportation to/from, 93, 151, 152–53, 338, 340–41, 343, 344, 499

Quality Inn & Suites by the Parks, 61

Renaissance Orlando Resort and Spa, 97, **177,** 197
rental homes and condominiums, 183–86
Residence Inn Orlando at Flamingo Crossings, **192,** 198
Riverside, Disney's Port Orleans Resort. *See* Port Orleans Resort—French Quarter and Port Orleans Resort—Riverside, Disney's
Riviera Resort, Disney's, 15, **142–43**
  amenities/services and recreation, 93, 95, 96, 142–43

See also the Restaurant Index on pages 525–528 and the Subject Index on pages 529–547.

ACCOMMODATIONS INDEX

contact information, 37
costs, 85, 94
dining, 143, 212, 217, 244, 282–83
information table, 196
lighting in, 105
map, 12–13, 141
noise, 99, 105
readers' report card, 108–9, 110
romantic getaways, 328
room diagram, 103
room quality/type, 89, 91, 142–43
room size, 99
theme, 98, 142–43
transportation to/from, 91, 93, 143, 338, 340–41, 344, 345, 405, 459
Royal Pacific Resort at Universal Orlando, Loews, **187,** 196

Sapphire Falls Resort at Universal Orlando, Loews, **187,** 196
Saratoga Springs Resort & Spa, Disney's, **143–47**
 amenities/services and recreation, 95, 96, 146
 contact information, 37
 costs, 61, 85, 94
 dining, 97, 203, 243, 284
 information table, 196, 198
 map, 12–13, 144
 noise, 99, 105
 older guests, 324
 readers' report card, 108–9
 room diagram, 102
 room quality/type, 89, 91, 145, 146
 theme, 96, 97, 98, 145
 transportation to/from, 93, 146, 338, 340–41, 343, 344, 499
Shades of Green, **126–29**
 amenities/services and recreation, 34, 79, 80, 95, 96, 126–29
 contact information, 37
 costs, 94
 dining and reservations, 127
 information table, 198
 map, 12–13, 128
 readers' report card, 108–9
 room quality/type, 89, 127
 transportation to/from, 8–9, 91, 128–29, 338, 340–41
Sheraton Vistana Resort Villas Lake Buena Vista/Orlando, 61, **190,** 198
Sheraton Vistana Villages Resort Villas, I-Drive/Orlando, 187, 199
Signia by Hilton Orlando Bonnet Creek, 12–13, 79, 80, 93, 190, 199
Sonesta ES Suites Lake Buena Vista, 79, 190, 199
SpringHill Suites Orlando at Flamingo Crossings, 192, 198

Stella Nova Resort, Universal's, **188,** 198
Surfside Inn & Suites, at Universal's Endless Summer Resort **188,** 198
Swan, Walt Disney World, **136–39**
 amenities/services and recreation, 79, 80, 95, 96, 136–38
 contact information, 37
 costs, 92, 94, 137
 dining and reservations, 97, 210, 212, 243–44, 259, 261–62, 264
 Early Theme Park Entry and, 34
 information table, 199
 map, 12–13, 138
 readers' report card, 108–9
 refurbishment, 137
 room quality/type, 89, 137, 139
 theme, 96, 97, 98
 transportation to/from, 9, 32, 91, 93, 136, 137, 338, 340–41, 344
Swan Reserve, Walt Disney World, **136–39**
 amenities/services and recreation, 79, 80, 95, 96, 136–38
 contact information, 37
 costs, 89, 92, 94
 dining, 97, 138, 210, 247
 Early Theme Park Entry and, 34
 information table, 199
 map, 12–13, 138
 readers' report card, 108–9
 room quality/type, 90, 139
 theme, 96, 97, 98
 transportation to/from, 9, 32, 93, 136, 338, 340–41

Terra Luna Resort, Universal's, **188,** 199
TownePlace Suites Orlando at Flamingo Crossings, **192,** 198
Treehouse Villas at Disney's Saratoga Springs Resort & Spa, **146–47**
 amenities/services and recreation, 96, 147
 costs, 85, 94, 147
 information table, 198
 map, 12–13, 145
 noise, 106
 room diagram, 102
 room quality/type, 147
 room size, 98
 transportation to/from, 147

Universal Orlando accommodations, 181–82
Universal's Aventura Hotel, **187,** 199
Universal's Cabana Bay Beach Resort, **187,** 199
Universal's Endless Summer Resort, **188,** 198, 199
Universal's Helios Grand Hotel, **188,** 198
Universal's Stella Nova Resort, **188,** 198

See also the Restaurant Index on pages 525–528 and the Subject Index on pages 529–547.

ACCOMMODATIONS INDEX

Universal's Terra Luna Resort, **188,** 199
US 192 (Irlo Bronson Memorial Highway) resort area, 180, 181, **190–91**
vacation rental homes, 182, 183–86
Villas at Disney's Grand Floridian Resort & Spa, The. *See* Grand Floridian Resort & Spa, Disney's, and The Villas at Disney's Grand Floridian Resort & Spa
Visit Orlando (website), 186
Vrbo (vacation rentals by owner), 182, 186

Waldorf Astoria Orlando, 12–13, 34, 79, 80, 93, **190,** 198
Wilderness Lodge, Boulder Ridge Villas, and Copper Creek Villas & Cabins, Disney's, 15, **119–23**
 amenities/services and recreation, 95, 96, 119–23
 as an author pick, 107
 contact information, 37
 costs, 85, 92, 94
 dining, 121, 216, 242, 278, 286
 information table, 194, 195, 197
 lighting in, 105
 map, 12–13, 120
 noise, 106
 readers' report card, 108–9, 110
 remodeling/refurbishments, 121
 romantic getaways, 328
 room diagram, 100, 102
 room quality/type, 89, 91, 119–23
 theme, 95, 98, 119–20
 transportation to/from, 8–9, 93, 121, 338, 340–41, 344, 365, 495
Wyndham Garden Lake Buena Vista, 12–13, 97, **178,** 198. *See also* Disney Springs Resort Area (DSRA)
Wyndham Grand Orlando Resort Bonnet Creek, 12–13, 93

Yacht Club Resort, Disney's, **129–32**
 amenities/services and recreation, 92, 95, 96, 129–32
 as an author pick, 107
 contact information, 37
 costs, 92, 94
 dining, 97, 131, 212, 242, 245, 247, 288
 dog policies, 362
 information table, 197
 map, 12–13, 130
 noise, 99, 105
 readers' report card, 108–9
 romantic getaways, 328
 room diagram, 100
 room quality/type, 83, 89, 90, 132
 theme, 98, 129–30
 transportation to/from, 9, 32, 93, 131, 338, 340–41, 344

See also the Restaurant Index on pages 525–528 and the Subject Index on pages 529–547.

RESTAURANT INDEX

Note: Page numbers in **bold** indicate a restaurant's main entry.

ABC Commissary, 224, **237**, 460, 466
Akershus Royal Banquet Hall, 209, 211, 216, 220, 245, **246-47**, 313, 407
Ale & Compass Restaurant, 242, **247**, 251
Aloha Isle, **229**, 367, 374
Amare, 138, 210, 244, **247**
Amorette's Patisserie, **239**, 503, 517-18
AmphiBar, 504
Artist Point, 215, 216, 242, **278**, 313
Atlantic Dance Hall, 510
Auntie Gravity's Galactic Goodies, 229
Avalunch, 488

Backlot Express, 224, **237**, 460
Bar Riva, 93, 143
BaseLine Tap House, 224, **228**
Basket, The, 287
B.B. Wolf's Sausage Co., 501
Beaches & Cream Soda Shop, 209, 242, **247-48**
Benihana, 177
Be Our Guest Restaurant, 218, 225, 243, 244, **248**, 367, 382
Biergarten Restaurant, 220, 225, 243, 244, **248-49**, 319-20, 407, 412, 425
Big River Grille & Brewing Works, 134
Blaze Fast-Fire'd Pizza, 20, 202, **239**
Boathouse, The, 202, 209, 210, 211, 245, **249**, 269, 278, 504
Boatwright's Dining Hall, 152, 201, 243, **249-50**
Boma—Flavors of Africa, 97, 155, 202, 242, 243, **250**
Bourbon Steak by Michael Mina, 246

Cake Bake Shop, The, 134, 210, **246**
California Grill, 124, 202, 212, 242, **250-51**, 326

Capa, 210, 211
Cape May Café, 216, 242, 243, **251**, 313
Captain Cooks, 93, 320
Casey's Corner, 219, **229**, 367, 374
Catalina Eddie's, 224, 237, 460, 466
Centertown Market, 204
Chef Art Smith's Homecomin', 202, 209, 242, **252**, 269, 278
Chef Mickey's, 124, 209, 215, 216, 243, **252-53**, 313
Chefs de France, 220, 244, **253**, 266, 319-20, 407
Cheshire Café, 229-30
Chicken Guy!, **239**
Chronos Club, 90, 158
Cinderella's Royal Table, 208-9, 215, 216, 218, 225, 243, **253-54**, 313, 367, 374
Citricos, 202, 212, 226, 242, **254**
City Works Eatery and Pour House, 242, **254**,
Columbia Harbour House, 219, **230**, 320, 356, 367
Connections Cafe and Connections Eatery, 221, **232-33**, 407
Contempo Café, 124
Cookes of Dublin, **239-40**, 271
Cooling Hut, 488
Coral Reef Restaurant, 220, 226, 245, **254-55**, 407, 420
Cosmic Ray's Starlight Café, 219, **230**, 320, 367, 386
Covington Mill, 177
Creature Comforts, **235**, 437
Crystal Palace, The, 216, 218, 243, **255-56**, 313, 367

Daily Poutine, The, 501
Diamond Horseshoe, The, 218, 367

See also the Accommodations Index on pages 519–524 and the Subject Index on pages 529–547.

RESTAURANT INDEX

Disney's Candy Cauldron, 504
D-Luxe Burger, 20, **240,** 320
Docking Bay 7 Food and Cargo, 223, **237-38,** 320, 460, 466, 478
Dockside Diner, 224, **238,** 460, 466
Dockside Margaritas, 504

Earl of Sandwich, **240**
Edison, The, 210, 242, **256,** 504
Eet by Maneet Chauhan, 202, 240
Eight Spoon Café, 222, 223, **235,** 437, 444
El Mercado de Coronado Food Court, 204
Enchanted Rose, 228
End Zone Food Court, 204
Enzo's Hideaway, 210, 504
Erin McKenna's Bakery NYC, 500
Everglazed Donuts & Cold Brew, 500
EverGreen Cafe, 175
Evergreens Sports Bar, 127
Everything POP, 204
Express Café, 127

Fairfax Fare, 224, **238,** 460
Fantasmic! Dining Package, 208-9, 467-68
Festival Favorites/Outdoor Kitchen—Florida Fresh, **233,** 407, 412
Fife & Drum Tavern, **233,** 407
50's Prime Time Cafe, 224, 226, 242, **256-57,** 460, 466
Flame Tree Barbecue, 223, **235,** 437, 444
Flying Fish, 210, 212, 245, **257**
Food Trucks at Exposition Park, 500
Fountain, The, 243, **257-58**
Friar's Nook, The, **230,** 367, 374
Frontera Cocina, 210, 245, **258,** 504
Front Porch/Smokehouse at House of Blues, The, 500
Frostbite Freddy's, 488

Ganachery, The, 503
Garden Gallery, 127
Garden Grill Restaurant, 203, 215, 216, 220, 242, 253, 256, **258-59,** 313, 327, 407, 412
Garden Grove, 243, 259
Gasparilla Island Grill, 320
Gaston's Tavern, **230,** 367, 382
Geo-82, 228
Geyser Point Bar & Grill, 121
Gideon's Bakehouse, 503
Golden Oak Outpost, **230,** 367
Grand Floridian Café, 202, 242, **259**

Harambe Market, 223, **235-36,** 437, 444
Hollywood Brown Derby, The, 224, 242, **260-61,** 460, 466
Hollywood & Vine, 216, 224, 226, 242, 243, 251, **260,** 313, 460, 466

Hoop-Dee-Doo Musical Revue, 208-9, 211, **226-27**
House of Blues Restaurant & Bar, 242, **261,** 504

Il Mulino New York Trattoria, 210, 212, 244, **261-62**
Intermission Food Court, 204

Jaleo by José Andrés, 203, 210, 245, **262,** 278, 282, 499
Java Café, 127
Jellyrolls, 510
Jiko—The Cooking Place, 97, 155, 202, 210, 212, 226, 242, **262-63,** 273-74
Jock Lindsey's Hangar Bar, 500
Joffrey's Coffee & Tea, 503
Jungle Navigation Co. Ltd. Skipper Canteen, 218, 242, 244, 245, 248, **263,** 367

Kat Saka's Kettle, 224
Katsura Grill, 221, **233,** 407
Kimonos, 210, 244, **264**
Kitchen + Bar, The, 175
Kona Cafe, 202, 245, **264,** 320
Kringla Bakeri og Kafe, **233,** 407, 412
Kusafiri Coffee Shop and Bakery, **236,** 437

La Cantina de San Angel, **232,** 407
La Cava del Tequila, 221, **221-22,** 228, 423
La Crêperie de Paris, 220, 244, **255,** 407
La Hacienda de San Angel, 220, 245, **259-60,** 407, 431
Landscape of Flavors, 168, 204
L'Artisan des Glaces, 221, **232,** 407
Leaning Palms, 491
Le Cellier Steakhouse, 211, 220, 245, **251-52,** 267, 320, 407, 412, 430
Le Petit Café, 143
Les Halles Boulangerie-Patisserie, 201, 220, **233,** 407, 412
LetterPress, 176
Liberty Square Market, 219, **230,** 367, 374
Liberty Tree Tavern, 218, 225, 242, 248, 253, 256, **264-65,** 367, 374
Lottawatta Lodge, 488
Lotus Blossom Café, **233-34,** 407
Lowtide Lou's, 491
Lunching Pad, The, 219, **231,** 367

Main Street Bakery, The (Starbucks), **231,** 367, 368, 374
Mainstreet Market, 177
Mangino's, 127, 128
Mara, The, 155
Maria & Enzo's Ristorante, 210, 244, **265**
Maya Grill, 243, 245, **265-66**
McGuffins, 500

See also the Accommodations Index on pages 519-524 and the Subject Index on pages 529-547.

RESTAURANT INDEX

Milk Stand, **238,** 460, 466, 478
Monsieur Paul, 208, 212, 220, 244, **266,** 407
Morimoto Asia, 210, 244, 245, **266-67,** 269, 278, 504
Mr. Kamal's, 222, **236,** 437, 444
Narcoossee's, 202, 211, 212, 226, 245, **267,** 319-20
Nine Dragons Restaurant, 220, 243, **267,** 407
1900 Park Fare, 202, 217, 242, 243, **267-68,** 313
Nomad Lounge, 15, 222, 223, **228,** 281, 321, 437

Oga's Cantina, 208, 224-25, **238,** 460, 478
'Ohana, 202, 217, 245, **268,** 313
Olivia's Cafe, 242, **268-69**

Paddlefish, 210, 243, 245, **269**
Palm Breezes Restaurant, 177
Paradiso 37, 210, 244, **269-70**
Pecos Bill Tall Tale Inn & Cafe, 219, **231,** 367
Pepe by José Andrés, 240
Pineapple Lanai, 93
Pinocchio Village Haus, **232,** 367
Pirate Tavern, 228
Pizza al Taglio, **234,** 407
Pizzafari, **236,** 437
Pizza Ponte, **240**
P & J's Southern Takeout, 204
Plancha, 210
Planet Hollywood, 210, 243, **270**
Plaza Restaurant, The, 218, 243, **270-71,** 367, 374, 398
Polar Pub, 488
Polite Pig, The, 234, **240-41**
Pongu Pongu, 222, 223, **236,** 437
Primo Piatto, 143
Princess Storybook Dining, 215

Raglan Road Irish Pub & Restaurant, 42, 202, 210, 244, **271,** 504
Rainforest Cafe, 212, 223, 243, **271-72**
Ravello, 210, 211, 215, 216, 313, 361
Refreshment Outpost, **234,** 407
Refreshment Port, **234,** 407
Regal Eagle Smokehouse, 220, **234,** 407, 412, 426
River Roost, 510
Riverside Mill Food Court, 152, 204
Rix Sports Bar & Grill, 510
Ronto Roasters, 223-24, **238,** 460, 466, 478
Rosa Mexicano, 210, 211, 244, **272**
Rose & Crown Dining Room, 243, **272,** 320, 407, 429, 431
Rose & Crown Pub, 220, **222,** 429, 431

Rosie's All-American Cafe, 224, **238-39,** 460
Roundup Rodeo BBQ, 211, 224, 242, **273,** 460, 466
Royal Anandapur Tea Company, **236,** 437

sake bars, 222
Salt & Straw, 202, **241**
Sanaa, 97, 155, 157, 202, 242, 244, **273-74**
San Angel Inn Restaurante, 220, 245, **274,** 407
Sassagoula Floatworks & Food Factory, 204
Satu'li Canteen, 205, 222, **236,** 437, 444
Scat Cat's Club, 510
Sci-Fi Dine-In Theater Restaurant, 224, 226, 243, **274-75,** 460
Sebastian's Bistro, 140, 211, 244, 245, **275**
Shades Bar & Grill, 176
Shiki-Sai: Sushi Izakaya, 220, 244, **275,** 407, 412
Sleepy Hollow, 219, **232,** 366, 374
Smiling Crocodile, The, 223
Smokehouse, The, 500
Snack Shack, 491
Sommerfest, 221, **234,** 407, 412
Space 220, 208, 209, 211, 220, 243, **276,** 407
Spice Road Table, 220, 245, **276,** 407, 412, 427, 431
Splitsville Dining Room, 210, 243, **277,** 504
Sprinkles, 501
Starbucks, 231, **241,** 368, 499
Starlight Café, 320
Steakhouse 71, 124, 245, **277**
STK Orlando, 210, 245, **277-78,** 504
Summer House on the Lake, 210, 245, **278-79,** 504
Sunshine Seasons, 204, **234-35,** 407

Takumi-Tei, 212, 220, 226, 244, 266, **279,** 407, 412
Tambu Lounge, 115
Tamu Tamu, 223
Tangierine Café, **235,** 407
Teppan Edo, 220, 226, 244, **279-80,** 407, 412
Terralina Crafted Italian Restaurant, 210, 244, **280**
Thirsty River Bar & Trek Snacks, 437
Three Bridges Bar & Grill, 158, 242, 245, **280-81**
Tiffins Restaurant, 15, 223, 226, 242, 245, **281,** 437, 444, 445
Todd English's Bluezoo, 210, 212, 245, **281**
Toledo—Tapas, Steak & Seafood, 158, 245, **282**
Tomorrowland Terrace Restaurant, **232,** 367, 395-96, 398

See also the Accommodations Index on pages 519-524 and the Restaurant Index on pages 525-526.

Tony's Town Square Restaurant, 218, 244, **282,** 367, 374, 398
Top of the World Lounge, 126, 510
Topolino's Terrace—Flavors of the Riviera, 211, 212, 215, 216, 244, **282–83,** 326
Tortuga Tavern, 219, **232,** 367
Trader Sam's Grog Grotto, 115, 510
Trader Sam's Tiki Terrace, 93
Trattoria al Forno, 244, **283**
T-Rex Restaurant, 243, **283–84**
Trolley Car Cafe, The, **239,** 460, 466
Tune-In Lounge, 228
Turf Club Bar & Grill, 243, **284**
Tusker House Restaurant, 215, 216, 223, 226, 242, **284,** 313, 437, 444
Tutto Gusto Wine Cellar, **222,** 426
Tutto Italia Ristorante, 220, 244, **284–85,** 319–20, 407, 412
Typhoon Tilly's, 491

Uzima Springs, 156

Via Napoli Ristorante e Pizzeria, 201, 220, 244, **285,** 407, 412, 426
Victoria & Albert's, 97, 202, 208, 211, 212, 226, 244, 254, 266, **285–86,** 326
Victoria Falls, 155
Vivoli il Gelato, 500

Warming Hut, 488
Weinkeller, 222
Whispering Canyon Cafe, 242, **286**
Wine Bar George, 202-3, 210, 245, 278, **286–87,** 504
Wolfgang Puck Bar & Grill, 242, **287**
Woody's Lunch Box, 224, **239,** 460, 466
World Premier Food Court, 204

Yachtsman Steakhouse, 212, 245, **288**
Yak & Yeti Local Food Cafes, **237**
Yak & Yeti Restaurant, 223, 226, **288,** 444
Yorkshire County Fish Shop, 221, **235,** 272, 407, 412, 429

See also the Accommodations Index on pages 519–524 and the Restaurant Index on pages 525–528.

SUBJECT INDEX

ABC Fine Wine & Spirits, 363
accessibility, 315–25. *See also* wheelchairs
   disabilities, guests with, 315–20
   ECV rentals, 318–19, 369, 398, 408, 462
   larger guests, 322–23
   older guests, 323–25
   pregnant guests, 321–22
   service animals, 316
   theme park, 316
accommodations, 77–199. *See also separate Accommodations index*
   accessibility, 315, 324
   Animal Kingdom, 153–69
   Bonnet Creek, 93, 94, 143–53
   campground, 169–73
   categories, 82
   check-in and checkout, 105–6
   contact information, 37–38
   costs, 77–81, 84–88, 91–92, 94, 183–86
   Disney's Hollywood Studios, 92, 93, 499
   Disney Springs, 35, 94, 173–78
   EPCOT, 92–93, 129–43
   families with kids, 81, 107, 186, 293
   housekeeping service, 106
   inside Disney World, 77–107
   inspection of, 99, 105–7
   Magic Kingdom, 92, 93, 110–29
   massages at, 515
   nightlife in, 510–11
   outside Disney World, 77–78, 180–93
   pools and amenities, 92–93, 95
   pros and cons of Disney resorts, 78–81
   rating/ranking, 88–91, 94, 107–10, 194–99
   readers' report card, 107–10
   reservations, 20, 25, 82–88
   returning for midday break, 41
   romantic getaways, 328
   room diagrams, 100–104
   room request service, 26
   room upgrades, 88
   themes, 95, 96–97, 98
   transportation to/from, 91, 329–34, 337–45
   Universal area, 187–88
   views from, 26
acronyms and abbreviations, 18
addresses, WDW, 38
admission, 60–76
   advance purchase of, 65
   Annual Passes, 68–69
   contact information, 73
   cost increases, 73
   costs, 60–76
   date-based pricing, 66–67
   discounts, 20, 61, 64–66, 70–72
   early, 34–36, 78
   expiration dates for, 68, 69, 70, 72
   Florida resident passes, 71, 72
   linking tickets to MDE profiles, 25
   online purchase of, 23–24, 69
   options for, 70–71
   Park Hopper/Park Hopper Plus add-ons, 67, 70–71, 343, 480
   park reservations for, 68
   purchasing, 69–70
   third-party wholesalers, 69, 71
   with travel packages, 178–79, 325
   unauthorized sellers, 69–70
   United Kingdom, purchasing in, 71, 72
   water parks, 70–71, 480
   Water Park and Sports add-on, 67
   where to buy, 69–70
   wristbands for, 23–24, 73–74, 355, 358
adult time, tips for, 326
Advance Dining Reservations, 80, 207–10
Advance Passenger Information and Secure Flight (APIS) process, 23
Advent Health Centra Care, 38, 359
Adventureland (Magic Kingdom), 377–79
   fright potential of attractions, 305
   Jungle Cruise, 304, 377
   Magic Carpets of Aladdin, The, 377
   map, 366–67
   not-to-be-missed attractions, 368
   Pirate's Adventure: Treasure of the Seven Seas, A, 378

See also the Accommodations Index on pages 519–524 and the Restaurant Index on pages 525–528.

SUBJECT INDEX

Adventureland *(continued)*
  Pirates of the Caribbean, 378
  Swiss Family Treehouse, 378-79
  Walt Disney's Enchanted Tiki Room, 379
Adventurers Outpost, 445
Aerophile (shop), 500-501
Affection Section, 449-50
Africa (Disney's Animal Kingdom), 447-50
  Conservation Station, 449-50
  Gorilla Falls Exploration Trail, 448
  Kilimanjaro Safaris, 448-49
  map, 436-37
  not-to-be-missed attractions, 440
  Rafiki's Planet Watch, 449-50
  Wildlife Express Train, 450
age, attraction suitability and, 291, 304-7
Airbnb, 61, 182
airports, 329-31, 336-37
Akershus Castle, 424
Aladdin, The Magic Carpets of, 377
Alamo (car rental), 332, 333, 334, 346
alcoholic beverages, 221-22, 363
Alcoholics Anonymous, Al-Anon, Alateen, 328
Aldridge, Justin (Jedi master), 518
Alien Swirling Saucers, 472-73
Allegiant Air, 337
allergies, 212, 319-20
alligators, in water bodies, 298
AMC Disney Springs 24 Dine-In Theatres, 500-501
America Gardens Theatre, 426
American Adventure Pavilion, The, 426
American Adventure, The (film), 426-27
American Heritage Gallery, 426
American Threads, 500-501
Amorette's Patisserie, 503, 517
AmphiBar (bar), 504
Animal Kingdom, Disney's, 435-57
  accommodations in or near, 153-69
  Africa, 447-50
  arriving at, 338, 439-40
  Asia, 450-53
  attractions
    Animation Experience at Conservation Station, The, 449
    Avatar Flight of Passage, 454-55
    fright potential, 306
    Discovery Island Trails, 445
    Expedition Everest, 450-51
    Feathered Friends in Flight!, 451-52
    Festival of the Lion King, 447-48
    Finding Nemo—The Big Blue . . . and Beyond!, 453
    Gorilla Falls Exploration Trail, 448
    height restrictions, 308
    Kali River Rapids, 48, 452
    Kilimanjaro Safaris, 448-49
    Lightning Lane passes, 440, 442-44
    Maharajah Jungle Trek, 452-53
    Na'vi River Journey, 441-43, 455
    not-to-be-missed, 439
    Pandora—The World of Avatar, 453-55
    pregnant guests and, 321
    ratings by age, 441
    Rider Switch, attractions offering, 309
    sample ride vehicles, 322
    Tree of Life, The, 446-47
    Valley of Mo'ara, 441, 443
    Wilderness Explorers, 446-47
    Wildlife Express Train, 450
  baby care in, 298
  behind the scenes, 496
  commuting time to/from, 341
  crowds, 456
  dining in, 222-23, 228, 235-37, 444
  Discovery Island, 444-47
  Disney characters in, 312, 455-56
  entertainment, 455-56
  first aid in, 298-99
  getting oriented, 440-44
  GPS coordinates, 346
  Guest Relations/information, 356, 440
  lost persons at, 303, 440
  map, 436-37
  Oasis, The, 444
  overview, 14, 435-39
  parking, 346-47
  Rafiki's Planet Watch, 449-50
  rope-drop procedures, 439-40
  services, 440
  shopping, 507
  strollers in, 300, 440
  touring plans, 440, 442-44, 457
  traffic patterns, 456
  transportation to/from, 439
  when to go, 40, 42
animals. *See also* Animal Kingdom
  Caring for the Giants (elephants), 496
  pet accommodations, 362
  in Seas with Nemo & Friends Pavilion, The, 420-21
  Starlight Safari, 496
  Up Close with Rhinos, 496
  Wild Africa Trek, 496
animation classes, 518
Animation Courtyard (DHS), 474-75, 479
Animation Experience at Conservation Station, The, 449-50
Anna and Elsa
  For the First Time in Forever: A Frozen Sing-Along Celebration, 470
  meet and greet, 424-25
Annual Passes, 68-69
Anthropologie, 503
aquariums, 420-21
archery lessons, 516
Arendelle, 424
Ariel's Grotto, 383
Armed Forces Recreation Center, 88
Arribas Brothers (shop), 502
arrival and departure days, 41-43

SUBJECT INDEX

Art Corner, The (shop), 500–501
Art of Disney, The (shop), 502, 506
Asia (Disney's Animal Kingdom), 450–53
  Expedition Everest, 450–51
  fright potential of attractions, 306
  Kali River Rapids, 48, 452
  Maharajah Jungle Trek, 452–53
  not-to-be-missed attractions, 440
assistive-technology devices, 320
Astro Orbiter, 390–91
Atlántic Dance Hall, 510
ATMs, 355, 369, 408, 440, 462
autism spectrum disorder, 316
autographs, of Disney characters, 313
AutoSlash (website), 28, 334
Avatar (film), 453
Avatar Flight of Passage, 454–55
Avis (car rental), 332
Awakenings (film), 446
Awesome Planet (film), 418

babies. *See* children
baby care facilities and services, 298–99
  Animal Kingdom, 440
  Disney's Hollywood Studios, 462
  EPCOT, 408
  and lost children, 302
  Magic Kingdom, 369
babysitting services, 313
banking services, 355–56, 369, 408, 440, 462
Barnstormer, The, 383
bars and nightlife. *See* nightlife
Basin (shop), 502
Bay Lake and Seven Seas Lagoon Electrical Water Pageant, 395
Bay Lake area, 337
Bay Slides, 490, 491
Beachcomber Shacks, 485
bears, at *Country Bear Musical Jamboree*, 380
Beast's Castle, 382
Beauty and the Beast—Live on Stage, 466
Beauty and the Beast Sing-Along, 428
behind the scenes
  Animal Kingdom, 496
  EPCOT, 495
  Magic Kingdom, 494–95
Behind the Seeds Tour (EPCOT), 419, 495
Belle, Enchanted Tales with, 384–85
Best Friends Pet Care, 362
beverages, 65, 221–22, 363
Bibbidi Bobbidi Boutique, 505, 515
Big Thunder Mountain Railroad, 44, 306, 379–80
Big Top Souvenirs, 505
Bijutsukan Gallery, 427
birds
  Feathered Friends in Flight!, 451–2
  Walt Disney's Enchanted Tiki Room, 379
  Winged Encounters—The Kingdom Takes Flight, 456

birthday celebrations, 314
Black History Month, 33
Black Spire Outfitters (shop), 478, 508
blisters, 297–98, 322, 359–60
Blizzard Beach, 14, 487–89
  attractions, 489
  commuting time to/from, 341, 342
  GPS coordinates, 346
  height restrictions, 308
  map, 488
boarding groups, 24, 52
BoardWalk, Disney's, 16
Boardwalk Ticketing, 69
Boathouse, The (bar at), 504
boat rides
  Frozen Ever After, 424
  Gran Fiesta Tour, 423
  It's a Small World, 304, 385
  Jungle Cruise, 304, 377
  Kali River Rapids, 48, 452
  Living with the Land, 304, 418–19
  Na'vi River Journey, 441–43, 455
  Pirates of the Caribbean, 378
  Tiana's Bayou Adventure, 15, 306, 381
boat transportation, 344, 422–23, 459
Bonnet Creek resorts, 143–53
bottlenecks, avoiding. *See* crowds
boutique hotels, 182
Bowes Signature Candles, 500–501
bowling, 277, 499
Box Office Gifts, 505
Braille guidebooks and menus, 320
breakfast, 66
breast feeding, 299
Budget (car rental), 332
Buena Vista Urgent Care, 359
buffets, 203
Build-A-Dino/Dino Store, 500–501
buses
  commuting times on, 339, 342
  Disney's Hollywood Studios, 459
  Disney Springs, 499
  Magical Express, 329
  Magic Kingdom, 365
  Mears Connect, 329–30
  shuttle buses from hotels, 353, 480
  to/from airport, 353
Buzz Lightyear's Space Ranger Spin, 391

cake decorating class, 517
calendar, Walt Disney World, 32–34
Camera Center, 506
cameras, memory cards and supplies, 506
campground, 169–73
Canada Far and Wide (film), 430
Canada Pavilion, 430, 508
cancellation policies, hotel, 82–83
Candlelight Processional (EPCOT), 510–11
Candy Cauldron, Disney's, 504
Car Care Center, 347
Caring for the Giants (elephants), 496

See also the Accommodations Index on pages 519–524 and the Restaurant Index on pages 525–528.

Carousel of Progress, Walt Disney's (show), 394
carousels
  Marketplace (Disney Springs), 499
  Prince Charming Regal Carrousel, 388
cars. *See also* parking
  auto club discounts, 88
  electric vehicle charging, 354
  lost, 358
  miniature, in Tomorrowland, 392–93
  rental, 28, 331–34, 346
  speeding tickets, 348
  town car service, 330-31
  travel in
    to and around Disney World, 80–81, 182, 346–53
    commuting time for, 182, 340–41
    directions for, 334–36
    vs. the Disney transportation system, 339, 340–41
    GPS locations for theme parks, 346
    sneak routes, 348–53
    to/from airport, 353–54
    to/from Disney Springs, 498–99
    to/from EPCOT, 405, 408
    to/from water parks, 480
  trouble with, 347
Casey Jr. Splash 'N' Soak Station, 383–84
cash and ATMs, 355, 369, 408, 440, 462
Castaway Creek, 490, 491
castles, 369, 382–83
cast members, 16–17
cavalcades. *See also* parades
  Disney's Hollywood Studios, 479
  Magic Kingdom, 394
¡Celebración Encanto!, 415
celebrations, tips for, 326
cell phones
  charging, 356, 408, 440, 462
  to occupy children in lines, 309
  reception problems with, 356
Central Plaza (Magic Kingdom), 369
chairlift to Summit Plummet, 487, 488, 489
Chapel Hats, 500–501
characters, Disney. *See* Disney characters
charging stations, for devices, 356
check-in and checkout, 105–6
child care centers/clubs, 313. *See also* Baby Care Centers and services
children, 289–314
  accommodations for, 81, 107, 186, 293
  active listening, 295
  attractions
    age for, 291, 304–7
    Animal Kingdom, 306
    Disney's Hollywood Studios, 306
    EPCOT, 305–6
    Magic Kingdom, 305
    suitability of, 304–7
  baby care facilities for, 298–99, 369, 408, 440, 462

  babysitting services, 313
  birthday celebrations, 314
  consistency with, 294
  discipline, 294–96
  endurance, 293–94
  expectations, 290
  favorite activities, 296–97
  flexibility with, 294
  frightening attractions, 304–7
  health considerations, 297–98
  height requirements, 307, 308–9
  Kidcot Fun Stops, 421, 423
  naps for, 292–93
  planning recommendations for, 290–94
  restaurants for, 226
  rest for, 292–93
  in restrooms, 303
  Rider Switch, 307, 309–10, 409
  school, missing, 291–92
  separation from parents, 302–3
  special programs, 313
  strollers for. *See* strollers
  touring plans for, 297, 401–2
  when to visit with, 29, 30, 291–92
  waiting-in-line strategies for, 307, 309–10
China Pavilion, 425, 506
Christmas
  events for, 34, 75
  planning visit for, 32
  shopping for, 502, 505
Cinderella Castle, 369, 375, 382–83
Cirque du Soleil, 499
City Hall (Magic Kingdom), 368
civil service employees, discounts for, 72
classes, 517–18
climate, Florida's, 29–30
clinics, for medical care, 359
closed-captioning, 320
closing time, 41
Club Cool, 415–16
Coach (shop), 503
Coca-Cola Store, 503
cognitive disabilities, visitors with, 316
Colors of Coronado Painting Experience, 517
Columbia Sportswear, 503
commuting time, 182, 340–41, 345
complaints, contacting Disney about, 360
concerts
  free Disney World, 510–11
  House of Blues, 511
condominiums, 66, 183–86
Conservation Station, 449–50
contactless payments, 74
conventions, 72
corporate sponsors, discounts for, 72
costs. *See also* discounts
  accommodations, 77–81, 84–88, 91–92, 94, 182–86
  admission tickets, 66–74
  Annual Passes, 68–69
  daily, 70–71

See also the Accommodations Index on pages 519–524 and the Restaurant Index on pages 525–528.

SUBJECT INDEX

increases in, 73
Lightning Lane passes, 55, 57
overall vacation, 60–66
parking, 347
rental cars, 332, 333–34
restaurants, 205–6, 213, 231, 241–45
RunDisney events, 513–14
special events, 74–76
stroller rental, 300
travel packages, 178–79, 325
water parks, 480
costumes, of characters, 311, 313
counter-service restaurants, 204, 213
   Animal Kingdom, 235–37
   Disney's Hollywood Studios, 237–39
   Disney Springs, 239–41
   EPCOT, 232–35
   Magic Kingdom, 229–30, 231–32
Country Bear Musical Jamboree, 380
couples, activities for, 325–28
Creations Shop, 506
credit cards, 355
Cross Country Creek, 487, 488, 489
crowd calendar, 26, 31–32
crowds. *See also* touring plans; traffic patterns
   Animal Kingdom, 456
   children lost in, 302–3
   Early Entry and, 35–36
   EPCOT, 431–33
   Future World, 431–33
   holiday and spring break, 31, 32
   live-entertainment effects on, 397–99
   off-season, 29, 30, 31
   opening procedures and, 399
   at parades, 397
   time of year for, 29–31
   waiting-in-line strategies for, 43–59, 307, 309–10
   water parks, 481
   World Showcase, 431–33
Crown & Crest, The, 508
Crush, Turtle Talk with, 421
Crush 'n' Gusher, 490, 491
Crystal Arts by Arribas Brothers (shop), 502
currency exchange, 356

dark rides, 307
   Haunted Mansion, The, 382
   Mickey & Minnie's Runaway Railway, 15, 458, 468
   Remy's Ratatouille Adventure, 15, 404, 428
   Rock 'n' Roller Coaster, 44, 468–69
   Space Mountain, 44, 48, 307, 392
   Spaceship Earth, 409, 413, 416–17
   Star Wars: Rise of the Resistance, 48–49, 458, 476, 477–78
   Toy Story Mania!, 473–74
   Under the Sea—Journey of the Little Mermaid, 389–90

Darkroom, The, 508
Das Kaufhaus, 507
David's Vacation Club Rentals, 86
Days of Christmas, Disney's, 502
deaf guests, services for, 320
dehydration, 297, 358
dental emergencies, 359
Department of Defense (DOD) employees, discounts for, 72
departure and arrival days, 41–43
DHS. *See* Disney's Hollywood Studios
diaper-changing facilities, 298, 369, 408, 440, 462
dietary restrictions, 212, 319–20
Die Weihnachts Ecke (shop), 506
dining, 200–288. *See also separate Restaurant Index*
   in accommodations, 97, 98, 202–3
   Advance Reservations, 207–10
   allergy considerations, 212, 319–20
   in Animal Kingdom, 222–23, 228, 235–37, 444
   best places to find good dining, 202–3
   breakfast, 66
   bringing your own food, 65–66, 213
   buffet, 203
   categories of Disney restaurants, 203–5
   for children, 226
   at closing time, 347
   contact information, 37–38
   costs, 205–6, 213, 231, 241–45
   counter-service, 204, 205, 213, 229–41
   dietary restrictions, 212, 319–20
   dining plans for, 205–7
   dinner theater, 226–27
   with Disney characters, 203, 214–18, 313
   Disney resort guests, early reservation access for, 78
   in Disney's Hollywood Studios, 223–25, 228, 237–39, 465, 466, 467–68, 478
   in Disney Springs, 202–3, 239–41
   in Disney World, 81, 200–288
   dress recommendations for, 212
   in EPCOT, 219–22, 228, 232–35, 412
   family-style, 203
   Fantasmic! Dining Package, 467–68
   fast food, 204–5
   full-service, 203, 212–13
      Advance Reservations for, 207–10
      for children, 225–26
      cuisine types in, 242–45
      profiles of (alphabetical), 246–88
   healthful food, 212
   international food, 219–22, 241–45
   in lounges, 221–22, 228
   in Magic Kingdom, 218–19, 228, 229–30, 231–32, 374
   mobile ordering, 213
   money-saving tips, 213
   new restaurants, 246
   noise, 217, 226

534 SUBJECT INDEX

dining *(continued)*
  for older guests, 325
  reader comments, 227, 228
  reservations for, 28, 207-10, 408
  restaurant ratings, 202, 241-46
  restaurant recommendations by type of dining, 211
  romantic and quiet restaurants, 226
  Star Wars: Galaxy's Edge, 478
  surveys and reviews, 200-202
  time-saving tips, 213
  theme park admission and access to restaurants, 212
  vendor food, 205
  in water parks, 482
  in World Showcase, 219-22
Dining Plans, Disney, 205-7
dinner theater, 226-27
Disability Access Service (DAS) card, 316-18
disabilities, visitors with, 315-20. *See also* wheelchairs
  contact information, 37, 38
  Disability Access Service, 316-18
  Disney resort amenities, 315
  guide for, 28
  service animals, 316
  theme park booklets and support, 316
discipline, of children, 294-96
discounts
  accommodations, 77-78, 84-88, 178-80, 182
  admission, 20, 70-72
  auto club, 88
  shopping, 508, 509-10
Discovery Island, 441, 444-47
Discovery Island Trails, 445
Discovery Trading Company, 507
discussion boards, online, 29
Disney, Walt, 475
Disney Adventure Friends cavalcade, 394
Disney characters, 310-13. *See also* meet and greets; *specific characters by name*
  in Animal Kingdom, 312, 455-56
  autographs from, 313
  in cavalcades, 394
  dining with, 203, 214-18, 313
  in Disney's Hollywood Studios, 312, 466, 471, 474, 479
  in EPCOT, 312, 416, 420-21, 424-25
  in *Fantasmic!*, 467-68
  in Fantasyland, 384-85, 388-89
  For the First Time in Forever: A Frozen Sing-Along Celebration, 470
  furry type, 311, 313
  lost children and, 302
  in Magic Kingdom, 312, 369, 376, 384-85, 388-89
  meeting, 302, 311-13
  and touring plans, 297
Disney Character Warehouse, 66, 509-10

Disney Dining Plans, 205-7
Disney Ever After (shop), 500-501
Disney Good Neighbor Hotels, 35, 80
Disney H2O Glow After Hours, 76
Disney Imagination Campus, 72
Disney Junior Play and Dance!, 474
Disney on Broadway (EPCOT), 511
Disney Parks Christmas Day Parade, 34
Disney & Pixar Short Film Festival, 417
Disney Princess Half Marathon, 513
Disney Reservation Center (DRC), 82
Disney Rewards Visa Card, 87
Disney's BoardWalk, 16
Disney's Candy Cauldron, 504
Disney's Days of Christmas, 502
Disney's Hollywood Studios (DHS), 458-79
  accommodations near, 92, 93, 499
  After Hours events, 76
  Animation Courtyard, 474-75, 479
  arriving at, 346, 459-62
  attractions
    Alien Swirling Saucers, 472-73
    Beauty and the Beast—Live on Stage / Theater of the Stars, 466
    for children, 306, 310-13
    Disney Junior Play and Dance!, 474
    Disney Villains: Unfairly Ever After, 15, 466
    Fantasmic!, 467-68
    For the First Time in Forever: A Frozen Sing-Along Celebration, 470
    height restrictions, 308
    Indiana Jones Epic Stunt Spectacular!, 470-71
    Lightning Lane passes, 54, 463-65
    Little Mermaid—A Musical Adventure, The, 474-75
    Meet Disney Stars at *Red Carpet Dreams*, 471
    Meet Olaf at Celebrity Spotlight, 471
    Mickey & Minnie's Runaway Railway, 15, 458, 468
    Millennium Falcon: Smugglers Run, 475, 476-77
    not-to-be-missed, 459
    pregnant guests and, 321
    ratings by age, 463
    Rider Switch, attractions offering, 309
    Rock 'n' Roller Coaster, 468-69
    sample ride vehicles, 322-23
    Slinky Dog Dash, 473
    Star Tours—The Adventures Continue, 471-72
    Star Wars: Rise of the Resistance, 48-49, 458, 476, 477-78
    Star Wars Launch Bay, 474
    time to allocate for, 459
    Toy Story Mania!, 473-74
    Twilight Zone Tower of Terror, The, 306-7, 469-70

See also the Accommodations Index on pages 519-524 and the Restaurant Index on pages 525-528.

SUBJECT INDEX

Vacation Fun at Mickey Shorts Theater, 472
Walt Disney Presents, 475
baby care in, 298
commuting time to/from, 340
dining in, 223-25, 228, 237-39, 465, 466, 467-68, 478
Disney characters in, 312, 466, 471, 474, 479
Echo Lake, 306, 459, 470-72
entertainment in, 479
first aid in, 298
getting oriented, 462-65
GPS coordinates, 346
Grand Avenue, 472
Guest Relations, 462
Hollywood Boulevard, 306, 459, 462, 465-70
map, 460-61
overview, 9, 458
rope-drop procedures, 459
parking, 346-47, 459
Pixar Place, 479
services, 462
shopping, 478, 508
Star Wars: Galaxy's Edge, 15, 306, 459, 475-79
strollers in, 300, 462
Sunset Boulevard, 306, 459, 462, 465-70
touring plans for, 479
when to go, 40
Disney's Keys to the Kingdom Tour, 494
Disney's Pin Traders, 500-501
Disney Skyliner gondola system, 15, 338, 344-45, 459
Disney Springs, 498-504
accommodations in or near, 94, 173-78
arriving at, 338-39, 498-99
commuting time to/from, 341, 342
getting oriented, 499
GPS coordinates, 346
height restrictions, 308
Landing, The, 503
map, 500-501
Marketplace, 502
Memory Maker service, 362
nightlife, 504
overview, 14, 498-499
restaurants, 202-3, 239-41
sneak routes to, 348, 350
Town Center, 499, 503
Toy Story Land, 15, 306, 459, 472-74
transportation to/from, 338-39, 498-99
Welcome Center, 356, 500-501
West Side, 499, 504
Disney Starlight Parade, 15, 395
Disney stars at *Red Carpet Dreams*, 471
DisneyStyle (shop), 504
Disney's Very Merry Christmas Party, 34, 75
Disney's Wonderful World of Memories (shop), 500-501

Disney transportation system (DTS), 337-45
Disney Vacation Club (DVC), 72, 85-86
Disney Villains: Unfairly Ever After, 15, 466
Disney Wine & Dine Half Marathon, 513
DiveQuest, 495
diversions (attraction type), 44
DiVine (stilt walker), 456
Dockside Margaritas (drinks to go), 504
doctors, 359
Dollar (car rental), 332
Downhill Double Dipper, 488, 489
Drawn to Life (Cirque de Soleil), 499
dress recommendations
   Disney "uniform," 302
   restaurants, 212
   water parks, 482
Drinking Around the World, 421-22
driving. *See* car(s)
Droid Depot, 478
drugstores and prescriptions, 359
DuckTales World Showcase Adventure (EPCOT), 422
Dumbo the Flying Elephant, 384
DVC Rental Store, 86

Ear for Each Other (Facebook group), 515
Early Theme Park Entry (ETPE), 15, 33-36, 40, 45, 51, 79, 80, 342, 459
Easter celebrations, 33
Eat to the Beat (concert series), 511
Echo Lake (DHS), 306, 459, 470-72
Edison, The (bar at), 504
Edward Beiner (shop), 500-501
Eiffel Tower replica, 428
elders. *See* older guests
electric conveyance vehicles (ECVs/scooters), 318-19, 369, 398, 408, 462
electric vehicle (car) charging locations, 354
elephants
   Caring for the Giants, 496
   Dumbo the Flying Elephant, 384
Elsa and Anna
   For the First Time in Forever: A Frozen Sing-Along Celebration, 470
   meet and greet, 424-25
Emporium, The (sundries shop), 358, 505
Enchanted Tales with Belle, 384-85
Enterprise (car rental), 332
entertainment. *See* dinner theater; films and animated shows; live entertainment; nightlife; shows, theater and stage
Enzo's Hideaway (bar at), 504
EPCOT, 404-34. *See also* Future World; World Showcase
   acronym meaning, 404
   After Hours events, 76
   arriving at, 338, 405, 408
   attractions, 406-7. *See also specific attractions by name*
   for children, 305-6
   Frozen Ever After, 424

See also the Accommodations Index on pages 519-524 and the Restaurant Index on pages 525-528.

SUBJECT INDEX

EPCOT *(continued)*
  attractions *(continued)*
    Guardians of the Galaxy: Cosmic Rewind, 15, 44, 304, 404, 413-14
    height restrictions, 308
    Journey of Water, Inspired by Moana, 404, 417-18
    Lightning Lane passes, 54, 408, 409-12
    not-to-be-missed, 405
    ratings by age, 409, 410
    Remy's Ratatouille Adventure, 15, 404, 429
    Rider Switch, attractions offering, 309
    sample ride vehicles, 322
  baby care in, 298
  behind the scenes, 495
  commuting time to/from, 340, 343
  crowds, 431-33
  dining in, 219-22, 228, 232-35, 412
  Disney characters in, 312, 416, 420-21, 424-25
  Festival of the Arts, 15, 33, 511
  Festival of the Holidays, 34, 419, 510-11
  fireworks, 15, 431-33
  first aid in, 298
  Flower & Garden Festival, 33, 511
  Food & Wine Festival, 33, 511
  getting oriented, 409-12
  GPS coordinates, 346
  Guest Relations/information, 356, 408
  hours of operation, 408
  Journey of Water, Inspired by Moana, 15
  live entertainment, 430-33
  Luminous, 15, 404, 431
  map, 406-7
  Odyssey Center, 406-7
  Outpost, 406-7
  overview, 9, 404-8
  parking, 346-47, 405
  physical size of, 9
  pregnant guests, tips for, 321
  resorts, 92-93, 129-43
  rope-drop procedures, 408
  Seas with Nemo & Friends Pavilion, The, 223, 226, 305, 357, 405, 408, 420
  services, 408
  shopping, 505-8
  strollers in, 300, 408, 418
  touring plans for, 433-34
  traffic patterns, 433
  transportation to/from, 346, 405, 408, 433
  when to go, 40
Everything but Water (shop), 500-501
exercise. *See* recreation
Expedia.com, 85, 182
Expedition Everest, 44, 450-51
expiration, of tickets, 68
Extended Evening Theme Park Hours (EETPH), 15, 36, 51, 79, 80, 342

Fabletics, 503
Fairytale Garden, Meet Mirabel at, 386
Fairy Tale Weddings & Honeymoons department, 325
family and friends, registration of, 25
family-style restaurants, 203, 215
Fantasia Gardens and Fairways Miniature Golf, 516-17
Fantasmic! (show), 467-68
Fantasy Faire (shop), 505
Fantasyland (Magic Kingdom), 382-90
  attractions
    Ariel's Grotto, 383
    Barnstormer, The, 383
    Casey Jr. Splash 'N' Soak Station, 383-84
    for children, 305
    Dumbo the Flying Elephant, 384
    Enchanted Tales with Belle, 384-85
    It's a Small World, 304, 385
    live entertainment, 394-99
    Mad Tea Party, 385-86
    Many Adventures of Winnie the Pooh, The, 386
    Meet Mirabel at Fairytale Garden, 386
    Mickey's PhilharMagic, 387
    not-to-be-missed, 368
    Peter Pan's Flight, 387
    Pete's Silly Sideshow, 388
    Prince Charming Regal Carrousel, 388
    Princess Fairytale Hall, 388-89
    Seven Dwarfs Mine Train, 48, 389
    Under the Sea—Journey of the Little Mermaid, 389-90
    Walt Disney World Railroad, 390
fast-casual restaurants, 204-5
fast food, 204-5. *See also* counter-service restaurants
FastPass+, 51-52, 53. *See also* Lightning Lane passes
Feathered Friends in Flight!, 451-52
ferry (to Magic Kingdom), 365
Festival of Fantasy Parade, 395
Festival of the Lion King, 447-48
festivals (EPCOT)
  Festival of the Arts, 15, 33, 511
  Festival of the Holidays, 34, 419, 510-11
  Flower & Garden Festival, 33, 511
  Food & Wine Festival, 33, 511
Figment, 307, 417
films and animated shows
  Awakenings, 446
  Awesome Planet, 418
  Beauty and the Beast Sing-Along, 428
  Canada Far and Wide, 430
  Disney & Pixar Short Film Festival, 417
  Impressions de France, 428-29
  Mickey's PhilharMagic, 387
  Reflections of China, 425
  Soarin' Around the World, 419-20
  Turtle Talk with Crush, 421

See also the Accommodations Index on pages 519-524 and the Restaurant Index on pages 525-528.

SUBJECT INDEX

Vacation Fun at Mickey Shorts
   Theater, 472
Walt Disney Presents, 475
Zootopia: Better Zoogether!, 15, 446
*Finding Nemo—The Big Blue . . . and
   Beyond!*, 453
fireworks
   EPCOT, 15, 430–33
   exit strategies after, 396–97
   Magic Kingdom, 397–99, 495
   viewing, 396–97
Fireworks Cruise, 396, 495
Fireworks Dessert Party, 395–96
first aid, 298–99, 358–59
   Animal Kingdom, 440
   Disney's Hollywood Studios, 462
   EPCOT, 408
   Magic Kingdom, 369
Fit2Run (shop), 500–501
Fjording, The (shops), 506
flag retreat event, 395
Flamingo Crossings (accommodations),
   192
flight-simulation rides
   Millennium Falcon: Smugglers Run, 475,
      476–77
   Mission: Space, 414–15
   Soarin' Around the World, 419–20
   Star Tours—The Adventures Continue,
      471–72
Florida Mall, The, 509
Florida resident passes, 71, 72
Flower & Garden Festival, EPCOT
   International, 33, 511
flume rides
   at Blizzard Beach, 489
   Tiana's Bayou Adventure, 15, 306, 381
   at Typhoon Lagoon, 490
food. *See* dining
food courts, 204
Food & Wine Festival, EPCOT International,
   33, 511
foot care, 297–98, 359–60
Forever Vintage, 510
*For the First Time in Forever: A Frozen
   Sing-Along Celebration*, 470
Fox shuttle service, 332, 333
France Pavilion, 404, 427–28, 507–8
Francesca's, 503
Free People, 503
friends and family, registering online, 25
Friendship Boats, 422–23
Friends of Bill W., 328
fright factors, 304–7
Fright-Potential Table, 305–6
Frontera Cocina (margaritas to go), 504
Frontierland (Magic Kingdom), 379–81
   Big Thunder Mountain Railroad, 44, 306,
      379–80
   for children, 305
   Country Bear Musical Jamboree, 380

   not-to-be-missed attractions, 368
   Tiana's Bayou Adventure, 15, 306, 381
   Walt Disney World Railroad, 381
Frozen Ever After (ride), 424
*Frozen Sing-Along Celebration, A (For the
   First Time in Forever)*, 470
Future World (EPCOT), 409, 413–21. *See
   also* Imagination! Pavilion; World
   Celebration; World Nature; World
   Discovery
   attractions
      for children, 305
      Lightning Lane passes, 408
      not-to-be-missed, 405
      ratings by age, 409
   crowds, 431, 433
   hours of operation, 408
   live entertainment, 415, 431
   meet and greets, 416
   services, 408
   traffic patterns, 433

Gala Street Band, 456
Gallery, Bijutsukan, 427
games, for waiting in line, 309
Ganachery, The, 503
Gangplank Falls, 490, 491
Garden Gate Gifts, 300
Garden Rocks (concert series), 511
Gay Days, 33
Genie, 24, 58–59
Genie+, 52
Germany Pavilion, 425–26, 506–7
Ghirardelli Soda Fountain & Chocolate
   Shop, 502
Gideon's Bakehouse, 503
gift cards, Disney, 355
Glaskunst (shop), 507
Glimmering Greenhouses, 419
golf, 67, 79
Goofy's Candy Co., 502
Google Maps, 346
Gorilla Falls Exploration Trail, 303, 441, 448
GPS coordinates, for theme parks, 346
Grand Avenue (DHS), 472
Gran Fiesta Tour Starring the Three
   Caballeros, 423
Grauman's Chinese Theatre replica, 462
greeting, Disney characters. *See* meet and
   greets
grocery stores, 362–63
Guardians of the Galaxy: Cosmic Rewind, 15,
   44, 304, 404, 413–14
Guerlain (shop), 507
Guest Relations
   Animal Kingdom, 356, 440
   Disney's Hollywood Studios, 462
   Disney Springs, 356
   EPCOT, 356
   Magic Kingdom, 356
Guide for Guests with Disabilities, 28

See also the Accommodations Index on pages 519–524 and the Restaurant Index on pages 525–528.

SUBJECT INDEX

Hall of Presidents, The, 381–82
Happily Ever After (show), 395
Harambe (Animal Kingdom), 447–50
Harambe Village Acrobats, 456
hard-of-hearing guests, services for, 320
Harley-Davidson, 503
Haunted Mansion, The, 382
Havaianas (shop), 500–501
headache remedies, 358
headliner attractions, 44
health considerations, 38, 358–59
healthful food, 212
heat and humidity, 357–58
height requirements, for attractions, 307, 308–9, 489, 490
Hertz, 332
holiday(s)
  attendance during, 32
  early arrival advantage during, 45
  special events during, 32–34
Hollywood Boulevard (DHS), 306, 459, 462, 465–70
homes, rental, 182, 183–86
honeymoon packages, 325–26
Hotel Room Views project, 83
hotels. *See* accommodations; *separate Accommodations index*
Hotels.com, 182
Hotwire, 85, 182
hours of operation, 40–41
  Animal Kingdom, 439
  Early Entry and, 35, 79, 80
  EPCOT, 408
  water parks, 481
House of Blues, 504, 511
House of Good Fortune, 506
Humunga Kowabunga, 486, 490, 491

I-4, Lake Buena Vista area, accommodations, 180, 188–90, 191
ice, restrictions on, 328
Il Bel Cristallo (shop), 507
ImageWorks, 506
Imagination! Pavilion, 417
Impressions de France (film), 428–29
Incredi-Pass, 66, 68
Indiana Jones Epic Stunt Spectacular!, 470–71
Indigenous Peoples' Day, 34
infants. *See* children
information. *See also* planning
  accommodations, 82–88
  admission, 60–76
  Animal Kingdom, 440
  EPCOT, 408–12
  live entertainment, 369, 462
  Magic Kingdom, 368–74
  parades, 368
  vacation-home rental, 182, 183–86
  water parks, 482–87
insurance, car-rental, 333
insurance, trip, 20
International Drive (I-Drive) area, 180, 187–88, 189, 350, 352, 353
international food, 219–22, 241–45
international visitors, tips for, 21
internet, information on
  accommodations, 82, 85, 106, 182–83
  admission tickets, 69
  discussion boards, 29
  My Disney Experience, 24–26
  TouringPlans.com, 26–27
  Wi-Fi connections in parks, 356
Interstate 4 (I-4), 180, 181, 188–90, 191, 334–37, 348, 351
Irlo Bronson Memorial Highway (US 192), 180, 190, 193, 348, 349
Island Mercantile, 507
Italy Pavilion, 426, 507
It's a Small World, 304, 385

Jaleo (bar at), 504
JAMMitors, 431
Japan Pavilion, 427, 507
Jedi Training, 518
Joffrey's Coffee & Tea Company, 503
Johnny Was (shop), 500–501
Johnston & Murphy (shop), 503
Jollywood Nights, 34, 75–76
Jo Malone (shop), 503
Journey into Imagination with Figment, 307, 417
Journey of Water, Inspired by Moana, 15, 404, 417–18
Jungle Cruise, 304, 377

Kali River Rapids, 48, 452
Karamell-Küche (shop), 425, 506
Kate Spade New York, 503
Keelhaul Falls, 490, 491
Kendra Scott (shop), 500–501
kennels, 362
Ketchakiddee Creek, 490, 491
Keystone Clothiers, 508
Key to the World (KTTW) Card, 73–74
Kidcot Fun Stops, 421, 423
kids. *See* children
Kilimanjaro Safaris, 448–49
Kingdom Strollers, 301
Kissimmee, accommodations near, 180
Kora Tinga Tinga (musician), 456
Kunstarbeit in Kristall (shop), 507

La Cava del Tequila (bar), 423
Lacoste, 500–501
Lake Buena Vista, accommodations, 180, 188–90, 191
Landing, The (Disney Springs), 16, 499, 503
Land Pavilion, The, 418–20
La Princesa de Cristal (shop), 505
larger guests, 322–23
La Signature (shop), 507

See also the Accommodations Index on pages 519–524 and the Restaurant Index on pages 525–528.

SUBJECT INDEX

lazy rivers, 486
Legends of Hollywood (shop), 508
Lego Store, The, 502
L'Esprit de la Provence, 508
Les Vins de Chefs de France, 508
Levi's, 503
Liberty Square, 381–82
  for children, 305
  Hall of Presidents, The, 381–82
  Haunted Mansion, The, 382
  not-to-be-missed attractions, 368
Lightning Lane passes, 15, 48–49, 53–57, 74
  Animal Kingdom, 440, 442–44
  DAS card use, 316, 318
  Disney resort early access, 78, 80
  Disney's Hollywood Studios, 54, 463–65
  EPCOT, 54, 408, 409–12
  Lightning Lane Multi Pass (LLMP), 24, 48, 52, 53–56
  Lightning Lane Premier Pass (PP), 57
  Lightning Lane Single Pass (LLSP), 24, 48–49, 52, 56–57
  Magic Kingdom, 54, 370–74
  touring plans and, 373–74
Lilly Pulitzer (shop), 503
lines. *See also* crowds; Lightning Lane passes; touring plans
  games for, 309
  single-rider lines, 59, 327
  waiting strategies in, 43–59, 307, 309–10
Lines app, 26, 27
Lion King, Festival of the, 447–48
Little Mermaid, Under the Sea—Journey of the, 389–90
Little Mermaid—A Musical Adventure, The, 474–75
live entertainment. *See also* Disney characters; shows, theater and stage
  Animal Kingdom, 455–56
  dinner theater, 226–27
  in Disney's Hollywood Studios, 467–68, 478–79
  in EPCOT, 430–33, 511
  in Fantasyland, 394–99
  fireworks, 15, 395–96, 397–99, 430–33, 495
  in Frontierland, 394–99
  in Future World, 430–33
  information on, 369, 462
  in Magic Kingdom, 394–99
  on Main Street, U.S.A., 375–76, 394–99
  music, 394–99, 430–33, 510–11
  parades. *See* parades
  in World Showcase, 430–33
Living with the Land, 304, 418–19
L'Occitane en Provence (shop), 500–501
lockers, 362
  Animal Kingdom, 440
  Disney's Hollywood Studios, 462
  Magic Kingdom, 369
  water parks, 483, 485

lodging. *See* accommodations
Lords and Ladies (shop), 508
lost and found, 358
  Animal Kingdom, 440
  contact information, 37
  Disney's Hollywood Studios, 462
  EPCOT, 408
  Magic Kingdom, 369
lost persons, 302–3
  Animal Kingdom, 440
  Disney characters and, 302
  Disney's Hollywood Studios, 462
  EPCOT, 408
  Magic Kingdom, 369
  water parks, 487
Lovepop, 503
Lululemon, 503
Luminous (fireworks), 15, 404, 431–32
Luxury of Time, 500–501
Lyft app, 331, 345
MAC Cosmetics, 503
Mad Tea Party, 385–86
MagicBand+ wristbands, 23–24, 73–74, 309, 355, 358, 483
Magic Carpets of Aladdin, The, 377
Magic Kingdom, 364–403. *See also* specific "lands" by name
  accommodations in or near, 92, 93, 110–29
  Adventureland, 377–79
  After Hours events, 76
  arriving at, 338, 364–65
  attractions, 366–67. *See also* specific attractions by name
    for children, 305
    height restrictions, 308
    Lightning Lane options, 54, 370–74
    not-to-be-missed, 368
    pregnant guests and, 321
    ratings by age, 369–70
    sample ride vehicles, 322
    Rider Switch, attractions offering, 309
  baby care in, 298
  behind the scenes, 494–95
  cavalcades, 394
  commuting time to/from, 340
  dining in, 218–19, 228, 229–30, 231–32, 374
  Disney characters in, 312, 369, 376, 384–85, 388–89
  Early Entry benefits, 34–35
  Extended Evening Theme Park Hours, 36
  Fantasyland, 382–90
  fireworks, 395–96, 397–99
  first aid in, 298
  Frontierland, 379–81
  GPS coordinates, 346
  Guest Relations, 356
  hard-ticket events, 399
  Liberty Square, 381–82
  live entertainment, 394–99
  Main Street. *See* Main Street, U.S.A.
  map, 366–67

See also the Accommodations Index on pages 519–524 and the Restaurant Index on pages 525–528.

540 SUBJECT INDEX

Magic Kingdom *(continued)*
  orientation, 368–74
  overview, 8–9, 364–68
  rope-drop procedures, 365, 368, 399
  parades, 396–97
  parking, 346–47, 365
  physical size of, 8
  services, 369
  shopping, 505
  strollers in, 300, 369
  Tomorrowland, 390–94
  touring plans, 373–74, 401–3
  traffic patterns, 399–400
  transportation to/from, 339, 364–65, 376–77
  when to go, 40
Maharajah Jungle Trek, 452–53
Main Street, U.S.A. (Magic Kingdom), 374–77
  attractions
    Cinderella Castle, 369, 375, 382–83
    Meet Mickey at Town Square Theater, 376
    Walt Disney World Railroad, 376–77
  cavalcades, 394
  City Hall, 368
  live entertainment, 375–76, 394–99
  services, 369
  vehicles, 376
Main Street Cinema, 505
Main Street Confectionery, 505
Main Street Jewelers, 505
major attractions, 44
makeovers, 515–16
Mall at Millenia, The, 509
Many Adventures of Winnie the Pooh, The, 386
maps
  Animal Kingdom, 436–37
  Blizzard Beach, 488
  Disney's Hollywood Studios, 460–61
  Disney Springs, 500–501
  EPCOT, 406–7
  Google Maps, 346
  I-4 and Walt Disney World area, 335
  list of, iv
  Magic Kingdom, 366–67
  South Orlando, 10–11
  Typhoon Lagoon, 491
  Walt Disney World, 12–13
marathons, 33, 512–13
Mardi Gras, 33
marine animals, in The Seas with Nemo & Friends Pavilion, 420–21
Marketplace (Disney Springs), 14, 499, 502
Marketplace carousel, 499
Marketplace Co-op, 502
Marketplace Train Express, 500–501
marriage license, 325
massages, 515
Matsuriza, 431
Mayday Falls, 490, 491

Mears Connect, 329–30, 353
Mears Transportation Group, 331
Medical Concierge, 359
medical problems, 358–59
medications, 299, 320
meet and greets, 311–13
  Adventurers Outpost, 445
  Anna and Elsa, 424–25
  Ariel's Grotto, 383
  Disney stars at *Red Carpet Dreams,* 471
  Enchanted Tales with Belle, 384–85
  Mickey & friends in World Celebration, 416
  Mickey Mouse at Town Square Theater, 376
  Mirabel at Fairytale Garden, 386
  Olaf at Celebrity Spotlight, 471
  Princess Fairytale Hall, 388–89
  Star Wars Launch Bay, 474
  venues for, 312
Melt-Away Bay, 487, 488, 489
Memory Maker service, 74, 360–61
merry-go-rounds
  Prince Charming Regal Carrousel, 388
  Marketplace carousel, 499
Mexico Pavilion, 423, 506
Mickey & Minnie's Runaway Railway, 15, 458, 468
Mickey Mouse meet and greets, 376, 416
Mickey Shorts Theater, 472
Mickey's Not-So-Scary Halloween Party, 33–34, 75
Mickey's of Hollywood, 508
Mickey's PhilharMagic (film), 387
military personnel, discounts for, 71, 72, 88
Millennium Falcon: Smugglers Run, 475, 476–77
miniature cars, 392–93
miniature golf, 516–17
Minnie Vans, 345
minor attractions, 44
Miss Adventure Falls, 490–91
Mission: Space, 44, 414–15
Mitsukoshi Department Store, 427, 507
M&M's (shop), 504
mobile ordering of food, 213
mobile payments, 355
Mombasa Marketplace, 508
moms-to-be, tips for, 321–22
money services
  Animal Kingdom, 440
  Disney's Hollywood Studios, 462
  EPCOT, 408
  Magic Kingdom, 369
monorail, 338, 343–44, 365
Monsters, Inc. Laugh Floor, 391–92
Monstropolis, 9, 472
Morimoto Asia (bar at), 504
Morocco Pavilion, 427, 507
motels. *See* accommodations; *separate Accommodations index*

See also the Accommodations Index on pages 519–524 and the Restaurant Index on pages 525–528.

motion sickness, 44
motion simulators
  Avatar Flight of Passage, 454–55
  Mission: Space, 414–15
  Soarin' Around the World, 419–20
  Star Tours—The Adventures Continue, 471–72
  Test Track, 415
MouseSavers, 28
movies. *See* AMC Disney Springs 24 Dine-In Theatres; films and animated shows
Mount Gushmore chairlift, 488
music. *See also* concerts
  Animal Kingdom, 456
  Garden Rocks concert series, 511
  Magic Kingdom, 394–99
My Disney Experience (MDE) app, 20, 24–26, 73–74, 106, 342, 360–62
MyMagic +, 23–24
Na Hoku (shop), 503
National (car rental), 332, 333
Na'vi River Journey, 441–43, 455
Nemo & Friends, 420–21
New Hope Confections, A, 516
New Year's events, 32
nightlife
  in accommodations, 510–11
  dining in lounges, 221–22, 228
  dinner theater, 226–27
  Disney Springs, 504
noise
  in accommodations, 100, 105, 106
  in restaurants, 217, 226
nonapparent disabilities, services for guests with, 316
Northwest Mercantile, 508
Norway Pavilion, 423–25, 506
not-to-be-missed attractions
  Animal Kingdom, 439
  Disney's Hollywood Studios, 459
  EPCOT, 405
  Magic Kingdom, 368
nursing of infants, 299

Oakley (shop), 500–501
Oasis, The (Animal Kingdom), 444
Odyssey Center (EPCOT), 406–7
off-season touring, 29, 30
off-site vs. on-site accommodations, advantages and disadvantages, 36, 53
Oktoberfest Musikanten, 425
Olaf, Meet at Celebrity Spotlight, 471
Olde Christmas Shoppe, 505
older guests, 323–25
Olukai (shop), 500–501
Once Upon a Toy (shop), 502
online information. *See* internet
online travel agencies (OTAs), 182
opening procedures. *See* rope-drop procedures
OpenTable restaurant reservations, 210

operating hours. *See* hours of operation
Orbitz, 182
Orlando International Airport (MCO)
  departing from, 353–54
  getting to Disney World from, 329–37
  shopping at, 510
Orlando Magical Rides, 330–31
Orlando Premium Outlets, 509
Orlando Stroller Rentals, 301
Oscar's Super Service, 300
Outpost (EPCOT), 506
overheating, of children, 297
package handling, 362
pagoda, Japanese, 427
painting class, 517
Pandora Jewelry (shop), 503
Pandora—The World of Avatar, 15, 439, 453–55
parades. *See also* cavalcades
  Disney Parks Christmas Day Parade, 34
  Disney Starlight Parade, 15, 395
  Festival of Fantasy Parade, 395
  lost children at, 303
  Magic Kingdom
    information on, 368
    leaving after fireworks, 397–99
    traffic patterns and, 400
    viewing, 396–97
Park Hopper/Park Hopper Plus, 67, 70–71, 343, 480
parking, 79, 107
  Animal Kingdom, 346–47
  costs, 347
  for disabled guests, 324
  Disney's Hollywood Studios, 346–47, 459
  EPCOT, 346–48, 405
  lot locations, 346
  Magic Kingdom, 346–47, 365
  water parks, 480, 487
partial-day option at theme parks, 41–42
parties
  Disney's Very Merry Christmas Party, 34, 75
  Magic Kingdom After Hours, 76
  Mickey's Not-So-Scary Halloween Party, 75
Payless (car rental), 332
Pelé Soccer (shop), 504
PeopleMover, Tomorrowland Transit Authority, 393
pet care, 362
Peter Pan's Flight, 387
Pete's Silly Sideshow, 388
pharmacies, 359
PhilharMagic, Mickey's, 387
phone numbers, 37–38. *See also specific service or attraction*
phones. *See* cell phones
PhotoPass, 360–62, 500–501
photos, for souvenirs, 74, 360–62
physicians, 359

See also the Accommodations Index on pages 519–524 and the Restaurant Index on pages 525–528.

SUBJECT INDEX

PIN codes, for discounts, 87
Pin Traders, Disney's, 500-501
pirate activities
  Pirate's Adventure: Treasure of the Seven Seas, A, 378
  Pirates of the Caribbean ride, 378
Pirate Pass, 68
Pixar Place, 479
Pixie Dust Pass, 68
planDisney website, 28
planning, 19-38. *See also* touring plans
  accommodations, 77-81, 179-80
  information resources, 23-29
  My Disney Experience issues, 24-26
  MyMagic+, 23-24
  timeline for, 19-23
  when to go, 29-36
Plaza de Los Amigos, 506
Plaza Gardens East and West, viewing fireworks from, 397
PlugShare, 354
Plume et Palette (shop), 507-8
Polar Patios, 485
ponchos, 65, 357
pools and amenities, 92-93, 95
Port of Entry (shop), 506
pregnant guests, tips for, 321-22
prescriptions, 359
Presidents, The Hall of, 381-82
Presidents' Day, 33
Priceline, 85, 182
Primark, 66, 509
Prince Charming Regal Carrousel, 388
princess(es). *See* meet and greets
Princess Fairytale Hall, 388-89
Pura Vida (shop), 500-501

quality ratings, accommodations, 88-91
Queen's Table, The (shop), 508
queues. *See* lines

rack rates, accommodations, 61
radio frequency identification (RFID) chip, 73, 74
Rafiki's Planet Watch, 449-50
raft rides
  Gangplank Falls, Keehaul Falls, Mayday Falls, Miss Adventure Falls (Typhoon Lagoon), 490
  Kali River Rapids (Animal Kingdom), 48, 452
  Na'vi River Journey (Animal Kingdom), 441-43, 455
  Runoff Rapids (Blizzard Beach), 488, 489
  Teamboat Springs (Blizzard Beach), 487-488, 489
Raglan Road (bar at), 504
railroads. *See* trains
rain/raingear, 356-57
reader comments, 5-6, 107-10
recreation

  accommodations and, 79
  classes, 517-18
  contact information, 37-38
  golf, 79
  miniature golf, 516-17
  RunDisney, 512-14
  spa services, 514-16
  wilderness adventures, 516
Reflections of China (film), 425
reflective captioning, 320
religious services, 362
Remy's Ratatouille Adventure, 15, 404, 429
rentals. *See also* wheelchairs
  car, 28, 331-34, 346
  condominium, 183-86
  ECV (scooter), 318-19, 369, 398, 408, 462
  locker, 362, 369, 440, 462, 483
  stroller, 300, 301, 369, 408, 440, 462
  vacation home, 183-86
reservations
  accommodations, 20, 25, 82-88, 182-83, 185-86
  for admission, 68
  contact information, 37-38
  online information on, 24-26
  restaurant, 25-26, 28, 207-10, 408
  ride. *See* Lightning Lane passes
restaurants. *See* dining; separate Restaurant Index
restrooms, 303
rest time during visit, 41
RFID (radio frequency identification) chip, 73, 74
Rider Switch, 47, 307, 309, 409
rides. *See also specific "lands" and parks by name*
  boat. *See* boat rides
  for children, 304-7
  dark. *See* dark rides
  flume, 381, 489, 490
  frightening, 304-7
  height requirements for, 307, 308-9
  last-minute cold feet at, 310
  lost children at, 303
  motion-sickness potential for, 44
  reservations. *See* Lightning Lane passes
  roller coaster. *See* roller coasters
  simulator. *See* simulator rides
  single-rider lines for, 59, 327
  unexpected closures of, 47-49
  visual impact of, 307
  waiting-in-line strategies for. *See* waiting-in-line strategies
ride-sharing services, 330, 331, 345, 365, 499
River Roost (bar), 510
Rix Sports Bar & Grill, 510
Rock 'n' Roller Coaster, 44, 468-69
roller coasters
  Barnstormer, The, 383
  Big Thunder Mountain Railroad, 44, 306,

See also the Accommodations Index on pages 519-523 and the Restaurant Index on pages 525-526.

SUBJECT INDEX

379–80
Expedition Everest, 44, 450–51
Guardians of the Galaxy: Cosmic Rewind, 404, 413–14
Rock 'n' Roller Coaster, 44, 468–69
Seven Dwarfs Mine Train, 48, 389
Slinky Dog Dash, 473
Space Mountain, 44, 48, 307, 392
Tron Lightcycle/Run, 393–94
romantic getaways, 226, 328
Ron Jon Surf Shop, 500–501
room-only reservation, 82
rope-drop procedures, 45–46
  Animal Kingdom, 439–40
  Disney's Hollywood Studios, 459
  Early Entry and, 35, 78, 80
  EPCOT, 408
  Magic Kingdom, 365, 368, 399
Rothy's (shop), 500–501
Royal Sommerhus meet and greet, 424–25
RunDisney, 512–14
Runoff Rapids, 488, 489

safaris. *See* Animal Kingdom
safety and security
  contact information, 38
  Orlando International Airport, 353–54
  for single travelers, 327
  on waterslides, 489, 490
Sanford International Airport, 336–37
Sangria University, 517
Savannah Bee Company, 500–501
Savi's Workshop (shop), 478
Savor the Savanna, 496
scams, accommodations, 183
Scat Cat's Club, 510
scavenger hunts (Wilderness Explorers), 446–47
Scooterbug Rentals, 501
scooters, electric, 318–19
seasons to visit WDW, 29–30, 84–85, 291–92
Seas with Nemo & Friends Pavilion, The, 420–21
security. *See* safety and security
Segway tour, 516
Selina Ashley (hairstylist), 515
seniors. *See* older guests
Senses Spa, 514–15
Sephora, 500–501
service animals, 316
services, 360–63
  Animal Kingdom, 440
  baby care, 298–99, 300, 369, 408, 440, 462
  babysitting, 313
  banking, 355–56, 369, 408, 440, 462
  camera memory cards and supplies, 506
  car trouble, 347
  cash and ATMs, 355, 369, 408, 440, 462
  cell phone charging, 356, 408, 440, 462
  check-in and checkout, 105–6

currency exchange, 356
for deaf and hard-of-hearing guests, 320
for disabled guests, 28, 316–19, 320, 369, 408, 440, 462
  Disney's Hollywood Studios, 462
  EPCOT, 408
first aid, 298–99, 358–59, 369, 408, 440, 462
grocery delivery, 362–63
information. *See* information
lockers, 362, 369, 440, 462, 483, 485
lost and found, 37, 358, 369, 408, 440, 462
lost persons, 302–3, 369, 408, 440, 462, 487
Magic Kingdom, 369
money, 408, 440, 462
pet care, 362
PhotoPass and Memory Maker, 360–62
religious, 362
reservations. *See* reservations
strollers. *See* strollers
for visually impaired guests, 320
wedding, 325
wheelchairs. *See* wheelchairs
Seven Dwarfs Mine Train, 48, 389
ShopDisney (online), 509
shopping
  in Animal Kingdom, 507
  discounts for, 508, 509–10
  in Disney Hollywood Studios, 478, 508
  in Disney Springs, 498–504
  in EPCOT, 505–8
  grocery stores, 362–63
  Magic Kingdom, 505
  in malls, 509
  in outlet stores, 509–10
  outside Disney World, 510
  pharmacies, 359
  souvenirs, 74, 360–62, 505, 507–10
  in World Showcase, 505–8
Shore (shop), 500–501
shows, theater and stage. *See also* dinner theater; films and animated shows; live entertainment
  American Adventure, The, 426–27
  Beauty and the Beast—Live on Stage, 466
  Disney Junior Play and Dance!, 474
  Disney's Hollywood Studios, 478–79
  Disney Villains: Unfairly Ever After, 15, 466
  Fantasmic!, 467–68
  Feathered Friends in Flight!, 451–52
  Festival of the Lion King, 447–48
  Finding Nemo—The Big Blue ... and Beyond!, 453
  For the First Time in Forever: A Frozen Sing-Along Celebration, 470
  Hall of the Presidents, The, 381–82
  Happily Ever After, 395

See also the Accommodations Index on pages 519–523 and the Restaurant Index on pages 525–526.

Little Mermaid—A Musical Adventure, The, 474-75
lost children at, 303
  traffic patterns and, 400
Walt Disney's Carousel of Progress, 394
Winged Encounters—The Kingdom Takes Flight, 456
shuttle service
  from accommodations, 339, 342, 353
  to/from airport, 332, 353
sign-language interpretations, 320
simulator rides
  Avatar Flight of Passage, 454-55
  Millennium Falcon: Smugglers Run, 475, 476-77
  Mission: Space, 414-15
  Soarin' Around the World, 419-20
  Star Tours—The Adventures Continue, 471-72
  Test Track, 415
single-rider lines, 59, 327
singles activities, 327, 328
Sixt (car rental), 332, 333
size, of accommodations, 92, 98-99, 100-104
Ski Patrol Training Camp, 487, 488, 489
Skyliner gondola system, 15, 338, 344-45, 459
slides, water. *See* water parks
Slinky Dog Dash, 473
Slush Gusher, 486, 487, 488, 489
Small World, It's a, 304, 385
smoking prohibition, 328
snacks, 65-66
sneak routes, for driving, 348-53
Snow Stormers, 488, 489, 490
Snow White, 121, 216-17, 312, 389
Soarin' Around the World, 419-20
Sol, A Wellness Company, 515
Sorcerer Pass, 68
Souk-al-Magreb (shop), 507
South Orlando map, 10-11
souvenirs, 66, 508-9
Souvenirs de France, 508
Space Mountain, 44, 48, 307, 392
Space Mountain Gift Shop, 505
Spaceship Earth, 409, 413, 416-17
spa services, 514-16
special deliveries, 516
special events, 32-34, 51, 74-76. *See also* live entertainment
Special Hours, 369
special kids' programs, 313-14
speeding, 348
Speedway, Tomorrowland, 392-93
Sperry (shop), 500-501
Spice & Tea Exchange, The, 502
Splitsville (bar at), 504
Splitsville bowling, 277, 499
Sportsman's Shoppe, 508
Springtime Surprise, 513
stage shows. *See* shows, theater and stage

Stance (shop), 500-501
standby queues, 48, 52
Starlight Parade, 15, 395
Starlight Safari, 496
Star Tours—The Adventures Continue, 44, 471-72
Star Wars: Galaxy's Edge, 15, 306, 459, 475-79
Star Wars: Rise of the Resistance, 48-49, 458, 476, 477-78
Star Wars Galactic Outpost, 504
Star Wars Launch Bay, 474
Star Wars Trading Post (shop), 502
Stein Haus (shop), 507
STK Orlando (bar at), 504
storage lockers. *See* lockers
Storm Slides, 490, 491
Storybook Circus, 382
street performers, Animal Kingdom, 456
strollers, 65, 299-301
  at Animal Kingdom, 300, 440
  banned from rides, 297
  at Disney's Hollywood Studios, 300, 462
  at EPCOT, 300, 408
  looking out for, 324
  at Magic Kingdom, 300, 369
  for older kids, 299-300
  at parades, 398
  taken or moved, 301
studios. *See* Disney's Hollywood Studios
stunt shows, 470-71
Sugarboo (shop), 503
Summer House on the Lake (cookie bar at), 504
Summit Plummet, 486, 487, 488, 489
sunburn, 297
Sun Country, 337
Sundries (shop), 500-501
sunglasses, 298
Sunglass Hut (shop), 504
Sunset Boulevard, 306, 459, 462, 465-70
Superdry (shop), 503
super-headliner attractions, 43
Super Hero Headquarters (shop), 504
surcharges, admission, 66-67
Surf Pool, 490, 491, 492
swimming, 92-93, 95. *See also* water parks
Swiss Family Treehouse, 378-79
switching off in lines, 307, 309, 409

Tampa International Airport (TPA), 337
Tam Tam Drummers of Harambe, 456
tantrums, 296
tattoos, temporary, 302
taxis, 331
TD Collectibles, 510
Tea Caddy, The, 508
teacup ride (Mad Tea Party), 385-86
Teamboat Springs, 487, 488, 489
Temple of Heaven replica, 425
Test Track, 15, 47, 415

See also the Accommodations Index on pages 519-524 and the Restaurant Index on pages 525-528.

SUBJECT INDEX

Thanksgiving, 34
Theater of the Stars, 466
theater shows. *See* shows, theater and stage
themed resort hotels, 95–97, 98. *See also separate Accommodations index*
TheUnofficialGuides.com, 27
third-party ticket wholesalers, 69, 71
Three Caballeros, 423
Thrifty (car rental), 332
Thrill Data, 28–29
thrill rides, 44
Tiana's Bayou Adventure, 15, 47, 306, 381
Ticket Price Comparison Tool, 70
tickets. *See* admission
Tike's Peak, 487, 488, 489
Tiki Birds, 379
time and timing
  allocating time at WDW, 39–43
  arrival and departure days, 41–43
  avoiding long waits in line, 43–59
  hours of operation, 40–41
  order of parks to see, deciding on, 40
  taking time out to rest, 41
  when to visit WDW, 29–36, 324
Tinker Bell's flight, 397
Toboggan Racers, 488, 489
tolls, 334
Tommy Bahama, 503
Tomorrowland (Magic Kingdom), 390–94
  Astro Orbiter, 390–91
  Buzz Lightyear's Space Ranger Spin, 391
  for children, 305
  Monsters, Inc. Laugh Floor, 391–92
  not-to-be-missed attractions, 368
  Space Mountain, 44, 48, 307, 392
  Tron Lightcycle/Run, 393–94
  Walt Disney's Carousel of Progress, 394
Tomorrowland Speedway, 392–93
Tomorrowland Transit Authority PeopleMover, 393
Top of the World, 510
touring plans
  Animal Kingdom, 440, 442–44, 457
  for children, 297, 401–2
  crowd level information, 26, 31–32
  customized, 26, 49–50
  Disney characters' effect on, 297
  Disney's Hollywood Studios, 479
  Early Entry and, 51
  EPCOT, 433–34
  Extended Evening Theme Hours and, 51
  Lightning Lane passes, 373–74
  Magic Kingdom, 373–74, 401–3
  online sources for, 26–28
  rejecting the plan, consequences of, 50–51
  reliability consideration in, 48–49
  special events and, 51
  as strategy for avoiding lines, 46–51
  variables affecting, 47–49

videos, 28
water parks, 482, 493
TouringPlans.com, 26–27, 49–50
Tower of Terror, The Twilight Zone, 306–7, 469–70
town car service, 330–31
Town Center, Disney Springs, 499, 503
Town Square Theater, Meet Mickey at, 376
Toy Soldier, The (shop), 508
Toy Story Land, 15, 306, 459, 472–74
Toy Story Mania!, 473–74
Trader Sam's Grog Grotto, 510
traffic (car), 66, 182
traffic patterns, in parks
  Animal Kingdom, 456
  EPCOT, 433
  Future World, 433
  Magic Kingdom, 399–400
  World Showcase, 433
trains
  Big Thunder Mountain Railroad, 44, 306, 379–80
  Seven Dwarfs Mine Train, 48, 389
  Walt Disney World Railroad, 297, 376, 381, 390
  Wildlife Express, 450
transportation. *See also* buses
  accommodations, as factor in choosing, 91
  boat, 344, 422–23, 459
  car rental, 28, 331–34, 346
  for disabled visitors, 318–19
  driving on I-4, 334–36
  driving vs. using the Disney transportation system, 339, 340–41
  inside Disney World, 8, 80–81, 337–54
  Magical Express, 329
  on Main Street, U.S.A., 376
  Mears Connect, 329–30
  monorail, 338, 343–44, 366–67
  for older guests, 324
  opening procedures, 46
  ride-sharing services, 330, 331, 345, 365, 499
  for single travelers, 327
  Skyliner, 15, 338, 344–45, 459
  taxis, 331
  to/from accommodations, 80–81, 182, 337–45
  to/from airport, 329–37, 353–54
  to/from Animal Kingdom, 439
  to/from Disney's Hollywood Studios, 459
  to/from Disney World, 329–37
  to/from Magic Kingdom, 364–65, 376
  Tomorrowland Transit Authority PeopleMover, 393
  town car service, 330–31
  WDW Railroad, 297, 376–77, 381, 390
  Wildlife Express Train, 450
Transportation and Ticket Center (TTC), 338, 365
travel agents, 82, 87, 182

See also the Accommodations Index on pages 519–524 and the Restaurant Index on pages 525–528.

SUBJECT INDEX

Travelocity, 85, 182
travel packages, 178–80, 325
treasure hunts, 378
Treehouse, Swiss Family, 378–79
Tree of Life, The, 446–47
Tren-D (shop), 502
Tri-Circle-D Ranch, 516
trip insurance, 20
Tripster (third-party ticket wholesaler), 69
Tron Lightcycle/Run, 15, 44, 393–94
Tropical Americas (Animal Kingdom), 435
TSA PreCheck, 353, 354
tubes, in water parks, 484
Turo (car-share service), 332, 333
Turtle Talk with Crush, 421
Twilight Zone Tower of Terror, The, 306, 307, 469–70
@two4art (vendor), 515
Typhoon Lagoon, 489–92
   commuting time to/from, 341, 342
   crowds, 481
   GPS coordinates, 346
   height restrictions, 308
   overview, 14
   Surf Pool, 491

Uber app, 331, 345
Under Armour, 500–501
Under the Sea—Journey of the Little Mermaid, 389–90
Uniqlo, 503
United Kingdom, ticket purchase in, 72
United Kingdom Pavilion, 429–30, 508
United States Pavilion (The American Adventure), 426
Universal Orlando, accommodations in or near, 181–82, 187–88
UNOde50 (shop), 500–501
"Unofficial Guides Newsletter," 27
Unofficial Guide to Disney Cruise Line, The, 4
Unofficial Guide to Universal Orlando, The, 4, 481
Unofficial Guide to Walt Disney World, The, 1–6
Up Close with Rhinos, 496
upgrades, for accommodations, 88
US 192 (Irlo Bronson Memorial Highway), 180, 190, 193, 348, 349

Vacation Fun at Mickey Shorts Theater, 472
vacation homes, rental, 66, 182, 183–86
Valley of Mo'ara, 453
vendor food, 205
Vera Bradley, 503
views, from accommodations, 83
Village Traders, 506
Vineyard Vines (shop), 500–501
Vintage Amphicar & Italian Water Taxi Tours, 249, 500–501
VIP tours, 496–97

virtual queues, 24, 52
Visit Orlando (website), 186
Visitor Toll Pass, 334
visually impaired guests, 320
Voices of Liberty, 426, 430
Volkskunst (shop), 507
Vrbo, 61, 182

waiting-in-line strategies, 43–59. *See also* Lightning Lane passes
   boarding groups/virtual queues, 52
   early arrival advantages, 44–45
   for rides, 43–44, 307, 309–10
   single-rider line, 59, 327
   standby queues, 48, 52
   tools for, 27
   touring plan strategy, 46–51
   water parks, 481
Walt Disney Presents (film), 475
Walt Disney's Carousel of Progress, 394
Walt Disney's Enchanted Tiki Room, 379
Walt Disney World Marathon, 33, 512–13
Walt Disney World Railroad, 297, 376–77, 381, 390
Walt Disney World (WDW)
   acronyms and abbreviations, 17–18
   contact information, 37–38
   electric-vehicle charging in, 354
   map, 12–13
   overview, 7–18
   size of, 8–9
   special events, 32–34
   travel packages, 178–80, 325
   what's new, 15
Wandering Reindeer, The, 506
water-flume rides. *See* flume rides
water parks, 480–93. *See also* Blizzard Beach; Typhoon Lagoon
   admission to, 67, 72, 480, 483
   as arrival-day option, 42
   attire for, 482
   dining at, 482
   height restrictions, 489, 490
   hours of operation, 481
   lazy rivers, 486
   lockers at, 483, 485
   overview, 7, 14, 480–82
   parking, 480, 487
   picnics, 482
   planning for, 482–87
   pregnant guests, tips for, 321
   ratings by age, 482
   slides, 486, 487
   touring plans, 482, 493
   tubes, 484
   waiting-in-line strategies, 481
   wave pools, 485, 487, 489
   weather conditions, 481, 486
   when to go, 481
waterslides, wave pools. *See* water parks
weather in Florida, 29–31, 65

See also the Accommodations Index on pages 519–524 and the Restaurant Index on pages 525–528.

SUBJECT INDEX

behind-the-scenes tours, 495
Fantasmic! cancellation, 467
heat and humidity, 357-58
rain/raingear, 356-57
ride closures, 49
water-park use, 481, 486
websites. *See* internet
weddings, commitment ceremonies, vow renewals, 325
Weinkeller (shop), 506-7
West Side (Disney Springs), 499, 504
wheelchairs, 318-19
  Animal Kingdom, 440
  Disney's Hollywood Studios, 462
  EPCOT, 408
  Magic Kingdom, 369
  at parades, 398
  water parks, 483
whitewater raft rides. *See* raft rides
Wi-Fi connections in parks, 356
Wild Africa Trek, 496
Wilderness Explorers, 446-47
wildlife, in water bodies, 298
Wildlife Express Train, 450
Windtraders, 507
Wine Bar George (bar at), 504
Wine & Dine Half-Marathon Weekend, 34
Winged Encounters—The Kingdom Takes Flight, 456
Winnie the Pooh, The Many Adventures of, 386
Winter Summerland Miniature Golf, 517
Wonderful World of Animation, 479
Wonderful World of Memories, Disney's, 500-501
World Celebration (EPCOT), 405, 415-417
  attractions
    ¡Celebración Encanto!, 415
    Club Cool, 415-16
    Spaceship Earth, 409, 413, 416-17
  map, 406-7
World Discovery (EPCOT), 405, 413-15
  attractions
    Guardians of the Galaxy: Cosmic Rewind, 15, 44, 304, 413-14
    Mission: Space, 414-15
    Test Track, 415
  map, 406-7
World Nature (EPCOT), 405, 417-421
  attractions, 417-21
    Awesome Planet, 418
    Journey of Water, Inspired by Moana, 417-18
    Living with the Land, 304, 418-19
    Seas with Nemo & Friends, The, 420-21
    Soarin' Around the World, 419-20
    Turtle Talk with Crush, 421
  Land Pavilion, The, 418-20
  map, 406-7
  Seas with Nemo & Friends Pavilion, The, 420-21
World of Disney (superstore), 499, 502
World Showcase (EPCOT), 42, 404, 409, 421-30
  attractions, 421-30
    American Adventure Pavilion, The, 426-27
    Canada Pavilion, 430, 508
    for children, 306
    China Pavilion, 425, 506
    France Pavilion, 427-29, 507-8
    Germany Pavilion, 425-26, 506-7
    Italy Pavilion, 426, 507
    Japan Pavilion, 427, 507
    Lightning Lane passes, 408
    Mexico Pavilion, 423, 506
    Morocco Pavilion, 427, 507
    Norway Pavilion, 423-25, 506
    Remy's Ratatouille Adventure, 15, 404, 429
    United Kingdom Pavilion, 429-30, 508
  crowds, 433
  Drinking Around the World, 421-22
  DuckTales World Showcase Adventure, 422
  Friendship Boats, 422-23
  hours of operation, 408
  Kidcot Fun Stops, 421, 423
  live entertainment, 421, 430-31
  map, 406-7
  meet and greets, 424-25
  restaurants, 412
  shopping, 505-8
  traffic patterns, 433
World Showcase Lagoon, 406-7
wristbands (MagicBand+), 23-24, 73, 74, 309, 358

Zara, 499, 503
Zootopia: Better Zoogether! (film), 15, 446
Zucker, Jason (animator), 518
Zuri's Sweets Shop, 507

See also the Accommodations Index on pages 519–524 and the Restaurant Index on pages 525–528.

TOURING PLANS

"Not a Touring Plan" TOURING PLANS

MAGIC KINGDOM

FOR ALL GUESTS If you're willing to purchase Lightning Lane Single Pass (LLSP), you should do so as soon as you are eligible to get the best selection of return times. If using Lightning Lane Multi Pass (LLMP), get the first available reservation for Tiana's Bayou Adventure, Big Thunder Mountain Railroad, Jungle Cruise, Peter Pan's Flight, or Space Mountain. Make two Tier 2 selections that fit with your plan. Fit those return-time windows into the plan. Throughout the day, continue obtaining the earliest available LLMP reservation for any of the next few attractions you're visiting.

FOR ALL GUESTS USING EARLY ENTRY Arrive at the Magic Kingdom entrance 40 minutes–1 hour before official opening. If you are driving and parking, add 20 minutes to get from the Transportation and Ticket Center to the entrance.

FOR ALL OFF-SITE GUESTS ARRIVING AT OFFICIAL OPENING Arrive at the park entrance 30–60 minutes before official opening.

FOR PARENTS WITH ONE DAY TO TOUR AND USING EARLY ENTRY Tour Fantasyland first, starting with Peter Pan's Flight. See Frontierland, then Adventureland. Consider a midday break at the hotel if the park is open past 8 p.m. Then tour Tomorrowland and (if your kids are interested in The Haunted Mansion) Liberty Square.

FOR PARENTS WITH ONE DAY TO TOUR AND ARRIVING AT OFFICIAL OPENING Begin a clockwise tour of the park in Fantasyland, skipping Seven Dwarfs Mine Train and Peter Pan's Flight. After Fantasyland, tour Tomorrowland, then Adventureland. Experience Seven Dwarfs Mine Train and Peter Pan's Flight in the late afternoon or evening, or use Lightning Lanes.

FOR ADULTS WITH ONE DAY TO TOUR AND USING EARLY ENTRY Start in Tomorrowland, at Space Mountain and then Tron, at official park opening. Tour the headliner attractions in Frontierland and Adventureland next, saving shows for the middle of the day. Tour Liberty Square around dinner. End the day with Fantasyland, saving Seven Dwarfs Mine Train for as late as possible, or use LLSP.

FOR ADULTS WITH ONE DAY TO TOUR AND ARRIVING AT OFFICIAL OPENING Start touring in Frontierland, then tour Adventureland and Liberty Square. Visit Fantasyland in the late afternoon and Tomorrowland after dinner.

FOR ALL GUESTS WITH TWO DAYS TO TOUR AND USING EARLY ENTRY On Day One, tour Fantasyland's headliner rides first, starting with Peter Pan's Flight and Seven Dwarfs Mine Train. Tour Frontierland next, then Liberty Square. Finish up with Fantasyland's secondary rides. Start Day Two in Tomorrowland, then tour Adventureland and any favorites you'd like to repeat.

FOR ALL GUESTS WITH TWO DAYS TO TOUR AND ARRIVING AT OFFICIAL OPENING On Day One, tour Frontierland first, then Liberty Square, followed by Fantasyland. Finish with Peter Pan's Flight and Seven Dwarfs Mine Train in Fantasyland. Start Day Two in Tomorrowland, then see Adventureland.

FOR ALL GUESTS WITH AN AFTERNOON AND A FULL DAY For the afternoon, tour Frontierland and Tomorrowland. On your full day of touring, see Fantasyland, Liberty Square, and Adventureland.

EPCOT

FOR ALL GUESTS If you're willing to purchase LLSP for Guardians of the Galaxy: Cosmic Rewind, do so as soon as you are eligible to get the best selection of return times. Likewise, if you're using LLMP, obtain the earliest possible reservation for Remy's Ratatouille Adventure or Test Track, along with two early Tier 2 selections. Throughout the day, continue obtaining the earliest available LLMP reservation for any of the next few attractions you're visiting.

FOR ALL GUESTS USING EARLY ENTRY Enter EPCOT at the main entrance if possible, and ride Guardians, followed by Test Track and Frozen Ever After. Tour World Discovery, then World Nature, then World Celebration. Begin a clockwise tour of World Showcase starting with Mexico. For dinner, snack at the food booths or quick-service spots in World Showcase. Try to ride Remy while other guests eat dinner. Finish the day by viewing *Luminous* and/or the light shows on Spaceship Earth. If you're entering from the International Gateway, start at Remy, saving Guardians for the late evening.

FOR ALL GUESTS ARRIVING AT OFFICIAL PARK OPENING Enter EPCOT at the main entrance and ride Guardians and Test Track as soon as you're admitted to the park. Tour World Nature, then visit World Discovery and World Celebration. Begin a clockwise tour of World Showcase at Mexico. For dinner, snack at the food booths or quick-service spots in World Showcase. Finish the day by viewing *Luminous* and/or the light shows on Spaceship Earth. Watch for wait-time drops at Frozen Ever After and Remy in the afternoon and evening.

DISNEY'S ANIMAL KINGDOM

FOR ALL GUESTS If you're willing to purchase LLSP for Avatar Flight of Passage, do so as soon as you are eligible. Likewise, if you're using LLMP, obtain the earliest possible reservation for either Na'vi River Journey or Kilimanjaro Safaris, plus two other selections. Throughout the day, continue obtaining the earliest available LLMP reservation for any of the next few attractions you're visiting. Don't use LLMP for shows unless it's a very crowded day and you'd like to see *Festival of the Lion King*.

FOR ALL GUESTS USING EARLY ENTRY Begin a land-by-land, clockwise tour of the park starting in Pandora. Work in shows like *Feathered Friends in Flight!* as you near them. If the park is open past dark, eat dinner, then end the night with *Awakenings* at the Tree of Life and a tour of the Valley of Mo'ara in Pandora.

FOR ALL GUESTS ARRIVING AT OFFICIAL PARK OPENING Begin a land-by-land, clockwise tour of the park starting at Kilimanjaro Safaris in Africa. Work in shows like *Feathered Friends in Flight* as you near them. Save the attractions in Pandora for last. If the park is open past dark, eat dinner, and then end the night with *Awakenings* at the Tree of Life and a tour of the Valley of Mo'ara in Pandora.

FOR ALL GUESTS ARRIVING IN LATE MORNING Begin a clockwise tour of the park, starting in Africa and saving Pandora for last. If the park is open past dark, eat dinner, and then end the night with *Awakenings* at the Tree of Life and a tour of the Valley of Mo'ara in Pandora.

DISNEY'S HOLLYWOOD STUDIOS

FOR ALL GUESTS If you're willing to purchase LLSP for Rise of the Resistance, do so as soon as you are eligible. Likewise, if you're using LLMP, obtain the earliest possible reservation for Slinky Dog Dash, along with two Tier 2 selections (one of them as early as possible). If Slinky isn't available, try *Millennium Falcon:* Smugglers Run, Rock 'n' Roller Coaster, or Mickey & Minnie's Runaway Railway. Throughout the day, continue to obtain the earliest available LLMP reservation for that same list of time-saving attractions.

FOR GROUPS WITH OLDER CHILDREN, TEENS, AND ADULTS USING EARLY ENTRY Ride Rise of the Resistance as soon as you're admitted into the park. It is usually the only attraction to open before Early Entry officially begins. Next, begin a clockwise tour of the Studios in Toy Story Land with Slinky and Toy Story Mania, followed by Runaway Railway, and then the attractions on Sunset Boulevard just before or after lunch. Spend the afternoon watching shows, and revisit Galaxy's Edge in the evening, when crowds start to thin. Finish the night at *Fantasmic!*

FOR ADULTS ARRIVING AROUND LUNCHTIME Begin a tour of the park in Galaxy's Edge, then visit the attractions on Sunset Boulevard. Ride Mickey & Minnie's Runaway Railway in midafternoon, and save Toy Story Land for last, when crowds have started to thin. Get in line for Rise of the Resistance during the last 2 hours the park is open. Use LLSP and/or LLMP as described above.

CLIP-OUT TOURING PLANS 551

The Magic Kingdom

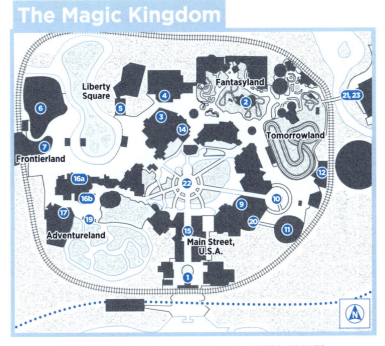

EARLY-ENTRY ONE-DAY TOURING PLAN FOR ADULTS

1. Arrive at the Magic Kingdom entrance 45 minutes before official opening on days of normal attendance, and 1 hour before official opening during holidays and other busy times. Take pictures on Main Street, U.S.A., before the park opens.
2. As soon as the park opens, ride Seven Dwarfs Mine Train in Fantasyland.
3. Fly through Neverland on Peter Pan's Flight.
4. Sail on It's a Small World.
5. Tour The Haunted Mansion in Liberty Square.
6. Ride Big Thunder Mountain Railroad in Frontierland.
7. Ride Tiana's Bayou Adventure. Use mobile ordering to order lunch while in line. The highest-rated spot is Columbia Harbour House.
8. Eat lunch.
9. Watch *Monsters, Inc. Laugh Floor* in Tomorrowland.
10. Ride the Tomorrowland Transit Authority PeopleMover.
11. Experience *Walt Disney's Carousel of Progress*.
12. Ride Space Mountain.
13. Watch the Festival of Fantasy Parade from Main Street or the castle area.
14. Enjoy *Mickey's PhilharMagic* in Fantasyland.
15. Explore Main Street, U.S.A., including shopping and catching performances by the Dapper Dans or the Casey's Corner Pianist.
16. If time permits, watch *Country Bear Musical Jamboree* (16a) or *Walt Disney's Enchanted Tiki Room* (16b).
17. Ride Pirates of the Caribbean in Adventureland.
18. Eat dinner.
19. Ride Jungle Cruise.
20. Ride Buzz Lightyear's Space Ranger Spin.
21. If there are two showings of the Starlight Parade, ride Tron during the first. Otherwise, grab spots for the parade.
22. See the *Happily Ever After* fireworks show.
23. If you haven't yet ridden Tron, get in line just before park closing.

To use Lightning Lane Multi Pass (LLMP) with this plan: The most useful LLMP reservations for this plan are for Tiana's Bayou Adventure, Space Mountain, Big Thunder Mountain Railroad, The Haunted Mansion, and Jungle Cruise. Get the first available reservation for one Tier 1 and two Tier 2 selections, and fit those return-time windows into the plan. Once you're able to get your next LLMP reservation, look for the earliest return time for any of the next few attractions in the plan. **If using Lightning Lane Single Pass,** try to get a reservation for Tron Lightcycle/Run with a return time in the early evening and/or a Seven Dwarfs Mine Train reservation for midmorning.

See **theugseries.com/free-touring-plans** to customize this plan at no charge, including the attractions and your walking speed, plus real-time updates while you're in the park.

The Magic Kingdom

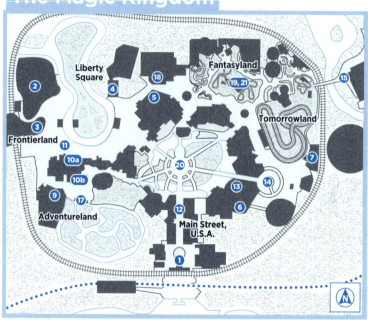

NON-EARLY-ENTRY ONE-DAY TOURING PLAN FOR ADULTS

1. Arrive at the entrance 30 minutes before official opening on days of normal attendance and 1 hour before official opening during holidays and busy times.
2. As soon as you're admitted to the park, ride Big Thunder Mountain Railroad in Frontierland.
3. Ride Tiana's Bayou Adventure.
4. Tour The Haunted Mansion in Liberty Square.
5. Fly through Neverland on Peter Pan's Flight in Fantasyland.
6. Experience Buzz Lightyear's Space Ranger Spin in Tomorrowland.
7. Ride Space Mountain. While in line, use mobile ordering for lunch. The highest-rated spot is Columbia Harbour House.
8. Eat lunch.
9. Ride Pirates of the Caribbean in Adventureland.
10. If time permits, watch *Country Bear Musical Jamboree* (10a) and/or *Walt Disney's Enchanted Tiki Room* (10b).
11. Watch the Festival of Fantasy Parade from Frontierland.
12. Explore Main Street, U.S.A., including shopping and catching performances by The Dapper Dans or the Casey's Corner pianist.
13. Watch *Monsters, Inc. Laugh Floor* in Tomorrowland.
14. Ride the Tomorrowland Transit Authority PeopleMover.
15. Ride Tron Lightcycle/Run.
16. Eat dinner.
17. Ride Jungle Cruise in Adventureland.
18. Ride It's a Small World in Fantasyland.
19. If there are two showings of the Starlight Parade, ride Seven Dwarfs Mine Train during the first. Otherwise, grab spots for the parade.
20. See the *Happily Ever After* fireworks show.
21. If you haven't yet ridden Seven Dwarfs Mine Train, get in line just before park closing.

To use Lightning Lane Multi Pass (LLMP) with this plan: The most useful LLMP reservations for this plan are for Tiana's Bayou Adventure, Big Thunder Mountain Railroad, Space Mountain, The Haunted Mansion, and Buzz Lightyear. Get the first available reservation for one Tier 1 and two Tier 2 selections, and fit those return-time windows into the plan. Once you're able to get your next LLMP reservation, look for the earliest return time for any of the next few attractions in the plan. **If using Lightning Lane Single Pass,** try to get a reservation for Tron Lightcycle/Run with a return time in the late afternoon and a Seven Dwarfs Mine Train reservation for late evening.

See **theugseries.com/free-touring-plans** to customize this plan at no charge, including the attractions and your walking speed, plus real-time updates while you're in the park.

CLIP-OUT TOURING PLANS

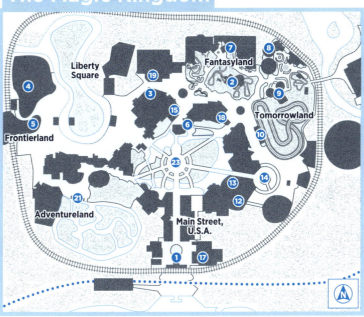

EARLY-ENTRY ONE-DAY TOURING PLAN FOR PARENTS WITH SMALL CHILDREN

Review the Small-Child Fright-Potential Table on pages 305–306. Attractions shown should be suitable for most children ages 5 and up. Interrupt the plan for snacks, rest, and bathroom breaks.

1. Arrive at the entrance 50 minutes before official opening on days of normal attendance, and at least an hour before official opening during holidays and busy times.
2. As soon as the park opens, head toward the right-hand side of Cinderella Castle and ride Seven Dwarfs Mine Train in Fantasyland.
3. Take Peter Pan's Flight.
4. Ride Big Thunder Mountain Railroad in Frontierland (if everyone is tall enough).
5. Ride Tiana's Bayou Adventure.
6. Meet one set of princesses in Princess Fairytale Hall.
7. Ride Under the Sea—Journey of the Little Mermaid.
8. Meet Disney Pals at Pete's Silly Sideshow.
9. Ride Dumbo the Flying Elephant.
10. Drive on Tomorrowland Speedway in Tomorrowland. Use mobile ordering to order lunch while in line.
11. Eat lunch.
12. Ride Buzz Lightyear's Space Ranger Spin.
13. Watch *Monsters, Inc. Laugh Floor*.
14. Ride the Tomorrowland Transit Authority PeopleMover.
15. See *Mickey's PhilharMagic* in Fantasyland.
16. Watch the Festival of Fantasy Parade from Main Street, U.S.A.
17. Meet Mickey at Town Square Theater.
18. Ride The Many Adventures of Winnie the Pooh in Fantasyland.
19. Float through It's a Small World.
20. Eat dinner.
21. Ride Jungle Cruise in Adventureland.
22. Watch the Starlight Parade from the castle area or Main Street, U.S.A.
23. See the *Happily Ever After* fireworks show.

Alternate plan: Leave the park after riding Buzz Lightyear for an afternoon rest, then return in time for It's a Small World.

To use Lightning Lane Multi Pass (LLMP) with this plan: The most useful LLMP reservations for this plan are Peter Pan's Flight, Big Thunder Mountain Railroad, Tiana's Bayou Adventure, Tomorrowland Speedway, Buzz Lightyear, Winnie the Pooh, and It's a Small World. Get the first available reservations for any of those, and fit those return-time windows into the plan. Once you're able to get your next LLMP reservation, look for the earliest return time for any of the next few attractions in the plan. **If using Lightning Lane Single Pass,** try to get a reservation for Seven Dwarfs Mine Train in the morning.

See **theugseries.com/free-touring-plans** to customize this plan at no charge, including the attractions and your walking speed, plus real-time updates while you're in the park.

The Magic Kingdom

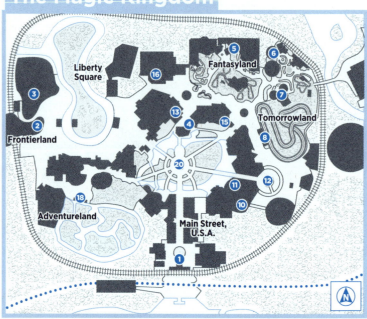

NON-EARLY-ENTRY ONE-DAY TOURING PLAN FOR PARENTS WITH SMALL CHILDREN

Review the Small-Child Fright-Potential Table on pages 305–306.
Interrupt the plan for snacks, rest, and bathroom breaks.

1. Arrive at the Magic Kingdom entrance 30 minutes before official opening on days of normal attendance, and 1 hour before official opening during holidays and busy times.
2. As soon as the park opens, head to Frontierland and ride Tiana's Bayou Adventure.
3. Ride Big Thunder Mountain Railroad (if everyone is tall enough).
4. Meet one of the princesses at Princess Fairytale Hall.
5. Ride Under the Sea—Journey of the Little Mermaid.
6. Meet Disney Pals at Pete's Silly Sideshow.
7. Ride Dumbo the Flying Elephant.
8. Drive on Tomorrowland Speedway in Tomorrowland. Use mobile ordering to order lunch while in line.
9. Eat lunch.
10. Ride Buzz Lightyear's Space Ranger Spin.
11. Watch *Monsters, Inc. Laugh Floor*.
12. Ride the Tomorrowland Transit Authority PeopleMover.
13. See *Mickey's PhilharMagic* in Fantasyland.
14. Watch the Festival of Fantasy Parade.
15. Ride The Many Adventures of Winnie the Pooh in Fantasyland.
16. Float through It's a Small World.
17. Eat dinner.
18. Ride Jungle Cruise in Adventureland.
19. Watch the Starlight Parade from the castle area or Main Street, U.S.A.
20. See the *Happily Ever After* fireworks show.

Alternate plan: Leave the park after riding Buzz Lightyear for an afternoon rest, then return in time for It's a Small World.

To use Lightning Lane Multi Pass with this plan: The most useful LLMP reservations for this plan are Peter Pan's Flight, Big Thunder Mountain Railroad, Tiana's Bayou Adventure, Tomorrowland Speedway, Buzz Lightyear, Winnie the Pooh, and It's a Small World. Get the first available reservations for any of those, and fit those return-time windows into the plan. Once you're able to get your next LLMP reservation, look for the earliest return time for any of the next few attractions in the plan. **If using Lightning Lane Single Pass,** try to get a reservation for Seven Dwarfs Mine Train in the morning to add it to your itinerary.

See **theugseries.com/free-touring-plans** to customize this plan at no charge, including the attractions and your walking speed, plus real-time updates while you're in the park.

CLIP-OUT TOURING PLANS 555

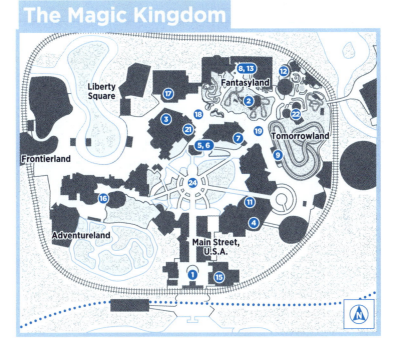

EARLY-ENTRY DUMBO-OR-DIE-IN-A-DAY TOURING PLAN FOR PARENTS WITH SMALL CHILDREN

Review the Small-Child Fright-Potential Table on pages 305-306.
Interrupt the plan for snacks and rest as needed.

1. Arrive at the entrance 50 minutes before official opening on days of normal attendance, and 1 hour before official opening during holidays and busy times.
2. As soon as the park opens, ride Seven Dwarfs Mine Train in Fantasyland.
3. Take Peter Pan's Flight.
4. Experience Buzz Lightyear's Space Ranger Spin in Tomorrowland.
5. Meet Princess Tiana in Princess Fairytale Hall.
6. Meet Cinderella in Princess Fairytale Hall.
7. Ride The Many Adventures of Winnie the Pooh.
8. Explore Under the Sea—Journey of the Little Mermaid.
9. Drive on the Tomorrowland Speedway. While in line, use mobile ordering to order lunch.
10. Eat lunch.
11. Watch *Monsters, Inc. Laugh Floor* in Tomorrowland.
12. Meet Disney Pals at Pete's Silly Sideshow in Fantasyland.
13. Take part in *Enchanted Tales with Belle*.
14. Watch the Festival of Fantasy Parade from Main Street, U.S.A.
15. Meet Mickey at Town Square Theater.
16. Ride The Magic Carpets of Aladdin in Adventureland.
17. Float through It's a Small World in Fantasyland.
18. Ride the Prince Charming Regal Carrousel.
19. Take a spin on Mad Tea Party.
20. Eat dinner.
21. Watch *Mickey's PhilharMagic* in Fantasyland.
22. Ride Dumbo the Flying Elephant.
23. Watch the Starlight Parade from the castle area or Main Street U.S.A.
24. See the *Happily Ever After* fireworks show.

To use Lightning Lane Multi Pass with this plan: The most useful LLMP reservations for this plan are Buzz Lightyear, Winnie the Pooh, Tomorrowland Speedway, and It's a Small World. But many of these attractions don't have long lines compared to other height-restricted headliners. If you choose to purchase and use LLMP, get the earliest available reservation for any of the listed attractions, and fit those return-time windows into the plan. Once you're able to get your next LLMP reservation, look for the earliest return time for any of the next few attractions in the plan. **Lightning Lane Single Pass reservations** shouldn't be needed for this plan.

See **theugseries.com/free-touring-plans** to customize this plan at no charge, including the attractions and your walking speed, plus real-time updates while you're in the park.

The Magic Kingdom

NON-EARLY-ENTRY **DUMBO-OR-DIE-IN-A-DAY TOURING PLAN FOR PARENTS WITH SMALL CHILDREN**

Review the Small-Child Fright-Potential Table on pages 305–306. Interrupt the plan for snacks and rest.

1. Arrive at the entrance 30 minutes before official opening on days of normal attendance, and 45 minutes before official opening during holidays and busy times.
2. As soon as you're admitted to the park, meet Princess Tiana in Princess Fairytale Hall.
3. Meet Cinderella in Princess Fairytale Hall.
4. Ride Seven Dwarfs Mine Train in Fantasyland.
5. Take part in *Enchanted Tales with Belle*.
6. Take a spin on Mad Tea Party.
7. Meet Disney Pals at Pete's Silly Sideshow.
8. Drive on Tomorrowland Speedway in Tomorrowland.
9. Experience Buzz Lightyear's Space Ranger Spin. While in line, use mobile ordering to order lunch.
10. Eat lunch.
11. Watch *Monsters, Inc. Laugh Floor*.
12. Ride Prince Charming Regal Carrousel in Fantasyland.
13. Watch *Mickey's Philharmagic*.
14. Watch the Festival of Fantasy Parade from Main Street, U.S.A.
15. Meet Mickey at Town Square Theater.
16. Ride The Magic Carpets of Aladdin in Adventureland.
17. Float through It's a Small World in Fantasyland.
18. Ride Under the Sea—Journey of the Little Mermaid.
19. Eat dinner.
20. Ride The Many Adventures of Winnie the Pooh.
21. Ride Dumbo the Flying Elephant.
22. Watch the Starlight Parade from the castle area or Main Street, U.S.A.
23. See the *Happily Ever After* fireworks show.

To use Lightning Lane Multi Pass (LLMP) with this plan: The most useful LLMP reservations for this plan are Buzz Lightyear, Tomorrowland Speedway, It's a Small World, Winnie the Pooh, and Dumbo. Get the first available reservations for any of those and fit those return-time windows into the plan. Once you're able to get your next LLMP reservation, look for the earliest return time for any of the next few attractions in the plan. **If using Lightning Lane Single Pass,** try to get a reservation for Seven Dwarfs Mine Train in the morning.

See **theugseries.com/free-touring-plans** to customize this plan at no charge, including the attractions and your walking speed, plus real-time updates while you're in the park.

CLIP-OUT TOURING PLANS

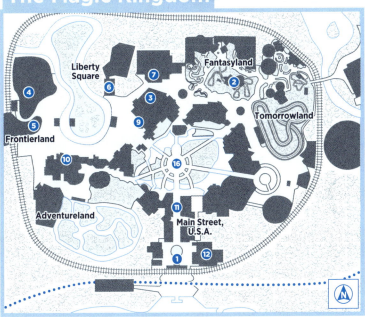

EARLY-ENTRY TWO-DAY TOURING PLAN FOR ADULTS: DAY ONE

1. Arrive at the entrance 50 minutes before official opening on days of normal attendance, and at least 1 hour before official opening during holidays and busy times.
2. As soon as the park opens, ride Seven Dwarfs Mine Train in Fantasyland.
3. Ride Peter Pan's Flight.
4. In Frontierland, ride Big Thunder Mountain Railroad.
5. Ride Tiana's Bayou Adventure.
6. In Liberty Square, ride The Haunted Mansion.
7. Ride It's a Small World in Fantasyland. Order lunch using mobile ordering. The best nearby spot is Columbia Harbour House.
8. Eat lunch.
9. Watch *The Hall of Presidents* in Liberty Square.
10. Work in a viewing of *Country Bear Musical Jamboree* in Frontierland.
11. Explore Main Street, U.S.A., including shopping and catching performances by The Dapper Dans or the Casey's Corner pianist.
12. Meet Mickey Mouse in Town Square Theater.
13. Watch the Festival of Fantasy Parade from Main Street, U.S.A.
14. Take an afternoon and evening break to return to your resort, take the monorail to explore lounges and eat dinner at one of the Deluxe resorts, or revisit favorites around the park.
15. Watch the Starlight Parade from the castle area or Main Street, U.S.A.
16. See the *Happily Ever After* fireworks show.

To use Lightning Lane Multi Pass (LLMP) with this plan: The most useful LLMP reservations for this plan are Tiana's Bayou Adventure, Peter Pan's Flight, Big Thunder Mountain Railroad, and The Haunted Mansion. But the pace of the plan is so relaxed that you shouldn't need any of them. If you do choose to purchase LLMP, get the first available reservations for any of the listed attractions and fit those return-time windows into the plan. Once you're able to get your next LLMP reservation, look for the earliest return time for any of the next few attractions in the plan. **Lightning Lane Single Pass reservations** shouldn't be needed for this plan.

See **theugseries.com/free-touring-plans** to customize this plan at no charge, including the attractions and your walking speed, plus real-time updates while you're in the park.

(see next page for Day Two)

The Magic Kingdom

EARLY-ENTRY TWO-DAY TOURING PLAN FOR ADULTS: DAY TWO

1. Arrive at the entrance 50 minutes before official opening on days of normal attendance, and at least 1 hour before official opening during holidays and busy times.
2. As soon as the park opens, ride Space Mountain.
3. At official park opening, ride Tron.
4. Ride Buzz Lightyear's Space Ranger Spin.
5. In Adventureland, take the Jungle Cruise.
6. See *Walt Disney's Enchanted Tiki Room*. Use mobile ordering to order lunch.
7. Tour the Swiss Family Treehouse.
8. Eat lunch.
9. Ride the Tomorrowland Transit Authority PeopleMover in Tomorrowland.
10. See *Walt Disney's Carousel of Progress*.
11. See *Monsters, Inc. Laugh Floor*.
12. Ride Under the Sea—Journey of the Little Mermaid.
13. Revisit any favorite attractions or tour the rest of the park.
14. If you've not already done so, see the Starlight Parade and the *Happily Ever After* fireworks show.

To use Lightning Lane Multi Pass with this plan: The most useful LLMP reservations for this plan are for Space Mountain, Jungle Cruise, and Buzz Lightyear. But the pace of the plan is so relaxed that you shouldn't need any of them. If you do choose to purchase LLMP, get the first available reservations for any of the listed attractions and fit those return-time windows into the plan. Once you're able to get your next LLMP reservation, look for the earliest return time for any of the next few attractions in the plan. **If using Lightning Lane Single Pass,** make reservations for Tron for in the morning.

See **theugseries.com/free-touring-plans** to customize this plan at no charge, including the attractions and your walking speed, plus real-time updates while you're in the park.

CLIP-OUT TOURING PLANS 559

EARLY-ENTRY ONE-DAY TOURING PLAN

1. Arrive at the main entrance 50 minutes before official opening (70 minutes on busy days and holidays).
2. Immediately join the line for Guardians of the Galaxy: Cosmic Rewind.
3. Ride Test Track. Use the single-rider line if possible.
4. Cross the park to The Land Pavilion and ride Soarin' Around the World.
5. Float along Living with the Land.
6. Take the back entrance into The Seas Main Tanks and Exhibits. Watch *Turtle Talk with Crush* if it interests you.
7. Walk through Journey of Water.
8. Ride Spaceship Earth.
9. Eat a light lunch. Opt for festival booths if they are open. Otherwise, Sunshine Seasons and Connections Eatery are nearby, or you could eat in Mexico to start your afternoon.
10. Begin a clockwise tour of World Showcase at Mexico, including Gran Fiesta Tour.
11. Tour the Norway Pavilion and ride Frozen Ever After.
12. See the China Pavilion. Skip the film—it's not rated highly by any age group.
13. Check out the Germany Pavilion.
14. Tour the Italy Pavilion.
15. Watch Voices of Liberty in The American Adventure Pavilion. If time allows, watch *The American Adventure*.
16. Tour the Japan Pavilion and exhibits. Watch Matsuriza.
17. Eat dinner now or sometime around the next few steps.
18. Tour the Morocco Pavilion.
19. Tour the France Pavilion and ride Remy's Ratatouille Adventure. Use the single-rider line if possible.
20. Tour the United Kingdom Pavilion.
21. Tour the Canada Pavilion and see the film.
22. See the *Luminous* fireworks show. Good viewing locations should be available around the Mexico Pavilion; in front of World Showcase where it meets Future World; and between Canada and France.

To use Lightning Lane Multi Pass (LLMP) with this plan: The most useful LLMP reservations for this plan are Remy's Ratatouille Adventure, Frozen Ever After, Test Track, and Soarin' Around the World (in that order). Those will likely all be Tier 1 selections, and very few Tier 2 selections are useful at EPCOT. If you opt to use LLMP anyway, pick the earliest tier 1 return time you can find and fit that return-time window into the plan. Once you're able to get your next LLMP reservation, look for the earliest return time for any of the next few attractions in the plan. **If using Lightning Lane Single Pass**, try to get a Guardians reservation for as close to park opening as possible, when the wait will be shortest.

See **theugseries.com/free-touring-plans** to customize this plan at no charge, including the attractions and your walking speed, plus real-time updates while you're in the park.

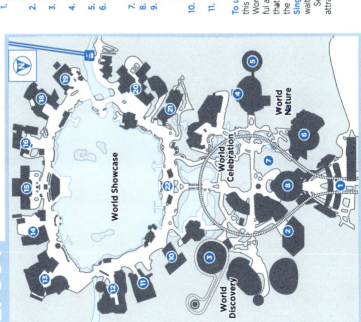

EPCOT

EPCOT

NON-EARLY-ENTRY ONE-DAY TOURING PLAN

1. Arrive at EPCOT's main entrance 30 minutes before official opening (50 minutes on busy days and holidays).
2. As soon as the park opens, ask a cast member if Test Track in World Discovery is operating. If yes, ride Test Track. You can use the single-rider line if it's open.
3. Cross the park to The Land Pavilion and ride Soarin' Around the World.
4. Float along Living with the Land.
5. Take the back entrance into The Seas Main Tanks and Exhibits. Watch *Turtle Talk with Crush* if it interests you.
6. Begin a clockwise tour of World Showcase at Mexico, including Gran Fiesta Tour.
7. Eat lunch at festival booths or at the Mexico Pavilion.
8. Tour the Norway Pavilion and ride Frozen Ever After.
9. See the China Pavilion. Skip the film—it's not rated highly by any age group.
10. Check out the Germany Pavilion.
11. Tour the Italy Pavilion.
12. Watch Voices of Liberty in The American Adventure Pavilion. If time allows, watch *The American Adventure*.
13. Tour the Japan Pavilion and exhibits. Watch Matsuriza.
14. Tour the Morocco Pavilion.
15. Tour the France Pavilion and ride Remy's Ratatouille Adventure. Use the single-rider line if possible.
16. Tour the United Kingdom Pavilion.
17. Tour the Canada Pavilion and see the film.
18. Eat dinner around the next few steps.
19. Walk through Journey of Water.
20. Ride Spaceship Earth.
21. Ride Guardians of the Galaxy: Cosmic Rewind.
22. See the *Luminous* fireworks show. Good viewing locations should be available around the Mexico Pavilion; in front of World Showcase where it meets Future World; and between Canada and France.

To use Lightning Lane Multi Pass (LLMP) with this plan: The most useful LLMP reservations for this plan are Remy's Ratatouille Adventure, Frozen Ever After, Test Track, and Soarin' Around the World (in that order). Those will likely all be Tier 1 selections, and very few Tier 2 selections are useful at EPCOT. If you opt to use LLMP anyway, pick the earliest Tier 1 return time you can find and fit that return-time window into the plan. Once you're able to get your next LLMP reservation, look for the earliest return time for any of the next few attractions in the plan. **If using Lightning Lane Single Pass,** try to get a Guardians reservation for as close to park opening as possible, when the wait will be shortest.

See **theugseries.com/free-touring-plans** to customize this plan at no charge, including the attractions and your walking speed, plus real-time updates while you're in the park.

CLIP-OUT TOURING PLANS 561

EPCOT

EARLY-ENTRY ONE-DAY TOURING PLAN FOR FAMILIES

1. Arrive at the International Gateway 50 minutes before official opening (70 minutes on busy days and holidays).
2. Immediately join the line for Remy's Ratatouille Adventure.
3. Ride Frozen Ever After.
4. Meet Mickey and Friends in CommuniCore Hall.
5. Ride Soarin' in The Land Pavilion.
6. Float along on Living with the Land.
7. Ride The Seas with Nemo & Friends.
8. Explore The Seas Main Tanks and Exhibits and participate in *Turtle Talk with Crush*.
9. Eat lunch at Sunshine Seasons or Connections Eatery.
10. Walk through Journey of Water.
11. Ride Spaceship Earth.
12. Begin a clockwise tour of World Showcase at Mexico, including Gran Fiesta Tour. At each country, find the Kidcot Fun Stop.
13. Meet Anna and Elsa at the Norway Pavilion if time allows.
14. See the China Pavilion. Skip the film—it's not rated highly by any age group.
15. Check out the Germany Pavilion.
16. Tour the Italy Pavilion.
17. Watch Voices of Liberty in The American Adventure Pavilion.
18. Tour the Japan Pavilion and exhibits. Watch Matsuriza.
19. Eat dinner now or sometime around the next few steps.
20. Tour the Morocco Pavilion.
21. Tour the France Pavilion.
22. Tour the United Kingdom Pavilion.
23. Tour the Canada Pavilion and see the film.
24. See the *Luminous* fireworks show. Good viewing locations should be available around the Mexico Pavilion; in front of World Showcase where it meets Future World; and between Canada and France.

To use Lightning Lane Multi Pass with this plan: The most useful LLMP reservations for this plan are Frozen Ever After, Soarin', The Seas, and Spaceship Earth. If you opt to use LLMP, pick the earliest Tier 1 return time you can find, along with two Tier 2 selections. Fit those return-time windows into the plan. Once you're able to get your next LLMP reservation, look for the earliest return time for any of the next few attractions in the plan. **If using Lightning Lane Single Pass**, try to get a Guardians reservation for anytime in the morning, when adults can go ride individually while others keep sticking to the plan.

See **theugseries.com/free-touring-plans** to customize this plan at no charge, including the attractions and your walking speed, plus real-time updates while you're in the park.

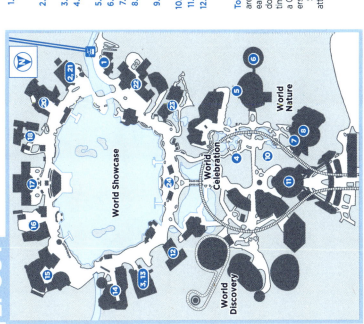

NON-EARLY-ENTRY ONE-DAY TOURING PLAN FOR FAMILIES

1. Arrive at the main entrance 50 minutes before official opening (70 minutes on busy days and holidays).
2. Ride Frozen Ever After.
3. Meet Mickey and Friends in CommuniCore Hall.
4. Ride Soarin' in The Land Pavilion.
5. Ride The Seas with Nemo & Friends.
6. Explore The Seas Main Tanks and Exhibits and participate in *Turtle Talk with Crush*.
7. Eat lunch at Sunshine Seasons or Connections Eatery.
8. Walk through Journey of Water.
9. Ride Spaceship Earth.
10. Begin a clockwise tour of World Showcase at Mexico, including Gran Fiesta Tour. At each country, find the Kidcot Fun Stop.
11. Meet Anna and Elsa at the Norway Pavilion if time allows.
12. See the China Pavilion. Skip the film—it's not rated highly by any age group.
13. Check out the Germany Pavilion.
14. Tour the Italy Pavilion.
15. Watch Voices of Liberty in The American Adventure Pavilion.
16. Tour the Japan Pavilion and exhibits. Watch Matsuriza.
17. Eat dinner now or sometime around the next few steps.
18. Tour the Morocco Pavilion.
19. Tour the France Pavilion and ride Remy's Ratatouille Adventure.
20. If time allows, tour the United Kingdom Pavilion and the Canada Pavilion.
21. See the *Luminous* fireworks show. Good viewing locations should be available around the Mexico Pavilion; in front of World Showcase where it meets Future World; and between Canada and France.

To use Lightning Lane Multi Pass with this plan: The most useful LLMP reservations for this plan are Remy's Ratatouille Adventure, Frozen Ever After, Soarin', The Seas, and Spaceship Earth. If you opt to use LLMP, pick the earliest Tier 1 return time you can find, along with two Tier 2 selections. Fit those return-time windows into the plan. Once you're able to get your next LLMP reservation, look for the earliest return time for any of the next few attractions in the plan. **If using Lightning Lane Single Pass,** try to get a Guardians reservation for anytime in the plan, when adults can go ride individually while others keep sticking to the plan.

See **theugseries.com/free-touring-plans** to customize this plan at no charge, including the attractions and your walking speed, plus real-time updates while you're in the park.

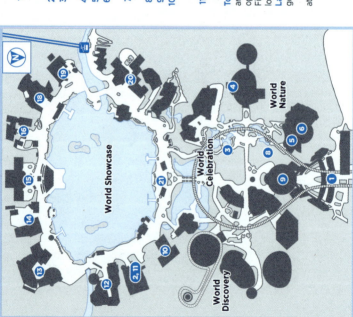

EPCOT

Disney's Animal Kingdom

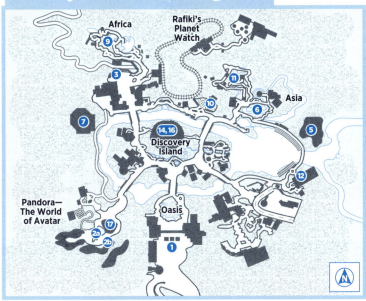

EARLY-ENTRY ONE-DAY TOURING PLAN

1. Arrive at the entrance 50 minutes before official opening on days of normal attendance (70 minutes during holidays and busy times). Follow cast member instructions to line up for Avatar Flight of Passage.
2. Ride Avatar Flight of Passage (**2a**), then Na'vi River Journey (**2b**) in Pandora.
3. Ride Kilimanjaro Safaris in Africa.
4. Sign up for Wilderness Explorers at any booth or dedicated space you pass that has booklets.
5. Ride Expedition Everest in Asia.
6. Get wet on Kali River Rapids, if temperatures permit.
7. Watch *Festival of the Lion King*. Use mobile ordering to order lunch while you wait for the show. Satu'li Canteen in Pandora and Flame Tree Barbecue on Discovery Island are both good options.
8. Eat lunch.
9. Walk the Gorilla Falls Exploration Trail.
10. Watch *Winged Encounters* and then *Feathered Friends in Flight!* in Asia (usually scheduled 15 minutes apart).
11. Tour the Maharajah Jungle Trek.
12. See *Finding Nemo: The Big Blue . . . and Beyond!*
13. On your way back to the front of the park, watch *Zootopia: Better Zoogether!*
14. Tour the Discovery Island Trails and any other animal exhibits that catch your interest.

If the park is open past dark:

15. Eat dinner in the park—try Nomad Lounge or book a meal at a table-service restaurant like Tusker House or Yak & Yeti.
16. See *Awakenings* at the Tree of Life. Check *Times Guide* for start time.
17. Tour the Valley of Mo'ara in Pandora.

To use Lightning Lane Multi Pass (LLMP) with this plan: The most useful LLMP reservations for this plan are for Na'vi River Journey and Kilimanjaro Safaris, then Expedition Everest and (during summer) Kali River Rapids. Get the first three available reservations for any of those, and fit those return-time windows into the plan. Once you're able to get your next LLMP reservation, look for the earliest return time for any of the next few attractions in the plan. **Lightning Lane Single Pass reservations** shouldn't be needed for Flight of Passage as long as you head there first thing during Early Entry.

See **theugseries.com/free-touring-plans** to customize this plan at no charge, including the attractions and your walking speed, plus real-time updates while you're in the park.

Disney's Animal Kingdom

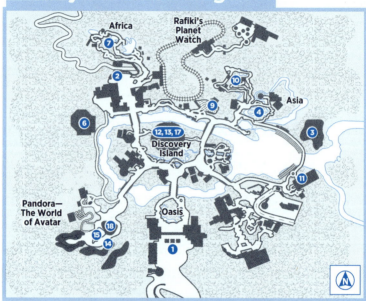

NON-EARLY-ENTRY ONE-DAY TOURING PLAN

1. Arrive at the main entrance 30 minutes before official opening on days of normal attendance (50 minutes during holidays and busy times).
2. As soon as you're admitted into the park, take the Kilimanjaro Safaris tour in Africa.
3. Ride Expedition Everest in Asia.
4. Get wet on Kali River Rapids, if temperatures permit.
5. Sign up for Wilderness Explorers at any booth or dedicated space that has booklets. Play along as you tour the rest of the park.
6. Watch *Festival of the Lion King*.
7. Walk the Gorilla Falls Exploration Trail. Use mobile ordering to order lunch in advance. The best restaurants in the park are Satu'li Canteen in Pandora and Flame Tree Barbecue on Discovery Island.
8. Eat lunch.
9. Watch *Winged Encounters* and then see *Feathered Friends in Flight!* in Asia (usually scheduled 15 minutes apart).
10. Walk the Maharajah Jungle Trek.
11. See *Finding Nemo: The Big Blue . . . and Beyond!*
12. On your way back to the front of the park, watch *Zootopia: Better Zoogether!*
13. Tour the Discovery Island Trails and any other animal exhibits that catch your interest.
14. Take the Na'vi River Journey boat ride.
15. Ride Avatar Flight of Passage in Pandora.

If the park is open past dark:

16. Eat dinner in the park.
17. See *Awakenings* at the Tree of Life. Check *Times Guide* for start time.
18. Tour the Valley of Mo'ara in Pandora.

To use Lightning Lane Multi Pass (LLMP) with this plan: The most useful LLMP reservations for this plan are for Na'vi River Journey and Kilimanjaro Safaris, then Expedition Everest and (during summer) Kali River Rapids. Get the first three available reservations for any of those and fit those return-time windows into the plan. Once you're able to get your next LLMP reservation, look for the earliest return time for any of the next few attractions in the plan. **If using Lightning Lane Single Pass,** obtain a reservation for Flight of Passage for around 4 p.m.

See **theugseries.com/free-touring-plans** to customize this plan at no charge, including the attractions and your walking speed, plus real-time updates while you're in the park.

CLIP-OUT TOURING PLANS **565**

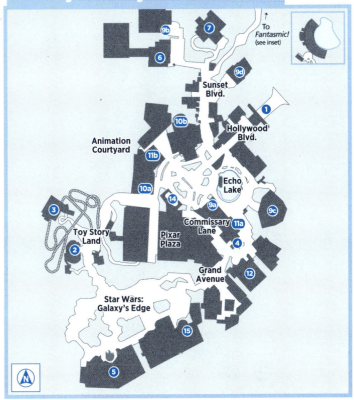

Disney's Hollywood Studios

EARLY-ENTRY ONE-DAY TOURING PLAN

1. Plan to arrive 60 minutes before official park opening on non-peak days (90 minutes during holidays and other busy times).
2. When the park opens, go straight to Slinky Dog Dash.
3. Ride Toy Story Mania!
4. Meet Mickey & Minnie at *Red Carpet Dreams* as close to official park opening as possible.
5. Ride *Millennium Falcon: Smugglers Run*.
6. Ride Rock 'n' Roller Coaster.
7. Ride the Tower of Terror. Use mobile ordering to order lunch. The highest-rated spots are Docking Bay 7 and Woody's Lunch Box.
8. Eat lunch.
9. Watch *For the First Time In Forever* (**9a**), *Disney Villains: Unfairly Ever After* (**9b**), *Indiana Jones Epic Stunt Spectacular!* (**9c**), and *Beauty and the Beast—Live on Stage* (**9d**) sometime in the afternoon.
10. If you have time between the showtimes above, see *Walt Disney Presents* (**10a**) in Animation Courtyard. If you have kids, try *Disney Junior Play and Dance!* (**10b**) instead.
11. Meet Olaf at Celebrity Spotlight (**11a**), or Darth Vader or Chewbacca at Star Wars Launch Bay (**11b**).
12. Ride Star Tours—The Adventures Continue.
13. Eat dinner.
14. Ride Mickey & Minnie's Runaway Railway.
15. Experience Rise of the Resistance.
16. End the night with *Fantasmic!*

To use Lightning Lane Multi Pass (LLMP) with this plan: The most useful LLMP reservations for this plan are Slinky Dog Dash, Tower of Terror, *Millennium Falcon: Smugglers Run*, Toy Story Mania!, and Rock 'n' Roller Coaster. (During summer and holidays, almost any LLMP reservation except Star Tours will save time.) Get the first available reservation for Slinky Dog Dash, plus two Tier 2 selections (at least one as early as possible) and fit those return-time windows into the plan. Once you're able to get your next LLMP reservation, look for the earliest return time for any of the next few attractions in the plan. **If using Lightning Lane Single Pass,** book one for Rise of the Resistance in the early evening.

See **theugseries.com/free-touring-plans** to customize this plan at no charge, including the attractions and your walking speed, plus real-time updates while you're in the park.

Disney's Hollywood Studios

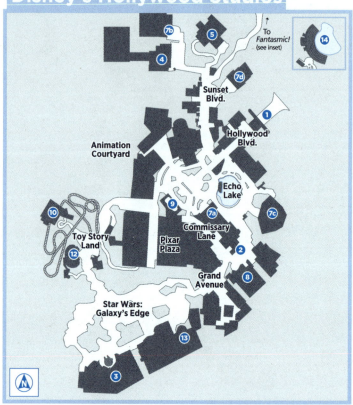

NON-EARLY-ENTRY ONE-DAY TOURING PLAN

1. Check official park hours the night before your visit, and plan to arrive 30 minutes before official park opening (45 minutes during holidays and other busy times).
2. As soon as you're admitted into the park, Meet Mickey & Minnie at *Red Carpet Dreams*.
3. Ride *Millennium Falcon: Smugglers Run*.
4. Ride Rock 'n' Roller Coaster on Sunset Boulevard.
5. Ride The Twilight Zone Tower of Terror. Use mobile ordering to order lunch. The highest-rated spots are Docking Bay 7 and Woody's Lunch Box.
6. Eat lunch.
7. Watch *For the First Time In Forever* (**7a**), *Disney Villains: Unfairly Ever After* (**7b**), *Indiana Jones Epic Stunt Spectacular!* (**7c**), and *Beauty and the Beast—Live on Stage* (**7d**) sometime in the afternoon.
8. If you have time between the showtimes above, ride Star Tours—The Adventures Continue.
9. Ride Mickey & Minnie's Runaway Railway.
10. Ride Toy Story Mania!
11. Eat dinner.
12. Ride Slinky Dog Dash.
13. Experience Rise of the Resistance.
14. End the night with *Fantasmic!*

To use Lightning Lane Multi Pass (LLMP) with this plan: The most useful LLMP reservations for this plan are for Slinky Dog Dash, Tower of Terror, *Millennium Falcon: Smugglers Run*, Toy Story Mania!, Runaway Railway, and Rock 'n' Roller Coaster. (During summer and holidays, almost any LLMP reservation except Star Tours will save time.) Get the first available reservation for Slinky Dog Dash, plus two Tier 2 selections, and fit those return-time windows into the plan. Once you're able to get your next LLMP reservation, look for the earliest return time for any of the next few attractions in the plan. **If using Lightning Lane Single Pass**, try to obtain one for Rise of the Resistance for the early evening.

See **theugseries.com/free-touring-plans** to customize this plan at no charge, including the attractions and your walking speed, plus real-time updates while you're in the park.

CLIP-OUT TOURING PLANS   567

Blizzard Beach

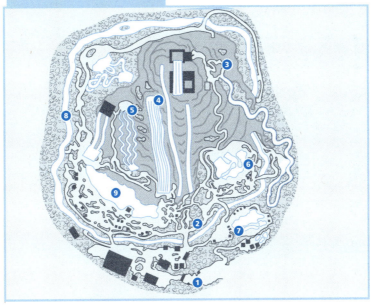

**BLIZZARD BEACH ONE-DAY TOURING PLAN
FOR PARENTS WITH SMALL CHILDREN**

1. Arrive at the park entrance 30 minutes before opening. Take care of locker and towel rentals at Lottawatta Lodge, to your left as you enter the park. Find a spot to stow the remainder of your gear, noting any nearby landmarks to help you find your way back.
2. Take the chairlift up Mount Gushmore to the Green Slope. *Note:* It might be faster—though more tiring—to walk to the top.
3. Raft down Teamboat Springs. Repeat as much as you like while the park is still uncrowded.
4. If your kids are up for it, try the Toboggan Racers.
5. If the kids enjoyed the Toboggan Racers, try the Snow Stormers next.
6. Visit the Ski Patrol Training Camp.
7. Visit Tike's Peak.
8. Grab some tubes and go floating in Cross Country Creek.
9. Swim in Melt-Away Bay's Wave Pool for as long as you like.

Typhoon Lagoon

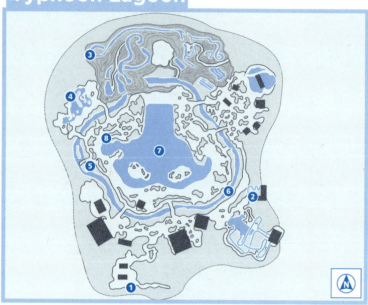

TYPHOON LAGOON ONE-DAY TOURING PLAN FOR PARENTS WITH SMALL CHILDREN

1. Arrive at the park entrance 30 minutes before opening. Take care of locker and towel rentals at Singapore Sal's, to your right after you've walked along the winding entrance path and emerged into the park. Find a spot to stow the remainder of your gear, noting any nearby landmarks to help you find your way back.
2. Ride Miss Adventure Falls as many times as you like.
3. Ride Gangplank Falls as many times as you like.
4. If your kids enjoyed Gangplank Falls, try Keelhaul Falls if it seems appropriate.
5. Enjoy the Ketchakiddee Creek kids' play area.
6. Grab some tubes and ride Castaway Creek. A complete circuit takes 20–25 minutes.
7. Swim in the Surf Pool as long as you like.
8. Ride the Bay Slides in the Surf Pool.
9. Repeat your favorite attractions as desired.

MAGIC KINGDOM TOURING PLAN COMPANION

ATTRACTION INFORMATION

Attraction | Location | When to Go | Authors' Rating | Comments

- Ariel's Grotto | Fantasyland | Early or late | ★★★
- Astro Orbiter | Tomorrowland | Before 11 a.m. or just before park closing | ★★ | Fright potential*
- The Barnstormer *(LLMP)* | Fantasyland | Early or late | ★★ | 35" minimum height
- Big Thunder Mountain Railroad *(LLMP)* | Frontierland | Early or late | ★★★★ | 40" minimum height; pregnant guests should not ride; motion sickness and fright potential*
- Buzz Lightyear's Space Ranger Spin *(LLMP)* | Tomorrowland | First or last hour the park is open | ★★★★ Fright potential*
- Casey Jr. Splash 'N' Soak Station | Fantasyland | When it's hot | ★★½
- Cinderella Castle | Main Street, U.S.A. | Anytime | ★★★★
- Country Bear Musical Jamboree | Frontierland | Anytime | ★★★½
- Dumbo the Flying Elephant *(LLMP)* | Fantasyland | Early or late | ★★★
- Enchanted Tales with Belle | Fantasyland | Early or late | ★★★★
- The Hall of Presidents | Liberty Square | Anytime | ★★½
- The Haunted Mansion *(LLMP)* | Liberty Square | Early or late | ★★★★ | Fright potential*
- It's a Small World *(LLMP)* | Fantasyland | Early or late | ★★★½
- Jungle Cruise *(LLMP)* | Adventureland | Early or late | ★★★½ | Fright potential*
- Mad Tea Party *(LLMP)* | Fantasyland | Anytime | ★★½ | Motion sickness potential; pregnant guests should not ride
- The Magic Carpets of Aladdin *(LLMP)* | Adventureland | Before noon or after dark | ★★
- Main Street Musical Acts | Main Street, U.S.A. | Check for showtimes | ★★★½
- Main Street Stage Shows | Main Street, U.S.A. | Check for showtimes | ★★★½
- Main Street Vehicles | Main Street, U.S.A. | Midmorning | ★★★
- The Many Adventures of Winnie the Pooh *(LLMP)* | Fantasyland | Early or late | ★★★½ | Fright potential*
- Meet Mickey at Town Square Theater | Main Street, U.S.A. | Early or late | ★★★★
- Meet Mirabel at Fairytale Garden | Fantasyland | Early or late | ★★★½
- Mickey's PhilharMagic *(LLMP)* | Fantasyland | Anytime | ★★★½
- Monsters, Inc. Laugh Floor *(LLMP)* | Tomorrowland | Anytime | ★★★ | Fright potential*
- Peter Pan's Flight *(LLMP)* | Fantasyland | First or last 30 minutes the park is open | ★★★★
- Pete's Silly Sideshow | Fantasyland | Early or late | ★★★★
- A Pirate's Adventure: Treasure of the Seven Seas | Adventureland | Afternoon | ★★½
- Pirates of the Caribbean *(LLMP)* | Adventureland | Anytime | ★★★★ | You'll get wet; fright potential*
- Prince Charming Regal Carrousel | Fantasyland | Anytime | ★★★
- Princess Fairytale Hall | Fantasyland | Early or late | ★★★½
- Seven Dwarfs Mine Train *(LLSP)* | Fantasyland | As soon as the park opens | ★★★★ | Fright potential*
- Space Mountain *(LLMP)* | Tomorrowland | At park opening or the last hour before closing | ★★★★ 44" minimum height; pregnant guests should not ride; motion sickness and fright potential*
- Swiss Family Treehouse | Adventureland | Anytime | ★★ | Fright potential*
- Tiana's Bayou Adventure *(LLMP)* | Frontierland | As early or late as possible | ★★★★ | 40" minimum height; pregnant guests should not ride; you'll get wet; fright potential*
- Tomorrowland Speedway *(LLMP)* | Tomorrowland | Not in the hot sun | ★★ | 54" minimum height for kids to drive unassisted, 32" to ride with a person age 14 or older
- Tomorrowland Transit Authority PeopleMover | Tomorrowland | Anytime | ★★★½
- Tron Lightcycle/Run *(LLSP)* | Tomorrowland | At park opening or just before closing | ★★★★ Fright potential*
- Under the Sea—Journey of the Little Mermaid *(LLMP)* | Fantasyland | Early or late | ★★★ Fright potential*
- Walt Disney's Carousel of Progress | Tomorrowland | Afternoon | ★★★
- Walt Disney's Enchanted Tiki Room | Adventureland | Afternoon | ★★★ | Fright potential*
- Walt Disney World Railroad | Multiple stations | Anytime | ★★★

See Small-Child Fright-Potential Table on pages 305–306.

DINING INFORMATION Counter Service

Restaurant | Location | Quality | Value | Selections

- Aloha Isle | Adventureland | Excellent | B | Soft-serve, ice-cream floats, pineapple juice
- Auntie Gravity's Galactic Goodies | Tomorrowland | Fair | D | Soft-serve, floats, churros, other desserts
- Casey's Corner | Main Street, U.S.A. | Good | B- | Hot dogs, plant-based "sausage" dogs, corn dogs, corn dog nuggets, fries, Baseball Brownie

DINING INFORMATION Counter Service *(continued)*

Restaurant | Location | Quality | Value | Selections

Cheshire Café | Fantasyland | Good | B | Seasonal snacks, such as the Cheshire Cat Tail cream-filled pastry

Columbia Harbour House | Liberty Square | Good | B | Grilled salmon, fried fish and shrimp, lobster roll, fried chicken, grilled shrimp, plant-based "crab" cake sandwich, salads, hush puppies

Cosmic Ray's Starlight Café | Tomorrowland | Poor-Fair | C | Burgers (including plant-based), hot dogs, Greek salad, chicken sandwich, chicken strips, seasonal dessert; some kosher

The Friar's Nook | Fantasyland | Good | B | Tots, hand pies, mac and cheese, breakfast sandwiches

Gaston's Tavern | Fantasyland | Good | B | Ham-and-Gruyère tart, cinnamon rolls, Grey Stuff, Crème Brûlée Croissant, LeFou's Brew

Golden Oak Outpost *(seasonal)* | Frontierland | Fair | C | Shrimp gumbo, hot honey chicken, beignets

Liberty Square Market | Liberty Square | Fair | C | Hot dogs, fresh fruit, pretzels, packaged drinks and snacks

The Lunching Pad | Tomorrowland | Poor | D | Hot dogs, pretzels, specialty frozen drinks

Main Street Bakery (Starbucks) | Main Street, U.S.A. | Good | B | Coffees, pastries, breakfast sandwiches

Pecos Bill Tall Tale Inn and Cafe | Frontierland | Fair | C | Burger, grilled masa flatbread, Caesar salad, tamale, create-your-own nacho and rice bowls

Pinocchio Village Haus | Fantasyland | Poor-Fair | D | Flatbread pizzas, chicken strips, fries, Caesar salad

Sleepy Hollow | Liberty Square | Fair-Good | B– | Large Mickey waffles, funnel cakes, corn dogs

Tomorrowland Terrace Restaurant *(seasonal)* | Tomorrowland | Fair | C– | Varies

Tortuga Tavern *(seasonal)* | Adventureland | Poor-Fair | C | Sandwiches, hot dogs, and more

DINING INFORMATION Table Service

Restaurant | Meals Served | Location | Price | Quality | Value | Selections

Be Our Guest Restaurant | L-D | Fantasyland | Expensive | ★★★ | ★★ | French onion soup, dry-aged Duroc pork chop, Grey Stuff; kids' menu

Cinderella's Royal Table | B-L-D | Fantasyland | Expensive | ★★★ | ★★ | *Breakfast:* Eggs, bacon, pastries, shrimp and grits, banana-stuffed French toast, beef tenderloin frittata, plant-based option. *Lunch and dinner:* Lamb chops, filet mignon, fish, grilled chicken, vegetarian pasta; kids' menu

The Crystal Palace | B-L-D | Main Street, U.S.A. | Expensive | ★★½ | ★★½ | Buffet with fried chicken, prime rib, Southern Fried Cauliflower, seasonal salads; character meals

Jungle Navigation Co. Ltd. Skipper Canteen | L-D | Adventureland | Moderate | ★★★½ | ★★★ | Char siu pork, Korean barbecue-inspired crispy fried chicken, grilled steak, corn pancakes with pork and avocado cream; chocolate cake with caramelized bananas; plant-based options; kids' menu

Liberty Tree Tavern | L-D | Liberty Square | Expensive | ★★★½ | ★★★½ | All-you-can-eat platter with roasted turkey, pork roast, mashed potatoes, stuffing, vegetables, and mac and cheese; Impossible Meatloaf; toffee cake

The Plaza Restaurant | L-D | Main Street, U.S.A. | Inexpensive | ★★½ | ★★½ | Old-fashioned diner and ice-cream shop fare: bacon cheeseburger, chicken sandwich, sundae; kids' menu

Tony's Town Square Restaurant | L-D | Main Street, U.S.A. | Moderate | ★★ | ★★ | Spaghetti with meatballs, fettuccine Alfredo, chicken parmigiana, garlic bread; kids' menu

Advance Reservations are recommended for most Magic Kingdom full-service restaurants; call ☎ *407-WDW-DINE (939-3463) or visit disneyworld.disney.go.com/reservations/dining.*

GOOD REST AREAS

Back of Storybook Circus, between Big Top Treats and the train station | Fantasyland | Covered plush seating with electrical outlets and USB phone-charging stations

Covered porch with rocking chairs on Tom Sawyer Island | Frontierland | Across the water from the *Liberty Belle* Riverboat dock; bring refreshments from Frontierland; closes at sunset

Cul-de-sac | Main Street, U.S.A. | Between the china shop and Main Street Bakery (Starbucks) on the right side of the street as you face the castle; refreshments nearby

Picnic tables | Fantasyland | Near the *Tangled*-themed restrooms, between Peter Pan's Flight and The Haunted Mansion; outdoors but has phone-charging stations

Quiet seating area | Tomorrowland | Near restrooms on the right as you approach Space Mountain. Near building to the right of Space Mountain's entrance, near the trees, there's a covered seating area farther back in that corridor; refreshments nearby

Second floor of train station | Main Street, U.S.A. | Refreshments nearby; crowded during fireworks and parades

Upstairs at Columbia Harbour House | Liberty Square | Grab a beverage and relax upstairs; restrooms available

CLIP-OUT TOURING PLAN COMPANIONS   571

EPCOT TOURING PLAN COMPANION
ATTRACTION INFORMATION

Attraction | Location | When to Go | Authors' Rating | Comments

The American Adventure | The American Adventure, World Showcase | Anytime | ★★★½
Awesome Planet | The Land Pavilion, World Nature | Anytime | ★★
Beauty and the Beast Sing-Along | France, World Showcase | 10 a.m.–6:30 p.m. | ★★
Canada Far and Wide | Canada, World Showcase | Anytime | ★★★
¡Celebración Encanto! | World Celebration | Anytime | ★★★
Club Cool | World Celebration | Anytime | ★★½
Disney & Pixar Short Film Festival (LLMP) | Imagination! Pavilion | Anytime | ★★
DuckTales World Showcase Adventure | World Showcase | Anytime | ★★½
Friendship Boats | World Showcase | Anytime | ★★
Frozen Ever After (LLMP) | Norway, World Showcase | At park opening or after 7 p.m. | ★★★★ | Fright potential*
Gran Fiesta Tour Starring the Three Caballeros | Mexico, World Showcase | Anytime | ★★½
Guardians of the Galaxy: Cosmic Rewind (LLSP) | World Discovery | When your boarding group is called | ★★★★★ | 42" minimum height; fright and motion sickness potential*
Impressions de France | France, World Showcase | 9–9:30 a.m. or 7–8:45 p.m. | ★★★½
Journey into Imagination with Figment (LLMP) | Imagination! Pavilion | Anytime | ★★½ | Fright potential*
Journey of Water, Inspired by Moana | World Nature | Anytime | ★★★★
Living with the Land (LLMP) | The Land Pavilion, World Nature | Anytime | ★★★★
Meet Anna and Elsa at Royal Sommerhus | Norway, World Showcase | At park opening, at lunch or dinner, or in the last hour the park is open | ★★★★
Meet Beloved Disney Pals at Mickey & Friends | World Celebration | Early or late | ★★★½
Mission: Space (LLMP) | World Discovery | Anytime | ★★★½ | Orange version not recommended for pregnant guests or anyone prone to motion sickness or claustrophobia; 44" minimum height for Orange version, 40" minimum height for Green version; fright potential*
Reflections of China | China, World Showcase | Anytime | ★★½
Remy's Ratatouille Adventure (LLMP) | France, World Showcase | At park opening | ★★★★ | Fright potential*
The Seas Main Tank and Exhibits | The Seas with Nemo & Friends Pavilion, World Nature | When you need a break from the elements | ★★★½
The Seas with Nemo & Friends (LLMP) | The Seas with Nemo & Friends Pavilion, World Nature | Anytime | ★★★ | Fright potential*
Soarin' Around the World (LLMP) | The Land Pavilion, World Nature | First 2 hours the park is open or after 4 p.m. | ★★★★½ | 40" minimum height
Spaceship Earth (LLMP) | World Celebration | Midday | ★★★★
Test Track (LLMP) | Test Track Pavilion, World Discovery | First 30 minutes the park is open or just before closing, or use the single-rider line | ★★★★ | 40" minimum height; pregnant guests should not ride; fright potential*
Turtle Talk with Crush (LLMP) | The Seas with Nemo & Friends Pavilion, World Nature | Anytime | ★★★★

*See Small-Child Fright-Potential Table on pages 305–306.

DINING INFORMATION Counter Service

Restaurant | Location | Quality | Value | Selections

L'Artisan des Glaces | France, World Showcase | Excellent | C | Gourmet ice cream and dairy-free sorbet
La Cantina de San Angel | Mexico, World Showcase | Good | B | Tacos, fried cheese empanada, nachos, grilled chicken, guacamole, churros, margaritas
Connections Café/Eatery | World Celebration | Good | C | Burgers, pizza, salads, plant-based options, cake
Festival Favorites/Outdoor Kitchen—Florida Fresh | World Celebration | Fair–Good | C | Varies
Fife & Drum Tavern | The American Adventure, World Showcase | Fair | C | Turkey legs, hot dogs, popcorn, soft-serve, slushies, beer, alcoholic lemonade, root beer floats
Les Halles Boulangerie-Pâtisserie | France, World Showcase | Excellent | B | Sandwiches (ham and cheese; Brie, cranberry, and apple), quiches, soups, bread, pastries
Katsura Grill | Japan, World Showcase | Good | B | Sushi; udon noodle bowls; pork ramen; chicken, beef, or shrimp teriyaki; chicken curry; edamame; miso soup; yuzu tea cheesecake; Kirin beer, sake, plum wine
Kringla Bakeri og Kafe | Norway, World Showcase | Good | B | Norwegian pastries and desserts, iced coffee, imported beers and wines
Lotus Blossom Café | China, World Showcase | Fair | C | Egg rolls, pot stickers, orange chicken, chicken fried rice, Mongolian beef with rice, caramel-ginger or lychee ice cream; plum wine, Tsingtao beer
Pizza al Taglio | Italy, World Showcase | Good | B | Pizza, tiramisu, alcoholic beverages
Refreshment Outpost | Between Germany and China, World Showcase | Good | B– | Typical festival offerings
Refreshment Port | Near Canada, World Showcase | Good | B | Soft-serve and other festival-related fare

DINING INFORMATION Counter Service *(continued)*
Restaurant | Location | Quality | Value | Selections

Regal Eagle Smokehouse | The American Adventure, World Showcase | Good–Excellent | A– | Regional barbecue specialties, burgers, salads, vegetarian options; beer, hard cider, wine, and specialty cocktails

Sommerfest | Germany, World Showcase | Fair | C | Bratwurst, pretzel bread pudding, jumbo pretzel, beer

Sunshine Seasons | The Land, World Nature | Fair–Good | B | Rotisserie and wood-fired meats and fish; soups, salads, sandwiches, flatbreads, grab-and-go options

Tangierine Café | Morocco, World Showcase | Fair–Good | B– | Festival offerings

Yorkshire County Fish Shop | United Kingdom, World Showcase | Good | A | Fish-and-chips, draft ale

DINING INFORMATION Table Service
Restaurant | Meals Served | Location | Price | Quality | Value | Selections

Akershus Royal Banquet Hall | B-L-D | Norway, World Showcase | Expensive | ★★★ | ★★★ | Norwegian meatballs, grilled salmon, chicken and dumplings, lefse; full bar; kids' menu; character meals

Biergarten | L-D | Germany, World Showcase | Expensive | ★★★ | ★★★★ | Buffet with schnitzel, German sausages, homemade spaetzle; kids' menu

Le Cellier Steakhouse | L-D | Canada, World Showcase | Expensive | ★★★★½ | ★★★ | Filet mignon with mushroom risotto, Canadian Cheddar soup, smoked Gouda mac and cheese, loaded mashed potatoes, poutine, maple crème brûlée; full bar with Canadian wines; kids' menu

Chefs de France | L-D | France, World Showcase | Expensive | ★★½ | ★★★ | Boeuf bourguignon, French onion soup topped with Gruyère; beer, wine, cocktails; kids' menu

Coral Reef Restaurant | L-D | The Seas with Nemo & Friends, World Nature | Moderate | ★★★ | ★★½ | Steak and seafood; chocolate mousse bar dessert; full bar; kids' menu

La Crêperie de Paris | B-L-D | France, World Showcase | Inexpensive | ★★★½ | ★★★½ | Savory crepe with chèvre, spinach, and walnut; banana-filled dessert crepe; full bar; kids' menu

Garden Grill Restaurant | B-L-D | The Land, World Nature | Expensive | ★★★½ | ★★★½ | Grilled steak, Mickey waffles; full bar; character meals; no kids' menu

La Hacienda de San Angel | D | Mexico, World Showcase | Expensive | ★★★ | ★★★½ | Guacamole, queso fundido, carne asada-style New York strip, osso buco; full bar; kids' menu

Monsieur Paul | D | France, World Showcase | Expensive | ★★★ | ★★★ | Black-truffle soup, snapper in potato "scales"; full bar; no kids' menu

Nine Dragons Restaurant | L-D | China, World Showcase | Moderate | ★★★ | ★★ | Crispy duck bao buns, honey-sesame chicken, smoked duck fried rice; full bar; kids' menu

Rose & Crown Dining Room | D | United Kingdom, World Showcase | Moderate | ★★★½ | ★★½ | Fish-and-chips, bangers and mash, shepherd's pie (with vegetarian option), Scotch egg, sticky toffee pudding; full bar; kids' menu

San Angel Inn Restaurante | L-D | Mexico, World Showcase | Moderate | ★★★ | ★★ | Queso fundido, rib eye tacos, vegetarian huarache; sweet corn ice cream; full bar; kids' menu

Shiki-Sai | L-D | Japan, World Showcase | Moderate | ★★★★ | ★★★★ | Sushi, octopus fritters, savory Japanese pancake, grilled Wagyu gyoza, ishiyaki beef rice; full bar with sake; kids' menu

Space 220 | L-D | World Discovery | Expensive | ★★½ | ★½ | Seared tuna, miso-glazed salmon, vegetarian stuffed shells, roasted chicken, burger, steak, pad Thai; full bar; kids' menu

Spice Road Table | L-D | Morocco, World Showcase | Inexpensive | ★★★★ | ★★★½ | Spiced shrimp, hummus fries, lamb kefta with tzatziki, spiced chicken; full bar

Takumi-Tei | D | Japan, World Showcase | Expensive | ★★★★★ | ★★★½ | Traditional kaiseki cuisine: Wagyu beef, sushi, plant-based menu; full bar; multicourse kids' menu

Teppan Edo | L-D | Japan, World Showcase | Expensive | ★★★★ | ★★★ | Chicken, shrimp, beef, scallops, and veggies stir-fried on teppanyaki grill; full bar; kids' menu

Tutto Italia Ristorante | L-D | Italy, World Showcase | Expensive | ★★★ | ★★½ | Pasta, steak, salmon, chicken Parmesan, gnocchi, fried calamari; full bar; kids' menu

Via Napoli Ristorante e Pizzeria | L-D | Italy, World Showcase | Moderate | ★★★½ | ★★★ | Wood-fired pizzas, pastas, filet, Mediterranean sea bass, chicken Parmesan; beer and wine; kids' menu

Advance Reservations recommended for most EPCOT full-service restaurants; call ☎ 407-WDW-DINE (939-3463) or visit disneyworld.disney.go.com/reservations/dining.

GOOD REST AREAS

Benches | Mexico, World Showcase | Inside the pavilion against the inside of the wall that forms the walking ramps to the retail space; air-conditioned

Benches | The Seas, World Nature | Air-conditioned

Japan gardens | Japan, World Showcase | To the left of Katsura Grill, a set of tables overlooking a lovely garden and koi pond; outdoors but shaded, with refreshments nearby

Rotunda and lobby | The American Adventure, World Showcase | Air-conditioned; refreshments nearby; usually quiet

UK Rose Garden benches | United Kingdom, World Showcase | Behind the pavilion

DISNEY'S ANIMAL KINGDOM TOURING PLAN COMPANION

ATTRACTION INFORMATION

Attraction | Location | When to Go | Authors' Rating | Comments

The Animation Experience at Conservation Station | Rafiki's Planet Watch | Check *Times Guide* | ★★★½
Avatar Flight of Passage (LLSP) | Pandora | At park opening or after 3 p.m. | ★★★★½ | 44" minimum height; pregnant guests should not ride; fright potential*
Awakenings | Tree of Life, Discovery Island | After sunset | ★★★
Conservation Station and Affection Section | Rafiki's Planet Watch | Morning | ★★★
Discovery Island Trails | Discovery Island | Anytime | ★★★
Expedition Everest (LLMP) | Asia | Early or late | ★★★★½ | 44" minimum height; motion sickness potential; pregnant guests should not ride; single-rider line available; fright potential*
Feathered Friends in Flight! (LLMP) | Asia | Anytime; check *Times Guide* for performance times. | ★★★★
Festival of the Lion King (LLMP) | Africa | Earlier or later showtimes | ★★★★½
Finding Nemo: The Big Blue . . . and Beyond! (LLMP) | Former DinoLand area | Check *Times Guide* | ★★★½
Gorilla Falls Exploration Trail | Africa | Before or after Kilimanjaro Safaris | ★★★★
Kali River Rapids (LLMP) | Asia | Before 11 a.m. or last hour the park is open | ★★★½ | 38" minimum height; pregnant guests should note that the ride is bouncy; you'll get wet; fright potential*
Kilimanjaro Safaris (LLMP) | Africa | At park opening or after 3 p.m. | ★★★★★
Maharajah Jungle Trek | Asia | Anytime | ★★★★ | Fright potential*
Meet Favorite Disney Pals at Adventurers Outpost | Discovery Island | First thing in the morning or after 5 p.m. | ★★★½
Na'vi River Journey (LLMP) | Pandora | Before 9:30 a.m. or in the last 2 hours before closing | ★★★½ | Fright potential*
Wilderness Explorers | Parkwide | Sign up in the morning and complete activities throughout the day | ★★★★
Wildlife Express Train | Africa | Anytime | ★★
Zootopia: Better Zoogether! (LLMP) | Tree of Life, Discovery Island | Check *Times Guide* | Too new to rate

*See Small-Child Fright-Potential Table on pages 305–306.

DINING INFORMATION Counter Service

Restaurant | Location | Quality | Value | Selections

Creature Comforts (Starbucks) | Discovery Island near Africa | Good | C | Coffee and espresso drinks, teas, sandwiches, pastries
Eight Spoon Café | Discovery Island | Good | B | Baked mac and cheese, typical Disney snacks, like churros
Flame Tree Barbecue | Discovery Island | Good | A− | Ribs, smoked half chicken, pulled-pork sandwich, mac and cheese with pulled pork, plant-based "sausage" sandwich; beer, frozen rum drink
Harambe Market | Africa | Good | B | Grilled chicken or shrimp over rice and salad greens; salads; plant-based "sausage"
Kusafiri Coffee Shop and Bakery | Africa | Good | B | Pistachio-honey croissant, sausage biscuits, colossal cinnamon rolls
Mr. Kamal's | Between Asia and Africa | Good | B | Small snacks, like dumplings and seasoned fries
Pizzafari | Discovery Island | Poor | D | Chicken pastas, personal pizzas, Caesar salad, cupcakes
Pongu Pongu | Discovery Island | Good | B | Stuffed pancakes, pineapple-cream cheese spring rolls, pretzels
Royal Anandapur Tea Company | Asia | Good | B | Hot and iced teas, hot chocolate, coffee and espresso drinks, frozen chai, pastries
Satu'li Canteen | Pandora | Good–Excellent | A− | Customizable bowls with chicken, beef, shrimp, or fried tofu; steamed "pods" (stuffed bao buns)
Yak & Yeti Local Food Cafes | Asia | Fair | B− | Honey chicken with steamed rice, cheeseburger, teriyaki chicken salad, vegetarian tikka masala, Korean-style fried-chicken sandwich, tempura shrimp, egg rolls, fried rice; American-style breakfast fare

DINING INFORMATION Table Service

Restaurant | Meals Served | Location | Price | Quality | Value | Selections

Rainforest Cafe | B-L-D | Park entrance | Moderate | ★½ | ★★ | Spinach-and-artichoke dip, coconut shrimp, burgers, brownie volcano with ice cream and sparklers; full bar; kids' menu
Tiffins Restaurant | L-D | Discovery Island | Expensive | ★★★★ | ★★★ | Charred octopus and pineapple-glazed pork belly appetizers, tamarind-braised short rib, burger; full bar; kids' menu
Tusker House Restaurant | B-L-D | Africa | Expensive | ★★★½ | ★★★ | Tandoori chicken, berbere-marinated pork, green curry shrimp, beef tagine, doro wat (Ethiopian chicken stew), salmon, plant-based options; character meals; full bar next door; kids' selections

DINING INFORMATION Table Service *(continued)*

Restaurant | Meals Served | Location | Price | Quality | Value | Selections

Yak & Yeti Restaurant | L-D | Asia | Moderate | ★★★ | ★★★ | Lo mein bowls, coconut shrimp, chicken tikka masala, Korean fried chicken tenders, firecracker shrimp; full bar; kids' menu

Advance Reservations recommended for most Animal Kingdom full-service restaurants; call ☎ 407-WDW-DINE (939-3463) *or visit* disneyworld.disney.go.com/reservations/dining.

GOOD REST AREAS

Gazebo behind Flame Tree Barbecue | Discovery Island | Follow the path toward the water, along the left side of Flame Tree Barbecue; gazebo has ceiling fans

Seating area adjacent to Dawa Bar | Africa | Refreshments nearby; outdoors and can be noisy from street performers

Walkway between Africa and Asia | Plenty of shaded rest spots, some overlooking streams; refreshments nearby; a favorite of *Unofficial Guide* researchers

DISNEY'S HOLLYWOOD STUDIOS TOURING PLAN COMPANION

ATTRACTION INFORMATION

Attraction | Location | When to Go | Authors' Rating | Comments

Alien Swirling Saucers *(LLMP)* | Toy Story Land | After 3 p.m. | ★★½ | 32" minimum height; motion sickness potential

Beauty and the Beast—Live on Stage / Theater of the Stars *(LLMP)* | Sunset Boulevard | Check *Times Guide* | ★★★★

Disney Junior Play and Dance! *(LLMP)* | Animation Courtyard | Check *Times Guide* | ★★½

Disney Villains: Unfairly Ever After / Sunset Showcase Theater | Sunset Boulevard | Check *Times Guide* | Too new to rate

Fantasmic! | Sunset Boulevard | Check *Times Guide*; if two shows are offered, the second will be less crowded | ★★★★½ Fright potential*

For the First Time in Forever: A Frozen Sing-Along Celebration *(LLMP)* | Echo Lake | Check *Times Guide* | ★★★½

Indiana Jones Epic Stunt Spectacular! *(LLMP)* | Echo Lake | Check *Times Guide* | ★★★½

The Little Mermaid—A Musical Adventure | Animation Courtyard | Check *Times Guide* | Too new to rate

Meet Disney Stars at Red Carpet Dreams | Echo Lake | First or last hour the park is open or during mealtimes | ★★★½

Meet Olaf at Celebrity Spotlight | Echo Lake | First or last hour the park is open or during mealtimes | ★★★½

Mickey & Minnie's Runaway Railway *(LLMP)* | Hollywood Boulevard | Early or late | ★★★★ | Fright potential*

Millennium Falcon: Smugglers Run *(LLMP)* | Galaxy's Edge | Before 10 a.m. or after 6 p.m. | ★★★★ | 38" minimum height; pregnant guests should not ride; single-rider line available; motion sickness and fright potential*

Rock 'n' Roller Coaster *(LLMP)* | Sunset Boulevard | Early or late | ★★★★ | 48" minimum height; pregnant guests should not ride; single-rider line available; motion sickness and fright potential*

Slinky Dog Dash *(LLMP)* | Toy Story Land | At park opening or just before closing | ★★★★ | 38" minimum height; fright potential*

Star Tours—The Adventures Continue *(LLMP)* | Echo Lake | Lunchtime or after 4 p.m. | ★★★★ | 40" minimum height; pregnant guests should not ride; motion sickness and fright potential*

Star Wars Launch Day Character Greetings | Animation Courtyard | Anytime | ★★★½

Star Wars: Rise of the Resistance *(LLSP)* | Galaxy's Edge | First thing or late at night | ★★★★★ | 40" minimum height; pregnant guests should not ride; motion sickness and fright potential*

Toy Story Mania! *(LLMP)* | Toy Story Land | Early or late | ★★★★½

The Twilight Zone Tower of Terror *(LLMP)* | Sunset Boulevard | Early or late | ★★★★★ | 40" minimum height; pregnant guests should not ride; fright potential*

Vacation Fun at Mickey Shorts Theater | Echo Lake | Anytime | ★★★

Walt Disney Presents | Animation Courtyard | Anytime | ★★½

* See Small-Child Fright-Potential Table on pages 305-306.

DINING INFORMATION Counter Service

Restaurant | Location | Quality | Value | Selections

ABC Commissary | Commissary Lane | Fair-Good | B- | Carnitas or shrimp tacos, Buffalo chicken grilled cheese, Mediterranean salad with or without chicken, chicken club sandwich, plant-based burger, beer

Backlot Express | Echo Lake | Fair | C | Bacon cheeseburger, chicken strips, Cuban sandwich, Southwest salad, with or without chicken, teriyaki chicken bowl, barbecue pulled-pork burger

Catalina Eddie's | Sunset Boulevard | Fair | C | Pizza, Caesar salad, meatball sub

Docking Bay 7 Food and Cargo | Galaxy's Edge | Good | A- | Smoked ribs served with blueberry corn muffins, roasted chicken salad, fried chicken cubes with mac and cheese and roasted veggies

Dockside Diner | Echo Lake | Fair | D | Hot dogs with over-the-top toppings, bacon mac and cheese

Fairfax Fare | Sunset Boulevard | Poor-Fair | C+ | Unimpressive bowls

Milk Stand | Galaxy's Edge | Fair | D | Frozen nondairy drinks, with or without alcohol

Oga's Cantina | Galaxy's Edge | Fair | D | Alcoholic and nonalcoholic cocktails, charcuterie board, flatbread, pretzel roll

Ronto Roasters | Galaxy's Edge | Good | B | Pita wrap filled with roasted pork, grilled pork sausage, and slaw; pork rinds; nonalcoholic fruit punch; breakfast wraps

Rosie's All-American Cafe | Sunset Boulevard | Poor | D | Burgers, hot dogs, chicken nuggets, fries, plant-based "lobster" roll

The Trolley Car Cafe (Starbucks) | Hollywood Boulevard | Good | C | Coffee and espresso drinks, tea, breakfast sandwiches, pastries

DINING INFORMATION Counter Service *(continued)*

Restaurant | Location | Quality | Value | Selections

Woody's Lunch Box | Toy Story Land | Good | B | *Breakfast:* Lunch Box Tarts; breakfast bowl with scrambled eggs, potato barrels, and country gravy *Lunch and dinner:* Sandwiches (BBQ brisket, smoked turkey, grilled three-cheese); tomato-basil soup; "totchos" with chili, queso, and corn chips

DINING INFORMATION Table Service

Restaurant | Meals Served | Location | Price | Quality | Value | Selections

50's Prime Time Café | L-D | Echo Lake | Moderate | ★★★ | ★★★ | Pot roast, meat loaf, fried chicken, meat loaf, PB&J milkshake, warm apple crisp, chocolate–peanut butter layer cake; full bar; kids' menu

Hollywood & Vine | B-L-D | Echo Lake | Expensive | ★★★½ | ★★★ | *Breakfast:* Bananas Foster French toast, eggs Benedict, chicken with Mickey waffles *Lunch and dinner:* Buffet with steak, salmon, chicken, tofu, ham, peel-and-eat shrimp, shepherd's pie and vegetables; character meals; full bar.

The Hollywood Brown Derby | L-D | Hollywood Boulevard | Expensive | ★★★★ | ★★½ | Cobb Salad (named after the owner of the original restaurant), pork, lamb, grapefruit cake; kids' menu. Patio lounge serves cocktails and small plates.

Roundup Rodeo BBQ | L-D | Toy Story Land | Expensive | ★★★ | ★★★½ | Family-style barbecue, cheddar biscuits with sweet pepper jelly, salmon, mac and cheese, corn on the cob, tots

Sci-Fi Dine-In Theater Restaurant | L-D | Commissary Lane | Inexpensive | ★★ | ★★ | Burgers (plant-based option available), milkshakes and sundaes; full bar; kids' menu

Advance Reservations recommended for DHS full-service restaurants; call ☎ 407-WDW-DINE (939-3463) or visit disneyworld.disney.go.com/reservations/dining.

GOOD REST AREAS

Animation Building | Animation Courtyard | Benches in and around Star Wars Launch Bay; refreshments nearby

Benches along Echo Lake | Some shaded; refreshments nearby

Covered seating behind Sunshine Day Bar | Sunset Boulevard | Refreshments nearby; ample seating